Dental Cementum in Anthropology

EDITED BY

STEPHAN NAJI
New York University
Commonwealth War Graves Commission

WILLIAM RENDU
Université Bordeaux, CNRS, PACEA, France
Institue of Archaeology and Ethnography SB RAS (ZooSCAn)

LIONEL GOURICHON
Université Côte d'Azur, CNRS, CEPAM, Nice, France

CAMBRIDGE
UNIVERSITY PRESS

University Printing House, Cambridge CB2 8BS, United Kingdom

One Liberty Plaza, 20th Floor, New York, NY 10006, USA

477 Williamstown Road, Port Melbourne, VIC 3207, Australia

314–321, 3rd Floor, Plot 3, Splendor Forum, Jasola District Centre,
New Delhi – 110025, India

103 Penang Road, #05–06/07, Visioncrest Commercial, Singapore 238467

Cambridge University Press is part of the University of Cambridge.

It furthers the University's mission by disseminating knowledge in the pursuit of
education, learning, and research at the highest international levels of excellence.

www.cambridge.org
Information on this title: www.cambridge.org/9781108477086
DOI: 10.1017/9781108569507

© Cambridge University Press 2022

This publication is in copyright. Subject to statutory exception
and to the provisions of relevant collective licensing agreements,
no reproduction of any part may take place without the written
permission of Cambridge University Press.

First published 2022

Printed in the United Kingdom by TJ Books Limited, Padstow Cornwall

A catalogue record for this publication is available from the British Library.

Library of Congress Cataloging-in-Publication Data
Names: Naji, Stephan, 1975– editor. | Rendu, William, 1979– editor. |
Gourichon, Lionel, 1972– editor.
Title: Dental cementum in anthropology / edited by Stephan Naji, William Rendu, Lionel Gourichon.
Description: Cambridge, United Kingdom ; New York, NY : Cambridge University Press, 2021. |
Includes bibliographical references and index.
Identifiers: LCCN 2021024982 (print) | LCCN 2021024983 (ebook) | ISBN 9781108477086
(hardback) | ISBN 9781108569507 (ebook)
Subjects: MESH: Dental Cementum – physiology | Paleodontology – methods. | Cementogenesis
Classification: LCC RK51.5 (print) | LCC RK51.5 (ebook) | NLM GN 209 | DDC 617.6/34–dc23
LC record available at https://lccn.loc.gov/2021024982
LC ebook record available at https://lccn.loc.gov/2021024983

ISBN 978-1-108-47708-6 Hardback

Additional resources for this publication at www.cambridge.org/naji.

Cambridge University Press has no responsibility for the persistence or accuracy of
URLs for external or third-party internet websites referred to in this publication
and does not guarantee that any content on such websites is, or will remain,
accurate or appropriate.

We would like to dedicate this book to wonderful colleagues and friends who paved the way of cementochronology for us, supported our endeavors, and brightened our lives.

Jean-Pierre Bocquet-Appel (1949–2018) – a mentor, a pioneer, a visionary scholar, and a generous friend. He was a true anthropologist. Farewell.

Anne Pike-Tay (1956–2020) – an inventive, challenging, and luminous archaeozoologist and paleoanthropologist. We owe her a lot.

Vicky Wedel (1974–2021) – a dedicated researcher who strived to use anthropology as a platform to speak for those who no longer had a voice. You were a gentle soul, and it was a privilege knowing you; we will miss you dearly.

****

To Galina A. Klevezal, whose publications are still the benchmarks of interdisciplinary studies on cementum – we thank you sincerely for your outstanding scientific rigor and dedication.

To Joël Blondiaux, who trained every anthropologist in France in cementochronology – thank you so much for your patience, generosity, and brilliant scientific intuitions.

Contents

List of Contributors		*page* x
Foreword by Daniel Antoine		xvii
	Introduction: Cementochronology in Chronobiology Stephan Naji	1
Part I	**The Biology of Cementum**	19
1	**A Brief History of Cemental Annuli Research, with Emphasis upon Anthropological Applications** Jane E. Buikstra	21
2	**Development and Structure of Cementum** Brian L. Foster, Francisco H. Nociti, Jr., and Martha J. Somerman	46
3	**Insights into Cementogenesis from Human Disease and Genetically Engineered Mouse Models** Brian L. Foster, Michael B. Chavez, Tamara N. Kolli, and Leigh Oldershaw	65
4	**A Comparative Genetic Analysis of Acellular Cementum** Amber E. Trujillo, Alex R. DeCasien, Mareike C. Janiak, Stephan Naji, and Todd R. Disotell	83
5	**Pattern of Human Cementum Deposition with a Special Emphasis on Hypercementosis** Emmanuel d'Incau, Bruno Maureille, and Christine Couture-Veschambre	94
6	**Recent Advances on Acellular Cementum Increments Composition Using Synchrotron X-Radiation** Stephan Naji, Stuart R. Stock, William Rendu, Lionel Gourichon, Thomas Colard, and Zhonghou Cai	110
7	**Incremental Elemental Distribution in Chimpanzee Cellular Cementum: Insights from Synchrotron X-Ray Fluorescence and Implications for Life-History Inferences** Adeline Le Cabec, Jan Garrevoet, Kathryn M. Spiers, and M. Christopher Dean	138

8	**Identifying Life-History Events in Dental Cementum: A Literature Review** Elis Newham and Stephan Naji	155
Part II	**Protocols**	**171**
9	**Cementochronology for Archaeologists: Experiments and Testing for an Optimized Thin-Section Preparation Protocol** Eric Pubert, Stephan Naji, Lionel Gourichon, Frédéric Santos, and William Rendu	173
10	**Optimizing Preparation Protocols and Microscopy for Cementochronology** Paola Cerrito, Stephan Naji, and Timothy Bromage	189
11	**Cementochronology Protocol for Selecting a Region of Interest in Zooarchaeology** William Rendu, Stephan Naji, Eric Pubert, Carlos Sánchez-Hernández, Manon Vuillien, Hala Alarashi, Emmanuel Discamps, Elodie-Laure Jimenez, Solange Rigaud, Randall White, and Lionel Gourichon	201
12	**Tooth Cementum Annulations Method for Determining Age at Death Using Modern Deciduous Human Teeth: Challenges and Lessons Learned** Vicki L. Wedel†, Kenneth P. Hermsen, and Mathew J. Wedel	215
13	**The Analysis of Tooth Cementum for the Histological Determination of Age and Season at Death on Teeth of US Active Duty Military Members** Nicholas Wilson and Katrin Koel-Abt	226
14	**Preliminary Protocol to Identify Parturitions Lines in Acellular Cementum** Thomas Colard, Stephan Naji, Amélie Debroucker, Sofiann El Ayoubi, and Guillaume Falgayrac	234
15	**Toward the Nondestructive Imaging of Cementum Annulations Using Synchrotron X-Ray Microtomography** Adeline Le Cabec, Nancy K. Tang, Valentin Ruano Rubio, and Simon Hillson	249
16	**Noninvasive 3D Methods for the Study of Dental Cementum** Elis Newham, Kate Robson Brown, Ian J. Corfe, Pamela G. Gill, Philippa Brewer, Priscilla Bayle, and Philipp Schneider	258
Part III	**Applications**	**273**
17	**Using Cementochronology to Discuss the Organization of Past Neanderthal Societies** William Rendu, Eric Pubert, and Emmanuel Discamps	275
18	**Investigating Seasonal Competition between Hominins and Cave Hyaenas in the Belgian Ardennes during the Late Pleistocene: Insights from Cementum Analyses** Elodie-Laure Jimenez and Mietje Germonpré	288

19	**Cementochronology to the Rescue: Osteobiography of a Middle Woodland Woman with a Combined Skeletal Dysplasia**	306
	Aviva A. Cormier, Jane E. Buikstra, and Stephan Naji	
20	**Estimating a Mortality Profile of Fisher-Gatherers in Brazil Using Cementochronology**	322
	Stephan Naji, Joël Blondiaux, Sheila Mendonça de Souza, Iris Zeng, and Jean-Pierre Bocquet-Appel†	
21	**Cementochronology: A Solution to Reconstructing Past Populations' Mortality Profiles Using Individual Age-at-Death Estimates**	338
	Laëtitia Lanteri, Bruno Bizot, Bérengère Saliba-Serre, and Aurore Schmitt	
22	**Assessing Age-Related Mortality at Petra, Jordan, Using Cementochronology and Hazard Modeling**	351
	Akacia Propst, Michael Price, and Megan Perry	
23	**Shaping Age-at-Death Distributions by Applying Tooth Cementum Analysis to the Early Medieval Graveyard of Lauchheim (Germany)**	364
	Ursula Wittwer-Backofen and Felix Engel	
24	**Back to the Root: The Coming of Age of Cementochronology**	379
	Stephan Naji and William Rendu	

Index 394

Color plates can be found between pages 172 and 173.

Contributors

Hala Alarashi
University of Côte d'Azur CNRS, CEPAM, Nice, France

Priscilla Bayle
Univ. Bordeaux, CNRS, MCC, PACEA, UMR 5199, Pessac, France

Bruno Bizot
Service Régional de l'Archéologie PACA, Ministère de la Culture et de la Communication, Aix-en-Provence, France

Joël Blondiaux
Centre d'Études en Paléopathologie du Nord, Walincourt-Selvigny, France

Jean-Pierre Bocquet-Appelt†
Université Aix-Marseille, Marseille, France

Philippa Brewer
Natural History Museum of London, London, UK

Timothy Bromage
Department of Biomaterials & Biomimetics, New York University College of Dentistry, NY, USA

Jane E. Buikstra
School of Human Evolution and Social Change, Center for Bioarchaeological Research, Arizona State University, Tempe, AZ, USA

Zhonghou Cai
Advance Photo Source, Argonne National Laboratory, Lamont, AZ, USA

Paola Cerrito
Department of Anthropology, New York University, NY, USA

List of Contributors

Michael B. Chavez
College of Dentistry, Biosciences Division, The Ohio State University, Columbus, OH, USA

Thomas Colard
Department of orthodontics, Lille University, Lille University Hospital, Lille, France. Univ. Bordeaux, CNRS, MCC, PACEA, UMR 5199, Pessac, France

Ian J. Corfe
University of Helsinki, Helsinki, Finland

Aviva A. Cormier
Department of Anthropology, Vassar College, NY, USA

Christine Couture-Veschambre
Univ. Bordeaux, CNRS, MCC, PACEA, UMR 5199, Pessac, France

M. Christopher Dean
Department of Cell and Developmental Biology, University College London, London, UK

Amélie Debroucker
Department of Oral Radiology, University of Lille, Lille University Hospital, Lille, France

Alex R. DeCasien
Department of Anthropology, New York University, NY, USA

Emmanuel Discamps
Université Toulouse Jean Jaurès, CNRS - TRACES Toulouse, France

Todd R. Disotell
Department of Anthropology, New York University, NY, USA

Sofiann El Ayoubi
Department of Oral Radiology, University of Lille, Lille University Hospital, Lille, France

Felix Engel
Faculty of Medicine, Albert-Ludwigs University Freiburg, Global Health Center for Medicine and Society, Freiburg, Germany

List of Contributors

Guillaume Falgayrac
Marrow Adiposity and Bone Lab, Littoral Côte d'Opale, Lille, France

Brian L. Foster
College of Dentistry, Biosciences Division, The Ohio State University, Columbus, OH, USA

Jan Garrevoet
Deutsches Elektronen-Sychrotron DESY, Hamburg, Germany

Mietje Germonpré
Royal Belgian Institute of Natural Sciences, Brussels, Belgium

Pamela G. Gill
Natural History Museum of London, Bristol, UK

Lionel Gourichon
University Côte d'Azur, CNRS, CEPAM Nice, France

Kenneth P. Hermsen
Creighton University, School of Dentistry, Omaha, NE, USA

Simon Hillson
Institute of Archaeology, University College London, London, UK

Emmanuel d'Incau
UFR des Sciences Odontologiques, University of Bordeaux, Bordeaux, France

Mareike C. Janiak
Department of Anthropology and Archaeology, University of Calgary, Alberta, Canada

Elodie-Laure Jimenez
Royal Belgian Institute of Natural Sciences, Brussels, Belgium ; University of Aberdeen, School of Geosciences, Scotland, UK

Katrin Koel-Abt
Forensic anthropologist; Kenyon International Emergency Services

Tamara N. Kolli
College of Dentistry, Biosciences Division, The Ohio State University, Columbus, OH, USA

List of Contributors

Laëtitia Lanteri
CNRS/Université Aix-Marseille, Marseille, France

Adeline Le Cabec
Department of Human Evolution, Max Planck Institute for Evolutionary Anthropology Leipzig, Germany/Univ. Bordeaux, CNRS, MCC, PACEA, UMR 5199, Pessac, France

Bruno Maureille
Univ. Bordeaux, CNRS, MCC, PACEA, UMR 5199, Pessac, France

Sheila Mendonça de Souza
Escola Nacional de Saùde Pùblica, Rio de Janeiro, Brazil

Stephan Naji
Department of Anthropology, New York University, NY, USA
Commonwealth War Graves Commission, Western Europe Area – FRANCE

Elis Newham
Queen Mary University of London, London UK

Francisco H. Nociti, Jr.
Department of Prosthodontics and Periodontics, Division of Periodontics, Piracicaba Dental School, University of Campinas-UNICAMP, São Paulo, Brazil

Leigh Oldershaw
Department of Anthropology, The Ohio State University, Columbus, OH, USA

Megan Perry
Department of Anthropology, East Carolina University, Greenville, NC, USA

Michael Price
Santa Fe Institute, Santa Fe, NM, USA

Akacia Propst
Department of Anthropology, McMaster University, Hamilton, Canada

Eric Pubert
Univ. Bordeaux, CNRS, MCC, PACEA, UMR 5199, Pessac, France

William Rendu
Univ. Bordeaux, CNRS, MCC, PACEA, UMR 5199, Pessac, France / ZooSCAn, CNRS, Institute of Archaeology and Ethnography SB RAS, Novosibirsk, Russia

Solange Rigaud
Univ. Bordeaux, CNRS, MCC, PACEA, UMR 5199, Pessac, France

Kate Robson Brown
University of Bristol, Bristol, UK

Valentin Ruano Rubio
Data Science Data Engineering, Broad Institute, Cambridge, MA, USA

Carlos Sánchez-Hernández
Institut Català de Paleoecologia Humana i Evolució Social, Tarragona, Spain

Bérengère Saliba-Serre
CNRS/Université Aix-Marseille, Marseille, France

Frédéric Santos
Univ. Bordeaux, CNRS, MCC, PACEA, UMR 5199, Pessac, France

Aurore Schmitt
CNRS/Université Aix-Marseille, Marseille, France

Philipp Schneider
University of Southampton, Southampton, UK

Martha J. Somerman
National Institute of Arthritis and Musculoskeletal and Skin Diseases (NIAMS), National Institutes of Health, Bethesda, MD, USA

Kathryn M. Spiers
Deutsches Elektronen-Synchrotron DESY, Hamburg, Germany

Stuart R. Stock
Northwestern University, Evanston, IL, USA

Nancy K. Tang
Independent Researcher

Amber E. Trujillo
Department of Anthropology, New York University, NY, USA

Manon Vuillien
University of Côte d'Azur, CNRS, CEPAM Nice, France

Mathew J. Wedel
Western University of Health Sciences, College of Dental Medicine, Pomona, CA, USA

Vicki L. Wedel†
Western University of Health Sciences, College of Dental Medicine, Pomona, CA, USA

Nicholas Wilson
Uniformed Services University, Bethesda, MD, USA

Ursula Wittwer-Backofen
Faculty of Medicine, Albert-Ludwigs University Freiburg, Global Health Center for Medicine and Society, Freiburg, Germany

Iris Zeng
Department of Anthropology, New York University, NY, USA

Foreword

Unlocking the Potential of Cementum Layering
Daniel Antoine, The British Museum, London

The world of dental histology opens up a wealth of information on human growth and development. My early insights into this world involved evaluating the periodicity of cementum layering using teeth with a known age of extraction as part of my undergraduate research. The results were mixed, in part due to the small sample size and the complexity of imaging cementum under a scanning electron microscope. Simon Hillson and I had hoped that this form of microscopy would facilitate the counting of cementum layers! To a certain extent, it did. In some teeth, counts were similar to the age of extraction (Hillson & Antoine 2003); in others, they differed from it, and some individuals had finer layers in between more defined ones. At the time of the study, the literature was relatively sparse and I was guided by a handful of key papers (e.g., Charles et al. 1986; Condon et al. 1986). By the time I was involved in another cementum project (Huffman & Antoine 2010), I had changed my focus to enamel microstructures. A chance meeting with Stephan at a poster symposium on cementum during the 2012 American Association of Physical Anthropology meetings in Knoxville (US) revealed to me how far the field had moved forward! Following a similarly successful symposium at the 2017 meetings in New Orleans, I am very pleased that Stephan, William, and Lionel followed through to produce this comprehensive, much-needed, and remarkably insightful volume. Although the periodicity and use of incremental structures in enamel and, to a lesser extent, dentine have benefited from more anthropological research (Antoine et al. 2018), it is clear that work on cementum layering, particularly in humans, has – until recently – been more sporadic. This, in part, reflects the fact that both cementum and dentine are more susceptible than enamel to diagenetic changes, affecting our ability to observe their growth structures in many archaeological and fossil teeth (Tang et al. 2016). The highly mineralized enamel offers some protection to the dentine immediately below its surface. This is not the case for the roots on which cementum is deposited.

Combining the latest research on cementum into this single book is a major achievement and represents a giant step forward. The volume is underpinned by several chapters that explore the biology of cementum and provide the crucial background for a fuller interpretation of the histological structures being observed. A range of preparation protocols, imaging methods, and applications are also clearly presented.

Questions regarding our ability to record such structures, as well as their periodicity, are discussed in some detail. However, some questions remain, offering avenues for future research (e.g., Chapter 1). The lessons learned from work on other hard tissues may offer some valuable insights. The interpretation of incremental structures in teeth not only requires a clear understanding of the biological processes that lead to their formation, but it must also account for the physics behind the imaging techniques used to analyze such complex tissues. In transmitted light microscopy, for example, structures are usually made visible by the scattering of light through a relatively thick 100 μm "thin section." Over such a thickness, many variables can impact what is being observed. For example, as the layers of cementum curve around the roots, they are unlikely to be perpendicular to the plane of section and some optical interference is likely. By assessing the impact of the preparation methods (e.g., different mounting resins and planes of section), by offering clear preparation protocols, and by using multiple imaging techniques on the same tooth (e.g., Chapters 10 and 14), this volume helps us understand some of the challenges involved in imaging cementum, particularly in diagenetically altered tissues. Moving forward, the narrower optical plane of laser confocal microscopy could, for example, be used to clarify some of the structures seen in transmitted light microscopy (both can be used to image the exact same area; see Antoine et al. 2009). Such multi-imaging approaches are likely to lead to a better interpretation of what is being observed, including any complex layering patterns (e.g., doubling, sublayering, and accentuated lines) and what may be impacting our ability to record such structures. Despite the time and labor often required to image dental microstructures, the development of more sophisticated imaging techniques should help overcome some of these difficulties. The insights gained are worth the effort! This much-needed volume offers an essential framework for future research that will, hopefully, act as a catalyst to a plethora of new work. Well done!

Antoine, D., Hillson, S., & Dean, M. C. (2009). The Developmental Clock of Dental Enamel: A Test for the Periodicity of Prism Cross-Striations in Modern Humans and an Evaluation of the Most Likely Sources of Error in Histological Studies of This Kind. *Journal of Anatomy* **214**, 45–55.

Antoine, D., FitzGerald, C. M., & Rose, J. C. (2018). Incremental Structures in Teeth: Keys to Unlocking and Understanding Dental Growth and Development. In M. A. Katzenberg & A. L. Grauer (eds.), *Biological Anthropology of the Human Skeleton*, 3rd ed. Oxford: John Wiley & Sons, 225–56.

Charles, D. K., Condon, K., Cheverud, J. M., & Buikstra, J. E. (1986). Cementum Annulation and Age Determination in Homo Sapiens. 1. Tooth Variability and Observer Error. *American Journal of Physical Anthropology* **71**, 311–20.

Condon, K., Charles, D. K., Cheverud, J. M., & Buikstra J. E. (1986). Cementum Annulation and Age Determination in Homo Sapiens. II. Estimates and Accuracy. *American Journal of Physical Anthropology* **71**, 321–30.

Hillson, S., & Antoine, D. (2003). Ancient Bones and Teeth on the Microstructural Level. In G. Grupe & J. Peters (eds.), *Deciphering Ancient Bones – The Research Potential of Bioarchaeological Collections*. Documenta Archaeobiologiae, Rahden/Westf.: Leidorf, 141–57.

Huffman, M., & Antoine, D. (2010). Analysis of Cementum Layers in Archaeological Material. *Dental Anthropology* **23** (3), 67–73.

Tang, N., Le Cabec, A. & Antoine, D. (2016). Dentine and Cementum Structure and Properties. In J. D. Irish & G. R. Scott (eds.), *A Companion to Dental Anthropology*. Oxford: John Wiley & Sons, 204–22.

Introduction: Cementochronology in Chronobiology

Stephan Naji

The purpose of this edited volume was to bring together specialists from various fields to present all the information needed to understand and implement cementochronology, the analysis of cementum growth. This interdisciplinary "Cementum Research Program" was initiated in 2010/2011 at a Paris workshop with Jean-Pierre Bocquet-Appel, Joël Blondiaux, Thomas Colard, and me. Initially, the goal was to develop a standardized cementum protocol for age estimation in anthropology (Colard et al. 2015). However, the program's scope expanded rapidly into an first poster symposium held at the 2012 annual meeting of the American Association of Physical Anthropology (AAPA) in Knoxville (USA). With the invaluable support of Jane Buikstra, selected presentations were published in a special issue of the *International Journal of Paleopathology* (Naji et al. 2016).

This event's positive feedback prompted our group to reach out even more broadly to the international community. Our purpose was to connect with zooarchaeologists who were implementing cementum analyses routinely and paleoanthropologists interested in evolutionary processes using dental remains. In collaboration with William Rendu and Lionel Gourichon, the second phase of our research program started in 2015 (Naji et al. 2015) funded by a sizable French grant (ANR CemeNTAA) dedicated to cementum analysis. The results were presented as a second poster symposium at the 2017 annual meeting of the AAPA in New Orleans (USA). This event was an ideal opportunity to meet new colleagues and motivated students. Consequently, prompted by many colleagues' support, in particular Daniel Antoine, we decided to publish our collaborative efforts in this edited volume.

This publication's premise is to reply to one of the first questions anthropologists ask when considering dental cementum as an age indicator: Why should cementum growth follow an annual/seasonal deposition pattern in distinct layers on the roots' surface?

This chapter is a short introduction to the field of chronobiology to present current theories explaining and interpreting cyclic growth marks observed in skeletal and dental tissues, specifically in cementum. The references are by no means comprehensive, but the reader should find adequate primary sources to explore the topic in greater detail in (Dunlap et al. 2003; Foster 2005; Kumar 2017; Lemmer 2009; Lincoln 2019).

Cementochronogly Nomenclature

First, I will briefly discuss the various labels used to name cementum growth deposits to ensure that all scientists, regardless of their field, are talking about the same histological structures. For a detailed history of cementum discovery in biology, see Foster (2017) and Buikstra (Chapter 1). According to the following definitions, we have tried to homogenize the nomenclature relative to cementum growth analysis throughout this volume.

As early as 1887, Black summarized contemporary cementum knowledge, describing its structure as individual "lamellae, layers, or strata" divided by distinct lines called "incremental lines of the cementum" and observing its chronological deposition pattern as "each lamellae being the results of a single period of activity [...] each successive lamella is younger than the preceding one" (Black 1887,105–6). Sixty years later, these incremental structures started to be tested for aging animals and humans under several different names describing the contrasting optical layers visible in histological sections.

For animals, Scheffer (1950) and Laws (1952) defined external "growth ridges" and internal "annual growth zones or rings," respectively, for dentin growth in sea mammals, but not cementum. Sergeant and Pimlott (1959) were the first to investigate the principle of growth layers for age estimation in cementum using moose as their study sample. They referred to "cement growth layers" to characterize the annual histological structure composed of the two seasonal "growth zones," one opaque and one translucent. Klevezal' and Kleinberg, in their first seminal review (Klevezal' & Kleinenberg 1967, 67), referenced "annual layers" composed of "bands" and "stripes."

In 1978, the conference on odontocete age estimation (Perrin et al. 1980) proposed standardizing dental growth markers' terminology. Every layer parallel to a tissues' formative surface, contrasting with the adjacent one, was defined as an "incremental growth layer." A repeatable pattern of growth layers counting as a time unit was then termed a "growth layer group (GLG)."

In terrestrial mammals, however, cementum growth layers have a slightly different interpretation: The "growth zones" (Baglinière et al. 1992) represent layers interpreted as a rapid deposition due to increased metabolic activity during the "favorable" season (Demars, Le Gall & Martin 2007, 109). Conversely, annuli (singular, annulus) are slow growth layers formed during a decrease of osteogenic activity. Annuli are thus thinner than zones. Also, in French terminology, "growth rest lines" (*ligne d'arrêt de croissance*) (Castanet 1980) were defined as a very thin structure, highly birefringent and often hypermineralized, that can be found within an annulus or alone and alternating with rapid growth zones (Baglinière et al. 1992, 444).

Finally, in her second seminal review, Klevezal' (1996) proposed a new definition for the cementum growth unit as a "growth layer of the first order" composed of an incremental cementum line (principal element counted for age estimation) and a cementum band (intermediate element).

In humans, the first use of cementum for age estimation specifically was published by Gustafson in 1950 with a nonspecific "cementum apposition" component, representing cementum width, not incremental counts, in his multicriteria dental method (Gustafson 1950). Three decades later, the pivotal publication of Stott and colleagues (1982) used the incremental count of cementum deposits for the first time and described them as "cemental annulations." Since then, cementum annuli (Stein & Corcoran 1994) was used preferentially.

In the influential first large-scale controlled study, Wittwer-Backofen and Buba (2002) labeled the use of cementum as the teeth cementum annulations (TCA) method. The acronym seems to be the most preferred among anthropologists today. However, this name can create confusion with the mammal's slow growth layer's "annulus." In forensic anthropology, Wedel proposed another descriptor, dental cementum increment analysis (DCIA) (Wedel 2007), which is entirely accurate.

Finally, following the 1992 publication of the symposium on vertebrate age estimation using hard tissues (Baglinière et al. 1992), another term, the French "*cémentochronologie*" was proposed to follow the larger context of chronobiology (Grosskopf 1996; Martin 1995). In the English literature, "cementochronology" was introduced during the 82nd annual conference of the American Association of Physical Anthropology in 2013 in a contributed poster symposium titled "Cementochronology," organized by Naji, Colard, and Bertrand (Naji et al. 2013). The purpose of this nomenclature shift was to reflect the broader multidisciplinary approach to a common biological growth process and move away from potentially confusing descriptors.

Chronobiology, the Cycles of Life

The periodicity of growth processes has a deep history, from the ancient Greeks' understanding of daily leaf movement to the first published demonstration of endogenous plants' periodicity in 1832 (cited in Schwartz & Daan 2017). Formally, the field of chronobiology, the study of biological rhythms, can be traced to the 1960 edition of the Cold Spring Harbor Biological Laboratory's annual symposium in Long Island, New York, titled "Biological Clocks" (Lemmer 2009).

Chronobiology rests on the premise that the regular rotation of the earth around its central axis and around the sun produces two fundamental periodicities to which all life, from unicellular organisms to primates, has become adapted. The hypothesis is that circadian clocks govern daily rhythmicity, and circannual clocks provide a seasonal endogenous calendar (Lincoln 2019). The various external stimuli (e.g., light cycle, food availability, temperature variation) provide a template for living organisms to anticipate cyclic environmental events by periodic and predictable internal adjustments in physiology and behavior, even where standard environmental cues are weak or ambiguous (Piccione et al. 2009). The frequencies of these rhythms have evolved to cover nearly every division of time (Lemmer 2009), from *intradian* – less than a day – oscillations of one per second (e.g., brain waves), or one per several seconds (e.g., heart rate); *circadian*, one within twenty-four hours (e.g., enamel cross-striations, dentine's von Ebner's lines); *multidien*, five-day rhythm (e.g., enamel of domestic pig, Bromage et al. 2016); *circaseptan*, near-seven-day periodicity (e.g., heart rate and pressure, Reinberg et al. 2017); *lunar*, once a month (e.g., ovulation); to *circannual*, one per year (e.g., reproduction, molt, migration, and cementum).

Today, chronobiology is incorporated into practically all fields of human and nonhuman endeavors, including ecology, biology, sociology, and psychology (Reinberg et al. 2017) to optimize sleep, diet, immune system response, or performances, among other factors.

Mechanisms Responsible for Annual Cycles

We will focus here on the mechanisms and consequences of the annual cycles (For a review of circadian cycles, see Panda et al. 2002; Weinert & Waterhouse 2017). Annual rhythms can be classified into three types (Lincoln 2019; Zucker et al. 1991).

Type 1 trans-generational annual rhythms are mostly observed in short-lived species with multiple generations throughout the year. The innate circannual timing mechanism passes from individual to offspring across the year and may be expressed at only one phase of the life cycle (Lincoln 2019). The presence of annual environmental cues such as annual variations in temperature and photoperiod influences the annual neuroendocrine rhythms via hormonal maturation, for example, puberty and reproduction (Zucker et al. 1991). This is a population/cohort response because an individual cyst only hatches once. A variant is a modular rhythm for longer-lived insects that transform from the egg, through larval instars, to pupation and hatching of the sexually mature adult (Lincoln 2019). Again, this rhythm is a population/cohort event because each animal pupates only once.

Type 2 seasonal (circannual) progressive rhythms recur under constant conditions with a period between ten and twelve months, more typical of long-lived species, including primates. The progressive development from juvenile to adulthood to old age and circannual timing generates cycles in multiple aspects of physiology and behavior (e.g., gonad size, body weight, food intake, gut morphology, immune function, molt, thermoregulation, hibernation, and migration) (Lincoln 2019). Type 2 persists in the absence of periodic light input (Zucker et al. 1991) but varies among and within individuals (Piccione et al. 2009). Animals have an individual annual chronotype (e.g., early rutting/late rutting). This circannual chronotype has been observed in humans with a seasonal affective disorder that could be interpreted as a natural adaptation to winter, where a change in appetite and increased body weight in autumn and the development of withdrawal behaviors in winter was once an advantage for our hunter-gatherer ancestors (Lincoln 2019). Also, mRNA expression levels indicated in one study that 23 percent of the genome showed significant seasonal differences with two distinct antiphase patterns: One set of genes up-regulated in summer and the other, approximately equal, up-regulated in winter (Dopico et al. 2015).

Type 3 annual rhythms are found in animals living in unpredictable environments (desert/equator) where the cue is rainfall and plant growth. In other words, type I rhythms are evoked by environmental cycles, while types II and III are synchronized to environmental cycles (Piccione et al. 2009).

The current working hypothesis to explain circannual cycles assumes that this timing first evolved in free-living eukaryote cells as an adaptation to survive the winter (Lincoln 2019). These organisms alternate between seasonal growth and dormancy across their life-history, which requires a genetically regulated, cell-autonomous, and transgenerational mechanism. Switching between growth in the circannual "summer" and dormancy in the circannual "winter" is a highly adaptive strategy that has thus been conserved in our evolution and is observable today in five of the eight eukaryotic kingdoms (Helm & Lincoln 2017).

The Clock-Shop Model: Combining plant models with animal models provides a general theoretical mechanism linking circadian (daily) modification to circannual rhythm timescale (Schwartz & Daan 2017). Knowledge of the physiological pathways governing time measurement mechanisms has been unfolding rapidly in the past decades through comparative studies that have uncovered the photoperiodic signal transduction cascades in birds, fish, and mammals (Foster 2005). These studies revealed the universality and diversity of photoperiodic mechanisms, such as the fact that molecules involved are conserved while the tissues responsible for these mechanisms are species-specific (Ikegami & Yoshimura 2017). The highly adaptive strategy of annual growth, irrespective of an organism's size and longevity, has determined the evolution of innate, genetically regulated timing processes, broadly encompassed by the clock-shop model (Lincoln 2019). In mammals, in particular, we now understand that the cyclic rhythms are controlled by the body's "central clock" located in the brain at the suprachiasmatic nuclei and supported by "peripheral clocks" located in several other tissues (Liu & Panda 2017; Zheng et al. 2014).

The clock-shop model proposes that environmental signals, notably photoperiod, are relayed by the sensory systems to the central pacemakers to synchronize physiology with the seasons using, among other mechanisms, melatonin-responsive thyrotropic cells in the *pars tuberalis* of the mammalian pituitary gland (Ganguly & Klein 2017). The conjecture is that long-term timing mechanisms reside in all tissues but with dominant pacemaker systems in the brain and pituitary gland orchestrating the circannual phenotype (Lincoln 2019). Circadian and circannual timing systems thus share formal properties: ancestry, cell autonomy, innateness, entrainment, temperature compensation, and ubiquity (Lincoln 2019).

At a molecular level, the favored model for circannual timekeeping proposes that the long-time domain is generated by the cyclical epigenetic regulation of chromatin structure (DNA and histone proteins), determining whether specific circannual timer genes are transcriptionally active or not. This regulation drives the oscillation between the two stable, operational states of subjective summer and subjective winter (Lincoln 2019; Stevenson & Lincoln 2017).

The consequence is that circannual timing mechanisms are more flexible and reprogrammable in the long term, which means if a consistent seasonal change is observed in any organism, it is most likely to be regulated by an endogenous timing mechanism rather than by a passive response to the environment.

Several cyclic mineralization pathways have been identified for bones, suggesting that bone deposition and mineralization are under direct circadian controls (Zheng et al. 2014). For example, the diurnal variation in the synthesis of type I collagen and osteocalcin is under a local circadian oscillator mechanism. Also, analyses in sheep and humans suggest that a single biological rhythm governs all lamellar bone formation within a given taxon (Bromage et al. 2009).

For teeth, there are daily variations in the rate of production and secretion of enamel proteins between early morning and late afternoon, suggesting that enamel protein secretion is under circadian control and that enamel matrix production and maturation are closely controlled by selectively regulating key enamel matrix proteins encoding genes (Zheng et al. 2014). Like enamel, dentin is formed incrementally, indicating the involvement of a circadian clock mechanism during dentinogenesis. This cyclic growth has been demonstrated using proline tracers that labeled collagen during dentin formation and showed that twice as much collagen is secreted during the daylight twelve hours as during the nocturnal twelve hours. These studies suggest that dentin, similar to bone and enamel, is controlled by a circadian clock mechanism (Zheng et al. 2014).

Unlike the other dental hard tissues, cementum does not seem to be controlled by circadian mechanisms but more likely by circannual ones. Stock and colleagues (2017) first identified second-order lines in Beluga whales between first-order (annual) increments in contrasting Ca and Zn variations. Dean and colleagues (2018) have also identified an average of twelve second-order increments (monthly), interpreted as menstrual within chimpanzee samples. Recent work on cementum presented in this volume (Chapter 1, Chapter 6, Chapter 7, Chapter 14) is starting to document specific pathways (e.g., pyrophosphate regulation, vitamin D absorption, hormonal variations) that might be involved in mammals' annual cycles, specifically.

Linking circadian mechanisms to annual ones across mammalian species of various body mass is a complex question. Lincoln argues that circannual rhythms are independent and cannot be explained by frequency demultiplication of circadian rhythms, although changes in the circadian system occur in parallel with the circannual cycle and are the basis of photoperiod entrainment of the circannual clock (Lincoln 2019, 4).

However, Bromage and colleagues (2016) have proposed a hypothesis that "a periodic rhythm longer than the daily biological clock regulates some aspects of metabolic variability that contribute to variability in body size and the pace and pattern of life" (Bromage 2016, 19). Their metabolome and genome analyses from blood plasma in thirty-three domestic pigs revealed that blood plasma metabolites and small noncoding RNA (sncRNA) strongly oscillate on a five-day multidien rhythm, as does the pig enamel.

The adaptive benefits for circannual timekeeping, especially for larger vertebrates, include two critical features. The first is its predictive power to anticipate and prepare for upcoming seasonal changes in the environment (Ball et al. 2017). In a highly seasonal habitat, where changes in food supply and other selective pressures can be predicted through photoperiod, the timing mechanism allows for precise regulation of the timing of cycles in physiology and behavior of fundamental significance in evolution (Helm & Lincoln 2017). The second is organisms' ability to express robust annual cycles, which at specific phases override the effects of proximate cues, including photoperiods, such as in cross-equatorial migratory birds or hibernating species (Helm & Lincoln 2017).

Circannual Rhythms Validation Studies

Even though, in theory, circadian and circannual rhythms are relatively well understood from an evolutionary perspective, seasonal rhythms are expressed at the individual level. Therefore, these cyclic growth markers still need to be identified by repeated measurements on documented individuals to understand the mechanism's geographical and temporal variability. Circannual rhythms can be observed in many biological or behavioral mechanisms (Ball et al. 2017). In wildlife biology or anthropology, identifying a seasonal pattern in hard tissues to define a precise and accurate marker to estimate age and season at death or any life event represents a powerful tool to explore topics such as demography and mobility patterns robustly.

To demonstrate hard tissue seasonal growth rate in animals, including humans, three lines of evidence can be sought from documented subjects: (1) Long term capture–recaptures and sampling; (2) chemical labeling; and (3) empirical identification (Baglinière et al. 1992). We will see that all three have been successfully used in skeletal and dental tissues to support the hypothesis of circannual incremental deposits.

Bone and Other Hard Tissues

Sclerochronology is the method that describes elapsed time from recorded hard tissue (Baglinière et al. 1992). Otholometry studies fish's otolith (inner ear bone), composed of accretion of calcium layers with two periodicities: a daily cycle influenced by water temperature and an annual period (Baillon 1992; Kimura 1977; Kimura & Chikuni 1987). The annual periodicity of growth has been validated using both injection of fluorochrome calcein and empirical observations (Baillon 1992; Mounaix 1992). Similarly, fish scale growth scalimetry has been empirically observed to have an annual deposition rhythm in various species (Mounaix 1992).

Skeletochronology is the use of periodic incremental growth structure in bones for age estimation studies. It has been applied in dinosaurs, reptiles, and mammals (Castanet et al. 1977; Woodward et al. 2013) as early as the 1930s (Clerc 1927). Long-term capture–recaptures have demonstrated the annual growth of one layer of new bone every year through successive amputations of the same limb in amphibians such as toads (Hemelaar 1985). The annual growth pattern has also been tracked in vivo bone labeling of fluorescent marker calcein or tetracycline and recaptures in crocodiles (de Buffrénil & Castanet 2000). For example, in the dermal scutes of Nile crocodiles, the laminae (the bone tissue between successive growth marks) are deposited by accretion/resorption phases so that the presence of one zone and one annulus marks the passage of one year (Woodward et al. 2013). Also related, cartilaginous shark bones present comparable circannual growth layers (Baglinière et al. 1992).

Mammals: The annual periodicity of bone growth has also been tested in mammals. An extensive study of the mouse lemur *Microcebus* assessed the number of annual growth layers in captive individuals of known age across the skeleton (Castanet et al. 1993). More recently, circannual cycles have also been empirically observed in forty species of ungulates of varied size, diet, and habitat from the Equator to near the Poles environments (Köhler et al. 2012). Results showed that lamellar bone growth is arrested during the unfavorable season and accompanied by decreases in body temperature, metabolic rate, and bone-growth-mediating plasma insulin-like growth factor-1 levels. This "growth arrest" forms part of a plesiomorphic metabolic strategy for energy conservation (Köhler et al. 2012). Conversely, at the beginning of the favorable season, phases of intense tissue growth coincide with peak metabolic rates and correlated hormonal changes, indicating an increased efficiency in acquiring and using seasonal resources (Köhler et al. 2012). These results from tachymetabolic mammals show unequivocally that annual growth layers are a universal pattern of homoeothermic endotherms and should not be regarded as anything more than endogenous markers of annual rhythms (Padian & Lamm 2013).

Human Studies: In humans, the use of bone remodeling patterns in age estimation is limited to growth stages of life because intracortical remodeling usually prevents any meaningful analysis in senescing individuals. In forensic contexts, however, the histological determination of adult age in cortical bone employs remodeling activity through the evaluation of osteon density, the number of primary vascular canals, the amount of unremodeled lamellar bone, the percent remodeled bone, and the average size of secondary osteons or Haversian canals (Streeter 2011). However, the correlation between observed age and estimated age in adults is poor at best since not all growth marks reflect environmental cues on growth. Some marks reflect temporary realignments of internal bone structure such as cortical drift; others may directly reflect environmental stresses (Woodward et al. 2013).

The timing of lamellar growth rates was measured using fluorescent labeling in the bones of rats, monkeys, sheep, and humans and revealed that the number of days needed to form one lamella is species-dependent: seven days for rats, twenty-eight days for macaques, thirty-five days for sheep, and fifty-six days for humans (Bromage et al. 2009). Further research based on the histological analyses of skeletal remains of twelve Bantu individuals of known sex and life-history discovered that incremental lamellar bone is deposited with long-period (five to six weeks) growth rate variability previously unobserved in humans (Bromage et al. 2011). Of greater interest to us, potential annual growth deposits have also been observed in some of the individuals (Bromage et al. 2011, 505).

Overall, there is ample evidence that skeletal growth markers that are periodic often occur annually (Woodward et al. 2013). It now also appears that in most vertebrates, including dinosaurs and mammals, cyclical growth markers resulting from the temporary cessation of growth simply reflect internal hormonal cues rather than direct environmental influence (Woodward et al. 2013).

Teeth

Odontochronology: With the advent of more powerful microscopes, dentin and enamel have also been explored to identify growth cycles (Hogg 2018) and, ultimately, cementum during the fifties (Chapter 1).

Enamel and Dentine: Mammalian teeth exhibit microanatomical incremental features representing successive forming fronts of enamel and dentine at varying timescales (Bromage et al. 2009; Dean 2006). The outcome is visible in light microscopy as a daily "cross-striation" and as a long period, "stria of Retzius," measured as the number of cross-striations between adjacent striae and is thus reported in units of whole days. The number of daily increments between striae is identical for all teeth of an individual yet variable between and occasionally within a species that reflects a positive relationship with body size (Padian & Lamm 2013).

Incremental dentin lines are termed von Ebner's lines, which delineate the amount of mineral deposited in a single day. The circadian mineralizing lines in dentine are distinguished by their characteristic appearance, where small spheres of mineralizing dentine increase in size until they eventually coalesce (Dean 2006). Using a biomarker on macaques, Bromage (1991) confirmed the daily rate of dentine von Ebner's lines formation. Later, Dean and Scandrett (1996) also used biomarkers on humans to correlate dentin and enamel formation. However, enamel and dentine have not been linked to any circannual growth patterns in mammals but have been in some species of toothed fish, where the annual growth lines were demonstrated by tetracycline labeling (Day et al. 1986).

Cementum: The benchmark of experimental studies involves using fluorochrome dyes to record cementum growth at precise intervals. In bears, epi-fluorescent photomicrography was used to date a chemical biomarker's exact position in cementum increments to the nearest year (Matson & Kerr 1998). Bosshardt and colleagues (1989) used tetracycline labeling and fluorescence mapping of acellular and cellular cementum in one macaque to demonstrate that acellular cementum formation is a tightly controlled biological phenomenon that occurs with the same regularity and speed wherever this type of tissue is needed.

Empirically, the presence of an endogenous growth rhythm based on growth mark formation in vertebrate skeletal tissues has been proposed by many researchers in a diversity of environments (Grue & Jensen 1979; Klevezal' & Kleinenberg 1967). For example, hibernating mammals form an annual increment despite being prevented from hibernating (i.e., in the absence of typical environmental influences) (Perrin et al. 1980). Also, Grue (1976) noted that mink raised on farms where they were fed a steady diet reduced their food intake during winter months. Likewise, cyclical cementum incremental growth is visible in tropical vertebrates and cannot be ascribed to marked seasonal fluctuations (Klevezal' 1996, 93). Logically, the early hypotheses formulated to interpret these observations included the presence of a genetic component for increment formation (Grue & Jensen 1979).

Finally, age and seasonal data obtained through the analysis of incremental growth structures corroborate similar data obtained through various other morphometric methods (e.g., teeth attrition) in living specimens. In many cases, these provide more accurate and precise age estimates (Matson et al. 1993; Miller 1974; Stallibrass 1982).

Overall, the annual cementum growth cycle has been observed in control groups of known age and season of death of terrestrial (Klevezal' & Kleinenberg 1967; Lieberman 1993) and marine mammals (Klevezal' & Myrick 1984; Perrin et al. 1980; von Biela et al. 2008). Additionally, cementum has been found in fossils and extant animals outside of the mammalian phylogeny, including reptiles (Enax et al. 2013; Luan et al. 2009), ichthyosaurs (Maxwell et al. 2011), mosasaurs (LeBlanc et al. 2017), dinosaurs (García & Zurriaguz 2016), and toothed fossil birds (Dumont et al. 2016). Similarly, in humans, more than thirty-five studies of known-age individuals have been repeatedly successful in demonstrating the strongest correlation between acellular cementum increment number and chronological age (for a full summary, see Chapter 1; Naji et al. 2016; Naji & Koel-Abt 2017).

Biological Aging and the Tempo of Senescence

Today, biologists have a strong hypothesis for interpreting cyclic growth patterns. The evolutionary clock-shop model is gaining rapid empirical validation in chronobiology, even though tissue-specific molecular/physiological pathways are not fully understood yet, and intermediate mechanisms between circadian and circannual patterns may still need exploring (Bromage et al. 2016).

For cementum, the annual/seasonal periodicity has been demonstrated repeatedly in documented collections by chemical labeling studies and the most extensive cross-species empirical validation tests probably ever produced for an age indicator (Chapter 1). Also, there is some evidence that the antiquity of the thecodont tooth attachment system that includes the alveolar bone, a periodontal ligament, and cementum has been hypothesized to be a plesiomorphic shared feature of all amniotes for the past 290 million years (LeBlanc et al. 2017; Newham et al. 2020) and is thus probably under tight genetic control (Chapter 3, Chapter 4, Chapter 16).

Not knowing the precise molecular and physiological mechanisms for cementogenesis should not lead anthropologists to dismiss cementochronology entirely. This is not a failure of the method; this is simply the state of our current knowledge. Today, we cannot explain most of the adult standard anthropological aging methods we have been using for more than a century. Fundamental research and validation studies have allowed us to tease out some variables responsible for the skeletal and dental changes we observe and use to model biological age.

For example, in skeletal estimators based on the ilium's auricular surface, the sternal rib end or the cranial sutures, the "age" component is the weakest to explain observed changes. Biomechanical wear and tear are the principal components of change for the first two, and we still do not fully understand the processes for the latter. Infections (e.g., septic arthritis), mineralization defects (e.g., osteoporosis), or genetic syndromes (e.g., craniosynostosis) will also have a compounding or leading influence in any degenerative age indicator. Of course, time is correlated to these changes because it creates a longer exposure to external stimuli.

In healthy individuals, mechanical loading is the primary driver. Theoretically, an anthropologist analyzing the remains of someone who has been immobilized for several decades (e.g., in a coma) using these standard age indicators should observe no or limited articular degeneration and conclude to a very young skeletal age, whereas we have ample evidence of young adult weight lifters with significant joint damage that an anthropologist could (mis)interpret as belonging to an elderly individual. Using these degenerative changes should thus be restricted to relative comparisons in similar environmental, social, or behavioral contexts and individual frailty. Therefore, this is not a promising area of research for precise and accurate age estimations. However, we are looking forward to recent developments of the transition analysis (www.statsmachine.net/software/TA3).

Conversely, growth mechanisms are part of a strong selective process. They are reliably used for age estimations in developing humans and animals, with indicators for the youngest age categories being the most accurate and precise since the exposure to environmental insults is the shortest. Of course, external (e.g., diet, pathogens, pollutants) variables can influence growth and maturation and, ultimately, adult height, but because we observe a reasonably stable species-wide mechanism, the principal component of growth is undoubtedly genetic, not environmental.

Cementum deposition is akin to, if not entirely, a growth process. As we will see in Part I, cementum is continuously produced throughout life to ensure proper dental attachment in the alveolar bone and constant occlusion. Moreover, cementum is avascular and is not remodeled by cementoblast activity once deposited, contrary to bone.

Chapters Presentation

In this volume, we argue that cementochronology should enjoy a privileged place among hard tissue age indicators, as it is the only one identified so far with such well-defined and permanent growth characteristics. To present our arguments, we have divided the chapters into three parts that cover (i) cementum biology, (ii) protocols, and (iii) applications.

In Part I, Buikstra contextualizes the discovery of cementum (Chapter 1) and our current understanding of cementum biology (Chapters 2–5). Chapters 6 and 7 present state-of-the-art analyses of cementum ultrastructure using synchrotron x-ray fluorescence and diffraction mapping. Today, synchrotron-level energy is the only available technique to analyze the composition of individual cementum increments. Finally, in Chapter 8, we summarize the current literature on one of the most exciting research avenues in cementochronology: identifying life-history events, specifically pregnancies.

Part II presents recent advances in cementum analysis protocols and starts with a proposal for a standardized method for ungulates and new options for human samples (Chapter 9). Chapters 10 and 11 complement this approach by testing specific steps to optimize published protocols. Wedel proposes expanding cementochronology to decidual teeth (Chapter 12), and Wilson expands season-at-death estimation to human remains (Chapter 13), specifically in a forensic context, a method pioneered by Wedel in 2007. Colard (Chapter 14) offers a robust yet straightforward multi-analyses protocol to identify cementum growth variations resulting from pregnancies and potentially other life-history events or stressors. This is a welcome contribution that reinforces other potential methods (see Chapter 8 for a review). The innovative breakthrough in cementum protocols comes with the use of 3D synchrotron micro-CT reconstruction of cementum. Two independent teams are leading the way. First, Le Cabec (Chapter 15) demonstrates the potential of nondestructive imaging in human samples. Then, Newham (Chapter 16) proposes for the first time a fully automated 3D analysis package tested on various species with unparalleled precision and accuracy to estimate the age-at-death noninvasively.

Finally, Part III offers a range of cementochronology applications. Using faunal remains to estimate season at death, Rendu (Chapter 17) discusses his work on Neandertal's residential mobility patterns in southern France. In contrast, Jimenez (Chapter 18) presents original data on human and hyaena seasonal settlements in Belgium during the Late Pleistocene. Cormier (Chapter 19) offers a robust osteobiography analysis of a Middle Woodland woman with a combined skeletal dysplasia and illustrates how cementochronology is effectively used for individual age at death while severe pathologies compromise other skeletal components. Naji (Chapter 20) publishes for the first time the age-at-death distribution of a hunter-fisherman shell-midden sample in Brazil, while Lanteri (Chapter 21), using a similar methodology, tests the accuracy of cementochronology death distribution with archival data of a sixteenth- to eighteenth-century French cemetery. Finally, the last two chapters offer new options for demographic studies using cementochronology. Propst (Chapter 22) illustrates the effectiveness of cementochronology in a complex Nabataean sample from Petra, Jordan, using a Gompertz-Makeham hazard model to contrast age-specific mortality risk. Wittwer-Backofen (Chapter 23) finishes the range of application by showing how cementochronology can help shape an early medieval age-at-death distribution based on standard skeletal age indicators. In conclusion, Naji and Rendu (Chapter 24) summarize the advances made in cementum studies in the last decade or so and address some of the remaining challenges to moving forward.

We hope that this collection of chapters, written by most of the leading authors in cementochronology today, will provide the necessary context to evaluate this method and stimulate future collaborative research.

Acknowledgments

I would like to thank Jane Buikstra, Brian Foster, Adeline Le Cabec, and Aaron Stutz for their helpful comments on earlier drafts. Unless otherwise stated, all chapters have been peer-reviewed anonymously by two specialists. Supplemental online materials are available at www.cambridge.org/naji.

References

Baglinière, J.-L., Castanet, J., Conand, F., & Meunier, F. J. (1992). *Tissus Durs et Âge Individuel des Vertébrés*. Paris: ORSTOM/INRA Editions.

Baillon, N. (1992). Otolithometrie, revue et problèmes. In J.-L. Baglinière, J. Castanet, F. Conand, & F. J. Meunier eds., *Tissus Durs et Age Individuel des Vertébrés*. Paris: ORSTOM-INRA Editions, 21–52.

Ball, G. F., Alward, B. A., & Balthazart, J. (2017). Seasonal changes in brain and behavior. In V. Kumar, ed., *Biological Timekeeping: Clocks, Rhythms and Behaviour*. New Delhi: Springer India, 571–88.

Black, G. V. (1887). *A Study of the Histological Characters of the Periosteum and Peridental Membrane*. Chicago: W. T. Keener.

Bosshardt, D., Luder, H. U., & Schroeder, H. E. (1989). Rate and growth pattern of cementum apposition as compared to dentine and root formation in a fluorochrome-labeled monkey (*Macaca fascicularis*). *Journal de Biologie Buccale*, **17**(1), 3–13.

Bromage, T. G. (1991). Enamel incremental periodicity in the pig-tailed macaque: A polychrome fluorescent labelling study of dental hard tissues. *American Journal of Physical Anthropology*, **86**, 205–14.

Bromage, T. G., Idaghdour, Y., Lacruz, R. S., ... Schrenk, F. (2016). The swine plasma metabolome chronicles "many days" biological timing and functions linked to growth. *PLOS ONE*, **11**(1), e0145919.

Bromage, T. G., Juwayeyi, Y. M., Smolyar, I., Hu, B., Gomez, S., Scaringi, V. J. C., Bondalapati, P., Kaur, K., & Chisi, J. (2011). Signposts ahead: Hard tissue signals on rue Armand de Ricqlès. *Comptes Rendus Palevol*, **10**(5), 499–507.

Bromage, T. G., Lacruz, R. S., Hogg, R., ... Boyde, A. (2009). Lamellar bone is an incremental tissue reconciling enamel rhythms, body size, and organismal life history. *Calcified Tissue International*, **84**(5), 388–404.

Castanet, J. (1980). La squelettochronologie chez les vertébrés supérieurs (Mammifères et Oiseaux). *Bulletins de la Société de Zoologie Française*, **105**, 347–54.

Castanet, J., Francillon-Vieillot, H., Meunier, F. J., & Ricqlès, A. (1993). Bone and individual aging. In B. K. Hall, ed. *Bone: A Treatise*. Boca Raton, CRC Press, 245–83.

Castanet, J., Meunier, F. J., & Ricqlès, A. de. (1977). L'enregistrement de la croissance cyclique par le tissu osseux chez les vertébrés poïkilothermes: Données comparatives et essai de synthèse. *Bulletin Biologique de la France et de la Belgique*, **111**(2), 183–202.

Clerc, W. (1927). Etude de la périodicité de la croissance d'après les plans isodynamiques des os. *Revue Suisse de Zoologie*, **34**, 477–96.

Colard, T., Bertrand, B., Naji, S., Delannoy, Y., & Bécart, A. (2015). Toward the adoption of cementochronology in forensic context. *International Journal of Legal Medicine*, **129**, 1–8.

Day, G. I., & Carrel, W. K. (1986). *Aging Javelina by Tetracycline Labeling of Teeth: A Final Report*. Research Branch, Arizona Game and Fish Department.

de Buffrénil, V., & Castanet, J. (2000). Age estimation by skeletochronology in the Nile Monitor (*Varanus niloticus*), a highly exploited species. *Journal of Herpetology*, **34**, 414.

Demars, P.-Y., Le Gall, O., & Martin, H. (2007). Saisonnalité, mobilité et spécialisation des sites: Une approche polythématique. In S. A. Beaune ed. *Chasseurs-Cueilleurs: Comment Vivaient les Hommes du Paléolithique Supérieur - Méthodes d'Analyse et d'Interprétation en Préhistoire*. Paris: CNRS, 99–115.

Dean, C. (2006). Tooth microstructure tracks the pace of human life-history evolution. *Proceedings of the Royal Society B: Biological Sciences*, **273**(1603), 2799–2808.

Dean, C., Le Cabec, A., Spiers, K., Zhang, Y., & Garrevoet, J. (2018). Incremental distribution of strontium and zinc in great ape and fossil hominin cementum using synchrotron X-ray fluorescence mapping. *Journal of the Royal Society, Interface*, **15**(138). https://doi.org/10.1098/rsif.2017.0626

Dean, M. C., & Scandrett, A. E. (1996). The relation between long-period incremental markings in dentine and daily cross-striations in enamel in human teeth. *Archives of Oral Biology*, **41**(3), 233–41.

Dopico, X. C., Evangelou, M., Ferreira, R. C., . . . Todd, J. A. (2015). Widespread seasonal gene expression reveals annual differences in human immunity and physiology. *Nature Communications*, 6. https://do.org/10.1038/ncomms8000

Dumont, M., Tafforeau, P., Bertin, T., . . . Louchart, A. (2016). Synchrotron imaging of dentition provides insights into the biology of *Hesperornis* and *Ichthyornis*, the "last" toothed birds. *BMC Evolutionary Biology*, **16**(1), 178.

Dunlap, J. C., Loros, J. J., & DeCoursey, P. J. (2003). *Chronobiology: Biological Timekeeping*. Sunderland, MA: Sinauer Associates.

Enax, J., Fabritius, H.-O., Rack, A., Prymak, O., Raabe, D., & Epple, M. (2013). Characterization of crocodile teeth: Correlation of composition, microstructure, and hardness. *Journal of Structural Biology*, **184**(2), 155–63.

Foster, B. L. (2017). On the discovery of cementum. *Journal of Periodontal Research*, **52**(4), 666–85.

Foster, R. G. (2005). *Rhythms of Life: The Biological Clocks that Control the Daily Lives of Every Living Thing*. New Haven, CT: Yale University Press.

Ganguly, S., & Klein, D. C. (2017). The timezyme and melatonin: Essential elements of vertebrate timekeeping. In V. Kumar, ed., *Biological Timekeeping: Clocks, Rhythms and Behaviour*. New Delhi: Springer India, 503–20.

García, R. A., & Zurriaguz, V. (2016). Histology of teeth and tooth attachment in titanosaurs (*Dinosauria*; *Sauropoda*). *Cretaceous Research*, **57**, 248–56.

Grosskopf, B. (1996). Cementochronologie – Eine methode zur bestimmung des individualalters. *Bulletin de la Société Suisse d'Anthropologie*, **2**, 27–31.

Grue, H. (1976). Nonseasonal incremental lines in tooth cementum of domestic dogs (*Canis familiaris* L.). *Danish Review of Game Biology*, **10**(2), 1–8.

Grue, H., & Jensen, B. (1979). Review of the formation of incremental lines in tooth cementum of terrestrial mammals. *Danish Review of Game Biology*, **11**, 1–48.

Gustafson, G. (1950). Age determination of teeth. *Journal of the American Dental Association*, **41**, 45–54.

Helm, B., & Lincoln, G. A. (2017). Circannual rhythms anticipate the earth's annual periodicity. In V. Kumar, ed., *Biological Timekeeping: Clocks, Rhythms and Behaviour*. New Delhi: Springer India, 545–69.

Hemelaar, A. (1985). An improved method to estimate the number of year rings resorbed in phalanges of *Bufo bufo* (L.) and its application to populations from different latitudes and altitudes. *Amphibia-Reptilia*, **6**(4), 323–41.

Hogg, R. (2018). Permanent record: The use of dental and bone microstructure to assess life history evolution and ecology. In D. A. Croft, D. F. Su, & S. W. Simpson, eds., *Methods in Paleoecology: Reconstructing Cenozoic Terrestrial Environments and Ecological Communities*. Cham: Springer International Publishing, 75–98.

Ikegami, K., & Yoshimura, T. (2017). Molecular mechanism regulating seasonality. In V. Kumar, ed., *Biological Timekeeping: Clocks, Rhythms and Behaviour*. New Delhi: Springer India, 589–605.

Kimura, D. K. (1977). Statistical assessment of the age-length key. *Journal of Fisheries Research Board of Canada*, **34**, 317–24.

Kimura, D. K., & Chikuni, S. (1987). Mixture of empirical distributions: An iterative application of the age-length key. *Biometrics*, **43**, 23–55.

Klevezal', G. A. (1996). *Recording Structures of Mammals: Determination of Age and Reconstruction of Life History*. Rotterdam: A. A. Balkema Series.

Klevezal', G. A., & Kleinenberg, S. E. (1967). *Age Determination of Mammals from Annual Layers in Teeth and Bones*. Akademiya Nauk SSSR.

Klevezal', G. A., & Myrick, A. C. (1984). Marks in tooth dentine of female dolphins (Genus *Stenella*) as indicators of parturition. *Journal of Mammalogy*, **65**(1), 103–10.

Köhler, M., Marín-Moratalla, N., Jordana, X., & Aanes, R. (2012). Seasonal bone growth and physiology in endotherms shed light on dinosaur physiology. *Nature*, **487**(7407), 358–61.

Kumar, V. (ed.). (2017). *Biological Timekeeping: Clocks, Rhythms and Behaviour*, Springer India. https://doi.org/10.1007/978-81-322-3688-7

Laws, R. M. (1952). A new method of age determination for mammals. *Nature*, **169**, 972–73.

LeBlanc, A. R. H., Brink, K. S., Cullen, T. M., & Reisz, R. R. (2017). Evolutionary implications of tooth attachment versus tooth implantation: A case study using dinosaur, crocodilian, and mammal teeth. *Journal of Vertebrate Paleontology*, **37**(5), e1354006.

Lemmer, B. (2009). Discoveries of rhythms in human biological functions: A historical review. *Chronobiology International*, **26**(6), 1019–68.

Lieberman, D. E. (1993). Life history variables preserved in dental cementum microstructure. *Science*, **261**, 1162.

Lincoln, G. (2019). A brief history of circannual time. *Journal of Neuroendocrinology*, **31**(3), e12694.

Liu, Y. H., & Panda, S. (2017). Circadian photoentrainment mechanism in mammals. In V. Kumar, ed., *Biological Timekeeping: Clocks, Rhythms and Behaviour*. New Delhi: Springer India, 365–93.

Luan, X., Walker, C., Dangaria, S., ... Rieppel, O. (2009). The mosasaur tooth attachment apparatus as paradigm for the evolution of the gnathostome periodontium. *Evolution & Development*, **11**(3), 247–59.

Martin, M. (1995). La Chasse au post-glaciaire: Les apports de la cémentochronologie, l'exemple de deux sites pyrénéens. *Etudes et Recherches Archéologiques de l'Université de Liège*, **68**, 284–86.

Matson, G. M., & Kerr, K. D. (1998). A method for dating tetracycline biomarkers in black bear cementum. *Ursus*, **10**, 455–58.

Matson, G., Van Daele, L., Goodwin, E., Aumiller, L., Reynolds, H., & Hristienko, H. (1993). *A Laboratory Manual for Cementum Age Determination of Alaska Brown Bear PM1 Teeth*. Milltown, MT: Alaska Department of Fish and Game; Matson's Laboratory.

Maxwell, E. E., Caldwell, M. W., & Lamoureux, D. O. (2011). Tooth histology in the cretaceous ichthyosaur *Platypterygius australis* and its significance for the conservation and divergence of mineralized tooth tissues in amniotes. *Journal of Morphology*, **272**(2), 129–35.

Miller, F. L. (1974). *Biology of the Kaminuriak Population of Barren-Ground Caribou. Part 2. Dentition as an Indicator of Age and Sex; Composition and Socialization of the Population*. Ottawa, ON: Canadian Wildlife Service.

Mounaix, B. (1992). Validation by calcein injection of ageing European eel *Anguilla unguilla* in the Vilaine river (Brittany) first results. In J.-L. Baglinière, J. Castanet, F. Conand, & F. J. Meunier, eds., *Tissus Durs et Âge Individuel des Vertébrés*. Paris: ORSTOM/INRA, 109–19.

Naji, S., Colard, T., & Bertrand, B. (2013). Cementochronology. *American Journal of Physical Anthropology*, S.56, 52.

Naji, S., Colard, T., Blondiaux, J., Bertrand, B., d'Incau, E., & Bocquet-Appel, J.-P. (2016). Cementochronology, to cut or not to cut? *International Journal of Paleopathology*, **15**, 113–19.

Naji, S., & Koel-Abt, K. (2017). Cementochronology – The still underestimated old "new" method for age-at-death assessment. *Journal of Forensic Sciences & Criminal Investigation*, **3**(5), 1–5.

Naji, S., Rendu, W., & Gourichon, L. (2015). La cémentochronologie. In M. Balasse, J.-P. Brugal, Y. Dauphin, E.-M. Geigl, & C. Oberlin, eds., *Message d'Os. Archéométrie du Squelette Animal et Humain*. Paris: Editions des Archives Contemporaines, 172–90.

Newham, E., Gill, P. G., Brewer, P., Benton, M. J., Fernandez, V., Gostling, N. J., Haberthür, D., et al. (2020). Reptile-like physiology in Early Jurassic stem-mammals. *Nature Communications*, **11**(1), 5121.

Padian, K., & Lamm, E.-T. (2013). *Bone Histology of Fossil Tetrapods: Advancing Methods, Analysis, and Interpretation*. Berkeley: University of California Press.

Panda, S., Hogenesch, J. B., & Kay, S. A. (2002). Circadian rhythms from flies to humans. *Nature*, **417**. https://doi.org/10.1038/417329a

Perrin, W. F., & Myrick, A. C. (1980). *Age Determination of Toothed Whales and Sirenians: Growth of Odontocetes and Sirenians: Problems in Age Determination: Proceedings of the International Conference on Determining Age of Odontocete Cetaceans (and Sirenians), La Jolla, California, September 5–19, 1978*. Cambridge: International Whaling Commission.

Piccione, G., Giannetto, C., Casella, S., & Caola, G. (2009). Annual rhythms of some physiological parameters in *Ovis aries* and *Capra hircus*. *Biological Rhythm Research*, **40**(6), 455–64.

Reinberg, A. E., Dejardin, L., Smolensky, M. H., & Touitou, Y. (2017). Seven-day human biological rhythms: An expedition in search of their origin, synchronization, functional advantage, adaptive value and clinical relevance. *Chronobiology International*, **34**(2), 162–91.

Scheffer, V. B. (1950). Growth layer on the teeth of *Pinnipedia* as an indication of age. *Science*, **112**, 309–11.

Schwartz, W. J., & Daan, S. (2017). Origins: A brief account of the ancestry of circadian biology. In V. Kumar, ed., *Biological Timekeeping: Clocks, Rhythms and Behaviour*. New Delhi: Springer India, 3–22.

Sergeant, D. E., & Pimlott, D. H. (1959). Age determination in moose from sectioned incisor teeth. *Journal of Wildlife Management*, **23**(3), 315–21.

Stallibrass, S. (1982). The use of cement layers for absolute ageing of mammalian teeth: A selective review of the literature, with suggestions for further studies and alternative applications. In B. Wilson, C. Grigson, & S. Payne, eds., *Ageing and Sexing Animal Bones from Archaeological Sites*. Oxford: British Archaeological Report, 109–26.

Stein, T. J., & Corcoran, J. F. (1994). Pararadicular cementum deposition as a criterion for age estimation in human beings. *Oral Surgery, Oral Medicine, Oral Pathology*. **77**(3), 266–70.

Stevenson, T. J., & Lincoln, G. A. (2017). Epigenetic mechanisms regulating circannual rhythms. In V. Kumar, ed., *Biological Timekeeping: Clocks, Rhythms and Behaviour*. New Delhi: Springer India, 607–23.

Stock, S. R., Finney, L. A., Telser, A., Maxey, E., Vogt, S., & Okasinski, J. S. (2017). Cementum structure in Beluga whale teeth. *Acta Biomaterialia*, **48**, 289–99.

Stott, G. G., Sis, R. F., & Levy, B. M. (1982). Cemental annulation as an age criterion in forensic dentistry. *Journal of Dental Research*, **61**(6), 814–17.

Streeter, M. (2011). Histological age-at-death estimation. In C. Crowder & S. Stout, eds., *Bone Histology: An Anthropological Perspective*. London: CRC Press LLC, 135–52.

von Biela, V. R., Testa, J. W., Gill, V. A., & Burns, J. M. (2008). Evaluating cementum to determine past reproduction in northern sea otters. *Journal of Wildlife Management*, **72**(3), 618–24.

Wedel, V. L. (2007). Determination of season at death using dental cementum increment analysis. *Journal of Forensic Sciences*, **52**(6), 1334–37.

Weinert, D., & Waterhouse, J. (2017). Interpreting circadian rhythms. In V. Kumar, ed., *Biological Timekeeping: Clocks, Rhythms and Behaviour*. New Delhi: Springer India, 23–45.

Wittwer-Backofen, U., & Buba, H. (2002). Age estimation by tooth cementum annulation: Perspective of a new validation study. In R. D. Hoppa & J. W. Vaupel, eds., *Paleodemography, Age Distributions from Skeletal Samples*. Cambridge: Cambridge University Press, 107–28.

Woodward, H. N., Padian, K., & Andrew, L. H. (2013). Skeletochronology. In K. Padian, & E.-T. Lamm, eds., *Bone Histology of Fossil Tetrapods: Advancing Methods, Analysis, and Interpretation*. Berkeley: University of California Press, 195–215.

Zheng, L., Ehardt, L., McAlpin, B., . . . Papagerakis, P. (2014). The tick-tock of odontogenesis. *Experimental Cell Research*, **325**(2), 83–9.

Zucker, I., Lee, T. M., & Dark, J. (1991). The suprachiasmatic nucleus and rhythms of mammals. In D. Klein, S. Reppert, & R. Moore, eds., *Suprachiasmatic Nucleus: The Mind's Clock*. Oxford: Oxford University Press, 246–59.

Part I

The Biology of Cementum

1 A Brief History of Cemental Annuli Research, with Emphasis upon Anthropological Applications

Jane E. Buikstra

> While cementum, from a purely histological point of view, is the least interesting of the three calcified dental tissues, chiefly on account of the fact that its structure and functions are of a simpler character than those of enamel and dentine, and therefore do not admit of the possibility of so many unsolved problems and so much controversy.
>
> (Hopewell-Smith 1920: 59–60)

Although the authors of this volume would doubtless dispute the notion that cementum is the least interesting of the dental tissues and that there are few unsolved problems concerning its formation, Hopewell-Smith's 1920 statement clearly reflects the storied history of cementum studies prior to the twentieth century. Cementum, due to its relative invisibility, was discovered a century after tooth enamel and dentin. Famous natural philosophers and anatomists debated nomenclature and function, as well as its presence across vertebrate species. Advances in imaging technology led to nineteenth-century debates about the presence of cells and the function of cementum, although texts of the period focused upon dentin and enamel as the primary – if not exclusive – dental structures.

Even without further knowledge of proximate causes, however, during the twentieth century, cementum's apparent age-related thickness and then its regular encircling deposits attracted the attention of wildlife ecologists, followed by archaeologists and forensic scientists. Key in the history of human applications was an article by Stott et al. (1982) that stimulated considerable anthropological interest. These researchers counted light-dark bands or "annuli" in three adults more than fifty years of age and showed close correspondence between annulus count added to tooth-specific eruption and chronological age.

Though interest in Stott's approach developed, it built slowly. Histological preparation methods presented few problems, and many techniques provided satisfactory results. Methods for counting annuli proved challenging, however, leading some workers to consider age estimations using annulus counts intractable, despite mounting evidence to the contrary. A number of validation studies, reviewed here, have proved encouraging, countering concerns about inaccuracy due to factors such as periodontal disease, slowed or erratic deposition in old age, and the impact of systemic health conditions, such as diabetes and tuberculosis. Today annulus counts, termed the Tooth Cementum Annulus or TCA method since the early twenty-first century, excite cautious optimism not only for age estimation in mammals, including humans, but also for recording other life-history events relating to gestation, health, and seasonality. Complete tooth or even tooth root destruction is not necessary, and the tooth can be recorded and modeled digitally. While mysteries remain, such as the proximate causes for the annuli, focused research should provide resolution in the near term.

The present volume is, therefore, timely, an interdisciplinary stocktaking of contemporary knowledge and future promise for these long overlooked and underappreciated cementum structures. We begin our historical treatment by focusing first upon the identification of cementum as a tissue distinct from dentin and enamel, followed by considerations of cemental annuli as they became accepted as normal annular dental structures, characteristic of mammals, including humans.

1.1 History of Cementum Discovery and Early Characterizations

Although earlier observers had explored dental structures, it was not until the development of magnifying lenses that cementum was identified. As recounted first by Denton (1941) and then by Foster (2017) in their excellent reviews of the discovery and characterization of cementum from the seventeenth through the nineteenth centuries, technological advances were necessary for this minor but important component of teeth to be recognized and studied (Figure 1.1).

The Greek physician Galen (130–200), writing during the second century AD, set the tone for knowledge of the oral cavity that would only be superseded by Renaissance and Enlightenment anatomists, whose communications benefited from the earlier development of the printing press during the mid-fifteenth century. Galen appreciated that adult humans developed thirty-two teeth, which he divided into incisors, canines, and molars, contrasting the sharp and cutting anterior teeth with those suited for grinding. Comparisons with animals, such as lions, dogs, and cattle, reinforced his discussions of functional associations. He recognized variations in the

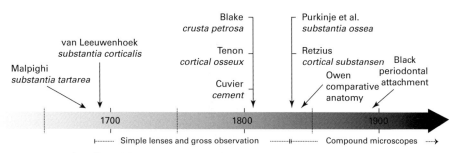

Figure 1.1 Time line of discovery of cementum discussed in detail in the text (based on data from Foster 2017: 2).

number of tooth roots, while also remarking upon "strong ligaments" that bound human teeth to the alveoli "especially at the roots" (Shklar and Brackett 2009: 26).

It was not until the mid-sixteenth century that anatomists added significant anatomical knowledge of the oral cavity. Among the most well-known was Andreas Vesalius (1514–1564), whose publication in 1543, *De humani corporis fabrica* contained an eleventh chapter of Book One, titled, *De Dentibus, qui etiam ossium numero ascribuntur*, translating to "On the Teeth, Which Are Also Counted as Bones" (Hast and Garrison 1995) or "On the Teeth, which are also included in the number of the bones" (Saunders and O'Mally 1944). Within this essay, he followed Galen's discussion of tooth numbers and variability in crown shape and numbers of roots (Figure 1.2A), although, in general, *De humani corporis fabrica* was designed to address many of the errors Vesalius perceived in Galen's work. Vesalius also perpetuated the interpretation of deciduous teeth exfoliating their "appendages," or crowns, while retaining the roots, upon which the permanent crowns would develop. Comparisons to the structure of bone also anchored his interpretations. Importantly, he described and illustrated the pulp cavity of a tooth, giving lie to the assumption that teeth are solid structures. Vesalius said that this cavity functioned to make the teeth lighter in weight and facilitated the delivery of nourishment (Hast and Garrison 1995).

Vesalius' contemporary and protagonist, Bartolomeo Eustachio (1520–1574), in his 1563 *Libellus de Dentibus* (Figure 1.2B), clearly illustrated and distinguished enamel and dentin, comparing these two components to the bark of a tree and its softer, more vulnerable inner portion (Bennett 2009; Trenouth 2014). Eustachio also corrected Vesalius' interpretations of the development of the "milk" dentition. He is credited with the detailed study of the dental pulp cavity and the periodontal ligament (Bennet 2009; Shklar and Chernin 2000). In chapter 4 (of thirty) in his treatise on the dentition, he notes that "there are extremely strong fibers attached to the roots, which provide a firm connection to the socket" (Shklar and Chernin 2000: 28). Thus, careful macroscopic observations had identified enamel, dentin, and the periodontal ligament. Microscopy and then histology would be required to establish the nature of cementum.

Marcello Malpighi (1628–1694) is cited for the first formal recognition of cementum (Denton 1941; Foster 2017). Employing a single-lens microscope, he observed a "substantia tartarea," covering the human tooth root (Figure 1.2C), distinct from the "substantia filamentosa," which he said enveloped the upper part of the tooth. His characterization is thought to date to approximately 1667, although published posthumously in 1700. A less clear, but possible seventeenth-century recognition of the cementum layer in a calf was termed "substantia corticalis" by the Dutch draper, Antoni Van Leeuwenhoek (1632–1723), whose observations were also aided by the simple magnifiers that he helped develop (Foster 2017; van Zuylen 1981).

Discoveries of cemental structures in nonhuman mammals have helped stimulate knowledge development of human cementum. For example, more than a century later, physician Robert Blake (1772–1822) identified a "crusta petrosa" covering the roots of

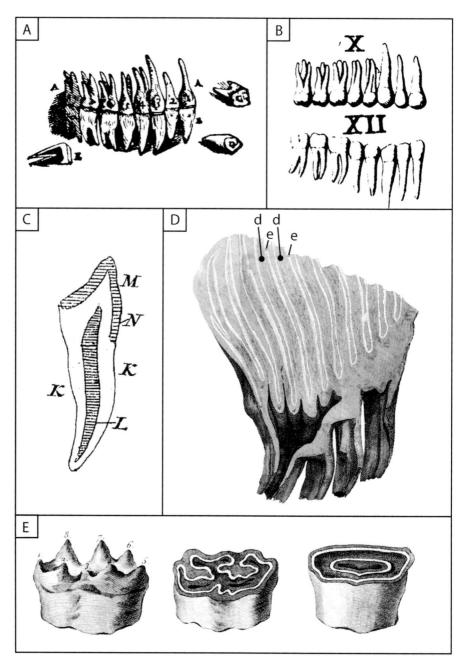

Figure 1.2 Discovery of cementum in the seventeenth to eighteenth centuries. (A) Diagram of the human dentition, including teeth in cross-section, by Andreas Vesalius (Vesalius, 1543). (B) Illustration of the human dentition from the *Libellus de Dentibus* (Eustachio, 1563). (C) Diagram of a human tooth by Marcello Malpighi (Malpighi, 1700; table 2, figure 4 from his *Opera Posthuma* – (M) *substantia filamentosa* = crown enamel; (K) *substantia tartarea* = cementum). (D) Elephant molar section by Robert Blake, showing the complex folded crown and root – (d) "bony part of the tooth" = dentin; (e) the cortex striatus = enamel; the *crusta petrosa* (cementum)

herbivorous mammals such as elephants and horses (Figure 1.2D), being especially thick in an elderly equid. Blake's 1798 thesis in Latin at the University of Edinburgh and its 1801 translation provided an overview of dental structure in humans and other animals (Trenouth 2014). Blake did mention this hardened layer in association with hypercementosis in a single human tooth, but he did not readily generalize his observations from grazers to humans. Cementum in equids was also recognized by Jacques Rene Tenon (1724–1816), a French surgeon and pathologist whose "cortical osseux" was indeed a specialized dental layer (Figure 1.2E). The term "cement," a precursor to "cementum," was coined by the eminent comparative anatomist Georges Cuvier (1769–1832) to reference the substance uniting the plates of elephant teeth. He recognized the presence of cement in many species but erred in arguing that the substance lacked a recognizable structure (Foster 2017).

Although most eighteenth-century researchers failed to identify cementum on human teeth, an exception was the dentistry text of Carl Joseph von Ringelmann (1776–1854), published in 1824. Ringelmann, a practitioner, argued that the "horny substance" previously reported by Blake and others as a pathological condition associated with tooth roots was instead ubiquitous across the human species (Foster 2017).

During the nineteenth century, the creation of compound microscopes facilitated observations of cementum details. The Czech anatomist Jan Purkinje (1787–1869) reported a "substantia ossea" as regularly present on human teeth, represented in the drawings of his student, Meyer Fränkel (1835), as laminated but otherwise unstructured (Figure 1.3). Anders Retzius (1796–1870) described a "cortical substansen" (1837) covering the human tooth root in greater detail, including its greater thickness at the apex and its increased thickness with age.

It was the extensive comparative studies of the British naturalist and paleontologist Richard Owen (1804–1892) that truly established the vertebrate patterning for "ciment," Cuvier's term that Owen embraced. Owen clearly recognized parallels between cementum and bone development, though the relationship between cementum and ligaments attaching the tooth to alveolus was not defined. His detailed volume, *Odontography*, compiled between 1840 and 1845, represented a monumental treatment of teeth across living and fossil vertebrates. In this, he coined the term dentine (Trenouth 2014).

A further contribution by American practitioner and researcher Greene Vardiman (G. V.) Black (1836–1915) established the nature of the periodontium, including

Caption for Figure 1.2 (cont.)

fills the space between adjacent enamel plates (Blake, 1798). (E) Diagrams of horse molars and incisor by Jacques Tenon, indicating the layers of cortical osseux (cementum; shaded area), enamel (whitish layers), and dentin (cross-hatched layers) (Tenon, 1797). Leftmost image indicates a lower third molar upon eruption, with cementum-covered cusps intact, while the middle image indicates the same tooth after attrition, revealing the complex layers. Right image indicates similar tissue layering in the incisor tooth (based on data from Foster 2017).

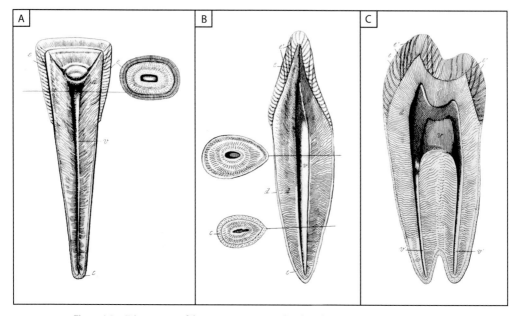

Figure 1.3 Discovery of human cementum in the nineteenth century. (A) Diagram of a longitudinal coronal section of a middle lower incisor by Fränkel (1835) showing dentin (d), enamel (e), and thin *substantia ossea* (acellular cementum) covering the root (c). Transverse cross-section shows the tissues of the crown. (B) Another section of an incisor (with a more sagittal orientation) by Fränkel shows another view of the *substantia ossea* (cementum) distribution, including two cross-sections through the root. (C) Longitudinal section of a lower premolar by Fränkel showing substantia ossea (cementum). Fränkel denotes the presence of *osseous corpuscula* (cementocytes) by dots within the *substantia ossea* (based on data from Foster 2017).

cementum, periodontal ligament, alveolus, gingiva, and supporting vessels and nerves (Garant 1995). The lamellar nature of cementum was established, along with parallels and distinctions between bone-forming and cementum-forming cells (Figure 1.4). Moreover, the alternating deposits of lamellae and incremental lines of the cementum were identified (Black 1887: 105–6).

Thus, by the twentieth century, cementum had been established as a fundamental part of the dental apparatus in vertebrates, with lamellar structure identified in humans and other mammals. The least visible of the three hard dental tissues, it presented cellular and acellular structure, the former more obvious in the thicker apical portion than in the thinned portion near the cervix. It was also intimately linked to the periodontal ligament. Many observations of cementum in humans developed following observations in other species. Most researchers emphasized inter individual variation in the development of cementum within human cohorts, Black's "utmost irregularity" (1887: 106). It would take a considerable part of the twentieth century for this argument to be countered, first by simply measuring cementum thickness across the human life span and also by incorporating comparative mammalian studies into annulus formation models.

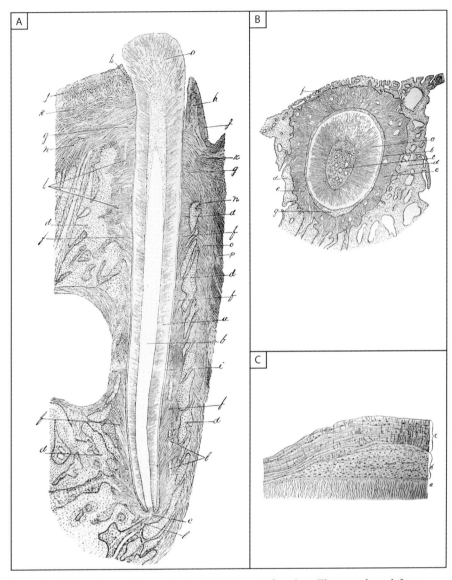

Figure 1.4 Elaboration of the periodontal attachment function. Figures adapted from G. V. Black's *A Study of the Histological Characters of the Periosteum and Peridental Membrane* (1887). (A) Section of a small incisor from a kitten showing the relationship of the tooth to the surrounding periodontia, including detailed depiction of the PDL and alveolar bone. Black noted this tooth was in total only 1/4-inch long. (B) Cross-section of a human incisor tooth illustrating the PDL fibers radiating from the tooth root cementum to the surrounding alveolar bone. (C) Cementum hypertrophy in the cellular cementum of a premolar tooth. Black noted that only the first cementum lamella appeared unusual (labeled by the author as b), while subsequent lamellae (c) presented normal thickness (based on data from Foster 2017).

1.2 Early Twentieth Century Knowledge of Cementum: 1900–1982

Correlation of Cemental Thickness with Age in Humans

By the beginning of the twentieth century, the basic anatomical structure of the tooth was known. Cementum had been described as cellular and acellular, encasing the tooth root, sometimes overlaying enamel at the cervix, linked to fibers that anchored the tooth to the crown, and more obvious in other mammals than in humans. For our purposes, the early observations made by Magitot (1878) and Black (1887) concerning the increasing thickness of cementum with age in humans were of special significance. This age-related pattern in humans was accepted by many other workers during the final years of the nineteenth and the first half of the twentieth centuries, e.g., Broomell (1898), Gottlieb (1943), Kronfeld (1938), and Stillson (1917).

Alternative positions also persisted into the twentieth century, with researchers such as Hopewell-Smith (1920: 64) maintaining that normal cementum was acellular and lacked "histological pattern or design." Even Hopewell-Smith, however, accepted the premise that cementum thickened with age but argued that bounding incremental lines were abnormal and not to be found in "perfectly formed tissue" (Hopewell-Smith 1920: 66).

Skeptics such as Weibusch (1957) persisted in arguing that the deposition of cementum was atypical. In response, Zander and Hürzeler (1958: 1035) developed one of the more rigorous quantifications of the relationship between cementum thickness and age in humans.

Zander and Hürzeler (1958) employed 233 single-rooted healthy teeth from individuals ages eleven to seventy-six. Decalcified and embedded in celloidin, the teeth were sectioned horizontally at eighty microns and stained with hematoxylin and eosin. Sections magnified twenty-five times via an overhead projector microscope were traced on file-folder paper, cut out, weighed, and measured. These observations, facing the methodological issues of characterizing the cementum, used a novel method that facilitated statistical treatment. The authors concluded that their results "showed a straight-line relationship between age and cementum thickness." The thickness of cementum was approximately tripled between the ages of eleven and seventy-six years. This rate was not the same for every area of the root. Cementum accrual was less near the cement-enamel junction and greater in the apical area (Zander and Hürzeler 1958: 1043).

Arguments also developed over the degree to which cementum thickness was a response to biomechanical stressors or associated with oral disease. Azaz and colleagues (1974), by studying cementum thickness in sixty impacted canines and premolars, observed cemental thickening with age in healthy teeth that were not biomechanically stressed, further reinforcing a relationship between cementum thickness and age.

Though it was generally accepted that cementum was thicker in older ages than in youth, the first attempt to explicitly use cementum thickness in estimating age was that of Gustafson (1950), who incorporated a four-stage gradation of cementum thickness (normal, slightly greater than normal, great, and heavy) as viewed in section within the apical portion. Noting that grading cementum was especially "difficult" (Gustafson 1950: 48), Gustafson summed across the six variables (attrition, secondary dentin, periodontosis, cementum apposition, root resorption, and root transparency), calibrated in terms of nineteen teeth from individuals of known age. He reported a standard error of 3.63 years. While each of these features has been critically evaluated and reservations expressed (e.g., Dalitz 1962), Gustafson's study remains a landmark effort, upon which other methods of forensic and bioarchaeological age estimation have been based.

Wildlife and Zoo Studies of Cementum Annulation

As in earlier centuries, twentieth-century studies of cementum were informed significantly by comparative studies of other vertebrates, especially mammals. Beginning at mid-century, a number of studies of marine and terrestrial mammals, including various species of pinnipeds, focused upon a hypothesized relationship between age and annulus counts.

Although the earliest studies of seals focused upon root dentine (Scheffer 1950; Laws 1952), cementum layers were soon added to the mix as it became clear that dentine development does not extend into older adult age groups for these marine mammals. Studies focused on large ungulates such as the moose (Sergeant and Pimlott 1959), red deer (Mitchell 1963; Keiss 1969), reindeer (McEwan 1963; Low and Cowan 1963), white-tailed deer (Ransom 1966; Gilbert 1966), mule deer (Erikson Seliger 1969), and bison (Novakowski 1965), all first synthesized by Klevezal' and Kleinenberg (1967, 1969).

Studies were designed to address age-at-death, reproductive status, growth and weight by age, and related issues. Periodicity was assumed to be related to factors such as migration and periods of fasting. Periods of fasting, hibernation, and migration were also hypothesized causes for terrestrial mammal cemental annuli, as well as seasonal rainfall.

By the end of the 1960s, many of these studies experienced validation problems, in that age-at-death or tooth extraction were not known but estimated through other means. Reference collections started to be built along with standardization of analyses (Saxon and Higham 1968; Klevezal' and Kleinenberg 1969; Morris 1972), which also prompted the first fossil implementation on Neolithic samples (Saxon and Higham 1969).

Several researchers who focused upon African animals reported line doubling (two lines per year), which they attributed to bimodal rainfall in the equatorial zone for buffalo, waterbuck, and two species of gazelle (Spinage 1973; Spinage 1976a, b). However, examples of doubling in animals such as greater kudu and bushbuck from unimodal rainfall areas suggested that the simple argument linking line doubling with rainfall patterning lacked explanatory power. Spinage's (1976b) results from a study of twenty-two buffalo first incisors, along with a miscellany of other teeth from areas with unimodal annual rainfall, generally supported the formation of one line per year.

Methodological issues were raised in recognition of doubling and a need for further controlled research endorsed (Spinage 1976b).

The range of species rapidly expanded in the next two decades to maritime mammals (Kasuya 1976, 1977; Kasuya and Matsui 1984); insectivores, such as the hedgehog, the mole, or the bat (Grue and Jensen 1979); and rodents, such as the beaver, ground squirrel, rats, mice, porcupines, rats, rabbits, and voles (summarized in Klevezal' 1996).

This development led to the first archaeological study on prehistoric hunting strategies in France (Spiess 1976). However, the protocol did not include embedding the teeth and was thus not suitable for archaeological remains. Stallibrass (1982) was the first to propose a dedicated method for ancient remains with resin embedding and polarized microscopy.

By the time of Stott et al.'s seminal publication (1982: 814), a range of animals had been studied, including bear, caribou, moose, elk, deer, bison, red fox, coyote, otter, squirrel, and two species of primates – one an Old World macaque and the other a marmoset from the Americas. Additional New World primates representing two species of *Saguinus* were reported by Yoneda (1982), who associated dark bands with possible environmental and endogenous factors, the former including the beginning of the rainy season and the latter being the coincident breeding season. Today, more than seventy-two species of terrestrial and maritime mammals across twenty-one families, and nine orders have been successfully documented.

Uncertainty concerning the proximate cause(s) for line formation has continued into the twenty-first century.

Late Twentieth- and Twenty-First Century Knowledge of Cementum Annuli and the Development of Dental Cementum Analysis

At the cusp of the twenty-first century, an authoritative review of contemporary knowledge about cementum was published in *Periodontology* (Bosshardt and Selvig 1997). We refer the reader to Foster et al. (Chapter 2) for a detailed summary of cementum biology and function. Thus, at this point in time, the anatomy of cementum was largely known, although the causes of annulus formation remained speculative. Comparative studies had suggested circannual season cycles of sunlight, nutrition, and related environmental factors (Introduction). Even without knowledge of proximate causes, the ultimate cause of annulus formation appeared securely tied to yearly cycles in humans, as in other mammals.

We now turn our focus to these annuli and their ability to monitor time and life histories in humans, as explored during the final decades of the twentieth century and the early portion of the twenty-first century.

Countable cemental annulations are present in human teeth. Cross-sections through undecalcified tooth roots can be properly stained and mounted so that cemental annulations can be photographed through a light microscope. Annulations counted from a photograph provide a close estimate of the actual age of the individual from which the tooth was extracted. This technique may be extremely valuable in forensic medicine, forensic dentistry, and anthropology. (Stott et al. 1982: 816)

The highly influential paper by Stott et al. (1982) stimulated considerable interest in using cemental annulus counts to estimate age-at-death in humans from medico-legal and archaeological contexts. Stott and colleagues, explicitly influenced by the annulus studies of pinnipeds and terrestrial mammals, demonstrated that annulus counts in teeth from three human beings, all in excess of fifty years of age (fifty-seven, sixty-seven, and seventy-six), could be used to estimate age-at-death when counts were added to age at eruption. In a detailed and systematic statement, they described the use of undecalcified, stained, transverse 100–150 μm tooth sections. Thus, they presented readily replicable methods for achieving impressive results for individuals more than fifty years of age, addressing the persistent problem of estimating age-at-death in human remains, whether from archaeological or medico-legal contexts.

Influenced by Stott et al. (1982), as well as the many mammal studies, Naylor and colleagues (1985: 197) presented a method designed to "develop a rapid, controlled technique to enhance and distinguish human cemental annulations with a significant degree of repeatability." Using single-rooted teeth extracted in blocks from cadavers, the authors removed a section 15 to 45 percent of the distance from the root apex to the neck. The most desirable section thickness, they said, was 100 microns, and etched undecalcified sections were preferred for a very practical reason. "Decalcification may require days or weeks depending on the solutions used and if not watched closely may dissolve the entire tooth resulting in complete loss of what may be an irreplaceable specimen" (Naylor et al. 1985: 198, 200). Stains recommended were, first, 0.1 percent cresyl fast (etch) violet in 70 percent alcohol for three minutes, with a second choice being a 5 percent toluidine blue in 70 percent alcohol for forty-five seconds. The authors recommended photomicrographs of the mounted sections, followed by photographic enlargements.

Validation Studies 1986–2001

Naylor's method had presented a refinement of Stott et al.'s protocol, which appeared to anticipate an orderly progression toward acceptance of TCA as an accurate method for estimating age-at-death in human skeletal remains. Further validation tests would be needed, of course, and these followed, with somewhat contradictory results. Table 1.1 summarizes key elements of TCA methodologies and results as they developed during the final decades of the twentieth century and the early portion of the twenty-first century. These tables extend and update earlier versions by Wittwer-Backofen and Buba (2002) and Naji et al. (2016).

Two linked studies directly stimulated by Stott et al. (1982) were explicitly designed to explore methodological best practices and accuracy (Charles et al. 1986; Condon et al. 1986). Our research team collected a relatively large sample of known age teeth from Midwestern US clinical and cadaver contexts. Canines and premolars were chosen from among single-rooted teeth due to availability, with a usable sample from approximately seventy individuals, with numbers varying by test. Both mineralized and demineralized sections were considered. The middle third of the tooth was chosen because of visualization difficulties nearer the crown due to thinned annuli and the obscuring effects of cellular remnants and resorption spaces nearer the apex. This

Table 1.1 List of validation studies. Column abbreviations: (1) S: single-rooted; all*: except M3; I: incisor; C: canine; P: premolar; M: molar; (2) 1. outlier; 2. no visible line; 3. poor quality; 4. fractured; 5. taphonomy; 6. ROI not suitable; (3) T: transverse; L: longitudinal; (4) M: middle 1/3; C: coronal 1/3; A: apical.

	Reference			Sample characteristics				
Authors	Year	Teeth[1]	N. Teeth	N. Subjects	N. Eliminated	Reason[2]	Age Range	Pathology
Aggarwal et al.	2008	All	30	20			13–69	Y
Avadhani et al.	2009		25	25	6	6	~16–73	N
Bertrand et al.	2018	C	200	200				N
Blondiaux et al.	2006		112	76			~12–85	
Bojarun et al.	2003		227	178			~11–78	N
Broucker et al.	2016	all	41	18	6	2;4;5	34–78	Y
Caplazi	2004	P	49	49	1	1	16–60	Both
Colard et al.	2015	I,C	9	9			35–76	N
Condon et al.	1986	C,P	73	80	7	1;2	~11–70	Both
Dias et al.	2010		55	42	24	6	17–77	Both
Gowda et al.	2014	P	15	15			20–60	
Grosskopf	1990	all	36	36	4	1	~11–45	Both
Gupta et al.	2014	all	100	100			25–60	Both
Jankauskas et al.	2001	all	51	49	8	1	~10–69	
Joshi et al.	2010		30	30	5	6	20–70	Both
Kagerer & Grupe	2001a,b	all	80	80			Avg = 57.5	N
Kasetty et al.	2010	I,C,P	200	200			17–60	Both
Kaur et al.	2015	all	60	60			Avg = 42.8	Both
Kvaal & Solheim	1995	C,P	95	95			13–89	Both
Lipsinic et al.	1986	P	31	31	1	1	~11–60	N
Lucas & Loh	1986	I,C,P	45	41			~11–80	?
Meinl et al.	2008	S	67	37			20–91	N
Miller et al.	1988	S	100	100	29	3	~10–78	
Padavala and Gheena	2015	all	20	20	4	2	32–72	Both
Pilloud	2004	P	42	24	8	3	21–90	N
Pundir et al.	2009	S	52	40	12	4	22–67	Y
Rao & Rao	1988	all*	15	15			14–56	N
Ristova et al.	2106	S	11	15	4	2;4	55–76	Y
Sousa et al.	1999	all	17	17			23–77	Both
Stein & Corcoran	1994	I,P	52	42			27–84	Y
Stott et al.	1982	all	3	3			57–76	
Shruthi et al.	2015	S	150	150			15–75	N
Swetha et al.	2018	I,C	80	80			22–60	Y
Wittwer-Backofen & Buba	2002	S	42	42			17–81	Both
Wittwer-Backofen et al.	2004	S	433	211	70	3;6	~10–96	Both

Table 1.1 (cont.)

	Thin-section preparation				Microscopy				Results		
Decal-cified	Cut[3]	Region[4]	Width (μm)	Multi. cuts	Light	Zoom	View mode	Multi. obs.	r max.	r min.	Accuracy
No	L	A;M		No	P;BF		Software	Yes	0.95		
No	Both	M		No	BF	×5	Enlarged	Yes	0.95		~2–3
No	T	M	100	Yes	BF	×200–400	Software		0.93		
No	T	all	80–100	Yes	BF	×20	Software	Yes	0.88		Avg = 4.29
No	T		33–35	Yes		×20–40	Software	Yes	0.95		5.58; 3.71 <50/X/7.86>50
No	T	A;M	100	Yes	BF	×200	Software		0.92	0.62	Avg = 2–3
No	T	A;M	60–100	Yes	Ph	×100–400	Projected		0.89	0.75	
No	T	M	100	Yes	P; BF	×400	Software	Yes	0.96		2.3–6.0
Yes	L		7	No	BF	×400	Projected	No	0.95	0.73	SE = 9.7/7.4; 4.7/9.4
No	T	M	30	No			Software	Yes	0.74	0.06	Avg = 9.7/1.6/22.6
No	T	M		?	Ph	×100	Software		0.97		
No	T	M;C	100	Yes	Ph	×200	Photo		0.84	0.75	Avg = 3.23/2.31
No	L	A;M		No			Software		0.99		
No	T	A	35–100	Yes	BF		Binoculars	Yes	0.88		Avg = 6.46
No	L	M		No			Photo		0.73	0.4	
No	T	C; M	70	Yes			Software	Yes			Avg 5.7/3.9
No	L		100	No	P	×100	Software	Yes	0.42		Predication ±12
No	L	M			P;BF;Ph		Photo		0.99	0.35	
Yes	L	all	5–7	Yes	Fl		Software	Yes	0.84	0.74	
Yes	T	M	5	Yes	BF	×100		Yes	0.93	0.51	SE = 8; 2.2 <30/8.5>30
No	T	M	≤150	No		×100–400		Yes	0.45		
No	T	M	90–100	Yes			Software	No	0.92		Avg = 6.9
No	T	M	350	Yes		×90	Projected	Yes			85% > ±10
No	L	A;M		No	P		Software		-0.015		
No	T	A;M	60–80	Yes	Ph	×100	Software		0.85	0.03	57–90 = 12.7 / 57–77= 8
No	L	A;M	80	Yes	P;BF;Ph		Software	Yes	0.98		
No	L	A;M	4–5	No	BF	×400	Screen	Yes	0.99		14/15 (93% between ±1–2)
No	L	all		No	SEM		SEM	Yes	0.95		±4%
both	T	M	100	Yes			Photo		0.97		
No	L		500	No		×100	Photo		0.98	0.93	
No	T	C;M	100–150	Yes	BF		Photo		0.998		
No	L	A;M	150	No	BF				0.98		3.6
No	L	C;M	80		Ph	×200	Software		0.96		2.6
No	T	M	70–80	Yes	BF	×400–500	Software	Yes	0.94		
No	T	M	70–80	Yes	BF		Software		0.98	0.97	2.5

Table 1.1 (cont.)

S: single-rooted	1. outlier	T: transverse	M: middle 1/3
all*: except M3	2. no visible line	L: longitudinal	C: coronal 1/3
I: incisor	3. poor quality		A: apical 1/3
C: canine	4. fractured		
P: premolar	5. taphonomy		
M: molar	6. ROI not suitable		

portion of the tooth continues to be preferred in TCA studies today (Naji et al. 2016). The Charles et al. (1986) paper concluded that repeatability was significantly greater than in other macroscopic methods, that demineralized sections of premolars performed best, and that efficiency was increased most by counting multiple sections and then by increasing observers. Demineralized sections, while performing well in validations tests, are generally considered less desirable than mineralized sections, due to the fragile nature of archaeologically recovered remains, as Naylor et al. (1985) had emphasized.

In a companion paper, Condon et al. (1986) explicitly considered accuracy. Using approximately the same sample, the researchers reported an r of 0.78 for the total sample ($N = 73$) and 0.86 for fifty-five individuals with no evidence of periodontal disease. Error estimates averaged 6.0 years, with notable sex differences ($M = 9.7$ and $F = 4.7$). Individuals with anomalous doubling (9 percent) and absence of lines (4 percent) were also noted. The authors concluded (Condon et al. 1986: 329) that the cemental annulation method "compares favorably with the summary age technique of Lovejoy et al. (1985) and is superior to any single macroscopic technique reported to date."

Two other studies published the same year, along with Miller et al. (1988), set a more pessimistic tone, however. Lucas and Loh (1986: 386), based upon a Pearson's r of 0.45, the difficulty in reading lines, and low inter-observer concordance, reported that the "accuracy of the use of cement lines to estimate age is unconfirmed." They also argued that annual cementum layers should not be anticipated in humans, even when documented in other mammals, as humans were buffered from the environmental stressors associated with seasonal dietary changes and migrations. Lucas and Loh's (1986) figure 1.2 shows that only four estimates fell above expected values for age-at-death in documented individuals, while the remainder is below. Lucas and Loh's (1986) figure 1 indicates that one of their problems involved the obscuring effects of cellular cementum. The systematic undercounting of this brief report from Singapore is therefore not surprising.

Lipsinic and colleague's (1986) research reported a sample of thirty-one, with an r of 0.84 after an outlier was removed. The r for individuals younger than thirty was 0.93 while, without the outlier, the r statistic for the older group was 0.64, again signaling significant undercounting of lines in sections from older individuals. Even with what some might conclude were encouraging results, the authors (Lipsinic et al. 1986: 988) asserted that TCA, due to systematic underprediction, was "not a reliable prediction method for humans."

Although undercounting appears not to have been a problem for Miller and colleagues (1988), the fact that nearly a third of their sample of 100 individuals were eliminated due to unreadable images suggests that a combination of section thickness

(350 μm) and observer inexperience may have influenced their remarkably inaccurate results, as 85 percent of the observable images produced counts that departed from the known ages by ten years or more.

The authors of subsequent twentieth-century studies (Rao and Rao 1988; Grosskopf 1990; Stein and Corcoran 1994; and Sousa et al. 1999) generally voiced more optimism about the TCA method. Grosskopf (1990) advocated for TCA in both unburned and incinerated teeth. Issues of accuracy in older age groups and diseased teeth were voiced by Kvaal and Solheim (1995), with doubling mentioned by Grosskopf (1990) and Stein and Corcoran (1994). In general, when outliers or individuals without visible lines are removed, these studies report r values of 0.84 and 0.99. Writing of research conducted late in the twentieth century, Jankauskas and colleagues (2001) reported an r of 0.88 for a clinical sample, also using a largely identified Stalin-era mass grave to evaluate TCA against macroscopic indicators such as Nemeskéri's "combined" method, endocranial suture ossification, and pubic symphysial changes (Garmus 1996). Though Condon and colleagues (1986) had concluded that TCA was as accurate as Lovejoy's summary age method and better than any single morphoscopic method, Jankauskas concluded that Nemeskéri's combined method was the best, the pubic symphysis method the worst, with TCA being intermediate. They further argued that TCA was useful as an independent test of macroscopic techniques and should be the method of choice for fragmentary materials.

Thus, by the turn of the twenty-first century, there was cautious optimism upon the part of a few workers concerning the utility of TCA for archaeological and forensic applications. Most focused on single-rooted teeth, although molars had been utilized. Third molars were difficult, due to frequent root fusion. While both longitudinal and transverse sections provided readable images, the middle portion of the root and to a lesser extent the coronal segment, above the cellular apical portion, were preferred in both sections. Unresolved issues continued to be debated: (1) Were the lines annual events and, if so, why? (2) Can we reliably count lines in older individuals, given knowledge of decreased cementum production in individuals older than approximately fifty years of age (Kvaal and Solheim 1995)? (3) What about the influence of sex? (4) Are lines formed predictably, without resorption, in diseased teeth? and (5) How do we identify "outliers" when dealing with samples of unknown age? These were key issues carried into the twenty-first century. Obviously, while creating readable sections remained challenging, with thicknesses varying between 5 and 500 μm, most agreed that creating undecalcified sections was more facile and less likely to damage fragile teeth. One great problem remained: how best to read the sections? From personal experience with the 1986 project, I can say that it takes training and experience to count annuli. Without multiple observers, multiple observations, and preferably multiple sections, the TCA method is unlikely to achieve its full potential. A further issue with these (and more recent) validation studies is the lack of systematic reporting of key variables that facilitates an evaluation of best practices. Many studies systematically report the number of observers, if not their experience. Such information is vital for a developing methodology.

1.3 Twenty-First Century Teeth Cementum Annulations

The Rostock Paleodemography Workshops (Hoppa and Vaupel 2002) focused attention upon many fundamental matters, including the need for methodologically and statistically rigorous approaches to estimating age-at-death for individual skeletons. Wittwer-Backofen and Buba (2002) presented the TCA method as maybe one of the "best and most reliable" age estimators (Wittwer-Backofen and Buba 2002: 107). In an attempt to review progress and define unresolved issues, Wittwer-Backofen and Buba posed the following questions:

> What methods produce the best results and are time-efficient and cost-effective?
> How can reproducible estimates by image analysis techniques be established?
> How can images be enhanced to improve results?
> How many observers are necessary to produce reliable results?
> How many counts are necessary to produce reliable results?
> Does periodontal reduction influence the TCA and, if so, to what extent?
> Can we calculate missing incremental lines by the amount of periodontal reduction?
> Does tooth type affect TCA age estimation?
> Do all teeth produce the same quality of results?
> Is there intra-individual variability between different teeth?
> How can confidence intervals be calculated properly?
> (Wittwer-Backofen and Buba 2002: 115)

Although the twenty-first century TCA studies summarized in Table 1.1 address many of these issues and, in general, are more supportive of the method, it appears that a clear consensus methodology was not developing. We will return to this issue.

Most of the equivocal twenty-first-century studies (Dias et al. 2010, Kasetty et al. 2010; Padavala and Gheena 2015; Pilloud 2004) do identify subsets, frequently the young and healthy, wherein the TCA works well. While several studies express concern about diseased teeth (Condon et al. 1986; Kagerer and Grupe 2001a; Dias et al. 2010), especially those from individuals suffering from periodontal disease, a number of these recent investigations find that periodontal disease did not significantly affect results (Aggarwal et al. 2008; de Broucker et al. 2016; Pundir et al. 2009; Ristova et al. 2018; Wittwer-Backofen et al. 2004). Age is voiced as a problem in several studies (Bojarun et al. 2003; Dias et al. 2010; Gupta 2014; Meinl et al. 2008; Pilloud 2004; Shruthi et al. 2015) associated with inferences of decreased deposition in older individuals (>50–55). Other studies reported positive results across the age span (Aggarwal et al. 2008; Pundir et al. 2009; Wittwer-Bachofen et al. 2004). Caplazi (2004), as with Condon et al. (1986), reports increased accuracy for females, though Caplazi's results are not statistically significant. Distinctive, enhanced bands perhaps associated with periods of pregnancy in females have been reported (Caplazi 2004; Kagerer and Grupe 2001b; Dean et al. 2018; Chapter 8), which could potentially explain the increased readability of lines in some skeletal series and not others. Until we know the true proximate cause of the line formation, we can report correlations with known life-history events, such as pregnancies, diseases such as tuberculosis (Blondiaux et al. 2006) and diabetes (Dias et al. 2010), and season of death (Klevezal' and Shishlina 2001; see Wedel and Wescott 2016 for an archaeological case study, and Chapter 13), but applications in unknown contexts must remain speculative. Comparative nonhuman mammal studies, such as those by Klevezal'

(1996) and Grue and Jensen (1979), will continue to provide important complementary data for those studying the human condition.

The most impactful methodological advance during the twenty-first century stems from digital technologies in real-time microscopic image recording, enhancement, and software processing (Wittwer-Backofen et al., 2004: 126). As someone who recalls the considerable eye strain of those "former studies," I can appreciate the manner in which the ability to digitally enlarge and enhance images will increase the ease and accuracy of TCA methods. Researchers have experimented with semiautomated (Klauenberg and Lagona 2007) and automated (Czermak et al. 2011) systems, which, while promising, are not yet beyond experimental stages (Chapters 15 and 16).

Several twenty-first-century authors have attempted to develop a system for estimating line numbers based upon the width of cementum and the measurement of one or a few obvious light-dark bands (Aggarwal et al. 2008; Gowda et al. 2014; Ristova et al. 2018; Struthi et al. 2015) with promising results. Such an adaptation needs to be sensitive to decreasing cementum deposition and, therefore, bandwidth with age. Therefore, the choice of a youthful band or bands will lead to age underestimation for individuals more than approximately fifty to fifty-five years of age. More knowledge of the pattern of decrease is necessary. If, for example, bands begin to decrease gradually to approximately fifty, a sampling of band width in the middle of the post-fifty unit would appear optimal. If there is a clear dichotomy, the sampling anywhere in the post-fifty unit would be satisfactory. If semiautomatic or automatic methods are to be used, then perhaps an inflection point in bandwidth can be identified digitally.

Other methodological issues include the type of microscope used for viewing images, with experimental evidence that phase contract outperforms polarized and light microscopes (Joshi et al. 2010; Kaur et al. 2015; Pundir et al. 2009). Maat et al. (2006) have argued that sections for observing annuli should be taken parallel to the outline of the root rather than oriented to the main axis of the tooth (Chapter 10).

An issue that has emerged from animal annulus studies is taphonomy as a factor that can complicate counts, a topic treated in Chapters 9 and 11. In previous research on mammalian teeth recovered from the archaeological record, Stutz (2002a) has demonstrated that postdepositional changes in tooth cementum can introduce crystal banding that mimics in vivo events. A method employing polarizing light microscopy coupled with a lambda plate has been proposed for identifying such diagenetic effects (Chapter 11).

As illustrated in columns D and E of Table 1.1, a number of studies eliminated teeth due to a variety of factors, which included breakage, unreadable cementum, cementum without definable lines, and statistical outliers. Although such reductions in sample size are to be expected in experimental work, as they would be in archaeological or forensic applications, only the statistical outliers pose a significant issue, especially in forensic contexts. The outliers are sufficiently rare that they are unlikely to bias paleodemographic inferences, but "doubling" or other perturbations of annual band development could negatively impact forensic casework. The biological profile generated for records search could be artificially elevated and a match unlikely. Therefore, if at all possible, especially in forensic contexts, more traditional gross morphological approaches should be considered along with TCA.

1.4 The Need for a Standard Approach and Why Hasn't It Happened?

After our team completed and published our study (Charles et al. 1986; Condon et al. 1986), I anticipated that the method would soon become a standard method for age-at-death estimation in bioarchaeology and forensic anthropology. I was obviously over-optimistic! Further applications during the 1980s were generally not supportive, and a body of research on humans did not develop. Given that the method was used more commonly in paleozoology and wildlife studies with a manual for Alaskan Brown Bears published by Matson and colleagues in 1993, the case for standard human cementum annuli studies seemed considerably overdue.

With the renewed interest stimulated by the Rostock Manifesto and the development of digital enhancement methods, ongoing resistance to the method is even more surprising. Wittwer-Backofen's scholarly publications surely should have started a groundswell (Wittwer-Backofen and Buba 2002; Wittwer-Backofen et al. 2004), or so I thought at the beginning of the twenty-first century. Yet, we have researchers such as Meinl et al. (2008:104) remarking that "TCA is an expensive, tedious but comparatively precise technique regarding the fact that the measurement depends principally on the absolute count of lines. Unfortunately, no standardized protocol of how to prepare the sections and how to count them exists which may lead to errors in the assessment of the line count." More recently, also publishing in *Forensic Science International,* Cunha and colleagues (2009: 6) in an evaluative overview of various estimators of age-at-death method argues that despite their being affected by taphonomy, the Lamedin dentin translucence method is preferable to TCA because TCA "is more time-consuming, expensive, not user-friendly and less accurate. Recently, its applicability has also been seriously questioned." There is no reference for the "less accurate" assertion, and in fact, Meinl et al.'s study (2008) demonstrates that TCA is more accurate than the Lamedin technique. The "serious questioning" occurred in the course of an article by Renz and Radlanski (2006) that begins with the assumption that the mechanisms for annulus formation in humans should be the same as those for tree rings. While the common nature of cemental annulus formation seems secure across Mammalia and Crocodilia (Introduction), an extension from the Animal Kingdom to the Plant Kingdom, while creative, would seem to be overly bold.

Obviously, the TCA method needs advocacy, which has been building, albeit slowly. This volume is one tangible outcome, as was a recent special issue of the *International Journal of Paleopathology* (2016, vol. 15: 113–63). Wittwer-Backofen and colleagues have advanced the field, including a recently published, detailed methodological protocol (Wittwer-Backofen 2012). As reported by Colard et al. (2015), an international research group (Cementochronology Research Program) has been formed recently (2010), and a protocol has been submitted and approved by the ISO-9000. This protocol (Figure 1.5) specifies equipment, supplies, and procedures that should be readily available in forensic or histology laboratories. As Colard and colleagues note (2015: 7), the cost of a single section would appear to be approximately US$20. Reading sections and counting lines is a learned skill; workshops and other training sessions should solve this problem.

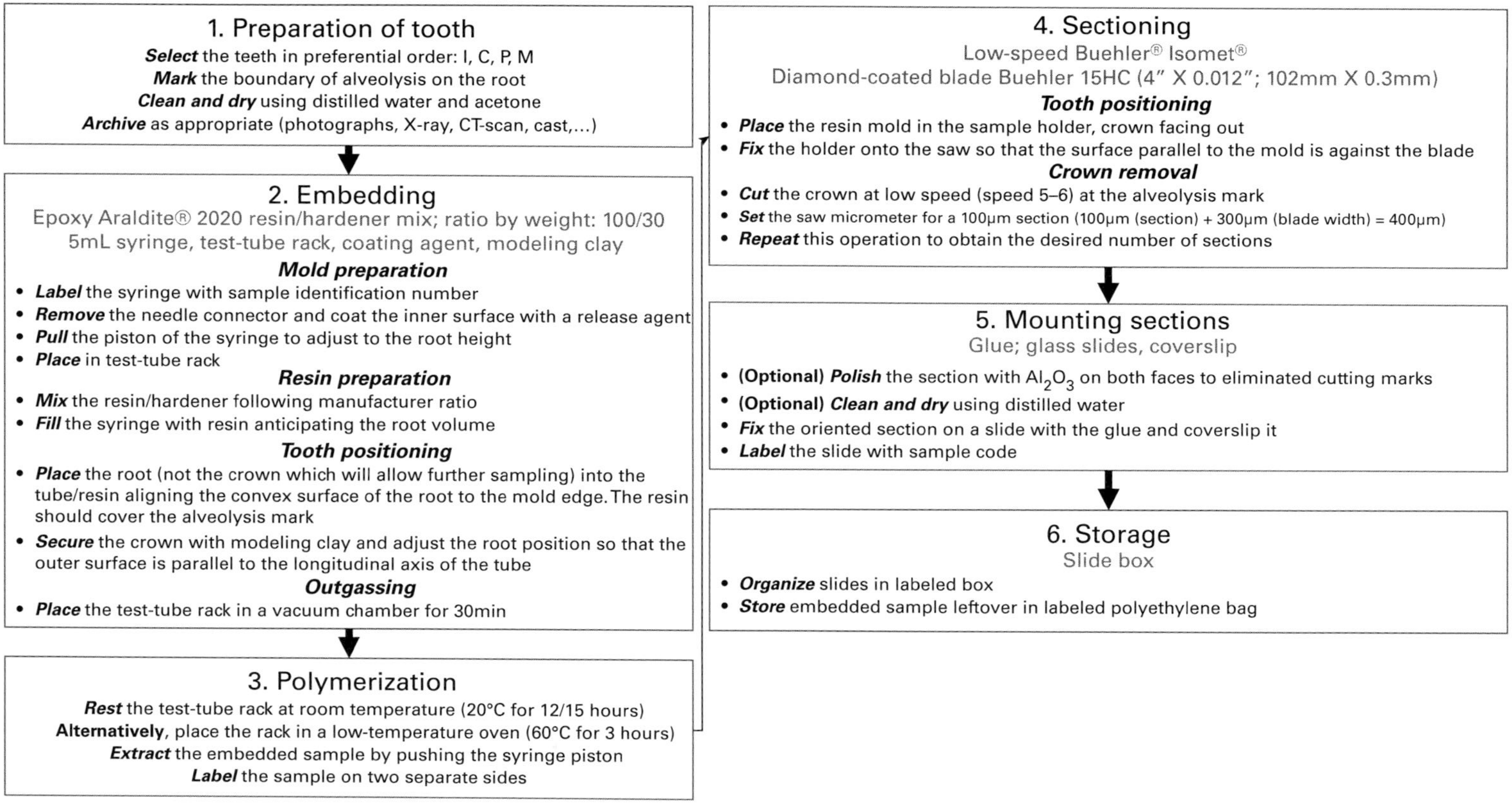

1. Preparation of tooth

Select the teeth in preferential order: I, C, P, M
Mark the boundary of alveolysis on the root
Clean and dry using distilled water and acetone
Archive as appropriate (photographs, X-ray, CT-scan, cast,....)

↓

2. Embedding

Epoxy Araldite® 2020 resin/hardener mix; ratio by weight: 100/30
5mL syringe, test-tube rack, coating agent, modeling clay

Mold preparation
- ***Label*** the syringe with sample identification number
- ***Remove*** the needle connector and coat the inner surface with a release agent
- ***Pull*** the piston of the syringe to adjust to the root height
- ***Place*** in test-tube rack

Resin preparation
- ***Mix*** the resin/hardener following manufacturer ratio
- ***Fill*** the syringe with resin anticipating the root volume

Tooth positioning
- ***Place*** the root (not the crown which will allow further sampling) into the tube/resin aligning the convex surface of the root to the mold edge. The resin should cover the alveolysis mark
- ***Secure*** the crown with modeling clay and adjust the root position so that the outer surface is parallel to the longitudinal axis of the tube

Outgassing
- ***Place*** the test-tube rack in a vacuum chamber for 30min

↓

3. Polymerization

Rest the test-tube rack at room temperature (20°C for 12/15 hours)
Alternatively, place the rack in a low-temperature oven (60°C for 3 hours)
Extract the embedded sample by pushing the syringe piston
Label the sample on two separate sides

↓

4. Sectioning

Low-speed Buehler® Isomet®
Diamond-coated blade Buehler 15HC (4" X 0.012"; 102mm X 0.3mm)

Tooth positioning
- ***Place*** the resin mold in the sample holder, crown facing out
- ***Fix*** the holder onto the saw so that the surface parallel to the mold is against the blade

Crown removal
- ***Cut*** the crown at low speed (speed 5–6) at the alveolysis mark
- ***Set*** the saw micrometer for a 100μm section (100μm (section) + 300μm (blade width) = 400μm)
- ***Repeat*** this operation to obtain the desired number of sections

↓

5. Mounting sections

Glue; glass slides, coverslip

- **(Optional)** ***Polish*** the section with Al_2O_3 on both faces to eliminated cutting marks
- **(Optional)** ***Clean and dry*** using distilled water
- ***Fix*** the oriented section on a slide with the glue and coverslip it
- ***Label*** the slide with sample code

↓

6. Storage

Slide box

- ***Organize*** slides in labeled box
- ***Store*** embedded sample leftover in labeled polyethylene bag

Figure 1.5 Cementochronology procedure for dental preparation, certified according to the ISO-9001 (based on data from Colard et al. 2015).

It is up to forensic anthropologists and bioarchaeologists to overcome their fear of laboratories and accept one of the most accurate methods for estimating age-at-death in human remains.

Acknowledgments

First of all, I would like to thank Stephan Naji for the invitation to write this chapter, which led me to a wonderful world of late Renaissance and Enlightenment science. Brian Foster was most generous with his illustrations from historical sources, for which I am most grateful. To all who are laboring in this challenging, but important field, do keep up the good work!!

References

Aggarwal, P., S. Saxena, and P. Bansal. 2008. Incremental Lines in Root Cementum of Human Teeth: An Approach to Their Role in Age Estimation Using Polarizing Microscopy. *Indian Journal of Dental Research* 19(4): 326–30.

Avadhani, A., J. V. Tupkari, A. Khambaty, and M. Sardar. 2009. Cementum Annulations and Age Determination. *Journal of Forensic Dental Sciences* 1(2): 73.

Azaz, B., M. Ulmansky, R. Moshev, and J. Sela. 1974. Correlation between Age and Thickness of Cementum in Impacted Teeth. *Oral Surgery, Oral Medicine, Oral Pathology* 38(5): 691–4.

Bertrand, B., E. Cunha, and V. Hédouin. 2018. Cementochronology: Too Precise to Be True or Too Precise to Be Accurate? *American Journal of Physical Anthropology* 165 (S66): 27.

Bennett, G. W. 2009. The Root of Dental Anatomy: A Case for Naming Eustachius the "Father of Dental Anatomy." *Journal of the History of Dentistry* 57: 85–8.

Black, G. V. 1887. *A Study of the Histological Characters of the Periostium and Peridental Membrane*. Chicago, IL: W. T. Keener.

Blondiaux, J., N. Gabart, A. Alduc-Le Bagousse, C. Niel, and E. Tyler. 2006. Relevance of Cement Annulations to Paleopathology. *Paleopathology Newsletter* 135: 4–13.

Bojarun, R., A. Garmus, and R. Jankauskas. 2003. Microstructure of Dental Cementum and Individual Biological Age Estimation. *Medicina (Kaunas)* 39(10): 960–4.

Bosshardt, D. D., and K. A. Selvig. 1997. Dental Cementum: The Dynamic Tissue Covering of the Root. *Periodontology* 13(1): 41–75.

Broomell, I. N. 1898. The Histology of Cementum. *Dent Cosmos* 40(9): 697–723.

Broucker, A. de, T. Colard, G. Penel, J. Blondiaux, and S. Naji. 2016. The Impact of Periodontal Disease on Cementochronology Age Estimation. *International Journal of Paleopathology* 15 (December): 128–33.

Caplazi, G. 2004. Eine Untersuchung über die Auswirkungen von Tuberkulose auf Anlagerungsfrequenz und Beschaffenheit der Zementringe desmenschlichen Zahnes. *Bulletin de la Société Suisse d'Anthropologie* 10(1): 35–83.

Charles, D. K., K. Condon, J. M. Cheverud, and J. E. Buikstra. 1986. Cementum Annulation and Age Determination in *Homo Sapiens*. 1. Tooth Variability and Observer Error. *American Journal of Physical Anthropology* 71: 311–20.

Colard, T., B. Bertrand, S. Naji, Y. Delannoy, and A. Bécart. 2015. Toward the Adoption of Cementochronology in Forensic Context. *International Journal of Legal Medicine* 129: 1–8.

Colard, T., G. Falgayrac, B. Bertrand, S. Naji, O. Devos, C. Balsack, Y. Delannoy, and G. Penel. 2016. New Insights on the Composition and the Structure of the Acellular Extrinsic Fiber Cementum by Raman Analysis. *PLOS ONE* 11(12): e0167316.

Condon, K., D. K. Charles, J. M. Cheverud, and J. E. Buikstra. 1986. Cementum Annulation and Age Determination in *Homo Sapiens*. II. Estimates and Accuracy. *American Journal of Physical Anthropology* 71(3): 321–30.

Cunha, E., E. Baccino, L. Martrille, F. Ramsthaler, J. Prieto, Y. Schuliar, N. Lynnerup, and C. Cattaneo. 2009. The Problem of Aging Human Remains and Living Individuals: A Review. *Forensic Science International* 193: 1–13.

Czermak, A., A. Czermak, H. Ernst, and G. Grupe. 2011. Age at Death Evaluation by Tooth Cementum Annulation (TCA) – A Software for an Automated Incremental Line Counting. Poster presented at the 80th annual meeting of the American Association of Physical Anthropologists, Minneapolis, MN.

Dalitz, G. D. 1962. *Age Determination of Adult Human Remains by Teeth Examination*. PhD thesis, University of Melbourne: Australia.

Dean, C., A. Le Cabec, K. Spiers, Y. Zhang, and J. Garrevoet. 2018. Incremental Distribution of Strontium and Zinc in Great Ape and Fossil Hominin Cementum Using Synchrotron X-Ray Fluorescence Mapping. *Journal of the Royal Society, Interface* 15 (138).

Denton, G. B. 1941. *The Discovery of Cementum*. Chicago: Northwestern University.

Dias, P. E. M., T. L. Beaini, and R. F. H. Melani. 2010. Age Estimation from Dental Cementum Incremental Lines and Periodontal Disease. *Journal of Forensic Odontostomatology* 28(1): 13–21.

Erickson, J. A., and W. G. Seliger. 1969. Efficient Sectioning of Incisors for Estimating Age of Mule Deer. *Journal of Wildlife Management* 33(2): 384–88.

Foster, B. L. 2017. On the Discovery of Cementum. *Journal of Periodontal Research* 52(4): 666–85.

Garant, P. R. 1995. G. V. Black's Contribution to the Structural Biology of the Periodontium. *Periodontal Clinical Investigation* 17: 16–20.

Garmus, A. 1996. *Lithuanian Forensic Osteology*. Vilnus, Lithuania: Baltic Medico-Legal Association.

Gilbert, F. F. 1966. Aging White-Tailed Deer by Annuli in the Cementum of the First Incisor. *Journal of Wildlife Management* 30(1): 200–2.

Gottlieb, B. 1943. Continuous Deposition of Cementum. *Journal of American Dental Association* 30: 842–7.

Gowda, C. B. K., P. Srinivasa Reddy, G. Kokila, and L. Pradeep. 2014. Cemental Annulation and Phase Contrast Microscope: Tool for Age Estimation. *Journal of South India Medicolegal Association* 6(1): 9–13.

Grosskopf, B. 1990. Individual Age Determination Using Growth Rings in the Cementum of Buried Human Teeth. *Zeitschrift für Rechtsmedizin* 103(5): 351–59.

Grue, H., and B. Jensen. 1979. Review of the Formation of Incremental Lines in Tooth Cementum of Terrestrial Mammals. *Danish Review of Game Biology* 11: 1–48.

Gupta, P. 2014. Human Age Estimation from Tooth Cementum and Dentin. *Journal of Clinical and Diagnostic Research* 8(4): 7–10.

Gustafson, G. 1950. Age Determination of Teeth. *Journal of American Dental Association* 41: 45–54.

Hast, M. H., and D. H. Garrison. 1995. Andreas Vesalius on the Teeth: An Annotated Translation from *De Humani Corporis Fabrica* 1543. *Clinical Anatomy* 8: 134–138.

Hopewell-Smith, A. 1920. *Concerning Human Cementum*. Philadelphia: Evans Dental Institute, University of Pennsylvania.

Hoppa, R. D., and J. W. Vaupel, eds. 2002. *Paleodemography: Age Distributions from Skeletal Samples*. Cambridge: Cambridge University Press.

Jankauskas, R., S. Barakauskas, and R. Bojarun. 2001. Incremental Lines of Dental Cementum in Biological Age Estimation. *HOMO – Journal of Comparative Human Biology* 52(1): 59–71.

Joshi, P. S., M. S. Chougule, and G. P. Agrawal. 2010. Comparison of Polarizing & Phase Contrast Microscopy for Estimation of Age Based on Cemental Annulations. *Indian Journal of Forensic Odontology* 3(3): 17–25.

Kagerer, P., and G. Grupe. 2001a. On the Validity of Individual Age-at-Death Diagnosis by Incremental Line Counts in Human Dental Cementum. Technical Considerations. *Anthropologischer Anzeiger* 59(4): 331–42.

———. 2001b. Age-at-Death Diagnosis and Determination of Life-History Parameters by Incremental Lines in Human Dental Cementum as an Identification Aid. *Forensic Science International* 118(1): 75–82.

Kasetty, S., M. Rammanohar, and T. R. Ragavendra. 2010. Dental Cementum in Age Estimation: A Polarized Light and Stereomicroscopic Study. *Journal of Forensic Sciences* 55(3): 779–83.

Kasuya, T. 1976. Reconsideration of Life History Parameters of the Spotted and Striped Dolphins Based on Cemental Layers. *Scientific Reports of the Whales Research Institute* 28: 73–106.

Kasuya, T. 1977. Age Determination and Growth of the Baird's Beaked Whale with a Comment of the Fetal Growth Rate. *Scientific Reports of the Whales Research Institute* 29: 1–20.

Kasuya, T., and S. Matsui. 1984. Age Determination and Growth of the Short-Finned Pilot Whale off the Pacific Coast of Japan. *Scientific Reports of the Whales Research Institute* 35: 57–91.

Kaur, P., M. Astekar, J. Singh, K. S. Arora, and G. Bhalla. 2015. Estimation of Age Based on Tooth Cementum Annulations: A Comparative Study Using Light, Polarized, and Phase Contrast Microscopy. *Journal of Forensic Dental Sciences* 7(3): 215–21.

Keiss, R. E. 1969. Comparison of Eruption-Wear Patterns and Cementum Annuli as Age Criteria in Elk. *Journal of Wildlife Management* 3(1): 175–80.

Klauenberg, K., and F. Lagona. 2007. Hidden Markov Random Field Models for TCA Image Analysis. *Computational Statistics & Data Analysis* 52(2): 855–68.

Klevezal', G. A. 1996. *Recording Structures of Mammals: Determination of Age and Reconstruction of Life History*. Rotterdam: A. A. Balkema Series.

Klevezal', G. A., and S. E. Kleinenberg. 1969. Age Determination of Mammals from Annual Layers in Teeth and Bones. Akademiya Nauk S.S.S.R, 1967. Translated 1969 from Russian by Israel Progr. Sci. Transl. Jerusalem.

Klevezal', G.A., and N. I. Shishlina. 2001. Assessment of the Season of Death of Ancient Human from Cementum Annual Layers. *Journal of Archaeological Science* 28(5): 481–6.

Kronfeld, R. 1938. The Biology of Cementum. *Journal of the American Dental Association* 25: 1451–61.

Kvaal, S. I., and T. Solheim. 1995. Incremental Lines in Human Dental Cementum in Relation to Age. *European Journal of Oral Sciences* 103(4): 225–30.

Laws, R. M. 1952. A New Method of Age Determination for Mammals. *Nature* 169: 972–3.

Lipsinic, F. E., D. G. Paunovich, D. G. Houston, and S. F. Robinson. 1986. Correlation of Age and Incremental Lines in the Cementum of Human Teeth. *Journal of Forensic Sciences* 31: 982–9.

Lovejoy, C. O., R. S. Meindl, R. P. Mensforth, and T. J. Barton. 1985. Multifactorial Determination of Skeletal Age at Death: A Method and Blind Tests of Its Accuracy. *American Journal of Physical Anthropology* 68: 1–14.

Low, W. A., and I. McT. Cowan. 1963. Age Determination of Deer by Annular Structure of Dental Cementum. *Journal of Wildlife Management* 27(3): 466–71.

Lucas, P. W., and H. S. Loh. 1986. Are the Incremental Lines in Human Cementum Laid Down Annually? *Annals of the Academy of Medicine, Singapore* 15(3): 384–6.

Maat, G. J. R., R. R. R. Gerretsen, and M. J. Aarents. 2006. Improving the Visibility of Tooth Cementum Annulations by Adjustment of the Cutting Angle of Microscopic Sections. *Forensic Science International* 159, Supplement (0): S95–99.

Magitot, E. 1878. *Experimental and Therapeutic Investigations*. Boston: Houghton, Osgood, and Company.

Matson, G., L. Van Daele, E. Goodwin, L. Aumiller, H. Reynolds, and H. Hristienko. 1993. *A Laboratory Manual for Cementum Age Determination of Alaska Brown Bear First Premolar Teeth*. Milltown, MT: Alaska Department of Fish and Game. Division of Wildlife Conservation and The Matson Laboratory.

McEwan, E. H. 1963. Seasonal Annuli in the Cementum of the Teeth of Barren Ground Caribou. *Canadian Journal of Zoology* 41: 111–13.

Meinl, A., C. D. Huber, S. Tangl, G. M. Gruber, M. Teschler-Nicola, and G. Watzek. 2008. Comparison of the Validity of Three Dental Methods for the Estimation of Age at Death. *Forensic Science International* 178(2–3): 96–105.

Miller, C. F., S. B. Dove, and J. A. Cottone. 1988. Failure of Use of Cemental Annulations in Teeth to Determine the Age of Humans. *Journal of Forensic Sciences* 33: 137–43.

Mitchell, B. 1963. Growth Layers in Dental Cement for Determining the Age of Red Seer (*Cervus elaphus* L.). *Journal of Animal Ecology* 36(2): 279–93.

Morris, P. A. 1972. A Review of Mammalian Age Determination Methods. *Mammal Review* 2 (3): 69–104.

Naji, S., T. Colard, J. Blondiaux, B. Bertrand, E. d'Incau, and J.-P. Bocquet-Appel. 2016. Cementochronology, to Cut or Not to Cut? *International Journal of Paleopathology* 15 (December): 113–9.

Naylor, J. W., W. G. Miller, G. N. Stokes, and G. G. Stow. 1985. Cemental Annulation Enhancement: A Technique for Age Determination in Man. *American Journal of Physical Anthropology* 68: 197–200.

Novakowski, N. S. 1965. Cemental Deposition as an Age Criterion in Bison, and the Relation of Incisor Wear, Eye-Lens Weight, and Dressed Bison Carcass Weight to Age. *Canadian Journal of Zoology* 43(1): 173–8.

Padavala, S., and S. Gheena. 2015. Estimation of Age Using Cementum Annulations. *Journal of Pharmaceutical Sciences & Research* 7(7): 461–3.

Pilloud, S. 2004. Läßt sich mittels der Altersbestimmung anhand Zahnzementes auch bei älteren Individuen ein signifikanter Zusammenhang zwischen histologischem und reellem finden? *Anthropologischer Anzeiger* 62(2): 231–9.

Pundir, S., S. Saxena, and P. Aggrawal. 2009. Estimation of Age Based on Tooth Cementum Annulations Using Three Different Microscopic Methods. *Journal of Forensic Dental Sciences* 1(2): 82.

Ransom, A. B. 1966. Determining Age of White-Tailed Deer from Layers in Cementum of Molars. *Journal of Wildlife Management* 30(1): 197–9.

Rao, N. G., and N. N. Rao. 1998. CCTV Study of Cemental Annulations in Determining the Age from a Single Tooth. *Indian Journal of Dental Research* 9: 41–5.

Renz, H., and R. J. Radlanski. 2006. Incremental Lines in Root Cementum of Human Teeth – A Reliable Age Marker? *HOMO – Journal of Comparative Human Biology* 57(1): 29–50.

Ristova, M., M. Talevska, and Z. Stojanovska. 2018. Accurate Age Estimations from Dental Cementum and a Childbirth Indicator – A Pilot Study. *Journal of Forensic Science & Criminology* 6: 1–12.

Saunders, J. B., and C. D. O'Malley. 1944. A Reading from the *De Humane Corporals Fabric* of Andreas Vesalius. *Journal of the American College of Dentists* 11: 211–18.

Saxon, A., and C. Higham. 1968. Identification and Interpretation of Growth Rings in the Secondary Dental Cementum of *Ovis aries*. *Nature* 219: 634–5.

1969. A New Research Method for Economic Prehistorians. *American Antiquity* 34(3): 303–11.

Scheffer, V. B. 1950. Growth Layer on the Teeth of Pinnipedia as an Indication of Age. *Science* 112: 309–11.

Sergeant, D. E., and D. H. Pimlott. 1959. Age Determination in Moose from Sectioned Incisor Teeth. *Journal of Wildlife Management* 23(3): 315–21.

Shklar, G., and C. A. Brackett. 2009. Galen on Oral Anatomy. *Journal of the History of Dentition* 57: 24–8.

Shklar, G., and D. Chernin. 2000. Eustachio *Libellus de Dentibus* the First Book Devoted to the Structure and Function of the Teeth. *Journal of the History of Dentition* 48: 25–30.

Shruthi, B. S., M. Donoghue, M. Selvamani, and P. V. Kumar. 2015. Comparison of the Validity of Two Dental Age Estimation Methods: A Study on South Indian Population. *Journal of Forensic Dental Sciences* 7(3): 189–94.

Sousa, E. M., G. G. Stott, and J. B. Alves. 1999. Determination of Age from Cemental Incremental Lines for Forensic Dentistry. *Biotechnic & Histochemistry: Official Publication of the Biological Stain Commission* 74(4): 185–93.

Spiess, A. 1976. Determining Season of Death of Archaeological Fauna by Analysis of Teeth. *Arctic* 29(1): 53–5.

Spinage, C. A. 1976a. Age Determination of the Female Grant's Gazelle. *African Journal of Ecology* 14(2): 121–34.

1976b. Incremental Cementum Lines in the Teeth of Tropical African Mammals. *Journal of the Zoological Society of London* 178: 117–31.

Spinage, C. A. 1973. A Review of the Age Determination of Mammals by Means of Teeth, with Special Reference to Africa. *East Africa Wildlife Journal* 11: 165–87.

Stallibrass, S. 1982. The Use of Cement Layers for Absolute Ageing of Mammalian Teeth: A Selective Review of the Literature, with Suggestions for Further Studies and Alternative Applications. In *Ageing and Sexing Animal Bones from Archaeological Sites*. B. Wilson, C. Grigson, and S. Payne, eds. BAR International Series 109. Oxford: British Archaeological Report, 109–26.

Stein, T. J., and J. F. Corcoran. 1994. Pararadicular Cementum Deposition as a Criterion for Age Estimation in Human Beings. *Oral Surgery, Oral Medicine, Oral Pathology* 77(3): 266–70.

Stillson, W. C. 1917. A Study of Cementum. *Dental Summary* 37: 30.

Stock, S. R., L. A. Finney, A. Telser, E. Maxey, S. Vogt, and J. S. Okasinski. 2017. Cementum Structure in Beluga Whale Teeth. *Acta Biomaterialia* 48 (January): 289–99.

Stott, G. G., R. F. Sis, and B. M. Levy. 1982. Cemental Annulation as an Age Criterion in Forensic Dentistry. *Journal of Dental Research* 61(6): 814–17.

Stutz, A. J. 2002a. Polarizing Microscopy Identification of Chemical Diagenesis in Archaeological Cementum. *Journal of Archaeological Science* 29(11): 1327–47.

Swetha, G., K. K. Kattappagari, C. S. Poosarla, L. P. Chandra, S. R. Gontu, and V. R. R. Badam. 2018. Quantitative Analysis of Dental Age Estimation by Incremental Line of Cementum. *Journal of Oral and Maxillofacial Pathology* 22(1): 138.

Trenouth, M. J. 2014. The Origin of the Terms Enamel, Dentine, and Cementum. *Faculty Dental Journal* 5(1): 26–31.

van Zuylen, J. 1981. The Microscopes of Antoni van Leeuwenhoek. *Journal of Microscopy* 121: 309–28.

Wedel, V. L., and D. J. Wescott. 2016. Using Dental Cementum Increment Analysis to Estimate Age and Season of Death in African Americans from an Historical Cemetery in Missouri. *International Journal of Paleopathology* 15 (December): 134–9.

Wiebusch, F. B. 1957. Periodontal Research: Problems Related to Practice. *Journal of the American Dental Association* 55: 612–16.

Wittwer-Backofen, U. 2012. Age Estimation Using Tooth Cementum Annulation. In *Forensic Microscopy for Skeletal Tissues: Methods and Protocols*. L. S. Bell, ed., Chapter 8. *Methods in Molecular Biology*, 915: 129–43.

Wittwer-Backofen, U., and H. Buba. 2002. Age Estimation by Tooth Cementum Annulation: Perspective of a New Validation Study. In *Paleodemography, Age Distributions from Skeletal Samples*. R .D. Hoppa and J. W. Vaupel, eds. Cambridge: Cambridge University Press, 107–28.

Wittwer-Backofen, U., J. Gampe, and J. W. Vaupel. 2004. Tooth Cementum Annulation for Age Estimation: Results from a Large Known-Age Validation Study. *American Journal of Physical Anthropology* 123(2): 119–29.

Yoneda, M. 1982. Growth Layers in Dental Cementum of Saguinus Monkeys in South America. *Primates* 23(3): 460–64.

Zander, H. A., and B. Hürzeler. 1958. Continuous Cementum Apposition. *Journal of Dental Research* 6: 1035–44.

2 Development and Structure of Cementum

Brian L. Foster, Francisco H. Nociti, Jr., and Martha J. Somerman

2.1 Introduction

Dental cementum, enveloping the tooth root and buried under the gingiva, was the last of the dental mineralized tissues to be discovered. Details of human cementum structure were not revealed until the advent of compound microscopes and the invention of advanced histology techniques in the laboratories of Anders Retzius and Jan Purkinje in the nineteenth century (Foster 2017; Chapter 1). The function of cementum in tooth attachment was not appreciated until nearer the end of the nineteenth century, when the anatomy of the periodontal complex was more fully realized in the work of G. V. Black and others.

Studies to date on the four mineralized tissues within the oral cavity indicate that some aspects of cementum formation, structure, and composition match those of bone, while enamel and dentin feature unique cell types, structures, and markers. There are several unanswered questions and controversies remaining about cementum biology; however, there is no question about its critical role in tooth retention and oral health and, by extension, in overall health and quality of life. In this brief chapter, we will summarize current knowledge of cementum biology, including cementum formation, types, composition, and clinical aspects. Chapter 3 will build on this foundation by discussing additional insights into cementum biology from inherited diseases and animal models.

2.2 Cementum Formation

Cementogenesis occurs during tooth root formation following completion of tooth crown morphogenesis. For a more detailed description of the cellular and molecular events directing root formation and cementogenesis, readers are directed to book chapters and more comprehensive reviews of the topic (Foster, Nociti, and Somerman 2013; Bosshardt 2005; Diekwisch 2001; Nanci 2018). Here we will describe establishment of cementum in broad strokes.

At initiation of root formation, the enamel organ responsible for producing the enamel matrix of the crown gives rise to a new structure that will guide root formation. Hertwig's epithelial root sheath (HERS), a cell bilayer composed of the inner and outer enamel epithelia, appears as a collar-like structure around the apical-most portion of the tooth (Figure 2.1A–C) (Luan, Ito, and Diekwisch 2006; Bosshardt and Schroeder 1992). HERS cells proliferate apically to define the contour of the root(s). The inner layer of HERS sends molecular signals to induce dental papilla cells to become odontoblasts, producing a layer of root dentin continuous with that of crown. The initial dentin layer is called mantle dentin, and mineralization of this region initiates as discrete hydroxyapatite crystal foci within odontoblast-derived matrix vesicles. The matrix vesicles burst, and foci merge into a unified mineralization front. Mantle dentin transitions to circumpulpal dentin that forms the bulk of the tooth and mineralizes under the influence of mineral regulating extracellular matrix (ECM) proteins including dentin matrix protein 1 (DMP1), dentin sialoprotein (DSP), and dentin phosphoprotein (DPP), as well as other factors like osteocalcin (OCN), osteopontin (OPN), proteoglycans, and others (Goldberg et al. 2011; Prasad, Butler, and Qin 2010; Butler 1998; Veis 1993; Embery et al. 2001).

HERS is a transitional structure that soon becomes disrupted as its apical edge continues to grow and define the developing root. Disruption of HERS reveals the underlying dentin surface, providing access for cementoblast precursors to extend cell processes or invade toward the exposed root dentin surface, upon which cementum will be formed (Figure 2.1D–G) (Cho and Garant 1988). Cementum forms on root dentin by actions of cementoblasts. The origin and nature of cementoblasts remain controversial, with a classic hypothesis suggesting mesenchymal origin and alternative hypothesis promoting epithelial cell transformation into cementoblasts (Bosshardt 2005; Diekwisch 2001; Huang et al. 2009; Foster et al. 2007).

The first step in cementum deposition is secretion of collagen fibers at the root surface. In humans, these initial cementum fibers intermingle with unmineralized collagen fibers of the dentin, creating a strong interphase that is mechanically competent to receive and distribute mechanical forces (Bosshardt and Schroeder 1991; Ho et al. 2004). Tightly packed "fringe fibers" of collagen extend in perpendicular fashion from the cementum surface and are continuous with collagen fibers of the periodontal ligament (PDL) (Bosshardt and Schroeder 1996). Fibroblast-like cementoblasts promote continued acellular cementum formation (Figure 2.1H). The slow appositional growth of acellular cementum throughout life is observed as a progressive mineralization and incorporation of fringe fibers into the cementum proper, becoming embedded Sharpey's fibers, bundles of mineralized collagen fibers incorporated into cementum.

During eruption, the root is partially completed and cementogenesis is altered to produce the thicker, more rapidly forming cellular cementum on the apical root. Cells producing cellular cementum are cuboidal in morphology, resembling osteoblasts (Figure 2.1I). A portion of these cells are embedded in the cementoid matrix, becoming cementocytes housed in lacunae, which feature a canalicular network of cell processes that reach toward the PDL interface (Figure 2.1J). The stimulus for the change from acellular to cellular cementum remains unknown. Cellular cementum formation is

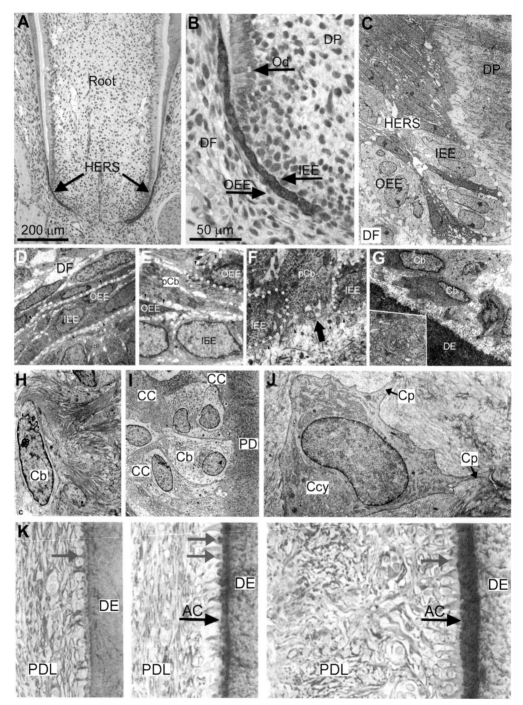

Figure 2.1 Cementum formation. (A, B) Decalcified section of mouse molar root at fourteen days postnatal. Box in panel A indicates area shown in panel B. Hertwig's epithelial root sheath (HERS) is positive for pan-keratin immunostaining (red-brown). HERS consists of inner and outer enamel epithelium (IEE and OEE, respectively) and separates the dental pulp (DP) and odontoblasts (Od) from the surrounding dental follicle (DF). **(C)** Transmission electron

initiated around the time the tooth enters occlusion, which is also when HERS cell proliferation is slowing. It has been hypothesized that slowing of HERS growth is a signal for cellular cementum (Thomas 1995) or changes in dentin mineralization affect the type of cementum (Takano et al. 2003), though precisely how these factors relate to cementogenesis still remains a matter of debate.

Embedded Sharpey's fibers remain continuous with collagen fiber bundles in the PDL. At the same time cementum is being deposited and PDL fibers are reorganizing during root elongation, the surrounding alveolar bone is increasing in height and also incorporating Sharpey's fibers (Sodek and McKee 2000; Fleischmannova et al. 2010; Alfaqeeh, Gaete, and Tucker 2013; Lungova et al. 2011). All of these activities prepare the cementum-PDL-bone periodontal attachment complex for the functional demands that accompany the tooth entering occlusion, as the alveolar bone becomes a highly responsive, remodeling support structure for the tooth (Ho et al. 2013; Sodek and McKee 2000).

Cementoblasts direct mineralization of cementum matrix on the root dentin by creating a local environment conducive to biomineralization. To accomplish this, cementoblasts secrete noncollagenous ECM proteins including bone sialoprotein (BSP), OPN, and OCN (discussed later under composition), which are deposited into spaces between collagen fibers and likely influence initiation and growth of hydroxyapatite crystals. The enzyme, tissue-nonspecific alkaline phosphatase (TNAP), promotes mineralization by hydrolysis of inorganic pyrophosphate, a hydroxyapatite crystal inhibitor. TNAP is a marker of cementoblasts and osteoblasts and is richly present in PDL tissues (Groeneveld et al. 1996; Groeneveld, Everts, and

---

Caption for Figure 2.1 (cont.)

microscope (TEM) image of a human mandibular premolar showing the HERS bilayer of IEE and OEE. Panels D–G show TEM images of apical edge of forming rat molar. (**D**) The intact IEE and OEE layers of HERS surrounded by DF cells. Epithelial cells are outlined by yellow stippled lines in panels D–G. (**E**) Precementoblasts (pCb) derived from the DF penetrate the OEE layer of HERS, though the inner layer remains intact. (**F**) pCb cells extend cytoplasmic processes (black arrow) between cells of the IEE to breach HERS and contact the forming root surface. (**G**) Differentiated cementoblasts (Cb) on the surface of root dentin (DE). Inset shows typical Cb Golgi complex with saccules, secretory granules, and lysosomes. Panels H–J show TEM images of cementum-associated cells of a forming human premolar. (**H**) Flattened, fibroblast-like Cb associated with acellular cementum (AC), secreting collagen fibers near developing root surface. (**I**) Cuboidal, osteoblast-like Cb associated with cellular cementum (CC), in the vicinity of the predentin (PD) matrix. (**J**) Newly embedded cementocyte (Ccy) forming cell processes (Cp) within the CC matrix. (**K**) Series of light microscope images of human premolar roots showing the root prior to AC formation (left panel), after two years of AC growth (middle panel), and after five years of AC growth (right panel). The fiber fringe (blue arrows) is observed to extend from the root surface at a perpendicular orientation into the PDL. Images in panels C and J adapted with permission from Bosshardt and Schroeder, *Cell Tissue Res* 267(2): 321–35, 1992. Images in panels D–G adapted with permission from Cho and Garant, *J Periodontal Res* 23(4): 268–76, 1988. Images in panels H, I, and K adapted with permission from Selvig and Bosshardt, *Periodontol 2000* 13: 41–75, 1997. (A black and white version of this figure will appear in some formats. For the color version, please refer to the plate section.)

Beertsen 1995; Beertsen, Van den Bos, and Everts 1990; Foster et al. 2012; Zweifler et al. 2014). Functions of cementum-associated ECM proteins and enzymes are discussed in more detail in Chapter 3.

Both acellular and cellular cementum are sometimes described as bone-like. Though bone is highly vascular and continuously remodels in response to loading, cementum is avascular, noninnervated, and grows by apposition, with no physiological turnover. Both acellular and cellular cementum grow by apposition throughout life. Acellular cementum thickness continues to increase by consistent appositional growth throughout life, with measured growth rates varying from about 3 µm per year in human premolars to 0.10 µm per day in deciduous teeth from *Macaca fascicularis* (Figure 2.1K) (Bosshardt, Luder, and Schroeder 1989; Bosshardt and Selvig 1997). Rates in other mammals likely vary greatly. The rate of cellular cementum apposition is initially 0.4–3.1 µm per day, later slowing to 0.1–0.5 µm per day, as measured in *Macaca fascicularis* (Bosshardt, Luder, and Schroeder 1989). Some aspects of cellular cementum homeostasis parallel those of bone. For example, in a mouse model of unopposed molar eruption, both cellular cementum and alveolar bone of the socket base responded with increased apposition (Luan et al. 2007; Holliday et al. 2005). Conversely, in a model of hyperocclusion (premature tooth contact that may result in occlusal trauma), cellular cementum apposition was disturbed and resorption was increased, a pattern matching the adjacent alveolar bone (Walker et al. 2008). The lack of physiological turnover in cementum, coupled with observations that osteoclasts more often target alveolar bone than cementum in most pathological situations, has led to the hypothesis that cementoblasts or cementum itself may have an antiresorptive role, serving as a protector of tooth root integrity. Although there may be some cementum-associated mechanism limiting root resorption, cementum does undergo many small resorption and repair events. Orthodontic tooth movement may lead to external root resorption, which can strike both types of cementum, depending on the forces involved (Wise and King 2008; Winter, Stenvik, and Vandevska-Radunovic 2009; Brezniak and Wasserstein 2002; Darendeliler et al. 2004; Ballard et al. 2009; Chan and Darendeliler 2006).

Observations that cementum grows with a circa-annual rhythm, which includes alternating translucent/opaque bands, has led to the counting of these tooth cementum annulations (TCA) as an approach to estimate ages of individuals from archaeological discoveries or forensic investigations, so-called dental cementum increment analysis or cementochronology (Naji et al. 2013). This topic will be the focus of several chapters in the book so will not be addressed further here.

2.3 Cementum Types

Cementum, located on the tooth root surfaces of human and many animal teeth, is classified into two major types, based on whether cells are included in the cementum matrix, and on the source of the major collagen fibers. Acellular cementum, located on the cervical part of the root, is also called primary cementum or acellular extrinsic fiber cementum (AEFC), with the latter term usually reserved for electron microscopy studies. Cellular cementum, located on the apical part of the tooth root, is also called secondary cementum or cellular intrinsic fiber (CIFC). The two cementum types are distinct from one another in their functions as well as their locations (Figure 2.2A).

Acellular cementum is a relatively thin tissue (approximately 50–200 µm) that contains no cells and is invested by extrinsically produced collagen fibers from the surrounding PDL (Figure 2.2B) (Sequeira, Bosshardt, and Schroeder 1992; Bosshardt and Schroeder 1996; Bosshardt and Selvig 1997; Yamamoto et al. 2016). Small diameter collagen fibers from the PDL insert into the acellular cementum surface at a high density, providing continuity between tooth root, PDL, and surrounding alveolar bone. These inserted collagen fibers, termed Sharpey's fibers (Figure 2.2C–E), serve to emphasize the important function of acellular cementum in attaching the tooth to manage the forces generated by occlusal loading.

Compared to acellular cementum, the thickness and volume of cellular cementum is much greater, coupled with more variability in size and shape (Figure 2.2F, G). Cellular cementum is sometimes called adaptive cementum, a name referring to its proposed function to maintain the tooth in its proper occlusal position after eruption, to compensate for enamel attrition through life. Cellular cementum is characterized by embedded cementocytes, cells that reside within lacunae in a matrix of intrinsically produced collagen fibers. Cementocytes parallel osteocytes in several regards. Both cell types reside in lacunae within their respective mineralized matrices and feature cell processes that extend through a canalicular system, and the two share expression of several markers, including DMP1 and sclerostin (SOST) among others (Zhao, Foster, and Bonewald 2016; Zhao et al. 2016). However, it remains unclear whether cementocytes function in tissue homeostasis in a comparable fashion to osteocytes of bone, which are implicated to be active cells in sensing and responding to mechanical loading, directing phosphate metabolism, and regulating bone formation and resorption (Bonewald 2011). Compared to osteocytes, cementocyte dendrites are fewer in number and density, and canalicular networks are not nearly as extensive as those from osteocytes. Mutations in the gene *SOST*, associated with Van Buchem disease, result in increased bone formation; however, changes in cellular cementum have been inconclusive (van Bezooijen et al. 2009). Ongoing studies attempt to better define the potential roles of cementocytes.

Though acellular and cellular types are the major varieties of cementum, there are at least two additional categories. Acellular afibrillar cementum (AAC) is sometimes found at the most cervical portion of the root, near the cementum-enamel junction (CEJ) or overlapping enamel, and without any known function (Figure 2.2H). Cellular mixed stratified cementum (CMSC) is a composite type comprised of alternating layers of acellular and cellular cementum and is found along with cellular cementum on the apical portions of molars. CMSC results from intermittent production of overlapping the two types, perhaps in response to changes in tooth function or other cues. Reparative cementum that forms after root resorption (described in more detail later) is often similar in structure to cellular cementum even when it is located on the

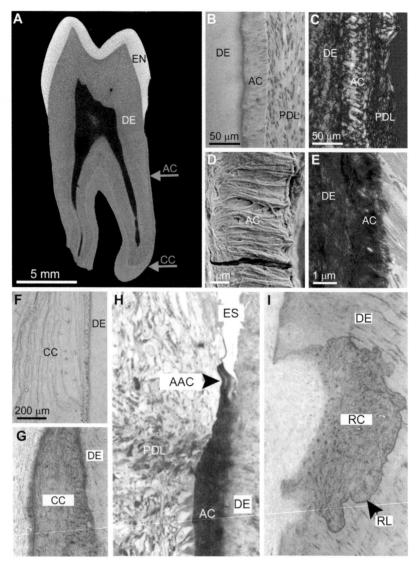

Figure 2.2 Types of cementum. (A) Microcomputed tomography reconstruction of human premolar showing localization of enamel (EN), dentin (DE), acellular cementum (AC), and cellular cementum (CC), with both cementum types shown in yellow. **(B)** Human AC in decalcified histology section stained by hematoxylin and eosin (H&E) or by **(C)** picrosirius red stain viewed under polarized light to emphasize inserted Sharpey's fibers. Mouse molar AC shown by **(D)** scanning electron microscopy and **(E)** transmission electron microscopy. **(F–G)** Human cellular cementum (CC) in decalcified histology section stained by H&E. **(H)** Human acellular afibrillar cementum (AAC) in decalcified histology section stained by H&E. Enamel space (ES) remains after decalcification of the enamel. **(I)** Reparative cementum (RP) of the CC type fills a resorption defect on the root surface. Note the reversal line (RL) marking the edge of the resorption left by odontoclasts. Image in B reproduced with permission from Foster, 2012. Image in C adapted from Thumbigere-Math et al., *J Dent Res* 97(4): 432–41, 2018, and used in accordance with STM permission guidelines. Image in D adapted from Foster et al., *J Dent Res* 92(2): 166–72, 2013, and used in accordance with STM permission guidelines. Image in

cervical root and repairs the acellular cementum layer (Figure 2.2I) (Bosshardt and Sculean 2009; Bosshardt and Selvig 1997).

Cementum discussed in the context of human teeth is an exclusively root tissue, though this is not the case across the animal kingdom. Coronal cementum forms on the crown enamel of some herbivores, including rabbits, guinea pigs, cows, horses, sheep, donkeys, and elephants. Coronal cementum varies from acellular to cellular depending on species, sometimes including vascular elements (Foster 2017).

2.4 Cementum Composition

Cementum is reported to be approximately 45 to 50 percent inorganic material by weight, with organic matrix making up the remainder (Nanci and Somerman 2008). The inorganic component is primarily hydroxyapatite, the mineral phase that is also present in enamel, dentin, and bone. The organic ECM features type I collagen as the major component, the fibrillar scaffold hosting deposition of additional ECM proteins and hydroxyapatite mineral deposition. Lesser amounts of collagens, including types III, V, VI, and XII are also present (Birkedal-Hansen, Butler, and Taylor 1977; Wang et al. 1980; Becker et al. 1991; Andujar et al. 1988; MacNeil et al. 1998). The remaining organic content of cementum is made up of a variety of noncollagenous proteins and proteoglycans, some of which are suspected to influence matrix properties and regulate the biomineralization process (Table 2.1) (Bosshardt 2005; Foster et al. 2007; Yamamoto et al. 2016; Arzate, Zeichner-David, and Mercado-Celis 2015; Ababneh, Hall, and Embery 1999, 1998).

BSP and OPN, members of the *S*mall *I*ntegrin-*B*inding *L*igand *n*-linked *G*lycoprotein (SIBLING) family of proteins, deserve special mention because of their presence in cementum and frequent use as markers of cementum. They are not cementum-specific, being found in bone, dentin, and some nonmineralized tissues (e.g., limited localization in placenta and platelets for BSP, wider and more robust expression in kidney, brain, and immune cells for OPN) (Ganss, Kim, and Sodek 1999; Sodek, Ganss, and McKee 2000). The *Ibsp* gene encoding BSP is highly and constitutively expressed by cementoblasts; BSP protein localizes to the root surface at initiation of cementogenesis and is found by immunostaining in the cementum matrix (Figure 2.3A–B) (Bosshardt et al. 1998; MacNeil et al. 1995; Foster 2012; McKee, Zalzal, and Nanci 1996; Foster et al. 2018; Foster et al. 2015). BSP is a multifunctional protein thought to promote mineralization through effects on cell differentiation and direct effects on hydroxyapatite mineral growth (Ganss, Kim, and Sodek 1999).

Caption for Figure 2.2 (cont.)

E adapted with permission from Foster et al., *Bone* 78: 150–64, 2015. Images in G–I reproduced and adapted with permission from Selvig and Bosshardt, *Periodontol 2000* 13: 41–75, 1997. (A black and white version of this figure will appear in some formats. For the color version, please refer to the plate section.)

A genetically engineered mouse model where the gene encoding BSP was deleted suggests an important function of BSP in cementogenesis, because in the absence of BSP, acellular cementum was limited and periodontal function was compromised (Foster et al. 2015; Foster et al. 2013). BSP is discussed in more detail in Chapter 3. The *Spp1* gene encoding OPN is expressed by cementoblasts, and OPN protein localizes to cementum matrix during formation and is produced locally by cementoblasts (along with osteoblasts and PDL fibroblasts), as well as being present at measurable levels in the blood (Van den Bos et al. 1999; Bosshardt et al. 1998; McKee, Zalzal, and Nanci 1996; Foster 2012; Foster et al. 2018) (Figure 2.3C–D). OPN has several functional domains and is thought to inhibit or negatively regulate hydroxyapatite mineral apposition. Mice where OPN was genetically ablated exhibit changes in bone and other mineralized tissues; however, cementum appeared normal, suggesting OPN is not a critical regulator of cementum formation or may be redundant with other regulatory factors (Boskey et al. 2002; Foster et al. 2018).

Another SIBLING member, dentin matrix protein 1 (DMP1), is expressed by cementocytes of cellular cementum, in parallel to bone osteocytes (Figure 2.3E) (Zhao, Foster, and Bonewald 2016; Zhao et al. 2016). DMP1 is sometimes reported in acellular cementum but is more consistently seen in cellular cementum associated with cementocytes (Ye et al. 2008; Toyosawa et al. 2004; Foster 2012; Sawada et al. 2012). Additional ECM proteins reported in cementum include DSP and OCN, though their roles remain unclear.

Table 2.1 summarizes cementum composition (and other properties) in comparison with bone, dentin, and enamel (Goldberg et al. 2011; Bartlett 2013; Hu et al. 2007; Embery et al. 2001; Sodek and McKee 2000). Chapter 3 presents a more detailed discussion on the impact of a number of genetic conditions, including the deletion of some of these genes, on the formation and function of the cementum.

2.5 Clinical and Environmental Considerations

When reading the following chapters highlighting TCA as a valuable method for determining age, it is important to realize that certain variables may influence the ability to accurately estimate age from TCA measurements. While most of these issues summarized in the following list relate to human teeth, environmental exposures in the wild may also alter tooth/cementum development in animals in a variety of ways. For example, trauma, self-inflicted or related to altercations with other animals, may damage the dental-oral region during tooth root development or in fully developed teeth. If whole skulls are recovered, these types of traumatic changes may be obvious and thus accounted for. However, this will not be possible for all situations, and thus environmental exposures should be suspected if substantial variations or abnormalities are observed. Another consideration for all species being examined by TCA is the marked diversity in patterns of tooth development, eruption, and replacement of teeth over a life span. For example, unlike humans that are diphyodont, elephants are polyphyodont, with cycles of tooth resorption and replacement throughout their life

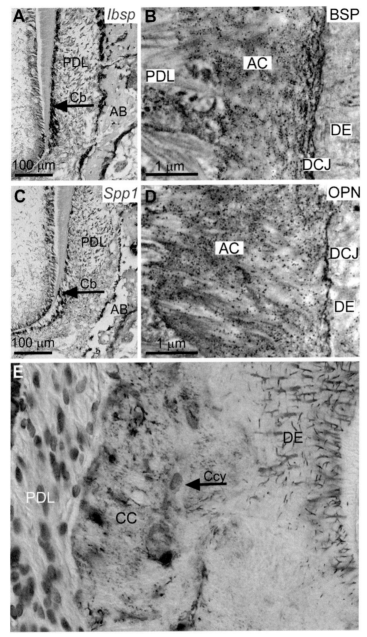

Figure 2.3 Composition of cementum. (A) In a developing mouse molar, *Ibsp* mRNA is expressed (red signal) by cementoblasts (Cb) lining the root dentin (DE) surface. **(B)** In a rat molar, BSP protein localizes to the acellular cementum (AC) layer by colloidal gold immunocytochemistry (black dots) imaged by transmission electron microscopy (TEM). AC is bounded by two tissues where BSP appears mostly absent, the periodontal ligament (PDL) and dentin (DE). Dentin-cementum junction (DCJ) is indicated. **(C)** *Spp1* mRNA (red signal) is expressed by some Cb in the developing mouse molar. **(D)** OPN protein labels rat AC by colloidal gold immunocytochemistry viewed by TEM. **(E)** DMP1 protein labels mouse molar

span; in such situations it may be difficult to capture age by measuring tooth root cementum (Marks and Schroeder 1996; Renvoise and Michon 2014).

In considering the use of tooth root cementum to estimate ages of human samples, a variety of circumstances may compromise cementum structure, growth, or other properties, leading to potentially inaccurate quantification of age (Chapter 5). Listed here are several categories of insults where cementum may be altered:

1. **Genetic modifications:** As discussed in detail in Chapter 3, there are several genetic mutations that affect cementum formation and stability (e.g., *PHEX*, *ALPL*, *ANKH* or *ENPP1* mutations).
2. **Dental diseases:** (Chapter 5)
   a. *Caries*: Tooth decay, a microbial-induced process, may cause destruction of crown enamel and dentin, as well as destruction of root cementum, the latter more often associated with the aging process and increased exposure of tooth roots (Arshad et al. 2020; Rajendran and Sivapathasundharam 2012).
   b. *Periodontal diseases*: Most periodontal diseases are caused by host-microbial interactions, which promote an inflammatory response, resulting in destruction of the periodontal complex, including cementum. As discussed earlier and in Chapter 3, some genetic disorders exhibit a periodontal/cementum phenotype (Newman et al. 2018; Foster et al. 2014; Foster, Nociti, and Somerman 2013).
   c. *Root resorption*: Root resorption is a progressive loss of radicular dentin and cementum through the continued action of osteoclastic/odontoclastic cells (that resorb mineralized tissues). Although root resorption is a normal physiological process essential for exfoliation of deciduous teeth, it is pathological in the adult dentition. Resorptive lesions can be most simply classified as external or internal (Darcey and Qualtrough 2013). In the former, the lesion occurs on the external aspect of the root and, therefore, cementum is severely compromised. In the latter, the lesion occurs within the dentin of the root canal and/or pulp chamber. Though the most common causes for root resorption include pulpal necrosis, trauma, periodontal treatment, orthodontic treatment, and tooth-whitening agents, there have been several reports of idiopathic tooth resorption where no etiological factor is evident (Neely et al. 2016; Aidos, Diogo, and Santos 2018; Schatzle, Tanner, and Bosshardt 2005).
   d. *Tumoral lesions*: Beyond the genetic disorders mentioned earlier and in Chapter 3, other rare conditions may affect the cementum macro structure, including odontogenic tumors and benign fibro-osseous lesions, where some of these lesions may have a genetic predisposition as well. Odontogenic tumors are

---

Caption for Figure 2.3 (cont.)

cellular cementum (CC) matrix around embedded cementocytes (Ccy) and is also present in dentin (DE). Images in B and D reproduced and adapted with permission from McKee and Nanci, 1995. Image in E reproduced with permission from Foster and Sanz, 2020. (A black and white version of this figure will appear in some formats. For the color version, please refer to the plate section.)

Table 2.1 The four mature mineralized tissues of the dentoalveolar complex.[1]

	Cementum	Bone	Dentin	Enamel
Mineralization	45–50%	50–60%	70%	> 95%
Inorganic composition	Hydroxyapatite	Hydroxyapatite	Hydroxyapatite	Hydroxyapatite
Organic composition	Collagens (predominantly collagen type I); highly phosphorylated and glycosylated proteins (e.g., BSP, OPN, DMP 1); proteoglycans & glycosaminoglycans (e.g., BGN, DCN, LUM, C4S)	Collagens (predominantly collagen type I); highly phosphorylated and glycosylated proteins (e.g., BSP, OPN, DMP 1); proteoglycans & glycosaminoglycans (e.g., BGN, DCN, C4S)	Collagens (predominantly collagen type I); highly phosphorylated and glycosylated proteins (dentin selective DSP, DPP); proteoglycans & glycosaminoglycans (e.g., BGN, DCN, FMOD, LUM, C4SDS)	No collagen Enamel selective, e.g., amelogenin, ameloblastin, enamelin, tuftelin (proteins removed during maturation stage)
Cell lineage	Mesenchymal*	Mesenchymal	Mesenchymal	Epithelial
Growth after maturation	Appositional	Remodeling	Appositional	None
Repair and remodeling	Limited repair	Extensive repair	Repair	None
Vascularity/nerves	No	Yes	No	No
References	Bosshardt and Selvig 1997; Bosshardt et al. 1998; Ababneh et al. 1998; Ababneh et al. 1999; Arzate et al. 2015; Yamamoto et al. 2016	Sodek et al. 2000	Veis 1993; Butler 1998; Embery et al. 2001; Prasad et al. 2010; Goldberg et al. 2011	Hu et al. 2007; Bartlett 2013

1. BGN, Biglycan; BSP, Bone sialoprotein; C4S, Chondroitin-4-sulfate; DCN, Decorin; DMP1, Dentin matrix protein 1; DPP, Dentin phosphoprotein; DSP, Dentin sialoprotein; FMOD, Fibromodulin; LUM, Lumican; OPN, Osteopontin.* The classical hypothesis proposes an ectomesenchymal origin for cementoblasts, while the alternative hypothesis suggests epithelial-mesenchymal transformation.

derived from the components of the tooth-forming apparatus and are relatively rare, with about 0.5 cases per 100,000 per year. Among the different types of odontogenic tumors, at least two lesions are characterized by a cementum overgrowth: cementoblastoma and cemento-ossifying fibroma (Barrios-Garay et al. 2020). Fibro-osseous lesions of the jaw include fibrous cemento-osseous dysplasia (COD), which is the most prevalent osseous-fibrous lesion. COD is further subclassified as focal, periapical, and florid COD based on the extent and distribution of lesions. Focal COD presents with a single lesion predominantly found in black African and East Asian females. Periapical COD presents with multiple lesions restricted to the anterior aspect of the mandible. The lesions are self-limiting and do not exhibit significant growth. In an African setting, periapical COD is prevalent in middle-age black females, suggesting a genetic predisposition. Florid COD presents with multifocal and multiquadrant involvement of tooth-bearing areas of the jaws. Florid COD can occur sporadically or be inherited as familial florid COD (Nel et al. 2020).
  e. *Trauma*: Any substantial trauma to the dental-oral region (e.g., sports, automobile accidents, and falls) may affect tooth roots and associated cementum structure (Chapter 5).
3. **Dental therapies:** Although not relevant for most ancient samples, effects of dental therapies may be pertinent to application of TCA to modern human samples.
   a. *Preventive care*: Routine prophylactic oral health care involves removal of plaque (biofilm) and calculus and, in some cases, may include scaling and root planing. This may result in removal of small amounts of cementum (Newman et al. 2018).
   b. *Caries therapy*: Treatment of dental diseases may alter the structure cementum. In mild caries, restorations are limited to the tooth crown; however, more severe caries may require restoration of tooth roots, which would affect cementum properties.
   c. *Periodontal treatment*: A variety of procedures are used to treat periodontal diseases based on severity of the disease, that is, extent of destruction of the periodontal complex. At early stages of disease, tooth roots are scaled and planed to remove biofilm from the root. This procedure also removes some of the tooth root cementum. In more severe disease, surgical procedures are used to gain access to deeper root infections and apply agents in attempt to restore lost tissues (Heitz-Mayfield et al. 2002; Liang, Luan, and Liu 2020). Interestingly, a cellular cementum-like layer is often found as part of the healing process after removal of diseased acellular cementum, and under those circumstances is referred to as reparative or regenerative cementum (Figure 2.2I) (Bosshardt and Sculean 2009; Bosshardt and Selvig 1997).
   d. *Orthodontic therapy*: Cells within the dentoalveolar region respond to tension and compression related to orthodontic treatment. In some situations, this may modify the structure of tooth roots, e.g., excessive root resorption affecting the composition of cementum (Proffit et al. 2018).
   e. *Endodontic therapy*: In certain situations, such as severe caries and/or trauma, the pulp becomes necrotic and must be removed (i.e., endodontic therapy) in

order to save the tooth. After removal of the pulp, the tooth becomes brittle and normal occlusal forces may compromise the cementum (Garg and Garg 2018).

4. **Drug-induced modifications:** Many drugs alter salivary flow, affecting the microbial environment and extent of caries and periodontal disease, if not carefully monitored. Further, there are several drugs used to treat systemic diseases (e.g., bone, kidney, and heart diseases) that may have direct effects on dental-oral tissues. These include antiresorptive agents (e.g., bisphosphonates, neutralizing antibodies that target osteoclast activities, forms of parathyroid hormone, and other hormonal agents) used to treat disorders of bone density, including osteoporosis. Although rare, antiresorptive therapies have been known to cause osteonecrosis of the jaw, especially high-dose, long-term treatment in the context of poor oral health (Wan et al. 2020; Thumbigere-Math et al. 2009).

2.6 Conclusions

In this chapter, we highlight important aspects of cementum biology, including development, mature cementum structure, different forms of cementum and associated cells, ECM composition, and pathologies and treatment effects that may warrant attention in the context of TCA. Some understanding of underlying cementum biology should be appreciated when employing and interpreting TCA measurements. Chapter 3 will delve deeper into hereditary disorders and how they provide insights into cementum biology.

Acknowledgments

The authors gratefully acknowledge those researchers who have provided critical insights into cementum summarized in this chapter, including especially Dr. Dieter Bosshardt, Dr. Thomas Diekwisch, Dr. Antonio Nanci, Dr. Moon-Il Cho, Dr. Philias Garant, Dr. Knut Selvig, Dr. Hubert Schroeder, Dr. Marc McKee, Dr. Lynda Bonewald, and Dr. Jian Q. Feng, as well as many others. This work was funded by grants DE028411, DE028632, and DE027639 (to BLF), CNPq grant #301086/2019-2 (to FHN), and NIAMS/NIH Intramural Research Program (to MJS).

References

Ababneh, K. T., R. C. Hall, and G. Embery. 1998. Immunolocalization of glycosaminoglycans in ageing, healthy and periodontally diseased human cementum. *Arch Oral Biol* 43 (3): 235–46.
1999. The proteoglycans of human cementum: Immunohistochemical localization in healthy, periodontally involved and ageing teeth. *J Periodontal Res* 34 (2): 87–96.
Aidos, H., P. Diogo, and J. M. Santos. 2018. Root resorption classifications: A narrative review and a clinical aid proposal for routine assessment. *Eur Endod J* 3 (3): 134–45.

Alfaqeeh, S. A., M. Gaete, and A. S. Tucker. 2013. Interactions of the tooth and bone during development. *J Dent Res* 92(12): 1129–35.

Andujar, M. B., D. J. Hartmann, H. Emonard, and H. Magloire. 1988. Distribution and synthesis of type I and type III collagens in developing mouse molar tooth root. *Histochemistry* 88 (2): 131–40.

Arshad, A. I., P. Ahmad, P. M. H. Dummer, M. K. Alam, J. A. Asif, Z. Mahmood, N. A. Rahman, and N. Mamat. 2020. Citation classics on dental caries: A systematic review. *Eur J Dent* 14 (1): 128–43.

Arzate, H., M. Zeichner-David, and G. Mercado-Celis. 2015. Cementum proteins: Role in cementogenesis, biomineralization, periodontium formation and regeneration. *Periodontol 2000* 67 (1): 211–33.

Ballard, D. J., A. S. Jones, P. Petocz, and M. A. Darendeliler. 2009. Physical properties of root cementum: Part 11. Continuous vs intermittent controlled orthodontic forces on root resorption. A microcomputed-tomography study. *Am J Orthod Dentofacial Orthop* 136 (1): 8.e1–8; discussion 8–9.

Barrios-Garay, K., L. Agudelo-Sanchez, J. Aguirre-Urizar, and C. Gay-Escoda. 2020. Analyses of odontogenic tumours: The most recent classification proposed by the World Health Organization (2017). *Med Oral Patol Oral Cir Bucal* 25(6): e732–8.

Bartlett, J. D. 2013. Dental enamel development: Proteinases and their enamel matrix substrates. *ISRN Dent* 2013: 684607.

Becker, J., D. Schuppan, J. P. Rabanus, R. Rauch, U. Niechoy, and H. R. Gelderblom. 1991. Immunoelectron microscopic localization of collagens type I, V, VI and of procollagen type III in human periodontal ligament and cementum. *J Histochem Cytochem* 39 (1): 103–10.

Beertsen, W., T. Van den Bos, and V. Everts. 1990. The possible role of alkaline phosphatase in acellular cementum formation. *J Biol Buccale* 18 (3): 203–5.

Birkedal-Hansen, H., W. T. Butler, and R. E. Taylor. 1977. Proteins of the periodontium. Characterization of the insoluble collagens of bovine dental cementum. *Calcif Tissue Res* 23 (1): 39–44.

Bonewald, L. F. 2011. The amazing osteocyte. *J Bone Miner Res* 26 (2): 229–38.

Boskey, A. L., L. Spevak, E. Paschalis, S. B. Doty, and M. D. McKee. 2002. Osteopontin deficiency increases mineral content and mineral crystallinity in mouse bone. *Calcif Tissue Int* 71 (2): 145–54.

Bosshardt, D. D., and H. E. Schroeder. 1992. Initial formation of cellular intrinsic fiber cementum in developing human teeth. A light- and electron-microscopic study. *Cell Tissue Res* 267 (2): 321–35.

1996. Cementogenesis reviewed: A comparison between human premolars and rodent molars. *Anat Rec* 245 (2): 267–92.

Bosshardt, D. D., and A. Sculean. 2009. Does periodontal tissue regeneration really work? *Periodontol 2000* 51: 208–19.

Bosshardt, D. D., and K. A. Selvig. 1997. Dental cementum: The dynamic tissue covering of the root. *Periodontol 2000* 13: 41–75.

Bosshardt, D., H. U. Luder, and H. E. Schroeder. 1989. Rate and growth pattern of cementum apposition as compared to dentine and root formation in a fluorochrome-labelled monkey (Macaca fascicularis). *J Biol Buccale* 17 (1): 3–13.

Bosshardt, D. D. 2005. Are cementoblasts a subpopulation of osteoblasts or a unique phenotype? *J Dent Res* 84 (5): 390–406.

Bosshardt, D. D., and H. E. Schroeder. 1991. Initiation of acellular extrinsic fiber cementum on human teeth. A light- and electron-microscopic study. *Cell Tissue Res* 263 (2): 311–24.

1996. Cementogenesis reviewed: A comparison between human premolars and rodent molars. *Anat Rec* 245 (2): 267–92.

Bosshardt, D. D., S. Zalzal, M. D. McKee, and A. Nanci. 1998. Developmental appearance and distribution of bone sialoprotein and osteopontin in human and rat cementum. *Anat Rec* 250 (1): 13–33.

Brezniak, N., and A. Wasserstein. 2002. Orthodontically induced inflammatory root resorption. Part I: The basic science aspects. *Angle Orthod* 72 (2): 175–9.

Butler, W. T. 1998. Dentin matrix proteins. *Eur J Oral Sci* 106 Suppl 1: 204–10.

Chan, E., and M. A. Darendeliler. 2006. Physical properties of root cementum: Part 7: Extent of root resorption under areas of compression and tension. *Am J Orthod Dentofacial Orthop* 129 (4): 504–10.

Cho, M. I., and P. R. Garant. 1988. Ultrastructural evidence of directed cell migration during initial cementoblast differentiation in root formation. *J Periodontal Res* 23 (4): 268–76.

Darcey, J., and A. Qualtrough. 2013. Resorption: Part 1: Pathology, classification and aetiology. *Br Dent J* 214 (9): 439–51.

Darendeliler, M. A., O. P. Kharbanda, E. K. Chan, P. Srivicharnkul, T. Rex, M. V. Swain, A. S. Jones, and P. Petocz. 2004. Root resorption and its association with alterations in physical properties, mineral contents and resorption craters in human premolars following application of light and heavy controlled orthodontic forces. *Orthod Craniofac Res* 7 (2): 79–97.

Diekwisch, T. G. 2001. The developmental biology of cementum. *Int J Dev Biol* 45 (5–6): 695–706.

Embery, G., R. Hall, R. Waddington, D. Septier, and M. Goldberg. 2001. Proteoglycans in dentinogenesis. *Crit Rev Oral Biol Med* 12 (4): 331–49.

Fleischmannova, J., E. Matalova, P. T. Sharpe, I. Misek, and R. J. Radlanski. 2010. Formation of the tooth-bone interface. *J Dent Res* 89 (2): 108–15.

Foster, B. L. 2012. Methods for studying tooth root cementum by light microscopy. *Int J Oral Sci* 4 (3): 119–28.

2017. On the discovery of cementum. *J Periodontal Res* 52 (4): 666–85.

Foster, B. L., M. Ao, C. R. Salmon, M. B. Chavez, T. N. Kolli, A. B. Tran, E. Y. Chu, K. R. Kantovitz, M. Yadav, S. Narisawa, J. L. Millan, F. H. Nociti, Jr., and M. J. Somerman. 2018. Osteopontin regulates dentin and alveolar bone development and mineralization. *Bone* 107: 196–207.

Foster, B. L., M. Ao, C. Willoughby, Y. Soenjaya, E. Holm, L. Lukashova, A. B. Tran, H. F. Wimer, P. M. Zerfas, F. H. Nociti, Jr., K. R. Kantovitz, B. D. Quan, E. D. Sone, H. A. Goldberg, and M. J. Somerman. 2015. Mineralization defects in cementum and craniofacial bone from loss of bone sialoprotein. *Bone* 78: 150–64.

Foster, B. L., K. J. Nagatomo, F. H. Nociti, H. Fong, D. Dunn, A. B. Tran, W. Wang, S. Narisawa, J. L. Millán, and M. J. Somerman. 2012. Central role of pyrophosphate in acellular cementum formation. *PLoS One* 7 (6): e38393.

Foster, B. L., F. H. Nociti, Jr., and M. J. Somerman. 2014. The rachitic tooth. *Endocr Rev* 35 (1): 1–34.

Foster, B. L., T. E. Popowics, H. K. Fong, and M. J. Somerman. 2007. Advances in defining regulators of cementum development and periodontal regeneration. *Curr Top Dev Biol* 78: 47–126.

Foster, B. L., M. S. Ramnitz, R. I. Gafni, A. B. Burke, A. M. Boyce, J. S. Lee, J. T. Wright, S. O. Akintoye, M. J. Somerman, and M. T. Collins. 2014. Rare bone diseases and their dental, oral, and craniofacial manifestations. *J Dent Res* 93 (7 Suppl): 7S–19S.

Foster, B. L., Y. Soenjaya, F. H. Nociti, Jr., E. Holm, P. M. Zerfas, H. F. Wimer, D. W. Holdsworth, J. E. Aubin, G. K. Hunter, H. A. Goldberg, and M. J. Somerman. 2013. Deficiency in acellular cementum and periodontal attachment in bsp null mice. *J Dent Res* 92 (2): 166–72.

Foster, B. L., F. H. Nociti, Jr., and M. J. Somerman. 2013. Tooth Root Formation. In *Stem Cells, Craniofacial Development and Regeneration*, eds. G. T. J. Huang and I. Thesleff. Hoboken, NJ: Wiley-Blackwell.

Ganss, B., R. H. Kim, and J. Sodek. 1999. Bone sialoprotein. *Crit Rev Oral Biol Med* 10 (1): 79–98.

Garg, N., and A. Garg. 2018. *Textbook of Endodontics*, 3rd ed. New Delhi: JayPee Brothers.

Goldberg, M., A. B. Kulkarni, M. Young, and A. Boskey. 2011. Dentin: Structure, composition and mineralization. *Front Biosci (Elite Ed)* 3: 711–35.

Groeneveld, M. C., V. Everts, and W. Beertsen. 1995. Alkaline phosphatase activity in the periodontal ligament and gingiva of the rat molar: Its relation to cementum formation. *J Dent Res* 74 (7): 1374–81.

Groeneveld, M. C., T. Van den Bos, V. Everts, and W. Beertsen. 1996. Cell-bound and extracellular matrix-associated alkaline phosphatase activity in rat periodontal ligament. Experimental Oral Biology Group. *J Periodontal Res* 31 (1): 73–9.

Heitz-Mayfield, L. J., L. Trombelli, F. Heitz, I. Needleman, and D. Moles. 2002. A systematic review of the effect of surgical debridement vs non-surgical debridement for the treatment of chronic periodontitis. *J Clin Periodontol* 29 (Suppl 3): 92–102; discussion 160–2.

Ho, S. P., M. Balooch, S. J. Marshall, and G. W. Marshall. 2004. Local properties of a functionally graded interphase between cementum and dentin. *J Biomed Mater Res A* 70 (3): 480–9.

Ho, S. P., M. P. Kurylo, K. Grandfield, J. Hurng, R. P. Herber, M. I. Ryder, V. Altoe, S. Aloni, J. Q. Feng, S. Webb, G. W. Marshall, D. Curtis, J. C. Andrews, and P. Pianetta. 2013. The plastic nature of the human bone-periodontal ligament-tooth fibrous joint. *Bone* 57 (2): 455–67.

Holliday, S., B. Schneider, M. T. Galang, T. Fukui, A. Yamane, X. Luan, and T. G. Diekwisch. 2005. Bones, teeth, and genes: A genomic homage to Harry Sicher's "Axial Movement of Teeth." *World J Orthod* 6 (1): 61–70.

Hu, J. C., Y. H. Chun, T. Al Hazzazzi, and J. P. Simmer. 2007. Enamel formation and amelogenesis imperfecta. *Cells Tissues Organs* 186 (1): 78–85.

Huang, X., P. Bringas, Jr., H. C. Slavkin, and Y. Chai. 2009. Fate of HERS during tooth root development. *Dev Biol* 334 (1): 22–30.

Liang, Y., X. Luan, and X. Liu. 2020. Recent advances in periodontal regeneration: A biomaterial perspective. *Bioact Mater* 5 (2): 297–308.

Luan, X., Y. Ito, and T. G. Diekwisch. 2006. Evolution and development of Hertwig's epithelial root sheath. *Dev Dyn* 235 (5): 1167–80.

Luan, X., Y. Ito, S. Holliday, C. Walker, J. Daniel, T. M. Galang, T. Fukui, A. Yamane, E. Begole, C. Evans, and T. G. Diekwisch. 2007. Extracellular matrix-mediated tissue remodeling following axial movement of teeth. *J Histochem Cytochem* 55 (2): 127–40.

Lungova, V., R. J. Radlanski, A. S. Tucker, H. Renz, I. Misek, and E. Matalova. 2011. Tooth-bone morphogenesis during postnatal stages of mouse first molar development. *J Anat* 218 (6): 699–716.

MacNeil, R. L., J. Berry, J. D'Errico, C. Strayhorn, B. Piotrowski, and M. J. Somerman. 1995. Role of two mineral-associated adhesion molecules, osteopontin and bone sialoprotein, during cementogenesis. *Connect Tissue Res* 33 (1–3): 1–7.

McKee, M. D., and A. Nanci. 1995. Post-embedding colloidal-gold immunocytochemistry of noncollagenous extracellular matrix proteins in mineralized tissues. *Microsc Res Tech* 31: 44–62.

MacNeil, R. L., J. E. Berry, C. L. Strayhorn, Y. Shigeyama, and M. J. Somerman. 1998. Expression of type I and XII collagen during development of the periodontal ligament in the mouse. *Arch Oral Biol* 43 (10): 779–87.

Marks, S. C., Jr., and H. E. Schroeder. 1996. Tooth eruption: Theories and facts. *Anat Rec* 245 (2): 374–93.

McKee, M. D., S. Zalzal, and A. Nanci. 1996. Extracellular matrix in tooth cementum and mantle dentin: Localization of osteopontin and other noncollagenous proteins, plasma proteins, and glycoconjugates by electron microscopy. *Anat Rec* 245 (2): 293–312.

Naji, S., T. Colard, B. Bertrand, E. D'Incau, L. Lanteri, E. Brandt, and J. Blondiaux. 2013. Cementochronology, to cut or not to cut? *Am J Phys Anthropol* 150: 204–5.

Nanci, A. 2018. Periodontium. In *Ten Cate's Oral Histology*. St. Louis, MO: Elsevier.

Nanci, A., and M. J. Somerman. 2008. Periodontium. In *Ten Cate's Oral Histology: Development, Structure, and Function*, ed. A. Nanci. St. Louis, MO: Mosby.

Neely, A. L., V. Thumbigere-Math, M. J. Somerman, and B. L. Foster. 2016. A familial pattern of multiple idiopathic cervical root resorption with a 30-year follow-up. *J Periodontol* 87 (4): 426–33.

Nel, C., Z. Yakoob, C. M. Schouwstra, and W. F. van Heerden. 2020. Familial florid cemento-osseous dysplasia: A report of three cases and review of the literature. *Dentomaxillofac Radiol* 50(1): 20190486.

Newman, M., H. Takei, P. Klokkevold, and F. Carranza. 2018. *Newman and Carranza's Clinical Periodontology*, 13th ed. Philadelphia: Elsevier.

Prasad, M., W. T. Butler, and C. Qin. 2010. Dentin sialophosphoprotein in biomineralization. *Connect Tissue Res* 51 (5): 404–17.

Proffit, W. R., H. W. Fields, B. E. Larson, and D. M. Sarver. 2018. *Contemporary Orthodontics*, 6th ed. Philadelphia: Elsevier.

Rajendran, A., and B. Sivapathasundharam. 2012. *Shafer's Textbook of Oral Pathology*, 7th ed. New Delhi: Elsevier.

Renvoise, E., and F. Michon. 2014. An Evo-Devo perspective on ever-growing teeth in mammals and dental stem cell maintenance. *Front Physiol* 5: 324.

Sawada, T., T. Ishikawa, S. Shintani, and T. Yanagisawa. 2012. Ultrastructural immunolocalization of dentin matrix protein 1 on Sharpey's fibers in monkey tooth cementum. *Biotech Histochem* 87 (5): 360–5.

Schatzle, M., S. D. Tanner, and D. D. Bosshardt. 2005. Progressive, generalized, apical idiopathic root resorption and hypercementosis. *J Periodontol* 76 (11): 2002–11.

Sequeira, P., D. D. Bosshardt, and H. E. Schroeder. 1992. Growth of acellular extrinsic fiber cementum (AEFC) and density of inserting fibers in human premolars of adolescents. *J Periodontal Res* 27 (2): 134–42.

Sodek, J., B. Ganss, and M. D. McKee. 2000. Osteopontin. *Crit Rev Oral Biol Med* 11 (3): 279–303.

Sodek, J., and M. D. McKee. 2000. Molecular and cellular biology of alveolar bone. *Periodontol 2000* 24: 99–126.

2000. Molecular and cellular biology of alveolar bone. *Periodontol 2000* 24: 99–126.

Takano, Y., H. Sakai, E. Watanabe, N. Ideguchi-Ohma, C. K. Jayawardena, K. Arai, Y. Asawa, Y. Nakano, Y. Shuda, Y. Sakamoto, and T. Terashima. 2003. Possible role of dentin matrix in region-specific deposition of cellular and acellular extrinsic fibre cementum. *J Electron Microsc (Tokyo)* 52 (6): 573–80.

Thomas, H. F. 1995. Root formation. *Int J Dev Biol* 39 (1): 231–7.

Thumbigere-Math, V., M. C. Sabino, R. Gopalakrishnan, S. Huckabay, A. Z. Dudek, S. Basu, P. J. Hughes, B. S. Michalowicz, J. W. Leach, K. K. Swenson, J. Q. Swift, C. Adkinson, and D. L. Basi. 2009. Bisphosphonate-related osteonecrosis of the jaw: Clinical features, risk factors, management, and treatment outcomes of 26 patients. *J Oral Maxillofac Surg* 67 (9): 1904–13.

Toyosawa, S., K. Okabayashi, T. Komori, and N. Ijuhin. 2004. mRNA expression and protein localization of dentin matrix protein 1 during dental root formation. *Bone* 34 (1): 124–33.

van Bezooijen, R. L., A. L. Bronckers, R. A. Gortzak, P. C. Hogendoorn, L. van der Wee-Pals, W. Balemans, H. J. Oostenbroek, W. Van Hul, H. Hamersma, F. G. Dikkers, N. A. Hamdy, S. E. Papapoulos, and C. W. Lowik. 2009. Sclerostin in mineralized matrices and van Buchem disease. *J Dent Res* 88 (6): 569–74.

Van den Bos, T., A. L. Bronckers, H. A. Goldberg, and W. Beertsen. 1999. Blood circulation as source for osteopontin in acellular extrinsic fiber cementum and other mineralizing tissues. *J Dent Res* 78 (11): 1688–95.

Veis, A. 1993. Mineral-matrix interactions in bone and dentin. *J Bone Miner Res* 8 (Suppl 2): S493–7.

Walker, C. G., Y. Ito, S. Dangaria, X. Luan, and T. G. Diekwisch. 2008. RANKL, osteopontin, and osteoclast homeostasis in a hyperocclusion mouse model. *Eur J Oral Sci* 116 (4): 312–8.

Wan, J. T., D. M. Sheeley, M. J. Somerman, and J. S. Lee. 2020. Mitigating osteonecrosis of the jaw (ONJ) through preventive dental care and understanding of risk factors. *Bone Res* 8: 14.

Wang, H. M., V. Nanda, L. G. Rao, A. H. Melcher, J. N. Heersche, and J. Sodek. 1980. Specific immunohistochemical localization of type III collagen in porcine periodontal tissues using the peroxidase-antiperoxidase method. *J Histochem Cytochem* 28 (11): 1215–23.

Winter, B. U., A. Stenvik, and V. Vandevska-Radunovic. 2009. Dynamics of orthodontic root resorption and repair in human premolars: a light microscopy study. *Eur J Orthod* 31 (4): 346–51.

Wise, G. E., and G. J. King. 2008. Mechanisms of tooth eruption and orthodontic tooth movement. *J Dent Res* 87 (5): 414–34.

Yamamoto, T., T. Hasegawa, T. Yamamoto, H. Hongo, and N. Amizuka. 2016. Histology of human cementum: Its structure, function, and development. *Jpn Dent Sci Rev* 52 (3): 63–74.

Ye, L., S. Zhang, H. Ke, L. F. Bonewald, and J. Q. Feng. 2008. Periodontal breakdown in the Dmp1 null mouse model of hypophosphatemic rickets. *J Dent Res* 87 (7): 624–9.

Zhao, N., B. L. Foster, and L. F. Bonewald. 2016. The cementocyte – An osteocyte relative? *J Dent Res* 95 (7): 734–41.

Zhao, N., F. H. Nociti, Jr., P. Duan, M. Prideaux, H. Zhao, B. L. Foster, M. J. Somerman, and L. F. Bonewald. 2016. Isolation and functional analysis of an immortalized murine cementocyte cell line, IDG-CM6. *J Bone Miner Res* 31 (2): 430–42.

Zweifler, L. E., M. K. Patel, F. H. Nociti, H. F. Wimer, J. I. Millan, M. J. Somerman, and B. L. Foster. 2014. Counter-regulatory phosphatases TNAP and NPP1 temporally regulate tooth root cementogenesis. *Int J Oral Sci*. In press.

3 Insights into Cementogenesis from Human Disease and Genetically Engineered Mouse Models

Brian L. Foster, Michael B. Chavez, Tamara N. Kolli, and Leigh Oldershaw

3.1 Introduction

Though cementum of the tooth root is critical for dental attachment and periodontal function, this tissue was the last of the dental mineralized tissues to be discovered, more than a century after microscopic structures of enamel and dentin had been described (Foster 2017). Previously published reviews (Bosshardt 2005; Foster and Somerman 2012; Foster et al. 2007), and other chapters in this book (Chapter 2), have provided detailed accounts of the formation, distribution, and composition of acellular cementum (primary cementum, acellular extrinsic fiber cementum) and cellular cementum (secondary cementum, cellular intrinsic fiber cementum) (Figure 3.1A). This chapter emphasizes how insights into the nature of cementum have been gained through human disease and experimental animal models. We focus primarily on the acellular cementum because, compared to cellular cementum, it is more slowly and consistently accumulated over time in humans (and potentially other species) making it more amenable to measurement; it is the variety most critical for tooth attachment; there is much greater information available regarding its genetic regulators; and, importantly, it is the type recommended for use in cementochronology in anthropology. However, the study of cellular cementum may also provide important insights for age estimates in wildlife biology and conditions of hypercementosis, as detailed elsewhere in this book.

The three areas of focus include phosphate metabolism, regulation by inorganic pyrophosphate, and the role of extracellular matrix proteins in cementum formation. This is by no means an exhaustive list, as other signaling pathways, morphogens, growth factors, and regulators have been documented (Foster and Somerman 2012; Bosshardt 2005; Ripamonti 2007; Tummers and Thesleff 2009). To close the chapter, we will consider how these insights may intersect with anthropological and evolutionary studies of cementum.

Though their discussion in an anthropology text may be unexpected, mice are the most commonly studied model research organisms in biology, used to provide insights into human development and disease and serve as experimental models for new therapies. While yeasts, worms, flies, and other species have been instrumental in

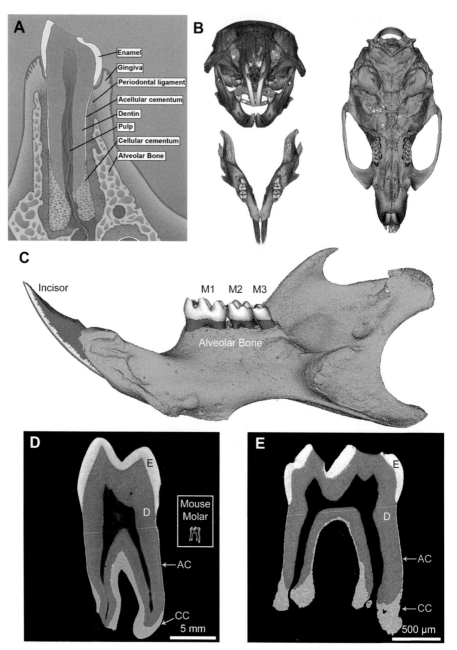

Figure 3.1 Cementum and the human and mouse dentition. (A) Schematic of mouse molar and supporting tissues. (B) Mouse skull (3D rendering from micro-CT scan). (C) The mouse hemi-mandible includes one incisor and three molars (M1–M3) (3D rendering from micro-CT scan). 2D renderings of (D) human premolar (with mouse molar to scale) and (E) mouse molar showing enamel (E), dentin (DE), pulp chamber (P), acellular cementum (AC), and cellular cementum (CC). (A black and white version of this figure will appear in some formats. For the color version, please refer to the plate section.)

studying basic cellular and developmental processes, the laboratory mouse has emerged as the foremost mammalian model system because of shared developmental processes, physiology, and disease progression, cost-effectiveness, and increasing knowledge of mouse genetics in recent decades. Based on discoveries in mouse genetics in the 1980s, the ability to inactivate specific genes emerged in the 1990s as a powerful strategy for testing the functions of the encoded proteins. Although the techniques available for gene editing have expanded in the last two decades, the most basic aim remains to produce a targeted change in a specific gene in order to ascertain its biological importance and function. Genome editing can achieve gene knock-out (disrupting the genomic DNA encoding a gene, deleting expression of the encoded protein), transgenic expression (inserting a gene into the genome, resulting in increased or ectopic expression of the encoded protein), or gene knock-in (inserting a gene into a specific location in the genome, either a "normal" gene or modified or "mutated" version) (Hall, Limaye, and Kulkarni 2009). More sophisticated techniques have since emerged that allow gene editing only in specific cell populations or at certain developmental time points. These gene-editing approaches provide powerful tools that reveal unique insights into developmental and pathological processes.

These genetic advances have led to mice becoming the most common models to study tooth development. Mice have three molar teeth and one incisor per quadrant, for a 1|3 dental formula (Figure 3.1B, C). In mice, teeth begin forming *in utero* at about embryonic day 11.5; molars erupt around postnatal day twenty and are complete and in occlusion by postnatal day twenty-five. Major events in odontogenesis are conserved from rodent to human (Tummers and Thesleff 2009), and anatomy of mouse molars is very similar to human molar teeth (Figure 3.1D, E), including acellular cementum on cervical root surfaces and cellular cementum covering the apical root. Some differences in mouse versus human teeth serve to introduce a note of caution in extrapolating between species. Continuously erupting mouse incisors are not ideal models for human odontogenesis, and mice have a simplified dentition with only incisors and molars compared to human incisors, canines, premolars, and molars. Mice develop one set of teeth (monophyodont), whereas humans develop primary and secondary dentitions (diphyodont). Mouse teeth form rapidly in a matter of weeks while human teeth take months to years to form, and differences in developmental timing and related ultrastructure have been documented across species (Bosshardt and Schroeder 1996; Bosshardt 2005). Despite these limitations, mice have served as model organisms for dental development, with more than 6,000 publications in the last fifty years.

3.2 Phosphate Metabolism

Inorganic phosphate (P_i) is abundant in the body, essential for many biological functions including bone and tooth mineralization where it precipitates with calcium as hydroxyapatite (HAP): $Ca_{10}(PO_4)_6(OH)_2$ or variations with carbonate, fluoride, and/or other chemical substitutions. Hydroxyapatite serves as the inorganic component of our dental and skeletal tissues. P_i metabolism/homeostasis, which maintains a circulating concentration of about 1.5 mM in adults, involves complex interactions of multiple systems that are beyond the scope of this chapter; detailed reviews are available elsewhere (Bergwitz and Jüppner 2010; Foster, Nociti, and Somerman 2014). P_i is typically abundant in the diet and efficiently absorbed in the small intestine, with some notable exceptions discussed later. Physiological levels of P_i (and ionic calcium; Ca^{2+}) are controlled by the kidney-parathyroid-bone axis and three major hormonal regulators (Figure 3.2A). Vitamin D (the active form being 1a, 25-dihydroxyvitamin D_3) promotes P_i and Ca^{2+} absorption in the intestine. Parathyroid hormone (PTH), produced in parathyroid glands and stimulated by hypocalcemia, readjusts Ca^{2+} levels by increasing vitamin D synthesis, increasing renal Ca^{2+} reabsorption, and increasing osteoclastic bone turnover to release Ca^{2+} into the bloodstream. Fibroblast growth factor 23 (FGF23), produced by osteocytes in bone, reduces circulating P_i by promoting renal excretion of P_i and reducing vitamin D levels. Notably, in addition to expressing FGF23, bone also serves as a vast reservoir of Ca^{2+} and P_i. HAP synthesis during bone formation requires absorption and uptake of large amounts of Ca^{2+}, P_i, and other mineral-phase components, while the resorption of bone mineral releases P_i and other components into the blood. Teeth do not undergo physiological turnover, though dental cells are influenced by vitamin D and PTH signaling (Foster, Nociti, and Somerman 2014; Foster and Hujoel 2018).

X-linked hypophosphatemia (XLH) is the most common form of hereditary rickets, having an incidence of about 1 in 20,000. Historically, it was recognized that there were cases of rickets resembling nutritional rickets (i.e., insufficient vitamin D intake or production) that were resistant to conventional treatment of vitamin D supplements or phototherapy, and these came to be classified as "refractory rickets." The rachitic bone pathology resulting from XLH, including short stature, leg bowing, and osteomalacia (Carpenter et al. 2011), results from mutations in the gene *PHEX* (phosphate regulating neutral endopeptidase, X-linked). PHEX is an enzyme with multiple functions secreted mostly by mineralized tissue cells, especially osteocytes (Ruchon et al. 2000). At the tissue level, PHEX cleaves some extracellular matrix (ECM) proteins that inhibit mineralization (those harboring acidic serine aspartate-rich MEPE-associated motifs; ASARMs) (Barros et al. 2013; Salmon et al. 2013). Systemically, PHEX loss-of-function increases FGF23, driving increased P_i excretion, hypophosphatemia, and decreased vitamin D. Treatment of XLH to date has been limited to vitamin D (and analogs) supplementation, though this intervention does not completely alleviate skeletal problems (Carpenter et al. 2011).

Dental case reports for XLH describe the most common manifestations to be enamel defects, thin and poorly mineralized dentin, spontaneous dental fractures and abscesses (infections of the pulp chamber), enlarged pulp chambers and pulp horns, root abnormalities, periodontal disease, and tooth loss due to pulp infections (Baroncelli et al. 2006; Boukpessi et al. 2006; Chaussain-Miller et al. 2003; Pereira et al. 2004; Foster, Nociti, and Somerman 2014; Foster et al. 2014). XLH enamel and dentin manifestations are shown in Figure 3.1B–F. The *Hyp* mouse harboring mutations in the murine *Phex* gene recapitulates skeletal and dental defects of XLH (Eicher et al. 1976; Sitara et al. 2004; Foster, Nociti, and Somerman 2014). Recognized for the first time in the *Hyp*

Insights into Cementogenesis from Human Disease   69

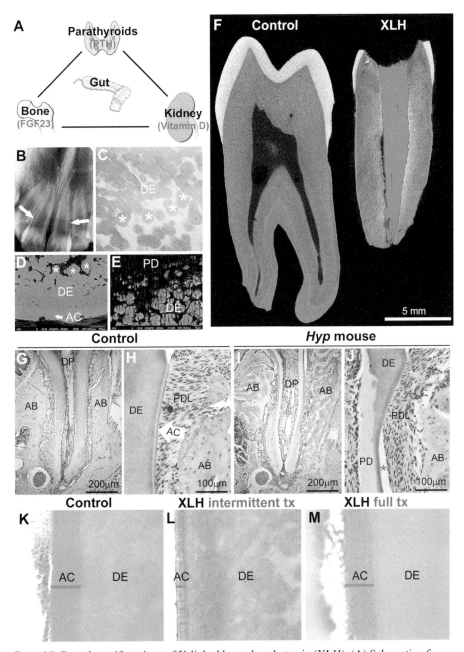

Figure 3.2 Dental manifestations of X-linked hypophosphatemia (XLH). (A) Schematic of kidney-parathyroid-bone axis major hormonal regulators, vitamin D, PTH, and FGF23. (B) Dental radiograph of juvenile with XLH revealing thin dentin and wide pulp chambers. (C) Histology of tooth from an adult with XLH showing excessive interglobular dentin (DE) patterns (*) indicating defective mineralization. (D, E) Scanning electron micrograph images of a tooth from an adult with XLH demonstrating hypomineralized interglobular DE (*), wide predentin (PD), and irregular PD margin. (F) Comparison of healthy control and XLH teeth highlighting hypomineralized interglobular DE (red) in the latter. XLH tooth has undergone endodontic

mouse, hypophosphatemia caused acellular cementum to be thin and hypomineralized, and regions of periodontal fiber detachment were evident (Figure 3.2G–J) (Fong et al. 2009; Coyac et al. 2017). Periodontal problems in human subjects with XLH were not methodically studied until a report on a cohort of individuals with XLH confirmed reduced acellular cementum and provided evidence that early and consistent intervention with vitamin D and P_i significantly improved periodontal parameters (Biosse Duplan et al. 2017) (Figure 3.2K–M).

Mineralization defects of enamel, dentin, and cementum in XLH likely arise from a combination of hypophosphatemia (reduced availability of P_i), elevated local levels of inhibitory peptides, and reduced vitamin D signaling. Defects in dentin apparent by radiograph, micro-CT, histology, and SEM seem to support that dentin is the most severely affected of the mineralized tissues, making it hypomineralized, fragile, and prone to fractures. Acellular cementum is thinner with disturbed mineralization; however, tooth loss from defective attachment is not widely reported in XLH, suggesting broad maintenance of periodontal attachment.

3.3 Pyrophosphate Regulation

The process of biomineralization of the skeleton and dentition minimally requires an extracellular matrix (ECM) scaffold (described in Section 3.4) and P_i and Ca^{2+} ions that precipitate as HAP. Mineralization of ECM anywhere except in bones and teeth is a pathological process referred to as ectopic calcification and is associated with a range of disorders including kidney stones, osteoarthritis, cardiovascular calcification, and more severe genetic conditions. Spatial restriction of ECM mineralization is critical and is regulated by multiple local and systemic factors that can inhibit or otherwise regulate hydroxyapatite formation, including proteins like matrix gla protein (MGP), fetuin-A (AHSG), and osteopontin (OPN).

While P_i functions as a building block for HAP, a closely related small molecule, inorganic pyrophosphate (PP_i; two phosphate ions joined by a phosphoanhydride bond), is a potent inhibitor of HAP crystal growth (Figure 3.3A) and functions as an important line of defense against ectopic calcification. PP_i metabolism is regulated by

---

Caption for Figure 3.2 (cont.)

treatment (blue in pulp). Compared to (G, H) healthy control mice, (I, J) *Hyp* mouse molars show DE hypomineralization, reduced AC, and PDL detachment from root surfaces. (K–M) Histological comparison of (K) healthy control tooth, (L) tooth from an XLH patient who received intermittent treatment (tx) in childhood and adulthood, and (M) tooth from an XLH patient receiving full treatment throughout childhood and adulthood. Panels A, D, and E adapted from Foster et al., *Endocr Rev* 35 (1): 1–34, 2014, and reproduced by permission. Panels B and C adapted from Pereira et al., *J Endod* 30 (4): 241–5, 2004, and reproduced by permission. Panels K–M adapted from Biosse Duplan et al., *J Dent Res* 96 (4): 388–95, 2017, and used in accordance with STM permission guidelines. (A black and white version of this figure will appear in some formats. For the color version, please refer to the plate section.)

Insights into Cementogenesis from Human Disease 71

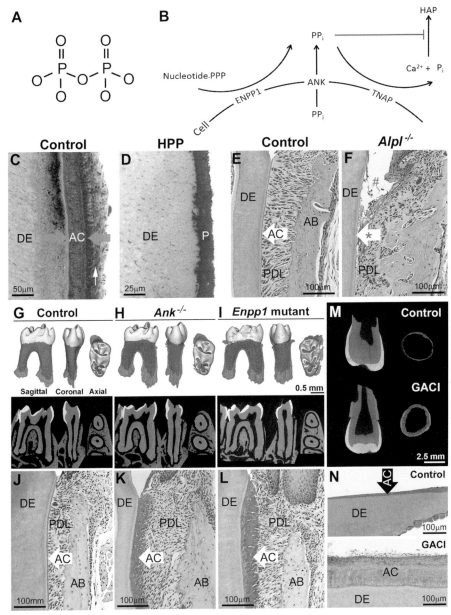

Figure 3.3 Effects of inorganic pyrophosphate (PP$_i$) on cementum. (A) Mineralization inhibitor, PP$_i$. (B) ENPP1, ANK/ANKH, and TNAP regulate levels of PP$_i$ that inhibits hydroxyapatite (HAP) precipitation by phosphate (P$_i$) and calcium (Ca^{2+}). (C, D) Compared to the well-developed acellular cementum (AC) on the dentin (DE) surface in a healthy control tooth, HPP inhibits AC formation allowing dental plaque (P) formation on root surfaces. (E, F) Compared to normal control mice, molars from *Alpl*-/- mice exhibit deficient AC (red * in F), PDL detachment (# in F), and accumulation of osteoid at the alveolar bone (AB) surface. (G–L) Compared to normal control mice, molars from *Ank*-/- or *Enpp1* mutant mice feature dramatically increased AC. 3D (G, top row) and 2D (G, bottom row) images from micro-CT scans show enamel in white, DE in gray, and cementum in yellow. Histology images in J–L show H&E stained

several proteins (Figure 3.3B) and loss-of-function of any of these causes genetic disorders of mineralization.

The first recognized genetic disorder affecting cementum was hypophosphatasia (HPP). Early case reports identified premature loss of deciduous teeth in children with HPP. The cause of tooth loss was identified as absence of the acellular cementum, resulting in weak periodontal attachment (Bruckner, Rickles, and Porter 1962). HPP is caused by mutations in *ALPL*, the gene for tissue-nonspecific alkaline phosphatase (TNAP), an enzyme produced by mineralizing cells of bones and teeth (Millan and Whyte 2016). Skeletal effects of HPP, including hypomineralization (generalized reduction of bone or tooth mineral content), rickets, and osteomalacia (softening of the bones, sometimes marked by accumulation of unmineralized osteoid), result from insufficient TNAP activity to deactivate PP_i and allow mineralization. Reports over several decades have underscored consistent defects in acellular cementum formation in individuals with HPP (Figure 3.3C, D) (van den Bos et al. 2005; Hu et al. 2000; Reibel et al. 2009; Luder 2015). This has been confirmed and further studied in the *Alpl* knock-out mice that mimic skeletal and dental aspects of the most severe forms of HPP, including cementum defects (Figure 3.3E, F) (Beertsen, van den Bos, and Everts 1999; McKee et al. 2011; Foster, Nagatomo, Nociti, et al. 2012). Defects in dentin and enamel have been documented in some human subjects with HPP (Foster et al. 2014; Foster, Nociti, and Somerman 2014; Reibel et al. 2009) and in the HPP mouse model (Foster, Nagatomo, Tso, et al. 2012; Yadav et al. 2012), though these tissues are not as universally or as severely affected by HPP as cementum.

The importance of PP_i metabolism in governing acellular cementum formation is further underscored by examination of two other PP_i regulating proteins (Figure 3.3B). The progressive ankylosis protein (ANK) controls PP_i transport from inside to outside of cells, and ectonucleotide pyrophosphatase phosphodiesterase I (ENPP1) is a cell surface enzyme that produces extracellular PP_i from nucleotide triphosphates like ATP. Therefore, both ANK and ENPP1 promote increased PP_i in tissues, working to inhibit ectopic calcification. Mutations in the human gene *ANKH* are associated with craniometaphyseal dysplasia (CMD) and chondrocalcinosis (CCAL2). Mutations in *ENPP1* cause generalized arterial calcification in infancy (GACI), an often lethal condition within the first year of life. Both disorders involve ectopic calcifications in distinct sites, and *Ank* and *Enpp1* mutant or knock-out mice replicate the major manifestations

---

Caption for Figure 3.3 (cont.)

sections. (M) Compared to an exfoliated primary incisor from a healthy control subject, the primary incisor from an individual with GACI from loss-of-function mutations in *ENPP1* exhibits increased AC (yellow), as shown in 2D reconstructions of the teeth and 3D images isolating only the AC. (N) H&E stained tooth sections from a control and GACI subject reveal the expanded AC. Panels C and D adapted from Luder, *Front Physiol* 6: 307, 2015, and reproduced with permission. Panels G, H, and K adapted from Ao et al., *Bone* 105:134–47, 2017, and reproduced by permission. Panels I, J, L, M, and N adapted from Thumbigere-Math et al., *J Dent Res* 97 (4): 432–41, 2017, and used in accordance with STM permission guidelines. (A black and white version of this figure will appear in some formats. For the color version, please refer to the plate section.)

of excessive mineralization (Ho, Johnson, and Kingsley 2000; Gurley et al. 2006; Okawa et al. 1998; Johnson et al. 2003).

Loss-of-function of either ANK or ENPP1 in mice causes dramatic expansion of acellular cementum thickness and volume (Figure 3.3G–L) (Thumbigere-Math et al. 2018; Ao et al. 2017; Foster, Nagatomo, Nociti, et al. 2012). Development and mineralization of dentin and enamel are not disturbed, in contrast to increased acellular cementum, and cellular cementum and alveolar bone are only modestly affected. Although effects of *ANKH* mutations in humans have yet to be demonstrated, loss-of-function of *ENPP1* has recently been proven to have a similar dramatic effect on human cementum (Figure 3.3M, N) (Thumbigere-Math et al. 2018).

Based on these human and mouse examples, "tuning" of cementogenesis by PP_i (via activities of proteins TNAP, ANK, and ENPP1) appears to be a powerful mechanism that is evolutionarily conserved across species.

3.4 Extracellular Matrix Proteins

Bones and teeth are composites of inorganic and organic elements. The inorganic component is predominantly the HAP that mineralizes enamel, dentin, cementum, bone, and calcified cartilage. The organic component is composed of cells and their secreted ECM, a collection of chemicals, proteins, and molecules. The ECM provides structural support and supplies biomechanical and biochemical cues to cells that direct development, homeostasis, remodeling, and response to injury and disease.

ECM composition of bones and teeth are largely composed of type I collagen (about 90 percent), smaller amounts of other collagens, and noncollagenous proteins. Enamel is the exception, produced by ameloblasts using a semi-specific suite of ECM proteins and proteinases rather than fibrillar collagens (e.g., amelogenin, ameloblastin, enamelin, matrix metalloproteinase 20, and kallikrein 4). Upon the isolation of many proteins from bone and tooth ECM, the hypothesis arose that these proteins closely associated with mineralized matrices might play an active role in regulating mineralization at these sites. This line of thinking was in part based on the observation that many tissues in the body are composed of fibrillar collagens, yet mineralization is generally restricted to bones and teeth. Some have argued that mineralization is spatially restricted by circulating inhibitors such as PP_i (described in detail earlier); however, growing recognition of hereditary mineralization disorders associated with ECM proteins, as well as numerous studies of genetically modified mouse models, provide increasing evidence that ECM proteins play significant roles in local regulation of normal mineralization.

The *S*mall *I*ntegrin-*B*inding *Li*gand, *N*-linked *G*lycoprotein (SIBLING) family of closely related ECM proteins includes some of the earliest discovered from bone and teeth (Fisher and Fedarko 2003). SIBLINGs include bone sialoprotein (BSP), osteopontin (OPN), dentin matrix protein 1 (DMP1), dentin sialoprotein (DSP), dentin phosphoprotein (DPP), and matrix extracellular phosphoglycoprotein (MEPE). BSP was identified as a potential positive regulator ("promoter") of HAP nucleation and

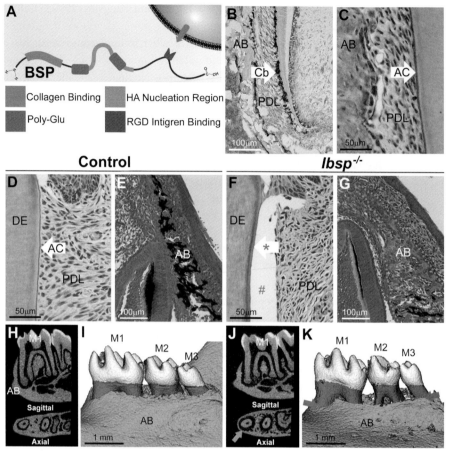

Figure 3.4 Defective cementum in mice lacking bone sialoprotein (BSP). (A) Schematic of BSP highlighting the collagen-binding domain, polyglutamic acid (polyE) motifs, hydroxyapatite (HAP) nucleation region, and arginine-glycine-aspartic acid (RGD) sequence. (B) During mouse molar development, the *Ibsp* gene is expressed (red color) by cementoblasts (Cb) and alveolar bone (AB) osteoblasts. (C) In the completed mouse molar, BSP protein (reddish-brown) is localized to acellular cementum (AC) and AB. (D, F) Compared to H&E stained sections of control mouse molars, *Ibsp-/-* mice feature reduced or absent AC (* in F) and PDL detachment (# in F). (E, G) Von Kossa staining of undecalcified histological sections indicates delayed mineralization (lack of black stain within yellow dotted region) in AB of *Ibsp-/-* mice versus controls. (H–K) 2D and 3D micro-CT scans of mandibles show reduced AB (yellow * and yellow and red arrows) around roots of *Ibsp-/-* mouse molars. Panel B adapted from Foster et al., *Bone* 107: 196–207, 2018, and reproduced by permission. Panel C adapted from Foster et al., *J Dent Res* 92 (2): 166–72, 2013, and used in accordance with STM permission guidelines. Panels D, F, and H–K adapted from Ao et al., *Bone* 105: 134–47, 2017, and reproduced by permission. Panels E and G adapted from Foster et al., *Bone* 78:150–64, 2015, and reproduced with permission. (A black and white version of this figure will appear in some formats. For the color version, please refer to the plate section.)

crystal growth by virtue of its evolutionarily conserved functional domains (Figure 3.4A) (Harris et al. 2000; Goldberg and Hunter 2012). BSP was also identified in cementum and came to be used as a primary marker for cementoblasts, the cells that produce cementum (Figure 3.4B, C) (Bosshardt et al. 1998; McKee, Zalzal, and Nanci 1996; Macneil et al. 1994). Though its function in both bone and dental tissues was unclear, it was proposed that BSP might contribute to proper mineralization of these tissues.

Genetic deletion of BSP in $Ibsp^{-/-}$ mice resulted in smaller long bones, thinner cortical bone, and delayed bone remodeling (Malaval et al. 2008; Holm et al. 2015), supporting the hypothesis that BSP plays an important and nonredundant role in skeletal development and physiology. $Ibsp^{-/-}$ mice featured a dramatic dental phenotype, where enamel and dentin appeared normal but acellular cementum was absent or dramatically reduced, and alveolar bone showed large delays in mineralization (Figure 3.4D–G) (Foster et al. 2015; Foster et al. 2013; Ao et al. 2017). As a result of this lack of acellular cementum, $Ibsp^{-/-}$ mice develop periodontal detachment and severe alveolar bone loss over time (Figure 3.4H–K), emphasizing the importance of the attachment function of cementum. Though the mechanism for cementum deficiency has not been definitively demonstrated in the absence of BSP, the defect is consistent with a role for BSP in initiation of cementum mineralization. No skeletal or dental hereditary condition in humans has yet been associated with BSP; however, several studies have linked *IBSP* polymorphisms to bone density and fracture risk. Genetic ablation of BSP has provided the most dramatic ECM-associated cementum phenotype in a mouse model; however, other ECM factors likely play important roles in cementogenesis. Undoubtedly, additional studies will uncover other ECM components essential for cementum.

3.5 Discussion

To date, anthropological studies of cementum have remained limited in their scope, focusing mainly on the use of cementum banding to determine age or season of death in human and nonhuman populations (Chapters 1, 17–23; Lieberman 1994; Wedel 2007; Kay, Rasmussen, and Beard 1984; Burke and Castanet 1995; Klevezal' and Shishlina 2001). Although mouse models may seem far removed from these applications, information gleaned from mice provides insights into cementum formation. This is especially timely as recent explorations of cementum are uncovering new potential applications for analysis. For example, cementum can potentially be used to identify events that influence Ca^{2+} and P_i biochemistry, including pregnancies, skeletal trauma, and renal dysfunction (Kagerer and Grupe 2001); trace element studies have identified variations in elemental content along bands, suggesting cementum could be used to explore metal exposure over the lifetime (Chapters 6–8; Stock et al. 2017; Martin et al. 2004), and synchrotron imaging has identified potential stress markers in cementum (Mani-Caplazi et al. 2017). This potential wealth of information is unsurprising given the fact that cementum does not remodel and therefore provides a continuous, unchanged, record of life from early childhood through death.

A number of lingering questions related to the origin of cementum banding should be addressed. Though current data suggest that visual differences are the result of differences in collagen fiber orientation and/or mineral content (Chapters 7 and 8), and that banding reflects season of cementum deposition (Colard et al. 2016; Naji et al. 2016; Stock et al. 2017), the exact mechanisms underlying these structures have yet to be verified (Naji et al. 2016). It is also unclear why different quadrants of the root may display different numbers of bands (Strott and Grupe 2003), why some individuals display band numbers significantly incongruous with their biological age, and how disease processes (Kagerer and Grupe 2001; Condon et al. 1986; Wittwer-Backofen, Gampe, and Vaupel 2004; Grosskopf 1990), masticatory loading (Grosskopf and McGlynn 2011), age (Condon et al. 1986; Klevezal' and Shishlina 2001; Pilloud 2004; Strott and Grupe 2003), and climate (Cipriano 2002) affect the formation of incremental lines.

Although more research is necessary in some cases to solidify links between mouse models and human remains, findings presented here highlight some of the potential areas where mouse models and human disease are providing a deeper understanding to anthropological research based on cementum. Some advances and lingering questions are summarized here.

Phosphate metabolism: The influence of P_i metabolism on cementum raises questions about mechanisms underlying cementum band thickness and variations in band mineralization. Hypophosphatemic rickets has been connected to decreased cementum thickness in mice and humans, suggesting that seasonal UV exposure (a stimulus for vitamin D synthesis), and its effects on P_i metabolism, may also influence cementum thickness. How this relates to seasonal banding is unclear, although current research suggests that dark, more mineralized, and possibly more organized bands are formed during winter rest periods (Colard et al. 2016). Interestingly, these periods may also be associated with lower UV exposure and a reduction in P_i absorption.

Mouse models raise questions about the systemic implications of vitamin D–related rickets, a disease that is commonly addressed in bioarchaeology but seldom linked to dental pathologies. If hypophosphatemic rickets results in thin, hypomineralized cementum and defective periodontal attachment, we may need to consider this as a potential factor in determining rates of antemortem tooth loss in past human populations where vitamin D–related rickets was prevalent. If rickets causes a reduced availability of P_i for mineralization, we may also want to test whether other elements substitute for missing P_i, as this may affect trace element content. These findings emphasize the need to question whether or not there are other systemic issues that we might be neglecting to consider when we examine dental pathologies.

Regulation by pyrophosphate: Mouse models and human disorders indicate that PP_i plays a profound role in acellular cementum formation. Loss-of-function of either ANK or ENPP1 in mice results in expanded acellular cementum thickness and volume. Interestingly, in humans with *ENPP1* mutations and GACI, acellular cementum was not only significantly thicker, but mineral density was increased compared to healthy subjects, suggesting the process of HAP deposition was more rapid and capable of increased packing of HAP crystals onto collagen fibrils. If ANK and ENPP1 vary in function, this may explain differences in cementum thickness across time, individuals, and populations.

Extracellular matrix proteins: Based on mouse models, one can speculate that differential deposition of cementum ECM proteins such as BSP and OPN (that may also accompany altered mineralization or collagen deposition) could alter the optical properties of cementum, leading to the appearance of light and dark bands. This hypothesis has not yet been posed or tested.

Evolutionary implications: In broader terms, animal studies can provide significant insight into the evolutionary origins of cementum. Cementum and cementum annuli have been identified in more than seventy-two species of mammals across twenty-one families and nine orders (Klevezal' and Kleĭnenberg 1969; Bosshardt, Luder, and Schroeder 1989; Grue and Jensen 1979; Stallibrass 1982; Klevezal' 1996). The human and mouse cementum phenotypes described in this chapter provide insights into fundamental influences on cementum initiation, growth, and its regulation. This speaks to a larger theme about how mineralization is regulated in the periodontal complex comprised of cementum-periodontal ligament-bone. The gomphosis, or tooth socket, of mammals is a unique form of thecodont tooth attachment shared only with crocodilians among the extant vertebrates (Gaengler 2000). In the gomphosis, the tooth root is separated from the alveolar bone of the socket by the unmineralized periodontal ligament in a three-layer "sandwich" arrangement that maintains tooth flexibility, distributes forces from occlusion, permits cellular activities including remodeling and repair, and maintains vascular, lymphatic, and nerve supply. However, the periodontal ligament, positioned between mineralized tissues, harboring osteoblast and cementoblast progenitor and stem cells and composed of ECM remarkably similar to those of bone and cementum, remains unmineralized, a phenomenon poorly understood at present. This question is both clinically relevant (to understand periodontal disease and repair) and lies at the heart of the evolution of the gomphosis, as the ability to promote and restrict mineralization in a site-specific fashion is key for maintaining hard–soft interfaces. *This evolutionary concept is supported by studies pointing to an ancient origin of cementum and documenting variable regulation of periodontal mineralization in extinct and extant species* (Fong et al. 2016; LeBlanc et al. 2016; LeBlanc and Reisz 2013; Luan et al. 2009; McIntosh et al. 2002).

3.6 Conclusions

Animal studies have long been a source of biological information, and the study of cementum is no exception. Although clear connections are still emerging, it is certain that future research using mouse models will improve methodological and interpretive approaches in many areas of anthropology, including cementum-related studies in paleopathology, cementochronology, and evolutionary biology.

References

Ao, M., M. B. Chavez, E. Y. Chu, K. C. Hemstreet, Y. Yin, M. C. Yadav, J. L. Millan, L. W. Fisher, H. A. Goldberg, M. J. Somerman, and B. L. Foster. 2017. Overlapping functions of bone sialoprotein and pyrophosphate regulators in directing cementogenesis. *Bone* 105: 134–47.

Baroncelli, G. I., M. Angiolini, E. Ninni, V. Galli, R. Saggese, and M. R. Giuca. 2006. Prevalence and pathogenesis of dental and periodontal lesions in children with X-linked hypophosphatemic rickets. *Eur J Paediatr Dent* 7 (2): 61–6.

Barros, N. M., B. Hoac, R. L. Neves, W. N. Addison, D. M. Assis, M. Murshed, A. K. Carmona, and M. D. McKee. 2013. Proteolytic processing of osteopontin by PHEX and accumulation of osteopontin fragments in Hyp mouse bone, the murine model of X-linked hypophosphatemia. *J Bone Miner Res* 28 (3): 688–99.

Beertsen, W., T. VandenBos, and V. Everts. 1999. Root development in mice lacking functional tissue non-specific alkaline phosphatase gene: Inhibition of acellular cementum formation. *J Dent Res* 78 (6): 1221–9.

Bergwitz, C., and H. Jüppner. 2010. Regulation of phosphate homeostasis by PTH, vitamin D, and FGF23. *Annu Rev Med* 61: 91–104.

Biosse Duplan, M., B. R. Coyac, C. Bardet, C. Zadikian, A. Rothenbuhler, P. Kamenicky, K. Briot, A. Linglart, and C. Chaussain. 2017. Phosphate and vitamin D prevent periodontitis in x-linked hypophosphatemia. *J Dent Res* 96 (4): 388–95.

Bosshardt, D., H. U. Luder, and H. E. Schroeder. 1989. Rate and growth pattern of cementum apposition as compared to dentine and root formation in a fluorochrome-labelled monkey (*Macaca fascicularis*). *J Biol Buccale* 17 (1): 3–13.

Bosshardt, D. D., and H. E. Schroeder. 1996. Cementogenesis reviewed: A comparison between human premolars and rodent molars. *Anat Rec* 245 (2): 267–92.

Bosshardt, D. D. 2005. Are cementoblasts a subpopulation of osteoblasts or a unique phenotype? *J Dent Res* 84 (5): 390–406.

Bosshardt, D. D., S Zalzal, M. D. McKee, and A. Nanci. 1998. Developmental appearance and distribution of bone sialoprotein and osteopontin in human and rat cementum. *Anat Rec* 250 (1): 13–33.

Boukpessi, T., D. Septier, S. Bagga, M. Garabedian, M. Goldberg, and C. Chaussain-Miller. 2006. Dentin alteration of deciduous teeth in human hypophosphatemic rickets. *Calcif Tissue Int* 79 (5): 294–300.

Bruckner, R. J., N. H. Rickles, and D. R. Porter. 1962. Hypophosphatasia with premature shedding of teeth and aplasia of cementum. *Oral Surg Oral Med Oral Pathol* 15: 1351–69.

Burke, A. M., and J. Castanet. 1995. Histological observations of cement growth in horse teeth and their applications to archaeology. *J Archaeol Sci* 22: 479–93.

Carpenter, T. O., E. A. Imel, I. A. Holm, S. M. Jan de Beur, and K. L. Insogna. 2011. A clinician's guide to X-linked hypophosphatemia. *J Bone Miner Res* 26 (7): 1381–8.

Chaussain-Miller, C., C. Sinding, M. Wolikow, J. J. Lasfargues, G. Godeau, and M. Garabédian. 2003. Dental abnormalities in patients with familial hypophosphatemic vitamin D-resistant rickets: Prevention by early treatment with 1-hydroxyvitamin D. *J Pediatr* 142 (3): 324–31.

Cipriano, A. 2002. Cold stress in captive great apes recorded in incremental lines of dental cementum. *Folia Primatol (Basel)* 73 (1): 21–31.

Colard, T., G. Falgayrac, B. Bertrand, S. Naji, O. Devos, C. Balsack, Y. Delannoy, and G. Penel. 2016. New insights on the composition and the structure of the acellular extrinsic fiber cementum by Raman analysis. *PLoS One* 11 (12): e0167316.

Condon, K., D. K. Charles, J. M. Cheverud, and J. E. Buikstra. 1986. Cementum annulation and age determination in *Homo sapiens*. II. Estimates and accuracy. *Am J Phys Anthropol* 71 (3): 321–30.

Coyac, B. R., G. Falgayrac, B. Baroukh, L. Slimani, J. Sadoine, G. Penel, M. Biosse-Duplan, T. Schinke, A. Linglart, M. D. McKee, C. Chaussain, and C. Bardet. 2017. Tissue-specific mineralization defects in the periodontium of the Hyp mouse model of X-linked hypophosphatemia. *Bone* 103: 334–46.

Eicher, E. M., J. L. Southard, C. R. Scriver, and F. H. Glorieux. 1976. Hypophosphatemia: Mouse model for human familial hypophosphatemic (vitamin D-resistant) rickets. *Proc Natl Acad Sci USA* 73 (12): 4667–71.

Fisher, L. W., and N. S. Fedarko. 2003. Six genes expressed in bones and teeth encode the current members of the SIBLING family of proteins. *Connect Tissue Res* 44 (Suppl) 1: 33–40.

Fong, H., E. Y. Chu, K. A. Tompkins, B. L. Foster, D. Sitara, B. Lanske, and M. J. Somerman. 2009. Aberrant cementum phenotype associated with the hypophosphatemic *hyp* mouse. *J Periodontol* 80 (8): 1348–54.

Fong, R. K., A. R. LeBlanc, D. S. Berman, and R. R. Reisz. 2016. Dental histology of *Coelophysis bauri* and the evolution of tooth attachment tissues in early dinosaurs. *J Morphol* 277 (7): 916–24.

Foster, B. L. 2017. On the discovery of cementum. *J Periodontal Res* 52 (4): 666–85.

Foster, B. L., M. Ao, C. Willoughby, Y. Soenjaya, E. Holm, L. Lukashova, A. B. Tran, H. F. Wimer, P. M. Zerfas, F. H. Nociti, Jr., K. R. Kantovitz, B. D. Quan, E. D. Sone, H. A. Goldberg, and M. J. Somerman. 2015. Mineralization defects in cementum and craniofacial bone from loss of bone sialoprotein. *Bone* 78: 150–64.

Foster, B. L., K. J. Nagatomo, F. H. Nociti, Jr., H. Fong, D. Dunn, A. B. Tran, W. Wang, S. Narisawa, J. L. Millan, and M. J. Somerman. 2012. Central role of pyrophosphate in acellular cementum formation. *PLoS One* 7 (6): e38393.

Foster, B. L., K. J. Nagatomo, H. W. Tso, A. B. Tran, F. H. Nociti, S. Narisawa, M. C. Yadav, M. D. McKee, J. L. Millán, and M. J. Somerman. 2012. Tooth root dentin mineralization defects in a mouse model of hypophosphatasia. *J Bone Miner Res* 28(2): 271–82.

Foster, B. L., F. H. Nociti, Jr., and M. J. Somerman. 2014. The rachitic tooth. *Endocr Rev* 35 (1): 1–34.

Foster, B. L., T. E. Popowics, H. K. Fong, and M. J. Somerman. 2007. Advances in defining regulators of cementum development and periodontal regeneration. *Curr Top Dev Biol* 78: 47–126.

Foster, B. L., M. S. Ramnitz, R. I. Gafni, A. B. Burke, A. M. Boyce, J. S. Lee, J. T. Wright, S. O. Akintoye, M. J. Somerman, and M. T. Collins. 2014. Rare bone diseases and their dental, oral, and craniofacial manifestations. *J Dent Res* 93 (7 Suppl): 7S–19S.

Foster, B. L., Y. Soenjaya, F. H. Nociti, Jr., E. Holm, P. M. Zerfas, H. F. Wimer, D. W. Holdsworth, J. E. Aubin, G. K. Hunter, H. A. Goldberg, and M. J. Somerman. 2013. Deficiency in acellular cementum and periodontal attachment in bsp null mice. *J Dent Res* 92 (2): 166–72.

Foster, B. L., and P. P. Hujoel. 2018. Vitamin D in dentoalveolar and oral health. In *Vitamin D*, eds. D. Feldman, J. W. Pike, and R. Bouillon. London: Academic Press.

Foster, B. L., and M. J. Somerman. 2012. Cementum. In *Mineralized Tissues in Oral and Craniofacial Science: Biological Principles and Clinical Correlates*, eds. L. K. McCauley and M. J. Somerman. Ames, IA: Wiley-Blackwell.

Gaengler, P. 2000. Evolution of tooth attachment in lower vertebrates to tetrapods. In *Development, Function and Evolution of Teeth*, eds. M. Teaford, M. Smith, and M. Ferguson. Cambridge: Cambridge University Press.

Goldberg, H. A., and G. K. Hunter. 2012. Functional domains of bone sialoprotein. In *Phosphorylated Extracellular Matrix Proteins of Bone and Dentin*, ed. M. Goldberg. France: Bentham Science Publishers.

Grosskopf, B. 1990. Individual age determination using growth rings in the cementum of buried human teeth. *Z Rechtsmed* 103 (5): 351–9.

Grosskopf, B., and G. McGlynn. 2011. Age diagnosis based on incremental lines in dental cementum: a critical reflection. *Anthropol Anz* 68 (3): 275–89.

Grue, H., and B. Jensen. 1979. Review of the formation of incremental lines in tooth cementum of terrestrial animals. *Dan Rev Game Biol* 11: 3–48.

Gurley, K. A., H. Chen, C. Guenther, E. T. Nguyen, R. B. Rountree, M. Schoor, and D. M. Kingsley. 2006. Mineral formation in joints caused by complete or joint-specific loss of ANK function. *J Bone Miner Res* 21 (8): 1238–47.

Hall, B., A. Limaye, and A. B. Kulkarni. 2009. Overview: Generation of gene knockout mice. *Curr Protoc Cell Biol,* Chapter 19, Unit 19.12, 19.12: 1–17.

Harris, N. L., K. R. Rattray, C. E. Tye, T. M. Underhill, M. J. Somerman, J. A. D'Errico, A. F. Chambers, G. K. Hunter, and H. A. Goldberg. 2000. Functional analysis of bone sialoprotein: Identification of the hydroxyapatite-nucleating and cell-binding domains by recombinant peptide expression and site-directed mutagenesis. *Bone* 27 (6): 795–802.

Ho, A. M., M. D. Johnson, and D. M. Kingsley. 2000. Role of the mouse ank gene in control of tissue calcification and arthritis. *Science* 289 (5477): 265–70.

Holm, E., J. E. Aubin, G. K. Hunter, F. Beier, and H. A. Goldberg. 2015. Loss of bone sialoprotein leads to impaired endochondral bone development and mineralization. *Bone* 71: 145–54.

Hu, J. C., R. Plaetke, E. Mornet, C. Zhang, X. Sun, H. F. Thomas, and J. P. Simmer. 2000. Characterization of a family with dominant hypophosphatasia. *Eur J Oral Sci* 108 (3): 189–94.

Johnson, K., J. Goding, D. Van Etten, A. Sali, S. I. Hu, D. Farley, H. Krug, L. Hessle, J. L. Millán, and R. Terkeltaub. 2003. Linked deficiencies in extracellular PP(i) and osteopontin mediate pathologic calcification associated with defective PC-1 and ANK expression. *J Bone Miner Res* 18 (6): 994–1004.

Kagerer, P., and G. Grupe. 2001. Age-at-death diagnosis and determination of life-history parameters by incremental lines in human dental cementum as an identification aid. *Forensic Sci Int* 118 (1): 75–82.

Kay, R. F., D. T. Rasmussen, and K. C. Beard. 1984. Cementum annulus counts provide a means for age determination in *Macaca mulatta* (primates, anthropoidea). *Folia Primatol (Basel)* 42 (2): 85–95.

Klevezal', G. A., and S. E. Kleĭnenberg. 1969. *Age Determination of Mammals from Annual Layers in Teeth and Bones [by] G. A. Klevezal' and S. E. Kleinenberg.* Jerusalem: Israel Program for Scientific Translations.

Klevezal', G. A. 1996. *Recording Structures of Mammals: Determination of Age and Reconstruction of Life History.* trans. M. V. Mina and A. V. Oreshkin. Rotterdam: A. A. Balkema.

Klevezal', G. A., and N. I. Shishlina. 2001. Assessment of the season of death of ancient human from cementum annual layers. *J Archaeol Sci* 28 (5): 481–86.

LeBlanc, A. R., and R. R. Reisz. 2013. Periodontal ligament, cementum, and alveolar bone in the oldest herbivorous tetrapods, and their evolutionary significance. *PLoS ONE* 8 (9): e74697.

LeBlanc, A. R., R. R. Reisz, K. S. Brink, and F. Abdala. 2016. Mineralized periodontia in extinct relatives of mammals shed light on the evolutionary history of mineral homeostasis in periodontal tissue maintenance. *J Clin Periodontol* 43 (4): 323–32.

Lieberman, D. E. 1994. The biological basis for seasonal increments in dental cementum and their application to archaeological research. *J Archaeol Sci* 21 (4): 525–39.

Luan, X., C. Walker, S. Dangaria, Y. Ito, R. Druzinsky, K. Jarosius, H. Lesot, and O. Rieppel. 2009. The mosasaur tooth attachment apparatus as paradigm for the evolution of the gnathostome periodontium. *Evol Dev* 11 (3): 247–59.

Luder, H. U. 2015. Malformations of the tooth root in humans. *Front Physiol* 6: 307.

Macneil, R. L., N. Sheng, C. Strayhorn, L. W. Fisher, and M. J. Somerman. 1994. Bone sialoprotein is localized to the root surface during cementogenesis. *J Bone Miner Res* 9 (10): 1597–606.

Malaval, L., N. M. Wade-Guéye, M. Boudiffa, J. Fei, R. Zirngibl, F. Chen, N. Laroche, J. P. Roux, B. Burt-Pichat, F. Duboeuf, G. Boivin, P. Jurdic, M. H. Lafage-Proust, J. Amédée, L. Vico, J. Rossant, and J. E. Aubin. 2008. Bone sialoprotein plays a functional role in bone formation and osteoclastogenesis. *J Exp Med* 205 (5): 1145–53.

Mani-Caplazi, G., G. Schulz, H. Deyhle, G. Hotz, V. Werner, U. Wittwer-Backofen, and B. Müller. 2017. Imaging of the human tooth cementum ultrastructure of archeological teeth, using hard x-ray microtomography to determine age-at-death and stress periods. Paper read at SPIE Optical Engineering and Applications, 2017, San Diego, CA.

Martin, R. R., S. J. Naftel, A. J. Nelson, A. B. Feilen, and A. Narvaez. 2004. Synchrotron X-ray fluorescence and trace metals in the cementum rings of human teeth. *J Environ Monit* 6 (10): 783–6.

McIntosh, J. E., X. Anderton, L. Flores-De-Jacoby, D. S. Carlson, C. F. Shuler, and T. G. Diekwisch. 2002. Caiman periodontium as an intermediate between basal vertebrate ankylosis-type attachment and mammalian "true" periodontium. *Microsc Res Tech* 59 (5): 449–59.

McKee, M. D., Y. Nakano, D. L. Masica, J. J. Gray, I. Lemire, R. Heft, M. P. Whyte, P. Crine, and J. L. Millán. 2011. Enzyme replacement therapy prevents dental defects in a model of hypophosphatasia. *J Dent Res* 90 (4): 470–76.

McKee, M. D., S. Zalzal, and A. Nanci. 1996. Extracellular matrix in tooth cementum and mantle dentin: Localization of osteopontin and other noncollagenous proteins, plasma proteins, and glycoconjugates by electron microscopy. *Anat Rec* 245 (2): 293–312.

Millan, J. L., and M. P. Whyte. 2016. Alkaline phosphatase and hypophosphatasia. *Calcif Tissue Int* 98 (4): 398–416.

Naji, S., T. Colard, J. Blondiaux, B. Bertrand, E. d'Incau, and J.-P. Bocquet-Appel. 2016. Cementochronology, to cut or not to cut? *Int J Paleopathol* 15:113–9.

Okawa, A., I. Nakamura, S. Goto, H. Moriya, Y. Nakamura, and S. Ikegawa. 1998. Mutation in Npps in a mouse model of ossification of the posterior longitudinal ligament of the spine. *Nat Genet* 19 (3): 271–3.

Pereira, C. M., C. R. de Andrade, P. A. Vargas, R. D. Coletta, O. P. de Almeida, and M. A. Lopes. 2004. Dental alterations associated with X-linked hypophosphatemic rickets. *J Endod* 30 (4): 241–5.

Pilloud, S. 2004. Can there be age determination on the basis of the dental cementum also in older individuals as a significant context between histological and real age determination. *Anthropol Anz* 62 (2): 231–9.

Reibel, A., M. C. Maniere, F. Clauss, D. Droz, Y. Alembik, E. Mornet, and A. Bloch-Zupan. 2009. Orodental phenotype and genotype findings in all subtypes of hypophosphatasia. *Orphanet J Rare Dis* 4 (6).

Ripamonti, U. 2007. Recapitulating development: A template for periodontal tissue engineering. *Tissue Eng* 13 (1): 51–71.

Ruchon, A. F., H. S. Tenenhouse, M. Marcinkiewicz, G. Siegfried, J. E. Aubin, L. DesGroseillers, P. Crine, and G. Boileau. 2000. Developmental expression and tissue distribution of Phex protein: Effect of the Hyp mutation and relationship to bone markers. *J Bone Miner Res* 15 (8): 1440–50.

Salmon, B., C. Bardet, M. Khaddam, J. Naji, B. R. Coyac, B. Baroukh, F. Letourneur, J. Lesieur, F. Decup, D. Le Denmat, A. Nicoletti, A. Poliard, P. S. Rowe, E. Huet, S. O. Vital, A. Linglart, M. D. McKee, and C. Chaussain. 2013. MEPE-derived ASARM peptide inhibits odontogenic differentiation of dental pulp stem cells and impairs mineralization in tooth models of X-linked hypophosphatemia. *PLoS One* 8 (2): e56749.

Sitara, D., M. S. Razzaque, M. Hesse, S. Yoganathan, T. Taguchi, R. G. Erben, H. Jüppner, and B. Lanske. 2004. Homozygous ablation of fibroblast growth factor-23 results in hyperphosphatemia and impaired skeletogenesis, and reverses hypophosphatemia in Phex-deficient mice. *Matrix Biol* 23 (7): 421–32.

Stallibrass, S. 1982. The use of cement layers for absolute ageing of mammalian teeth: A selective review of the literature, with suggestions for further studies. In *Ageing and Sexing Animal Bones from Archaeological Sites*, eds. B. Wilson, C. Grigson, and S. Payne. London: BAR Publishing.

Stock, S. R., L. A. Finney, A. Telser, E. Maxey, S. Vogt, and J. S. Okasinski. 2017. Cementum structure in Beluga whale teeth. *Acta Biomater* 48: 289–99.

Strott, N., and G. Grupe. 2003. Structural characteristics of dental cementum of skeletal remains of the first Catholic cemetery in Berlin (St. Hedwig's Cemetery, Central Berlin; 1777–1834). *Anthropol Anz* 61 (2): 203–13.

Thumbigere-Math, V., A. Alqadi, N. I. Chalmers, M. B. Chavez, E. Y. Chu, M. T. Collins, C. R. Ferreira, K. FitzGerald, R. I. Gafni, W. A. Gahl, K. S. Hsu, M. S. Ramnitz, M. J. Somerman, S. G. Ziegler, and B. L. Foster. 2018. Hypercementosis associated with ENPP1 mutations and GACI. *J Dent Res* 97 (4): 432–41.

Tummers, M., and I. Thesleff. 2009. The importance of signal pathway modulation in all aspects of tooth development. *J Exp Zool B Mol Dev Evol* 312B (4): 309–19.

van den Bos, T., G. Handoko, A. Niehof, L. M. Ryan, S. P. Coburn, M. P. Whyte, and W. Beertsen. 2005. Cementum and dentin in hypophosphatasia. *J Dent Res* 84 (11): 1021–5.

Wedel, V. L. 2007. Determination of season at death using dental cementum increment analysis. *J Forensic Sci* 52 (6): 1334–7.

Wittwer-Backofen, U., J. Gampe, and J. W. Vaupel. 2004. Tooth cementum annulation for age estimation: Results from a large known-age validation study. *Am J Phys Anthropol* 123 (2): 119–29.

Yadav, M. C., R. C. de Oliveira, B. L. Foster, H. Fong, E. Cory, S. Narisawa, R. L. Sah, M. Somerman, M. P. Whyte, and J. L. Millan. 2012. Enzyme replacement prevents enamel defects in hypophosphatasia mice. *J Bone Miner Res* 27 (8): 1722–34.

4 A Comparative Genetic Analysis of Acellular Cementum

Amber E. Trujillo, Alex R. DeCasien, Mareike C. Janiak, Stephan Naji, and Todd R. Disotell

4.1 Introduction

Dental cementum is a calcified substance that anchors the tooth root to the bony alveolar canals (Chapter 2). Though not much is known about the origin of cementoblasts – the cells responsible for the deposition of cementum – extensive work has been done to describe its depositional patterns and genetic regulation (Chapters 2 and 3).

Dental cementum has a long evolutionary history (Chapters 1 and 3). As the vertebrate clade initially began to differentiate, teeth, originally derived from mandibular protrusions, quickly developed into a separate tissue that is attached to the alveolar canals by periodontal fibers. The presence of teeth set in sockets, also known as thecodonty, arose in the Permian period about 250 million years ago (Chapter 16). Not only has thecodonty been identified in recently extinct reptiles, but periodontal ligaments and cementum attachments are present in dinosaurs (LeBlanc, Brink, et al. 2017), Mosasaurs (LeBlanc, Lamoureux, et al. 2017), the earliest tetrapods (LeBlanc and Reisz 2013), and many extinct mammalian relatives (LeBlanc et al. 2016). Across these groups, there appear to be only small differences where cementum is generally located on the root (Garcia and Zurriaguz 2016; Yamamoto et al. 2009). However, we still lack a firm understanding of the external drivers and the genetic mechanisms underlying variation in cementum deposition across this wide array of animals.

In the late nineteenth century, Magitot (1878) found that acellular cementum – as opposed to cellular cementum – could be used as a direct proxy of age due to its predictable pattern of deposition (Chapter 1). Nonetheless, it was not until 1982 that researchers were able to use cementum incremental growth pattern as a reliable age indicator in humans following earlier development in zooarchaeology (Laws 1952; Stott et al. 1982; Chapter 1). The use of cementum growth layers has generally been referred to as the tooth cementum annulations (TCA) method in biological anthropology; however, we prefer the term "cementochronology" as defined in skeletochronology (Baglinière et al. 1992; Introduction). Cementochronology has been validated in more than twenty studies and across seventy-two species of mammals, representing twenty-one families and nine orders (Klevezal' 1996; Grue and Jensen 1979; Spinage

1976), as well as in some extinct and extant reptiles (Gaengler and Metzier 1992; Garcia and Zurriaguz 2016; LeBlanc and Reisz 2013).

Although cementum has been used for decades to estimate age and season at death in multiple mammal families (Naji et al. 2016; Chapter 1), the evolutionary genetic history of this tissue remains poorly understood. Researchers have found that, unlike enamel, which ceases to grow, or dentine, which is not deposited seasonally, acellular cementum (AC) does both (Chapter 2); however, taxon-specific factors may also influence AC deposition via alterations to relevant genes.

Contrary to previous hypotheses (Lieberman 1994), several recent studies have evidenced that the variation of AC deposition visible as contrasted opaque/translucent increments in transmitted bright field light is due to relative mineralization (Colard et al. 2016; Stock et al. 2017, and Chapters 6, 7, and 14). There are endogenous and exogenous factors that likely influence AC deposition and its underlying genetic architecture, such as (1) diet in relationship to nutrition and potential deficiencies leading to mineralization variations; (2) biomechanical stress stimulating cementogenesis (King and Hughes 2001; Chapter 5); (3) pathological conditions affecting mineralization or cementum production (Chapters 3, 4, and 5); and (4) hormonal cycles and processes associated with circadian clocks influencing cementogenesis rate (Zheng et al. 2014; Introduction and Chapter 3).

Here, we conducted a comparative analysis of four candidate genes associated with cementum deposition across more than forty species of mammals, reptiles, and birds. In order to investigate the evolutionary importance of these genes, we determined the overall type of selection (purifying, neutral, or positive) that has acted on them throughout their evolutionary histories. We also identified which type of selection best describes the recent evolutionary histories of all species included. Finally, we tested for significant correlations between lineage-specific selection pressures and four external factors that may influence the selection pressure on cementum genes: diet, radicularity (number of roots), total number of teeth, and life span.

4.2 Candidate Genes

ALPL encodes a member of the alkaline phosphatase family of proteins (alternatively referred to as tissue-nonspecific alkaline phosphatase – TNSALP, TNALP, or TNP) and is expressed in bone, teeth, liver, kidney, the central nervous system, and fibroblasts (Millán 2006). Experimentally caused loss-of-function mutations in *ALPL* result in hypophosphatasia (HPP), which leads to defects in skeletal and dental mineralization (Millán and Whyte 2016; Whyte 2016). Recent studies have also demonstrated that loss-of-function mutations to *ALPL* in osteoblasts and specific dental cells result in knock-out mice with "short molar roots with thin dentin, lack of acellular cementum, and osteoid accumulation in alveolar bone" (Foster et al. 2012; Foster et al. 2017; Chapter 3). Although homozygous or compound heterozygous expressions of HPP are relatively rare in humans – 1:100,000 in Canada and 1:300,000 in Europe (Mornet 2017) – the most severe cases lead to death *in utero* (Whyte 2017). Other clinical forms often manifest as rickets, muscle weakness, vitamin B_6–dependent seizures, and skeletal deterioration (Millàn and Whyte 2016). Children with HPP prematurely lose their deciduous teeth due to insufficient mineralization of cementum, specifically acellular cementum (van den Bos et al. 2005; Reibel et al. 2009; Bloch-Zupan 2016). Due to its influence on the development of dental alveolar tissues, specifically AC, we included *ALPL* as a candidate gene.

We predict that *ALPL* will be characterized by purifying selection overall. This is because *ALPL* plays such an essential role in the healthy deposition of cementum, and any deleterious mutations may result in death or a reduction in reproductive success. However, we also predict that lineages that have undergone recent, rapid evolutionary changes in dental anatomy will show positive selection on *ALPL* because morphological changes necessitate nonsynonymous mutations in relevant genes. Finally, we predict that tooth count and radicularity will be positively correlated with selection pressure on *ALPL* because species with more teeth and/or roots require a larger amount of cementum deposition as well as the mutations necessary to impact the change in *ALPL* expression. A negative association would imply that an increase in "purifying" selection has acted on this gene as tooth/root number increased, which would suggest that the gene does not contribute to the genetic basis of phenotypic change

BMP-2 and *-7* are two members of the bone morphogenetic protein (BMP) gene family that are expressed in various mineralized tissues throughout the body. However, specifically regarding dental-alveolar tissues, *BMP-7* is expressed in alveolar bone, cementum, and the periodontal ligaments while *BMP-2* is expressed solely in alveolar bone (Yamashiro et al. 2003; Thesleff 2003). Although *BMP-2* is not expressed in cementum, it stimulates alkaline phosphatase activity during osteoblast differentiation (Zeichner-David 2006), thereby influencing cementum development. Molar furcation defects in baboons treated with *BMP-7* result in significant cementogenesis while *BMP-2* treatment leads to limited cementum formation but increased bone mineralization (Zeichner-David 2006). In addition, *BMP-2* enhances bone and cementum formation compared to untreated or carrier-only-treated controls in a rat model of periodontal regeneration (King et al. 1997).

Interestingly, the effects of BMPs on dental development may also be influenced by external factors, including masticatory forces (King and Hughes 2001). Specifically, experimentally induced masticatory hypofunction stimulates early bone growth, and the addition of *BMP-2* treatment leads to increased ankylosis, or stiffening of the joint, due to bone fusion. Furthermore, occlusal loading stimulates remodeling and enhances *BMP-2*–induced cementogenesis (King and Hughes 1999), in line with the secondary determinants of cementum deposition as identified by Lieberman (1994).

We predict that the BMPs will be under purifying selection overall, due to their role in tooth and root formation; that positive selection will characterize lineages with recent, substantial alterations to dental anatomy; and that lineage-specific selection pressure on the BMPs will be positively correlated with tooth number and radicularity. In addition, we predict that lineage-specific selection pressure will be increased in species with herbivorous diets, since these rough foods (e.g., roots and barks) exert relatively higher levels of masticatory pressure.

The Aryl hydrocarbon receptor nuclear translocator-like (*ARNTL*) gene has been identified as an essential vertebrate clock gene (Zheng et al. 2014; Yan et al. 2014). Clock genes are a family of molecular elements that control circadian functions such as the dental mineralization of tissue formation. More specifically, *ARNTL* functions by binding enhancer elements upstream of other clock genes to control their activation (Murphy et al. 2018). Given that *ARNTL* influences the expression of other circadian rhythm genes, this gene may affect the development of tissues that are regulated by circadian clocks, including cementum. Although researchers have not yet linked specific genes to the circadian deposition of cementum, *ARNTL* may be a good candidate because it plays a role in the deposition of enamel and dentine, which are developmentally similar to cementum with comparable incremental cyclic growth patterns.

We predict that *ARNTL* will be characterized by purifying selection overall because it plays such a critical role in regulating circadian biological processes across vertebrates. Given that longer-lived species need to maintain regular cementum deposition for an extended period of time, we also predict that species with recent evolutionary increases in life span will demonstrate branch-specific positive selection, and that species maximum life span will be positively correlated with lineage-specific selection pressure.

4.3   Results

We first obtained the human sequences for our candidate genes, namely *ALPL, BMP-2, BMP-7,* and *ARNTL*. These sequences were then used as queries (sequences searched against in the National Center from Biotechnology Information (NCBI) database) to both run standard nucleotide BLAST (BLASTN – fully assembled genomes) and Sequence Read Archive BLAST (BLAST suite-SRA – unassembled portions of genomes) searches of forty-nine to fifty-six vertebrate species (species sample size per gene depended on sequence availability and quality). These species included four vertebrate classes (*Mammalia, Reptilia, Aves,* and *Amphibia*) and twenty vertebrate orders whose genomes are included in the NCBI database. Only sequences that matched the query by more than 75 percent were used. Protein coding regions were downloaded, concatenated, and aligned using pairwise global alignment with the MAFFT alignment server (Katoh et al. 2019) and Geneious analysis software (Kearse et al. 2012). Using a codon-based maximum likelihood model, PAML (Yang, 1997), in which the nonsynonymous to synonymous mutation rate (dN/dS) ratios are averaged across all sites and lineages, overall or global selection was analyzed. Unsurprisingly, global purifying selection was found in all candidate genes, presumably due to the necessity of cementum in all thecodonts and subsequent removal of deleterious mutations.

We examined branch-specific selection patterns using the adaptive branch-site random effects likelihood (aBSREL) model in the HyPhy software package (Smith et al. 2015), incorporating a maximum likelihood tree created in IQ-TREE. These analyses identified multiple branch-specific instances of positive selection for *ALPL, BMP-2*, and *BMP-7*. Specifically, positive selection on *ALPL* was detected for the branches leading to the large flying fox (*Pteropus vampyrus*), Weddell seal (*Leptonychotes weddellii*),

Australian saltwater crocodile (*Crocodylus porosus*), gharial (*Gavialis gangeticus*), the Chinese (*Alligator sinensis*), and American (*Alligator mississippiensis*) alligators. Positive selection on *BMP-2* was found for branches leading to the Arabian camel (*Camelus dromedarius*), American alligator, Australian saltwater crocodile, gharial, bald eagle (*Haliaeetus leucocephalus*), and emperor penguin (*Aptenodytes forsteri*). Positive selection on *BMP-7* was detected for branches leading to the domestic cat (*Felis catus*), great roundleaf bat (*Hipposideros armiger*), Weddell seal, rabbit (*Oryctolagus cuniculus*), and alpaca (*Vicugna pacos*). Interestingly, many of these species (i.e., crocodiles, alligators, and gharials) exhibit polyphyodonty (i.e., continual replacement of teeth). Furthermore, given that tooth dwarfism (and the genetic mutations that accompany it) is usually linked to domestication (Zeuner 1963), it is not surprising to see positive selection on these genes in domesticated lineages. Finally, no instances of branch-specific positive selection on *ARNTL* were identified.

To test how lineage-specific selection pressure may be influenced by exogenous factors, we first used the HyPhy software package (Smith et al. 2015) to calculate root-to-tip dN/dS ratios (lineage-specific selection pressure) for each species and candidate gene. The dN/dS ratio considers the number of nonsynonymous (mutations that change the amino acid) to synonymous (mutations that do not change the amino acid) mutation rates across each gene in order to classify whether it is under positive, neutral, or purifying selection (dN/dS > 1, ~1, and < 1, respectively). Whereas positive selection indicates that the gene is changing (possibly in response to an exogenous factor), neutral and purifying selection implies that the gene is not changing or has become fixed. The correlation between lineage-specific selection pressure and the various behavioral/morphological characteristics discussed earlier, including diet type, tooth count, radicularity, and maximum life span, was then explored using phylogenetic generalized least squares (PGLS) regression models. These analyses were carried out in R 3.2.2 (R Core 2017).

Our prediction that species with coarser diets would exhibit increased selection pressure on cementum genes was not supported. Specifically, selection pressure on *BMP-7* was significantly higher for insectivores compared to all other diet types (carnivores, frugivores, herbivores, and omnivores) after a strong outlier, the rabbit, was removed ($p < 0.0001$ for each comparison; Figure 4.1). In contrast to other lagomorphs, rabbits and hares experienced an evolutionary increase in molar number, the development of molarized upper premolars, and retention of the upper M3. This unique evolutionary history likely explains their extremely high dN/dS ratio. An insectivorous diet does not require high mastication strength because they pierce their prey using extremely sharp dentition; rather, the increased selection pressure in insectivores may be due to their evolved and highly specialized dentition, such as their degenerate incisors and "less robust anteroposterior [dental] diameters" (Samuels 2009). Overall, these results suggest that, though diet may be influencing selection pressure on *BMP-7* (as is reflected in the separation of insectivore dN/dS ratios in Figure 4.1), masticatory forces in particular may not be the driving factor. The influence of diet or food coarseness seems to only be affecting cementum distribution on the root morphology via mastication variations in associated biomechanical loadings (Chapter 5).

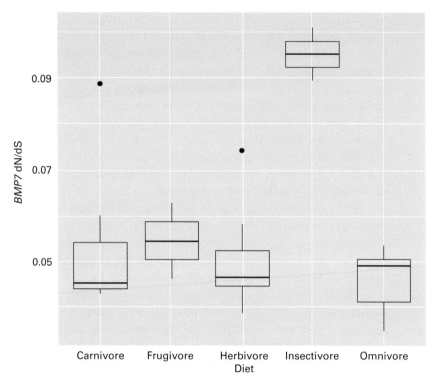

Figure 4.1 Compared to other diet types, insectivores exhibit significantly higher *BMP-7* dN/dS ratios (when excluding *O. cuniculus*; $p < 0.001$). Box and whisker plots show interquartile ranges (rectangles), medians (solid black lines), and outliers (black dots).

Our prediction that longer-lived species would exhibit increased selection pressure on the clock gene *ARNTL* was also supported ($p = 0.04$; Figure 4.2). This suggests that life span influences selection pressure on this gene, which may reflect the fact that longer-lived species require periodic cementum deposition to continue for longer periods of time.

Our predictions that selection pressure would be increased on genes associated with cementum deposition in species with more teeth and radicularity were supported. Specifically, selection pressure on *BMP-2* is positively correlated with total number of teeth ($p = 0.04$; Figure 4.3), even after the birds, which do not have teeth, were removed from the analysis. The bird species in our study exhibit a wide range of dN/dS ratios. Two of these species, the bald eagle and emperor penguin, exhibit the highest ratios of any species and are also characterized by recent positive selection on *BMP-2* (Figure 4.3).

Although birds do not require cementum deposition, their evolution is characterized by extreme alterations to their skeletons that aid in flight (Dumont 2010); therefore, their high dN/dS ratios likely reflect the fact that *BMP-2* is involved in bone growth and osteoblast differentiation (Zeichner-David 2006).

Finally, we found a positive correlation between selection pressure on *ALPL* and the number of polyradicular teeth ($p = 0.01$; Figure 4.4).

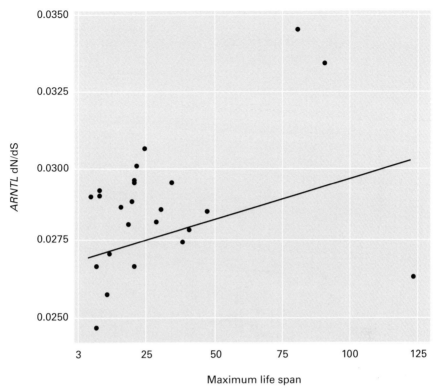

Figure 4.2 Phylogenetic generalized least squares (PGLS) regression between the dN/dS of *ARNTL* and maximum life span ($p = 0.04$).

4.4 Conclusion

Cementum has been utilized as a proxy for age in multiple subfields of anthropology, including forensics, zooarchaeology, and bioarchaeology. We have used analytical approaches from evolutionary genetics to deepen our understanding of the biological mechanisms that control cementum deposition. In particular, we examined (1) patterns of selection on multiple genes associated with cementum deposition; and (2) behavioral and morphological characteristics that have influenced the evolution of these genes.

Our results demonstrate that meaningful changes to these genes have occurred in lineages that have recently experienced rapid changes to their dental anatomy. Furthermore, we demonstrate that both behavioral and morphological characteristics, including diet type, tooth number, radicularity, and life span, influence the selection pressure on genes associated with the development of cementum. This increase in selection pressure suggests that these genes are evolving to accommodate behavioral niches that may require alterations to cementum deposition. Though cementum deposition is a universal mechanism that occurs in all thecodonts, our results suggest that certain behavioral and morphological characteristics may

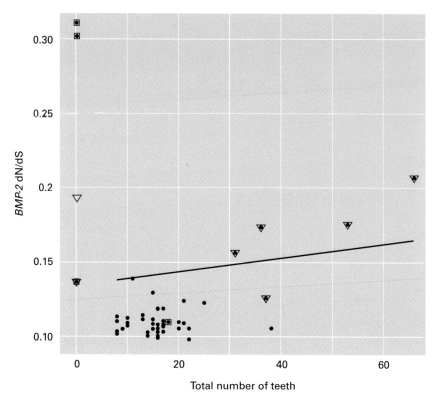

Figure 4.3 PGLS regression between dN/dS ratio of *BMP-2* and total number of teeth, excluding species with no teeth ($p = 0.04$). Mammals, aves, and reptiles are denoted as circles, squares, and triangles, respectively.

influence the structure of genes and proteins associated with cementum. It is essential to note that, although the candidate genes examined here are associated with the deposition of cementum, none of these genes is solely responsible for cementogenesis, and all are pleiotropic.

In the future, our understanding of the genetic architecture underlying cementum deposition will be deepened by additional knock-out experiments that identify other genes involved. Furthermore, additional phylogenetic comparative analyses on genes that have already been experimentally linked to the development of cementum, such as *Rsk2* (Koehne et al. 2016), bone sialoprotein (*BSP*), and ectonucleotide pyrophosphatase phosphodiesterase 1 (*ENPP1*), should be conducted.

Acknowledgments

We thank Dr. Ryan Raaum for statistical advice, which was integral to the betterment of this chapter.

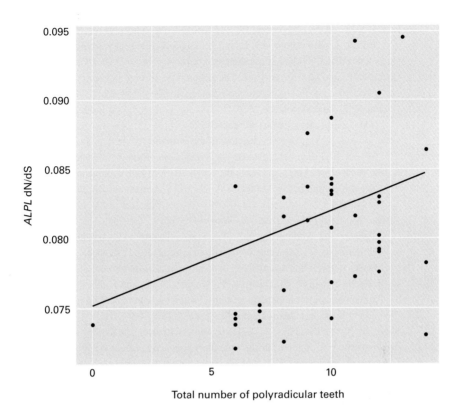

Figure 4.4 PGLS regression between the dN/dS ratio of *ALPL* and the total number of polyradicular teeth ($p = 0.01$).

References

Baglinière, J.-L., Castanet, J., Conand, F. and Meunier, F. J. 1992. Terminologie en sclérochronologie chez les Vertébrés. In J.-L. Baglinière, J. Castanet, F. Conand, and F. J. Meunier, eds. *Tissus durs et âge individuel des vertébrés*, Paris: ORSTOM/INRA Editions, 443–47.

Bloch-Zupan, A. 2016. Hypophosphatasia: Diagnosis and clinical signs – A dental surgeon perspective. *International Journal of Paediatric Dentistry*, 26(6): 426–38.

Colard, T., Falgayrac, G., Bertrand, B., Naji, S., Devos, O., Balsack, C., Delannoy, Y., and Penel, G. 2016. New insights on the composition and the structure of the acellular extrinsic fiber cementum by Raman analysis. *PloS One*, 11(12): e0167316.

Dumont, E. R. 2010. Bone density and the lightweight skeletons of birds. *Proceedings of the Royal Society of London B: Biological Sciences*, 277(1691): 2193–8.

Foster, B. L., Nagatomo, K. J., Nociti Jr, F. H., Fong, H., Dunn, D., Tran, A. B., Wang, W., Narisawa, S., Millán, J. L. and Somerman, M. J. 2012. Central role of pyrophosphate in acellular cementum formation. *PLoS One*, 7(6): e38393.

Foster, B. L., Kuss, P., Yadav, M. C., Kolli, T. N., Narisawa, S., Lukashova, L., Cory, E., Sah, R. L., Somerman, M. J., and Millán, J. L. 2017. Conditional ALPL ablation phenocopies dental defects of hypophosphatasia. *Journal of Dental Research*, 96(1): 81–91.

Gaengler, P., and E. Metzier. 1992. The periodontal differentiation in the phylogeny of teeth–an overview. *Journal of Periodontal Research*, 27(3): 214–25.

Garcia, R. A., and Zurriaguz, V. 2016. Histology of teeth and tooth attachment in titanosaurs (*Dinosauria*; *Sauropoda*). *Cretaceous Research*, 57: 248–56.

Grue, H., and Jensen, B. 1979. Review of the formation of incremental lines in tooth cementum of terrestrial mammals. *Danish Review of Game Biology* (*Denmark*), 11(1979): 1–48.

Katoh, K., Rozewicki, J., and Yamada, K. D. 2019. MAFFT online service: multiple sequence alignment, interactive sequence choice and visualization. *Briefings in Bioinformatics*, 20(4): 116–66.

Kearse, M., Moir, R., Wilson, A., Stones-Havas, S., Cheung, M., Sturrock, S., Buxton, S., Cooper, A., Markowitz, S., Duran, C., Thierer, T., Ashton, B., Mentjies, P., and Drummond, A. 2012. Geneious Basic: an integrated and extendable desktop software platform for the organization and analysis of sequence data. *Bioinformatics*, 28(12): 1647–49.

King, G. N., King, N., Cruchley, A. T., Wozney, J. M., and Hughes, F. J. 1997. Recombinant human bone morphogenetic protein-2 promotes wound healing in rat periodontal fenestration defects. *Journal of Dental Research*, 76(8): 1460–70.

King, G. N., and Hughes, F. J. 1999. Effects of occlusal loading on ankylosis, bone, and cementum formation during bone morphogenetic protein-2-stimulated periodontal regeneration in vivo. *Journal of Periodontology*, 70(10): 1125–35.

King, G. N., and Hughes, F. J. 2001. Bone morphogenetic protein-2 stimulates cell recruitment and cementogenesis during early wound healing. *Journal of Clinical Periodontology*, 28(5): 465–75.

Klevezal', G. A. 1996. *Recording Structures of Mammals: Determination of Age and Reconstruction of Life History*, Rotterdam: A. A. Balkema.

Koehne, T., Jeschke, A., Petermann, F., Seitz, S., Neven, M., Peters, S., Luther, J., Schweizer, M., Schinke, T., Kahl-Nieke, B., and Amling, M. 2016. Rsk2, the kinase mutated in Coffin-Lowry syndrome, controls cementum formation. *Journal of Dental Research*, 95(7): 752–60.

Laws, R. M. 1952. A new method of age determination for mammals. *Nature*, 169(4310): 972.

LeBlanc, A. R., and Reisz, R. R. 2013. Periodontal ligament, cementum, and alveolar bone in the oldest herbivorous tetrapods, and their evolutionary significance. *PLoS One*, 8(9): e74697.

LeBlanc, A. R., Reisz, R. R., Brink, K. S., and Abdala, F. 2016. Mineralized periodontia in extinct relatives of mammals shed light on the evolutionary history of mineral homeostasis in periodontal tissue maintenance. *Journal of Clinical Periodontology*, 43(4): 323–32.

LeBlanc, A. R., Lamoureux, D. O. and Caldwell, M. W. 2017. Mosasaurs and snakes have a periodontal ligament: Timing and extent of calcification, not tissue complexity, determines tooth attachment mode in reptiles. *Journal of Anatomy*, 231(6): 869–85.

LeBlanc, A. R., Brink, K. S., Cullen, T. M., and Reisz, R. R. 2017. Evolutionary implications of tooth attachment versus tooth implantation: A case study using dinosaur, crocodilian, and mammal teeth. *Journal of Vertebrate Paleontology*, 37(5): e1354006.

Lieberman, D. E. 1994. The biological basis for seasonal increments in dental cementum and their application to archaeological research. *Journal of Archaeological Science*, 21: 525–25.

Magitot, E. 1878. *Treatise on Dental Caries: Experimental and Therapeutic Investigations.* Houghton: Osgood and Company.

Millán, J. L. 2006. Alkaline phosphatases: Structure, substrate specificity and functional relatedness to other members of a large superfamily of enzymes. *Purinergic Signal*, 2(2): 335–41.

Millán, J. L., and Whyte, M. P. 2016. Alkaline phosphatase and hypophosphatasia. *Calcified Tissue International*, 98(4): 398–416.

Mornet, E., 2017. Genetics of hypophosphatasia. *Archives de Pédiatrie*, 24(5): 5S51–6.

Murphy, M., Brown, G., Wallin, C., Tatusova, T., Pruitt, K., Murphy, T., and Maglott, D. 2018. Gene help: Integrated access to genes of genomes in the reference sequence collection. In *Gene Help [Internet]*. National Center for Biotechnology Information (US). www.ncbi.nlm.nih.gov/books/NBK3841

Naji, S., Colard, T., Blondiaux, J., Bertrand, B., d'Incau, E., and Bocquet-Appel, J.-P. 2016. Cementochronology, to cut or not to cut? *International Journal of Paleopathology*, 15: 113–9.

Reibel, A., Manière, M. C., Clauss, F., Droz, D., Alembik, Y., Mornet, E., and Bloch-Zupan, A. 2009. Orodental phenotype and genotype findings in all subtypes of hypophosphatasia. *Orphanet Journal of Rare Diseases*, 4(1): 6.

Samuels, J. X. 2009. Cranial morphology and dietary habits of rodents. *Zoological Journal of the Linnean Society*, 156(4): 864–88.

Smith, M. D., Wertheim, J. O., Weaver, S., Murrell, B., Scheffler, K., and Kosakovsky Pond, S. L. 2015. Less is more: An adaptive branch-site random effects model for efficient detection of episodic diversifying selection. *Molecular Biology and Evolution*, 32(5): 1342–53.

Spinage, C. A. 1976. Incremental cementum lines in the teeth of tropical African mammals. *Journal of Zoology*, 178(1): 117–31.

Stock, S. R., L. A. Finney, A. Telser, E. Maxey, S. Vogt, and J. S. Okasinski. 2017. Cementum structure in Beluga whale teeth. *Acta Biomaterialia*, 48(2017): 289–99.

Stott, G. G., Sis, R. F., and Levy, B. M. 1982. Cemental annulation as an age criterion in forensic dentistry. *Journal of Dental Research*, 61(6): 814–17.

Thesleff, I. 2003. Developmental biology and building a tooth. *Quintessence International*, 34(8).

van den Bos, T., Handoko, G., Niehof, A., Ryan, L. M., Coburn, S. P., Whyte, M. P., and Beertsen, W. 2005. Cementum and dentin in hypophosphatasia. *Journal of Dental Research*, 84(11): 1021–25.

Whyte, M. P. 2016. Hypophosphatasia – Aetiology, nosology, pathogenesis, diagnosis and treatment. *Nature Reviews Endocrinology*, 12(4): 233.

Whyte, M.P. 2017. Hypophosphatasia: An overview for 2017. *Bone*, 102: 15–25.

Yamamoto, H., Niimi, T., Yokota-Ohta, R., Suzuki, K., Sakae, T., and Kozawa, Y. 2009. Diversity of acellular and cellular cementum distribution in human permanent teeth. *Journal of Hard Tissue Biology*, 18(1): 40–44.

Yamashiro, T., Tummers, M., and Thesleff, I. 2003. Expression of bone morphogenetic proteins and Msx genes during root formation. *Journal of Dental Research*, 82(3): 172–6.

Yan, J., Ma, Z., Xu, X., and Guo, A. Y. 2014. Evolution, functional divergence and conserved exon–intron structure of bHLH/PAS gene family. *Molecular Genetics and Genomics*, 289 (1): 25–36.

Yang, Z. 1997. PAML: A program package for phylogenetic analysis by maximum. *Computer Applications in the Biosciences: CABIOS*, 13(5): 555–6.

Zeichner-David, M. 2006. Regeneration of periodontal tissues: Cementogenesis revisited. *Periodontology 2000*, 41(1): 196–217.

Zeuner, F. E. 1963. *A History of Domesticated Animals*. London: Harper & Row.

Zheng, L., Ehardt, L., McAlpin, B., About, I., Kim, D., Papagerakis, S., and Papagerakis, P. 2014. The tick tock of odontogenesis. *Experimental Cell Research*, 325(2): 83–9.

5 Pattern of Human Cementum Deposition with a Special Emphasis on Hypercementosis

Emmanuel d'Incau, Bruno Maureille, and Christine Couture-Veschambre

5.1 Physiological Factors Modulating Cementum Deposition

Various physiological parameters influencing the deposition of certain cementum types are proposed here, mainly eruption, function, root anatomy, and dentoalveolar compensations. The relationship with age can be reviewed in Introduction and Chapter 1. We will only emphasize that cementum annual apposition rate has been demonstrated to be the lowest (1.13 µm/year) at the coronal third of the root, which consists essentially of acellular cementum. In contrast, the middle third (2.55 µm/year) and the apical third (6.09 µm/year) consisting essentially of cellular cementum have much faster rates (Zander and Hürzeler 1958).

Eruption and Function

Contrary to what Geppert and Müller (1951) claimed, the deposition of cementum does not depend solely on teeth eruption and function. Azaz et al. (1974) demonstrated that cementum deposition was certainly lower on impacted teeth than functional ones but still continuous. These results were later confirmed by Azaz, Michaeli, and Nitzan (1977), who also demonstrated that cementum deposition of impacted canines was again correlated with individuals' age. In addition to these results, there is a significant deposition of cellular cementum in the furcations and sometimes a significant apical thickness of cellular intrinsic fiber cementum (CIFC), especially in the presence of hypercementosis (Azaz et al. 1974; d'Incau 2012), on impacted or nonfunctional teeth (Figure 5.1). These impacted teeth studies confirm that function is not a prerequisite for CIFC genesis (Bosshardt and Selvig 1997).

Root Anatomy

According to Bosshardt and Schroeder (1992), cellular cementum tends to concentrate in mesial or distal root concavities during the prefunctional and functional phases of development. Several studies showed that the thickness of cellular cementum is

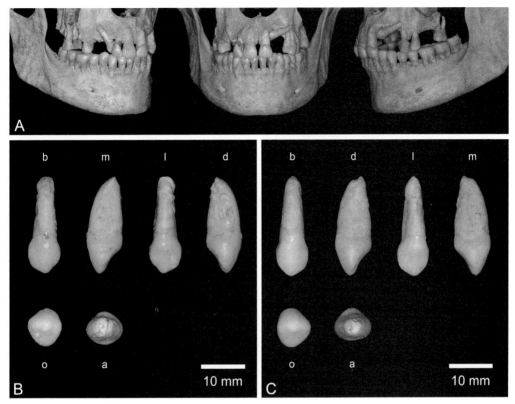

Figure 5.1 Impacted teeth frequently present hypercementosis. #755 (female > 20 y.o., Middle Ages, Sains-en-Gohelle, France). A: Maxillo-mandibular overview. B: Maxillary right canine partially impacted. C: Maxillary left canine fully impacted (b, buccal; m, mesial; l, lingual; d, distal; o, occlusal; a, apical). Based on data from d'Incau (2012).

significantly greater in root concavities (developmental depressions) (Štamfelj et al. 2008), which can lead to hypercementosis (d'Incau 2012) (Figure 5.2).

Dentoalveolar Compensations

The dentoalveolar compensatory mechanism helps to maintain a functional occlusion throughout life, despite the progression of occlusal and interproximal tooth wear (d'Incau, Rouas, and Couture-Veschambre 2015). The dental movements related to these compensations are accompanied by a remodeling of cementum in all three planes of space. These migrations are of three kinds: a continuous eruption at the level of each tooth in the vertical direction; a mesial drift of the posterior teeth and a lingual tilting of the anterior ones in the sagittal direction; and finally, a verticalization of the posterior teeth in the transverse direction (d'Incau, Couture, and Maureille 2012; Kaifu et al. 2003).

The idea that functional teeth (as opposed to antagonistic teeth) undergo a continuous eruption throughout life is old (Murphy 1959). Recent craniometric,

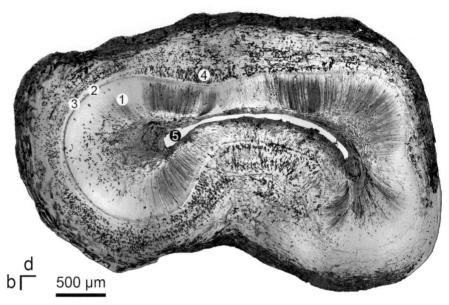

Figure 5.2 Ground section of a maxillary left second premolar presenting with a hypercementosis, belonging to individual 833 (male > 20 y.o., Middle Ages, Sains-en-Gohelle, France). Cellular cementum deposition is increased in root concavities (1: Dentin with tubules; 2: Granular layer of Tomes; 3: Hyaline layer of Hopewell-Smith; 4: Cellular cementum featuring numerous cementocyte lacunae; 5: Pulp cavity; b, buccal; d, distal). Based on data from d'Incau (2012).

radiological, and histological studies confirmed these results (d'Incau, Couture, and Maureille 2012; Kaifu et al. 2003), but few quantitative data were proposed. The study by Whittaker et al. (1990) showed, however, that in forty years, the molars erupted by 2.8 mm while the apex migrated coronally by only 2.2 mm. This means that in one year, the eruption of these teeth was 0.07 mm and that in forty years, 0.60 mm of cementum had been physiologically deposited at the apex.

The origin of the physiological mesial drift of the posterior teeth is not fully elucidated. However, the contraction of the transseptal fiber system is often mentioned (Moxham and Berkovitz 1995), resulting in bone (Saffar, Lasfargues, and Cherruau 1997) and cementum (Dastmalchi et al. 1990) remodeling with distal deposition in areas under tension and mesial resorption in areas under compression. Dastmalchi et al. (1990) showed that the thickness of cementum measured at mid-height of the distal root surface was significantly greater than the thickness measured on the mesial surface. Thus, it is possible to determine the annual deposition rate of premolars and molars cementum during the physiological mesial drift. It is on average equal to 2.9 μm/year with a faster deposition on the distal surfaces (4.3 μm/year) compared to the mesial surfaces (1.4 μm/year). This same idea of differential cementum deposition according to the origin of the stress is also reported by Polson et al. (1984) on *Macacus rhesus* (but see Štamfelj et al. (2008) for opposite results).

In addition, the lingual tilting of the anterior teeth in the sagittal plane is likely to influence the deposition of cellular cementum. Selmer-Olsen (1937) initially observed this change in axis and then confirmed it by metric studies (d'Incau, Rouas, and Couture-Veschambre 2015; Kaifu et al. 2003). From a biomechanical point of view, two types of movements are theoretically possible (Siatkowski 1974). The first has its center of rotation more apical than the center of resistance of the tooth. It causes a slight outward movement of the apex only while the free edge's inward migration is more important. A weak cementum deposition is therefore expected at the apex if this type of movement prevails. The second has its center of rotation at the center of resistance of the tooth. It draws the apex outward and the free edge inward. Therefore, significant lingual cementum deposition at the apex is expected on the upper and lower teeth undergoing this type of movement. This pattern is precisely what some human (d'Incau 2012) and *Pan troglodyte* (Villmoare et al. 2013: 803) case reports seem to confirm.

Finally, in the transversal direction, a tendency for more cementum deposition occurs on the lingual surfaces of the roots of the mandibular molars compared to the buccal surfaces, whereas the opposite was true for the maxillary ones (Solheim 1990; Štamfelj et al. 2008).

We can conclude that cementum thickness increases physiologically throughout life at all levels. Cementum deposition speed is faster at the apex, essentially composed of cellular mixed stratified cementum (CMSC) or CIFC alone, particularly for multi-rooted teeth. At the neck, cementum is essentially composed of acellular extrinsic fiber cementum (AEFC) and has a slower growth, especially for mandibular incisors. Physiological deposition of cellular cementum is also modulated by the root anatomy (concavities), the dentoalveolar compensatory mechanisms, and to a lesser extent by eruption and function.

5.2 Pathological Factors Modulating Cementum Deposition

Certain local pathological oral conditions (i.e., periodontal disease, occlusal trauma and pathological tooth displacement, apical periodontitis, root caries, and antemortem loss of antagonistic teeth) are widespread in past populations. They may influence the deposition of certain types of cementum. The pathologies related to pyrophosphate metabolism (e.g., X-linked hypophosphatemia) are not detailed here because Chapter 3 is specifically devoted to this issue.

Periodontal Disease

Most studies evaluating the effects of periodontitis on cementum show that as the disease progresses, the density of collagen fibers decreases significantly and that the thickness of cementum is typically less important than that found on healthy teeth (Bilgin et al. 2004). This loss is particularly true at the neck level where periodontitis begins and where AEFC is likely to wear out when directly exposed to the oral environment. However, Müller and Zander (1960) point out that significant local variations exist at the apex and between individuals. Kato et al. (1992) also show that the thickness of cellular cementum increases at the apical level of teeth that present periodontal disease in individuals more than sixty years of age.

Occlusal Trauma and Pathological Tooth Displacement

Kronfeld (1938) was one of the first authors to report that occlusal trauma and pathological tooth displacement were likely to generate axial and lateral forces that sometimes exceeded the root adaptation limit and induced cementum loss in the form of external root resorptions. This situation has subsequently been widely demonstrated, particularly in orthodontic therapies (Chan and Darendeliler 2006; Sreeja et al. 2009). In a more general way, external root resorptions can be considered as physiological because they are found isolated or grouped on the root surface of most (>90 percent) human temporary and permanent teeth (Jones and Boyde 1972). They most often take the form of well-defined oval lacunae (Henry and Weinmann 1951). These resorption areas, essentially present on the surface of AEFC or the acellular part of CMSC (Bercy and Frank 1980), are not irreversible because, during repair episodes, they are filled by neoformed cementum (Bosshardt and Schroeder 1994). In some situations (30 percent of cases), the depth of external root resorption is such that the dentin is exposed (Henry and Weinmann 1951).

Apical Periodontitis

Pathological external root resorptions are also found in inflammatory lesions of the periapical region, that is, apical periodontitis (Sreeja et al. 2009). These resorptions are the consequence of aggressions (caries, tooth wear, occlusal trauma) that alter the dental pulp, leading to bacterial infection of the endodontium. As the bone and cementum are resorbed, the lesion (granuloma that sometimes evolves into a cyst) increases in size. It induces a rarefaction of extrinsic fibers at the apex and a deposition of CMSC at a distance from the infected site (Eberhard and Plagmann 1999). Finally, for some authors (Malueg, Wilcox, and Johnson 1996; Sreeja et al. 2009), certain pulp necroses are likely to induce a granuloma that pressure on the cementum would cause resorption. This mechanism would be similar to lesions caused by occlusal trauma.

Root Caries

Like any mineralized dental tissue, the cementum is susceptible to caries when the dental roots are exposed in the oral cavity. The earliest carious lesions, histologically visible as small clefts traversing cementum and extending into peripheral dentin, are clinically not detectable (Schüpbach, Guggenheim, and Lutz 1989). If the demineralization mechanism continues, small vacuoles of 0.5 µm in diameter arranged in a honeycomb pattern are observable. As the disease progresses, substance losses widen, and many calcified peaks separated by deep depressions appear. Large multilocular cavities with splitting partitions can then be observed (Bercy and Frank 1980).

Antemortem Loss of Antagonistic Teeth

Hunter (1778: 110) was the first to state that human teeth would continue to erupt if they were no longer opposed to antagonistic teeth. This hypothesis was confirmed repeatedly (Craddock et al. 2007; Lindskog-Stokland et al. 2012). Two studies compared the cementum thicknesses of functional and contralateral teeth without antagonists on the same arch. They observed in humans (Kellner 1931) and mice (Holliday et al. 2005) that eruption increases cellular cementum deposition on teeth with no contralateral.

Thus, the thickness of cementum decreases (particularly AEFC) or increases (particularly CMSC or CIFC alone) in response to local conditions considered pathological. Under certain conditions, the response to these local factors or other general conditions is at the origin of hypercementosis.

5.3 Hypercementosis

Under certain conditions, the production of certain varieties of cementum becomes "excessive." The term "hypercementosis" is then used in the literature (Consolaro, De Oliveira, and Vasconcelos 1987; Pinheiro et al. 2008; Schroeder 1986: 119–24). This cementum hyperplasia exists in different categories (d'Incau et al. 2015). The first one is the diffuse form, which is a large deposit of cementum that gives the root a distinctive appearance in the form of a "club" or a "bulb" shape (Figure 5.3). Certain focal forms (i.e., cementum ridges and nodules), very minute in substance and not at all prominent, also exist but are significantly less frequent than the diffuse form (d'Incau et al. 2015).

The diffuse form is associated with an accumulation of successive layers of CMSC or CIFC alone (Comelli et al. 1978; Schroeder 1993). Apposition is irregular and occurs in isolated layers with many physiological or pathological resorption lacunae at the surface (Schroeder 1986: 121). A histometric study performed on thirty-one teeth with hypercementosis (d'Incau 2012) showed that the average thickness of *moderate* diffuse hypercementosis (d'Incau et al. 2015) at the apex is close to 500 μm (511.7 μm ± 261 μm). This value corresponds to the limit value (500 μm) set by von Sponholz, Kühne, and Hämmerling (1986) to define hypercementosis. On the other hand, the average thickness of *marked* diffuse hypercementosis (d'Incau et al. 2015) is about 900 μm (908 ± 442.63 μm) (d'Incau 2012) (Figure 5.4). This value is largely above the threshold determined at the apex by previous authors (Geppert and Müller 1951; Zander and Hürzeler 1958; Štamfelj et al. 2008), regardless of age group. Note that the high value of the standard deviation is explained by the sample's heterogeneity, which consists of five incisors, three canines, nine premolars, and fourteen molars. In terms of etiology, diffuse hypercementosis is more often considered the result of

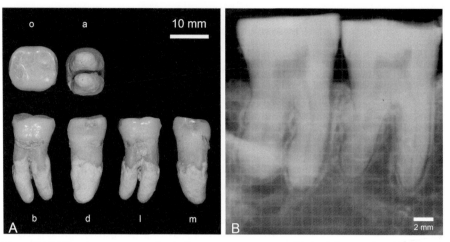

Figure 5.3 Diffuse hypercementosis. A: Gross appearance, mandibular left second molar (#1172; Middle Ages, Sains-en-Gohelle, France). (b, buccal; d, distal; l, lingual; m, mesial; o, occlusal; a, apical). B: Radiological appearance, mandibular right second molar #MXT-109-5R3, Mirgissa, Nubia (ca 2180 to 1552 BC). Based on data from d'Incau (2012).

a general pathology (thyroid goiter, Paget's disease, acromegaly, other rare diseases) or a specific local pathology (d'Incau et al. 2015).

A goiter is a diffuse hypertrophy of the body of the thyroid gland. Gardner and Goldstein (1931) were the first authors to establish a link between this general pathology and the presence of hypercementosis. To reevaluate this relationship, Kupfer (1951) subsequently studied the association between hypercementosis and the presence of a toxic goiter. In the first group affected by this benign thyroid tumor, he showed that 80 percent of its population had at least one hypercementosis (twenty-nine individuals out of thirty-six). In comparison, only 19 percent of individuals in both control groups had hypercementosis (seven out of thirty-six individuals in both cases). Kupfer (1954) subsequently demonstrated an association between hypercementosis and certain thyroid diseases without an actual causal link. More recently, this link was evidenced by Leider and Garbarino (1987), whose longitudinal study made it possible to follow a patient's evolution with generalized hypercementosis, affecting all teeth.

Paget's disease is a deforming osteopathy (*osteitis deformans*) of poorly known origin, characterized by an intense and uncontrolled reworking of bone tissue. Fox (1933) was the first author to notice in a patient that it could be associated with a generalized form of hypercementosis. Similar results have subsequently been reported in numerous studies involving many individuals (see d'Incau 2012 for a review). These studies also revealed a preferential localization of hypercementosis in the maxillary teeth and confirmed its generalized form and diffuse aspect.

Acromegaly is a rare chronic pathology, a singular noncongenital hypertrophy of the upper, lower, and cephalic extremities. It is linked to a hypersecretion of growth hormone (GH) by the pituitary gland. At the cephalic level, it is associated with

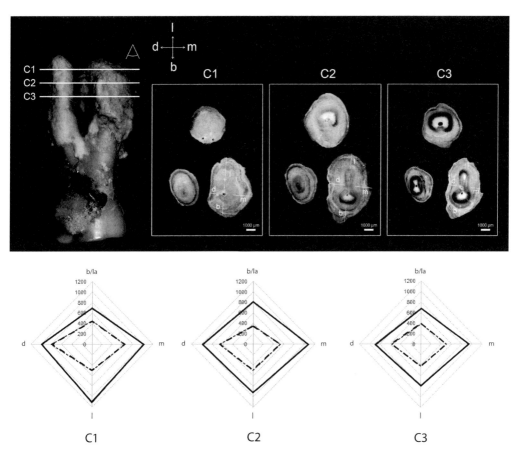

Figure 5.4 Thickness (in microns) of cellular mixed stratified cementum (CMSC) measured at different apical levels (C1 to C3) on 55 roots with diffuse hypercementosis (Middle Ages, Sains-en-Gohelle, France). Upper part: Methodological principles of measurement. C1: measurement made at 1.5 mm from the anatomical apex; C2: measurement made at 3.0 mm from the anatomical apex; C3: measurement made at 4.5 mm from the anatomical apex (b/la, buccal or labial; d, distal; l, lingual; m, mesial). Lower part: Results. Dotted lines represent the values of moderate hypercementosis and solid lines those of marked hypercementosis. Cementum is significantly thicker ($p < 0.05$) for the marked form than for the moderate one. Based on data from d'Incau (2012).

a dysmorphic syndrome, progressive dental malocclusion, and some cases of hypercementosis have been reported (Gardner and Goldstein 1931; Kashyap et al. 2011; Künzler and Farmand 1991). Künzler and Farmand (1991) found multiple hypercementosis in both upper and lower jaws in 61 percent of their thirty-one patients. According to Kashyap et al. (2011), the presence of hypercementosis in individuals with acromegaly is induced by occlusal constraints related to dental movements rather than the general pathology itself. This opinion is often shared in the literature, but it is always based on assumptions (d'Incau 2012). On the other hand, Smid et al. (2004) objectively show that mouse cellular cementum is highly dependent on GH status.

The presence of generalized hypercementosis affecting many or all the teeth has also been reported in individuals suffering from rare diseases such as Pendred syndrome, Gardner syndrome, enamel dysplasia with hamartomatous atypical follicular hyperplasia, enamel renal syndrome, calcinosis, chronic sclerosing osteomyelitis, renal osteodystrophy, pycnodysostosis, idiopathic hypoparathyroidism, and systemic lupus erythematosus (d'Incau et al. 2015).

The link between diffuse hypercementosis and certain specific pathologies or local conditions, prevalent in past populations, has also been described widely, but mainly through case reports. Factors most often blamed are continuous eruption being linked with the antemortem loss of antagonistic teeth (Brau 1986; Consolaro et al. 1987; d'Incau 2012; Kim, Hwang, and Lee 1991; Kronfeld 1938; Schroeder 1986: 121; Sicher and Bhaskar 1972: 174–7); apical periodontitis caused by dental caries; occlusal wear or traumas (Consolaro et al. 1987; d'Incau 2012; Humerfelt and Reitan 1966; Kronfeld 1938; Lacy et al. 2012; Sicher and Bhaskar 1972: 174); periodontal disease (Comuzzie and Steele 1989; Corruccini et al. 1987; d'Incau 2012; Hanihara et al. 1994; Seed and Nixon 2004; Sharma and Pradeep 2007; Suter et al. 2011; Zhou et al. 2012); overloading and occlusal traumas (Comuzzie and Steel 1989; Kim et al. 1991); impaction (Azaz et al. 1974; d'Incau 2012; Kim et al. 1991; Kronfeld 1938); arrested dental eruption (Humerfelt and Reitan 1966; Israel 1984); and dilaceration (Prabhakar, Reddy, and Bassappa 1998).

As we have seen previously, these different dentoalveolar conditions are likely to induce cellular cementum production. The potential etiologies of diffuse hypercementosis are therefore numerous, sometimes contradictory (e.g., hyper- or hypofunction), and mainly documented in the literature through case reports concerning a single tooth in an individual (i.e., localized hypercementosis). However, the study by d'Incau (2012) realized in different French medieval series allows us better to appreciate the relative involvement of these potential etiological factors. Different local factors seem to be predominant. The primary factor is continuous eruption due to antemortem loss of antagonistic teeth, followed by apical periodontitis linked to pulp necrosis and finally periodontal disease. To highlight the molecular and genetic mechanisms involved in these etiological factors, we can turn to the animal model. In a study conducted on mice, Holliday et al. (2005) compared cementum thickness to the apex of functional and contralateral teeth without antagonists. Their results show that cementum deposition is significantly higher in nonfunctional teeth (37 percent increase of CIFC in twelve days). According to Holliday et al. (2005), nonfunctional teeth's dental eruption resets the tissue deposition process that occurs during root development and initial eruption. This process is disrupted as long as the tooth is in occlusion and cementum growth is inhibited. As soon as the teeth lose their antagonists, the expression of specific genes is activated in order to ensure the synthesis of proteins from the extracellular matrix (elastin and tenascin C), proteoglycans (brevican, lumican, biglycan), and a fibroblast growth factor (FGF-9). On the other hand, the expression of other proteins (laminin, cathepsin D, MMP11) is significantly reduced. The supraposition of unopposed molars (in rats) is considerably facilitated when the antagonistic teeth are lost early (Fujita et al. 2009) or when the periodontium is inflammatory (Craddock et al. 2007; Lindskog-Stokland et al. 2012). Other potential etiological factors such as dental impaction, occlusal overloading, or dilaceration seem to be involved in the development of diffuse hypercementosis only slightly, even in the Neanderthal lineage (d'Incau 2012). Finally, some idiopathic hypercementosis must be related to cementum deposition increase with age (Gardner and Goldstein 1931; Kim, Hwang, and Lee 1991; Schehl 1966).

Cementum ridges are described as small spike-like projections or spurs ("sawtooth" or "cock's comb" hypercementosis) on the lateral and interradicular root surfaces (d'Incau 2012; d'Incau et al. 2015; Pinheiro et al. 2008). They result from the mineralization of Sharpey's fibers' insertions at the AEFC surface, which could be under considerable tension (Brau 1986; Sicher and Bhaskar 1972: 174–7; Schroeder 1986: 120–1). This hypothesis seems to be confirmed in the medieval sample of Sains-en-Gohelle (France), in which 16.61 percent of teeth with hypercementosis present this type of ridges, mainly located at the apex of maxillary central incisors with marked and sometimes atypical tooth wear, of the "Lingual Surface Attrition of the Maxillary Teeth – LSAMAT" type (d'Incau 2012) (Figure 5.5).

Nodular forms, first described by Shmamine (1910), are associated with the presence of various sizes of cementicles that give the root surface an irregular appearance.

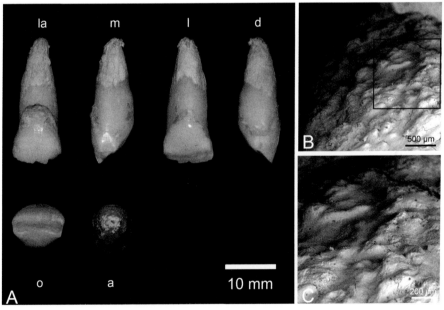

Figure 5.5 Hypercementosis in the form of spike-like projections. A: Gross appearance of a moderate stage, maxillary right central incisor (#603, Middle Ages, Sains-en-Gohelle, France). Note that tooth wear is of the type "Lingual Surface Attrition of the Maxillary Teeth – LSAMAT" (la, labial; m, mesial; l, lingual; d, distal; o, occlusal; a, apical). B: Scanning electron microscopic observation of the spike-like projections localized at the tooth apex mentioned earlier. C: View at higher magnification of the area delimited in B (black square). Based on data from d'Incau (2012).

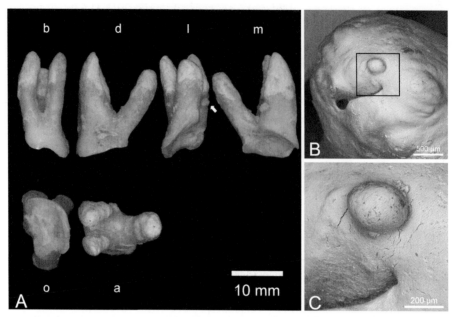

Figure 5.6 Nodular hypercementosis. A: Gross appearance of a marked nodular focal hypercementosis (white arrow) on the maxillary left first molar (#144, Middle Ages, Sains-en-Gohelle, France). (b, buccal; m, mesial; l, lingual; d, distal; o, occlusal; a, apical). B: Scanning electron microscopy observation of a moderate nodular focal hypercementosis on the maxillary left second molar of individual 26 (same series). C: View at higher magnification of the area delimited in B (black square). Based on data from d'Incau (2012).

These abnormal spherical or hemispherical formations with an initial diameter ranging from 100 to 200 μm are initially free in the periodontal ligament (Moskow 1971). With the subsequent depositions of cementum, cementicles adhere to the root surface and eventually are embedded (Figure 5.6). Nodular forms consist mainly of AEFC and are sometimes covered with CIFC (Bosshardt and Nanci 2003; Schroeder 1986: 122–4). Their origin is debated and may be linked with the presence of epithelial rests of Malassez, cementoblast fragments, degenerate and mineralized Sharpey's fibers, or phleboliths (Brau 1986; Moskow 1971).

5.4 Conclusion

Cementum deposition depends on various physiological factors, including age, root shape, and eruptional and functional history. However, the actual contribution of any of these factors is still ill-defined. Some bucco dental pathologies are also likely to modulate the deposition of specific varieties of cementum. Generally speaking, AEFC tends to resorb, leaving marks characteristic of such pathologies that are particularly frequent in past populations. Therefore, it is essential to take these stress markers (reduction in cementum thickness due to periodontal disease, presence of resorption lacunae related to occlusal trauma, demineralization due to caries) into account when assessing the oral health of these individuals but also when assessing their age-at-death counting cementum annulus. On the other hand, because CMSC and CIFC are adaptive tissues, their deposition is likely to accelerate to respond to specific pathological conditions and become excessive (hypercementosis). This tissue hyperplasia is regarded as a favorable and protective reaction to irritation. The diffuse form is associated with extensive root concavities, missing or extracted antagonists, periodontal disease, periapical inflammation, delayed tooth eruption, impacted teeth, root laceration, and probably age. As we have demonstrated in various medieval samples, hypercementosis frequency is directly related to bucco-dental pathologies or their consequences (d'Incau 2012). Therefore, hypercementosis frequency could be used as a general indicator of an archaeological sample's oral health. Furthermore, the presence of a generalized hypercementosis in an individual could suggest specific systemic pathologies (e.g., Paget's disease, thyroid problems, acromegaly, or specific rare syndromes). The studies and use of hypercementosis, so far largely understudied, potentially offer new research perspectives for past population health.

Acknowledgments

The authors would like to thank P. Hannois (Service régional de l'archéologie, région Nord-Pas-de-Calais, France) and C. Beauval (Archéosphère, Bordeaux, France) for providing access to Sains-en-Gohelle sample. Thanks are also due to P. Courtaud (UMR 5199 PACEA, Pessac, France) for his support to study the Mirgissa sample, to Y. Lefrais (IRAMAT-CRP2A, Pessac, France) for SEM micrograph, and finally to B. Bertrand and S. Coisnon (Direction de l'Archéologie de la communauté d'agglomération du Douaisis, LAPCM, France) for histological slice.

References

Azaz, B., Y. Michaeli, and D. Nitzan. 1977. Aging of tissues of the roots of nonfunctional human teeth (impacted canines). *Oral Surgery, Oral Medicine, Oral Pathology* 43(4): 572–8.

Azaz, B., M. Ulmansky, R. Moshev, and J. Sela. 1974. Correlation between age and thickness of cementum in impacted teeth. *Oral Surgery, Oral Medicine, Oral Pathology* 38(5): 691–4.

Bercy, P., and R. M. Frank. 1980. Microscopie électronique à balayage de la surface du cément humain dans diverses conditions physiologiques et pathologiques. *Journal de Biologie Buccale* 8(4): 353–73.

Bilgin, E., C. A. Gürgan, M. N. Arpak, H. S. Bostanci, and K. Güven. 2004. Morphological changes in diseased cementum layers: A scanning electron microscopy study. *Calcified Tissue International* 74(5): 476–85.

Bosshardt, D. D., and A. Nanci. 2003. Immunocytochemical characterization of ectopic enamel deposits and cementicles in human teeth. *European Journal of Oral Science* 111(1): 51–9.

Bosshardt, D. D., and H. E. Schroeder. 1992. Initial formation of cellular intrinsic fiber cementum in developing human teeth. *Cell & Tissue Research* 267(2): 321–35.

1994. How repair cementum becomes attached to the resorbed roots of human permanent teeth. *Acta Anatomica* 150(4): 253–66.

Bosshardt, D. D., and K. A. Selvig. 1997. Dental cementum: The dynamic tissue covering of the root. *Periodontology 2000* 13: 41–75.

Brau, E. 1986. Pathologie du cément. *Actualités Odonto-Stomatologiques* 40(156): 603–17.

Chan, E., and M. A. Darendeliler. 2006. Physical properties of root cementum: Part 7. Extent of root resorption under areas of compression and tension. *American Journal of Orthodontics and Dentofacial Orthopedics* 129(4): 504–10.

Comelli, L., R. Carlos, F. Lauand, E. Marcantonio, and C. B. Neto. 1978. A contribution to the histological study of hypercementosis using metal staining. *Journal of Dental Research* 57 (1): 146–52.

Comuzzie, A. G., and D. Gentry Steele. 1989. Enlarged occlusal surfaces on first molars due to severe attrition and hypercementosis: Examples from prehistoric coastal populations of Texas. *American Journal of Physical Anthropology* 78(1): 9–15.

Consolaro, A., L.U. De Oliveira, and M. H. F. Vasconcelos. 1987. Determinação da prevalência da hipercementose e suas implicações etiopatogênicas. *Odontologia Moderna* 14(3): 6–14.

Corruccini, R. S., K. P. Jacobi, J. S. Handler, and A. C. Aufderheide. 1987. Implications of tooth root hypercementosis in a Barbados slave skeletal collection. *American Journal of Physical Anthropology* 74(2): 179–84.

Craddock, H. L., C. C. Youngson, M. Manogue, and A. Blance. 2007. Occlusal changes following posterior tooth loss in adults. Part 1: A study of clinical parameters associated with the extent and type of supraeruption in unopposed posterior teeth. *Journal of Prosthodontics* 16(6): 485–94.

Dastmalchi, R., A. Polson, O. Bouwsma, and H. Proskin. 1990. Cementum thickness and mesial drift. *Journal of Clinical Periodontology* 17(10): 709–13.

d'Incau, E. 2012. Hypercementosis: Definition, classification and frequency. Application of these results to the Neanderthal line. PhD dissertation, University of Bordeaux, Talence. [In French.]

d'Incau, E., C. Couture, and B. Maureille. 2012. Human tooth wear in the past and the present: Tribological mechanisms, scoring systems, dental and skeletal compensations. *Archives of Oral Biology* 57(3): 214–29.

d'Incau, E., P. Rouas, and C. Couture-Veschambre. 2015. Tooth wear and compensatory modification of the dentoalveolar complex in a Nubian sample. *Journal of Craniomandibular Function* 7(4): 315–36.

d'Incau, E., C. Couture, N. Crépeau, F. Chenal, C. Beauval, V. Vanderstraete, and B. Maureille. 2015. Determination and validation of criteria to define hypercementosis in two medieval samples from France (Sains-en-Gohelle, AD 7th-17th; Jau-Dignac-et-Loirac, AD 7th-8th century). *Archives of Oral Biology* 60(2): 293–303.

Eberhard, J., and H.-C. Plagmann. 1999. Changes in the periodontal membrane due to apical periodontitis. *Journal of Endodontics* 25(7): 486–9.

Fox, L. 1933. Paget's disease (*osteitis deformans*) and its effect on maxillary bones and teeth. *The Journal of the American Dental Association* 20(10): 1823–29.

Fujita T., X. Montet, K. Tanne, and S. Kiliaridis. 2009. Supraposition of unopposed molars in young and adult rats. *Archives of Oral Biology* 54(1): 40–4.

Gardner, B. S., and H. Goldstein. 1931. The significance of hypercementosis. *The Dental Cosmos* 73(11): 1065–69.

Geppert, E.-G., and K.-H. Müller. 1951. Die wurzelzementapposition als meßbarer ausdruck der kaudruckbelastung des zahnes. *Deutsche Zahn-, Mund-, und Kieferheilkunde mit Zentralblatt für die Gesamte*, 15 (1–2/3–4): 30–48, 97–119.

Hanihara, T., H. Ishida, N. Ohshima, O. Kondo, and T. Masuda. 1994. Dental calculus and other dental disease in a human skeleton of the Okhotsk Culture unearthed at Hamanaka-2 site, Rebun Island, Hokkaido, Japan. *International Journal of Osteoarchaeology* 4(4): 343–51.

Henry, J. L., and J. P. Weinmann. 1951. The pattern of resorption and repair of human cementum. *The Journal of the American Dental Association* 42(3): 270–90.

Holliday, S., B. Schneider, M.T. S. Galang, T. Fukui, A. Yamane, X. Luan, and T. G. H. Diekwisch. 2005. Bones, teeth, and genes: A genomic hommage to Harry Sicher's "axial movement of teeth." *World Journal of Orthodontics* 6(1): 61–70.

Humerfelt, A., and K. Reitan. 1966. Effects of hypercementosis on the movability of teeth during orthodontic treatment. *The Angle Orthodontist* 36(3): 179–89.

Hunter, J. 1778. *The Natural History of the Human Teeth: Explaining Their Structure, Use, Formation, Growth, and Diseases.* 2nd ed. London: J. Johnson.

Israel, H. 1984. Early hypercementosis and arrested dental eruption: Heritable multiple ankylodontia. *Journal of Craniofacial Genetics and Developmental Biology* 4(3): 243–46.

Jones, S. J., and A. Boyde. 1972. A study of human root cementum surfaces as prepared for and examined in the scanning electron microscope. *Zeitschrift für Zellforschung und Mikroskopische Anatomie* 130(3): 318–37.

Kaifu, Y., K. Kasai, G. C. Townsend, and L. C. Richards. 2003. Tooth wear and the "design" of the human dentition: A perspective from evolutionary medicine. *American Journal of Physical Anthropology* 122(Suppl. 37): 47–61.

Kashyap, R. R., G. S. Babu, and S. R. Shetty. 2011. Dental patient with acromegaly: A case report. *Journal of Oral Science* 53(1): 133–36.

Kato, S., H. Nakagaki, H. Kunisaki, N. Sugihara, T. Noguchi, F. Ito, I. Yoshioka, J. A. Weatherell, and C. Robinson. 1992. The thickness of the sound and periodontally diseased human cementum. *Archives of Oral Biology* 37(8): 675–76.

Kellner, E. 1931. Das verhältnis der zement-und periodontalbreiten zur funktionellen beanspruchung der zähne. *Zeitschrift für Stomatologie* 29: 44–62.

Kim, S. H., E. H. Hwang, and S. R. Lee. 1991. A radiographic study of hypercementosis. *Korean Journal of Oral and Maxillofacial Radiology* 21(2): 249–59. [In Korean.]

Kronfeld, R. 1938. The biology of cementum. *The Journal of the American Dental Association* 25(9): 1451–61.

Künzler, A., and M. Farmand. 1991. Typical changes in the viscerocranium in acromegaly. *Journal of Cranio-Maxillo facial Surgery* 19(8): 332–40.

Kupfer, C. 1954. Relationship of hypercementosis to the exophtalmos of hyperthyroidism. *AMA Archives of Ophthalmology* 52(6): 942–5.

Kupfer, I. J. 1951. Correlation of hypercementosis with toxic goiter; a preliminary report. *Journal of Dental Research* 30(5): 734–6.

Lacy, S. A., Xiu-Jie Wu, C.-Z. Jin, D.-G. Qin, Y.-J Cai, and E. Trinkaus. 2012. Dentolveolar paleopathology of the early modern humans from Zhirendong, South China. *International Journal of Paleopathology* 2(1): 10–18.

Leider, A. S., and V. E. Garbarino. 1987. Generalized hypercementosis. *Oral Surgery, Oral Medicine, Oral Pathology* 63(3): 375–80.

Lindskog-Stokland, B., K. Hansen, C. Tomasi, M. Hakeberg, and J. L. Wennström. 2012. Changes in molar position associated with missing opposed and/or adjacent tooth: A 12-year study in women. *Journal of Oral Rehabilitation* 39(2): 136–43.

Malueg, L. A., L. R. Wilcox, and W. Johnson. 1996. Examination of external apical root resorption with scanning electron microscopy. *Oral Surgery, Oral Medicine, Oral Pathology, Oral Radiology and Endodontics* 82(1): 89–93.

Moskow, B. S. 1971. Origin, histogenesis and fate of calcified bodies in the periodontal ligament. *Journal of Periodontology* 42(3): 131–43.

Moxham, B. J., and B. K. B. Berkovitz. 1995. The periodontal ligament and physiological tooth movements. In *The Periodontal Ligament in Health and Disease*. 2nd ed. B. K. B. Berkovitz, B. J. Moxham, and H. N. Newman, eds. Barcelona: Mosby-Wolfe, 183–214.

Müller, G., and H. A. Zander. 1960. Cementum of periodontally diseased teeth from India. *Journal of Dental Research* 39(2): 385–90.

Murphy, T. 1959. Compensatory mechanisms in facial height adjustment to functional tooth attrition. *Australian Dental Journal* 4(5): 312–23.

Pinheiro, B. C., T. N. Pinheiro, A. L. Capelozza, and A. Consolaro. 2008. A scanning electron microscopic study of hypercementosis. *Journal of Applied Oral Science* 16(6): 380–84.

Polson, A., J. Caton, A. P. Polson, S. Nyman, J. Novak, and B. Reed. 1984. Periodontal response after tooth movement into intrabony defects. *Journal of Periodontology* 55(4): 197–202.

Prabhakar A. R., V. V. Reddy, and N. Bassappa. 1998. Duplication and dilaceration of a crown with hypercementosis of the root following trauma: A case report. *Quintessence International* 29(10): 655–7.

Saffar, J.-L., J.-J. Lasfargues, and M. Cherruau. 1997. Alveolar bone and the alveolar process: The socket that is never stable. *Periodontology 2000* 13: 76–90.

Schehl, S. 1966. Röntgenologisch-statistische untersuchungen über hyperzementosen. *Wissenschaftliche Zeitschrift der Ernst-Moritz-Arndt-Universität Greifswald* 15: 279–83.

Schroeder, H. E. 1986. *The Periodontium*. Berlin: Springer-Verlag.

——— 1993. Human cellular mixed stratified cementum: A tissue with alternating layers of acellular extrinsic and cellular intrinsic fiber cementum. *Schweizerische Monatsschrift für Zahnmedizin* 103(5): 550–60.

Schüpbach, P., B. Guggenheim, and F. Lutz. 1989. Human root caries: Histology of initial lesions in cementum and dentin. *Journal of Oral Pathology & Medicine* 18(3): 146–56.

Seed, R., and P. P. Nixon. 2004. Generalised hypercementosis: A case report. *Primary Dental Care* 11(4): 119–22.

Selmer-Olsen, R. 1937. The normal movement of the mandibular teeth and the crowding of the incisors as a result of growth and function. *The Dental Records* 57(9): 465–77.

Sharma, C. G. D., and A. R. Pradeep. 2007. Localized attachment loss in Pendred syndrome: Incidental? *Journal of Periodontology* 78(5): 948–54.

Shmamine, T. 1910. *Das sekundäre Zement: (Cementhyperplasie, Cementhypertrophie, Hypercementitis USW)*. Deutsche Zahnheilkunde in Vorträgen, Heft 13. Leipzig: Thieme.

Siatkowski, R. E. 1974. Incisor uprighting: Mechanism for late secondary crowding in the anterior segments of the dental arches. *American Journal of Orthodontics* 66(4): 398–410.

Sicher, H., and S. N. Bhaskar. 1972. *Orban's Oral Histology and Embryology*. 7th ed. St Louis: Mosby.

Smid, J. R., J. E. Rowland, W. G. Young, T. J. Daley, K. T. Coschigano, J. J. Kopchick, and M. J. Waters. 2004. Mouse cellular cementum is highly dependent on growth hormone status. *Journal of Dental Research* 83(1): 35–9.

Solheim, T. 1990. Dental cementum apposition as an indicator of age. *Scandinavian Journal of Dental Research* 98(6): 510–19.

Sponholz, von H., W. Kühne, and H.-U. Hämmerling. 1986. Anatomisch-histologische untersuchungen zur zementapposition unter besonderer berücksichtigung funktioneller reize. *Zahn-Mund und Kieferheilkunde mit Zentralblatt* 74(6): 563–6.

Sreeja, R., C. Minal, T. Madhuri, P. Swati, and W. Vijay. 2009. A scanning electron microscopic study of the patterns of external root resorption under different conditions. *Journal of Applied Oral Science* 17(5): 481–6.

Štamfelj, I., G. Vidmar, E. Cvetko, and D. Gašperšič. 2008. Cementum thickness in multirooted human molars: A histometric study by light microscopy. *Annals of Anatomy* 190(2): 129–39.

Suter, V. G. A., P. A. Reichart, D. D. Bosshardt, and M. M. Bornstein. 2011. A typical hard tissue formation around multiple teeth. *Oral Surgery, Oral Medicine, Oral Pathology, Oral Radiology, and Endodontology* 111(2): 138–45.

Villmoare, B., K. Kuykendall, T. C. Rae, and C. S. Brimacombe. 2013. Continuous dental eruption identifies Sts 5 as the developmentally oldest fossil hominin and informs the taxonomy of *Australopithecus africanus*. *Journal of Human Evolution* 65(6): 798–805.

Whittaker, D. K., S. Griffiths, A. Robson, P. Roger-Davies, G. Thomas, and T. Molleson. 1990. Continuing tooth eruption and alveolar crest height in an eighteenth-century population from Spitalfields, East London. *Archives of Oral Biology* 35(2): 81–5.

Zander, H. A., and B. Hürzeler. 1958. Continuous cementum apposition. *Journal of Dental Research* 37(6): 1035–44.

Zhou, J., Y. F. Zhao, C. Y. Xia, and L. Jiang. 2012. Periodontitis with hypercementosis: Report of a case and discussion of possible aetiologic factors. *Australian Dental Journal* 57(4): 511–14.

6 Recent Advances on Acellular Cementum Increments Composition Using Synchrotron X-Radiation

Stephan Naji, Stuart R. Stock, William Rendu, Lionel Gourichon, Thomas Colard, and Zhonghou Cai

6.1 Introduction

Dental cementum is a component of the tooth and the periodontium that serves primarily to attach the root to the alveolar bone via the principal periodontal ligament fibers (Chapter 2). Several studies have reported on the overall composition and classification of cementum (Chapters 2–4).

This chapter considers acellular extrinsic fiber cementum (AEFC), which has a regular growth rate, continuous throughout life (Chapter 2). This regular addition of cementum can be observed as an incremental deposition pattern, especially when 100 μm undecalcified thin sections are observed under transmitted/polarized light (Colard et al. 2015; Naji et al. 2016; Rendu 2010; Chapter 1). The incremental growth is strongly correlated with age in several mammals, including humans (Chapter 1). This unique property of circannual growth deposit has fundamental implications in human and animal biology (Introduction) and is now used with increasing success for estimating age and season of death (Chapter 1) in various fields (Part III).

However, various studies of the composition and nature of AEFC increments have provided contradictory conclusions (Colard et al. 2016; Cool et al. 2002; Dean et al. 2018; Lieberman 1994; Pike-Tay 1995; Renz et al. 1997; Smith et al. 1994; Stock et al. 2017), and the subject remains a matter of debate (Chapter 2; Yamamoto et al. 2016, and the Discussion section). Because of the renewed interest in the analysis of dental cementum growth, or cementochronology (Introduction), it is increasingly important to address the issue of the nature and composition of these circannual AEFC deposits (Chapter 8).

This study used synchrotron x-radiation (simultaneous x-ray diffraction and x-ray excited x-ray fluorescence mapping) to investigate acellular cementum increments' composition within human and ungulate dental thin sections. The goal is to investigate the extent to which the alternating dark–bright acellular increment pattern, observed in optical micrographs in transmitted light, is the product of varying mineral changes, in particular, changing Ca, P, and Zn elemental composition as well as carbonated (hydroxy)apatite (cAp) mineral content, or changes in orientation of the mineral

Supplemental online materials are available at www.cambridge.org/naji.

phase and underlying collagen fibrils. This is the first attempt to address this issue on samples of four different species of mammals.

6.2 Materials and Methods

Material

Two reference collections and three archaeological sites were sampled for this study (Table 6.1), and twelve individuals were selected (Table 6.2) for analysis.

The estimated age for the archaeological human (23_S82 & 56_S46-La Granède) and red deer (40_CL302-Covalejos) remains were estimated using cementochronology (Supplemental Figures SF.6.10–SF.6.12, respectively) following standardized protocols (Colard et al. 2015). The ages of the Kaminuriak-White reindeer (Pike-Tay 1995) and the Camargue cattle (Gourichon, personal communication) are based on documented modern observations.

Table 6.1 Summary of collections used in this study.

Collection	Species	Name	Period
Kaminuriak	*Rangifer tarandus*	Reindeer	Modern (1966–1968)
Camargue	*Bos taurus*	Cattle	Modern (2005)
Covalejos	*Cervus elaphus*	Red Deer	Archaeological (Middle Paleolithic: 40–35 ky. BP)
Pertus II	*Bos taurus*	Cattle	Archaeological (Neolithic)
La Granède	*Homo sapiens*	Human	Archaeological (Middle Ages: AD 600–1200)

Table 6.2 List of samples analyzed at the Advanced Photon Source.[1]

Species	Ref #	Tooth	Tooth eruption age	Date of birth	Date of death	Age at death (years; months)	Number of cementum increments
Reindeer	017_78	M2	10–15 m.	June–62	Apr–68	5; 10	5
Reindeer	36_108	M2	10–15 m.	June–60	Jun–67	7	6 or 7
Reindeer	46_38	P3	21–28 m.	June–60	Apr–67	6; 10	5
Reindeer	70_181	M2	15–15 m.	June–60	Jun–67	7	6 or 7
Reindeer	014_257	M2	10–15 m.	July–59	Nov–68	9; 4	8 or 9
Reindeer	022_256	P4	21–28 m.	July–61	Nov–68	7; 4	6
Reindeer	047_361b	M2	10–15 m.	June–62	Apr–68	5; 10	5
Cattle	050_PIIB1034	M2	15–18 m.	N/A	N/A	N/A	6 or 7*
Cattle	28_94261	I1	20–22 m.	June–95	May–05	9; 11	8
Red deer	40_CL302	M2	10–12 m.	N/A	N/A	N/A	3*
Human	23_S82	UC	11–13 y.	N/A	N/A	N/A	48 to 50*
Human	56_S46	LI2	6–7 y.	N/A	N/A	N/A	10 to 12*

1. M: molar; P: premolar; I: incisor; C: canine; m = months; y = years; (*) observed increments.

Methods

Thin-Section Preparation and Optical Microscopy

For the human samples, teeth were processed using a standardized protocol with no grinding steps (Colard et al. 2015; Chapter 2). For the animal samples, teeth were processed following another protocol with grinding and polishing steps (Chapter 9).

Regions of interest (ROI) showing highly visible AEFC were recorded using a Canon EOS-T5i camera mounted on a Leica DM2700P optical microscope (Chapter 9). A 10× or 20× objective lens was used for imaging; the resulting depth-of-field was around 5–9 μm (Nikon 2021). All micrographs were recorded with transmitted or polarized light to identify the number and type of AEFC increments (Figure 6.1A–C). Focus was set about 15 μm below the top surface of the section. In each micrograph, the AEFC increments were counted manually using the Image-J/FIJI platform version 1.51a (Schindelin et al. 2012) "counting tool" and the "luminescence plot profile" function (Figure 6.1B).

Synchrotron Sample Preparation and Microbeam Sampling

Samples were examined at beamline 2-ID-D of the Advanced Photon Source (APS) at Argonne National Laboratory (Illinois, USA). Transmission diffraction requires that the thin section be removed from the slides on which they were mounted for transmitted light microscopy; this was done by one of the authors (SRS). At the APS, micrographs were recorded of the freestanding thin sections to confirm the location of AEFC ROIs identified previously. Each sample was then glued to a holder with clear nail polish so that the x-ray beam could pass through the ROI(s) and transmission diffraction patterns could be recorded. Real-time radiography of each specimen mounted within the 2-ID-D instrument was used to position the x-ray beam within the previously identified ROI.

The experiments at 2-ID-D measured transmission diffraction patterns *simultaneously* with zinc (Zn), calcium (Ca), and phosphorous (P) fluorescent x-ray intensities using the geometry described previously (Figure 6.2A) (Stock et al. 2011). The incident 10.1 keV, 250 nm diameter beam was normal to the thin section. The transmission diffraction pattern was recorded by a CCD area detector placed behind the specimen (and normal to the incident beam). The fluorescence signal was recorded by an energy-sensitive detector viewing the specimen at a shallow angle ~10° from the specimen's plane. This viewing angle is not ideal for fluorescence mapping but was dictated by the limited space around the specimen at 2-ID-D, and the experimental geometry affects the interpretation of the different signals. Note that the cementum was always on the edge of the section closest to the detector.

The long acquisition times required for the diffraction patterns (Table 6.3) dictate that collecting area maps was impractical. Instead, the available experimental time was concentrated on collecting a small number of high-sensitivity, high-spatial-resolution line scans across each experimental ROI. Initially, a coarse scan (short count times, large translation steps) collected only Zn, Ca, and P fluorescent intensities. Subsequently, the high-resolution scans were recorded from just within dentin to air/

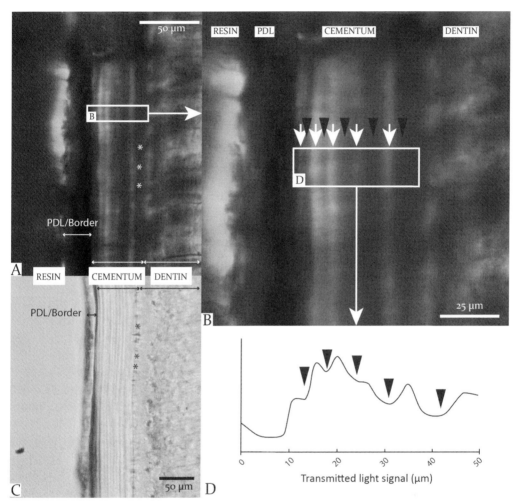

Figure 6.1 Optical micrographs illustrating cementum band contrast and determination of the number of band periods and their positions. (A) Polarized light micrograph of sample 070_181 (reindeer). The asterisks show the position of the CDJ. The box labeled B shows the area over which optical transmissivity versus position (plot in panel D) was measured. (B) Enlargement of panel A with the black arrowheads labeling dark bands and the white arrows light bands. The labeled box D shows the optical transmissivity measurement area. (C) Unpolarized light micrograph of specimen 046-S56 (human) showing cementum and transition zones similar to that shown for reindeer. (D) Optical transmissivity profile at the boxes' position in panels A and B with black arrowheads indicating dark band positions. One counts five light and five dark bands with a light band closest to the surface. (A black and white version of this figure will appear in some formats. For the color version, please refer to the plate section.)

plastic. Different step sizes and acquisition times were used (Table 6.3) depending on what was observed in preliminary scans.

Energy windows were set encompassing the K-emission lines of Zn, Ca, P, and the total number of counts within each window was taken as the fluorescent intensity of

Table 6.3 Parameters for the x-ray scans.[1]

Sample	N Δx columns	Step size Δx (μm)	N Δy points	Step size Δy (μm)	Scan length (μm)	Fluorescence count time (s)	Diffraction count time (s)
017_78	5	0.5	241	0.5	120	20	30
36_108	5	2	426	0.2	85	10	15
46_38	3	2	201	0.2	40	12	15
70_181	10	2	271	0.2	54	14	15
014_257	3	10	225	0.25	56	20	30
022_256	5	5	257	0.25	64	20	35
047_361b	3	5	131	0.5	65	15	25
050_PIIB1034	8	10	401	0.5	200	15	20
28_94261	2	10	334	0.6	200	20	30
40_CL302	21	5	171	0.5	85	15	20
23_S82	2	5	667	0.3	200	30	60
56_S46	12	2	173	0.5	86	10	20

1. N. Δ_x = number of line scans across the sample. N. Δ_y = number of points per line scan.

that element. Allowance was made for detector dead-time. The observed fluorescent intensity depends on several factors: (1) the number of atoms encountered by the incident beam, (2) the efficiency of the exciting photons at exciting the characteristic x-rays, (3) the number of incident photons, (4) the specimen volume sampled, (5) experimental geometry (mentioned earlier), and (6) acquisition time.

The cAp 00.2 and unresolved 21.1, 11.2, 30.0, and 20.2 quadruplet (abbreviated hereafter as "21.1+") reflections were observed from both cementum and dentin.[1] During setup, the investigators observed that the azimuthal distribution of 00.2 intensity was relatively constant for different positions within cementum. Accordingly, the 00.2 intensity was measured by diffraction pattern ROIs set either: (a) (before mapping was begun) on the CCD detector at the 00.2 intensity maximum at azimuth χ_{max}, at the 00.2 azimuth 90° from χ_{max} and at χ_{max} for 21.1+ (ROI 1, 2 and 3, respectively, in Figure 6.2B); or (b) (after the experiment) on the recorded diffraction patterns at various azimuths (Figure 6.2). The variation of 00.2 intensity as a function of position is a measure of mineral content and was determined for three azimuthal ROIs: (a) at χ_{max}, (b) where the intensity was about one half of that at χ_{max}, (c) near the end of the 00.2 diffraction arc (Figure 6.2B). The azimuthal variation of 00.2 intensity was measured every 15° around the diffraction ring. Taken together, the 00.2 diffracted intensity and the azimuthal variation of intensity around this ring provide a simultaneous assessment of mineral content and the crystallographic texture (preferred orientation) of the cAp nanoplatelets, as well as the underlying collagen fibrils (Stock et al. 2011) of cementum and dentin (see Results and Discussion sections).

After synchrotron microbeam scanning, the sections were reexamined with optical microscopy. In some sections, the x-ray exposures produced optically visible discoloration of the specimen ("burn" marks) that we used as fiducials for directly comparing

[1] The Miller-Bravais nomenclature for diffraction indices is used in order to emphasize that a hexagonal crystal system is being described; see (Cullity & Stock 2001).

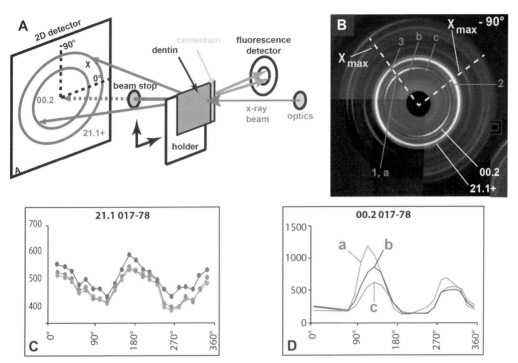

Figure 6.2 (A) Experimental setup for synchrotron x-ray fluorescence and diffraction mapping at beamline 2-ID-D, APS. (B) Typical diffraction pattern from cementum. The labels (azimuthal angles χ in yellow and different diffraction ROIs in red) are defined in the text. (C and D) Reindeer 017_78: variation of cAp 21.1 and 00.2 diffracted intensities, respectively, versus azimuthal angle. Each curve represents a different position within the specimen. (A black and white version of this figure will appear in some formats. For the color version, please refer to the plate section.)

x-ray scans with bands seen in optical micrographs (Supplemental Figures SF.6.13–SF.6.15). Such discoloration is not uncommon for bone and tooth specimens at the beamline in question. However, it is obscure why one sample is affected, and another nominally identical specimen remains unaffected. Whatever the origin of the optical contrast change, the cAp content (and diffracted intensity) and crystallographic texture remain unaltered by this x-ray exposure (Almer & Stock 2007). Similarly, the Ca and Zn elemental compositions do not change.

6.3 Results

The results are presented in three subsections. The first presents the x-ray signals characteristic of cementum compared to the adjacent dentin and describes the cementum mineralization front. The second describes the x-ray data for the cementum bands. The third describes the optical contrast and compares band structure from x-rays and optical microscopy. Readers should refer to Figure 6.1 to identify microstructural zones discussed here in typical optical micrographs with polarized or unpolarized light.

X-Ray Signals and the Dental Structures

Interpretation of variations in fluorescent and diffracted intensities associated with the AEFC increments requires identifying the CDJ and the cementum's outer surface. Based on optical micrographs of the ROIs and earlier work (Stock et al. 2017), Zn fluorescent intensity varies between cementum and dentin but also can be elevated at positions of active mineralization. In nine samples (Supplemental Figures SF.6.1; SF.6.4–SF.6.9; SF.6.11; SF.6.12), changes in the Zn signal clearly demark four regions illustrated in Figure 6.3:

- In *region 1*, the beam encounters air or resin; fluorescent and diffracted intensities are at background.
- In *region 2*, all signals rise simultaneously with a quasi-vertical slope. This transition is the sample's cementum border, including the periodontal ligament (PDL) remnants and the cementum mineralization front (MF). The MF often exhibits a sharp Zn intensity peak, which drops within the bulk of the cementum.
- Within cementum (*region 3*), Zn presents a moderate and relatively constant intensity plateau. This plateau may slope with decreasing Zn intensities as one moves away from the cementum MF.
- *Region 4* (dentin) is found where the Zn signal transitions into a second plateau with average intensity lower than that in cementum but much higher than the "region 1" background. The gradual slope between regions 3 and 4 is interpreted as the CDJ.

The Ca signal is much less consistent or sensitive than the Zn signal and creates three main patterns: (1) variations of Ca signal with position can parallel that of Zn in regions 2 and 3 (Figure 6.3B); (2) Ca intensity remains high without a distinct MF peak (Figure 6.3A) ; (3) Ca can gradually drop through cementum until reaching the dentin level (Figure 6.3C). Note that as the P fluorescent intensity always tracks that of Ca in all the samples (Supplemental Figures SF.6.1–SF.6.12), the P intensity is not plotted.

Determining the border between cementum and dentin is robust using the Zn fluorescent intensity. However, determining the boundary between the PDL/MF and cementum is not as clear using only Zn and Ca intensities because they can be present in both the mineral and the PDL. Instead, the MF–cementum boundary is best defined by the cAp diffracted intensity. This signal tracks only the mineral, and because the PDL is an unmineralized tissue, the cAp signal must drop sharply at the edge of the cementum–PDL transition. As the cAp diffracted intensity is integrated over the entire sample thickness and the experiment was optimized for collection of diffraction patterns and not fluorescence signals, it is a robust measure of when (mineralized) cementum begins. Table 6.4 summarizes the extents of the four regions for ten samples as defined earlier. Specifically, the cementum boundary with air/PDL/MF is taken to be where the cAp 00.2 diffracted intensity rises to one-half the level within the bulk of cementum (e.g., $x = 16$ µm in Figure 6.3A). The transition from cementum to dentin (center of the CDJ) is defined at the midpoint in Zn intensity change between the respective plateaus (e.g., $x = 56$ µm in Figure 6.3A).

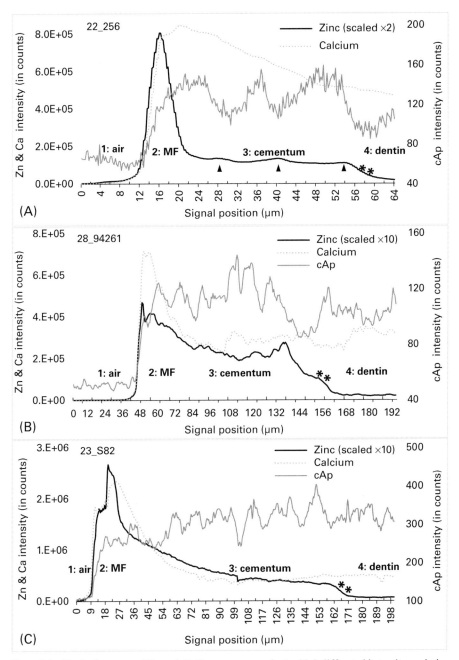

Figure 6.3 Typical pattern of Zn and Ca fluorescence and cAp 00.2 diffracted intensity variation extending from plastic to dentin (from left to right). (A) Reindeer 22_256. The black arrowheads indicate three local maxima in Zn intensity. (B) Bovine 28_94261. (C) Human 23_S82. MF: mineralization front; **: cementum–dentin junction.

Figure 6.4 compares the mean Ca, Zn, and cAp intensities for cementum and dentin. Note that for the fluorescence intensity means, the MF peak and the CDJ are not

Table 6.4 Limits (in μm) for each region defined in the text, based on fluorescence or diffracted intensities.[1]

X-Ray Signals (in μm)	All		Zn & Ca			cAp		All
Sample	Air	MF	Cem.	CDJ	Air	Cem.	CDJ	Dentin
017_78	0–1	1–16	16–65	65–77	0–4	4–70	70–77	77–120
46_38*	0–3	3–7	7–24	24–28	0–8	8–28	28–34	34–40
014_257	0–1	1–15	15–36	36–48	0–2	2–44	44–46	44–56
022_256	0–12	12–21	21–56	56–60	0–15	15–56	56–60	56–64
047_361	0–7	7–20	30–51	51–55	0–9	9–51	51–55	51–65
050_PIIB1034	0–22	22–32	32–172	172–180	0–26	26–172	172–178	178–200
28_94261	0–37	37–45	37–135	135–162	0–39	39–135	135–150	150–200
40_CL302*	0–4	4–19	19–54	54–72	0–19	19–60	60–72	72–85
23_S82	0–9	9–27	27–162	162–170	0–13	13–160	160–170	170–200
56_S46	0–20	20–30	30–73	73–77	0–23	23–64	64–77	77–86

1. MF: mineralization front; Cem.: cementum; CDJ: cementum–dentin junction; *: samples with some experimental geometry issues

included. For the four species studied, the Zn intensity averages a factor of five times greater for cementum than dentin, with a range of two to fifteen. The mean Ca intensities are comparable for cementum and dentin, as are the mean 00.2 cAp diffracted intensities. However, the range of intensity variation for 00.2 cAp is substantially greater for cementum than dentin (Figure 6.4D) and reflects the presence of annual bands in cementum but not in dentin. Supplemental Table ST.6.1 lists mean values for all specimens.

The 00.2 cAp diffraction rings from cementum consisted of arcs on opposite sides of the beam stop (Figure 6.2A) while the rings from dentin were uniform, that is, with little azimuthal intensity variation. For cementum, χ_{max} and $\Delta\chi$ (the azimuthal orientation of the maximum intensity of the 00.2 diffraction arcs and the full width at half-maximum intensity (FWHM) of the arc's azimuthal angular width, respectively) are measures of the crystallographic texture of the volume sampled by the beam. Each of the seven reindeer, two bovine, one red deer, and two human tooth sections had nearly constant χ_{max} and $\Delta\chi$ for all positions across the cementum. However, these quantities varied significantly between specimens. Supplemental Figures SF.6.1–SF.6.12 show typical diffraction patterns for different positions on the twelve specimens. Values of χ_{max} for the different sections varied over 180° (Table 6.5), and there was no relationship between χ_{max} and the cementum growth direction. Similarly, $\Delta\chi$ ranged considerably for the different sections, from 30° to 86°. In these cementum specimens, subtle changes in cAp texture manifest as small azimuthal rotations of 00.2 diffraction arcs (see Section 6.4).

X-Ray Signals and Band Structure in Cementum

Identification of peaks/valleys in fluorescent intensity is straightforward, but the determination of cAp diffracted intensity variation with position is more complex.

Supplemental Table ST.6.1 Average count value and standard deviation (SD) in cementum and dentin, based on fluorescence or diffracted intensities (00,2 cAp).

Intensity counts	Cementum							Dentin						
	Zinc		Calcium		00,2 cAp		Zinc		Calcium		00,2 cAp	
	Average	SD	Average	SD	Average	SD	Average	SD	Average	SD	Average	SD
017_78	372788	80361	3396459	399284	23131	5930	39720	9676	3947718	360384	6330	583
36_108	1063192	846228	1013787	217851	3297	1948	46675	23729	660568	20797	548	58
46_38	77860	64120	75636	4388	1345	395	20056	502	70784	1724	1432	123
70_181	372353	96538	684093	203025	2020	980	67640	31474	307292	43955	318	102
014_257	713561	125901	7192242	800486	8106	3724	169762	71537	8569862	184883	3238	743
022_256	1180786	142649	13415796	2340277	9828	3098	337094	140378	9754568	182036	3412	123
047_361b	760296	87890	5452733	1450792	5346	1235	220238	104501	6615886	166537	3004	248
050_PIIB1034	343342	125342	4820189	4343395	2780	520	21777	3681	1088318	167119	1680	1120
28_94261	440027	100930	5850625	598915	3450	807	66879	44672	6035438	731287	3090	174
40_CL302	239943	31370	5699294	718974	2083	372	109122	27437	5899599	106172	2063	111
23_S82	1855760	973512	19261368	12682865	12440	1244	210119	37021	14434290	1049540	11496	397
56_S46	265059	54088	569423	293663	1892	222	42354	32720	169161	18781	2416	306

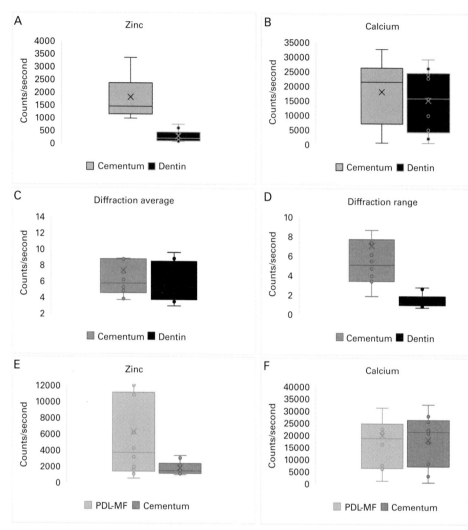

Figure 6.4 Mean fluorescent and cAp 00.2 diffracted intensities per unit counting time for all samples' cementum and dentin. Panels (A) and (E) compare mean Zn signal for dentin versus cementum and cementum plateau versus PDL/MF peak, respectively. Panels (B) and (F) make the same comparison for mean Ca signal. Panels (C) and (D) compare mean 00.2 diffracted intensity and the 00.2 intensity oscillation range, respectively, for cementum and dentin.

Figure 6.2D plots cAp 00.2 intensity variation as a function of azimuthal angle for reindeer specimen 17_78; each colored curve, from a different position within cementum, shows significant azimuthal intensity variation, the amplitude of which changes with position. For 21.1+, the diffraction ring is always complete and exhibits little azimuthal or positional intensity variation (Figure 6.2C for diffraction pattern ROI 3 of Figure 6.2A). The structure of the 00.2 and 21.1+ diffraction rings is typical of cAp mineralized tissues (Stock 2015; Stock et al. 2017). Prior diffraction mapping of cementum banding (Stock et al. 2017) leads the authors to expect similar band-related

Table 6.5 Numbers of bands observed with different modalities and 00.2 cAp mean crystallographic texture.[1]

	Number of peaks				00.2 arc		Notes
	Optical	Ca	Zn	cAp	χ_{max} (°)	$\Delta\chi$ (°)	
017_78	5	5	3	6	126	52	a
36_108	6	3	–	3	125	50	b
46_38	5	4	2?	3 or 4	45	30	c
70_181	6	4	3	5	80	30	d
014_257	8	5	4	3	95	54	e
022_256	6	4	3	3 or 5	100	40	f
047_361b	5	3	2	6	120	54	g
050_PIIB1034	6 or 7*	3	7	6 or 7	45	80	h
28_94261	8	"6–10"	8	7 or 8	20	40	i
40_CL302	3*	3	1	2	100	74	j
23_S82	48 to 50*	–	–	"8–12"	3	86	k
56_S46	10 to 12*	3	3	4	85	70	l

1. The expected value is that determined with optical microscopy, which agrees with documented age at death; asterisks label those specimens without documented age-at-death data. The azimuthal angle of the maximum intensity of the 00.2 cAp diffraction arc, χ_{max}, is measured counterclockwise from the three o'clock azimuth. Both χ_{max} and the full width at half maximum of this arc, $\Delta\chi$, are given in degrees. The notes a–j describe observations beyond the number of bands for each specimen.

Notes

a. An additional Zn peak may be buried in the high-intensity PDL/MF Zn peak.
b. The CDJ may or may not have been captured in these scans. The Zn signal consists of one large, broad peak, and peaks from cementum bands cannot be reliably ascertained.
c. The high-intensity PDL/MF zone may mask an additional Ca peak. The "?" indicates that the only evidence of Zn peaks is two weak inflection points in the strongly sloping Zn line scans.
d. The Ca peaks are relatively weak. There may be an additional Zn peak buried in the PDL/MF peak.
e. Multiple Ca peaks are unclearly defined. An additional Zn peak buried in the PDL/MF zone.
f. An additional Zn peak buried in the PDL/MF zone. Two of the cAp peaks are very broad, and each may be composed of two peaks, bringing the total cAp peaks to five.
g. There may be additional peaks in the broad PDL/MF zone.
h. The Ca intensity profiles are highly sloped, and this obscures some peaks.
i. The Ca peaks have weak intensity, and one is unsure whether there are as few as six or as many as ten peaks.
j. The broad Zn peak may contain a couple more peaks. The cAp peaks are indistinct and broad.
k. Ca and Zn peaks cannot be resolved. The cAp peaks may reflect the number of groups of closely spaced peaks.
l. The Ca intensity slopes sharply from the PDL/MF zone to the CDJ. Peaks are difficult to resolve.

intensity variation in this study's specimens if the sampling or analysis were sensitive enough.

Depending on how the cAp diffracted intensities are measured, the cementum band structure can be highly visible or obscure (Figure 6.5A–B). For example, the integrated intensity of the entire 00.2 diffraction ring versus position does not reveal band structure in Figure 6.5B (50_PIIB1034, bovine cementum). However, in Figure 6.5A (17_78, reindeer cementum), the integrated ring intensity variation suggests that structure exists. The magnitude of cementum's 00.2 integrated intensity peaks and valleys is comparable with those in dentin for specimen 17_78 (positions greater than 70 μm in Figure 6.5A), where bands would not be present. Therefore, the variation of the total 00.2 integrated intensity in cementum in this specimen cannot be reliably interpreted as a microstructural variation. In addition to 00.2 intensity variation across each band period, the crystallographic texture may also change systematically with position and potentially confound detection of individual bands.

The small arc rotations mentioned here suggest that use of diffraction ROI with small azimuthal extents might reveal subtle effects of texture that were not visible when using the entire ring's integrated intensity. Plots of the 00.2 rings' minimum intensities (i.e., CCD detector ROI 2, Figure 6.2) do not reveal cementum bands. However, 00.2 diffraction pattern ROIs 1/a, b, and c (diffraction arc maximum, intermediate, and tail intensities, respectively) clearly show a series of intensity maxima (Figure 6.5A–B), that is, cementum bands. Because the 00.2 maxima positions change depending on where the diffraction arcs are sampled, a subtle effect, crystallographic texture varies slightly but systematically across the cementum bands, an interpretation covered in the Discussion section.

For the reindeer specimen (Figure 6.5A), six cAp intensity maxima are visible; for the bovine specimen (Figure 6.5B), five maxima are definitely present, and probably one or two more that are not clearly seen. Note that the most recently formed diffraction maxima in Figure 6.5A (i.e., that closest to the surface) for the ROI plotted in gold occurs subsurface with a short plateau of intermediate intensity (i.e., a band minimum) before the intensity drops precipitously to zero outside the cementum. A similar effect (cAp band maximum beginning to drop toward a minimum) may be present in Figure 6.5B.

Figure 6.5C–D shows variation of Ca and Zn fluorescent intensities collected simultaneously with the diffraction patterns in Figure 6.5A–B. Five peaks in Ca intensity are labeled for 17_78 (gray shaded vertical bands), but none are visible for 050_PIIB1034. The band labeled "4" in Figure 6.5C has a much smaller height and width than the other identified bands, comparable with Ca fluctuations labeled in cementum peak 2 and in dentin; the authors are skeptical, therefore, that "4" represents a cementum band. Peaks 1–5 in Ca intensity match peaks 2–6 in 00.2 diffracted intensity, but varying amounts of shifts depend on the diffraction ROI used. The origin of the Ca peak at the CDJ in Figure 6.5C (vertical dashed line) and the other intensity variations in dentin are obscure.

The three peaks in Zn intensity in reindeer sample 17_78 (Figure 6.5C) have positions and widths that match those of Ca; any Zn peaks in the position range 5–20 μm are buried in the strong PDL/MF peak. In bovine specimen 050_PIIB1034 (Figure 6.5D), there are five or six clear peaks in Zn intensity and probably another peak adjacent to the surface; Zn peaks 1, 3, 4, 5, 6 and the arrowed near-surface position correspond to 00.2 peaks, but there are shifts of cAp relative to Zn. There may be a peak 2 in the cAp data, but this "peak" barely rises above the mean diffracted intensity, and peak 2 is also relatively weak in the Zn data. The authors have also shaded a weak Zn peak ("6") at position 50 μm that mirrors a slight increase in cAp intensity at the same position.

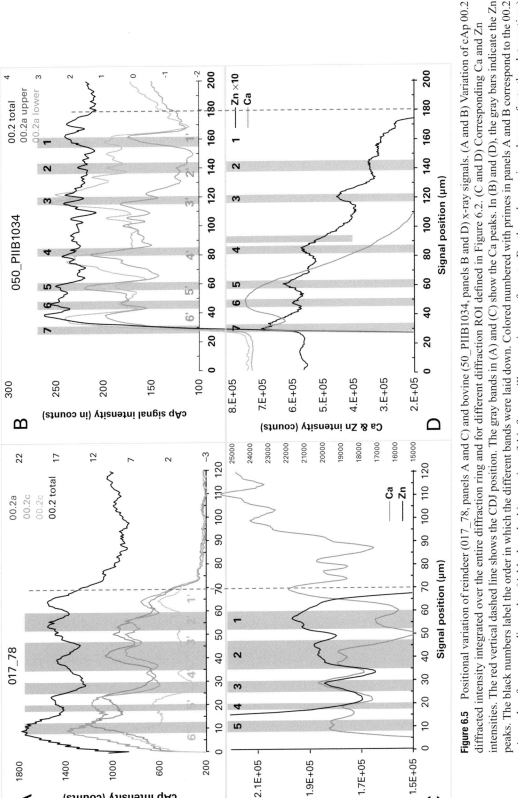

Figure 6.5 Positional variation of reindeer (017_78, panels A and C) and bovine (50_PIIB1034, panels B and D) x-ray signals. (A and B) Variation of cAp 00.2 diffracted intensity integrated over the entire diffraction ring and for different diffraction ROI defined in Figure 6.2. (C and D) Corresponding Ca and Zn intensities. The red vertical dashed line shows the CDJ position. The gray bands in (A) and (C) show the Ca peaks. In (B) and (D), the gray bars indicate the Zn peaks. The black numbers label the order in which the different bands were laid down. Colored numbered with primes in panels A and B correspond to the 00.2 cAp peaks of corresponding color. (A black and white version of this figure will appear in some formats. For the color version, please refer to the plate section.)

Plots of Ca, Zn, and cAp intensity for the remainder of samples are presented in the electronic supplemental materials. Even though the Ca, Zn, and cAp line scans of Figure 6.5 were collected simultaneously, each specimen's number and position of peaks do not always coincide. The registration with optical microscopy band positions is uncertain except for the three samples covered in the following subsection. Comparison of the observed number of bands is, therefore, the first step in synthesizing the results. Table 6.5 lists the number of expected bands in each specimen, based either on the individual's documented age at death or on optical microscopy and the number of Ca, Zn, and cAp peaks visible. The note for each specimen provides additional qualitative observations on the band patterns, such as the possibility that the PDF/MF may mask peaks or that a broad peak may contain unresolved peaks.

These data show that none of the x-ray signals always produce the best agreement with band numbers from optical microscopy and expected from documented age at death. This suggests that there are confounding factors that sometimes affect the cAp and Ca and Zn fluorescent signals differently. An additional complication is that it is difficult to know precisely where the x-ray data were collected relative to the optical micrograph. Only three specimens, where the x-ray beam produced burn marks on the samples, allowed for precise comparison, despite recording micrographs before the scan and translating to a position matching roughly that initially observed in the optical micrographs. Before examining the data for these three sections, it is essential to establish that we have reproducible data for a given specimen. Multiple parallel line scans were collected for each specimen, and not all showed Ca, Zn, or cAp peaks equally well. For clarity, Figures 6.3 and 6.5 show data for only one line per specimen.

Figure 6.6 (bovine specimen 50_PIIB1034) shows that the peaks and valleys in 00.2 diffracted intensity and in Zn fluorescent intensity are quite reproducible. The slight shift in absolute in Zn positions in scans represents a steady but small drift of the specimen relative to the beam, something often seen in 12–24 h long scans at 2-ID-D.

Comparison of AEFC Increments in Optical Micrographs with X-Ray Signals

Three specimens (reindeer 17_78, bovine 50_PIIB1034, and red deer 40_CL302) have x-ray scanning-induced discoloration that permits detailed comparison of optical and x-ray band positions (Supplemental Figures SF.6.13–SF.6.15). Registration of the optical and x-ray modalities was done by aligning each air-cementum and CDJ transition.

Optical contrast (e.g., light and dark cementum bands) consists of variation in the amount of light transmitted through the specimen, that is, variations in optical transmissivity. In polarized light micrographs, optical transmissivity is low outside the tooth (dark contrast, Figure 6.7, left side). Cementum begins when the optical transmission reaches that of the mineralized tissue. In conventional light micrographs, contrast outside the tooth matches that within (light contrast in Figures 6.8 and 6.9), and the transition into the tooth cementum is marked by a dip in light transmission at the PDL. Optical transmission also exhibits a slight dip at the CDJ. For the x-ray measurements, the most robust indicators of the air (plastic)–cementum interface and the CDJ are the

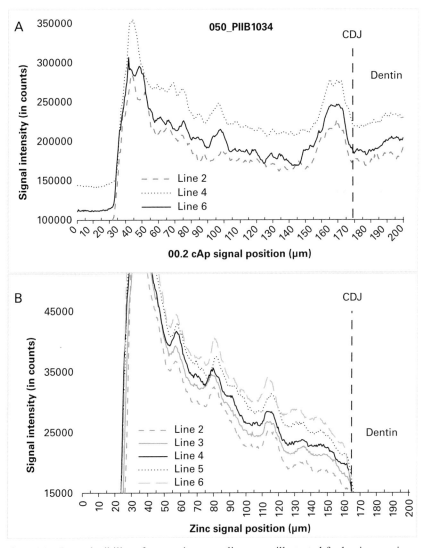

Figure 6.6 Reproducibility of successive x-ray line scans illustrated for bovine specimen 050_PIIB1034. (A) cAp 00.2 intensity, three lines shown. (B) Zn intensity, five lines shown.

rise in cAp diffracted intensity and the transition in Zn fluorescent intensity between cementum and dentin plateaus, respectively.

Figure 6.7A shows a polarized light micrograph of reindeer specimen 17_78. The optical absorption profile (white line) was recorded at the position of the inset panel B and averaged over the height of this box; this is the position where the x-ray "burns" were observed (Supplemental Figure SF.6.13). The positions of the light bands are peaks in the white line profile. All four profiles (Ca and Zn fluorescence, 00.2 cAp intensity, and optical transmission) are compared in Figure 6.7C, where the gray vertical bands indicate the dark optical bands'

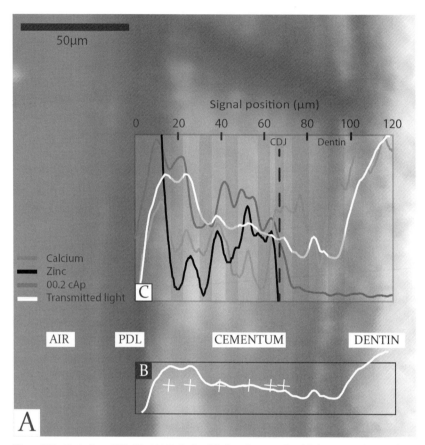

Figure 6.7 Reindeer 017_78. (A) Polarized light micrograph with inset panels B and C. (B) ROI for synchrotron mapping (black box) with positions of the optical light bands marked with "+," that is, the peaks in the optical transmission profile are shown in white. (C) Comparison of optical transmission (white), Zn fluorescent intensity (black), Ca fluorescent intensity (blue), and 00.2 cAp diffracted intensity (red). The gray vertical bands match the dark optical bands. PDL: periodontal ligament. (A black and white version of this figure will appear in some formats. For the color version, please refer to the plate section.)

position for box B. The Ca and Zn peaks coincide with the peaks in optical transmission, and, in this specimen, the light bands are positions with elevated Ca and Zn content. No particular relationship appears between the peaks in 00.2 cAp diffracted intensity and the optically visible bands.

Figure 6.8A shows an optical micrograph of red deer specimen 40_CL302 onto which optical transmission and x-ray intensity profiles have been superimposed. Box B indicates the area covered by the x-ray line scans, and box C marks the portion of the micrograph covered by the optical transmission measurement. The x-ray intensity profiles (Zn and 00.2 cAp diffracted intensity shown in panel B) were collected at the red arrowheads' position. The relatively gradual rise of cAp and Zn intensities is different from that observed for the previous specimens but can be seen to some extent in scans of other specimens (see the supplemental figures). The Ca intensity plot is not included in Figure 6.8 but appears in Supplemental Figure SF.6.10. The gradual rise of cAp diffracted intensity is not the product of crystallographic texture as all of the diffraction ROIs show the same rise. However, it represents a gradual increase in the amount of cAp intercepted by the beam during its path through the specimen thickness. Note also that the rise of Zn intensity "lags" that of cAp diffracted intensity, that is, it occurs at positions further from the start of the scans and further into the cementum. As covered in the Discussion section, the data are best interpreted as resulting from the tilt of the plastic–cementum interface from normal to the section in the orientation shown in Figure 6.8D. The white disks at the bottom of the micrograph label cementum bands. The three leftmost bands are clear in both the micrograph and the optical transmission plot (white). The two rightmost white disks mark positions where the authors believe they can discern two additional bands with very low contrast.

Figure 6.9 compares optical band positions with x-ray peaks for bovine specimen 50_PIIB1034. The optical bands are extremely difficult to see in the micrograph. However, the band positions in the optical transmission scan (white curve within the top boxed area, which matches the position of the synchrotron x-ray scans) agree with what was seen by the observer scanning the focal plane through the specimen. Panel B is inset over the lower portion of the micrograph; it compares optical band positions (minima in the white curve) represented as vertical gray bands with Zn fluorescence and with 00.2 cAp diffracted intensity. The Ca signal is not shown because it is not informative. Though there are multiple cAp and Zn maxima, their number and position do not agree particularly well with the optical bands.

6.4 Discussion

The two main novel findings (cementum and dentin's elemental signature; and the crystallographic texture within cementum) are essential in discussing why the number and positions of bands revealed from peaks in Ca and Zn fluorescent intensities and cAp 00.2 diffracted intensities are not in perfect agreement with those determined from optical micrographs.

Cementum Elemental Signature

The plateau in Zn intensity in cementum is always significantly greater than that in dentin. Normalizing the Zn intensity by the Ca intensity in each plateau (i.e., calculating I_{Zn}/I_{Ca} for cementum and for dentin) reveals that, in these specimens, the Zn signal in cementum is about five times higher on average than that of dentin, with a range of ratios spanning 1.9 to nearly 15. Clearly, one signature of cementum is a higher Zn content than dentin, which was also observed in Beluga whale teeth (Stock et al. 2017).

In most reindeer specimens (17_78, 46_38, 14_257, 22_256, 47_361, Supplemental Figures), fluorescent intensity profiles matched that identified as the PDL/MF zone in Figure 6.3. In one reindeer sample (70_181), the authors interpret the pattern as

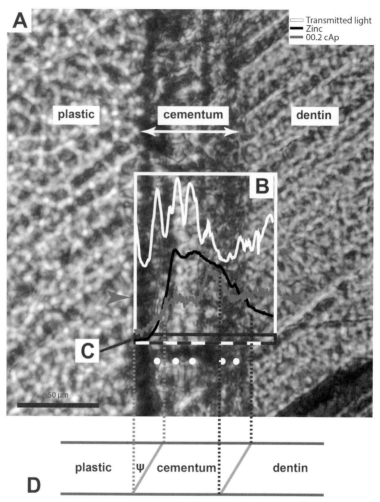

Figure 6.8 Red deer section 40_CL302. (A) Unpolarized light micrograph with scanning ROI for synchrotron mapping (B, white box) and the optical transmissivity ROI (C, black box). A black-white dashed line indicates the position where the two boxes overlap. The white disks below the x-ray ROI indicate band positions. The inset profiles within the x-ray ROI are for optical transmission (white), cAp 00.2 diffracted intensity (red), and Zn fluorescent intensity (black). The red arrowheads indicate the approximate position of the x-ray line scan. (D) Diagram of hypothetical tilted plastic–cementum and cementum–dentin interfaces. PDL: periodontal ligament. (A black and white version of this figure will appear in some formats. For the color version, please refer to the plate section.)

a seasonal band very close to the plastic cementum interface. In one case, a short plateau, with intensity matching that of the bulk of the cementum, exists between the high-intensity Zn peak nearest the surface and the drop-off to background in the mounting plastic (e.g., 23_S82, human, Figure 6.3C, and Supplemental Figure SF.6.11). The appreciable cAp diffracted intensity (Supplemental Figure SF.6.11) demonstrates that the Zn plateau is definitely within cementum. The presence of the

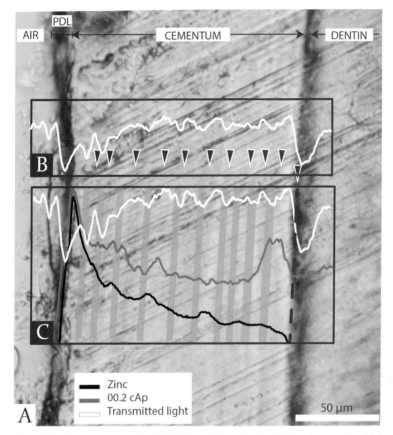

Figure 6.9 Bovine section 50_PIIB1034. (A) Unpolarized light micrograph with box (B) showing the ROI for synchrotron and transmission optical mapping. The optical transmission profile is superimposed in white in box B. The black arrowheads and gray vertical lines mark the optical microscopy positions of dark cementum bands. Box C contains the optical, Zn, and cAp profiles (white, black and red, respectively). PDL: periodontal ligament. (A black and white version of this figure will appear in some formats. For the color version, please refer to the plate section.)

near-surface Zn intensity plateau indicates that the last portion of cementum laid down was during a season where the minimum Zn concentration was being deposited, suggesting the season of death. Note that without the diffraction signal, the season of death determination for 23_S82 would have been problematic (see the anomalous Zn peak outside of the cAp zone in Supplemental Figure SF.6.4, 70_181).

Cementum Crystallographic Texture

The overall crystallographic texture (the macrotexture) revealed by the orientation and azimuthal width of the 00.2 diffraction arcs (Figure 6.2, Table 6.5) was nearly constant within a given specimen's cementum. Azimuthal arc orientations χ_{max} for all specimens cover 360° and have no specific relationship with the direction of cementum growth. For reindeer, the azimuthal 00.2 FWHM was in the range $30° \leq \Delta\chi \leq 54°$, and $\Delta\chi$ for the other three species was mostly larger; whether this is coincidence related to sampling or interspecies differences is unclear. At the micrometer scale, Figure 6.5A shows that 00.2 intensity maps across cementum had shifted peak positions when 00.2 intensity was measured at different diffraction arc positions (e.g., at χ_{max}, at the tails of the diffraction arc and at an arc position midway between the two); this indicates the existence of a subtle and difficult to detect seasonal variation in cAp crystallographic texture and in collagen orientation.

The various x-ray signals arise from different sampling volume elements (voxels) within the specimen, affecting the signals' measurements and comparisons. In x-ray fluorescence analysis, the incident x-rays excite electron transitions between shells in the atoms encountered, and K emission lines are characteristic of that element. The characteristic x-rays are emitted in all directions, but only those on paths to the energy-sensitive detector are measured. Note that incident x-ray photons are absorbed on their way to the voxel in question, and the characteristic x-rays are absorbed on their way out of the sample and by the air between the specimen and the detector. Here we ignore the effect of air absorption. X-ray attenuation is governed by the equation $I = I_0 \exp(-(\mu/\rho) * \rho * t)$, where μ/ρ is the mass attenuation coefficient (a function of the absorbing material and x-ray wavelength), ρ is the density of the absorber, I_0 is initial x-ray intensity, and I is the intensity of x-rays observed after passing through length t of the absorber. Table 6.6 gives the mass attenuation coefficients for bone (cementum and dentin have cAp contents and hence attenuation coefficients quite close to that of cortical bone) for the different energies (P, Ca, and Zn K-lines and the 10.1 keV incident radiation). Note also that the energy of diffracted x-rays is the same as that of the incident radiation.

The diffracted x-rays from all depths contribute to the signal reaching the area detector behind the specimen; the 10.1 keV radiation is not very heavily attenuated (Table 6.6). The energy-sensitive detector samples only fluorescent x-rays emitted from the front surface and close to parallel to the sample's surface (Figure 6.10A).

Table 6.6 gives reduction intensity as a function of depth for Ca and Zn signals emerging from cementum or dentin at an angle of 10°. Characteristic radiation from Ca ($E_{K\alpha} = 4$ keV) emerges from much smaller depths than that from Zn ($E_{K\alpha} = 8.6$ keV):

Table 6.6 Photon energies E and mass attenuation coefficients μ/ρ of bone for the incident radiation and the $K\alpha$ characteristic lines for P, Ca, and Zn.

			\% Intensity Escaping from Depth (μm)***				
Radiation E (keV)	μ/ρ (cm^2/g)	1	2	5	10	40
P	2.0*	587					
Ca	4.0**	133	87	90	49	24	0.3
Zn	8.6	46	95	75	77	59	12
Incident	10.1	28	99	99	97	95	81

1. The columns under "% Intensity Escaping from Depth (μm)" are relative to intensities emitted from the surface; the column headings give the depths. *Very heavily attenuated by air; **Heavily attenuated by air; *** For the incident radiation, this is the % transmitted through the sample of the given thickness.

Recent Advances on Acellular Cementum Increments Composition 131

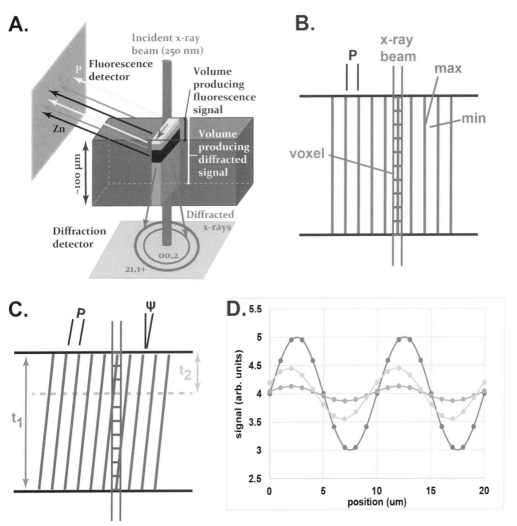

Figure 6.10 Illustration of depth from which signals originate in these experiments (A) and of the effect of band tilt (B–D). (A) Experimental geometry and volumes contributing to measured intensities. Table 6.6 lists the effect of attenuation on the different signals. (B) For purposes of discussion, the following characteristics of the band "contrast" are assumed. The contrast (00.2 cAp diffracted intensity) varies sinusoidally with a greatly exaggerated amplitude; the cementum band period is P = 10 μm. The x-ray microbeam, incident at 90°, is divided into ten volume elements (voxels). The maximum signal is from the positions indicated by solid blue lines and the minimum by the midpoint between blue lines. In (B), the bands lie perpendicular to the section ($\psi = 0°$). In (C), the bands are tilted at angle $\psi = 5.6°$ (chosen so that the beam samples one period of band structure as it traverses 100 μm thickness). Two specimen thickness $t_1 = 100$ μm and $t_2 = 30$ μm are considered. The blue curve in (D) is a variation of signal with position for the bands with $\psi = 0°$. For band tilt $\psi = 5.6°$ and thickness t_1, the different voxels sample different portions of the band's period. The result is the orange profile in (D), that is, greatly reduced band visibility and a slight shift in the band maxima and minima position. For $\psi = 5.6°$ and thickness t_2, bands are more visible (gold curve in D) but still substantially less visible than for the case of no tilt. (A black and white version of this figure will appear in some formats. For the color version, please refer to the plate section.)

From a depth 5 μm below the surface, the Ca signal is 49 percent of that from the surface and for Zn, 77 percent; at 10 μm depth, these values drop to 24 percent and 59 percent, respectively. If the interfaces and bands run through the specimen normal to the section's plane, the different depths combining to produce the measured signal would not matter except if one were using fluorescent intensity to calculate relative amounts of Ca and Zn within cementum or dentin. If, however, an interface is tilted, then the position and apparent interface width could differ between signals. Band tilts might also produce different apparent band positions for the different signals or band contrast might be suppressed due to through-depth averaging.

As mentioned in the Results section for red deer sample 40_CL302 (Figure 6.8), the gradual rise of cAp 00.2 diffracted intensity suggests a gradual transition between positions where only the plastic is sampled to positions where only cementum is sampled. If the plastic–cementum interface were tilted as the authors suggest in Figure 6.8D, then cAp signal would begin to rise at lower position values than those for Zn or Ca (whose signals, arising from the bottom of the specimen, do not emerge from the specimen and reach the detector). Similarly, the larger escape depth for Zn than Ca means that the rise of Zn signal would occur at lower position values than Ca. If the apparent position of the plastic–cementum interface is defined at the position where the intensity rises to one-half of the intensity typical of cementum, then the cAp defined interface is at position 18.5 μm, that of Zn at position 21.5 μm, and that of Ca at position 25 μm. Therefore, the three signals' results are consistent with the geometry of Figure 6.6D, that is, the presence of a tilted interface.

The distance over which the cAp intensity rises to the value characteristic of cementum can be used to calculate the tilt of the plastic–cementum interface, assuming the interface is flat and does not curve. The distance for 40_CL302 is 19 μm. If the section thickness is 100 μm, then the tilt angle ψ equals about 11°. Similar gradually rising cAp intensities at the interface with mounting plastic are observed in other specimens (possibly 36_108, 70_181, and 14_257, shown in the supplemental materials). Shifts of band positions with optical focal depth have been observed in some of the present specimens. It is essential to examine how much this might affect the x-ray measurements and their agreement with optical measures.

Because the different signals originate from different subvolumes of the specimen depth, the apparent positions of tilted bands may differ with different signals or band contrast may be washed out through depth averaging. In optical microscopy, objective lenses of 10X or 20X in air produce a depth of field of 5–10 μm (Nikon 2021), and this is the range of sample depths contributing to the micrographs, not the entire sample thickness. Typically, the investigators recorded micrographs with the optical focal plane located about 15 μm below the section's top surface. Consider the situation of 40_CL302 (tilt angle $\psi = 11°$) and, for simplicity of discussion, consider all of the Ca and Zn signals to originate from the thin layer at the top of the section. Trigonometry dictates that the optical band positions are displaced about 3 μm from those at the top surface.

The effect of tilt is even more severe on the diffraction signal (Figure 6.10B–D). In the transmission diffraction geometry, each pattern averages contributions through the entire sample thickness, and about 60 percent of 10.1 keV photons emerge from the exit surface of 100 μm thick section of cementum or dentin. For illustration purposes, assume that the diffracted intensity varies sinusoidally from band maximum to band maximum with a period (P) = 10 μm. The bands are not tilted in Figure 6.10B, and the voxels along the beam path all sample the same band position. Figure 6.10D (blue curve) shows the band contrast is strong; note that the relative contrast between band maxima and minima is much smaller than shown in reality. Consider a tilt $\psi = 5.6°$ (about one-half of that inferred for sample 40_CL032) and section thickness $t_1 = 100$ μm, enough tilt so that the column of voxels along the beam path, which samples the band maxima at the top surface, also samples the maxima of the adjacent band at the bottom surface (Figure 6.10C). If the signal were limited to the top voxel (red box, 10 μm depth), something that might represent the volume originating Ca or Zn intensities or the optical depth of field, the pattern of band maxima and minima would still be visible. The orange curve in Figure 6.10D results from summing the contributions from the entire column of voxels, that is, the diffraction depth integration; the maxima positions are shifted (relative to the blue curve), and contrast is significantly suppressed. For a thinner section, $t_2 = 30$ μm, the gold curve of Figure 6.10D results, and bands are more visible and have shifted less than in the case of the 100 μm thickness.

Table 6.4 gives widths of the CDJ, that is, the Zn intensity transition between the cementum and dentin plateaus, and these widths vary from about 5 μm to more than 25 μm. It is unlikely that the CDJ width varies this much, even between species. The most likely reason for this apparent variability is different tilts of the interface relative to the plane of the section or waviness of the CDJ through the thickness sampled, a variation analogous to that seen for the dentinoenamel junction (Oliviera et al. 2001; Stock et al. 2008; Whittaker 1978). For example, in the 17_78 sample area mapped in this study, optical micrographs show waviness: The CDJ deviates 15 μm from planarity over 375 μm distance, and waviness on the order of 5 μm occurs over lengths comparable to the section's thickness.

Collection of transmission diffraction patterns requires removing the thin section from the slides on which they were polished. Such removal sometimes warps sections (i.e., through the release of polished related residual stresses or through handling during removal from stubbornly adhering glue), and section curvature or surface waviness would affect Ca and P signals much more than Zn but should not affect the diffracted intensity. The specimen's tilt more toward the detector (counterclockwise in Figure 6.2A) would allow P and Ca signals to be detected from deeper within the specimen. The tilt of the specimen away from the detector (clockwise in Figure 6.2A) would tend to suppress P and Ca signals, and Zn would be less affected. Unusual Ca and P profiles (very broad maxima trailing off into dentin, e.g., samples 36_108 and 56_S82 in Supplemental Figures SF.6.2 and SF.6.12, respectively) may result from section curvature. It is also possible that unfavourable curvature or adherent glue is the reason why some specimens not reported here unexpectedly did not produce useful fluorescence intensities.

The present study shows cementum growth band contrast reflects both composition and cAp nanoplatelet and collagen fibril orientations. This may explain why various studies reached contradictory conclusions because the different techniques employed have different sensitivities to the different components of band contrast. Lieberman (1994), using SEM and fractured specimens, attributed band contrast variations to average collagen fibril orientation and changes in relative mineral density, resulting from a differential rate of collagen matrix formation, with a constant rate of mineralization. Employing SEM-based electron-dispersive x-ray analysis (EDX), Smith and colleagues (1994) also found no difference in mineralization between bands. The reader should note that SEM-EDX is relatively insensitive to small gradients in Ca content (SEM imaging with backscattered electrons, BSE, is far superior) and to the Zn compositions encountered in most mineralized tissues. Renz et al. (1997) identified minor variations of Ca, P, and K between individual cementum black bear increments using SEM. However, sampling precision hindered the interpretation. Another study (Cool et al. 2002) concluded that band contrast was not related to mineral density, chemistry, or collagen orientation but rather to altered mineral crystal orientations or mineral properties. Using polarized Raman spectroscopy (pRS), Colard and colleagues (2016) determined that mineralized collagen fibers are less aligned/organized in the bright layers than in the dark ones. However, pRS spatial resolution has limited interpretation at the level of individual bands (but see Chapter 14).

In Beluga whale cementum, which displays widely spaced cementum bands, synchrotron microbeam x-ray fluorescence and diffraction mapping revealed variations in Ca and Zn fluorescent intensities, and cAp diffracted intensities matched the cementum light-dark increment pattern visible in transmitted light (Stock et al. 2017). Crystallographic texture also varied with position but was not correlated with banding. Stock and colleagues (2017) also observed that Zn is elevated where mineralization is active and predicted that a peak in Zn intensity should be present at the outer cementum surface. Synchrotron x-ray fluorescence mapping of Ca, P, Sr, and Zn intensities in great apes and fossil hominins showed peaks in Ca, Sr, P, and Zn (i.e., mineral) corresponded with bright lines in transmitted light microscopy (Dean et al. 2018; Chapter 7) and confirmed that Zn appears to mark either the bouts of mineralization or slower periods of cementogenesis and is the best proxy for identifying and counting cementum annulations.

Protocol Improvements for Microstructure Analysis

The authors have specific recommendations for improving the protocols used in this study. It is important to remember that x-ray scanning will always be a supplement to optical microscopy; beam time is relatively scarce, and scan times are quite long, limiting the number of specimens that can be scanned. Nonetheless, simultaneous x-ray fluorescence and x-ray diffraction mapping provide enormously valuable information, as demonstrated by this study. Before implementing x-ray diffraction scanning, optical microscopy should be used to triage specimens for the interface's tilt (plastic–cementum and Cemento-Dentin-Junction or CDJ) hence of cementum bands. Prior quantification of tilts could be essential in avoiding less informative scanning sessions. As described earlier, tilts of even 5–6° for 100 μm thick sections can obscure bands' x-ray diffraction contrast while having much smaller effects on P, Ca, and Zn band intensities. The low depth of focus for 10× or 20× objectives means that band tilt has little effect on those results. That is not to say that x-ray diffraction should be abandoned because the present experiments show crystallographic texture is present albeit very subtle. Such mapping could greatly inform our understanding of seasonal effects on biomineralization processes. In the context of cementum bands' microtexture, however, more advanced analyses must be developed.

The use of ~40 μm instead of 100 μm thick sections might help x-ray diffraction mapping and minimize tilt effects. However, it would produce a 2.5× decrease in the number of cAp nanoplatelets sampled (and a matching decrease in diffracted intensity). This could be more than balanced by using a slightly larger x-ray beam, say 0.5 μm diameter: The number of nanoplatelets sampled (and signal) would increase by 4×. If the dark (or light) band spacing was 10 μm, a 0.5 μm diameter beam would divide each period into 20 increments, which would be more than adequate for comparison with optical micrographs.

One of the authors (SRS) routinely produces ~30 μm thick sections by careful hand polishing of freestanding sections originally cut to thicknesses of ~200 μm. This procedure, however, is not universally successful and often results in warped sections. Instead, polishing thick sections attached to glass slides with easily removed adhesive might be preferable and should be examined in future studies.

In addition to determining the number and location of cementum bands and their associated changes in cAp content and microtexture, improved diffraction and fluorescence mapping may be critical to a quantitative and nonsubjective determination of season of death and perhaps even to finer seasonal increments. Suppose that Zn intensity peaks correspond to more intense mineralization periods. In that case, the short Zn intensity plateau, observed at the cementum's outer surface in specimen 23_S82 (Figure 6.3C) and the spatially truncated Zn peak in specimen 28_94261 (Supplemental Figure SF.6.9), could indicate that these specimens might have diametrically opposed seasons of death. Optimizing specimen preparation and better design of data collection should, therefore, lead to an improved understanding of what cementum bands tell us about the individual age and season at death.

6.5 Conclusion

This study's results on four species (reindeer, red deer, bovine, and human) show that Ca or Zn x-ray fluorescent intensities and cAp diffracted intensity, all measures of compositional differences, reveal cementum band structure. Average crystallographic texture (reflecting cAp nanoplatelets' orientation and the underlying collagen fibril orientations) is constant for each specimen. However, microtextural variation is also present across individual bands, demonstrating that the overall collagen fibril orientation undergoes subtle changes with season. Patterns of "feast or famine" and concomitant changes in amount and intensity of PDL loading might produce altered collagen (and cAp) orientations between the "good" and the "bad" seasons for ungulates. Such interpretation might not apply to some modern human populations.

Acknowledgments

We would like to thank the collections managers for the express use of samples as follows: Christophe Saint-Pierre for the archaeological site of La Granède (Millau-France); Randal White for the Kaminuriak reindeer reference collection in New York University; Carlos Sànchez-Hernàndez for the Covalejos archaeological samples; Cédric Lepère for the archaeological sample from Pertus II; Emilie Blaise for the Camargue reference samples. We would also like to thank E. Newham and A. Le Cabec for constructive discussions of earlier drafts.

This work was supported by the "Agence National de la Recherche" [project CemeNTAA, ANR-14-CE31-0011]. This research used the Advanced Photon Source resources, a US Department of Energy (DOE) Office of Science User Facility operated for the DOE Office of Science by Argonne National Laboratory under Contract No. DE-AC02-06CH11357.

References

Almer, J., & Stock, S. R. (2007). Micromechanical response of mineral and collagen phases in bone. *Journal of Structural Biology*, **157**, 365–70.

Colard, T., Bertrand, B., Naji, S., Delannoy, Y., & Bécart, A. (2015). Toward the adoption of cementochronology in forensic context. *International Journal of Legal Medicine*, **129**, 1–8.

Colard, T., Falgayrac, G., Bertrand, B., . . . Penel, G. (2016). New insights on the composition and the structure of the acellular extrinsic fiber cementum by Raman analysis. *PLOS One*, **11**(12): e0167316.

Cool, S. M., Forwood, M. R., Campbell, P., & Bennett, M. B. (2002). Comparisons between bone and cementum compositions and the possible basis for their layered appearances. *Bone*, **30**(2): 386–92.

Cullity, B. D., & Stock, S. R. (2001). *Elements of X-Ray Diffraction*, 3rd ed. Upper Saddle River, NJ: Pearson.

Dean, C., Le Cabec, A., Spiers, K., Zhang, Y., & Garrevoet, J. (2018). Incremental distribution of strontium and zinc in great ape and fossil hominin cementum using synchrotron X-ray fluorescence mapping. *Journal of the Royal Society, Interface*, **15**(138): 20170626.

Lieberman, D. E. (1994). The biological basis for seasonal increments in dental cementum and their application to archaeological research. *Journal of Archaeological Science*, **21**, 525–39.

Naji, S., Colard, T., Blondiaux, J., Bertrand, B., d'Incau, E., & Bocquet-Appel, J.-P. (2016). Cementochronology, to cut or not to cut? *International Journal of Paleopathology*, **15**, 113–19.

Nikon. (2021). Depth of field and depth of focus. www.microscopyu.com/microscopy-basics/depth-of-field-and-depth-of-focus

Oliviera, C., Bergqvist, L., & Line, S. (2001). A comparative analysis of the structure of the dentinoenamel junction in mammals. *Journal of Oral Science*, **43**, 277–81.

Pike-Tay, A. (1995). Variability and synchrony of seasonal indicators in dental cementum microstructure of the Kaminuriak caribou population. *Archaeofauna*, 4: 273–84.

Rendu, W. (2010). Hunting behavior and Neanderthal adaptability in the Late Pleistocene site of Pech-de-l'Azé I. *Journal of Archaeological Science*, **37**(8): 1798–1810.

Renz, H., Schaefer, V., Duschner, H., & Radlanski, R. J. (1997). Incremental lines in root cementum of human teeth: An approach to their ultrastructural nature by microscopy. *Advances in Dental Research*, **11**(4): 472–7.

Schindelin, J., Arganda-Carreras, I., Frise, E., ... Cardona, A. (2012). Fiji: An open-source platform for biological-image analysis. *Nature Methods*, **9**(7): 676–82.

Smith, K. G., Strother, K. A., Rose, J. C., & Savelle, J. M. (1994). Chemical ultrastructure of cementum growth-layers of teeth of black bears. *Journal of Mammalogy*, **75**(2): 406.

Stock, S. R. (2015). The mineral–collagen interface in bone. *Calcified Tissue International*, **97**(3): 262–80.

Stock, S. R., Finney, L. A., Telser, A., Maxey, E., Vogt, S., & Okasinski, J. S. (2017). Cementum structure in Beluga whale teeth. *Acta Biomaterialia*, **48**, 289–99.

Stock, S. R., Veis, A., Telser, A., & Cai, Z. (2011). Near tubule and intertubular bovine dentin mapped at the 250 nm level. *Journal of Structural Biology*, **176**(2): 203–11.

Stock, S. R., Vieira, A. E. M., Delbem, A. C. B., Cannon, M. L., Xiao, X., & Carlo, F. D. (2008). Synchrotron microcomputed tomography of the mature bovine dentinoenamel junction. *Journal of Structural Biology*, **161**(2): 162–71.

Whittaker, D. K. (1978). The enamel–dentine junction of human and *Macaca irus* teeth: A light and electron microscopic study. *Journal of Anatomy*, **125**(Pt 2): 323–35.

Yamamoto, T., Hasegawa, T., Yamamoto, T., Hongo, H., & Amizuka, N. (2016). Histology of human cementum: Its structure, function, and development. *Japanese Dental Science Review*, **52**(3): 63–74.

7 Incremental Elemental Distribution in Chimpanzee Cellular Cementum: Insights from Synchrotron X-Ray Fluorescence and Implications for Life-History Inferences

Adeline Le Cabec, Jan Garrevoet, Kathryn M. Spiers, and M. Christopher Dean

Dental hard tissues contain periodic incremental markings that can be used as an absolute temporal archive to reconstruct their growth (Chapter 8). They also incorporate trace elements into their chemical structure during tooth formation that reflect diet, the environment, metabolism, and health. The temporal history of tooth tissue growth can be recovered from teeth using either classical or virtual tooth histology (e.g., Dean 2010; Le Cabec, Dean, and Begun 2017). When this is combined with the changing distribution of trace elements in enamel, dentine, or cementum, it becomes possible to resolve a continuous record of fine variation in trace element composition within each of the mineralized dental tissues. This, in turn, can contribute to our understanding of past life-history events in extant and extinct taxa. Enamel and dentine form relatively quickly, and their growth is completed by adulthood. Cementum, however, forms much more slowly and is the only dental tissue to leave an incremental record of its growth through adulthood until the time of death (Chapter 15). As such, it may contain a record of late life-history events that other dental tissues do not.

Based on bulk samples of bone, enamel, or dentine, stable and nonconventional isotope studies have revealed invaluable information about diet, migration pattern, or trophic level (Richards et al. 2008; Britton et al. 2011; Jaouen et al. 2016; 2018). High-resolution elemental analysis by laser ablation-inductively coupled plasma-mass spectrometry (LA-ICPMS) is now also widely used to reveal elemental variation with a greater temporal and spatial resolution (e.g., Humphrey et al. 2008; Austin et al. 2013; Humphrey 2014; Smith et al. 2018; Joannes-Boyau et al. 2019). However, both bulk sampling of dental tissues and LA-ICPMS are destructive techniques, which can become an issue when precious fossil material is to be sampled. Neither of these analytical techniques is able to provide fast, nondestructive continuous spatial mapping at both low and high resolution. LA-ICPMS requires that a thin tooth section be repeatedly sampled, partially or completely, to full section thickness with continuous tracks or individual spot dwells to collect multiple tissue samples (Humphrey et al. 2008; Humphrey, Jeffries, and Dean 2008; Müller et al. 2019). Moreover, the data collected do not allow measurements of absolute elemental concentration. On the contrary, data are most often standardized and expressed as a ratio, usually to calcium, often only in the form of look-up table (LUT) color maps with arbitrary units of measurement that have been extrapolated from these ratios (Austin et al. 2013; Joannes-Boyau et al. 2019; Smith et al. 2018).

Synchrotron x-ray fluorescence (SXRF) overcomes some of these disadvantages and is nondestructive to the polished ground sections that often already exist from previous histological studies of living and fossil specimens. However, it also has its own limitations: The range of elements detectable at low energy is more limited than with LA-ICPMS or bulk sampling. Maps of absolute elemental concentration are nonetheless possible at both low (e.g., 25 µm) and high (e.g., 0.25 µm) spatial resolution.

To date, there have been no studies of cellular cementum microstructure and chemistry in living great apes nor has cementum microanatomy been routinely employed in studies of human evolution in the way it has in archeology. Though acellular cementum forms slowly and regularly on the tooth root surface and has been regarded as ideal for making counts of annular growth increments (Chapters 1 and 2), cellular cementum tends to accumulate at the root tips and usually forms at irregular rates as teeth erupt and move in the alveolar bone in response to wear (Dean, Jones, and Pilley 1992; Chapter 5). Despite this, some physiological changes in anterior tooth inclination occur during life in a gradual way over many years. The lingual tilt of great ape, and some fossil hominin, anterior teeth is particularly marked and is mirrored by the formation of regular compensatory cellular cementum at the tooth root apex (Kaifu 2000; Villmoare et al. 2013; Le Cabec et al. 2017). This more regular and faster forming cellular cementum, which contains more widely spaced growth increments, lends itself to elemental mapping at a microstructural level. Our intention here is to show the potential of documenting the elemental distribution in cellular cementum using nondestructive SXRF on existing polished longitudinal thin-ground sections of teeth.

7.1 Trace Elements in Cementum

Because cementum grows continuously and incrementally after tooth emergence and over an individual's lifetime (Chapter 1), the distribution of chemical elements such as calcium (Ca), phosphorus (P), zinc (Zn), and strontium (Sr) in primate cementum may record valuable chronological information about diet, geographical location, and even late nursing history.

Because the mineral phase of cementum is largely made up of hydroxyapatite ($Ca_{10}(PO_4)_6(OH)_2$), it contains fluctuating concentrations of Ca and P within what are presumed to be hypo- and hypermineralized bands forming the yearly increments or annulations (Chapter 2). Phosphorus concentrations are not often reported, but since biological apatite contains carbonate ions (CO_3^{2-}) that may substitute for phosphate ions (PO_4^{3-}) in the hydroxyapatite lattice, any measure or pattern of P variability or fluctuation across incremental markings in cementum is of particular interest.

Information about absolute concentrations of both Ca and P, and gradients in forming cementum are, therefore, of considerable interest.

Among living great apes, nursing history and diet are extremely diverse, especially between gorillas and orang-utans in their natural habitats (Smith et al. 2017). Both Sr and barium (Ba) are incorporated into growing tooth tissues, but Ba levels are much lower (Smith et al. 2017; Humphrey et al. 2008; Humphrey 2014; ~<10 ppm in Trueman and Tuross 2002) than for Sr (~200 ppm). Sr and Ba have similar chemical properties to Ca as they both belong to the alkaline earth metals. Recently, enriched regions of Ba in orangutan teeth have been linked to elevated levels of Ba, initially reported in the breast milk and teeth of experimental macaques prior to weaning (Smith et al. 2017; 2018; Austin et al. 2013). Strontium, on the other hand, is reported to be depleted in breast milk relative to circulating plasma Sr levels (Humphrey 2014) but is also known to mirror both background environmental levels and diet (e.g., Beard and Johnson 2000). It has also been argued that sequestered Sr is preferentially released from the skeleton during periods of nutritional stress (Smith et al. 2017, 2018; Joannes-Boyau et al. 2019). In humans, it has been previously noted that Sr concentrations are higher in cementum (158 ppm) than in dentine (where they are 1.1 fold less; Martin et al. 2004).

A number of studies have identified zinc in bone and dental tissues (e.g., Chapter 6; Anné et al. 2014; Humphrey, Jeffries, and Dean 2008; Stock et al. 2017). Cementum is particularly zinc-rich (407 ppm) compared to dentine and bone (Martin et al. 2007). High levels of Zn occur at active mineralizing fronts in bone and slow-forming peritubular dentine. Although this appears to be transitory in bone (Stock et al. 2014; Gomez et al. 1999), Zn persists in peritubular dentine where it may, in fact, continue to accumulate through life (Stock et al. 2014). It is perhaps to be expected, therefore, that Zn would be strongly concentrated at the forming cementum surface in all apatitic vertebrate teeth (Stock et al. 2017). Besides cementum, higher Zn levels have been found in slow-growing secondary dentine surrounding the pulp chamber than in primary dentine (e.g., Martin et al. 2004; Stock et al. 2017). In each case, it remains unclear if Zn substitutes largely for Ca in the hydroxyapatite lattice or is to some extent also retained in the noncollagenous protein matrix or both, and/or indeed if Zn exists interstitially in mineralized tooth tissues (Stock et al. 2014). Zinc was found to be the most sensitive indicator of changes in mineralization in fast-forming cellular cementum in cetacean teeth (Stock et al. 2017). In Beluga whale cementum, maximum intensity peaks in Zn and Ca fluorescence (as well as in the carbonated hydroxyapatite fraction) occurred together and corresponded with the bright bands visible in transmitted light microscopy (TLM) as they did in both cellular and acellular great ape cementum (Dean et al. 2018). It has thus been suggested that Zn may provide a more reliable way of visualizing cementum growth increments than TLM (Stock et al. 2017).

7.2 Synchrotron X-Ray Fluorescence (SXRF)

For more than a decade, synchrotron imaging has paved the way to nondestructively access microstructural information contained in teeth, especially growth increments in enamel and dentine using phase-contrast micro-computed tomography (PPC-SR-µCT). Nonetheless, the yearly (first-order) increments in cementum have only seldom been investigated using PPC-SR-µCT in permanent and deciduous teeth (Chapters 15 and 16).

Synchrotron x-ray fluorescence provides a complementary approach to bulk isotope and LA-ICPMS analyses that seeks to access the chemical information retained in dental tissues. X-ray fluorescence can be roughly defined as the reemission of secondary x-rays (emitted beam) by a material when it has absorbed high-energy x-rays (incident beam). The measured x-ray absorbance comprises the individual element-specific absorbancies (Dik et al. 2008). The distribution of several elements can be recorded simultaneously, as long as their reemitted absorption line belongs to the range of energy of the incident beam cast on the sample. SXRF may provide quantitative data (in ppm) covering the whole sample area continuously in space (no need for extrapolation between isolated sampling spots as with LA-ICPMS). This approach has been successfully used on thin sections of extant great ape and fossil teeth to map the distribution of several elements in dental tissues, including cellular cementum (Dean et al. 2018, 2019).

Here we explored the Ca, P, Sr, and Zn distributions in cellular cementum of chimpanzee (*Pan*) teeth that had been sectioned for a previous study (see Dean and Cole 2013). We also investigated the effects of diagenesis in a fossil hominin tooth (*Paranthropus boisei*) and assessed the potential for including cementum microanatomy and chemistry in future studies of human evolution.

7.3 Samples, Experimental Setup, and Data Acquisition

We selected two ground sections of worn central incisors (permanent lower and upper central incisors [LI1 and UI1]) from a female *Pan* (UCL-CA-14E) housed in the Elliot Smith Research Collection at University College London. We also selected a 1.55–1.65 million-year-old fossil hominin canine root section attributed to *Paranthropus boisei* (KNM-ER 1817, from Koobi Fora, Kenya; Dean 2012). All teeth showed thick deposits of regular compensatory cellular cementum on the lingual aspect of their root apex, which is interpreted as resulting from the lingual tipping, or tilting, of anterior teeth to compensate for wear or continuous eruption during the long adult life span of those primates (Kaifu 2000; Villmoare et al. 2013).

Longitudinal thin sections of the teeth (thickness: 80–100 µm) were previously prepared, and laser confocal and transmitted light micrographs served to identify specific regions of interest (ROI) where cementum growth increments were best visible. Experiments were performed on the Beamline P06 (Boesenberg et al. 2016), Petra III, at DESY (Deutsches Elektronen-Synchrotron), Hamburg, Germany. Details about the sample preparation and acquisition parameters can be found in Dean et al.

(2018). The beamline setup includes a Maia detector (used in backscattered geometry). Elements of primary interest were Ca (Kα = 3.692 keV, all Kα energy values are from X-Ray Data Booklet 2009), P (Kα = 2.014 keV), Sr (Kα = 14.165 keV), and Zn (Kα = 8.639 keV); therefore, the primary energy (monochromatized) of 17 keV was chosen. Barium, by way of explanation, was not detected in this study, as the primary energy used of 17.0 keV was too low to excite electrons belonging to the Ba K-shell (Kα = 32.194 keV) and the signal from Ba L-lines (Ba L3 at 4.467 keV) was below minimum detection limits.

Data is acquired in "flyscanning" mode by continuously moving the sample relative to the x-ray beam. Spectral analysis, deconvolution, and initial image analysis of the fluorescence data were performed using GeoPIXE 7.4f, and subsequent image analysis was carried out using in-house software based on the PyFAI library (Ashiotis et al. 2015). The x-ray yield calculations were performed assuming cementum has a hydroxyapatite matrix ($Ca_{10}(PO_4)_6(OH)_2$) with a density close to 3.1 g/cm^3 (Weidmann, Weatherell, and Hamm 1967) and a final sample thickness of ~80 μm. Glass slides or Kapton polyimide film substrates were included in the overall sample model as appropriate. Concentrations were determined using a conversion factor (photon counts to equivalent charge) through measurement of a standard Ni foil with an areal density of 50.0 μg/cm^2 (Micromatter Technologies Inc. Canada). Elemental distribution maps were normalized to the incoming x-ray flux. SXRF concentrations are reported as ppm (by weight).

Overview scans (resolution: 25 μm) of the incisor roots were first acquired to assess the overall quality of the fluorescence signal. In combination with transmitted light microscopy (TLM), these overview scans served to identify ROIs with exceptionally well-defined incremental markings for later higher resolution scans. Those ROI reported here were both on the lingual aspects of the *Pan* incisors root apex in cellular cementum (UCL-CA-14E/UI1 at 5 μm, and UCL-CA-14E/LI1 at 1 μm).

7.4 Calcium and Phosphorus: Relatively Weak Trackers of Incremental Mineralization across Cementum

Figure 7.1 shows UCL-CA-14E/UI1 (scan at 5 μm). Cellular cementum is barely distinguished from dentine, with only a slight Ca gradient from the CDJ (~220,000 ppm) to the cementum surface (250,000 ppm). Phosphorus concentration across cellular cementum remains almost constant (~130,000 ppm) and does not follow the Ca gradient.

In UCL-CA-14E/LI1, cellular cementum shows widely spaced incremental markings and at a higher resolution (scan at 1 μm, Figure 7.2.), it is possible to better define the elemental contributions to the incremental markings visible in TLM (Figure 7.3). Cementocyte lacunae and unmineralized or hypomineralized Sharpey's fibers are most easily visible in the Ca, P, and Sr maps. Calcium concentration shows a slight peak at the CDJ and a weaker gradient from CDJ to cementum surface than in the upper incisor. Each incremental marking is associated with a slight rise in Ca concentration. Phosphorus concentration is more variable at ~115,000 ppm, slightly lower than in the chimpanzee upper incisor (~130,000 ppm, Figure 7.1). Thus, P concentrations in general

Incremental Elemental Distribution in Chimpanzee Cellular Cementum 143

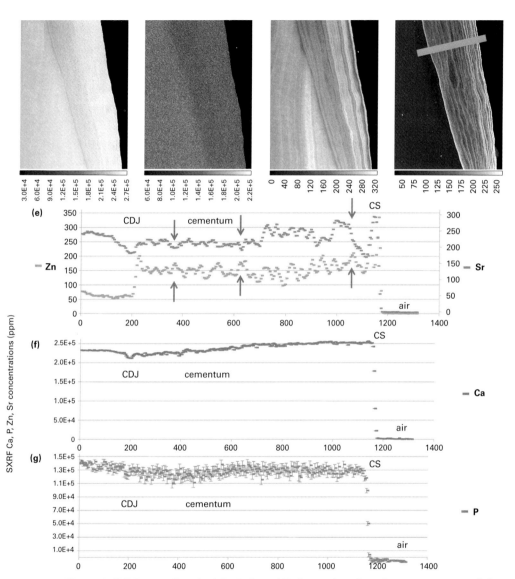

Figure 7.1 SXRF scans (5 μm) of Ca, P, Sr, and Zn in a region of regular compensatory cellular cementum in the chimpanzee UCL-CA-14E/UI1. The green bar (1350 μm long) on the Zn map (d) indicates the plane of SXRF Ca, P, Zn, and Sr concentrations (ppm) plots. The red arrows in (e) show regions where Zn and Sr concentrations are reciprocal. Color scales beneath each image denote concentration (ppm). Based on data from Dean et al. (2018). (A black and white version of this figure will appear in some formats. For the color version, please refer to the plate section.)

appear to be remarkably constant and show little clear sign of incremental fluctuation. They are, however, more variable than Ca, for example. This may suggest that P exists not only in the hydroxyapatite component of dentine and cementum but also in their organic components, whose distribution may be more homogenous. Irregular substitution of carbonate ions (CO_3^{2-}) is another potential factor that might underlie this greater

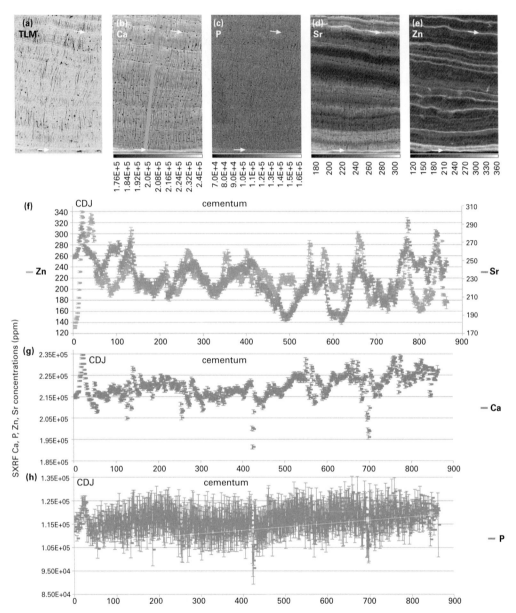

Figure 7.2 SXRF scans (1 μm) of Ca, P, Sr, and Zn (b–e) in regular compensatory cellular cementum in UCL-CA-14E/LI1 with the corresponding TLM on the left (a). The lower white arrows denote the first formed bright (dense) cementum layer at the CDJ. The upper white arrow denotes another clear, bright marking in the TLM. The green bar (860 μm long) on the Ca map indicates the plane of SXRF Zn, Sr, and Ca, P concentrations (ppm) plots (f, g, and h, respectively). There is a poor correspondence between Zn and Sr levels. Color scales beneath each image denote concentration (ppm). Based on data from Dean et al. (2018). (A black and white version of this figure will appear in some formats. For the color version, please refer to the plate section.)

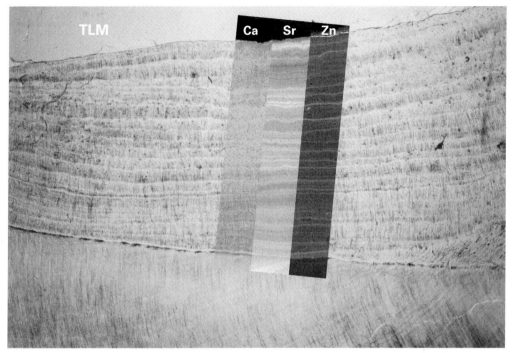

Figure 7.3 Calcium, strontium, and zinc in cellular cementum of UCL CA14E/LI1: Transmission light micrograph (TLM) overlain with SXRF map of calcium (Ca; left), strontium (Sr; middle), and zinc (Zn; right) distributions (5 μm resolution). Based on data from Dean et al. (2018).

variation in P concentration, but should this be the case, there is little evidence of any incremental fluctuation across the cellular cementum to match that seen here in Ca, Sr, and Zn. A further thought to bear in mind is that Ca and P may exist not only as hydroxyapatite in cementum but also in small quantities as calcium triphosphate and calcium octaphosphate as well as interstitially. These data show that for cellular cementum at least, Ca and P concentrations do not always covary in the same proportions, nor can P concentrations be assumed to track gradients in Ca concentration through cementum (Figure 7.2).

7.5   Strontium: A Potential Marker for Shifts in Diet and Seasonality

In the two chimpanzee incisors, Sr was incorporated into both primary and secondary dentine during growth, with strong alternating regions of Sr depletion and enrichment that follow the growth pattern of the dentine over ~10 years (overview at 25 μm, not shown, see figure 2 in Dean et al. (2018)). This observation confirms previous findings on modern humans (Martin et al. 2004). Fluctuating Sr concentrations were also incorporated into cellular cementum during its apposition.

Figure 7.1 shows that strontium concentration fluctuates around ~225 ppm throughout the whole thickness of cellular cementum at the root apex of UCL-CA-14E/UI1 and, in general, tracks Ca concentrations. Minima and maxima of Sr and Zn concentrations also track each other quite tightly through the thickness of the cementum, but there are places where they are out of phase with reciprocal concentrations (arrows in Figure 7.1e). In UCL-CA-14E/LI1 (scan at 1 μm, Figure 7.2), cementocyte lacunae and Sharpey's fibers are identifiable in the Sr map, as clearly as they are in the Ca and P maps. Additionally, peaks of Sr concentrations seem to correspond well with bright lines on the TLM. There is, however, no perfect match as the Sr lines appear thicker and/or may diffuse over several cementum increments (Figure 7.2). As in UCL-CA-14E/UI1, there is poor correspondence between peaks in Sr and Zn, although they do sometimes match. Overlying this general pattern of Sr distribution are bands or zones of Sr enrichment and depletion that are not mirrored by Ca, P, or Zn distribution.

Strontium levels in mineralized hard tissues are thought to mirror physiological levels in tissue fluid (Anné et al. 2014; Humphrey 2014). This, in turn, reflects geographical and geological location (Beard and Johnson 2000; Britton et al. 2011) and dietary intake, especially because some plants, nuts, and fruits (and seafood) concentrate Sr (Bowen and Dymond 1955) and perhaps because dust from soil on vegetation and other foodstuffs can vary between seasons. Strontium concentrations also depend upon many metabolic processes that discriminate against or favor Sr relative to Ca (Humphrey 2014). Specifically, Sr is excluded from breast milk (Humphrey 2014; Humphrey et al. 2008), but breastfeeding finishes long before ten years of age in *Pan* when cementum formation is well underway in all incisor roots. It seems most likely, however, that fluctuation in Sr levels in great ape cementum of the kind identified in this study would result from seasonal fluctuations in diet. Whether this reflects a simple volumetric increase, a decrease in a single dietary component, a shift from one dietary component to another, or rather reflects a seasonal rainfall pattern remains unknown. Because cementum potentially preserves a record of these seasonal fluctuations of diet over a period of up to twenty or thirty years, it is significant for future retrospective studies of primate life history.

7.6 Zinc: Recording Slow Growth and Resistance to Resorption

At low power (25 μm), Dean et al. (2018: see figure 2) detected Zn mostly in the dental hard tissues that form during (sub-)adult life, that is, the slow-formed secondary dentine surrounding the pulp cavity and the cementum on the root surface. This confirms previous findings in humans and other animals (e.g., Martin et al. 2004; Stock et al. 2017).

Figure 7.1 shows the root apex of UCL-CA-14E/UI1 (scan at 5 μm); Zn concentration in the cellular cementum (~150 ppm at the CDJ) is twice that of dentine (~75 ppm) and reaches its highest levels, as does Sr, at the cementum surface (mineralizing front). In UCL-CA-14E/LI1 (scan at 1 μm, Figures 7.2 and 7.3), higher concentrations in Zn correspond well to the bright lines in TLM, thus displaying fine and well-defined zinc increments (fluctuations across cementum: 160,000–300,000 ppm). This supports the conclusion that Zn appears to be the clearest proxy for the bright increments observed in TLM, even at the low concentrations expected of trace elements (Stock et al. 2017; Chapter 6). Between twenty-five and thirty wider-spaced cementum increments can be counted between the CDJ and the cementum surface in this chimpanzee LI1, which is compatible with an estimate of age at death during late adulthood. Zinc fluctuations mostly track those of Sr throughout the cementum thickness, although they may be out of phase in some places.

Cementum appears to retain unusually high levels of Zn compared with other mineralized tissues, such as bone or primary dentine, where its presence during active mineralization may be more temporary (Stock et al. 2017). Zinc readily substitutes for calcium in hydroxyapatite and confers greater resistance to acid dissolution (Dedhiya, Young, and Higuchi 1973). Cementum has the known property to resist resorption in a dynamic environment where the PDL and alveolar bone are constantly remodeling in response to masticatory forces and tooth movements. Zinc both inhibits osteoclast cell formation and function (Moonga and Dempster 1995) and reduces the acid solubility of carbonated hydroxyapatite (Featherstone and Nelson 1980). Both Zn and, to a lesser extent, Sr substitutions in hydroxyapatite may, along with other factors (Berkovitz, Holland, and Moxham 2018), have a primary role in protecting tooth root cementum from resorption.

Besides Zn, cementum (and especially acellular cementum) contains higher levels of fluoride than any other mineralized tissue (Berkovitz, Holland, and Moxham 2018). This might result from constant contact with circulating tissue fluid in the periodontal ligament space. Closer direct contact with the extracellular fluid (Sánchez-Quevedo et al. 1992) may not, however, be enough to explain the presence and distribution of Zn in cementum. Many Zn-containing enzymes (such as matrix metalloproteinases) are involved in the mineralization process, and as has been proposed for enamel (Müller et al. 2019; Dean, Spiers, et al. 2019), it may be Zn is retained in cementum after these enzymes have become inactive and their other degradation products removed. Higher Zn concentrations in some cementum layers may then reflect either the initiation of bouts of mineralization and/or proliferation and initiation of cementoblast secretory activity or, alternatively, as suggested earlier, regions of slower mineralization where a greater amount of Zn from all sources is able to exchange with Ca over time. The latter suggestion would, of course, not be incompatible with the narrower brighter markings seen in TLM that are both Ca- and Zn-rich being formed more slowly, although there is no evidence at all from this study for rates of formation of the alternating bright and dark bands of different thickness seen in TLM.

7.7 Second-Order Incremental Markings Revealed in Chimpanzee Cellular Cementum

Using high-resolution (1 μm) SXRF mapping, finer second-order (subannual) growth increments were identified between the wider-spaced first-order increments of cellular cementum in the root apex of *Pan* UCL-CA-14E/LI1 (Figures 7.2 and 7.3). These, presumably subannual, markings were also observed on the TLM but best detected as contrasting variations in Ca and Sr and to a lesser extent in Zn levels. Second-order lines have previously been reported in Beluga whales, where yearly (first-order) increments were even found to split or merge (Stock et al. 2017); in macaque monkeys with males having more numerous lines than females (Kay and Cant 1988), and in male (even castrated) black bears (Coy and Garshelis 1992), although those secondary lines were more difficult to discriminate from yearly increments than in females. However, the *Pan* specimen in this study was female. An average of ~12 second-order increments can be seen between what may be annual first-order lines, which, to speculate, is perhaps suggestive of a monthly menstrual cycle being expressed in hominid cementum. Small physiological changes in blood pH and core temperature might well, in theory, influence mineralization. Clearly, future studies on modern humans and great ape material of known age and well-documented life histories are required to test this hypothesis.

7.8 Diagenesis versus Biological Signal in 1.6 Ma Fossil Hominin Cementum

Taphonomic and diagenetic processes may affect cementum in fossil teeth (Stutz 2002). However, even very old fossil teeth may preserve a biological elemental distribution (Figures 7.4 and 7.5). Although the diagenetic changes to the cementum of the KNM-ER 1817 fossil canine root section (*P. boisei*, 1.55–1.65 Ma) may be very specific to the fossilization process within the volcanic tuff deposits at Koobi Fora (Kenya), TLM reveals good preservation of its cementum microstructure. These diagenetic changes include hypercalcification of cementum (~400,000 ppm) and the filling of cavities (i.e., pulp cavity, PDL space, and cracks) with exogenous (taphonomic) calcite (Ca > 450,000 ppm). Strontium seems to have followed the Ca diffusion – thus overprinting any biological Sr signal – and is more uniformly distributed in the cementum, reaching very high concentrations ~3,000 to 4,000 ppm. Surfaces, probably at one time in contact with groundwater, have accumulated iron (Fe Kα = 6.405 keV). However, neither iron nor calcite seems to have penetrated the deeper, denser dental tissues or filled cementocyte lacunae and canaliculi or dentine tubules (Figures 7.4 and 7.5).

Interestingly, Zn still distributes incrementally in cementum (Figure 7.4) as it might have been incorporated during life at ~140 ppm, and 20- to 25-cementum growth increments can be counted in some places. Thus, taphonomic processes do not seem to have affected the Zn distribution by loss or substitution in this particular fossil tooth. Zn may still then serve as a marker of cementum growth increments in fossil teeth. This might prove useful in future life-history studies of early hominins, especially from other archeological and fossil sites more favorable to trace element preservation (Anné et al. 2014).

7.9 Conclusions and Future Directions

Using high-resolution synchrotron x-ray fluorescence, we have mapped the calcium, phosphorus, zinc, and strontium distributions in regular compensatory cellular cementum of chimpanzee anterior teeth. Cellular cementum forms faster than acellular cementum and contains clear, widely spaced incremental markings. Although Ca

Incremental Elemental Distribution in Chimpanzee Cellular Cementum 149

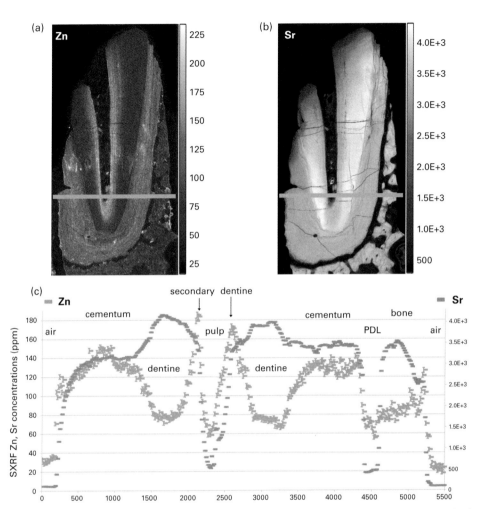

Figure 7.4 SXRF maps of zinc (a) and strontium (b) distribution in fossilized root dentine and cementum of KNM-ER 1817 (15 μm resolution). Plots (c) show Zn levels rising in cementum and in secondary dentine. Both Sr and Zn levels fall to near zero in air, the pulp space, and periodontal ligament space, both now filled with calcite. Color scales alongside each image denote concentration (ppm). Based on data from Dean et al. (2018). (A black and white version of this figure will appear in some formats. For the color version, please refer to the plate section.)

and P in hydroxyapatite predominate, trace elements are also incorporated into cementum during its apposition. Interestingly, finer second-order growth increments were resolved between presumed cementum annulations. Clear fluctuations in both Zn and Sr are preserved in cellular cementum. The fluctuations in Zn and Sr do not always correspond exactly. Fluctuations in Sr concentrations may more likely be related to seasonal shifts of diet and/or geographical location. Zinc in cementum may more likely coincide with either the initiation of bouts of mineralization as a reflection of the many Zn-containing enzymes and growth factors involved in this process or with slower periods of cementogenesis when greater amounts of mineral, particularly Ca and Zn as

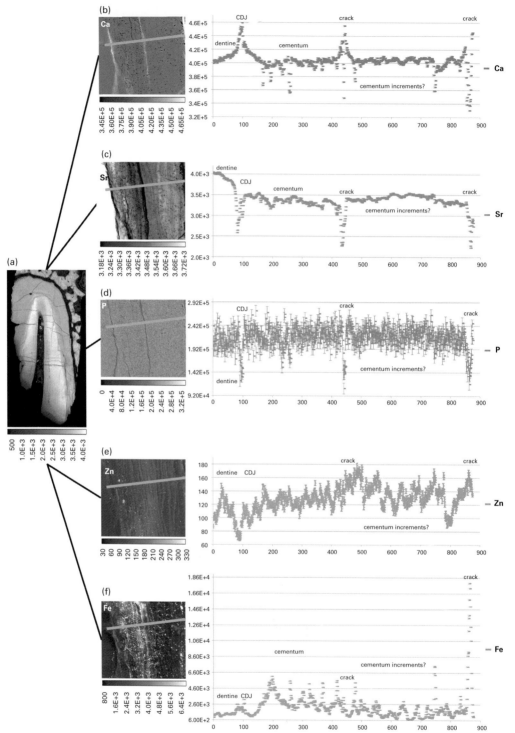

Figure 7.5 SXRF map of Sr in KNM-ER 1817 at 15 μm resolution (a) with green boundary box representing the location of SXRF maps of Ca (b), Sr (c), P (d), Zn (e), and Fe (f) at 1 μm resolution. Plots show Ca and Fe levels rise in the calcite-containing cracks, but P, Sr, and Zn levels in cracks fall to very low levels. Fluctuations in Ca, P, and Sr levels may correspond with cementum increments visible in the transmitted light micrograph. Color scales beneath each image denote concentration (ppm). Based on data from Dean et al. (2018). (A black and white version of this figure will appear in some formats. For the color version, please refer to the plate section.)

studied here, are able to accumulate over time. In the specimens studied here, the narrower, brighter incremental markings visible in TLM match the peaks in mineral concentration, but Zn lines, in particular, are finer and better defined and may prove to be the best proxy for identifying and counting cementum annulations. However, no data for changing rates of cellular cementum formation are available to elucidate further when and for how long these narrower, brighter bands might have formed in comparison with the broader, darker intervening bands. Although diagenetic changes to tooth tissues during fossilization are many and complex, cementum still appears to retain Zn, which distributes incrementally in cellular cementum.

Future directions of using XRF on fossil cementum may include one or more of the following:

(1) To perform the same type of analyses totally nondestructively, that is, on intact teeth (not on thin sections) using another type of fluorescence detector;
(2) To investigate extant specimens with known-life histories to build a reliable comparative framework with which to interpret fossils;
(3) To keep the delivered dose as low as possible for fossils potentially preserving exploitable ancient DNA (e.g., Neanderthals; see the dose calculator provided in Immel et al. 2016);
(4) To capture a broader range of elements (using the appropriate beam energy, for instance, for barium);
(5) To explore the elemental distribution in the cementum of deciduous teeth to document late childhood life history;
(6) To better characterize taphonomic and diagenetic modifications of dental tissues, which may have valuable implications for other biochemical analyses.

Acknowledgments

We are very grateful to Stephan Naji, William Rendu, and Lionel Gourichon for inviting us to contribute to this book. We thank the Government of Kenya and the National Museums of Kenya for continued access to precious fossil material in their care. We thank Drs. Emma Mbua and Meave Leakey, Tim Arnett, Jean-Jacques Hublin (MPI-EVA), the curators of the Elliot Smith Research Collection at University College London, the DESY User Office, Dr. Gerald Falkenberg, Dr. Yi Zhang, and those who have developed techniques employed in this study. We are grateful for the helpful comments of the editor and two reviewers. Parts of this research were carried out at Petra III at DESY, a member of the Helmholtz Association (HGF).

References

Anné, Jennifer, Nicholas P. Edwards, Roy A. Wogelius, Allison R. Tumarkin-Deratzian, William I. Sellers, Arjen van Veelen, Uwe Bergmann, et al. 2014. "Synchrotron Imaging

Reveals Bone Healing and Remodeling Strategies in Extinct and Extant Vertebrates." *Journal of the Royal Society Interface* 11 (96).

Ashiotis, Giannis, Aurore Deschildre, Zubair Nawaz, Jonathan P. Wright, Dimitrios Karkoulis, et al. 2015. "The Fast Azimuthal Integration." *Journal of Applied Crystallography*, 48: 510–19.

Austin, Christine, Tanya M. Smith, Asa Bradman, Katie Hinde, Renaud Joannes-Boyau, David Bishop, Dominic J. Hare, Philip Doble, Brenda Eskenazi, and Manish Arora. 2013. "Barium Distributions in Teeth Reveal Early Life Dietary Transitions in Primates." *Nature* 498 (7453): 216–19.

Beard, Brian L., and Clark M. Johnson. 2000. "Strontium Isotope Composition of Skeletal Material Can Determine the Birth Place and Geographic Mobility of Humans and Animals." *Journal of Forensic Science* 45 (5): 1049–61.

Berkovitz, Barry K. B., Graham R. Holland, and Bernard J. Moxham, eds. 2018. *Oral Anatomy, Histology, and Embryology*, 3rd ed. Mosby: New York, Edinburgh.

Boesenberg, Ulrike, Christopher G. Ryan, Robin Kirkham, D. Peter Siddons, Matthias Alfeld, Jan Garrevoet, Teresa Nunez, Thorsten Claussen, Thorsten Kracht, and Gerald Falkenberg. 2016. "Fast X-Ray Microfluorescence Imaging with Submicrometer-Resolution Integrating a Maia Detector at Beamline P06 at PETRA III." *Journal of Synchrotron Radiation* 23 (6): 1550–60.

Bowen, H. J. M., and J. A. Dymond. 1955. "Strontium and Barium in Plants and Soils." *Proceedings of the Royal Society of London B: Biological Sciences* 144 (916): 355–68.

Britton, Kate, Vaughan Grimes, Laura Niven, Teresa E. Steele, Shannon McPherron, Marie Soressi, Tegan E. Kelly, Jacques Jaubert, Jean-Jacques Hublin, and Michael P. Richards. 2011. "Strontium Isotope Evidence for Migration in Late Pleistocene *Rangifer*: Implications for Neanderthal Hunting Strategies at the Middle Palaeolithic Site of Jonzac, France." *Journal of Human Evolution* 61 (2): 176–85.

Coy, Pamela L., and David L. Garshelis. 1992. "Reconstructing Reproductive Histories of Black Bears from the Incremental Layering in Dental Cementum." *Canadian Journal of Zoology* 70 (11): 2150–60.

Dean, M. Christopher. 2010. "Retrieving Chronological Age from Dental Remains of Early Fossil Hominins to Reconstruct Human Growth in the Past." *Philosophical Transactions of the Royal Society B: Biological Sciences* 365 (1556): 3397–410.

―――. 2012. "Daily Rates of Dentine Formation and Root Extension Rates in *Paranthropus Boisei*, KNM-ER 1817, from Koobi Fora, Kenya." In *African Genesis. Perspectives on Hominin Evolution.* Sally C. Reynolds and Andrew Gallagher, eds. Cambridge, UK: Cambridge University Press, pp. 268–79.

Dean, M. Christopher, and T. J. Cole. 2013. "Human Life History Evolution Explains Dissociation between the Timing of Tooth Eruption and Peak Rates of Root Growth." *PLoS One* 8 (1): e54534.

Dean, M. Christopher, Martin E. Jones, and J. Richard Pilley. 1992. "The Natural History of Tooth Wear, Continuous Eruption and Periodontal Disease in Wild Shot Great Apes." *Journal of Human Evolution*, 22: 23–39.

Dean, M. Christopher, Adeline Le Cabec, Kathryn Spiers, Yi Zhang, and Jan Garrevoet. 2018. "Incremental Distribution of Strontium and Zinc in Great Ape and Fossil Hominin Cementum Using Synchrotron X-Ray Fluorescence Mapping." *Journal of the Royal Society Interface* 15 (138): 20170626.

Dean, M. Christopher, Kathryn Spiers, Jan Garrevoet, and Adeline Le Cabec. 2019. "Synchrotron X-Ray Fluorescence Mapping of Ca, Sr and Zn at the Neonatal Line in

Human Deciduous Teeth Reflects Changing Perinatal Physiology." *Archives of Oral Biology*. Amsterdam: Elsevier, pp. 90–102.

Dedhiya, Mahendra G., Fudah Young, and William I. Higuchi. 1973. "Mechanism for the Retardation of the Acid Dissolution Rate of Hydroxyapatite by Strontium." *Journal of Dental Research* 52 (5): 1097–109.

Dik, Joris, Koen Janssens, Geert Van Der Snickt, Luuk van der Loeff, Karen Rickers, and Marine Cotte. 2008. "Visualization of a Lost Painting by Vincent van Gogh Using Synchrotron Radiation–Based X-Ray Fluorescence Elemental Mapping." *Analytical Chemistry* 80 (16): 6436–42.

Featherstone, J. D. B., and D. G. A. Nelson. 1980. "The Effect of Fluoride, Zinc, Strontium, Magnesium, and Iron on the Crystal–Structural Disorder in Synthetic Carbonated Apatites." *Australian Journal of Chemistry* 33 (11): 2363–8.

Gomez, S., R. Rizzo, M. Pozzi-Mucelli, E. Bonucci, and F. Vittur. 1999. "Zinc Mapping in Bone Tissues by Histochemistry and Synchrotron Radiation–Induced X-Ray Emission: Correlation with the Distribution of Alkaline Phosphatase." *Bone* 25 (1): 33–8.

Humphrey, Louise T. 2014. "Isotopic and Trace Element Evidence of Dietary Transitions in Early Life." *Annals of Human Biology* 41 (4): 348–57.

Humphrey, Louise T., M. Christopher Dean, Teresa E. Jeffries, and Malcolm Penn. 2008. "Unlocking Evidence of Early Diet from Tooth Enamel." *Proceedings of the National Academy of Sciences* 105 (19): 6834–9.

Humphrey, Louise T., Teresa E. Jeffries, and M. Christopher Dean. 2008. "Micro Spatial Distributions of Lead and Zinc in Human Deciduous Tooth Enamel." In *Technique and Application in Dental Anthropology*. Joel D. Irish and Greg. C. Nelson, eds. Studies in Biological Anthropology. Cambridge, UK: Cambridge University Press, pp. 87–110.

Immel, Alexander, Adeline Le Cabec, Marion Bonazzi, Alexander Herbig, Heiko Temming, Verena J. Schuenemann, Kirsten I. Bos, et al. 2016. "Effect of X-Ray Irradiation on Ancient DNA in Sub-Fossil Bones – Guidelines for Safe X-Ray Imaging." *Scientific Reports* 6 (September): 32969.

Jaouen, Klervia, Melanie Beasley, Margaret Schoeninger, Jean-Jacques Hublin, and Michael P. Richards. 2016. "Zinc Isotope Ratios of Bones and Teeth as New Dietary Indicators: Results from a Modern Food Web (Koobi Fora, Kenya)." *Scientific Reports* 6: 26281.

Jaouen, Klervia, Rozenn Colleter, Anita Pietrzak, Marie-Laure Pons, Benoît Clavel, Norbert Telmon, Éric Crubézy, Jean-Jacques Hublin, and Michael P. Richards. 2018. "Tracing Intensive Fish and Meat Consumption Using Zn Isotope Ratios: Evidence from a Historical Breton Population (Rennes, France)." *Scientific Reports* 8 (1): 5077.

Joannes-Boyau, Renaud, Justin W. Adams, Christine Austin, Manish Arora, Ian Moffat, Andy I. R. Herries, Matthew P. Tonge, Stefano Benazzi, Alistair R. Evans, and Ottmar Kullmer. 2019. "Elemental Signatures of *Australopithecus Africanus* Teeth Reveal Seasonal Dietary Stress." *Nature* 572 (7767): 112–15.

Kaifu, Yousuke. 2000. "Tooth Wear and Compensatory Modification of the Anterior Dentoalveolar Complex in Humans." *American Journal of Physical Anthropology* 111: 369–92.

Kay, Richard F., and John G. H. Cant. 1988. "Age Assessment Using Cementum Annulus Counts and Tooth Wear in a Free-Ranging Population of *Macaca Mulatta*." *American Journal of Primatology* 15 (1): 1–15.

Le Cabec, Adeline, M. Christopher Dean, and David R. Begun. 2017. "Dental Development and Age at Death of the Holotype of *Anapithecus hernyaki* (RUD 9) Using Synchrotron Virtual Histology." *Journal of Human Evolution* 108: 161–75.

Martin, Ronald R., Steven J. Naftel, Andrew J. Nelson, Andrea B. Feilen, and Alfredo Narvaez. 2004. "Synchrotron X-Ray Fluorescence and Trace Metals in the Cementum Rings of Human Teeth." *Journal of Environmental Monitoring* 6 (10): 783–6.

Martin, Ronald R., Steven J. Naftel, Andrew J. Nelson, and William D. Sapp III. 2007. "Comparison of the Distributions of Bromine, Lead, and Zinc in Tooth and Bone from an Ancient Peruvian Burial Site by X-Ray Fluorescence." *Canadian Journal of Chemistry* 85 (10): 831–6.

Moonga, Baljit S., and David W. Dempster. 1995. "Zinc Is a Potent Inhibitor of Osteoclastic Bone Resorption in Vitro." *Journal of Bone and Mineral Research* 10 (3): 453–7.

Müller, Wolfgang, Alessia Nava, David Evans, Paola F. Rossi, Kurt W. Alt, and Luca Bondioli. 2019. "Enamel Mineralization and Compositional Time Resolution in Human Teeth Evaluated via Histologically Defined LA-ICPMS Profiles." *Geochimica et Cosmochimica Acta* 255 (June): 105–26.

Richards, M. P., M. Pacher, M. Stiller, J. Quilès, M. Hofreiter, S. Constantin, J. Zilhão, and E. Trinkaus. 2008. "Isotopic Evidence for Omnivory among European Cave Bears: Late Pleistocene *Ursus Spelaeus* from the Peștera Cu Oase, Romania." *Proceedings of the National Academy of Sciences* 105 (2): 600.

Sánchez-Quevedo, M. C., P. V. Crespo, J. M. García, and A. Campos. 1992. "X-Ray Histochemistry of Zinc in Dental Tissues." *European Archives of Biology* 103 (1): 47–9.

Smith, Tanya M., Christine Austin, Daniel R. Green, Renaud Joannes-Boyau, Shara Bailey, Dani Dumitriu, Stewart Fallon, et al. 2018. "Wintertime Stress, Nursing, and Lead Exposure in Neanderthal Children." *Science Advances* 4 (10): eaau9483.

Smith, Tanya M., Christine Austin, Katie Hinde, Erin R. Vogel, and Manish Arora. 2017. "Cyclical Nursing Patterns in Wild Orangutans." *Science Advances* 3 (5).

Stock, S. R., A. C. Deymier-Black, A. Veis, A. Telser, E. Lux, and Z. Cai. 2014. "Bovine and Equine Peritubular and Intertubular Dentin." *Biomineralization* 10 (9): 3969–77.

Stock, S. R., L. A. Finney, A. Telser, E. Maxey, S. Vogt, and J. S. Okasinski. 2017. "Cementum Structure in Beluga Whale Teeth." *Acta Biomaterialia* 48 (January): 289–99.

Stutz, Aaron Jonas. 2002. "Polarizing Microscopy Identification of Chemical Diagenesis in Archaeological Cementum." *Journal of Archaeological Science* 29 (11): 1327–47.

Trueman, Clive N., and Noreen Tuross. 2002. "Trace Elements in Recent and Fossil Bone Apatite." *Reviews in Mineralogy and Geochemistry* 48 (1): 489–521.

Villmoare, B., K. Kuykendall, T. C. Rae, and C. S. Brimacombe. 2013. "Continuous Dental Eruption Identifies Sts 5 as the Developmentally Oldest Fossil Hominin and Informs the Taxonomy of *Australopithecus Africanus*." *Journal of Human Evolution* 65 (6): 798–805.

Weidmann, S.M., J. A. Weatherell, and S. M. Hamm. 1967. "Variations of Human Enamel Density in Sections of Human Teeth." *Arch Oral Biol* 12: 85–97.

X-Ray Data Booklet. 2009. Lawrence Berkeley National Laboratory, University of California. http://xdb.lbl.gov

8 Identifying Life-History Events in Dental Cementum: A Literature Review

Elis Newham and Stephan Naji

8.1 Introduction

The circum-annual rhythm and continuous growth of cementum throughout life offer an exciting window of potential life-history information recorded in the shape, texture, and chemistry of its increments. A host of studies have examined the relationship between these factors and various mammalian life-history variables, most notably pregnancy and parturition.

Here, we review the cementum literature to isolate the predominant patterns in cementum incrementation related to pregnancy and other life-history variables and the clinical literature relating hormonal physiology to oral health to offer novel hypotheses regarding the relationship among physiology, oral health, and cementum growth.

8.2 The Relationship between Hormonal Physiology, Pregnancy, and Oral Health

Pregnancy is an intensive life-history event and creates substantial pressure on a mother's metabolism. This pressure is manifest in various hormonal changes (Boggess, 2008), increased nutritional demand on the mother (Bucher et al., 1996), and the harvesting of various minerals from calcified tissues (Surarit et al., 2016).

Hormonal changes in the blood and changes to oral bacterial flora in the saliva can cause adverse effects on dental and oral health during pregnancy. The most significant hormonal change during pregnancy is the increased production of estrogen and progesterone. This is mainly due to the development of the placenta, which becomes the main source of both hormones from the second trimester in humans. Estrogen and progesterone serve important roles during pregnancy: increasing basal metabolic rate, modulating the immune system, and affecting the vascular system. Concurrent damage to the gingiva and oral tissue is proportional to this significant influx of hormones. Silk et al. (2008) outline the three most common pathologies that affect the gingiva, teeth, and periodontal tissue in pregnant women. Gingivitis is the most common oral disease in pregnancy (60 percent to 75 percent prevalence found in Silk et al., 2008). During pregnancy, inflammation of the superficial gum tissue is aggravated by fluctuations in estrogen and progesterone levels (key hormones involved in the maintenance of pregnancy) as well as changes in oral bacterial flora and suppressed immune response. These factors have also been attributed to increased levels of periodontitis during pregnancy, the destructive inflammation of the periodontium. This process involves bacterial infiltration of the periodontium, producing toxins that stimulate a chronic inflammatory response. The periodontium is eventually broken down and destroyed and teeth loosen. Tooth loosening is the third common pathology known during pregnancy and can occur without prominent levels of gingivitis or periodontitis. This phenomenon has frequently been attributed to increases in estrogen and progesterone during pregnancy, although the mechanisms for increased movement in the absence of gum disease are poorly understood.

Damage and inflammation to gingival tissue also release macrophages. These are important immune cells that play a significant part in tissue remodeling by inhibiting tissue breakdown through proteolysis. Pregnant women with clinical gingivitis have low concentrations of plasminogen activator inhibitor type 2 (PAI-2), the proteolysis inhibitor produced by macrophages, relative to nonpregnant women. This reduces the protection of periodontal connective tissue in pregnant women (Kinnby et al., 1996).

In addition to progesterone and estrogen, prolactin is an important calciotropic hormone responsible for the resorption of bone and the donation of calcium to the fetus. In a recent in-vitro study by Surarit et al. (2016), prolactin receptors were found within the periodontal ligament (PDL). Further, when the PDL is exposed to concentrations of prolactin similar to those experienced during pregnancy, the stemness potential of PDL cells (that can usually proliferate into a wide range of cells including cementoblasts) is heavily reduced and the formation of osteoblasts heavily selected for, as opposed to other tissues including cementoblasts.

Several studies on populations of laboratory animals have revealed that instances of dental disease increase proportionally with increasing levels of estrogen and progesterone (Muhler and Shafer, 1955; Persson et al., 1998). Conversely, increases in androgen levels, the gonadal hormones responsible for promoting male secondary sexual characteristics, have no significant effect on oral health (Legler and Menaker, 1980). The root cause of the relationship between estrogen and dental health was believed to have been identified by Muhler and Shafer (1955), who found that increased levels of estrogen led to decreased thyroid activity and a reduction in saliva flow rate. Saliva plays several important roles in promoting oral health, including physically protecting tooth crowns, buffering pH levels, and neutralizing bacterial acids (Lenander-Lumikari and Loimaranta, 2000) as well as hosting antimicrobial agents that break down pathogenic organisms (Marsh, 1999). Further, clinical studies on both animals and humans have revealed sex differences in the composition and flow rate of saliva (Percival et al., 1994; Dodds et al., 2005). Females are consistently found to have lower rates of saliva production than males, and this is resistant to other factors known to affect saliva production including disease, medical procedures, and medications. The negative impacts of estrogen on oral health have been shown to significantly accelerate during puberty and pregnancy and fluctuate through the menstrual cycle

(Lukacs and Largaespada, 2006). These effects extend to the periodontium as well as caries in teeth (Silk et al., 2008). The dramatic rise in the production of estrogen and progesterone during puberty is accompanied among females by a proportional increase in gingival inflammation and bleeding. Several studies have also shown a concomitant increase in subgingival bacteria during puberty in females. Such microbial changes have been suggested to be due to preferential enhancement of these bacteria by female sex hormones. Further, significant and observable gingival inflammatory changes have been documented in association with the menstrual cycle. Bleeding, swollen gingiva, and increased tooth mobility have all been reported during ovulation. For example, Hugoson (1971) described an increase in gingival disease of at least 20 percent during ovulation in more than 75 percent of a sample of twenty-six women. The extracellular matrix, gingival vessels, and periodontal fibroblasts are all affected by hormonal changes. Interaction with various growth hormones and steroids causes activation of proteolytic enzymes from fibroblasts and epithelial cells, which break down connective tissue extracellular components of the gingiva, including primary collagen. Increased concentrations of estrogen and progesterone have also been shown to stimulate several signaling proteins (cytokines) involved in gingival inflammation and so may exacerbate symptoms of gingivitis. Finally, the conversion of estrone to estradiol (two of the primary forms of estrogen) has been shown to increase inflamed gingiva, and estradiol is known to negatively impact collagen metabolism (Silk et al., 2008). Fluctuations in female sex hormone levels are thus expressed directly and indirectly as damage to the gingiva, periodontium, and tooth crowns. Because these effects include the disruption of growth and breakdown of both periodontal and cementum cells, this damage has the potential to extend to the cementum.

It is clear that the substantial changes to hormone levels during pregnancy considerably alter a mother's gingival biology. In particular, the destruction, suppression of growth, and resorption of periodontal connective tissue may significantly affect the cementum. The growth of acellular cementum is triggered and sustained by fibroblasts and cementoblasts originating in the PDL. Damage to these cells and a reduction of their proliferation from periodontal stem cells during pregnancy are highly likely to have a direct impact on the growth of cementum and quality of the cementum matrix. Further, a primary component of the acellular extrinsic fiber cementum is collagenous Sharpey's fibers. Because these originate from within the PDL, the joint effects of proteolytic enzymes and estradiol on periodontal collagen formation may add to the negative effects of pregnancy on cementum growth. The effects of pregnancy can thus be expected to extend to cementum growth.

8.3 Cementum Growth and Hormonal Physiology in Animal Studies

There have been relatively few studies exploring possible sexual dimorphism in cementum structure. Kolb (1978) identified significant differences in the timing of formation and proportion of dark "slow growth" bands in the cementum of male and female foxes (*Vulpes vulpes*). Males showed a consistently thicker slow growth band that was initiated earlier in the year than females. This was also shown in the cementum of European lynxes (*Lynx lynx*) by Kvam (1984).

Correspondence between increment width and opacity with pregnancy have been found in the Atlantic walrus (*Odobenus rosmarus*; Klevezal, 1996), black bears (*Ursus americanus*; Coy and Garshelis, 1992), ringed seals (*Phoca hispida*; Stewart et al., 1996), northern sea otters (*Enhydra lutris*; von Biela et al., 2008), and most recently polar bears (*Ursus maritimus*; Medill et al., 2010). In each study, increments formed during pregnancy were found to be significantly thinner and less well defined than surrounding increments. Further, a study by Klevezal and Stewart (1994) found a significant change in the production rate of cementum coeval with the advent of sexual maturity in female northern elephant seals (*Mirounga angustirostris*), where an average production of two thin, chaotic increments per year is changed to one more morphologically stable increment deposited per year. This body of research suggests that there is a relationship between flux in female hormone regimes and cementum growth. However, the cause of this phenomenon during pregnancy is rarely discussed beyond increased metabolic demand (Medill et al., 2010).

The only study known to use cementum measurements to generate a predictive model for pregnancy events was by Medill et al. (2010). Analysis of cementum increments was performed on a large sample (more than 300) of individual polar bears from a monitored population in Western Hudson Bay, Canada. Pregnancy events and subsequent periods of parturition were recorded in the field, using evidence of females with cubs that appeared less than one year old. The differences between the "growth layer groups" (GLGs; one thick light increment and its corresponding thin dark increment) formed during pregnancy and the previous GLG was measured, along with the difference between the two previous GLGs (when applicable). These measurements were then input into a logistic regression model. The GLG width difference estimated to provide even (1:1) odds between "cub" (pregnant) and "noncub" (nonpregnant) was then used as a threshold in a predictive model subsequently used to estimate other pregnancy events in a blind test. This model predicted known pregnancy events with 71 percent accuracy in females with recorded life histories. However, when the model was applied to male polar bears, 40.6 percent had similar reductions in GLG growth as those seen during pregnancy. This identifies a substantial shortfall in this model because it is not yet refined enough to determine sex in a population of unknown demographic. The fact that similar results can be generated in both male and breeding female individuals also suggests that further refinement of this methodology is needed before pregnancy can be confidently estimated in populations and samples of unknown life-history and demographics.

The most recent studies to use cementum increment morphology as a proxy for life-history variables have adopted the methodology of Medill and colleagues (2009, 2010) to record changes in GLG width through time quantitatively and compare patterns to those seen in recorded environmental and ecological variables (Nguyen et al., 2017; Wittmann et al., 2016).

Wittman and colleagues (2016) quantified the relative width of the acellular extrinsic fiber cementum (AEFC) and its constituent GLGs recorded in longitudinal stained thin sections of the postcanine teeth in 158 (123 females and 35 males) New Zealand fur seals (*Arctocephalus forsteri*). Transverse AEFC width measurements (of the entire cementum tissue) were related to a series of body size morphometric measurements (body mass, bodily length, girth), and patterns in individual GLG widths were compared to temporal patterns in dominant climatic variables over the fifteen years before capture (sea surface temperatures, southern oscillation index). Using mixed-effects modeling (that also accounted for the potential effects of internal variables) on GLG width through time, the authors showed a significant negative correlation between both sea surface temperature and southern oscillation index with GLG width and somatic growth. This was suggested to reflect the effect of sea-level temperature on complex trophic interactions that limit the somatic growth of fur seals during periods of increased temperature with increases in seawater temperature known to decrease primary productivity, reduce food availability and increase foraging area.

Most recently, Nguyen and colleagues (2017) used the methodology of Medill and colleagues (2009, 2010) to generate a proportional width index (PWI) of AEFC increments in the cementum of seventy-five ringed seals (*Pusa hispida*) to compare patterns in PWI with independently sourced information regarding their breeding histories and local environmental conditions. PWI width here significantly correlated with a series of climatic variables (date of sea ice breakup and rate of open water gain). Increases in ovulation rate also correlated strongly with increases in increment PWI. The authors suggested that these correlations with PWI width may be used in future studies as a proxy for population health.

8.4 Cementum Growth and Hormonal Physiology in Human Studies

For humans, empirical observations used to match known physiological events to observed "irregular" annual AEFC layers have helped to generate the hypothesis and prediction that AEFC growth is sensitive to life-history events. This is the first step toward generating a larger theory of individual dental and skeletal growth variation in relation to environmental and physiological constraints under which we already operate for enamel (Bromage et al., 2011; Tang et al., 2015) and dentin growth (Dean, 2006); Zazzo, Balasse, and Patterson, 2006). For the past twenty years, several researchers have examined the relationship between AEFC variation and life-history parameters in documented human subjects, specifically looking at environmental (pathologies, traumas, lifestyle) and physiological (pregnancies, malnutrition) factors.

The most comprehensive experiment (Kagerer and Grupe, 2001) analyzed a large sample of eighty teeth with complete anamnestic protocols. Increments were visually counted in transverse thin sections, and individual increments of anomalous thickness and optical properties were noted and aged. Comparisons between increment counts and known chronological age suggested a small negative influence (2.5 percent) of oral pathologies on age estimation precision. However, the most interesting results were the identification of "broad and translucent layers among the post-eruptive incremental lines" (Kagerer and Grupe, 2001a, p. 79 and figures 1–5). Even though these broad and translucent annulations (BTAs) were not explicitly or quantitatively defined (in terms of width or luminescence contrast, for example), the authors identified them systematically in "all the sections taken from the same tooth" (Kagerer and Grupe, 2001a, p. 9). Also, twenty out of eighty teeth were from women with recorded pregnancies. In all cases, BTAs corresponded exactly with the age of pregnancy and interbirth intervals (Kagerer and Grupe, 2001a, p. 79). Finally, other life-history events were recorded such as skeletal trauma (Kagerer and Grupe, 2001a, figure 4) and one case of renal disorder (Kagerer and Grupe, 2001a, figure 5). BTAs were interpreted as being due to insufficiencies/disturbances of calcium/mineral deposition during cementogenesis at the time of the event. However, other recorded events such as osteoporosis, diabetes, or thyroid disorders were not observed.

Caplazi (2004) presented a validation study on thirty-four individuals from a documented nineteenth-century medical hospital cemetery in Basel Spitalfriedhod (Switzerland) to examine the influence of tuberculosis on cementum growth. A second goal was to explore potential sexual dimorphism observed in histological ground sections. In both cases, no differences were found. However, Caplazi estimated that qualitative changes of the optical properties of incremental cementum layers both at the cementum PDL border and within the cementum thickness were higher (36 percent) in females than in males (17 percent). In one case, a thick and dark (in bright-field transmitted light) cementum layer was deposited between twenty-four and twenty-eight and was linked to a known pregnancy at twenty-nine years of age (Caplazi, 2004, p. 61 and figure 16).

Following the protocol developed by Kagerer and colleagues (Kagerer and Grupe, 2001a, b) for preparing sections of AEFC and their definition of BTA, Blondiaux and colleagues (2006: 5) examined fifteen teeth from a modern human sample as well as sixteen teeth from the medieval site of Magnicourt (France) and compared them to a sample of twenty-three medieval teeth from individuals with articular tuberculosis. The purpose of the study was to simultaneously examine the incidence of BTA in individuals with tuberculosis lesions and to determine if pregnancies were visible in incremental cementum deposits. Blondiaux recorded the presence and year of BTA development and the number of BTA was interpreted as "frequent if over 50 percent, and rare if under 50 percent" (Blondiaux et al., 2006: 5). Results suggested that BTA were more frequent in individuals with chronic bone and joint tuberculosis lesions associated with early onset of BTAs and presumed acute thoracic infections with late-onset of BTA (Blondiaux et al., 2006: 6).

In the modern sample, BTAs in two women with recorded pregnancies were observed at or around the time of pregnancies. In comparison, "short clusters of BTA" (lasting one to two years) were scattered predominantly for females in years of peak fertility (Blondiaux et al., 2006: 6). Unfortunately, illustrations of the BTA are only available in one archaeological and one modern figure, which does not allow for critical evaluation. Further, the claim of a higher frequency of BTA associated with tuberculosis was not supported by any statistical tests.

In 2008, a presentation at the American Association of Physical Anthropologists presented data from thirty-nine women of known pregnancy history (Kuenzie &

Wittwer-Backofen, 2008). Results showed that the age of pregnant women was a strong influence on their susceptibility to "record" the event in cementum, with a higher proportion of BTAs corresponding with pregnancy events with increasing age of the pregnancy. In contrast, pregnancies were more visible when there was less chronological spacing between them. One of the most interesting results was that all miscarriages and stillbirth events were visible, while the signal became less pronounced for second and third pregnancies.

More recently, Mani-Caplazi and colleagues (2017) used synchrotron radiation-based micro-computed tomography (SRµCT) to analyze cementum variations in seven human teeth (six women and one man) from the same Swiss documented collection presented earlier. This preliminary study was able to identify cementum increments virtually and specifically identify broader increments that were interpreted as stress events. At this stage, the resolution and imaging contrast was not sufficient to accurately estimate age at death, let alone the age of the stress event. However, this article is the first publication that uses SRµCT to analyse cementum increments (Le Cabec et al., 2018; Chapters 15 and 16). Following this study, the same team published a protocol to measure incremental AEFC width and appearance to identify irregularities, as a first technical step to observe life-history events in cementum in a standardized way (Mani-Caplazi et al., 2019).

Two pilot studies tried to identify documented pregnancies in women using innovative imaging technologies. The first used a scanning electron microscope to accurately count cementum increments (Ristova et al., 2018). In addition to providing a 95 percent accurate age estimates for 15 individuals, the authors identified in one tooth an anomalously thick AEFC increment of significantly higher mineralization, compared to the surrounding increments. This increment corresponded to the age of this woman's single pregnancy. Edinborough and colleagues (2019) used a Time-of-Flight Secondary Ion Mass Spectrometry to identify a significantly lower level in calcium for the entire decades covering the six recorded pregnancies of one 65-year-old woman.

The latest study was presented by Cerrito et al. (2020), who examined cementum from forty-seven modern humans from Malawi (Central Africa) with documented information chronicling a range of life-history (e.g., pregnancy, menopause, serious illness) and lifestyle events (e.g., relocation, prison time). The authors departed from standardized cementochronology protocols (Chapter 1) by implementing one designed for enamel studies. This included using MMA embedding instead of epoxy and a longitudinal cutting axis instead of transverse. The authors failed to find discernable annual cementum increments and, instead, examined undefined optical cementum bands when viewed under cross-polarized light (XPL). XPL bands were assumed to be birefringent AEFC layers that each corresponds to a physiological event. With no circum-annual increments to rely on, the authors estimated the age at which each XPL band was deposited by dividing the total radial width of the cementum by the known age of the individual minus the average age of eruption for the respective tooth-type. The width between the cemento-dentine boundary and the XPL event was then divided by this value to provide its age estimate and compare it to the known ages at which life-history events occurred. A highly significant ($r^2 = 0.92$) positive correlation was found between estimated ages of formation for alternating XPL bands and known ages for a wide range of life-history events, leading the authors to conclude that cementum faithfully records such events.

With no comparable embedding and imaging modality used in previous physiological cementochronology studies, it is uncertain what XPL bands represent in comparison to increments and physiological records in other studies. It is therefore unclear how differences in birefringence under XPL are related to physiological events and which birefringent bands represent a change to cementum growth related to physiological stress versus "regular" cementum growth (i.e., which bands represent life history events and why). Thus, the temporal range of each XPL band for capturing known life-history events is not evident, which is a crucial factor for assessing their accuracy and precision given their subannual periodicity. Although dating of XPL bands was performed blindly, it is also unclear whether their match with life-history events was performed post hoc, *a priori*, or ad hoc, and whether every physiological life-history event known for each individual was recorded in XPL banding. Because the full life-history record of the Malawi sample is not presented in the supplement, it is unclear how many "significant" events (not defined by the authors) were recorded for each individual. The results thus seem data-driven and reinforce a perception of confirmation bias by selecting documented events to the estimated age.

Finally, there are several confusing points. First, the authors provided no protocol for the two measurements described in the methods or any interobserver test to validate the method. The resulting documented age-at-event standard deviation is large (Cerrito et al. 2020, supp. table 1), ranging from 0.5 to 6.4. This is a major limit to identifying events that may be occurring within that time frame, such as repeated pregnancies. Also, the authors state that they do not assume AEFC growth rate to be constant within a species but that the rate is constant within an individual. However, age estimation is not based on *total rates of growth*, but *seasonal deposits*. Validation studies largely evidenced that the *number* of layers is constant, not their *individual thickness* (Chapter 1). In this chapter, we hypothesize that individual band growth variation is one indicator to test for, whether optically (individual increment width measurement) or chemically (individual increment composition).

Although this study provides novel exploration of a previously unappreciated form of cementum incrementation, there is unfortunately no way to truly evaluate its accuracy as a physiological record (see Mani-Caplazi, 2019), which unfortunately undermines its title and conclusion.

8.5 Discussion: The Future of Cementochronology

The starting hypothesis of all the cementochronological studies discussed here is that any variations to the growth process during life should affect AEFC chemical composition or optical/material properties. The corollary questions are as follows: Which external or internal factors influence cementum growth, how, and why?

Cementum Mineralization

Recent understanding of cementum biology shed some light on these question (see Part I of this volume). In particular, Foster and colleagues (2015) directly tested the effect of mineralization defects on cementum growth from loss of bone sialoprotein (BSP), an anionic extracellular matrix protein associated with mineralized tissues of the skeleton and dentition. Mice null for the Bsp gene had severe defects in cementum and craniofacial bones, particularly affecting mineralization (hydroxyapatite deposition and growth). Also, Foster and colleagues (2012) identified the central role of inorganic pyrophosphate (PPi) as a regulator of cementum mineralization by inhibiting hydroxyapatite mineral precipitation in knock-out mice featuring PPi dysregulation. Specifically, only AEFC growth, not cellular cementum, seems to relate inversely to PPi production (Foster et al., 2012, p. 7, figure 14). Furthermore, other genetic disorders directly affect cementum mineralization, the first being hypophosphatasia (HPP) as observed in cases of rickets (both nutritional and refractory) and osteomalacia (Chapter 3).

This recent development in the understanding of long-term mineral variations/mobilization due to pathological factors, genetic variation, or environmental stressors strongly supports the hypothesis that life-history events, pregnancies, and skeletal trauma, in particular, should be "visible" in AEFC growth patterns.

Chemical Composition

Another approach is the direct study of chemical differences between individual AEFC increments in animals and modern/archaeological hominid samples (Dean et al., 2018; Stock et al., 2017; Chapters 6 and 7). This is a promising avenue for objectively distinguishing individual life-history events from other growth processes.

Dean and colleagues (2018) used synchrotron radiation-based x-ray fluorescence (SR XRF) to map changes in several chemical elements through the cementum of extant great apes, modern humans, and a 1.65 million-year-old fossil attributed to *Paranthropus boisei*. They found that peak/trough patterns in calcium (Ca), strontium (Sr), and zinc (Zn) all follow optical cementum increments seen in SEM micrographs in recent teeth. Sr levels in mineralized tissues are believed to reflect both geographical location and dietary intake, and patterns in Sr within the cementum may reflect seasonal changes in diet. Fluctuations in Zn show the strongest correlation with optical increments in SEM micrographs. Further, SR XRF revealed secondary, high-frequency incremental changes in Zn between annual increments. The finding of twelve such secondary Zn increments between two annual increments in female great apes was suggested as potentially recording menstrual cycling.

A major finding of this and a previous study by Stock and colleagues (2017) is that Zn is found in unusually high proportions in cementum, compared to other mineralized tissues. Zn is known to block demineralization of hydroxyapatite actively and inhibits the formation of osteoclasts. Therefore, its elevated presence is hypothesized by Dean and colleagues as a major factor in the resistance of cementum to resorption. Further, the presence of Zn in bone is known to stimulate osteoblast proliferation, collagen synthesis, and alkaline phosphate activity (which in turn mediates pyrophosphate activity). Dean and colleagues thus posit that fluctuations in Zn concentrations found in XRF data may represent changing rates of mineralization.

Another recent study was performed using Time-of-Flight Secondary Ion Mass Spectrometry (ToF-SIMS) to measure the degree and distribution of mineralization of cementum growth layers (Edinborough et al., 2019). ToF-SIMS was specifically applied to one tooth extracted from a 65-year-old woman with six documented pregnancies. Mass spectrometry could not resolve individual AEFC layers. Instead, the authors calculated the approximate width of incremental lines, given the theoretical maximum width of AEFC layers for that particular sex, age, and tooth and the observed total width of AEFC (Edinborough et al., 2019: 182). Using elemental and molecular maps of calcium and hydroxyapatite along the AEFC surface, the authors identified "obvious variation in Ca+ intensity across the AEFC width, but not for hydroxyapatite" (Edinborough et al.: 183, figure 2b, figure 3). They concluded that "[...] pregnancies are more likely to influence AEFC in terms of relatively reduced mineralization," as demonstrated by a lower rate of Ca starting with the first pregnancy and ending with the last.

The further study of discrete chemical changes in the cementum of samples of known life-history may elucidate more distinct chemical changes in cementum that correlate with specific life-history events and variables. For instance, Sr and Ba present contrasting patterns in concentration during parturition (Ba is enriched in breast milk, whereas Sr is depleted) (Smith et al., 2017). These patterns may be recorded in cementum increments produced during and immediately after pregnancy and parturition.

Virtual Cementochronology

When reviewing the results of previous studies regarding the relationship between cementum growth and a series of specific life-history variables, it becomes clear that the phenotypic expression of these variables differs between taxa and probably sexes. Previous metrics used to study increment morphology may not provide the necessary sensitivity to distinguish variables from one another. For instance, the finding of thin, poorly defined cementum increments formed during pregnancy relative to surrounding increments in all animal studies directly contrasts with the "broad, translucent annulations" (BTAs) formed during pregnancy in humans. BTAs, defined by the two-dimensional thickness and qualitative luminance of increments under study (i.e., the observer subjectively decides which line is different), are also seen in the same human sample to represent instances of bodily injury and renal disease, and there is no effort made to distinguish between the morphologies representing each life-history event.

This issue is reflected in the results of Medill and colleagues (2010), who discovered that the same difference in 2D thickness between increments formed during pregnancy and surrounding increments in 71 percent of female polar bears was also found in 40 percent of males. These results suggest that the metrics of 2D thickness and/or optical luminance of individual increments may not be sufficient for confidently distinguishing individual life-history variables in cementum.

The expanding use of nondestructive synchrotron radiation-based x-ray tomographic (SRμCT) imaging methods for studying cementum may in turn provide new ways of examining and comparing the morphology, contrast, and structure of cementum increments. The 3D nature of SRµCT imaging has permitted the quantitative study and comparison of several aspects of bone architecture, including volumetric and structural aspects of pore networks within long bones (Pratt et al., 2015). These comparisons have provided new information on the effects of various pathologies on the 3D structure of bone, from the effects of microcracking on bone fragility to changes in subchondral bone structure during the development of osteoporosis (Larrue et al., 2011; Chappard et al., 2013). A series of novel techniques for comparing individual and group cementum increments are presented by Newham et al. in this volume (Chapter 16). The proliferation of such techniques for comparing increments formed under differing life-history events and variables may provide a more confident estimation of such factors than using 2D methods alone.

8.6 Concluding Thoughts

Identifying life-history events within cementum is probably the most stimulating area of current research in cementochronology. We have here outlined several promising avenues of research that are currently being explored. However, a conclusively reliable and accurate protocol to identify and quantify AEFC variations linked to life-history events remains illusive. Two major hurdles need to be cleared before the use of cementum variations can move forward reliably.

The first hurdle is methodological. Today, two main approaches are being explored to identify the changes related to life-history events in cementum growth layers: optical and chemical.

- Optical methods of AEFC increment analysis include (a) a traditional 2D histology evaluation of AEFC layers, whether qualitative (luminescence, translucency, sharpness) or quantitative (width, tortuosity). This approach is by far the most practical because it is based on standard histology and imaging protocols, but methodological improvements are still much needed to objectively define "irregular" AEFC increments. Mani-Capalazi and colleagues (2019) started to propose one approach, and we are looking forward to future developments; (b) an innovative 3D SRµCT volumetric analysis that integrates morphological and optical variations of individual AEFC increments in a fully automated algorithm (Chapter 16). This 3D model is probably the most promising (noninvasive, subjective, automated), subject to access to a synchrotron.
- Future chemical methods should be more objective in quantifying individual AEFC increments' elemental variations, given that the definition of a "normal" AEFC band can be achieved first by measuring levels of zinc or calcium. Furthermore, with a better understanding of cementum growth and regulation, these variations could be directly interpreted in terms of specific life-history events (e.g., pregnancies versus trauma). However, these analyses imply both the destruction of the sample and access to very expensive analytical equipment.

The second hurdle is theoretical: How do we account for individual frailty? The recent global theory of biological aging departs from the customary view that the phenotypes of aging result from a failure of homeostasis in the body (Johnson et al., 1999). Several recent studies suggest that aging is a phylogenetically independent adaptation and that destruction of the body proceeds under strong control of the genome (Mitteldorf, 2016)(Horvath and Raj, 2018). Nine endogenous physiological dysregulations associated with aging (genomic instability, telomere attrition, epigenetic alterations, loss of proteostasis, deregulated nutrient-sensing, mitochondrial dysfunction, cellular senescence, stem cell exhaustion, and altered intercellular communication) that are common in different organisms including in mammals have been identified as central pathways to aging and longevity (López-Otín et al., 2013). Some of these mechanisms have been directly linked to bone growth variations that drive skeletal fragility (Farr and Almeida, 2018: table 1). It is reasonable to hypothesize that the same mechanisms should affect dental maintenance and thus cementum mineralization and growth, but to what extent remains unclear.

Finally, these intrinsic biological determinants (epigenetic clock), in combination with extrinsic behavioral (e.g., lifestyle/ecology, nutrition) and social factors (e.g., exposure to disease vectors, pollutants), have direct and significant effects on the heterogeneity of health outcomes, especially of older individuals. All of these factors need to be considered when dealing with documented collections built from teeth extracted from living patients or recently deceased individuals. These samples are very different from historical skeletons from archaeological sites that represent an aggregate of dead individuals with several potential biases summarized in the osteological paradox (DeWitte & Stojanowski, 2015; Wood et al., 1992). Selective mortality probably acted very differently to produce either robust survivors (strong selective mortality) or frail survivors (weak selective mortality).

Regardless of the method, if the link between cementum variations and life-history events can be formally demonstrated across species, it will be a key finding to address broad questions in anthropology, archaeology, zoology, and palaeontology.

Acknowledgments

We would like to thank the ANR CemeNTAA (CE3001), the Natural Environmental Research Council (UK), and Engineering and Physical Sciences Research Council (UK) for partial funding of this project, and two anonymous reviewers.

References

Blondiaux, J., Gabart, N., Alduc-Le Bagousse, A., Niel, C., & Tyler, E. (2006). Relevance of Cement Annulations to Paleopathology. *Paleopathology Newsletter*, **135**, 4–13.

Boggess, K. A. (2008). Maternal Oral Health in Pregnancy. *Obstetrics and Gynecology*, **111**(4), 976–86.

Bromage, T. G., Juwayeyi, Y. M., Smolyar, I., . . . Chisi, J. (2011). Signposts Ahead: Hard Tissue Signals on Rue Armand de Ricqlès. *Comptes Rendus Palevol*, **10**(5–6), 499–507.

Bucher, H. C., Guyatt, G. H., Cook, R. J., Hatala, R., Cook, D. J., Lang, J. D., & Hunt,D. (1996). Effect of Calcium Supplementation on Pregnancy-Induced Hypertension and Preeclampsia: A Meta-Analysis of Randomized Controlled Trials. *JAMA* **275**(14), 1113–17.

Caplazi, G. (2004). Eine Untersuchung über die Auswirkungen von Tuberkulose auf Anlagerungsfrequenz und Beschaffenheit der Zementringe des Menschlichen Zahnes. *Bulletin Der Schweizerischen Gesellschaft Für Anthropologie*, 35–83.

Cerrito, P., Bailey, S. E., Hu, B., &Bromage, T.G. (2020). Parturitions, Menopause and Other Physiological Stressors Are Recorded in Dental Cementum Microstructure. *Sci Rep. 2020*, **10**(1),5381.

Chappard, C., Bensalah, S., Olivier, C., Gouttenoire, P.J., Marchadier, A., Benhamou, C., & Peyrin, F. (2013). 3D Characterization of Pores in the Cortical Bone of Human Femur in the Elderly at Different Locations as Determined by Synchrotron Micro-Computed Tomography Images. *Osteoporos*, **147**(24), 1023–33.

Coy, P. L., & Garshelis, D. L. (1992). Reconstructing Reproductive Histories of Black Bears from the Incremental Layering in Dental Cementum. *Canadian Journal of Zoology*, **70**(11), 2150–60.

Dean, C. (2006). Tooth Microstructure Tracks the Pace of Human Life-History Evolution. *Proceedings of the Royal Society B: Biological Sciences*, **273**(1603), 2799–2808.

Dean, C., Le Cabec, A., Spiers, K., Zhang, Y., & Garrevoet, J. (2018). Incremental Distribution of Strontium and Zinc in Great Ape and Fossil Hominin Cementum Using Synchrotron X-Ray Fluorescence Mapping. *Journal of the Royal Society, Interface*, **15**(138). http://doi.org/10.1098/rsif.2017.0626

DeWitte, S. N., & Stojanowski, C. M. (2015). The Osteological Paradox 20 Years Later: Past Perspectives, Future Directions. *Journal of Archaeological Research*, **23**(4), 397–450.

Dodds, M. W. J., Johnson, D., & Yeh C.-K. (2005). Health Benefits of Saliva: A Review. *J Dent* **33**, 223–33.

Edinborough, M., Fearn, S., Pilgrim, M., . . . Edinborough, K. (2019). Life History Parameters in Acellular Extrinsic Fiber Cementum Microstructure. *BioRxiv*, 528760.

Farr, J. N., & Almeida, M. (2018). The Spectrum of Fundamental Basic Science Discoveries Contributing to Organismal Aging. *Journal of Bone and Mineral Research*, **33**(9), 1568–84.

Foster, B. L., Ao, M., Willoughby, C., . . . Somerman, M. J. (2015). Mineralization Defects in Cementum and Craniofacial Bone from Loss of Bone Sialoprotein. *Bone*, **78**, 150–64.

Foster, B. L., Nagatomo, K. J., Nociti, F. H., Fong, H., Dunn, D., Tran, A. B., Wang, W., Narisawa, S., Millán, J. L., & Somerman, M. J. (2012). Central Role of Pyrophosphate in Acellular Cementum Formation, *PLoS ONE* **7**(6).

Horvath, S., & Raj, K. (2018). DNA Methylation-Based Biomarkers and the Epigenetic Clock Theory of Ageing. *Nature Reviews Genetics*, **19**(6), 371–84.

Hugoson, A. (1971). Gingivitis in Pregnant Women. A Longitudinal Clinical Study. *Odontol Revy*, **22**(1), 65–84.

Johnson, F. B., Sinclair, D. A., & Guarente, L. (1999). Molecular Biology of Aging. *Cell*, **96**(2), 291–302.

Kagerer, P., & Grupe, G. (2001). Age-at-Death Diagnosis and Determination of Life-History Parameters by Incremental Lines in Human Dental Cementum as an Identification Aid. *Forensic Science International*, **118**(1), 75–82.

Kinnby, B., Matsson, L. & Astedt, B. (1996). Aggravation of Gingival Inflammatory Symptoms during Pregnancy Associated with the Concentration of Plasminogen Activator Inhibitor Type 2 (PAI-2) in Gingival Fluid. *Journal of Periodontal Research*, **31**, 271–7.

Klevezal, G. A. (1996). *Recording Structures of Mammals: Determination of Age and Reconstruction of Life History*. Rotterdam: A. A. Balkema Series.

Klevezal, G. A., & Stewart, B. S. (1994). Patterns and Calibration of Layering in Tooth Cementum of Female Northern Elephant Seals, Mirounga angustirostris. *Journal of Mammalogy*, **75**(2), 483–7.

Kolb, M. (1978). The Formation of Lines in the Cementum of Premolar Teeth in Foxes. *Journal of Zoology*, **185**, 259–63.

Kuenzie, M., & Wittwer-Backofen, U. (2008). Stress Markers in Tooth Cementum Caused by Pregnancy. *American Journal of Physical Anthropology*, **46**, 135.

Kvam, T. (1984). Age Determination in European Lynx Lynx l. lynx by Incremental Lines in Tooth Cementum. *Acta Zool Fenn*, **171**, 221–3.

Larrue, A., Rattner, A., Peter, Z. A., et al. (2011). Synchrotron Radiation Micro-CT at the Micrometer Scale for the Analysis of the Three-Dimensional Morphology of Microcracks in Human Trabecular Bone. *PLoS ONE*, **6**(7), e21297.

Le Cabec, A., Tang, N. K., Rubio, V. R., & Hillson, S. (2018). Nondestructive Adult Age at Death Estimation: Visualizing Cementum Annulations in a Known Age Historical Human Assemblage Using Synchrotron X-Ray Microtomography. *American Journal of Physical Anthropology*. http://doi.org/10.1002/ajpa.23702

Legler, D. W., & Menaker, L. (1980). Definition, Etiology, Epidemiology and Clinical Implication of Dental Caries. In L. Menaker, ed. *The Biological Basis of Dental Caries*. New York: Harper and Row, 217.

Lenander-Lumikari, M., & Loimaranta, V. (2000). Saliva and Dental Caries. *Advances in Dental Research*, **14**(1), 40–7.

López-Otín, C., Blasco, M. A., Partridge, L., Serrano, M., & Kroemer, G. (2013). The Hallmarks of Aging. *Cell*, **153**(6), 1194–1217.

Lukacs, J. R., & Largaespada, L. L. (2006). Explainnig Sex Differences in dental Caries Prevalence: Saliva, Hormones and "Life-History" Etiologies. *American Journal of Human Biology*, **18**, 540–55.

Mani-Caplazi, G., Hotz, G., Wittwer-Backofen, U., & Vach, W. (2019). Measuring Incremental Line Width and Appearance in the Tooth Cementum of Recent and Archaeological Human Teeth to Identify Irregularities: First Insights Using a Standardized Protocol. *International Journal of Paleopathology*, **27**, 24–37.

Mani-Caplazi, G., Schulz, G., Deyhle, H., Hotz, G., Vach, W., Wittwer-Backofen, U., & Müller, B. (2017). Imaging of the Human Tooth Cementum Ultrastructure of Archeological Teeth, Using Hard X-Ray Microtomography to Determine Age-at-Death and Stress Periods. 10391:103911C-10391-98. http://dx.doi.org/10.1117/12.2276148

Marsh, P. D. (1999). Microbiologic Aspects of Dental Plaque and Dental Caries. *Dent Clin North Am*, **43**, 599–615.

Medill, S., Derocher, A. E., Stirling, I., & Lunn, N. (2010). Reconstructing the Reproductive History of Female Polar Bears Using Cementum Patterns of Premolar Teeth. *Polar Biology*, **33**(1), 115–24.

Medill, S., Derocher, A. E., Stirling, I., Lunn, N., & Moses, R. A. (2009). Estimating Cementum Annuli Width in Polar Bears: Identifying Sources of Variation and Error. *Journal of Mammalogy*, **90**(5), 1256–64.

Mitteldorf, J. (2016). An Epigenetic Clock Controls Aging. *Biogerontology*, **17**(1), 257–65.

Muhler, J. C., & Shafer, W. G. (1955). Experimental Dental Caries. VII. The Effect of Various Androgens and Estrogens on Dental Caries in the Rat. *Journal of Dental Research*, **34**(5), 661–5.

Nguyen, L., Pilfold, N. W., Derocher, A. E., Stirling, I., Bohart, A. M., & Richardson, E. (2017). Ringed Seal (Pusa hispida) Tooth Annuli as an Index of Reproduction in the Beaufort Sea. *Ecological Indicators*, **77**, 286–92.

Percival, R. S., Challacombe, S. J., & Marsh, P. D. (1994). Flow Rates of Resting Whole and Stimulated Parotid Saliva in Relation to Age and Gender. *J Dent Res*, **73**, 1416–20.

Persson, R. E., Persson, G. R., Kiyak, H. A., & Powell, L. V. (1998). Oral Health and Medical Status in Dentate Low-Income Older Persons. *Special Care in Dentistry: Official Publication of the American Association of Hospital Dentists, the Academy of Dentistry for the Handicapped, and the American Society for Geriatric Dentistry*, **18**(2), 70–7.

Pratt, I. V., Belev, G., Zhu, N., et al. (2015). In Vivo Imaging of Rat Cortical Bone Porosity by Synchrotron Phase Contrast Micro Computed Tomography. *Phys Med Biol*, **60**, 211–32.

Ristova, M., Talevska, M., & Stojanovska, Z. (2018). Accurate Age Estimations from Dental Cementum and a Childbirth Indicator – A Pilot Study. *Journal of Forensic Science & Criminology*, **6**, 1–12.

Silk, H., Douglass, A. B., Douglass, J. M., & Silk, L. (2008). Oral Health during Pregnancy. *American Family Physician*, **77**(8), 1139–44.

Smith, T. M., Austin, C., Hinde, K., Vogel, E. R., & Arora, M. (2017). Cyclical Nursing Patterns in Wild Orangutans. *Science Advances*, **3**(5), e1601517.

Stewart, R. E. A., Stewart, B. E., Stirling, I., & Street, E. (1996). Counts of Growth Layer Groups in Cementum and Dentine in Ringed Seals (phoca Hispida). *Marine Mammal Science*, **12**(3), 383–401.

Stock, S. R., Finney, L. A., Telser, A., Maxey, E., Vogt, S., & Okasinski, J. S. (2017). Cementum Structure in Beluga Whale Teeth. *Acta Biomaterialia*, **48**, 289–99.

Surarit, R., Krishnamra, N., & Seriwatanachai, D. (2016). Prolactin Receptor and Osteogenic Induction of Prolactin in Human Periodontal Ligament Fibroblasts. *Cell Biology International*, **40**(4), 419–27.

Tang, N., Le Cabec, A., & Antoine, D. (2015). Dentine and Cementum Structure and Properties. In *A Companion to Dental Anthropology*, J. D. Irish & G. R. Scott, eds., Hoboken, NJ: John Wiley & Sons, Inc., 204–22.

von Biela, V. R., Testa, J. W., Gill, V. A., & Burns, J. M. (2008). Evaluating Cementum to Determine Past Reproduction in Northern Sea Otters. *Journal of Wildlife Management*, **72**(3), 618–24.

Wittmann, T. A., Izzo, C., Doubleday, Z. A., McKenzie, J., Delean, S., & Gillanders, B. M. (2016). Reconstructing Climate–Growth Relations from the Teeth of a Marine Mammal. *Marine Biology*, **163**(4), 71.

Wood, J. W., Milner, G. R., Harpending, H. C., & Weiss, K. M. (1992). The Osteological Paradox: Problems of Inferring Prehistoric Health from Skeletal Samples. *Current Anthropology*, **33**(4), 343–70.

Zazzo, A., Balasse, M., & Patterson, W. P. (2006). The Reconstruction of Mammal Individual History: Refining High-Resolution Isotope Record in Bovine Tooth Dentine. *Journal of Archaeological Science*, **33**(8), 1177–87.

Part II

Protocols

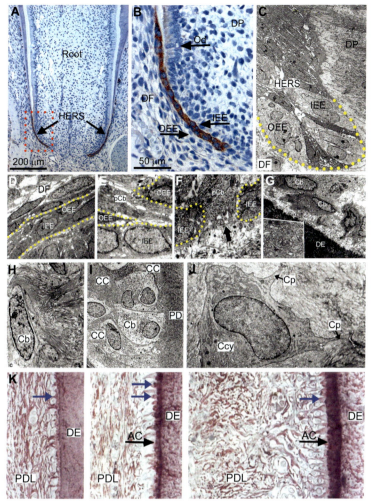

Figure 2.1 Cementum formation. (A, B) Decalcified section of mouse molar root at fourteen days postnatal. Box in panel A indicates area shown in panel B. Hertwig's epithelial root sheath (HERS) is positive for pan-keratin immunostaining (red-brown). HERS consists of inner and outer enamel epithelium (IEE and OEE, respectively) and separates the dental pulp (DP) and odontoblasts (Od) from the surrounding dental follicle (DF). (C) Transmission electron microscope (TEM) image of a human mandibular premolar showing the HERS bilayer of IEE and OEE. Panels D–G show TEM images of apical edge of forming rat molar. (D) The intact IEE and OEE layers of HERS surrounded by DF cells. Epithelial cells are outlined by yellow stippled lines in panels D–G. (E) Precementoblasts (pCb) derived from the DF penetrate the OEE layer of HERS, though the inner layer remains intact. (F) pCb cells extend cytoplasmic processes (black arrow) between cells of the IEE to breach HERS and contact the forming root surface. (G) Differentiated cementoblasts (Cb) on the surface of root dentin (DE). Inset shows typical Cb Golgi complex with saccules, secretory granules, and lysosomes. Panels H–J show TEM images of cementum-associated cells of a forming human premolar. (H) Flattened, fibroblast-like Cb associated with acellular cementum (AC), secreting collagen fibers near developing root surface. (I) Cuboidal, osteoblast-like Cb associated with cellular cementum (CC), in the vicinity of the predentin (PD) matrix. (J) Newly embedded cementocyte (Ccy) forming cell processes (Cp) within the CC matrix. (K) Series of light microscope images of human premolar roots showing the root prior to AC formation (left panel), after two years of AC growth (middle panel), and after five years of AC growth (right panel). The fiber fringe (blue arrows) is observed to extend from the root surface at a perpendicular orientation into the PDL. Images in panels C and J adapted with permission from Bosshardt and Schroeder, *Cell Tissue Res* 267(2): 321–35, 1992. Images in panels D–G adapted with permission from Cho and Garant, *J Periodontal Res* 23(4): 268–76, 1988. Images in panels H, I, and K adapted with permission from Selvig and Bosshardt, *Periodontol 2000* 13: 41–75, 1997. (A black and white version of this figure will appear in some formats.)

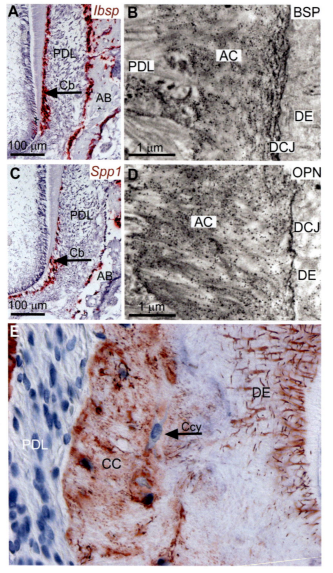

Figure 2.2 Types of cementum. (A) Microcomputed tomography reconstruction of human premolar showing localization of enamel (EN), dentin (DE), acellular cementum (AC), and cellular cementum (CC), with both cementum types shown in yellow. **(B)** Human AC in decalcified histology section stained by hematoxylin and eosin (H&E) or by **(C)** picrosirius red stain viewed under polarized light to emphasize inserted Sharpey's fibers. Mouse molar AC shown by **(D)** scanning electron microscopy and **(E)** transmission electron microscopy. **(F–G)** Human cellular cementum (CC) in decalcified histology section stained by H&E. **(H)** Human acellular afibrillar cementum (AAC) in decalcified histology section stained by H&E. Enamel space (ES) remains after decalcification of the enamel. **(I)** Reparative cementum (RP) of the CC type fills a resorption defect on the root surface. Note the reversal line (RL) marking the edge of the resorption left by odontoclasts. Image in B reproduced with permission from Foster, 2012. Image in C adapted from Thumbigere-Math et al., *J Dent Res* 97(4): 432–41, 2018, and used in accordance with STM permissions guidelines. Image in D adapted from Foster et al., *J Dent Res* 92(2): 166–72, 2013, and used in accordance with STM permissions guidelines. Image in E adapted with permission from Foster et al., *Bone* 78: 150–64, 2015. Images in G–I reproduced and adapted with permission from Selvig and Bosshardt, *Periodontol 2000* 13: 41–75, 1997. (A black and white version of this figure will appear in some formats.)

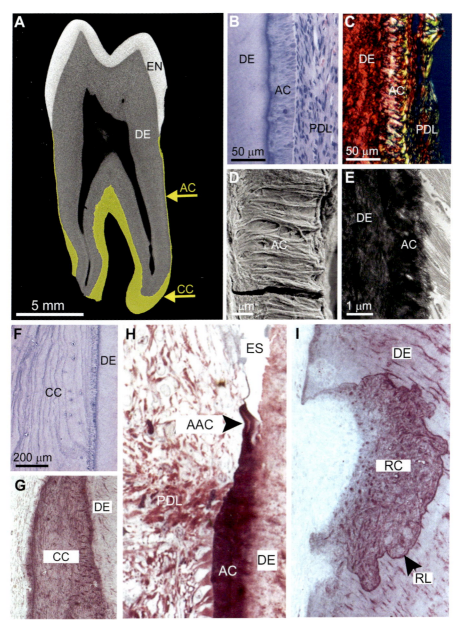

Figure 2.3 Composition of cementum. (A) In a developing mouse molar, Ibsp mRNA is expressed (red signal) by cementoblasts (Cb) lining the root dentin (DE) surface. **(B)** In a rat molar, BSP protein localizes to the acellular cementum (AC) layer by colloidal gold immunocytochemistry (black dots) imaged by transmission electron microscopy (TEM). AC is bounded by two tissues where BSP appears mostly absent, the periodontal ligament (PDL) and dentin (DE). Dentin-cementum junction (DCJ) is indicated. **(C)** Spp1 mRNA (red signal) is expressed by some Cb in the developing mouse molar. **(D)** OPN protein labels rat AC by colloidal gold immunocytochemistry viewed by TEM. **(E)** DMP1 protein labels mouse molar cellular cementum (CC) matrix around embedded cementocytes (Ccy) and is also present in dentin (DE). Images in B and D reproduced and adapted with permission from McKee and Nanci, 1995. Image in E reproduced with permission from Foster and Sanz, 2020. (A black and white version of this figure will appear in some formats.)

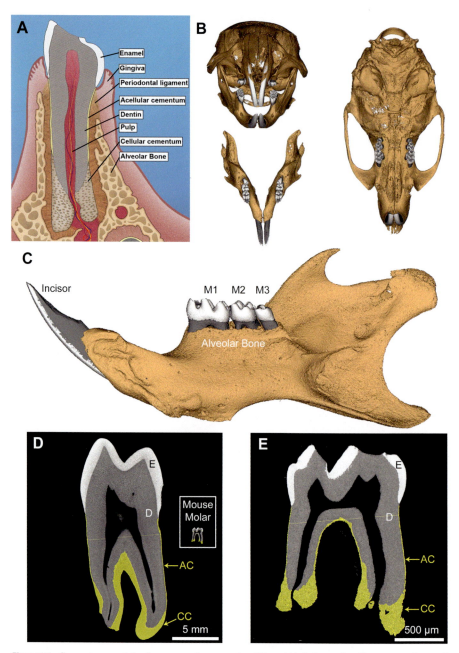

Figure 3.1 Cementum and the human and mouse dentition. (A) Schematic of mouse molar and supporting tissues. (B) Mouse skull (3D rendering from micro-CT scan). (C) The mouse hemi-mandible includes one incisor and three molars (M1-M3) (3D rendering from micro-CT scan). 2D renderings of (D) human premolar (with mouse molar to scale) and (E) mouse molar showing enamel (E), dentin (DE), pulp chamber (P), acellular cementum (AC), and cellular cementum (CC). (A black and white version of this figure will appear in some formats.)

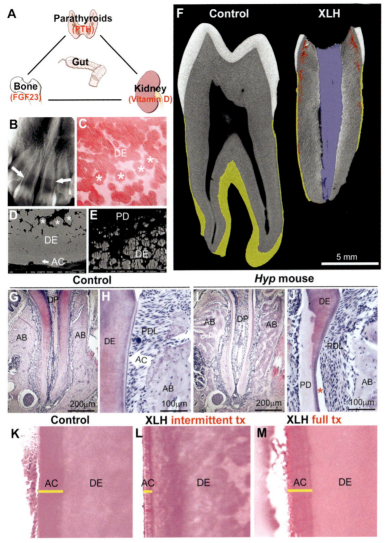

Figure 3.2 Dental manifestations of X-linked hypophosphatemia (XLH). (A) Schematic of kidney-parathyroid-bone axis major hormonal regulators, vitamin D, PTH, and FGF23. (B) Dental radiograph of juvenile with XLH revealing thin dentin and wide pulp chambers. (C) Histology of tooth from an adult with XLH showing excessive interglobular dentin (DE) patterns (*) indicating defective mineralization. (D, E) Scanning electron micrograph images of a tooth from an adult with XLH demonstrating hypomineralized interglobular DE (*), wide predentin (PD), and irregular PD margin. (F) Comparison of healthy control and XLH teeth highlighting hypomineralized interglobular DE (red) in the latter. XLH tooth has undergone endodontic treatment (blue in pulp). Compared to (G, H) healthy control mice, (I, J) Hyp mouse molars show DE hypomineralization, reduced AC, and PDL detachment from root surfaces. (K–M) Histological comparison of (K) heathy control tooth, (L) tooth from an XLH patient who received intermittent treatment (tx) in childhood and adulthood, and (M) tooth from an XLH patient receiving full treatment throughout childhood and adulthood. Panels A, D, and E adapted from Foster et al., *Endocr Rev* 35 (1): 1–34, 2014, and reproduced by permission. Panels B and C adapted from Pereira et al., *J Endod* 30 (4): 241–5, 2004, and reproduced by permission. Panels K–M adapted from Biosse Duplan et al., *J Dent Res* 96 (4): 388–95, 2017, and used in accordance with STM permissions guidelines. (A black and white version of this figure will appear in some formats.)

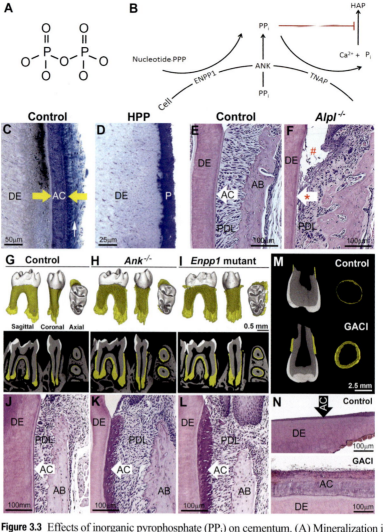

Figure 3.3 Effects of inorganic pyrophosphate (PP$_i$) on cementum. (A) Mineralization inhibitor, PP$_i$. (B) ENPP1, ANK/ANKH, and TNAP regulate levels of PP$_i$ that inhibits hydroxyapatite (HAP) precipitation by phosphate (P$_i$) and calcium (Ca^{2+}). (C, D) Compared to the well-developed acellular cementum (AC) on the dentin (DE) surface in a healthy control tooth, HPP inhibits AC formation allowing dental plaque (P) formation on root surfaces. (E, F) Compared to normal control mice, molars from Alpl$^{-/-}$ mice exhibit deficient AC (red * in F), PDL detachment (# in F), and accumulation of osteoid at the alveolar bone (AB) surface. (G-L) Compared to normal control mice, molars from Ank$^{-/-}$ or Enpp1 mutant mice feature dramatically increased AC. 3D (G, top row) and 2D (G, bottom row) images from micro-CT scans show enamel in white, DE in gray, and cementum in yellow. Histology images in J–L show H&E stained sections. (M) Compared to an exfoliated primary incisor from a healthy control subject, the primary incisor from an individual with GACI from loss-of-function mutations in ENPP1 exhibits increased AC (yellow), as shown in 2D reconstructions of the teeth and 3D images isolating only the AC. (N) H&E stained tooth sections from a control and GACI subject reveal the expanded AC. Panels C and D adapted from Luder, *Front Physiol* 6: 307, 2015, and reproduced with permission. Panels G, H, and K adapted from Ao et al., *Bone* 105:134–47, 2017, and reproduced by permission. Panels I, J, L, M, and N adapted from Thumbigere-Math et al., *J Dent Res* 97 (4): 432–41, 2017, and used in accordance with STM permissions guidelines. (A black and white version of this figure will appear in some formats.)

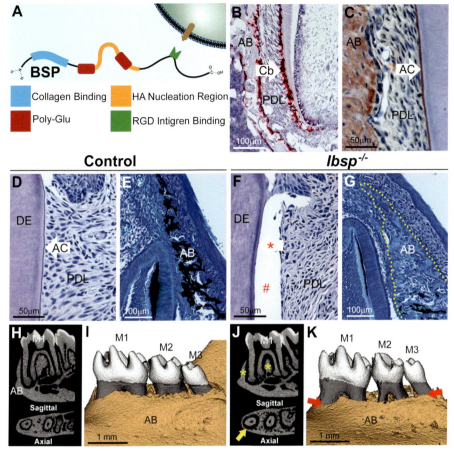

Figure 3.4 Defective cementum in mice lacking bone sialoprotein (BSP). (A) Schematic of BSP highlighting the collagen-binding domain, polyglutamic acid (polyE) motifs, hydroxyapatite (HAP) nucleation region, and arginine-glycine-aspartic acid (RGD) sequence. (B) During mouse molar development, the Ibsp gene is expressed (red color) by cementoblasts (Cb) and alveolar bone (AB) osteoblasts. (C) In the completed mouse molar, BSP protein (reddish-brown) is localized to acellular cementum (AC) and AB. (D, F) Compared to H&E stained sections of control mouse molars, Ibsp$^{-/-}$ mice feature reduced or absent AC (* in F) and PDL detachment (# in F). (E, G) Von Kossa staining of undecalcified histological sections indicates delayed mineralization (lack of black stain within yellow dotted region) in AB of Ibsp$^{-/-}$ mice versus controls. (H–K) 2D and 3D micro-CT scans of mandibles show reduced AB (yellow * and yellow and red arrows) around roots of Ibsp$^{-/-}$ mouse molars. Panel B adapted from Foster et al., *Bone* 107: 196–207, 2018, and reproduced by permission. Panel C adapted from Foster et al., *J Dent Res* 92 (2): 166–72, 2013, and used in accordance with STM permissions guidelines. Panels D, F, and H–K adapted from Ao et al., *Bone* 105: 134–47, 2017, and reproduced by permission. Panels E and G adapted from Foster et al., *Bone* 78:150–64, 2015, and reproduced with permission. (A black and white version of this figure will appear in some formats.)

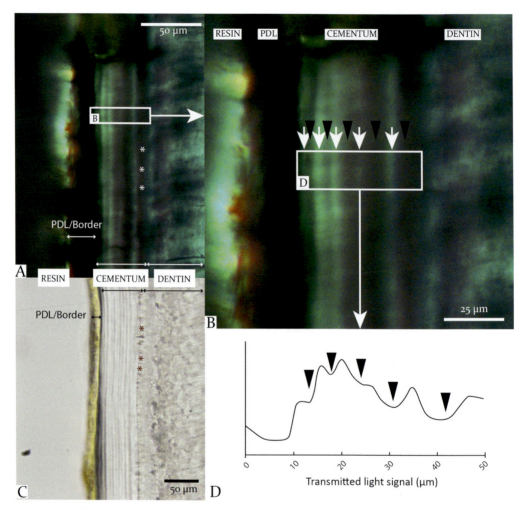

Figure 6.1 Optical micrographs illustrating cementum band contrast and determination of the number of band periods and their positions. (A) Polarized light micrograph of sample 070_181 (reindeer). The asterisks show the position of the CDJ. The box labeled B shows the area over which optical transmissivity versus position (plot in panel D) was measured. (B) Enlargement of panel A with the black arrowheads labeling dark bands and the white arrows light bands. The labeled box D shows the optical transmissivity measurement area. (C) Unpolarized light micrograph of specimen 046-S56 (human) showing cementum and transition zones similar to that shown for reindeer. (D) Optical transmissivity profile at the boxes' position in panels A and B with black arrowheads indicating dark band positions. One counts five light and five dark bands with a light band closest to the surface. (A black and white version of this figure will appear in some formats.)

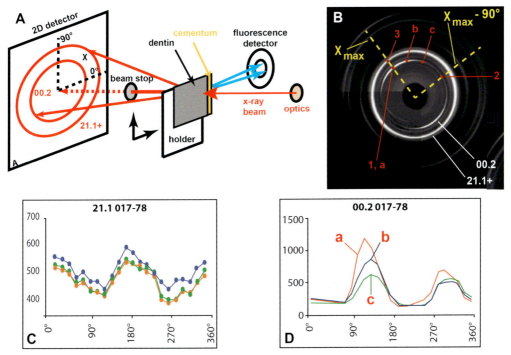

Figure 6.2 (A) Experimental setup for synchrotron x-ray fluorescence and diffraction mapping at beamline 2-ID-D, APS. (B) Typical diffraction pattern from cementum. The labels (azimuthal angles χ in yellow and different diffraction ROIs in red) are defined in the text. (C and D) Reindeer 017_78: variation of cAp 21.1 and 00.2 diffracted intensities, respectively, versus azimuthal angle. Each curve represents a different position within the specimen. (A black and white version of this figure will appear in some formats.)

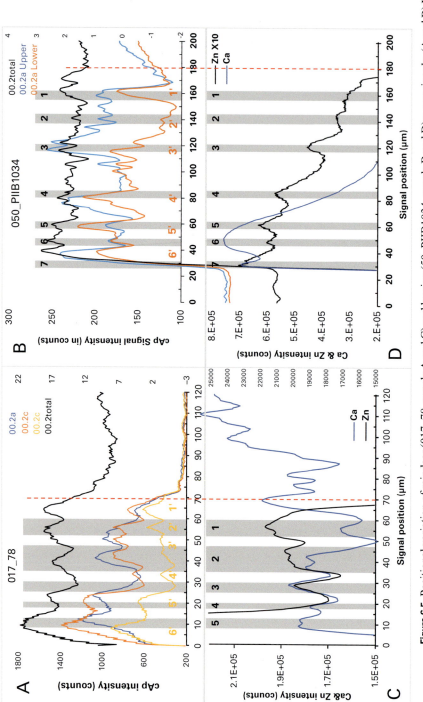

Figure 6.5 Positional variation of cAp 00.2 diffracted intensity integrated over the entire diffraction ring and for different diffraction ROI defined in Figure 6.2. (C and D) Corresponding Ca and Zn intensities. The red vertical dashed line shows the CDJ position. The gray bands in (A) and (C) show the Ca peaks. In (B) and (D), the gray bars indicate the Zn peaks. The black numbers label the order in which the different bands were laid down. Colored numbered with primes in panels A and B correspond to the 00.2 cAp peaks of corresponding color. (A black and white version of this figure will appear in some formats.)

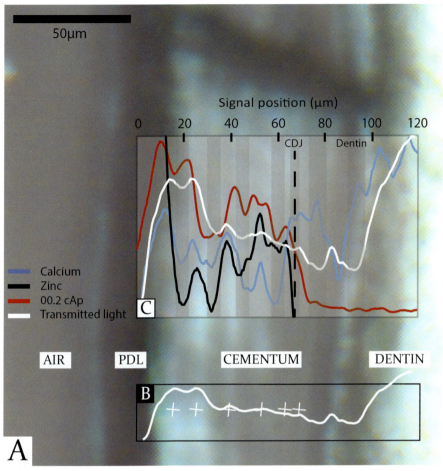

Figure 6.7 Reindeer 017_78. (A) Polarized light micrograph with inset panels B and C. (B) ROI for synchrotron mapping (black box) with positions of the optical light bands marked with "+," that is, the peaks in the optical transmission and optical transmission profile are shown in white. (C) Comparison of optical transmission (white), Zn fluorescent intensity (black), Ca fluorescent intensity (blue), and 00.2 cAp diffracted intensity (red). The gray vertical bands match the dark optical bands. PDL: periodontal ligament. (A black and white version of this figure will appear in some formats.)

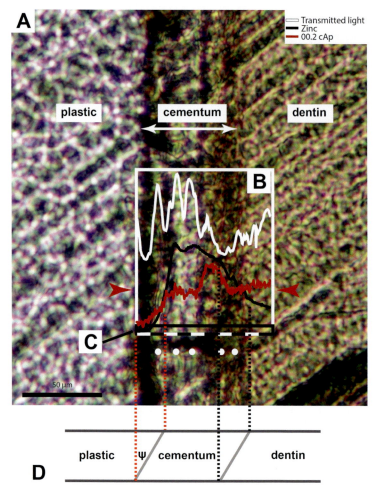

Figure 6.8 Bovine section 50_PIIB1034. (A) Unpolarized light micrograph with scanning ROI for synchrotron mapping (B, white box) and the optical transmissivity ROI (C, black box). A black-white dashed line indicates the position where the two boxes overlap. The white disks below the x-ray ROI indicate band positions. The inset profiles within the x-ray ROI are for optical transmission (white), cAp 00.2 diffracted intensity (red), and Zn fluorescent intensity (black). The red arrowheads indicate the approximate position of the x-ray line scan. **(D)** Diagram of hypothetical tilted plastic–cementum and cementum–dentin interfaces. PDL: periodontal ligament. (A black and white version of this figure will appear in some formats.)

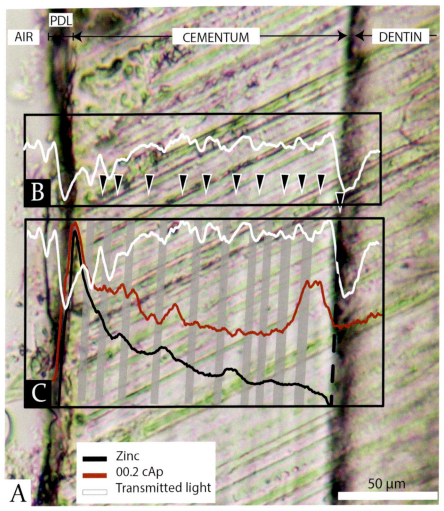

Figure 6.9 Red deer section 40_CL302. (A) Unpolarized light micrograph with box (B) showing the ROI for synchrotron and transmission optical mapping. The optical transmission profile is superimposed in white in box B. The black arrowheads and gray vertical lines mark the optical microscopy positions of dark cementum bands. Box C contains the optical, Zn, and cAp profiles (white, black and red, respectively). PDL: periodontal ligament. (A black and white version of this figure will appear in some formats.)

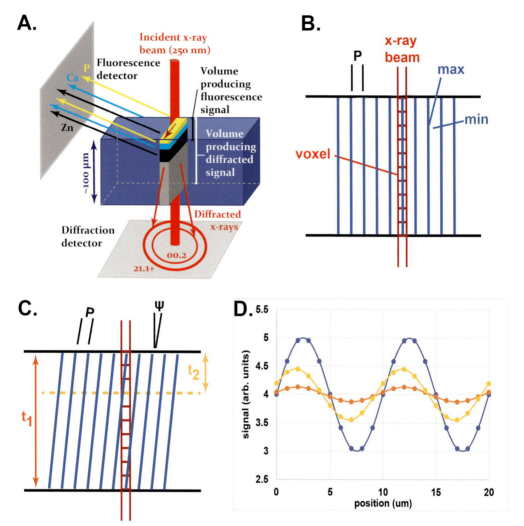

Figure 6.10 Illustration of depth from which signals originate in these experiments (A) and of the effect of band tilt (B–D). (A) Experimental geometry and volumes contributing to measured intensities. Table 6.6 lists the effect of attenuation on the different signals. (B) For purposes of discussion, the following characteristics of the band "contrast" are assumed. The contrast (00.2 cAp diffracted intensity) varies sinusoidally with a greatly exaggerated amplitude; the cementum band period is P = 10 μm. The x-ray microbeam, incident at 90°, is divided into ten volume elements (voxels). The maximum signal is from the positions indicated by solid blue lines and the minimum by the midpoint between blue lines. In (B), the bands lie perpendicular to the section (ψ = 0°). In (C), the bands are tilted at angle ψ = 5.6° (chosen so that the beam samples one period of band structure as it traverses 100 μm thickness). Two specimen thickness t_1 = 100 μm and t_2 = 30 μm are considered. The blue curve in (D) is a variation of signal with position for the bands with ψ = 0°. For band tilt ψ = 5.6° and thickness t_1, the different voxels sample different portions of the band's period. The result is the orange profile in (D), that is, greatly reduced band visibility and a slight shift in the band maxima and minima position. For ψ = 5.6° and thickness t_2, bands are more visible (gold curve in D) but still substantially less visible than for the case of no tilt. (A black and white version of this figure will appear in some formats.)

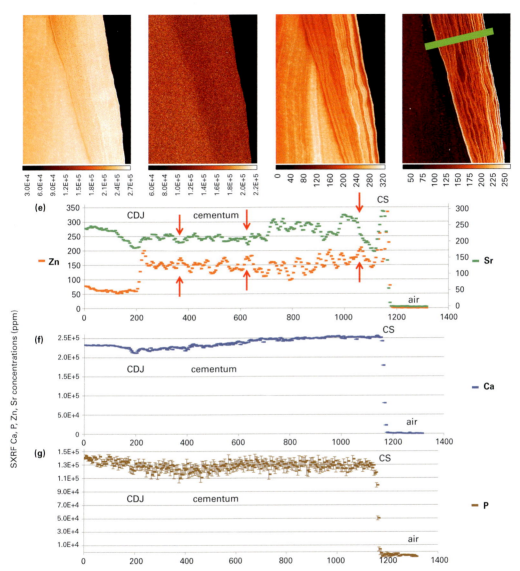

Figure 7.1 SXRF scans (5 μm) of Ca, P, Sr, and Zn in a region of regular compensatory cellular cementum in the chimpanzee UCL-CA-14E/UI1. The green bar (1350 μm long) on the Zn map (d) indicates the plane of SXRF Ca, P, Zn, and Sr concentrations (ppm) plots. The red arrows in (e) show regions where Zn and Sr concentrations are reciprocal. Color scales beneath each image denote concentration (ppm). Based on data from Dean et al. 2018. (A black and white version of this figure will appear in some formats.)

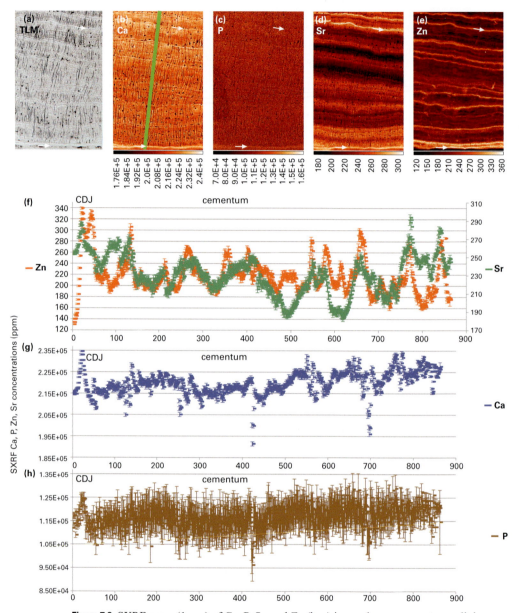

Figure 7.2 SXRF scans (1 μm) of Ca, P, Sr, and Zn (b–e) in regular compensatory cellular cementum in UCL-CA-14E/LI1 with the corresponding TLM on the left (a). The lower white arrows denote the first formed bright (dense) cementum layer at the CDJ. The upper white arrow denotes another clear, bright marking in the TLM. The green bar (860 μm long) on the Ca map indicates the plane of SXRF Zn, Sr, and Ca, P concentrations (ppm) plots (f, g, and h, respectively). There is a poor correspondence between Zn and Sr levels. Color scales beneath each image denote concentration (ppm). Based on data from Dean et al. 2018. (A black and white version of this figure will appear in some formats.)

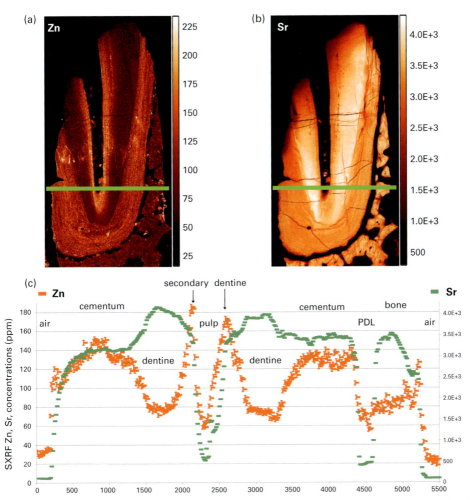

Figure 7.4 SXRF maps of zinc (a) and strontium (b) distribution in fossilized root dentine and cementum of KNM-ER 1817 (15 μm resolution). Plots (c) show Zn levels rising in cementum and in secondary dentine. Both Sr and Zn levels fall to near-zero in air, the pulp space and periodontal ligament space both now filled with calcite. Color scales alongside each image denote concentration (ppm). Based on data from Dean et al. 2018. (A black and white version of this figure will appear in some formats.)

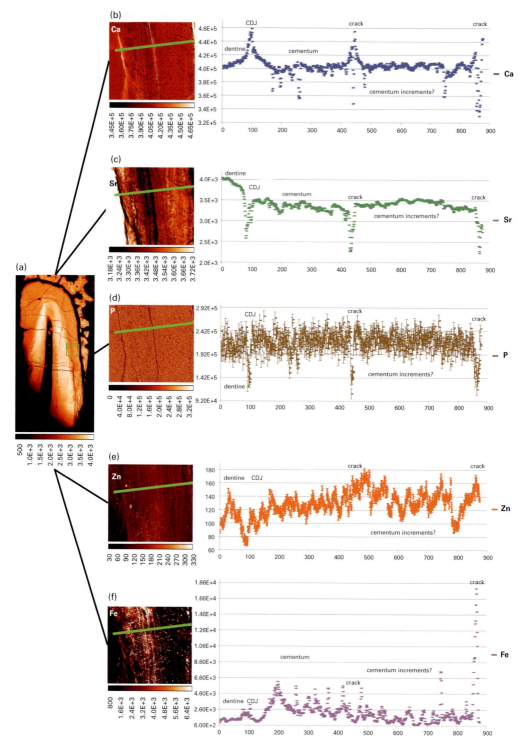

Figure 7.5 SXRF map of Sr in KNM-ER 1817 at 15 μm resolution (a) with green boundary box representing the location of SXRF maps of Ca (b), Sr (c), P (d), Zn (e), and Fe (f) at 1 μm resolution. Plots show Ca and Fe levels rise in the calcite-containing cracks, but P, Sr, and Zn levels in cracks fall to very low levels. Fluctuations in Ca, P, and Sr levels may correspond with cementum increments visible in the transmitted light micrograph. Color scales beneath each image denote concentration (ppm). Based on data from Dean et al. 2018. (A black and white version of this figure will appear in some formats.)

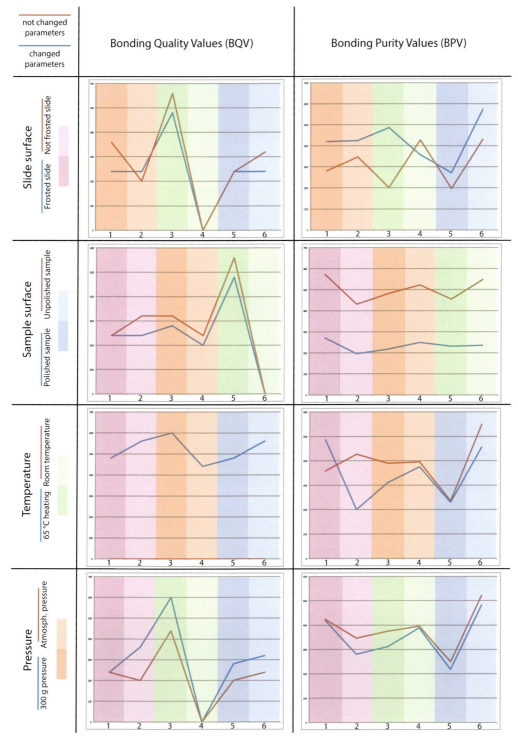

Figure 9.3 Comparison of the bonding quality with a series of unfrosted slide mounts (XPbo1) and a series of frosted glass slide mounts (XPbo2). For each graph, the colored columns show the interactions with other variables. Each color corresponds to a darker shade for the unchanged values and a lighter shade for the modified values. According to the related column, the values in ordinates correspond to an index of quality or purity; the lower this value is, the better the pasting. (A black and white version of this figure will appear in some formats.)

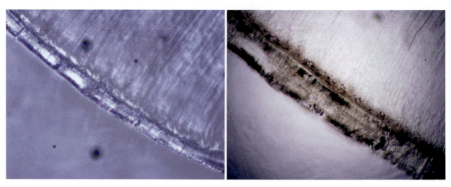

Figure 12.2 Photomicrograph of Haddix 16 under polarized light at 100x magnification (left) and in bright-field illumination at 200x magnification (right). The very high contrast caused by polarized light is obscuring at least some annulations, which can be seen on the right. (A black and white version of this figure will appear in some formats.)

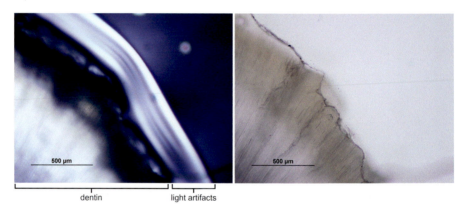

Figure 12.4 Photomicrographs of Haddix 19 in polarized light (left) and the same ROI in bright-field illumination (right). The light and dark bands visible around the edge of the tooth in the left image are not cementum annulations, as we originally thought. They are artifacts of polarization. This specimen was undergoing rhizolysis, and the cementum layers had already been resorbed, leaving only dentin. (A black and white version of this figure will appear in some formats.)

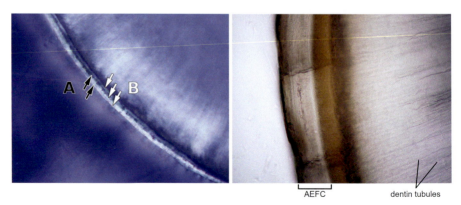

Figure 12.5 Photomicrographs of Haddix 39 in polarized light and at 40x magnification (left) and in bright-field illumination at 200x (right). The left image shows high contrast and low magnification that make identification of the cementum annulations (A, B) and the edge of mineralized tissues extremely difficult. The image on the right shows that many more annulations are present in the AEFC, even though the total count cannot be determined from this image. (A black and white version of this figure will appear in some formats.)

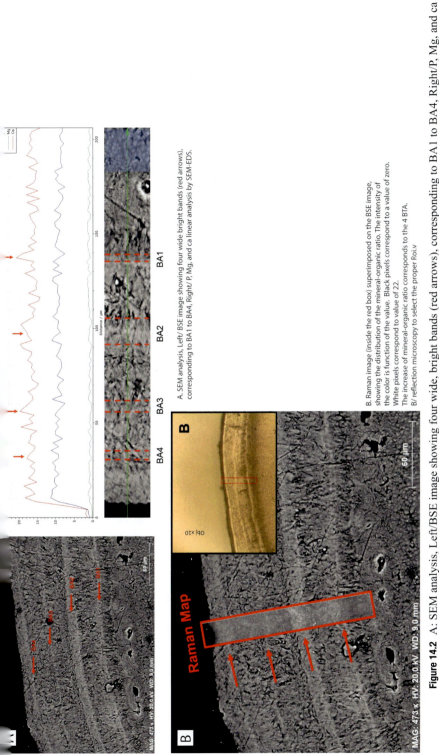

Figure 14.2 A: SEM analysis, Left/BSE image showing four wide, bright bands (red arrows), corresponding to BA1 to BA4, Right/P, Mg, and ca linear analysis by SEM-EDS; B: Raman image (inside the red box) superimposed on the BSE image, showing the distribution of the mineral–organic ratio. The intensity of the color is a function of the value. Black pixels correspond to a value of zero. White pixels correspond to the value of 22. The increase of mineral–organic ratio corresponds to the 4 BTA. B-insert: reflection microscopy to select the proper Roi. (A black and white version of this figure will appear in some formats.)

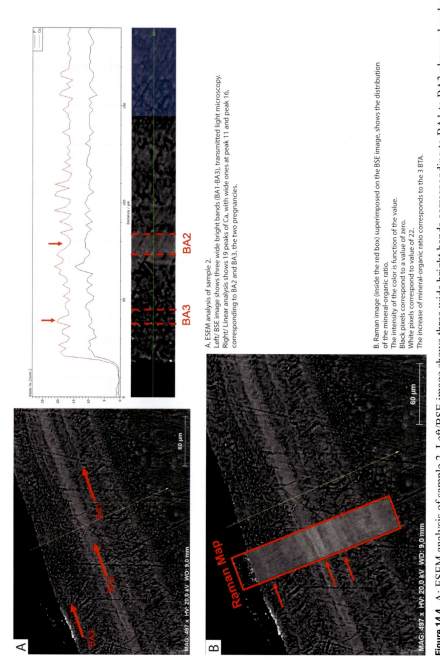

Figure 14.4 A: ESEM analysis of sample 2. Left/BSE image shows three wide bright bands corresponding to BA1 to BA3 observed under transmitted light microscopy. Right/Linear analysis shows 19 peaks of Ca, with wide ones at peak 11 and peak 16, corresponding to BA2 and BA3, the two pregnancies; B: Raman image (inside the red box) superimposed on the BSE image shows the distribution of the mineral–organic ratio. The intensity of the color is a function of the value. Black pixels correspond to a value of zero. White pixels correspond to the value of 22. The increase of mineral–organic ratio corresponds to the 3 BTA. (A black and white version of this figure will appear in some formats.)

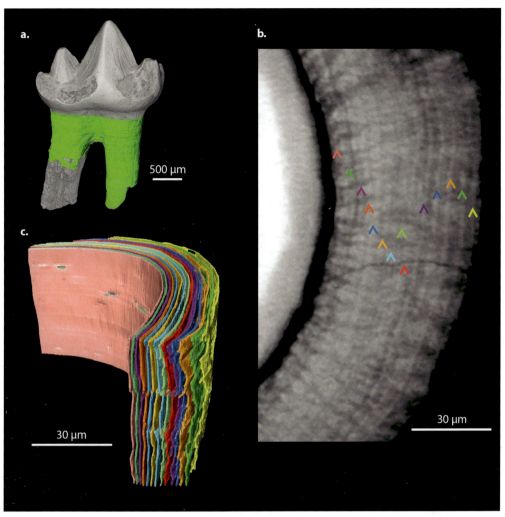

Figure 16.1 2D and 3D analyses of cementum structure using CT imaging. (a) 3D volume rendering of the m2 tooth of Early Jurassic fossil mammal Morganucodon (NHMUK PV M104134; voxel size 2 μm, laboratory-based μCT). (b) PPSRCT slice of Morganucodon cementum (specimen NHMUK PV M104127) with 14 circum-annual increments highlighted using colored arrows. (c) 3D segmentation of increments highlighted in b (colors of increments correspond to arrows in (b) through the fossilized cementum tissue. (A black and white version of this figure will appear in some formats.)

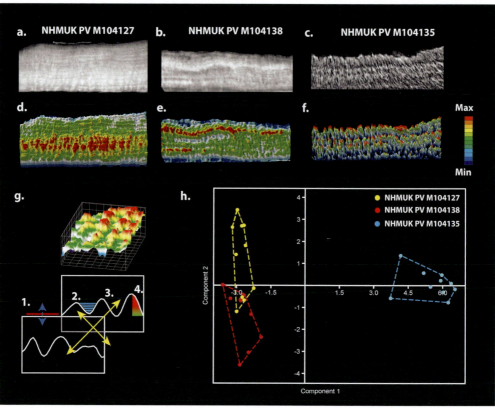

Figure 16.2 Analysis of cementum "texture" using PPSRCT grayscale values as a third dimension. (a–c) Straightened cementum data from the three Morganucodon fossil specimens. (d–f) 3D blue-red heat maps of each straightened image, with 3D height and color representing grayscale values in a–c (created using the "3D surface plot" tool in ImageJ/Fiji; Schneider et al., 2012). (g) Schematic diagram highlighting the nature of measures that can be applied to 3D heat maps of cementum increments. Numbers correspond to the four principal types of measures outlined in Table 16.1 [1: height measures that estimate grayscales above and below (blue arrows) the mean value of the surface (red line); 2: functional measures that characterize volumetric information based on the material ratio of the surface in question (the ratio between the intersecting area of a hypothetical plane passing through the surface at a given height, and the cross-sectional area of the surface – highlighted by blue infill into trough); 3: spatial measures that estimate the direction and anisotropy of grayscale values across the surface highlighted with yellow arrows; 4: hybrid measures that combine spatial and height measures.] (h) Principal components analysis of values for all measures in Table 16.1 performed for 10 PPSRCT slices for each specimen. PCA scores for measures performed for each specimen cluster in their own region of "texture space," with the specimen showing the most significant diagenetic alteration of original cementum microstructure (NHMUK PV M104135) significantly separated from the two other specimens. (A black and white version of this figure will appear in some formats.)

9 Cementochronology for Archaeologists: Experiments and Testing for an Optimized Thin-Section Preparation Protocol

Eric Pubert, Stephan Naji, Lionel Gourichon, Frédéric Santos, and William Rendu

9.1 Introduction

In the field of human dental cementum research, the protocol for sample preparation is now widely tested, validated, and standardized (Colard et al., 2015; Chapter 1). This standardization was facilitated by the low variability in the shape and size of the teeth studied. For work on nonhuman mammalian teeth, the problem is more complex. The minimum number of individuals (MNI) is usually calculated from the lower jugular teeth, which allows an estimate of age based on tooth wear. This is why posterior teeth are most often chosen for cementochronological analyses on wildlife (Naji et al., 2015). However, the taxa diversity implies a significant variation in the teeth's morphology with sometimes specific histological characteristics for species such as equids (Burke and Castanet, 1995) or suids (Klevezal', 1996).

Since the first studies on archaeological mammalian teeth (Saxon and Higham, 1969), preparation techniques, observation methods, and even the vocabulary used have varied significantly (Naji et al., 2015). Despite this diversity, the basis for making a thin section remains the same and includes four main steps: (1) consolidation (embedding in resin), (2) cutting, (3) gluing, and (4) finishing. Based on the standard procedures used by the PACEA laboratory (CNRS, UMR 5199, Bordeaux – France) and with the support of colleagues using slightly different procedures, we propose that a finer understanding of each protocol's variables could optimize the quality of the thin sections. For steps 1–3, we first conducted preliminary experiments to define a measurement protocol specific to this chapter and then tested several variables to produce thin sections. The last step (finishing) will only be addressed briefly in the discussion. The objective is to improve the protocol by optimizing the parameters to minimize the risk of errors and offer an easily reproducible quality of thin sections. This work required a total of twenty-six experiments, each of which generated a significant number of operations and the production of a large volume of data (Table 9.1). Because of the limited space available in the chapter, most figures and tables will be presented in online supplemental format.

Supplemental online materials are available at www.cambridge.org/naji.

Table 9.1 Detail of the operations for all the experimental designs

Experimental Plan	Experiment	Embedding	Cutting	Bonding	Polishing	Measurement	Analysis
Measurement (XPme)	4	NA	4	NA	2	180	NA
Consolidation (XPco)	7	94	304	NA	760	304	76
Cutting (XPcu)	13	NA	360	NA	NA	5,740	NA
Bonding (XPbo)	2	NA	NA	48	120	NA	48
Finish (XPfi)	0	0	0	0	0	0	0
TOTALS	26	94	668	48	882	6,224	124

9.2 Experimental Design Measures: Intraobserver Error

The preliminary experiments' objective was to test the variables that can influence the intraobserver errors of thin-sections preparation steps.

As our preparations required numerous section thickness controls with a digital flat-tip micrometer (HMI, measuring range: 0–25 mm; resolution: 0.001 mm; accuracy: 0.002 mm), we first evaluated the variability of these measurements (Supplemental Table ST.9.1).

For the first one (XPme1), we used a glass slide of 45 mm length, 30 mm width, and 1.2 mm thickness (manufacturer's data) as a standard sample. On this calibrated slide, we defined approximately nine measuring zones (Supplemental Figure SF.9.1a). For the second experiment (XPme2), we drew on the sample a grid consisting of fifteen 8 mm squares (Supplemental Figure SF.9.1b) and performed measurements on nine of these distinct zones.

The other two experiments (XPme3 and XPme4) involved an uncalibrated sample corresponding to a resin block cut to the exact dimensions as the previous glass slide and reduced to a thickness of 1.2 mm by manual polishing. This manual shaping does not always guarantee an even thickness of the sample, which brings us closer to the conditions we encounter when cutting the teeth into thin sections and those tested in future experiments. The same measurement protocols as in the XPme1 and XPme2 experiments were applied for XPme3 and XPme4, respectively. For these four experiments, each of the nine measurement zones was recorded five times (Supplemental Tables ST.9.2 and ST.9.3).

A statistical study of these data (Supplemental Appendix 9.1) has shown a high homogeneity of glass slide measurements. There is almost no variability between the measurements made with or without a grid. On the other hand, measurements made on the resin slide with an irregular surface showed a higher variability, especially when measurements were made without the grid. Statistical analyses showed a significant decrease by a factor of 10 in the measurement's variance taken with a grid on a resin slide compared to measurements without a grid.

Despite these unambiguous statistical results, analysis of the raw data (Supplemental Table ST.9.3) shows that across the entire slide areas, the maximum thickness difference between a measure without a marking grid and the measurement's average does not exceed 8 μm, that is, the thickness of a sheet of cigarette paper. By comparison, the thickness variation measured with a marking grid drops to 4 μm. Given the slight deviation and despite the statistical significance of the grid's improvement, we have chosen to carry out our experiments without a grid to speed up the process. Still, we acknowledged and integrated these results in our experiments.

Consequently, we have chosen to carry out nine measurements on our samples (except for some very narrow samples). The measure is repeated five times, and the average thickness is used. Also, we considered a variation of +/–10 μm as normal due to the slide's irregularity because we did not use a marking grid.

9.3 Plan of Experiments: Consolidations

This experimental design aims to test seventeen variables (Supplemental Table ST.9.4). To avoid the integration of an uncontrolled factor, we did not embed any object. We focused only on the technical procedure involving resin, molds, and vacuum processes so that only blank resin blocks were tested (but see Section 9.6 for observations on embedding teeth).

Seven experiments (Xpco1-7, Supplemental Table ST.9.4) totaling ninety-four consolidation tests were conducted. For the mixing mode, manual mixing (not precisely quantifiable by definition) consisted of mixing by hand at a moderate speed (about 100 rpm) until a homogeneous product was obtained (2 minutes) at an ambient temperature between 18° and 23°C. For the mechanical mixing, we used an Anchor stirrer model and a Viscojet stirrer model suitable for viscous liquids and gels, specially designed to mix while limiting the introduction of air into the preparation.

To control the consolidation quality after the resin was cured, a 1.6 cm x 1.6 cm wide and 2.4 mm thick lamella was taken from the center of each cylindrical indurated block (Figure 9.1). These samples, produced with an Isomet 5000 cutting saw, were then reduced to 1 mm thickness and polished on both sides with five successive abrasives (54, 18, 9, 3, and 1 μm) to make them transparent.

During the consolidation phase, the primary defect was bubbles produced by mixing the two fluids (turbulence) before polymerization and trapped once the resin had solidified. The bubbles were observed in all experiments, creating a background noise potentially obscuring some cementum increment's observations. Therefore, we

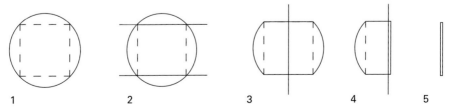

Figure 9.1 Cutting procedure for consolidation quality analysis

evaluated the quality of the consolidations based on the detection and characterization of bubbles within the cured resin block.

The samples were observed using a microscope (Olympus BH-2) at low magnification (X20) under cross-polarized transmitted light with an inserted quarter-wave plate increasing contrast to detect bubbles more precisely. Based on a visual examination of the sample's entire surface, we classified the bubbles according to their size (diameter) and frequency (total number). For each parameter, five categories were defined (Supplemental Table ST.9.5).

Consequently, we calculated a score for each bubble class with the formula "Size Category x Frequency Category." The sum of the five classes' scores in the same sample gives a global quality value (GQV) used as a quality measure of the consolidations. A high GQV indicates poor quality.

Consolidation Quality according to the Mixing Mode (XPco1, XPco2, and XPco3)

Mechanical mixing did not allow the catalyst to mix homogeneously, resulting in highly variable polymerization times. This is probably due to overly regular movements, which do not mobilize the entire volume of the liquids. Conversely, manual mixing with more ample movements allowed for a better mix of the two products. Therefore, the results obtained with manual mixing are better overall (Supplemental Figure SF.9.2).

Consolidation Quality according to Flow Velocity (XPco1, XPco2, and XPco3)

We varied the mixture's vertical flow velocity using a pipette under two discharge modes at room temperature. The first (Ex) used natural gravity, and the second used a blowout system with adjustable force.

We chose to test only the pouring by gravity effect and three blowing forces (1, 3, and 5) among the five proposed by the device for our experimental design. Resin poured by simple gravitational effect (Supplemental Figure SF.9.3, "Ex" mode) resulted in a better cumulative quality index than those obtained with blowing, regardless of the force.

Quality of Consolidation according to the Flow Height (XPco1, XPco2, and XPco3)

We applied five pouring heights of the resin into the molds: 18, 27, 36, 45, and 54 mm from the containers' bottoms.

The quality indices obtained are better with pouring at intermediate heights (27 and 36 mm, Supplemental Figure SF.9.4). This may be because if the pouring height is too low, the resin does not outgas as well during casting. Whereas if the pouring height is too high, the resin produces bubbles by touching the bottom of the mold or the already cast resin's surface more violently.

Inclusion Quality with or without Vacuum (XPco4)

We tested the influence of vacuum curing by casting two blocks of virgin resin at atmospheric pressure and two blocks under vacuum with the vacuum cycle recommended by the vacuum inclusion stand manufacturer. The results (Supplemental Figure SF.9.5) show that the use of the vacuum pump increases the resin's quality by reducing the presence of bubbles.

Resin Quality according to the Vacuum Cycle (XPco4, XPco5, XPco6, and XPco7)

Regardless of the type of inclusion, bubbles may form when pouring the resin into the sample mold and during vacuum outgassing. These bubbles are not a problem if they are not in contact with the tooth. However, the bubbles usually will find a point of attachment on the tooth surface. We made three series of two virgin resin blocks by modifying the vacuum cycles each time (Supplemental Table ST.9.6). During each experiment, we also cast two blocks at atmospheric pressure to serve as a reference. The vacuum cycle recommended by the manufacturer gives the best results (lowest index, Supplemental Figure SF.9.6).

9.4 Experimental Design: Cutting

The cutting tests were carried out with a Buehler Isomet 5000 saw, equipped with a sample-holder arm with micrometric feed. The automation of the machine also allows for serial cuts of predefined thickness. We conducted nine cutting experimental tests (Supplemental Table ST.9.7).

The criteria observed to evaluate the cutting operations were the flatness of the objects produced (uniformity of thickness over the entire surface) and the cut's precision (thickness obtained versus thickness expected).

The data are presented in matrices created using the PAST software package v.3.14 (Hammer et al., 2001) with nine colored areas corresponding to the measurement zones (Figure 9.2). The color scale illustrates the difference between the expected and the observed thicknesses, from blue (−400 μm minimum) to red (+400 μm maximum), through green (minimal difference). The color differences are perceptible as soon as a gap between two contiguous zones exceeds 5 μm. The zones containing no value (in the case of incomplete cuts) remain white. Under each matrix, one value indicates the standard deviation between the nine measuring points' values. A second value indicates the deviation of the mean of these nine points from the cut thickness.

Test Experiments: Variability of Cutting with Fixed Parameters (XPte1, XPte2, XPte3, and XPte4)

Before measuring the cut's variability on several series, a test was carried out on sections of different thicknesses. For this purpose, four experiments were carried out

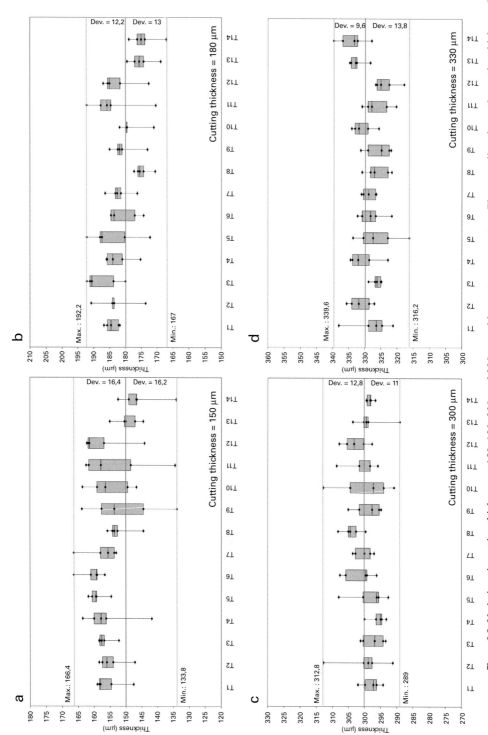

Figure 9.2 Variations in cutting thickness at 150, 180, 300, and 330 μm with constant parameters. The centerline shows the cutting thickness. The upper and lower lines indicate the minimum and maximum values of the series. The differences between these two values and the cut thickness are shown along each graph's right edge.

on fourteen sections each, at 150, 180, 300, and 330 µm thickness, respectively. The thickness was measured only at each angle and in the central part. The measurements were repeated five times, and the average was used as a reference for each point. The results show some variation in the cutting thickness of these samples (Figure 9.2). These variations are relatively well distributed in both positive and negative directions and range from −16.2 to +16.4 µm.

Comparing each series' deviations from the expected thickness also demonstrates that these deviations decrease (from 32 to 22 µm) with increasing cut thickness (from 150 to 330 µm, respectively).

Quality of the Cut according to the Resin Used (XPcu1 and XPcu2)

To test the type of resin's influence, we first used a block of Epoxy MA2+ (Presi) resin with a 10 percent catalyst by weight (manufacturer's recommendations). We then used a block of Epoxy EC157 (Polymir) resin with 20 percent catalyst by weight (manufacturer's recommendation). The two blocks were of the same dimensions, and the cutting parameters were identical (Supplemental Table ST.9.7). Here, we produced two series of 150 µm thick sections by varying the blade's rotation and feed speeds.

The results (Supplemental Figure SF.9.7) showed that with EC157 (XPcu2) resin, the cuts are always incomplete, with the blade deflecting outward and rapidly coming out of the block due to the thinness of the cuts. The same deflection phenomenon is visible with MA2+ (XPcu1) resin. Still, it is less frequent and less marked, which leads us to believe that it may be caused – or at least accentuated – by the mechanical characteristics of the resin used.

Therefore, resin's choice seems to be an essential criterion for the cuts' quality, especially for the thinnest cuts. Preliminary tests should thus be carried out for each resin used to determine its proprieties and limitations.

Quality of the Cut according to the Resin and Catalyst Dosages (XPcu3 and XPcu4)

We wanted to understand the effects of a change in the resin/catalyst ratio on the resulting resin block quality. We used Epoxy resin EC157 by modifying the recommended dose (20 percent) to 10 percent and 30 percent. For the first test (XPcu3), the resin catalyzed by forming a block, which, despite a moderately high hardness (79 Shore D), presented such a high resistance to cutting that we could not cut a single sample. The block was constantly breaking obliquely under the pressure of the cutting disc.

For the 10 percent polymerized block (XPcu4), it was necessary to put it in an oven at 50°C for two months to cure the resin fully. The block had a shore hardness of 70 Shore D, and none of the cuts made on this resin block could be completed, as the resin folded on itself during cutting and fractured before the end of the work.

The results of these two experiments underline the need to respect the dosages recommended by the manufacturer to obtain constant hardness and, therefore, reproducible results.

Cutting Quality according to the Cutting Settings (XPcu5)

The influence of variable cutting blade rotation and feed speeds was evaluated simultaneously (Supplemental Table ST.9.4). The two criteria had a significant impact on both the accuracy and flatness of the cut (Supplemental Figure SF.9.8). The high rotation speeds (3000 and 4000 rpm) yielded consistent results regardless of feed speed. However, we recommend cutting at 3000 rpm because the faster the rotation, the more violent the sample's ejection will be, thus increasing the breakage risk. We can also note that a feed speed of 8 mm/minute gives excellent results regardless of the blade's speed in the 1000 to 4000 rpm range.

Quality of the Cut according to Sample Position (XPcu6)

We tested the impact of the sample position in relation to the blade during cutting. We used a small and multiposition sample holder (Single Saddle Chuck, Buehler) to make four serial cuts at each position on a 24 x 17 mm MA2+ resin block: top, middle, and bottom.

Although the results obtained with a sample in the upper or intermediate position are similar, those obtained with a lower position sample are significantly more irregular (Supplemental Figure SF.9.9).

Cutting Quality according to the Model of the Cutting Disc Used (XPcu2 and XPcu5)

We evaluated the influence of the size and possible deformation of the cutting disc by comparing the XPcu2 and XPcu5 experiments (Supplemental Figure SF.9.7b and Supplemental Figure SF.9.8). For the XPcu2 and XPcu5 experiments, we used a Buehler blade N°114267 (178 x 0.6 mm) and N°114276 (152 X 0.5 mm), respectively.

All the sections made with the blade N°114267 are mostly incomplete. The blade is coming out of the resin block before reaching the cut's end, whereas the cuts made with the same parameters but using a blade 114276 are of much better quality. These results indicate that the smaller diameter blades undergo minimal deformation during cutting and are therefore more suitable for thinner sections.

Quality of the Cut according to the Diameter of the Flanges Used (XPcu7)

Cutting blades are used with holding flanges. The smaller the flange diameter (FD), the larger the free part of the blade is, which thus increases the maximum depth of cut (MCD), which we can calculate as follow: $MCD = (BD - FD)/2$, with BD corresponding to the blade diameter. We can assume that the lower the MCD, the more the blade will gain in rigidity and cutting quality. The XPcu7 experiment aimed to test this hypothesis using two blades (127 mm and 152 mm diameter) and four flanges of different diameters while keeping the other variables unchanged (Supplemental Table ST.9.7).

Contrary to our expectations, the relatively homogeneous results (Supplemental Figure SF.9.10) did not evidence a significant influence of the flange diameter on the cuts' quality.

Cutting Quality according to the Cutting Plane: Height (XPcu8)

For this experiment, we made four blocks of MA2+ Epoxy resin of identical length ($x = 20$ mm) and different heights ($y = 20, 17, 13$, and 10 mm). We then sectioned five $z = 250$ µm-thick samples in each block (Supplemental Table ST.9.7). The block was oriented so that the contact plane with the blade was the blocks' zy height plane (Supplemental Figure SF.9.11a).

We evaluated our samples' thickness by averaging five measurements over nine zones, except for the 13 mm and 10 mm cuts, with small dimensions allowing for only six measurement points. Thickness analysis (Supplemental Figure SF.9.11b) revealed the samples' thinning from the cut's front to end. This phenomenon is more accentuated on the smallest samples (Supplemental Figure SF.9.12). Moreover, the reduction in height leads to a substantial decrease in cuts' quality with significant irregularities.

Cutting Quality according to the Cutting Plane: Length (XPcu9)

Next, we wanted to know what happens with a reduction in the length of the sample. To explore this relationship, we made four blocks of MA2+ Epoxy resin of identical height ($y = 20$ mm) and variable lengths ($x = 20, 17, 13$, and 10 mm). In each sample, we sectioned five 250 µm-thick samples (Supplemental Table ST.9.7). The block was oriented so that the contact plane with the blade was the blocks' zx length plane (Supplemental Figure SF.9.13a).

The measurements were carried out following the usual protocol, but the shortest samples in our experiment were measured in only six areas. The thinning of the cut between the beginning and the end is less visible (Supplemental Figure SF.9.13b) than in the previous experiment, which the sample's smaller size may explain.

The matrix representations (Supplemental Figure SF.9.14) show homogeneous thicknesses on all cuts except on the longest 20 mm sample. Thus, the cut's quality decreases as soon as the cut length is greater than or equal to the sample's height.

9.5 Experimental Design: Gluing

The equipment used for the bonding tests was a heated bonding press (Brot Technologies), which controls the heating temperature of the stage and exerts a constant pressure through vertical loadings. Besides, we also tested a nonheated press that could be used with the gluing press's weights.

We used the sections from the XPte1 to XPte4 test designs measuring 1.6 x 1.6 cm, with thicknesses of 300 and 330 µm. The 330 lamellae were polished on one side to a thickness of 300 µm. Polishing was carried out in five steps: abrasive cloth (P240), polishing plate 54 μm and 18 μm, and then three diamond suspensions of 9, 3, and 1 μm each. The two experiments totaled twenty-four tests each. We tested nine variables, four of which had two possible values (Supplemental Table ST.9.8): "without modification" (unfrosted blade, unpolished rough sawing sample, ambient temperature, and atmospheric pressure) and "modified" (frosted blade, polished sample, heating to 65°C, and pressure of 300 g on the sample). The mixing of the bonding resin and its catalyst was done by hand.

The results were analyzed according to two criteria: bonding quality value (BQV) and bonding purity value (BPV). The BQV is calculated from the macroscopic condition of the sample and the bonded sample's surface (Supplemental Table ST.9.9). The BPV is established on the presence of bubbles (score 3) and air pockets. These can be distinguished from bubbles by their irregular shape and lumpy internal appearance. All the results are summarized in Figure 9.3, in which two superimposed curves indicate that the change in the tested variable had no impact. In comparison, a deviation of the two curves on the *y*-axis indicates a significant influence of the variable. The figure also enables identifying correlations between variables, for example, when the lines of the same figure deviate from each other in part of their trajectory only.

Bonding Quality according to the Surface Condition of the Slide and the Specimen (XPbo1 and XPbo2)

To test the influence of the polishing of the sample cutting surface, we used the results of the XPbo1 and XPbo2 experiments. The first experiment (XPbo1) was performed with unfrosted glass blades and the second (XPbo2) used 37 micrometers silicon-carbide ground-slides.

Concerning the bonding quality (BQV), the curves (Figure 9.3a and c) overlap almost entirely, showing a low incidence of the slide and the specimen surface condition on the bonding quality. On the other hand, the data on the gluing's purity (Figure 9.3b and d) show a significant influence on the specimen surface condition, with polished specimens showing a lower GVW. Concerning the GVW of the slide surface, unfrosted slides show slightly better results, and this difference is more pronounced when gluing on a hot plate (reduced setting time).

Gluing Quality according to Temperature (XPbo1 and XPbo2)

The data concerning the use of a heating plate set at 65°C (manufacturer's setting for Epoxy Geofix) indicate a strong influence of this parameter on the quality of the bond (Figure 9.3e and f), especially with regard to the quality of the bond (Figure 9.3e). However, this result should be nuanced because our experiments have been carried out on thin samples and that our previous personal experience has never allowed us to encounter such a phenomenon on thick (several millimeters) samples. Concerning the purity of the bond, we note that the curves tend to be superimposed but with a moderate incidence of pressure and a substantial incidence of the slide's surface state.

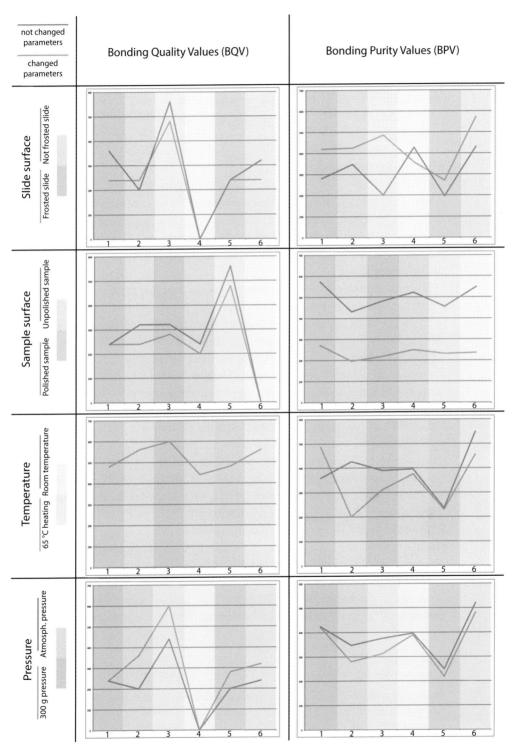

Figure 9.3 Comparison of the bonding quality with a series of unfrosted slide mounts (XPbo1) and a series of frosted glass slide mounts (XPbo2). For each graph, the colored columns show the

Gluing Quality according to Pressure (XPbo1 and XPbo2)

The curves for using a press are almost superimposed (Figure 9.3g and h), whether it is the GQV or the GMP. However, at atmospheric pressure, the bond's quality is better, whereas the bond's purity is slightly lower than with press bonding. This was not controlled in this study, but the use of a gluing press likely helps to provide thin sections with a homogeneous and constant glue interface thickness.

9.6 What about the Finishing?

For the finishing step, the thin section may or may not be covered with a coverslip.

Using a coverslip offers the advantage of protecting the specimen's surfaces by trapping it between two walls of glass. The disadvantage of the method is that it requires mechanical removal of the slide when the sample needs thickness reduction or additional analysis.

It is important to note that for human protocols, the cut is made directly at 100 µm without grinding or polishing steps (Chapter 1). In some zooarchaeology protocols (LG), the sample is just abraded mechanically until the expected thickness (60–80 µm) using a diamond grinding cup wheel (e.g., PetroThin, Buehler). Therefore, the only visible marks are those caused by the saw, and these are easily identifiable because they are regular and always in the same plane. The glue and the lamella allow the sample's surface to be optically homogenized, resulting in most cases in the visual suppression of saw marks. In cases where the marks are very pronounced, a light polishing with a diamond paste is usually sufficient to clean the blade before gluing the coverslip.

The second method that leaves the sample accessible for future analyses is preferably used by the other authors (EP, WR). The polishing protocol developed at the PACEA Laboratory comprises six steps: abrasive cloth 58 µm (Reflex NAC P240 type M, Presi), diamond polishing plates 54 and 18 µm (I-Max R, Presi), and finally diamond suspensions 9, 3, and 1 µm (Reflex LDP, Presi) on woven supports (Reflex PAD-MAG, Presi). This procedure produces uncovered slides with an almost complete absence of striae and a quasi-perfect transparence. Compared to the latter, the primary constraint of polished slides is the time/effort factor.

Each of the two techniques, therefore, has its qualities and disadvantages. It will be necessary to choose the most suitable finishing method according to the technical possibilities, the time available, and the thin sections' final analytical use.

Caption for Figure 9.3 (cont.)

interactions with other variables. Each color corresponds to a darker shade for the unchanged values and a lighter shade for the modified values. According to the related column, the values in ordinates correspond to an index of quality or purity; the lower this value is, the better the pasting. (A black and white version of this figure will appear in some formats. For the color version, please refer to the plate section.)

9.7 Production of Sections with Embedded Objects

The inclusion of a tooth in the resin will inevitably introduce new variables. We will cover some of the most recurring issues we have experienced.

Embedding

Several polymers are available to consolidate a sample before cutting. In anthropology, the most common inclusion process is done with methyl methacrylate (MMA). This slow setting polymer (> 24 h) allows a complete embedding of the sample, that is, all the voids present in the tooth will be filled by the MMA, making the sample completely inert. The use of MMA is tricky because it requires a series of cleaning and dehydration processes over several weeks, the use of a smoke extractor at all stages, and can potentially alter some tissues' optical properties, in particular the cementum. Chapter 10 tested this aspect and suggested using rapid-curing epoxy resins (the combination of an epoxy monomer with a hardener) for cementochronology. These resins are less harmful and cure within a few hours. In this case, the specimen will be embedded in several possible ways, depending on the objective.

It is essential for fragile archaeological teeth to ensure that the resin can penetrate the apical foramen to strengthen the tooth from the inside and avoid cracks or dislocations during cutting. In this case, it is therefore recommended to cut the root apex to widen the canal opening. The risk of dislocation may be accentuated by the thinness of the section and the specimen's size. In addition, thin cuts often lead to disassociation of the resin's specimen and may cause tissue damage, especially with monoradicular teeth cut transversely. It is advisable to use moderately thick cuts and thin the specimen once glued onto a glass slide. If the sectioned sample still has defects, it is still possible to strengthen it by applying resin to the cut surface before polishing.

For recent teeth, a simple coating is sufficient to guarantee quality cuts.

Air Bubbles

Regardless of the type of inclusion, bubbles may form when pouring the resin into the sample mold and during vacuum outgassing. These bubbles are not a problem if they are not in contact with the tooth. However, the bubbles usually will find a point of attachment on the tooth surface. A good cleaning of the tooth with alcohol and embedding in a vertical position and under vacuum can limit this phenomenon.

More problematic, bubbles may form when a coverslip is glued to the tooth's surface and cover the cementum sample, thus altering its reading under microscopy. To avoid this issue, it is imperative not to glue the coverslip directly flat on the slide, but to first position an edge of the coverslip on the slide and then gradually apply it to the whole section to remove any bubbles.

9.8 Conclusion: Animal and Human Protocol Proposal

The histology platform dedicated to cementochronology has been in use in the PACEA laboratory since the early 1990s. It has enabled us to perform all the tests presented here and clarify the main points potentially impacting the production of thin sections for cementum analysis synthesized in Table 9.2.

Table 9.2 Summary of recommendations based on the different experiments performed for this study

Embedding recommendations	
Resin type	The resin must be chosen according to the objectives and sample quality (embedding or complete impregnation)
Resin and catalyst proportions	The respect of manufacturer's proportions is crucial unless you wish to alter the resin qualities
Mixing method	Manual mixing is better than mechanical
Pouring speed	Slower speed is best (choose gravitational pouring if you use a pouring device)
Pouring height	Intermediate height is better (about 3 cm from the surface)
Vacuum or not	Vacuum embedding is much more efficient when the device manufacturer instructions are strictly followed
Cutting recommendations	
Blade speed rotation and feed speed	For Buehler Isomet 5000 or higher, use 3000 rd/min speed rotation and 8 mm/min feed speed; for Buehler low speed saw, select speed "5" or "6"
Sample position	If using a cutting machine with the disc running toward the sample, don't place the sample against the lower part of the blade
Blade diameter	Use a blade diameter suitable for the sample size
Blade condition	For best results, regularly sharpen the blade with the manufacturer's stone stick
Flange diameter	With high-speed cutting machine, the flange diameter does not seem to change the quality of the cut; it does for the low-speed machine
Sample length and height	The sample should be placed with the longest side vertically (portrait format)
Bonding recommendations	
Slide surface condition	Using a nonfrosted slide doesn't change the quality of bonding, but it can offer a better purity of bonding (fewer bubbles and air pockets)
Sample surface condition	Using a polished sample doesn't change the quality of bonding, but it can offer a better purity of bonding (fewer bubbles and air pockets), as well as higher optical resolution
Heating or not?	Using a heating plate for bonding is best for the purity of bonding but detrimental to the quality of bonding when working with samples that are too thin because corners often straighten up (probably not with thicker samples); to avoid this problem, place a wide intermediate piece on the specimen's surface and additional pressure with weights to ensure that the entire surface of the specimen stays in contact with the glass slide during the entire polymerization process
Atmospheric pressure or more?	Atmospheric pressure bonding is better for the quality of bonding but not as good for the purity of bonding

Cementochronology for Archaeologists

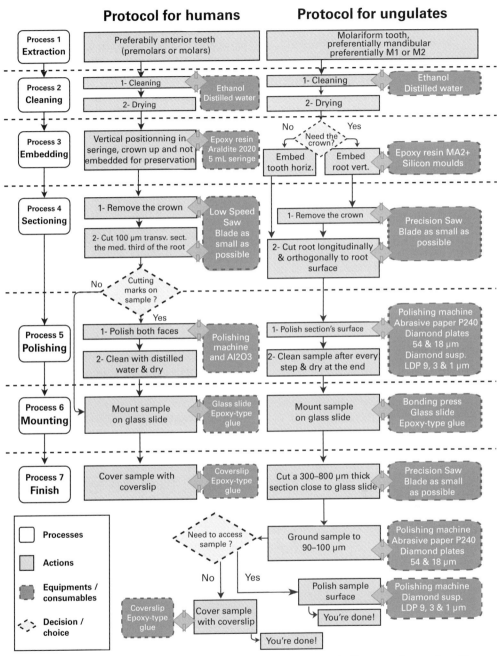

Figure 9.4 PACEA cementochronology decision tree for molariform ungulate teeth and human anterior teeth

Today, in France, there are six histology platforms for cementochronology. The one in Bordeaux (CNRS UMR 5199-PACEA, E. Pubert, and W. Rendu) deals with human and animal samples; the ones in Nice (CNRS UMR 7264-CEPAM, L. Gourichon) and Toulouse (CNRS UMR 5608-TRACES, M. Discamps) are dedicated to animals. At the same time, the laboratories of Lille (Université de Lille EA4490, T. Colard), Marseille (CNRS UMR 7268-ADES), and Caen (CNRS UMR6273-CRAHAM, C. Niel) are specialized in human samples.

The combined experience of the coauthors, enriched by the collaborations between these laboratories, allows us to propose standardized human (Chapter 1; Colard et al., 2015) and ungulate (large teeth) protocols for the systematic analysis of dental research collections (Figure 9.4).

Acknowledgments

This research was partially funded by the French National Agency for Research (ANR), as part of the CemeNTAA (ANR-14-CE31-0011) and DeerPal (ANR-18-CE03-0007) projects.

References

Burke, A., & Castanet, J. (1995). Histological observations of cementum growth in horse teeth and their application to archaeology. *Journal of Archaeological Science*, **22**, 479–93.

Colard, T., Bertrand, B., Naji, S., Delannoy, Y., & Bécart, A. (2015). Toward the adoption of cementochronology in forensic context. *International Journal of Legal Medicine*, **129**, 1–8.

Hammer, Ø., Harper, D. A. T., & Ryan, P. D. (2001). PAST: Paleontological Statistics Software Package for Education and Data Analysis. *Palaeontologia Electronica*, **4**, 1–9.

Klevezal', G. A. (1996). *Recording Structures of Mammals: Determination of Age and Reconstruction of Life History*. A. A. Balkema Series, Rotterdam.

Naji, S., Gourichon, L., & Rendu, W. (2015). La cémentochronologie. In M. Balasse, J.-P. Brugal, Y. Dauphin, E.-M. Geigl, C. Oberlin, & I. Reiche (eds.), *Messages d'os. Archéométrie Du Squelette Animal et Humain, Sciences Archéologiques*. Edition des Archives Contemporaines, France, 217–40.

Saxon, A., & Higham, C. (1969). A new research method for economic prehistorians. *American Antiquity*, **34**, 303–11.

10 Optimizing Preparation Protocols and Microscopy for Cementochronology

Paola Cerrito, Stephan Naji, and Timothy Bromage

10.1 Introduction

The count of dental cementum annulations or, more accurately, of acellular extrinsic fiber cementum (AEFC) layers is a histological method used to estimate age at death in forensic and archaeological contexts. This method, known as tooth cementum annulation (TCA) or cementochronology (Naji et al. 2016), typically requires embedding the tooth, sectioning the root, and imaging the resulting semi-thin sections to identify and count AEFC increments (Chapter 1). However, the different embedding and imaging protocols implemented in various labs render data comparability often impracticable (Wittwer-Backofen 2012). Consequently, authors have raised several criticisms toward the method itself (Huffman & Antoine 2010; Lucas & Loh 1986; Miller et al. 1988; Obertova & Francken 2009; Renz & Radlanski 2006). Although several validation studies on known-age samples have tested the accuracy and precision of the method (Aggarwal et al. 2008; Wittwer-Backofen et al. 2004; Wittwer-Backofen & Buba 2002), and two standardized cutting protocols have been published (Colard et al. 2015; Wittwer-Backofen 2012), there are still protocol steps that would benefit from additional experiments (Maat et al. 2006).

In this study, we carried out a systematic comparison between three standard illumination techniques (differential interference contrast, transmitted bright field, and transmitted polarized) by imaging sections with the same thickness, the same field of view, and with the same microscope, camera, and screen. Moreover, we performed this comparison on three different types of samples: freshly extracted teeth embedded in both MMA and epoxy, and on archeological samples embedded in epoxy. Finally, we compared the quality of AEFC increment visibility on longitudinal and hemi-transversal sections of the same root. The purpose is to evaluate which technical variables generate the optimal quality of AEFC micrographs for age-at-death estimation in anthropology, not to test the accuracy or precision of aging.

Supplemental online materials are available at www.cambridge.org/naji.

10.2 Imaging (Bright Field, Polarized Light, and Phase-Contrast)

The most commonly used optical microscopy illumination techniques to visualize cementum growth structures in histology are transmitted bright field (Colard et al. 2015; Wittwer-Backofen 2012), transmitted polarized light (Aggarwal et al. 2008; Blondiaux et al. 2006; Kasetty et al. 2010), and phase-contrast (Kagerer & Grupe 2001). Some authors have noted that the best results are yielded using phase-contrast illumination (Joshi et al. 2010; Kaur et al. 2015; Natesan et al. 2017; Pundir et al. 2009). However, these results' comparability is problematic because each laboratory does not follow the same embedding and preparation techniques.

10.3 Embedding (Epoxy and Methyl Methacrylate)

There are two possible embedding techniques for cementum section preparation. The first one requires the decalcification of the tooth, embedding in paraffin wax, and sectioning with a microtome (thin section); the resulting section is then stained to highlight the cementum lights. This is the preferred method in wildlife biology laboratories (Matson et al. 1993), and it yields excellent results. The second method involves embedding an undecalcified tooth in resin (e.g., epoxy or methyl methacrylate), sectioning it with a precision saw (semi-thin or ground section), and mounting it on a slide for grounding and polishing or direct observation. In archaeological contexts, because teeth have lost part of their organic component, decalcification is simply not possible without damaging the sample. Because of decalcified thin-section preparation constraints, only three studies employed this method for validation experiments (Condon et al. 1986; Kvaal & Solheim 1995; Lipsinic et al. 1986). Since 1995 every validation study adopted the more straightforward ground or semi-thin section approaches (Chapter 1, Table 1.1; Chapter 9). Today, published standardized methods have adopted undemineralized sectioning methods in forensic and archaeological settings (Colard et al. 2015; Wittwer-Backofen 2012; Part III of this volume for various examples).

The two most frequently used compounds to embed dental remains for sectioning are epoxy resin and methylmethacrylate (MMA). Occasionally, sections from freshly extracted teeth are prepared without prior embedding. However, this can cause cracks in the teeth and separation between the different dental tissues (Allen & Melfi 1985; Caropreso et al. 2000). Currently, no comparative data has been published regarding these two embedding materials. Because the compounds used may affect the optical properties of the mineralized tissue under examination, it is of paramount importance to rule out preparation interference and assess the least disruptive way to prepare the teeth for imaging. A high interobserver error and generally poor results in TCA counting were reported for teeth that have been embedded using MMA (Huffman & Antoine 2010), whereas consistently positive results have been obtained by imaging sections of teeth fixed with epoxy resin (Wittwer-Backofen et al. 2004).

10.4 Plane of Sectioning (Longitudinal and Transverse)

Acellular cementum increments are identifiable in both longitudinal and transverse sections of teeth. Longitudinal sections are standardly used in zoological samples (for a summary, see Klevezal' 1996), while transverse or longitudinal sections are equally used on human samples (Chapter 1, Table 1.1). Even though most experiments on human samples have used cross-sections, some obtained better results in longitudinal sections (Mallar et al. 2015; Stein & Corcoran 1994), while others advocate for transverse cut (Naji et al. 2016; Wedel & Wescott 2016).

In animal experiments, premolars and molars are most commonly used in cementochronology (Chapter 9). There is a preservation aspect for this choice in archaeological samples where anterior teeth are often missing. There is also a technical motivation because most posterior teeth have a relatively large flat root, as opposed to the conical shape of anterior teeth. This shape allows for a more precise cut perpendicular to the surface with higher consistency. Furthermore, AEFC is primarily distributed in the cervical half of the root (Yamamoto et al. 2009). However, the actual size of the AEFC region proper is more random than in human teeth. A longitudinal section ensures that the cut will go through AEFC if done in the longitudinal plane of the root.

The use of longitudinal sections in humans stems from the histology tradition in dentin and enamel studies. In contrast, the recognition that AEFC is primarily distributed in the middle third of the root in humans, with cellular cementum dominating the apical third, promoted the use of transverse cuts to optimize the maximum number of observable regions. Cervical thirds are usually avoided in case oral pathologies are impacting cementum deposition.

However, Maat and colleagues (2006) noted that typical cementum cross-sections are done perpendicular to the (cone-shaped) root's central axis. The authors argue that this angulation creates an optical superimposition of in-focus and out-of-focus tangentially positioned to the cementum layers (Chapter 6). The solution advocated by the authors is to perform the cuts perpendicular to the outside surface of the root rather than to its axis (Maat et al. 2006, figure 4: 97). This specification has been integrated into most current protocols (Colard et al. 2015), including this study.

10.5 Materials and Methods

Our sample includes fifty-one *H. sapiens* monoradicular and pluriradicular permanent and deciduous teeth (Table 10.1), with no observed radicular pathology. Thirty-one teeth are freshly extracted, and twenty are from the archeological site of La Granède, France (Saint-Pierre 2010).

Before imaging the sections, we made preliminary assessments of the cementum using a Leica® DM5000 at 5x or 10x magnification to determine a suitable region of interest (ROI). All counts of the AEFC increments were recorded for each of the

Table 10.1 Samples and preparation

Sample	Size ($n =$)	Embedding	Sectioning	Sections/Tooth	Polished	Cover Slip
Archaeological	20	Epoxy	Transverse	5/anterior	no	yes
Modern	20	MMA	Longitudinal & hemi-transverse	2/anterior and posterior	yes	no
Modern	11	Epoxy & MMA	Transverse	2/anterior and posterior	yes	no

selected ROI, at a distance of at least one week between each observation, using the multipoint tool in FIJI Image J® (Schindelin et al. 2012).

Sample Preparation for Imaging Comparison

The twenty monoradicular teeth comprising the archaeological sample were prepared following a standardized protocol (Colard et al. 2015). Five AEFC sections were produced for each tooth, and one optimal ROI of AEFC was selected for imaging for each section. Images were acquired using the three illumination techniques: transmitted bright field (BF) and differential interference contrast (DIC), using a Leica® DM5000 microscope; polarized light (POL), using a Leica® DMRXE microscope. We could not locate a suitable ROI for three teeth, effectively reducing our sample size to seventeen. Six blind counts of the AEFC increments were recorded for each of the selected ROI.

For each set of six counts, we calculated the relative standard error (RSE) to assess the precision (not the accuracy, as the individual's age was not known) of the counts for each specimen in each illumination method. The relative standard error of a sample is the standard error divided by the mean and expressed as a percentage. This measure of error effectively permits to control for the correlation between increased absolute error and increase number of TCA layers (hence, of age). The lowest the RSE, the highest the accuracy of the measurements. We then performed an analysis of variance (ANOVA) and a pairwise t-test on the RSE grouped by illumination category to detect the most precise method.

Sample Preparation for the Comparison between MMA and Epoxy Embedding

Prior to embedding, eleven teeth were transversely sectioned at the cervical third of the root using a Buehler® IsoMet® Low-speed precision saw with a wafering diamond blade. One portion was embedded in a two-component epoxy resin, while the other one was embedded in MMA following the protocol developed at the Hard Tissue Research Unit (HTRU) of NYU's College of Dentistry by Dr. Bin Hu (Bromage et al. 2016).

All blocks of hemi-teeth were grounded down and polished with 600, 800, and 1200 grit sandpapers on a wet circular polisher. Samples were then mounted on EXAKT® microscope plastic slides using cyanoacrylate, sectioned to approximately 130 μm using a Buehler® IsoMet® 1000 precision saw with diamond wafering blade, and ground/polished to a thickness 100+/−10 μm. To control for section thickness, each sample was measured using the micrometer calibrated z-plane stand of an Edge R400 Realtime 3D microscope. Exact thickness was then measured by focusing on the bottom and top of the thin section and recording the z-elevation of the stand in between.

The resulting thin sections represented, for each tooth, either side of the original transverse cut minus the thickness of the blade (200 μm) and the final polish. This enabled us to compare the two different compounds' effects while controlling for sample preparation and thickness. Each ROI was imaged using three imaging methods: BF, DIC, and POL. Six blind counts of the AEFC increments were recorded for each of the selected ROI. For each set of six counts, we calculated the RSE and performed a t-test between MMA- and epoxy-embedded sections.

Sample Preparation for the Comparison between Longitudinal and Transverse Sections

A sample of twenty freshly extracted teeth was used to compare AEFC increment counts on longitudinal and transverse sections. We embedded seventeen specimens following the same MMA protocol. Instead, the remaining three were embedded in fluorescent material as an exploratory attempt to increase the cementum annuli contrast.

The embedded teeth were sectioned along their mid-longitudinal plane (Figure 10.1a).

One of the two hemiblocks was then sectioned perpendicular to the root surface at the mid-cervical third of the root (Figure 10.1b) following Maat and colleagues' (2006) recommendation.

Following the procedure described in the previous section, we created one thin section of the longitudinal surface of the tooth and one of half of the transverse surface

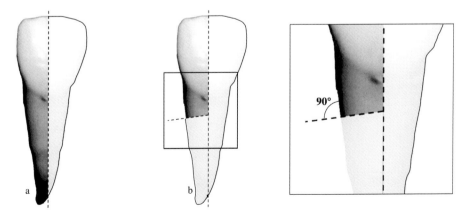

Figure 10.1 (a) Mid-longitudinal plane of sectioning (a); (b) Transverse plane of sectioning perpendicular to the root surface

(hemi-transverse) of the root. Each pair of corresponding sections was then compared for the clarity and visibility of the AEFC layers. Suitable ROIs were imaged in BF, DIC, and POL, and counts were performed for each set of six counts. We calculated the RSE and performed a t-test between transverse and longitudinal sections.

10.6 Results

IMAGING

Our comparison of the different illuminating techniques carried out on the archeological specimens is summarized in Figure 10.2 and described as follows (see online Appendix 10.1 for illustrations).

The RSE provides a measure of the precision achieved in counting the AEFC increments, irrespectively of observer training, as all counts were performed by the same author (PC).

The ANOVA results on the three imaging methods indicate a significant difference (p = 0.006) between them in terms of their RSE. The null hypothesis that the accuracy in TCA counting is independent of imaging type is thus rejected. Furthermore, we performed a pairwise t-test to assess which of the three is significantly different from the others. The results indicate that DIC measurements have significantly lower RSE (p = 0.005).

We also carried out an ANOVA and a pairwise t-test on the three imaging methods using pooled data from the archeological specimens and the modern sample (excluding the three specimens embedded in fluorescent material) (forty-eight specimens per imaging method), thus including specimens embedded in both MMA and epoxy (for a comparison between the two, see Section 10.7). The observation that DIC provides significantly best results (p = 2.2 * 10^{-6}) also holds in this case (Figure 10.2).

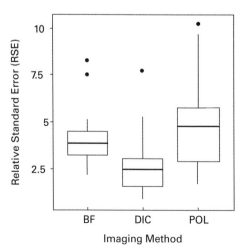 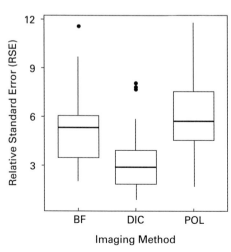

Figure 10.2 Boxplots of the relative standard error by imaging method. Left: Archeological sample. Right: Archeological and modern samples pooled

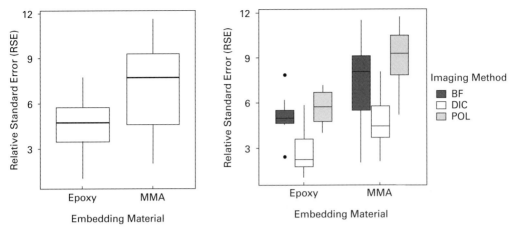

Figure 10.3 Boxplots of the relative standard error by embedding materials, irrespective of imaging method (left), by imaging method (right)

EMBEDDING

Of the eleven teeth sampled and imaged, two did not present any distinct AEFC layers in the MMA embedded section. Results of the comparison between sections embedded in epoxy or MMA clearly indicate that epoxy embedding yields much clearer sections for the identification of AEFC increments, as the RSE for epoxy-embedded specimens is significantly lower (p = 0.0006) than the one for MMA embedded sections (Figure 10.3, left). The results were valid irrespective of the imaging method (Figure 10.3, right, and online Appendix 10.2 for illustrations).

Furthermore, we used ANOVAs and pairwise t-tests to assess the effect of the imaging method separately on each embedding material. We found that in both cases, DIC provides significantly better results (p = 0.08 for the MMA-embedded samples; p = 0.001 for the epoxy-embedded samples).

PLANE OF SECTIONING

The twenty specimens used to test the differences in cementum increments visibility depending on the sectioning plane were embedded using MMA. However, as discussed in the previous section, TCAs are poorly visible in specimens embedded in MMA medium (see online Appendix 10.3 for illustrations). Therefore, the absence of a significant difference (p = 0.9) between the RSE of the transverse and longitudinal sections (Figure 10.4) is likely due to the results being swamped by the overall negative effects that MMA has on TCA visibility.

10.7 Discussion

One of the enduring problems in cementochronology is the perceived notion that there is a lack of standard protocols for human samples, even though two have been

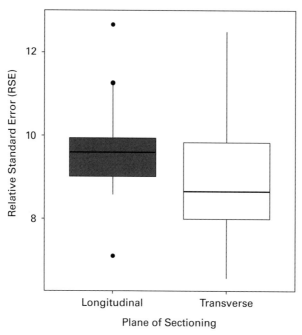

Figure 10.4 Boxplots of the relative standard error by planes of sectioning

published, and one has been certified ISO–9001 (Colard et al. 2015; Wittwer-Backofen 2012; Chapters 1 and 9). The confusion comes partly from the absence of explicit experimental tests performed for diverse protocol variables such as equipment (e.g., saw, microscope), consumable (e.g., resin, slides), or techniques (e.g., angulation of the cut, illumination) available to histologists (Chapter 9). Also, the motivation to use cementum in forensic or archaeological contexts usually comes from scientists or students not trained in histology who view cementochronology as a simple tool and not a complex histological method. Some researchers have naturally turned to histology laboratories for help in their initial training. However, hard material histology laboratories are usually set up for bone, dentin, and enamel, not cementum, which is the least studied dental tissue (Foster 2017, Chapter 1). Unfortunately, there are several key differences between cementum and other hard tissues in histology preparation and analytical stages. The purpose of this chapter was to explore some of the variables specific to cementochronology.

Even though at least two comparable standardized methods for producing semi-thin sections have been published (Colard et al. 2015; Wittwer-Backofen 2012), the reality of histological experiments demands constant testing and improvement to reduce methodological errors at every step. Comparing illumination techniques suggested that DIC might produce more contrasted micrographs than BF or POL and, therefore, should be used to optimize results. However, DIC is not a common type of microscope, while BF and POL are widely available in anthropology, geology, and biology departments, among others. Considering that validation studies with some of the highest accuracy and precision rates relied on BF or POL lights, it will be necessary to quantify, in a larger validation study, the higher contrast of DIC observed here and weigh it against the lower cost and availability of BF or POL.

The result is straightforward regarding the embedding medium, however. Epoxy is consistently more efficient than MMA. This could seem counterintuitive because MMA embedding produces a much higher quality plastic bloc. The complete penetration of the sample with MMA during the two-week-long infiltration stage might be what inhibits our observation of incremental bands in cementum. Contrast is diminished when "clearing" hard tissues. MMA has a refractive index very similar to cementum, and if it fills the minute nanoscale air spaces at boundaries between compositionally different cementum layers where the light would typically scatter; the light instead propagates through the tissue. This difference in the embedding medium might explain our third results. When comparing longitudinal and transverse sections, all embedded in MMA, no statistical differences are found. Even though we lack the comparative longitudinal sections from epoxy-embedded samples and therefore cannot make a stronger statement, our result supports a more significant trend observed in published experiments. Based on sixteen validation studies where at least fifty known-age teeth were sectioned and analyzed for age at death, transverse sections consistently produced more precise results, even though the accuracy was statistically comparable to longitudinal sections (Figure 10.5).

The main reason for this difference is probably related to the variation in AEFC distribution on the dental root, mainly on the cervical third in animals and mostly in the middle third in humans (Yamamoto et al. 2009), and the type of teeth typically used in cementochronology (multiradicular for animals, monoradicular for humans). The

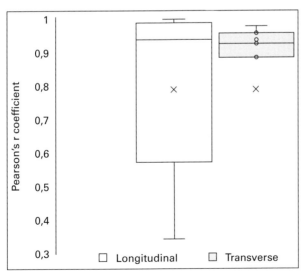

Figure 10.5 Boxplots of Pearson's r between observed number of cementum lines and known age, from studies with a sample size greater than fifty teeth, observed in longitudinal ($n = 9$), and transverse ($n = 7$) sections (Chapter 1, Table 1.1)

main advantage of transverse sections is to observe the entire perimeter of the root, which increases the chances of identifying optimal areas of interest. Furthermore, multiple thin sections per tooth can be produced in transverse cuts easily following the cementum-specific standardized protocol (Colard et al. 2015; Wittwer-Backofen 2012) to increase the probability of identifying an optimal AEFC region.

10.8 Conclusion

Our preliminary attempt to test and optimize some protocol variables in cementochronology suggests that differential interference contrast microscopy might be the ideal illumination method for cementochronology. However, brightfield is consistently providing a decent image. We demonstrated that epoxy resin with quick polymerization time does not affect cementum structure and allows for higher contrast micrographs than traditional MMA. Finally, our observations support that transverse sections are more suitable for identifying AEFC layers consistently.

To conclude, our results support the currently published protocol for human cementochronology and emphasize the need to use cementum-specific embedding and cutting procedures not compatible with traditional enamel or dentin histomorphology analyses.

Acknowledgments

This work was supported in part by the "Agence National de la Recherche" [project CemeNTAA, ANR-14-CE31-0011]. We would also like to thank Dr. Bin Hu for his assistance and help in NYU's HTRU dental histology laboratory.

References

Aggarwal, P., Saxena, S., & Bansal, P. (2008). Incremental lines in root cementum of human teeth: An approach to their role in age estimation using polarizing microscopy. *Indian Journal of Dental Research*, **19**(4), 326–30.

Allen, D. S., & Melfi, R. C. (1985). Improvements in techniques for aging mammals by dental cementum annuli. *Proceedings of the Iowa Academy of Science*, **92**(3), 100–2.

Blondiaux, J., Gabart, N., Alduc-Le Bagousse, A., Niel, C., & Tyler, E. (2006). Relevance of cement annulations to paleopathology. *Paleopathology Newsletter*, **135**, 4–13.

Bromage, T. G., Idaghdour, Y., Lacruz, R. S., ... Schrenk, F. (2016). The swine plasma metabolome chronicles "many days" biological timing and functions linked to growth. *PLoS ONE*, **11**(1), e0145919.

Caropreso, S., Bondioli, L., Capannolo, D., Cerroni, L., Macchiarelli, R., & Condò, S. G. (2000). Thin sections for hard tissue histology: A new procedure. *Journal of Microscopy*, **199**(3), 244–7.

Colard, T., Bertrand, B., Naji, S., Delannoy, Y., & Bécart, A. (2015). Toward the adoption of cementochronology in forensic context. *International Journal of Legal Medicine*, **129**, 1–8.

Condon, K., Charles, D. K., Cheverud, J. M., & Buikstra, J. E. (1986). Cementum annulation and age determination in *Homo sapiens*. II. Estimates and accuracy. *American Journal of Physical Anthropology*, **71**(3), 321–30.

Foster, B. L. (2017). On the discovery of cementum. *Journal of Periodontal Research*, **52**(4), 666–85.

Huffman, M., & Antoine, D. (2010). Analysis of cementum layers in archaeological material. *Dental Anthropology*, **23**(3), 67–78.

Joshi, P. S., Chougule, M. S., & Agrawal, G. P. (2010). Comparison of polarizing and phase-contrast microscopy for estimation of age based on cemental annulations. *Indian Journal of Forensic Odontology*, **3**(3), 17–25.

Kagerer, P., & Grupe, G. (2001). Age-at-death diagnosis and determination of life-history parameters by incremental lines in human dental cementum as an identification aid. *Forensic Science International*, **118**(1), 75–82.

Kasetty, S., Rammanohar, M., & Raju Ragavendra, T. (2010). Dental cementum in age estimation: A polarized light and stereomicroscopic sStudy. *Journal of Forensic Sciences*, **55**(3), 779–83.

Kaur, P., Astekar, M., Singh, J., Arora, K. S., & Bhalla, G. (2015). Estimation of age based on tooth cementum annulations: A comparative study using light, polarized, and phase-contrast microscopy. *Journal of Forensic Dental Sciences*, **7**(3), 215–21.

Klevezal', G. A. (1996). *Recording Structures of Mammals: Determination of Age and Reconstruction of Life History*. Rotterdam: A. A. Balkema Series.

Kvaal, S. I., & Solheim, T. (1995). Incremental lines in human dental cementum in relation to age. *European Journal of Oral Sciences*, **103**(4), 225–30.

Lipsinic, F. E., Paunovich, D. G., Houston, D. G., & Robinson, S. F. (1986). Correlation of age and incremental lines in the cementum of human teeth. *Journal of Forensic Sciences*, **31**, 982–9.

Lucas, P. W., & Loh, H. S. (1986). Are the incremental lines in human cementum laid down annually? *Annals of the Academy of Medicine, Singapore*, **15**(3), 384–6.

Maat, G. J. R., Gerretsen, R. R. R., & Aarents, M. J. (2006). Improving the visibility of tooth cementum annulations by adjustment of the cutting angle of microscopic sections. *Forensic Science International*, **159**, (Supplement), S95–S99.

Mallar, K. B., Girish, H. C., Murgod, S., & Kumar, B. Y. (2015). Age estimation using annulations in root cementum of human teeth: A comparison between longitudinal and cross-sections. *Journal of Oral and Maxillofacial Pathology: JOMFP*, **19**(3), 396–404.

Matson, G., Van Daele, L., Goodwin, E., Aumiller, L., Reynolds, H., & Hristienko, H. (1993). *A Laboratory Manual for Cementum Age Determination of Alaska Brown Bear PM1 Teeth*. Milltown, MT: Alaska Department of Fish and Game, and Matson's Laboratory.

Miller, C. F., Dove, S. B., & Cottone, J. A. (1988). Failure of use of cemental annulations in teeth to determine the age of humans. *Journal of Forensic Sciences*, **33**, 137–43.

Naji, S., Colard, T., Blondiaux, J., Bertrand, B., d'Incau, E., & Bocquet-Appel, J.-P. (2016). Cementochronology, to cut or not to cut? *International Journal of Paleopathology*, **15**, 113–19.

Natesan, S., Krishnapillai, R., Ramakrishnan, B., & Thomas, P. (2017). Phase-contrast microscopy: An adjuvant tool to assess cementum annulation in forensic dentistry. *Oral & Maxillofacial Pathology Journal*, **8**(1), 5–8.

Obertova, Z., & Francken, M. (2009). Tooth cementum annulation method: Accuracy and applicability. *Frontiers of Oral Biology*, **13**, 184–9.

Pundir, S., Saxena, S., & Aggrawal, P. (2009). Estimation of age based on tooth cementum annulations using three different microscopic methods. *Journal of Forensic Dental Sciences*, **1**(2), 82.

Renz, H., & Radlanski, R. J. (2006). Incremental lines in root cementum of human teeth – A reliable age marker? *HOMO – Journal of Comparative Human Biology*, **57**(1), 29–50.

Saint-Pierre, C. (2010). Millau, La Granède (Aveyron): Une église paléochrétienne anonyme sur un éperon barré. *Archéologie du Midi Médiéval*, **28**(1), 181–91.

Schindelin, J., Arganda-Carreras, I., Frise, E., … Cardona, A. (2012). Fiji: An open-source platform for biological-image analysis. *Nature Methods*, **9**(7), 676–82.

Stein, T. J., & Corcoran, J. F. (1994). Pararadicular cementum deposition as a criterion for age estimation in human beings. *Oral Surgery, Oral Medicine, Oral Pathology*, **77**(3), 266–70.

Wedel, V. L., & Wescott, D. J. (2016). Using dental cementum increment analysis to estimate age and season of death in African Americans from a historical cemetery in Missouri. *International Journal of Paleopathology*, **15**, 134–9.

Wittwer-Backofen, U. (2012). Age estimation using tooth cementum annulation. In L. S. Bell, ed., *Forensic Microscopy for Skeletal Tissues*, Vol. 915, Totowa, NJ: Humana Press, 129–43.

Wittwer-Backofen, U., & Buba, H. (2002). Age estimation by tooth cementum annulation: Perspective of a new validation study. In R. D. Hoppa and J. W. Vaupel, eds., *Paleodemography, Age Distributions from Skeletal Samples*, Cambridge: Cambridge University Press, 107–28.

Wittwer-Backofen, U., Gampe, J., & Vaupel, J. W. (2004). Tooth cementum annulation for age estimation: Results from a large known-age validation study. *American Journal of Physical Anthropology*, **123**(2), 119–29.

Yamamoto, H., Niimi, T., Yokota-Ohta, R., Suzuki, K., Sakae, T., & Kozawa, Y. (2009). Diversity of acellular and cellular cementum distribution in human permanent teeth. *Journal of Hard Tissue Biology*, **18**(1), 40–4.

11 Cementochronology Protocol for Selecting a Region of Interest in Zooarchaeology

William Rendu, Stephan Naji, Eric Pubert, Carlos Sánchez-Hernández, Manon Vuillien, Hala Alarashi, Emmanuel Discamps, Elodie-Laure Jimenez, Solange Rigaud, Randall White, and Lionel Gourichon

11.1 Introduction

Since the middle of the previous century, cementum analyses were developed for aging and assessing the season of death of varied taxa (Klevezal' 1996, Chapter 1). The method has been used mainly in archaeology since the 1960s to discuss subsistence strategies (Pike-Tay 1991; Rendu 2010), animal migrations (Burke 1993), mobility pattern (Rendu 2007; Delagnes and Rendu 2011), and livestock management (Gourichon 2004). More recently, applications on humans were conducted notably to estimate the age at death and demographic variables (Naji, Gourichon, and Rendu 2015; Part III). Although the method is now the most used for studying seasonality in archaeological contexts, some methodological issues still limit part of the interpretations.

Even though most of the authors seem to agree on the general conditions of observation of the cementum increments, very few explicit criteria are defined to accept or reject an observation precisely. In particular, the criteria to select a region of interest (ROI) for observation are rarely detailed. Instead, only a general description is usually proposed, such as the "first third of the root" or "just below the enamel–cementum junction" (Pike-Tay 1991; Klevezal' 1996), where acellular cementum is best observed. Because only a fraction of the tooth is analyzed, the proper selection of the ROI is a critical initial step in the protocol. This is a central issue when dealing with archaeological teeth of ungulates since the minimum number of individuals (MNI) is generally established on cheek teeth, which are thus preferentially selected for age and season-of-death analyses (Gordon 1988; Pike-Tay 1995; Naji, Gourichon, and Rendu 2015). For practical reasons, histological sections of molar and premolar roots are usually made longitudinally, following a mesio-distal axis (Chapter 9). However, the curvature of the root prevents the cutting plane from being strictly perpendicular to the increment deposits (as measured from the surface of the root), a necessary condition to avoid the superposition doubling effect of increments (Chapter 6; Naji, Gourichon, and Rendu 2015; Cool et al. 2002). Consequently, contrary to the limited ROI obtained in transverse sections primarily used for anterior human teeth (Naji et al. 2016; Chapter 1), the portion of cementum observable on an ungulate longitudinal thin section can be very large, although only part of it is suitable for the analysis.

Objective

To solve this common issue (Roksandic et al. 2009), we decided to assess the interobserver reliability of the three main steps of the microscopical analytical protocol in cementochronology: step 1, the selection of an optimal ROI; step 2, the estimation of the age at death; and step 3, the identification of the season of death estimations.

For the first step, we collectively discussed optimal criteria to define the best ROI that will be tested for clarity and reproducibility. For the second and third steps, agreement rates will be evaluated between documented age and season at death and the estimations proposed by the observers.

To define our criteria, we used the White-Kaminuriak collection composed of teeth of 999 members of the extant population of barren-ground caribou (*Rangifer tarandus groelandicus*) from Kaminuriak (Canada), with precise information about sex, age, and date of death of each individual. These animals were killed in the late 1960s by the Canadian Wildlife Service in spring, summer, and fall (namely, April, May, June, July, September, November, and December). Thin sections were produced in the 1990s by the Department of Anthropology at New York University and were analyzed in a previous study (Pike-Tay 1995).

From this study, fifty thin sections were selected for observation by four experienced analysts (LG, SN, WR, EP). The aim was to share our experience, acquired on different taxa and contexts, in order to describe the minimum number of standard criteria for including or rejecting an ROI (Figure 11.1) suitable for age and season at death estimation (Table 11.1).

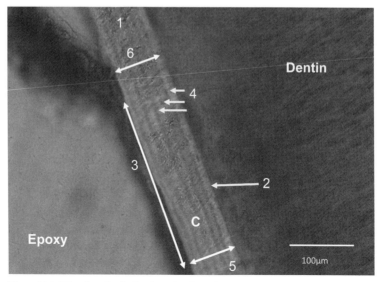

Figure 11.1 The six criteria for the selection of an ROI. Numbers refer to the criteria (Table 11.1). Picture from the White-Kaminuriak collection (W. Rendu)

Table 11.1 Criteria for the inclusion of a region of interest, White-Kaminuriak collection

#	Criteria – Definition	Goal
1	The observation must be made within the acellular extrinsic fiber cementum (AEFC), located generally *in the cervical third* of the root (see definition in Chapter 2).	avoids confusion with cellular intrinsic fiber cementum (CIFC) structures
2	Good visibility of the main histological structures in the cementum and the dentin: (i) Tomes' granular layer, (ii) hyaline layer of Hopewell-Smith (aka hyaline line), and (iii) dentin tubules.	confirms the nature of the AEFC; confirms that first and last increments are observable
3	Continuity of the AEFC increments on the whole ROI.	minimizes the presence of artifacts, increment splits, or convergence
4	Comparable thickness for all increments: directly observed or measured with an image processing software (see Lieberman, Deacon, and Meadow 1990).	excludes CIFC inclusions (mixed cementum), or diagenetic changes
5	ROI should be at least twice as large as thick.	allows for repetitive observations and measurements
6	Edges of cementum (outer border and inner hyaline line) should be equidistant for the whole ROI.	confirms the expected shape of AEFC regular seasonal growth, as opposed to irregular CIFC reactive growth

11.2 Material and Method

Sample Set

To test our criteria, we prepared a new set of thin sections from the White-Kaminuriak collection. To reduce the number of parameters, the sample was composed of eighty teeth from the same caribou population. Ten teeth for each recorded seven months of death represented in the corpus were selected to account for all potential growth stages of the last AEFC increment. One or two thin sections were then produced for each tooth by one of us (EP) following the protocol described by Pubert and colleagues (Chapter 9).

The teeth were embedded in epoxy resin using a vacuum chamber and then cut transversally in the mesio-distal plane with a Buehler Isomet 5000 saw. After polishing the cut surface, the embedded teeth were glued on a 30X45 mm glass. Finally, the samples were ground to a thickness of 100 μm and polished. A total of 115 thin sections were produced.

For the blind test, thirty thin sections were sampled by two of us (WR, LG) based on the presence of acellular cementum alone, identified with a polarized microscope at low magnification (X40).

Testing an Optimal ROI Selection

Four observers with different skill levels in cementum analysis (A and B: experienced; C: intermediate; D: beginner) were asked to conduct the observation of the three-step goals:

1. Identification of all the possible ROIs in each section
2. Counting the number of light incremental deposits (to evaluate the age at death)
3. Determination of the nature and stage of growth of the last increment for estimating the season of death

Regarding the last step, the procedure followed the method usually applied in zooarchaeology for the identification of the nature and growth stage of the last increment (Pike-Tay 1995; Gourichon 2004; Naji, Gourichon, and Rendu 2015; Sánchez-Hernández et al. 2019).

First, the *nature of the last deposit* is identified as either (i) a growth "*zone*," usually formed during the summer (wide, translucent in natural light, or light in cross-polarized light); or (ii) a rest layer or "*annulus*," usually formed in winter (thin, opaque in natural light or dark in cross-polarized light) (Chapter 6).

Second, the *growth stage* of the last deposit is estimated. For a *growth zone*, three stages are defined by comparing the thickness of the last increment proportionally to the previous growth zone: Z1 – *beginning* (width lesser than 1/3 of the previous one); Z2 – *middle* (width lesser than 2/3 and greater than 1/3); and Z3 – *late* (width greater than 2/3). For an *annulus*, the increment's width is usually too thin to subdivide.

During the blind test, observations have been performed under the same conditions for all analysts, with the same Leica DM2500P microscope and Leica MC120HD camera. Analysts were asked to examine each of the thirty thin sections with an X400 magnification. Following Stutz (2002), pictures had to be recorded using three illuminations: bright field ("natural," henceforth), cross-polarized, and cross-polarized with a full-wave retardation plate (λ-plate). The observation under the λ-plate was required to identify diagenetic transformations, which is recommended for all cementum analyses applied to archaeological context (Naji, Gourichon, and Rendu 2015).

For the first goal, the analysts identified the ROIs' coordinates using a mechanical XY stage, based on the six criteria defined in Figure 11.1. Analysts systematically photographed the ROI for an interobserver comparison. The *number* of identified ROIs and their *locations* for each thin section were compared using their coordinates as well as visual histological features on the micrograph.

For the second and third goals, the increment *count* and the identification of the nature and *stage of growth* of the last increment were compared between the analysts and checked against the information available for each caribou. Analysis of all the collected data was done by one of the authors (WR).

11.3 Results

Step 1: Selection of the ROI

All thirty thin sections were observed by the four analysts blindly (Table 11.2). One of the thin sections (#716) was rejected by all analysts because criteria 2, 3, 4, and 6 were not met.

The number of identified ROIs (Tables 11.2 and 11.3) does not strictly reflect the analysts' degree of experience because one of the most experienced (B) identified a total of forty-three ROIs while the other observers identified only thirty-seven or thirty-eight ROIs. Between one and three ROIs were identified per thin section, with a mean of 1.4.

For twenty-six thin sections, all analysts found at least one common ROI (Table 11.2 and Figure 11.2).

In two cases (#608A and #667), analyst A considered that criterion 1 was not respected, and in one of these cases (#608A), analyst D selected an ROI rejected by the three other observers based on the absence of criteria 4 and 6.

Finally, for thin section 608B, analyst D selected a different ROI than analysts B and C, which appeared to disregard criteria 1 (Table 11.2 and Figure 11.3).

Step 2: Age Estimation

Although the ROIs were successfully identified most of the time, the different analysts could not propose a valid increment count in every case. For these specific cases, the analysts identified some problems in the thin-section preparation (e.g., grounding too intense) that limited their confidence in counting the increments. Results presented here are thus proposed for sections with identified ROIs only.

Out of the twenty-nine thin sections in which the analysts selected one or more ROIs, twenty-six to twenty-nine provided increment counts (i.e., 108 observations that can estimate the individual age). The observed counts were compared to the expected number of increments for each tooth, calculated by subtracting the tooth's eruption age from the documented age of the individual. Considering the variability in the eruption dates (Canadian Wildlife Service and Miller 1974), and considering that most of the biologists agree that a margin of error of ±1 year is acceptable for the age estimation based on cementum count (Matson et al. 1993), we have defined a "success" when the estimation is equal to the expected increment number or has a deviation of only one unit (above or below) from the latter.

Table 11.4 shows large variability in the results with a total of 86 percent (93/108) increment counts in agreement with the expected age. Overestimations are more frequent (12 percent, 13 cases) that underestimations (1.9 percent, 2 cases).

The discrepancies between the analysts are of interest because their reliability is ranked by experience, with the most experienced observers (A and B) scoring very high success rates (> 95 percent); the intermediate observer (C) scoring 85 percent, and the least experienced (D) scoring 65 percent. This ranking confirmed previously published recommendations that proper training should be set up before data observation (Naji et al. 2016, Chapter 23). If we only include the experienced analysts, the success rates are 96 percent and 97 percent for analysts A and B, respectively, with no undervaluation and only a 1.9 percent overestimation by one or two years only above the usual confidence interval.

Based on the recorded observations on problematic ROIs, the one- to two-year underestimations seem to be linked to the first increment's misidentification after the

Table 11.2 Results of the blind test by thin section and analyst. Age is expressed in years; the season is expressed by the theoretical last stage of AEFC increment growth (Z1: zone beginning of growth; Z2: zone middle of growth; Z3: zone end of growth; A: annulus; R: rejected; N/A: no answer). Age estimation for each analyst represents the deviation from known age.

	Sample Information			Analyst A			Analyst B			Analyst C			Analyst D			Comparisons	
tth	NB	Age	SEASON	Number of ROI	Age	Season C	Number of ROI	Age	Season B	Number of ROI	Age	Season A	Number of ROI	Age	Season D	Analysts finding the same ROI	Nb Age Disagreement	Nb Season Disagreements
P4	304	8,42	Z3	2	0	Z3	1	0	Z3	1	1	A	1	N/A	N/A	ABCD	0	0
P3	310	7,42	Z3	2	0	Z3	2	0	Z3	1	0	Z1	1	1	Z	ABCD	0	1
P4	436	7	Z1	3	0	Z1	1	0	Z1	1	0	A	2	1	Z1	ABCD	0	1
P4	437	5	Z1	1	0	Z1	3	0	Z1	2	0	Z	1	2	N/A	ABCD	1	0
P4	440	7	Z1	2	−1	Z1	2	0	Z1	1	N/A	Z1	3	N/A	A	ABCD	0	2
M2	441	7	Z1	1	0	Z1	1	−1	Z1	1	0	Z1	1	1	Z1	ABCD	0	0
M2	441B	7	Z1	2	0	Z3	2	0	Z3	1	0	Z3	3	2	Z3	ABCD	1	0
P4	500	7	Z1	1	0	Z1	1	0	Z1	1	−1	A	1	1	A	ABCD	0	0
P4	507	6	Z1	1	0	Z1	4	0	Z1	1	0	Z	2	1	A	ABCD	0	1
M2	521	6,25	Z2	1	0	Z2	1	0	Z2	1	−1	A	1	−1	Z3	ABCD	0	2
P3	566A	2,25	Z2	2	1	Z2	3	1	Z2	2	0	Z	3	3	N/A	ABCD	1	2
M2	602	6,42	Z3	1	0	Z3	1	1	Z3	1	−1	A	1	−1	N/A	ABCD	0	0
P4	607	4,42	Z3	1	1	Z3	2	1	Z3	2	0	Z(3)	1	3	N/A	ABCD	1	0
P4	608A	3,42	Z3	R			1	1	Z3	2	3	A	1	4	N/A	BC	2	0
P4	608B	3,42	Z3	1	3	A	1	1	Z3	1	3	A	1	3	Z1	ABC	3	0
M2	652	8,42	A	1	−1	A	1	0	A	1	0	Z	1	−1	N/A	ABCD	0	1

M2+P4	657	3,42	A	1	0	Z3	2	0	A	2	0	A	1	0	A	ABCD	0	2
M2	667	4,42	A	R	0		1	0	A	1	0	Z1	1	0	N/A	BCD	0	1
M2	684	4,42	A	2	0	A	1	0	A	1	0	Z1	1	−1	Z3	ABCD	0	1
M2	704	4,42	A	2	0	A	1	1	A	2	0	A	1	1	N/A	ABCD	0	0
M2	716	6,83	A	R			R			R			R		R		0	0
M2	754	8,83	A	1	−1	Z	1	1	A	1	1	Z	1	2	N/A	ABCD	1	2
P4	774	5,83	A	1	1	A	1	2	A	1	2	A	3	N/A	N/A	ABCD	2	0
P4	777	5,83	A	1	1	A	1	1	A	2	N/A	N/A	2	N/A	N/A	ABCD	0	1
M2	783	6,93	A	1	1	A	1	1	A	2	1	A	1	2	Z1	ABCD	1	0
M2	793b	9,83	A	1	−1	Z1	1	−1	Z1	1	−2	Z1	1	−2	Z3	ABCD	2	1
P4	920	9,08	Z2	2	1	Z2	3	0	Z2	1	0	Z1	2	0	N/A	ABCD	0	1
M2	926	10,08	Z2	1	0	Z2	1	−1	Z2	1	0	Z1	1	1	A	ABCD	0	2
P4	935	5,08	Z2	1	0	Z2	1	0	Z2	1	1	Z	1	0	N/A	ABCD	0	0
P4	992	7,08	Z2	1	0	Z2	1	0	Z2	1	−1	Z1	1	−1	N/A	ABCD	0	2

Table 11.3 Number of occurrences of agreements for all analysts and per specific analyst

	Analyst A	Analyst B	Analyst C	Analyst D
4 agreements	26	26	26	26
3 agreements	1	2	2	1
2 agreements		1	1	
Rejected teeth	3	1	1	1

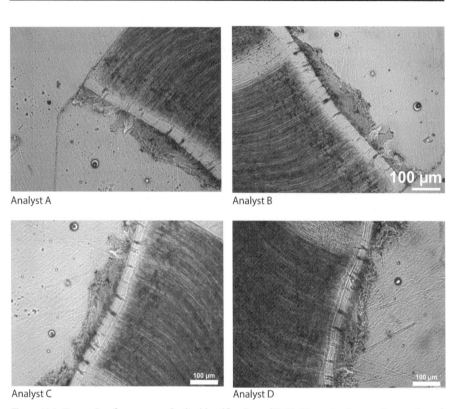

Figure 11.2 Example of agreement in the identification of ROI. Here, the four analysts selected the same portion of the thin section to make their analysis.

hyaline line, when it is a thin summer band (i.e., when teeth are in occlusion at the end of the root formation).

The count overestimations systematically occurred with the same thin sections. Based on the micrographs, it was possible to evaluate that in at least half of the cases, there was a microscope focus problem that led to a doubling optical effect due to the increment superposition throughout the thickness of the section (Naji, Gourichon, and Rendu 2015; Naji et al. 2014; Cool et al. 2002). This focus issue happened for the thin section 608B, where analysts C and D both overestimated by more than three years.

For 608A, two analysts selected the same ROI, which does not follow criteria 1 and 4 (presence of cellular cementum appositions) (Figure 11.4).

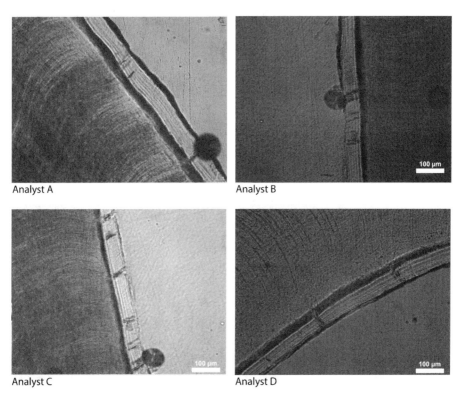

Figure 11.3 Example of disagreement in the identification of ROI. Here, three analysts selected the same portion of the thin section to analyze, while analyst D selected another region rejected by the others.

Moreover, analyst D frequently used low magnifications for some observations, contrary to the test requirements. Thus, the original criteria definition appears not to have been clear enough for inexperienced analysts, which led to misinterpretations and inaccurate observations.

Step 3: Identification of the Season of Death

Identifying the last increments for the season of death estimate is known to be a difficult task that directly depends on the observer's experience (Naji, Gourichon, and Rendu 2015; Lubinski and O'Brien 2001). Unsurprisingly, the season-of-death estimations was made in only 86 percent (98/114) of the selected ROI. However, this result masks a significant disparity because analysts A, B, and C proposed a season estimation for most of the ROIs selected (up to 100 percent for analyst B), whereas analyst D, probably less confident than the others, barely reaches 50 percent.

Annulus

Between the two seasonal appositions (growth/rest), the annulus (rest band) was misidentified more often, specifically by the two least experienced analysts

Table 11.4 Number of discrepancies between the observed and the expected numbers of increments per analyst

Difference between the Counting and the Expected Results	−2	−1	0	1	2	3	4	NA	Success rate
Analyst A		4	16	6		1		3	96 percent
Analyst B		2	16	10	1			1	97 percent
Analyst C	1	4	15	4	1	2		3	85 percent
Analyst D	1	5	4	8	4	3	1	4	65 percent

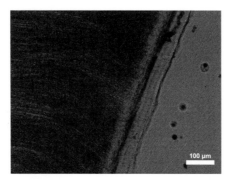 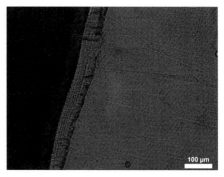

Analyst B   Analyst D

Figure 11.4 Thin section 608A. Analyst D selected an ROI with an extra apposition of cellular cementum, leading to an overestimation of the age at death. Analyst B, who selected an ROI by properly following the guidelines, obtained the right estimated age.

(Table 11.5). In two cases, analyst C identified a complete growth zone instead of an annulus for an animal that died in early December at the time of initiation of the annulus period (Pike-Tay 1995). Similarly, for sample 793 that died in the same period, three analysts identified the last increments as a first stage growth zone (Z1). In this case, the cementum cycle of this specific individual may be slightly in advance compared to the theoretical patterns. Indeed, minor variations exist within a population, and the transition from one phase of cementum deposit to the other can be spread over several weeks (for this specific population, see Pike-Tay 1995). This difference is a well-documented phenomenon in chronobiology in populations adapted to cold climates. This "synchronous chronotype" is characterized by significant rutting variations between individuals, with "front runners" targeting the prime females with the earliest estrus (Lincoln 2019).

Zone

The growth zones were accurately identified by the two experienced (A and B) analysts (error rate: A: 1/18 = 5.6 percent; B: 0 percent; Table 11.2 and Table 11.6). The two least experienced observers (C and D) had a significantly higher error rate (C: 7/19 = 36.8 percent; D: 4/10 = 40 percent; Tables 11.2 and 11.6) and even higher when

Table 11.5 Number of errors made by the analyst identifying the last increment (which is estimated for each tooth on the theoretical growth pattern established on the same collection by Pike-Tay 1995). NTO: Number of teeth observed. No estimation: Tooth for which no estimation was given.

	NTO	Analyst A	Analyst B	Analyst C	Analyst D
Annulus	11	3	1	5	3
Growth zone	19	1	0	7	4
No estimation		4	1	2	16

Table 11.6 Number of errors made by the analyst identifying the growth stage of the last increment when it was a growth zone (estimated for each tooth on the expected growth pattern identified on the same collection by Pike-Tay 1995). NTO: Number of teeth observed. No estimation: Teeth for which no estimation was given.

Growth Stage	NTO	Analyst A	Analyst B	Analyst C	Analyst D
Z1	7	1	1	5	4
Z2	6	0	0	6	2
Z3	6	1	0	5	2
No estimation		1	0	0	9

Table 11.7 Number of agreements and disagreements with the expected results of the nature and stage of growth of the last increments. Cases when a zone was correctly identified but without evaluation of its stage of growth are added in parentheses.

	Nb without Estimation	Nb Agreement	Nb Disagreement	Success Rate
Analyst A	3	22	5	**81 percent**
Analyst B	1	27	2	**93 percent**
Analyst C	2	7 (+4)	17	**23 percent**
Analyst D	16	3 (+1)	10	**21 percent**

considering the estimation of the growth stage (C: 11/19 = 58 percent; D: 7/10 = 70 percent).

However, we have to emphasize that one shared misinterpretation of a Z1 stage is related to tooth 441B, which all analysts interpreted as a Z3 stage. Because everyone agreed on the observation, we can hypothesize that we may be dealing with an individual deviating from the expected cementum deposition pattern.

The error rate in identifying the nature and stage of growth of the last increments is relatively high for the two least experimented analysts (C and D). As mentioned earlier, it appears that analyst D did not apply the protocol rigorously and made several observations using a low magnification (X100) instead of the recommended X400. This difference probably explains the high number of thin sections rejected or for which no estimation could be proposed (Table 11.7).

Similarly, analyst C tried to estimate the season of death systematically, even though in five cases, all the criteria were not met, and doubts about the estimation were expressed. For these cases, results were in disagreement with the expected pattern.

Because most of the analysts found the same ROIs, the choice of the ROIs does not seem to influence the agreement rate for this final step. The disagreements seem to be mostly about the winter increment (annulus), frequently not recognize by the least experienced analysts.

11.4 Discussion

Step 1, ROI: The criteria proposed for identifying optimal ROIs were based on the aggregated experiences of various specialists and relied on the proper identification of optical and histological structures. In most cases, the implementation of the six criteria allowed for the identification of the same ROIs (26/29 ≈ 90 percent success rate). This is a central point. First, this result attests to the reproducibility of the observations, even for analysts with limited experience. Second, because the selected region is strictly the same, the criteria allow for results comparison. In 10 percent of the cases, however, one observer made a decision different from the others. In these three cases, criteria 4 (same thickness of the increments) and 6 (equidistant cementum edges) were not followed. This deviation could indicate that these two criteria are less likely to be understood or simply implemented, while the observers easily integrate the other four.

Thus, by applying the criteria rigorously and following the protocol precisely, optimal ROI selection can be obtained systematically. Documentation including images of typical or problematic cases would support initial training for this fundamental step.

Step 2, age at death: The agreement rates for the age estimation, based on the number of growth zones observed, were very high for the most experienced (A and B) analysts with 96 percent and 97 percent, respectively. For the least experienced observers (C and D), the rates were significantly lower (85 percent and 65 percent, respectively). The difference in success is clearly due to experience, even when the optimal ROI is accurately selected at the previous step. Miscounting seemed to have been influenced mainly by microscope focal adjustments leading to blurred lines.

Step 3, season of death: As expected, identifying the nature and stage of growth of the last increment was more difficult. The two most experienced analysts obtained the correct success rate (>80 percent). Conversely, the two least trained analysts departed from the protocol and reached a poor agreement rate (<24 percent).

11.5 Conclusion

In conclusion, applying the criteria rigorously and following the protocol precisely solve the initial step of selecting an optimal ROI. Following that step, our interobserver test confirms previous reports (Lubinski and O'Brien 2001; Colard et al. 2015; Charles et al.

1986; Naji et al. 2016, and Chapter 23), emphasizing that accurately identifying and counting the cementum increments requires *proper training on a documented collection* before the analysis. However, as shown by the results obtained by the "beginner" and "intermediate" analysts, increment counting seems to be a relatively straightforward task to perform correctly and one in which improvements, in addition to training, can also be achieved by adjusting the microscopic focus and using image-processing software. Conversely, the identification and interpretation of the last cementum increment for estimating the season at death, which is critical information for zooarchaeology and other disciplines, probably remain the most challenging steps to control. This conclusion suggests that if the first parts of the cementochronology analytical procedure can be carried out by relatively inexperienced observers, extra precautions should be taken for the last step. Given the error rate observed with modern specimens, this caveat is even relevant when dealing with archaeological material with the additional taphonomic issues.

Acknowledgments

This research was carried out as part of CemeNTAA project – funded by the French National Agency for Research ANR (ANR-14-CE31-0011) and by the DeerPal project (ANR-18-CE03-0007).

References

Burke, A. 1993. "Applied Skeletochronology: The Horse as Human Prey during the Pleniglacial in Southwestern France." *Archaeological Papers of the American Anthropological Association* 4 (1): 145–50.
Charles, D. K., K. Condon, J. M. Cheverud, and J. E. Buikstra. 1986. "Cementum Annulation and Age Determination in *Homo Sapiens*. I. Tooth Variability and Observer Error." *American Journal of Physical Anthropology* 71: 311–20.
Colard, T., B. Bertrand, S. Naji, Y. Delannoy, and A. Bécart. 2015. "Toward the Adoption of Cementochronology in Forensic Context." *International Journal of Legal Medicine* 129: 1–8.
Cool, S. M., M. R. Forwood, P. Campbell, and M. B. Bennett. 2002. "Comparisons between Bone and Cementum Compositions and the Possible Basis for Their Layered Appearances." *Bone* 30 (2): 386–92.
Delagnes, A., and W. Rendu. 2011. "Shifts in Neandertal Mobility, Technology and Subsistence Strategies in Western France." *Journal of Archaeological Science* 38 (8): 1771–83.
Gordon, B. C. 1988. *Of Men and Reindeer Herds in French Magdalenian Prehistory*. BAR International Series 390. Oxford: BAR Publishing.
Gourichon, L. 2004. "Faune et Saisonnalité. L'Organisation Temporelle des Activités de Subsistance dans l'Epipaléolithique et le Néolithique Précéramique du Levant Nord (Syrie)." Ph.D. Dissertation. Lyon: Université Lumière-Lyon, 2.
Klevezal', G. A. 1996. *Recording Structures of Mammals: Determination of Age and Reconstruction of Life History*. Rotterdam: A. A. Balkema Series.

Lieberman, D. E., T. W. Deacon, and R. H. Meadow. 1990. "Computer Image Enhancement and Analysis of Cementum Increments as Applied to Teeth of *Gazella Gazella*." *Journal of Archaeological Science* 17: 519–33.

Lincoln, G. 2019. "A Brief History of Circannual Time." *Journal of Neuroendocrinology* 31 (3): e12694.

Lubinski, P. M., and C. J. O'Brien. 2001. "Observations on Seasonality and Mortality from a Recent Catastrophic Death Assemblage." *Journal of Archaeological Science* 28 (8): 833–42.

Matson, G., L. Van Daele, E. Goodwin, L. Aumiller, H. Reynolds, and H. Hristienko. 1993. *A Laboratory Manual for Cementum Age Determination of Alaska Brown Bear First Premolar Teeth*. Matson' Lab. Alaska Department of Fish and Game. Juneau: Division of Wildlife Conservation.

Miller, F. L. 1974. *Biology of the Kaminuriak Population of Barren-Ground Caribou, Part 2: Dentition as an Indicator of Age and Sex; Composition and Socialization of the Population*. Ottawa: Canadian Wildlife Service.

Naji, S. S., T. T. Colard, J. J. Blondiaux, B. B. Bertrand, E. E. d'Incau, and J-P. Bocquet-Appel. 2014. "Cementochronology, to Cut or Not to Cut?" *International Journal of Paleopathology*.

———. 2016. "Cementochronology, to Cut or Not to Cut?" *International Journal of Paleopathology* 15: 113–19.

Naji, S., L. Gourichon, and W. Rendu. 2015. "La Cémentochronologie." In *Messages d'Os. Archéométrie du Squelette Animal et Humain*. M. Balasse, J-P. Brugal, Y. Dauphin, E-M. Geigl, C. Oberlin, and I. Reiche (eds.). 217–40. Sciences Archéologiques. Edition des Archives Contemporaines.

Pike-Tay, A.. 1991. *Red Deer Hunting in the Upper Paleolithic of Southwest France: A Study in Seasonality*. British Archaeological Reports International Series S569. Oxford: Tempus Reparatum.

———. 1995. "Variability and Synchrony of Seasonal Indicators in Dental Cementum Microstructure of the Kaminuriak Caribou Population." *Archaeofauna* 4: 273–84.

Rendu, W. 2010. "Hunting Behavior and Neanderthal Adaptability in the Late Pleistocene Site of Pech-de-l'Aze I." *Journal of Archaeological Science* 37: 1789–1810.

Rendu, W. 2007. "Planification Des Activités de Subsistance Au Sein Du Territoire Des Derniers Moustériens. Cémentochronologie et Approche Archéozoologique de Gisements Du Paléolithique Moyen (Pech-de-l'Azé I, La Quina, Mauran) et Paléolithique Supérieur Ancien (Isturitz)." Bordeaux: Université de Bordeaux I.

Roksandic, M., D. Vlak, M. A. Schillaci, and D. Voicu. 2009. "Technical Note: Applicability of Tooth Cementum Annulation to an Archaeological Population." *American Journal of Physical Anthropology* 140 (3): 583–8.

Sánchez-Hernández, C., L. Gourichon, E. Pubert, W. Rendu, R. Montes, andF. Rivals. 2019. "Combined Dental Wear and Cementum Analyses in Ungulates Reveal the Seasonality of Neanderthal Occupations in Covalejos Cave (Northern Iberia)." *Scientific Reports* 9 (1): 14335.

Stutz, A. J. 2002. "Polarizing Microscopy Identification of Chemical Diagenesis in Archaeological Cementum." *Journal of Archaeological Science* 29 (11): 1327–47.

12 Tooth Cementum Annulations Method for Determining Age at Death Using Modern Deciduous Human Teeth: Challenges and Lessons Learned

Vicki L. Wedel†, Kenneth P. Hermsen, and Mathew J. Wedel

12.1 Introduction

Validating new methods is a hallmark of the scientific method. The tooth cementum annulation (TCA) method has been shown to provide reliable estimates of age at death in adult humans and other mammals (Naji et al. 2016; Chapter 1). Validating TCA for deciduous teeth could provide bioarchaeologists and forensic anthropologists with an independent estimate of age at death for teeth that may not be in occlusion or even in the alveolus. However, no published studies have determined whether TCAs in deciduous teeth reliably and accurately predict age at death in human subadults (but see Chapter 21). The original purpose of this chapter was to test age estimates derived from TCA and the London Atlas of Human Tooth Development and Eruption (AlQahtani et al. 2010, 2014) against known ages of extraction for a modern sample of deciduous teeth collected with consent from pediatric patients at Creighton University's School of Dentistry in Nebraska.

However, none of these samples is a perfect capture of cementum annulations in a deciduous tooth. Some are underground. Some are overground. Some exhibit rhizolysis where the cementum and dentil tubules are being resorbed. Some led us to record as cementum annulations alternating dark and light artifacts of light.

Nevertheless, this is the process of science: When a hypothesis is rejected, it is the researchers' responsibility to troubleshoot their work and reattempt the study. In this paper, the initial study results, which attempted to validate the use of tooth cementum annulations in deciduous teeth that had intact root apices, failed to statistically significantly correlate TCA with biological age at extraction, a proxy for age at death. With the help of an anonymous reviewer, we have identified the following issues: (1) inadequate magnification; (2) polarized light created light artifacts mistaken for cementum; (3) inadequate contrast (overexposure), among others. Due to the deadline constraints, we could not reevaluate our work entirely. Instead, we decided to publish various dental microstructures and light artifacts commonly mistaken for cementum deposits in deciduous teeth. Our goals are to discuss these sampling challenges and to provide guidelines, from sample preparation to microscopy, so that other researchers can avoid making the same errors.

12.2 Review of Literature

Using TCA to determine age at death in mammals is a long-practiced science in wildlife studies and zooarchaeology (Introduction, Chapter 1). More recently, bioarchaeological studies of human subadults have applied the method to anterior deciduous teeth (Chapter 21). However, the use of TCA to age human subadults has not been validated with modern teeth of known age at death or age at extraction. Several other established methods are much more frequently used to age subadult humans. These include dental eruption, crown development, and epiphyseal closure (AlQahtani et al. 2010, 2014; Cunningham et al. 2016).

Dental eruption charts have been in use since the 1940s (Schour and Massler 1941, 1944). Some previous TCA studies used the dental eruption chart developed by Ubelaker (1978). That chart was based on archaeological samples, which lacked definitive ages at death (as determined by demographic data or dental records). More recently, the London Atlas of Human Tooth Development and Eruption (AlQahtani et al. 2010, 2014) has provided a new standard of evidence for assessing human dental development. AlQahtani et al. (2010) provided a spectrum of morphological characters for assessing tooth development, including root formation, apex closure, and root resorption. Most important for this study is the scoring category "Ac" (apex closed with normal periodontal ligament width) (AlQahtani et al. 2010, modified from Moorrees et al. 1963a, b), the developmental stage corresponding to the samples described herein.

Although TCA is often applied in archaeological or forensic contexts (e.g., Wedel et al. 2013; Wedel and Westcott 2016, Chapters 17–23), constant validation of the method on diverse modern dental samples should continue. One major factor in conducting a validation study is the source of the samples (e.g., from dental clinics, historical archaeological sites with good data, or forensic cases).

12.3 Sampling Limitations

Cementochronologists face two unavoidable sampling problems when trying to understand the development and loss of dental cementum in deciduous teeth. First, readable cementum is not present for the entire life span of a deciduous tooth, and second, we have fewer opportunities to acquire nonpathological deciduous teeth than adult teeth.

The life span of a deciduous tooth can be grossly divided into three phases: (1) formation of the tooth and its root, (2) the period when the tooth is complete, with closed root apices, and (3) resorption of the root leading to eventual loss (Nanci 2018). Mineralized cementum starts to be laid down when a tooth erupts (Chapter 2), and the cementum record of a deciduous tooth starts to be destroyed when resorption of the root begins. Cementum from the cervical parts of the root may still be readable even as the root apices are being resorbed (to our knowledge, this possibility has been little explored), but normal root resorption sets an inexorable countdown for the very existence of cementum annulations. The best window of opportunity for a tooth to have readable cementum is during the middle period, between formation and resorption when

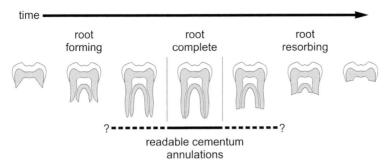

Figure 12.1 The development and loss of deciduous teeth restrict cementochronology to the interval in which the root apex is complete.

a tooth has complete roots (Figure 12.1). Unfortunately, this is the period when deciduous teeth from living populations are least likely to become available to investigators.

Teeth available for cementum increment analysis come from four sources: dental extractions, forensic cases, cemeteries, and other archaeological sources. Each of these sources poses a challenge in terms of sampling. Simply put, dentists do not typically extract healthy deciduous teeth. If deciduous teeth are surgically extracted, it is typically because their lack of root resorption and corresponding retention in the jaw were inhibiting the growth of the underlying permanent teeth. By definition, these retained deciduous teeth do not represent normal processes of tooth development and loss. Developing teeth are even less likely to be extracted than complete teeth, and teeth undergoing normal root resorption typically do not need to be extracted because they will soon fall out. So normal, healthy deciduous teeth are unlikely to be extracted, and extracted deciduous teeth are therefore unlikely to be normal.

The other source for teeth from extant populations is forensic cases, but such cases will probably never be a significant contributor to TCA's science in deciduous teeth for several reasons. First, the samples from forensic cases involving children and adolescents will always be small and uncontrollably random compared to dentists' samples. More importantly, issues of privacy and respect for grieving relatives of the decedents will understandably limit forensic material availability from children and adolescents.

Nonpathological deciduous teeth from extant populations fall into a perceptual blind spot for cementochronology researchers. Although hundreds of millions of children and adolescents worldwide have deciduous teeth, those teeth are generally unavailable for TCA analysis. The normally developing teeth are destined to lose their cementum records as their roots are resorbed, leaving primarily pathologically retained teeth as the primary source of complete teeth with known extraction dates.

12.4 Materials

Our study sample consisted of thirty-three deciduous teeth with intact root apices collected between March 2014 and June 2016 from twenty-seven children between the ages of four and fourteen who live in and around Omaha, Nebraska, in the American Midwest. Some children donated multiple teeth. The teeth were collected with informed consent and with the Institutional Review Board's oversight at the Creighton University School of Dentistry. The sample included maxillary and mandibular central and lateral incisors, canines, and first and second molars. Even though the results did not support our hypothesis, we are reporting the sampling results in case they are useful to other researchers considering a similar study in the future.

In total, six incisors, five canines, eight first molars, twelve second molars, and two indeterminate molars were available for the study (Table 12.1).

The age distribution of the children is listed in Table 12.2. Also, the patient's month of birth and month of extraction were recorded. Tooth fairy vouchers were given to the children who donated their teeth to this study.

Each donor was assigned a unique specimen number, prefaced with the letter H, in recognition of the Dr. George F. Haddix President's Faculty Research Grant, which funded this study. Multiple teeth from a single individual are distinguished with letters (e.g., H38A and H38B for the two teeth from donor H38). The deciduous teeth used in this study are just a subset of a larger, mixed collection that includes permanent teeth, so the H numbers of the teeth used in this study are not consecutive, and there are gaps in the numbering.

Table 12.1 Deciduous teeth used in this study

	Maxillary	Mandibular	Total
Central incisor	1	5	6
Canine	3	2	5
1st molar	3	5	8
2nd molar	5	7	12
Indeterminate molar	0	2	2
Total	12	21	33

Table 12.2 Ages at extraction for the donors and the teeth included in this study

Age in Years	Number of Individuals	Number of Teeth
4	1	1
5	2	3
6	6	7
7	6	6
8	2	6
9	1	1
10	3	3
11	2	2
12	1	1
13	1	1
14	2	2
Total	27	33

12.5 Methods

Each tooth was embedded in Sylmar© resin, a quick polymerization epoxy resin, sectioned at the middle third of the root, ground, and polished to 100 microns in thickness. The thin sections were examined using an Olympus BX41 microscope under polarized light at 100x magnification in the original analysis. TCAs were observed while the thin sections were under the microscope, and with polarization active; photomicrographs were taken using an Olympus DP71 digital camera.

Annulations were identified and counted starting at the dentin–cementum junction and continuing to the edge of mineralized tissues. In previous studies, each pair of annulations (light and dark) has been shown to correspond to one year of retention for each tooth (Wittwer-Backofen et al. 2004; Chapter 1, Table 1.1).

One age estimate was derived for each tooth. The number of pairs of annulations was added to the estimated age range at apex closure to derive the age estimate. According to the data presented in AlQahtani et al. (2010: table 4), the root apices close between the ages of two and four for incisors and molars and between ages three and four for canines (Table 12.3).

Consequently, we added two to four years to the number of pairs of annulations for incisors and molars and three to four years to the number of pairs of annulations for canines. We then scored whether the dental age (at extraction) fell within the estimated age range derived from TCA. Following the reviewer's comments, we reevaluated some of the samples under bright-field illumination at 200x magnification.

12.6 Results

Originally, we thought that alternating dark and light cementum annulations were visible on all of the teeth, though some annulations were more obvious and easily countable than others. The smallest number of annulations we initially identified in any of the sample teeth was three (nine teeth), and the largest number was eleven (two teeth).

Because all of what we thought were increments (light and dark) were counted, the TCA age estimate is the number of annulations divided by two to get an age since root

Table 12.3 Ages of root apex closure for deciduous teeth, based on data from AlQahtani et al. (2010). For each tooth, two ages are given: the earliest age of root apex closure (Ac) and the age at which all root apices were closed.

	Maxillary and Mandibular Teeth	
	Earliest Ac	All Ac
i^1	2–3 yrs	3–4 yrs
i^2	2–3 yrs	3–4 yr
c	3–4 yrs	3–4 yr
m^1	2–3 yrs	3–4 yr
m^2	2–3 yrs	3–4 yr

apex completion, plus the age ranges for root apex completion for each tooth type (see AlQahtani et al. 2010). For example, a molar with six cementum annulations represents three years of cementum deposition, plus two to four years for the age at root apex closure, when cementum deposition is inferred to have started so that it would have a TCA age estimate of five to seven years.

In the original analysis, the actual age at extraction fell within the resulting range of estimated ages for only nine of the thirty-three teeth in the sample (27 percent). For only one tooth, sample H35, did the predicted age range overestimate the actual age (actual age seven years, eleven months; predicted range 8.5–9.5 years). The predicted age range for the remaining twenty-three teeth underestimated the actual age by anywhere from three months to 108 months. For four of those twenty-three teeth, the predicted age range was off by only one season ([observed age – maximum predicted age] = 1–6 months), and for an additional three teeth, the predicted age range was off by two seasons ([observed age – maximum predicted age] = 7–12 months). For the final sixteen teeth, the difference between the actual age and the predicted age range was fifteen months or more.

Our initial results differed strongly by age at extraction. For teeth from 4- and 5-year-old donors, actual ages fell within the predicted range in all samples (four out of four, 100 percent). In 6-year-olds, actual ages fell within the predicted range in four out of seven samples (57 percent), and in 7-year-olds, in only one out of six samples (17 percent). For ages eight and above, the actual age always fell above the predicted age, in most cases by more than one year, and in the maximum (specimen H41), by nine years.

TCA's discordant results were the first clue that our method, developed for permanent teeth, did not produce comparable results on deciduous teeth. Furthermore, when we reanalyzed the samples under bright-field illumination and at 200x magnification (versus polarized at 100x initially), we identified several confounding factors leading to these miscounts. These factors are discussed next.

12.7 Discussion

After the draft's review, we revisited the samples to document the different sources of error, some of which were compounded in a single tooth: lack of familiarity with deciduous teeth, using polarized light versus bright-field illumination, using insufficient magnification, examining mixed ROIs with both CIFC and AEFC tissues, cloudy cementum, and insufficient ROIs per tooth (Figures 12.2–12.5). Each of these sources of error is expanded on here:

- An overarching problem is that we had not previously analyzed deciduous teeth, and we assumed that transposing a method validated on adult teeth (e.g., Naji et al. 2016; Wedel 2007) would work as effectively on deciduous teeth. The relative thinness of the AEFC in deciduous teeth threw us off, and in some cases, roots that had looked complete at a gross level were, in fact, compromised by rhizolysis.

- Insufficient magnification: One pervasive issue is that in our original data collection, we used 100x magnification, which was insufficient to resolve all the AEFC annulations.
- Polarized versus bright-field illumination: The combination of polarized light and low magnification created very high contrast in several samples, which obscured some of the annulations (Figure 12.2 and Figure 12.5). In some samples, the more alarming problem was that polarization created concentric light artifacts around the edge of the root, which we initially mistook for cementum annulations (Figure 12.2 and Figure 12.5). In one case, H19, there were no cementum annulations to count because the cementum had been entirely destroyed by rhizolysis (Figure 12.4).
- Mixed ROI with CIFC and AEFC: Another confounding factor following from the low magnification was that many of our ROIs included both CIFC and AEFC

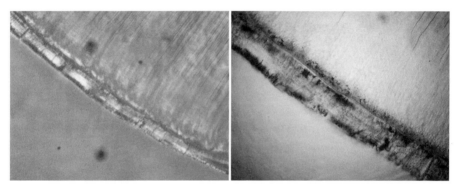

Figure 12.2 Photomicrograph of H16 under polarized light at 100x magnification (left) and in bright-field illumination at 200x magnification (right). The very high contrast caused by polarized light is obscuring at least some annulations, which can be seen on the right. (A black and white version of this figure will appear in some formats. For the color version, please refer to the plate section.)

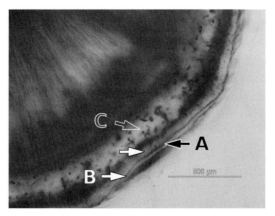

Figure 12.3 Photomicrograph of H7 under polarized light, showing an area of mixed cementum at low magnification (100x). Annulations are visible in the AEFC (A, B), but CIFC is also visible (C). Higher magnification and bright-field illumination might reveal more annulations.

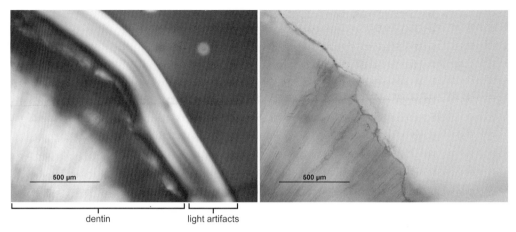

Figure 12.4 Photomicrographs of H19 in polarized light (left) and the same ROI in bright-field illumination (right). The light and dark bands visible around the edge of the tooth in the left image are not cementum annulations, as we originally thought. They are artifacts of polarization. This specimen was undergoing rhizolysis, and the cementum layers had already been resorbed, leaving only dentin. (A black and white version of this figure will appear in some formats. For the color version, please refer to the plate section.)

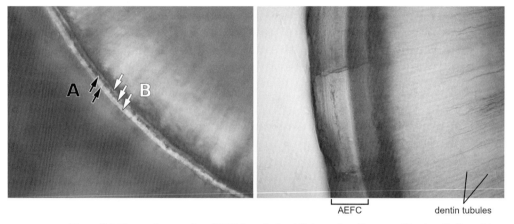

Figure 12.5 Photomicrographs of H39 in polarized light and at 40x magnification (left) and in bright-field illumination at 200x (right). The left image shows high contrast and low magnification that make identification of the cementum annulations (A, B) and the edge of mineralized tissues extremely difficult. The image on the right shows that many more annulations are present in the AEFC, even though the total count cannot be determined from this image. (A black and white version of this figure will appear in some formats. For the color version, please refer to the plate section.)

(Figure 12.3). In some cases, visualizing the CIFC under polarized light created opaque areas that obscured the annulations in the AEFC.
- Cloudy cementum: In several cases, the AEFC annulations appeared cloudy and were difficult to read. Some of these specimens were possibly cut at an oblique angle to the root's axis rather than orthogonally. Nonorthogonal cuts can make cementum

annulations more challenging to read because adjacent annulations can be stacked in the field of view (see Chapter 6, Figure 6.10).
- Not enough ROIs per tooth: Given these challenges, it is perhaps unsurprising that we had difficulty finding regions of each tooth where the cementum annulations could be read. In the original analysis, we only used one ROI per tooth. Multiple ROIs would have helped us avoid some of our errors.

These errors should serve as a warning that even experienced observers can be misled when the experiment's settings are changed, such as analyzing a different age group or a different species. Consequently, we have identified four main variables essential for a proper protocol: (1) Make sure that samples are cut and ground orthogonally to the tooth root; (2) use high magnification (200x–400x); (3) use bright-field illumination, and (4) use multiple ROIs, which show proper AEFC exclusively. This checklist should help to guide researchers attempting cementochronology on deciduous teeth.

12.8 Directions for Future Research

1. To limit the variability within the validation sample, this study only included teeth in which the root apices were closed from donors of ages four to fourteen. However, because root apices of most deciduous teeth start to close as early as the age of two, TCA might help determine age at death (or age at extraction) in even younger children. Further validation studies applying TCA to teeth in which the root apex has not yet closed have the potential to broaden the applicability of the method.
2. The appearance of cementum annulations during root resorption is understudied, but it could yield additional insights.
3. All of the teeth in this study came from a source population in the American Midwest and children and adolescents treated by dentists in a single city (Omaha, Nebraska). Further validation of the method using samples from populations at varying latitudes, under varying seasonal regimes, and varying levels of access to nutrition and care would help test the universality of TCA study findings.

12.9 Conclusion

One parameter biological anthropologists often want to estimate from subadult remains is the age of the individual. Epiphyseal appearance, epiphyseal union, and dental development help provide these answers when the correct elements are present, but when they are not, additional methods are needed. To that end, this study's original goal was to validate the use of the TCA method in deciduous teeth. To ensure we were reliably transposing the adult method (Naji et al. 2016) to subadult teeth, we collected only teeth in which the root apex was closed so that we could identify the middle third of the root. This variable limited our sample size to thirty-three teeth collected from a dental school's pediatric clinic over more than two calendar years. We failed to correlate the estimated ages at extraction with the actual chronological age of each child because of the methodological errors identified earlier.

We, therefore, turned our attention to reevaluating our results with the help of the review comments. This chapter's value lies in the results and process transparency, mostly with microscopy, although possibly with sample preparation, which illustrates how we initially evaluated the thin section and how we now view it. Our original hypothesis that TCA does significantly correlate with age at extraction in deciduous teeth from modern dental settings thus remains and will be tested and reported on in a future experiment. By showing how much difference magnification and bright-field light can make in assessing the number of increments in deciduous teeth, and more importantly, by depicting rhizolysis in cementochronology, our understanding of TCA studies moves forward. We hope that more work with an expanded sample size and age range will help clarify the relationship between cementum annulations and age in deciduous teeth.

Acknowledgments

We are grateful for the George F. Haddix President's Research Award and the patients of the Creighton University School of Dentistry clinic, who made this study possible. We thank Britnee Campos and David Rosette for laboratory support. We are especially grateful to an anonymous reviewer for constructively helping us to identify the sources of error in our original analysis.

References

AlQahtani, S. J., M. P. Hector, and H. M. Liversidge. 2010. Brief communication: The London Atlas of Human Tooth Development and Eruption. *American Journal of Physical Anthropology*, 142: 481–90.

2014. Accuracy of dental age estimation charts: Schour and Massler, Ubelaker, and the London Atlas. *American Journal of Physical Anthropology*, 154(1): 70–8.

Cunningham, C., L. Scheuer, and S. M. Black. 2016. *Developmental Juvenile Osteology*, 2nd ed. Amsterdam: Elsevier/AP.

Moorrees, C. F., E. A. Fanning, and E. E. Hunt, Jr. 1963a. Age variation of formation stages for ten permanent teeth. *Journal of Dental Research*, 42: 490–502.

1963b. Formation and resorption of three deciduous teeth in children. *American Journal of Physical Anthropology*, 21: 205–13.

Nanci, A. 2018. *Ten Cate's Oral Histology: Development, Structure, and Function*, 9th ed. St. Louis, MO: Mosby.

Naji S., T. Colard, J. Blondiaux, B. Bertrand, E. d'Incau, and J.-P. Bocquet-Appel. 2016. Cementochronology, to cut or not to cut? *International Journal of Paleopathology*, 15: 113–19.

Schour I., and M. Massler. 1941. The development of the human dentition. *Journal of the American Dental Association*, 28(7): 1153–60.

1944 *The Development of Human Dentition*, 2nd ed. Chicago: American Dental Association.

Ubelaker, D. H. 1978. *Human Skeletal Remains: Excavation, Analysis, Interpretation*. Aldine Manuals on Archeology. Chicago: Aldine Publishing Company.

Wedel, V. L. 2007. Determination of season at death using dental cementum increment analysis. *Journal of Forensic Sciences*, 52(**6**): 1334–7.

Wedel, V. L., G. Found, and G. L. Nusse. 2013. A 37-year-old cold case identification using novel and collaborative methods. *Journal of Forensic Identification*, 63(1): 5–21.

Wedel, V. L., and D. Wescott. 2016. Using dental cementum increment analysis to determine age and season at death in African Americans from a historical cemetery in Missouri. *International Journal of Paleopathology*, 15: 134–39.

Wittwer-Backofen, U., J. Gampe, and J. W. Haupfel. 2004. Tooth cementum annulation for age estimation: Results from a large known-age validation study. *American Journal of Physical Anthropology*, 123(2): 121–9.

13 The Analysis of Tooth Cementum for the Histological Determination of Age and Season at Death on Teeth of US Active Duty Military Members

Nicholas Wilson and Katrin Koel-Abt

13.1 Introduction

The aim of this project was to support the United States (US) government's Prisoner of War/Missing in Action (POW/MIA) recovery missions and to aid in the identification of US service members who did not come back home from past wars in which the United States was involved and who were declared MIA. When a US service member volunteers for the military, he or she understands that they may be required to give the ultimate sacrifice, meaning giving their life. Until this day, the US government claims that it is the government's responsibility to make sure that, if a service member has to give their life, their remains will be properly identified and returned to their family members. There are still nearly 83,000 Americans missing from past conflicts today.

In the field of forensic science, many disciplines work together to solve these cases and reach a positive identification of the service member. Unfortunately, no current technique is the magic bullet for identifications, and it takes the combination of various methods to build a profile of an individual that allows investigators to make positive identifications. Such a profile includes age and sex determination, stature estimation, trauma analysis, and an assessment of health status of the deceased. Two groups that frequently collaborate to reach this goal are forensic odontologists and anthropologists.

The developing technique of cementochronology has been gaining interest over recent years due to its potential to provide both an accurate age and season at time of death of an individual (Naji and Koel-Abt, 2017; Chapter 1). This technique is based on counting tooth cementum annulations, which is similar to the aging of trees by counting annual growth rings (Chapter 1). Throughout life, cementum is continuously deposited on the roots of our teeth in two major histological forms: Cellular cementum is formed in a faster process that leads to highly variable annulations, while acellular cementum is laid down slower and more steadily and therefore has well-defined rings (Chapter 2). The annulations are seen to occur in a light and dark pattern under light-microscopic view. The set of one light and one dark ring has been well correlated to

The views expressed in this chapter are those of the author(s) and do not reflect the official policy or position of the Department of the Army, Department of Defense, or the US Government.

represent one year of an individual's life (Stott et al., 1982; Condon et al., 1986; Charles et al., 1986; Wedel, 2007; Naji et al 2016) after tooth eruption. When applied to the teeth of humans, this had led multiple research groups to accurately determine the true chronological age of an individual to within two or three years with a high degree of certainty (Chapter 1, Table 1.1). In mammals, the light and dark cementum lines have also been correlated to specific seasons (Introduction and Chapter 1). Under transmitted light microscopy, the light bands are seen to represent spring/summer, while the dark bands are of fall/winter (Lieberman, 1994). The exact mechanism for this phenomenon is not fully understood yet (see the Introduction for current hypotheses).

Currently, the only published journal article to find a seasonality factor in cementum annulations of humans is Wedel 2007. In this study, Wedel stated that she could accurately determine the season in 99 percent of samples.

The purpose of this pilot study is to determine the utility of tooth cementum annulation analysis to assist in the identification of unaccounted-for US service members from past conflicts. It is our interest to improve upon previous techniques and to establish a reproducible method to be included into the standard operating procedures of forensic laboratories, such as the Defense POW/MIA Accounting Agency (DPAA), to help determine the age and season at time of death. Our hypothesis is that tooth cementum annulations can be used to accurately determine both the chronological age and season of death and thus has tremendous potential across many jurisdictions of forensic sciences, as well as in bioarchaeology or paleoanthropology (Chapter 24).

This project was conducted in collaboration with the US Army and DPAA in order to support their mission of "Providing the fullest possible accounting for our missing personnel to their families and the nation."

13.2 Materials and Methods

To determine if a relationship exists between cementum and the age and season at time of death a total of fifty-eight teeth from forty US service members were collected for analysis. These service members were all stationed in Hawaii at time of tooth extraction. The extracted teeth were previously treatment planned[1] for extraction due to dental diseases or for orthodontic care.

The age and season at time of tooth extraction here are equivalent to the age and season at time of death because, in both cases, cementum deposit is stopped. The exact age of patient, month and day of extraction, sex, tooth number, and reason for the extraction were recorded.

Once extracted, the teeth were rinsed with sterile saline and stored in 10 percent formalin until processing. The following steps were utilized for processing the samples (see Chapter 1 for a comparable protocol):

---

[1] Previously treatment planned: Teeth utilized in this study were from individuals who required the teeth to be removed due to dental disease or for a specific treatment plan. The teeth were not removed solely for the sake of this research project.

1. Teeth were cleaned, photographed, and embedded in a mixed solution of epoxy resin and hardener. Once the tooth was embedded, the middle third of the root was identified for proper sampling of acellular cementum.
2. Three transverse sections with a thickness of 100 μm in the middle third of the root were made using a linear precision saw (IsoMet™ 5000 Precision Saw).
4. Specimens were mounted on microscope slides using a mixed solution of epoxy resin and hardener.

Optimal areas of each root section were photographed under normal light and with a polarization filter at 200x using a microscope coupled with a digital camera. Each photo was processed with Adobe Photoshop® to enhance image quality and analyzed by two independent observers.

5. The estimated season at time of death was evaluated by correlating the color of the outermost band to spring/summer or fall/winter.
6. Age assessment was completed by counting all dark bands and adding the total to the average age range of eruption for the individual tooth.

13.3　Results

The utility of tooth cementum annulations (TCA) was evaluated through the full evaluation of fifty teeth. Table 13.1 describes the characteristics of the teeth analyzed and the age distribution of the patients. Eight teeth could not be fully evaluated (Table 13.1). The images of the root sections of these teeth exhibited "errors" so that cementum annulations could not be evaluated. Errors included cutting debris masking the annulations, samples containing mainly cellular cementum, and specimens that were too thin and fragile, leading to sample fracturing during processing. The distribution by sex is heavily skewed toward males. Finally, with 94 percent of the samples coming from (mainly male) US service members between the ages of twenty to thirty-nine, his distribution accurately represents the population of interest in the recovery mission of the DPAA.

Table 13.2 describes the teeth distribution by type. It is important to note that more than half of all samples were premolars. Unlike the other teeth that were extracted, the

Table 13.1 Right panel: number of sampled teeth used in this study and distribution by sex; Left panel: age distribution of sample

Total teeth processed	58	Age distribution	Total
Teeth fully evaluated	50	20–29	34
Number of individuals	40	30–39	13
Male	34	40–49	2
Female	6	50–59	1

Table 13.2 Tooth type distribution of evaluated teeth

	Maxillary	Mandibulary
Central incisor	2	1
Lateral incisor	7	2
Canine	1	0
1st premolar	9	14
2nd premolar	1	1
1st molar	2	6
2nd molar	1	3

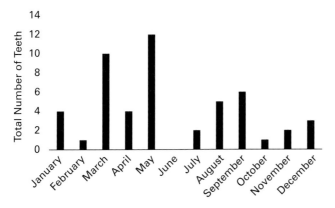

Figure 13.1 Distribution of teeth by month of extraction

premolars had been removed for orthodontic treatment and had no disease or pathologic conditions associated with them.

The number of teeth analyzed for each month of a calendar year is accounted for in Figure 13.1. The difference in the number of teeth collected for each month was simply due to the number of people who required treatment.

When separated into seasons, 58 percent of the teeth were from spring/summer, defined as April 15–October 14. For these teeth, the last band of cementum was expected to be dark (opaque). The remaining 42 percent of teeth were extracted from a period ranging from October 15–April 14 and defined as fall/winter. The last band was expected to be light (translucent).

The remaining graphs characterize the data collected from the analyzed teeth. In Figure 13.2A, one can see the accuracy of TCA for determining the true chronological age at time of tooth extraction. During the study, all samples were coded, so the observers had no knowledge of age of patient or month of tooth extraction for each specimen. The samples were also analyzed independently by each observer. The accuracy of age estimation of ±2 years of 76 percent for observer 1 and 62 percent for observer 2 is of high interest for application to future forensic identifications.

When expanding out to ±4 years as seen in Figure 13.2B, one must note the 86 percent and 84 percent accuracy of age estimation for observer 1 and observer 2,

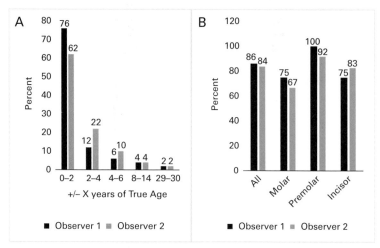

Figure 13.2 A: Observer accuracy of true chronological age estimation; B: Percent estimated within ±4 years of true chronological age per observer

respectively. It is also of interest to see that, within this data set, samples from premolars that had no history of disease had the highest accuracy of any tooth type.

The evaluation of season at time of death from TCA is a more difficult and sensitive technique. It can be difficult to clearly determine the border between cementum and periodontal ligament, meaning to distinguish where the cementum ends and where the periodontal ligament begins. The extension of Sharpey's Fibers into cementum can further confound analysis.

Figure 13.3A shows that the fall/winter season was correctly identified 20 percent higher than the spring/summer time frame. The overall correct season identification of 72/76 percent differs significantly from the 99 percent season accuracy found in Wedel, 2007.

This study is the first of its kind to be published, demonstrating an interobserver agreement of 78 percent for a correct season identification. This agreement was further analyzed by establishing a Cohen's Kappa Coefficient. The calculated value of 0.68 shows a significant interobserver agreement. Even though there was an overall correct season identification of 72/76 percent, the p-value was 0.057.

As seen in Figure 13.3B the individual tooth type did not have much of a factor in determining season; however, the premolars with no previous disease had the highest accuracy.

13.4 Discussion

Protocol: The processing of samples has a rather high initial technique sensitivity and must be accounted for (see Chapters 11 and 24 for a discussion). Different variants of TCA are currently being evaluated to determine a common standard, including the thickness of specimen, area of root to be analyzed, type of image enhancement through software

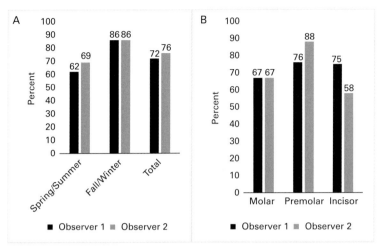

Figure 13.3 A: Correct season identified per observer; B: Correct season identified per tooth type and observer

programs, counting lines in images versus counting lines under real-time live view, and so forth. The two comparable standardized protocols introduced by Wittwer-Backofen (2012) and Colard and colleagues (2015) are trending to be the leading techniques; however, what once was thought to be minor differences in lab equipment between research groups may be leading to larger than anticipated discrepancies in collected data (Chapters 9 and 10). For example, there are many variances in types of precision saws, blade rotation speed, and feed rate. These seemingly simple parameters are proving to be vital in reliably producing cementum sections of 100 μm thickness that are smooth and free of defects. Samples that are 20 μm thicker (120 μm) were seen to display a doubling effect of cementum annulations due to depth of field complications within the microscope

Age-at-death: The hypothesis that tooth cementum annulations can be used to determine the chronological age of an individual accurately is supported in this study. The accuracy of our samples within ±0–4 years of chronological age (84–86 percent) is similar to results from other research groups (Wittwer-Backofen et al., 2004; Kagerer and Grupe, 2001). This accuracy is better than many other aging techniques, such as ±7–9 years with the pubic symphysis and ±15–20 years in cranial suture closure (Buikstra and Ubelaker, 1994; Brooks et al., 1990; Lovejoy et al., 1985). With an increased accuracy and precision to chronological age, TCA could provide investigators with very helpful information in narrowing down a pool of unidentified remains in forensic anthropology.

Season at time of death: In relation to season at time of death, the accuracy of tooth cementum annulations is partially supported in this study. A significant interobserver agreement was seen with Cohen's Kappa Coefficient of 0.68. This demonstrates the two independent observers were consistently identifying the same annulation as the last visible line before the periodontal ligament. Despite agreement, the p-value of 0.057 suggests the technique is not as accurate in identifying the true season at time of death for this study. One key factor in the accuracy discrepancy could be artifacts within the micrographs discussed earlier. The interface between the epoxy resin and the cementum has been noted to create an optically visible white line. By using transmitted polarized light and through real-time analysis under the microscope, this interface can be more successfully accounted for (Chapter 11). The observer can adjust the depth of focus of the microscope to bypass the image artifacts. Real-time analysis might not be as beneficial for overall age analysis because image enhancement within several software programs allows for much better contrast between light and dark bands.

With a collection of teeth from individuals with a known dental history, it is important to note that dental disease can affect the visibility of cementum annulations, at least within certain areas of the sample (Chapters 3 and 5). Other research groups have noted conflicting views on this topic (de Broucker et al. 2016). In this study, both observers identified one tooth incorrectly of being twenty-nine to thirty years older than the chronological age. This tooth had a history of localized severe chronic periodontitis with 90 percent bone loss at time of extraction. A further review of the patient's dental records would be required to assess the reason for the discrepancy between estimated and true age of the patient at time of tooth extraction; however, it was noted that the patient had a history of bone loss extending to the apical 1/3 of the root for more than a decade and already had multiple different dental therapies completed. The combination of long-standing bone loss and dental treatment could have led to alterations in the integrity of the cementum and the rate of cementum deposition.

13.5 Conclusion

With the continued refinement of tooth cementum annulation analysis, this method could be of value for forensic identification laboratories and more broadly in biological anthropology. Age estimation via TCA is already a well-developed technique and is a simpler method for a novice examiner than the assessment of season at time of death. Age estimation through TCA gives a more precise and accurate value to the chronological age of an individual than many other currently utilized forensic methods. Season at time of death estimation requires more validation studies and is an advanced method that is very sensitive to both processing and microscopic errors but would have significant value once a protocol is fully validated. Future research studies will focus on larger sampling sizes and more observers to help assess the technique on a broader spectrum.

13.6 Acknowledgments

A special thank you is extended to the clinicians of Schofield Barracks and Tripler Army Medical Center for helping collect all the extracted teeth. An endless amount of gratitude is also given to DPAA for forging this new collaborative research partnership, and to anyone at DPAA who contributed to this research in one way or another, especially to Tina Lopez-Schmidt for assisting with data collection. This project was funded through an ORISE postdoctoral fellowship while one of the authors was affiliated with DPAA as an ORISE postdoctoral fellow. This project was a research collaboration between the Hawaii Army 2-Year Advanced Education in General Dentistry Residency and DPAA.

References

Brooks, S., and J. M. Suchey. 1990. Skeletal age determination based on the os pubis: A comparison of the Acsádi-Nemeskéri and Suchey-Brooks methods. *Human Evolution* 5: 227–38.

Broucker A. de, T. Colard, G. Penel, J. Blondiaux, and S. Naji. 2016. The impact of periodontal disease on cementochronology age estimation. *International Journal of Paleopathology*.

Buikstra, J. E., and D. H. Ubelaker. 1994. Standards for data collection from human skeletal remains. *Research Series (44)*. Fayetteville, AR: Arkansas Archaeological Survey.

Charles, D. K., K. Condon, J. M. Cheverud, and J. E. Buikstra. 1986. Cementum annulation and age determination in *Homo sapiens*. I. Tooth variability and observer error. *American Journal of Physical Anthropology* 71: 311–20.

Colard, T., B. Bertrand, S. Naji, Y. Delannoy, and A. Becart. 2015. Toward the adoption of cementochronology in forensic context. *International Journal of Legal Medicine* 129: 1–8.

Condon, K., D. K. Charles, J. M. Cheverud, and J. E. Buikstra. 1986. Cementum annulation and age determination in *Homo sapiens* II. Estimates and accuracy. *American Journal of Physical Anthropology* 71: 321–30.

Kagerer, P., and G. Grupe. 2001. Age-at-death diagnosis and determination of life-history parameters by incremental lines in human dental cementum as an identification aid. *Forensic Science International* 118: 75–82.

Lieberman, D. E. 1994. The biological basis for seasonal increments in dental cementum and their application to archaeological research. *Journal of Archaeological Science* 21: 525–39.

Lovejoy, C. O., R. S. Meindl, R. P. Mensforth, and T. J. Barton. 1985. Multifactorial determination of skeletal age at death: A method and blind tests of its accuracy. *American Journal of Physical Anthropology* 68: 1–14.

Naji, S., and K. Koel-Abt. 2017. Cementochronology – The still underestimated old "new" method for age-at-death assessment. *Journal of Forensic Sciences & Criminal Investigation* 3(5): 1–5.

Naji, S., T. Colard, J. Blondiaux, B. Bertrand, E. d'Incau, and J.-P. Bocquet-Appel. 2016. Cementochronology, to cut or not to cut? *International Journal of Paleopathology* 15: 113–19.

Stott, G. G., R. F. Sis, and B. M. Levy. 1982. Cemental annulation as an age criterion in forensic dentistry. *Journal of Dental Research* 61: 814–17.

Wedel, V. L. 2007. Determination of season at death using dental cementum increment analysis. *Journal of Forensic Science* 52(6): 1334–37.

Wittwer-Backofen, U. 2012. Age estimation using tooth cementum annulation. 2012. In *Forensic Microscopy for Skeletal Tissues*, ed., L. S. Bell. Totowa, NJ:Humana Press, 129–43.

Wittwer-Backofen, U., J. Gampe, and J. W. Vaupel. 2004. Tooth cementum annulation for age estimation: results from a large known-age validation study. *American Journal of Physical Anthropology* 123: 119–29.

14 Preliminary Protocol to Identify Parturitions Lines in Acellular Cementum

Thomas Colard, Stephan Naji, Amélie Debroucker, Sofiann El Ayoubi, and Guillaume Falgayrac

14.1 Introduction

Dental tissues have the remarkable property of recording their development history as histological growth markers (e.g., Boyde, 1963, 1990; Dean, 1987, 2000; Reid and Dean, 2006). Most notably, numerous studies have shown that "stresses" of various kinds can alter the formation of dentin and enamel incremental layers, such as Retzius lines in the latter, with an enlarged and darker appearance in transmitted light microscopy (Dean, 2000). These modifications, if significant enough, can even be observed on the enamel surface by modifying the shape of the perikimata, the extremity of these Retzius striae, producing linear enamel hypoplasias LEH (e.g., Guatelli-Steinberg et al., 2004). Recent studies on animal have shown that many "stresses" such as infectious diseases or nutritional deficiencies, but also life-history events such as birth (neonatal line) or weaning, are capable of generating these lines (e.g., Schwartz et al., 2006; Dean et al., 2018; Skinner and Byra, 2019; Ristova et al., 2018).

In this regard, enamel and dentin offer a retrospective view of significant events occurring in growth but are limited in time to the end of the permanent dentition growth and development. Recent progress in the histological analysis of cementum in biological anthropology (Introduction) offers new perspectives for the analysis of "stresses" or life-history events throughout life (Lieberman, 1993; Dean et al., 2018; Chapters 7 and 8). Like other dental tissues, AEFC has an incremental growth, with an annual apposition of a light and a dark band when observed by transmitted light optical microscopy (Chapters 1, 2 and 6). Reasonably, we can thus hypothesize that certain events that may disrupt the cementum deposit will leave a chemical signal in the mineralized matrix, as it occurs in enamel and dentin and in bones (Introduction).

Recent publications have tried to explore this topic with mixed outcomes. Although some authors are testing ad hoc experiments (Cerrito et al., 2020), others (Mani-Caplazi et al., 2019) are adopting a more rigorous methodological approach based on extensive experience in producing and counting acellular extrinsic fibers cementum (AEFC) increments lines. In this study, we concur with the latter, and we test whether a pregnancy is a biological event that leaves a visible optical change in transmitted light microscopy as well as a chemical signal in the incremental layers of AEFC, using light microscopy, Raman spectrometry, and scanning electron microscopy equipped with an EDS probe.

14.2 Materials and Methods

Experimental Design

We adopted the following methodological steps:

1. Collection of modern teeth from women whose number and timing of pregnancies were known.
2. Analysis of AEFC thin sections by transmitted light optical microscopy (TLM) to identify potential regions of interest (ROI).
3. Analysis via Image J of the AEFC ROI grayscale profile to identify automatically outstanding layers, sometimes referred to as "broad, translucent annulations" (BTA) (Kagerer and Grupe, 2001; Blondiaux et al., 2006). We will refer to such lines as "broad annulation" (BA) to remain descriptive in TLM, which is our preferred method of analysis in cementochronology, and neutral regarding the increment's actual physical properties.
4. Linear analysis of the acellular cement in ESEM-EDS to characterize changes in the BA's elements mass or proportion.
5. Mapping analysis of the same ROI in Raman spectrometry to characterize molecular composition differences between regular AEFC and BA increments.

Sample Collection

Two human teeth were used for this preliminary study. Teeth were extracted from two distinct patients in the oral surgery department of Lille University Hospital. The patients gave informed written consent to participate, and the study was approved by an institutional review board (DC-2008–642, French Ministry of Education and Research, DGRI/05). The initial treatment included the extraction of one or several teeth.

The first tooth was a right mandibular second premolar (#45), extracted from a 66-year-old woman with a single pregnancy documented at 27. The second tooth was a right mandibular first molar (#46), extracted from a 42-year-old woman with two pregnancies documented at 28 and 37.

Samples Histological Preparation

Teeth were cleaned, dried with acetone, embedded in an epoxy resin (Araldite 20/20), and sectioned following the ISO-9001 protocol for human cementochronology (Colard et al., 2015; Buikstra, 2022) to produce two sequential 100 μm nondecalcified transverse sections. Histological observations of AEFC BA were identified in TLM with a Nikon Eclipse 50i microscope at 200X and 400X magnifications. Regions of interest showing contrasted AEFC lines and potential BAs were selected and recorded with a Nikon DS Fi1 fitted on the microscope. Finally, ROIs were optimized for contrasts using FIJI software (Schindelin et al., 2012).

Grayscale Profile Analysis by Fiji

Grayscale scaled micrographs of the selected ROIs were analyzed to identify AEFC light/dark layers using the Fiji software's "PlotProfil" option (Schindelin et al., 2012).

This tool displays a two-dimensional graph of pixel intensity along a one-pixel-wide line within the image. For rectangular selections, the plot displays a "column average plot," where the x-axis represents the horizontal distance through the selection and the y-axis the vertically averaged pixel intensity. Consequently, peaks and troughs on the profile plot were recorded and counted automatically with the "FindPeak" tool from the "BAR" package (Ferreira 2015).

To identify outstanding bands, the average distance and intensity of all peaks were used to define how many standard deviations from the average were necessary to filter out regular variations. Even though this method is sensitive to optical artifacts on a micrograph, it allows for objective identification of outstanding increments necessary to proceed to the composition analysis.

Raman Spectroscopy and Imaging Analysis

Raman microspectrometry allows the analysis of the molecular composition of calcified biological samples. The microspectrometer used was a LabRAM HR800 (HORIBA, Jobin-Yvon, France), equipped with a laser HeNe (λ = 633 nm) and air-cooled CDD (1024 × 256 pixels). The laser beam was focused perpendicularly to the sample surface by an ×100 objective (NA = 0.90, Olympus, France). The spot size was about one μm. Spectral acquisitions were made in the 300–1700 cm^{-1} range. The sample was mounted on an XYZ motorized stage, which allows micrometric displacements. The spectrometer uses a high-precision Piezo translator and feedback signal to automatically track and adjust the laser focus on the sample, ensuring a perfect focus for each measurement. A Raman peak intensity is sensitive to the compositional variation and orientation of the active group within the sample (Colard et al., 2015). A scrambler was used to eliminate variations in intensity related to molecules' orientation during the Pt-Img analysis. Therefore, the intensity variations were related only to the compositional variations within the active group. Two acquisition modes were available: the conventional mode, which allows the user to aim at a specific location manually and get one single spectrum, and the point-by-point imaging mode, in which an area was delimited on the surface sample by the user. Then, the laser beam was stepped automatically in two dimensions (x and y), with a spectrum being recorded at each position (x, y) within the delimited area. For this study, Raman images were done with a step size of 1 μm.

The physicochemical parameters (PCP) were evaluated from each Raman spectrum. The PCP allows us to assess semiquantitatively the modifications of the molecular composition. Three parameters were evaluated: the mineral/organic ratio, the type-B carbonate content, and crystallinity. These three band reports have been validated on bone and acellular cementum (Falgayrac et al., 2010, Colard et al., 2015).

- The mineral/organic ratio, which corresponded to the intensity ratio between the v1 PO_4^{3-} (960 cm^{-1}) to the δ (CH_2) collagen molecules (1450 cm^{-1}), peaks. The mineral/organic ratio reflected the amount of mineral per amount of organic matrix.
- The type-B carbonate substitution corresponded to the intensity ratio between B-type CO_3^{2-} and the v1 PO_4^{3-} (1070 cm^{-1}) peak (960 cm^{-1}). The type-B carbonate substitution reflected the amount of B-type CO_3^{2-} per amount of mineral.
- The crystallinity corresponded to the inverse of the full width of PO_4^{3-} (960 cm^{-1}) and reflected the mineral crystal size and perfection. This parameter is increased during mineralization from initial amorphous calcium phosphate phases to well-ordered apatite forms.

Environmental Scanning Electron Microscopy

Before analysis, samples were carbon-coated under vacuum evaporation. An environmental scanning Electron Microscopy (Quanta 200 FEI) coupled with an Energy Dispersive X-rays analysis detector (EDS, QuanTax Bruker) were used. The electron beam's accelerating voltage was adjusted to 20 kV, and the working distance at 10 mm. A ×400 nominal magnification corresponding to a pixel resolution of 1 µm/pixel was used.

14.3 Results

Sample 1

The first sample was a second right mandibular premolar. The age of the subject was 66 years, the age of the only pregnancy was 27 years, followed by breastfeeding. The age of alveolar emergence was estimated at 11 years following AlQahtani et al.'s (2010) chart. The number of expected pairs of AEFC increments in TLM is thus 55 for the age at extraction and 16 for the age at pregnancy.

Light Microscopy Analysis
For this sample, the AEFC width was measured from the CDJ to the surface and was estimated at 170 microns. The number of pairs of light and dark increments counted by two observers from the granular layer of Tomes to the outermost band following the cementum deposition direction was 53 (+/− 1.8), giving a "cementochronology" estimated age at extraction of 64 years (age of eruption plus the number of pairs of increments) (Figure 14.1A).

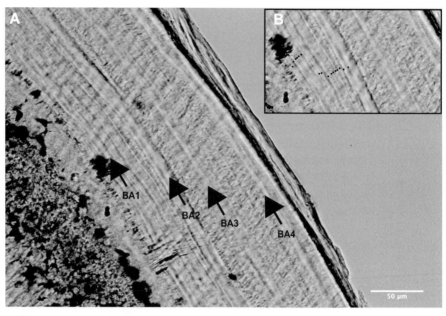
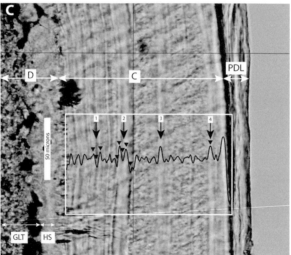

Figure 14.1 A: Sample 1 transmitted light microscopy showing four accentuated incremental layers BA1 to BA4; B: AEFC counts from the cemento-dentin junction to BA2, the documented pregnancy, showing the 16 dark increments; C: Sample 1. Plot profile of gray values in the cementum region (C). Arrows represent outstanding oscillations greater than 1.5 standard deviations. D: dentin; PDL: periodontal ligament border; GLT: granular layer of Tomes; HS: Hopewell-Smith line. The white box is the area used to generate the profile with the PlotProfile option.

Table 14.1 Sample 1. Selected outstanding peaks and troughs (BAs 1-4); distance X1 & X2 (in microns) of maxima (Y1) and minima (Y2) gray values in cementum

	Maxima		Minima	
	X1	Y1	X2	Y2
AL1	23.627	146.9765	26.54	123.3137
	29.129	150.6745		
AL2			43.37	123.9686
	45.636	161.0471	48.225	134.8588
	50.814	155.6235	54.698	113.9882
AL3	79.943	160.3569	107.778	131.0471
AL4	122.666	161.3294	128.816	134.9922

Optical tracking of the accentuated lines was performed, looking for a difference in width or color compared to the other incremental layers. The two observers found a very wide accentuated line corresponding to the 16th pair of rings, named BA2, and perfectly corresponding to the pregnancy's documented age. Three other smaller accentuated lines were identified, corresponding to the 4th, 30st, and 50th annulations (Figure 14.1B).

Grayscale Profile Analysis by Fiji

The optical choice of the broad annulations on the micrograph is relatively subjective and very dependent on the observer in the absence of a precise definition. Therefore, we used the image's grayscale profile variations to identify the BAs more objectively. A 140X80 microns box was used to count peaks and troughs (Figure 14.1C) automatically. Thirty maxima and minima were identified. The last peak on the left represented the mineralization front and was not selected. To automatically filter out regular peaks, we set the minimum value for the peak's gray value at 1.5 standard deviations (SD) because, at 2SDs, no peaks were selected. Four regions comprising successive peaks and valleys were selected (Figure 14.1A and C: numbers 1–4; Table 14.1), corresponding to BA1-4.

ESEM Analysis

ESEM analysis shows four bright wide bands with BSE analysis corresponding to BA1 to BA4. These bands appear much clearer and correspond to a denser area, which returns more electrons to the detector (Figure 14.2A: left). Figure 14.2A (right) shows wider peaks of calcium that also match BAs 1-4.

Raman Imaging

The selection of the ROI analyzed in Raman spectrometry is done by reflection microscopy. The image is much more challenging to read because the incremental pattern is not visible, and it is necessary to use landmarks (like cementum surface defects) to select the ROI located by transmitted light microscopy. Nevertheless, in Figure 14.1, we note the presence of a large bright band visible at 80 microns from the cementum surface. This band corresponds perfectly to the wide BA2 (16 pairs of

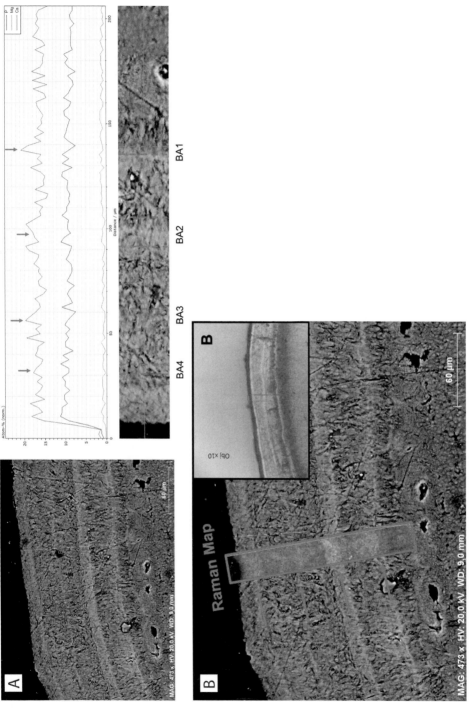

Figure 14.2 A: SEM analysis, Left/BSE image showing four wide, bright bands (red arrows), corresponding to BA1 to BA4, Right/P, Mg, and ca linear analysis by SEM-EDS; B: Raman image (inside the red box) superimposed on the BSE image, showing the distribution of the mineral–organic ratio. The intensity of the color is a function of the value. Black pixels correspond to a value of zero. White pixels correspond to the value of 22. The increase of mineral–organic ratio corresponds to the 4 BTA. B-insert: reflection microscopy to select the proper Roi. (A black and white version of this figure will appear in some formats. For the color version, please refer to the plate section.)

incremental layers) also recorded at 80 microns from the cementum surface on the light transmitted image.

The physicochemical analysis of the ROI (red box in Figure 14.2B) shows an increase in the mineral–organic ratio between 80 and 95 microns, which corresponds to the wide BA2 observed under transmitted light microscopy and thus to the estimated period of pregnancy. We note that the three other small BAs observed in transmitted light caused less intense physicochemical changes in our spectrometric analysis.

Sample 2

The second sample was a right mandibular first molar. The age of the subject was 43 years, the patient reported two pregnancies at the ages of 28 and 37, and the age of alveolar emergence was estimated at 6 years following AlQahtani et al.'s (2010) chart. The number of expected pairs of AEFC increments is thus 37 for the age at extraction and 22 and 31 for the two pregnancies.

Light Microscopy Analysis
For this sample, the acellular cementum width was measured from the CDJ to the cementum surface at 130 microns. The number of increments recorded (two experimenters) was 36 pairs of bright and dark layers, giving a "cementochronology" estimated age of 42.

Optical tracking of the accentuated lines was performed, looking for a difference in width or color compared to the other incremental layers. The two observers found three wide, broad annulations corresponding to the 7th, 21st, and 32nd pairs of rings, named BA1 to BA3. BA2 and BA3 corresponded to the documented age of the pregnancies perfectly (Figure 14.3A).

Grayscale Profile Analysis by Image J
A 140X80 microns box was used to count peaks and troughs (Figure 14.3B) automatically. Thirty maxima and minima were identified. To filter out outstanding peaks, we set the minimum value for the peaks' gray values at 3 SDs, because at four SDs, no peaks were selected. Three significant regions comprising a succession of peaks and valleys were identified (Figure 14.3B, numbers 1–3; Table 14.2).

ESEM Analysis
ESEM analysis shows three bright wide bands with BSE analysis, corresponding to BA1 to BA3. These bands appear much clearer and correspond to a denser area, which returns more electrons to the detector (Figure 14.4A, left). Figure 14.4A (right) shows wider calcium peaks that match BA2 and BA3 and correspond to the recorded pregnancies.

Raman Imaging
The selection of the ROI analyzed in Raman spectrometry is done by reflection microscopy. The physicochemical analysis of the ROI (Figure 14.4B, red box) shows an increase in the organo–mineral ratio between 60 and 70 microns, which

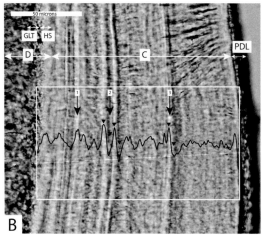

Figure 14.3 A: Sample 2 transmitted light microscopy showing three accentuated incremental layers BA1 to BA3. BA2 (21st pair of rings) and BA3 (32nd pair of rings) both correspond to the two documented pregnancies as indicated by the dots; B: Plot profile of gray values in the cementum region (C) of sample 2. Arrows represent outstanding oscillations greater than 3 standard deviations. D: dentin; PDL: periodontal ligament border; GLT: granular layer of Tomes; HS: Hopewell-Smith line.

corresponds to the BA observed in transmitted light at the level of the 21st ring pair (and thus to the estimated period of the first pregnancy). A second zone with an

Table 14.2 Distance X1 & X2 (in microns) of automatically selected maximum (Y1) and minimum (Y2) gray values in cementum

3SD	Maxima		Minima	
	X1	Y1	X2	Y2
AL1	28.869	178.6877	36.2593	130.8739
AL2	47.114	189.3266	50.5783	117.9771
	54.735	181.8567	57.5069	103.0516
AL3	92.611	181.8252	96.3067	115.6562

increase in the organo–mineral ratio between 100 and 115 microns is noted, which corresponds to the BA of ring pair 32 (i.e., the second pregnancy). The third one, smaller, is located near the cementum surface.

14.4 Discussion and Conclusion

About the Methodology

The central part of our approach is the capacity to demonstrate that we can identify hypothesized "stress lines" objectively in a micrograph and link them to documented events that theoretically should result in such a visible physiological change. Observing broad annulations can then be used as a starting hypothesis to test a large sample blindly to assess this proposed method's precision and accuracy. Such observations are possible because about a decade of works on cementochronology (e.g., Colard et al., 2016; Naji et al., 2016, 2016; Wittwer-Backofen, 2012; Mani-Caplazi et al., 2019), synthesized in various parts of this volume, has provided the necessary histology protocols and contextual, theoretical understanding of AEFC circannual growth, to move forward toward more interpretative hypotheses such as proposed in this chapter. We also need to work with rigorous and standardized tools such as those published by Mani-Caplazi and colleagues (2019) and contrary to more hazardous ones (Cerrito et al., 2020). Therefore, automatic counting and identification of outstanding AEFC peaks and troughs in a cementum micrograph are central to our approach. We decided to use the open-source software Fiji and its associated gray value intensity peaks counting tools to ensure the most extensive use possible.

Chemical Signal of Pregnancies

Our results showed a perfect concordance between documented pregnancy events and BA identified either in the form of a wide broad light annulation or, sometimes, in the form of two or more increments. In both samples, the Raman microspectrometry and ESEM-EDS analyses of the BA identified optically revealed *an increase in the BA's mineral/organic ratio*. In other words, the amount of mineral (carbonated hydroxyapatite) is higher in the BA when compared to the adjacent AEFC increments.

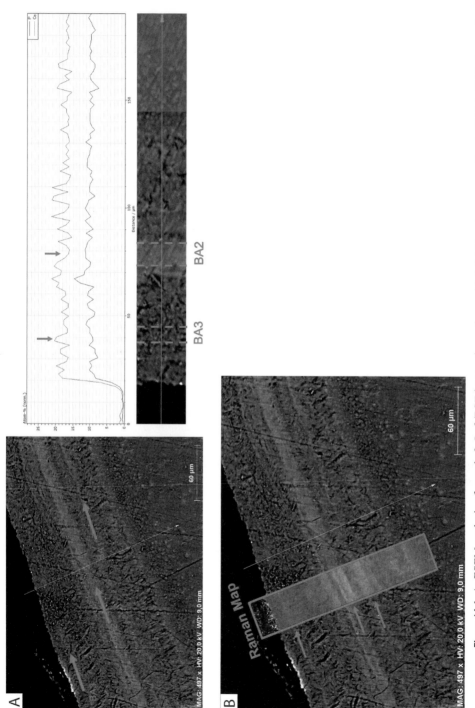

Figure 14.4 A: ESEM analysis of sample 2. Left/BSE image shows three wide bright bands corresponding to BA1 to BA3 observed under transmitted light microscopy. Right/Linear analysis shows 19 peaks of Ca, with wide ones at peak 11 and peak 16, corresponding to BA2 and BA3, the two pregnancies; B: Raman image (inside the red box) superimposed on the BSE image shows the distribution of the mineral–organic ratio. The intensity of the color is a function of the value. Black pixels correspond to a value of zero. White pixels correspond to the value of 22. The increase of mineral–organic ratio corresponds to the 3 BTA. (A black and white version of this figure will appear in some formats. For the color version, please refer to the plate section.)

Carbonated hydroxyapatite is the major component of the mineral in the cementum. More than 99 percent of calcium (Ca) and about 85 percent of phosphorus (P) are found in the hydroxyapatite crystals that form the calcified tissues (Courbebaisse and Souberbielle, 2011). Calcium homeostasis is significantly altered during pregnancy and lactation. The mother adapts differently during these two periods, while calcium demands are similar (Kovacs, 2005). During pregnancy, the proportion of calcium transferred to the fetus corresponds to 2 to 3 percent of the mother's total calcium (Salari and Abdollahi, 2014) and may represent up to 300 to 350 mg of calcium transferred per day. Lactation is another mechanism that modifies calcium metabolism. A newborn requires, on average, 200 mg of calcium per day in milk for the first 6 months and 120 mg of calcium in milk for the next 6 months (Kovacs, 2016, 2017; Surarit et al., 2016). The fact that the cementum is affected by pregnancies and lactation is an exciting hypothesis that will require further testing.

Our preliminary work showed that other significant variations are observed during cementum deposition in addition to documented pregnancies. This is not surprising because any physiological response, such as life-history event or external insults, is a trade-off that would require the organism to divert mineralization resources from growth and that should be visible in cementum (Chapter 8). One of these major physiological transitions is the onset of puberty. In our two samples, we have identified BAs at 13 and 14 years old. These estimates correspond to the variation that includes the onset of sexual hormones and the cascading consequences such as the adolescent growth spurt. Reliably testing the hypothesis of cementum growth variations in this framework is currently underway in an upcoming large-scale experiment.

On the Physical Nature of Broad Annulations

Our work shows that BAs are identified as large rings, ranging from light gray to white in TLM (hence the name "BTA," proposed by Kagerer and Grupe, 2001). Intuitively, several authors have assumed that these bright increments must be "less mineralized" because they seem to allow more light to pass through (translucent). Several authors favor this interpretation (e.g., Cool, 2002; Klevezal', 1996) based on the observed tissue's optical properties alone.

The nature of these bands has never been explored explicitly, however. In a previous polarization Raman spectrometry study (Colard et al., 2016), we have proposed that dark AEFC increments (from dark gray to black in TLM) had better-organized collagen fibers than lighter AEFC increments and were "more mineralized." In contrast, three recent articles matched dark AEFC increments to *minima of mineral* (calcium, phosphorous, zinc) *and apatite crystals intensities*, using synchrotron x-ray fluorescence mapping in ungulates, primates, and human samples (Dean et al., 2018; Stock et al., 2017; Chapter 6). Finally, in this chapter, new results of ESEM and Raman imaging of wide bright AEFC increments identified in TLM, and corresponding to known pregnancies, suggest *a higher mineral* content when compared to adjacent cementum deposits.

These potentially paradoxical results need to be tested within a broader hypothesis of periodical growth and metabolic trade-offs. One hypothesis predicts that a rapid growth period during the "good" season (i.e., spring/summer) mobilizes a large quantity of minerals and will produce a *wide hypomineralized* translucent band. The logic here is that the rapid growth rate allows for a large collage matrix to be laid out, but because the mineralization rate is constant, the mineral density (number of cAP crystals on the collagen matrix) is low. In TLM, light can thus go through cementum in greater quantity, resulting in a translucent band. Conversely, the "rest" period (fall/winter) of slow growth and metabolic rates will produce a *thin hypermineralized* opaque increment (Introduction) because of the reverse process of higher mineral density (same number of cAp crystals, but more limited space).

This contrasts with another hypothesis that predicts that during good seasons, the mineralization rate increases along with intense bouts of organic matrix growth. The mineral organization, however, is less organized because of the rapid growth rate. Light can thus pass through, resulting in a translucent rendering in TLM. Conversely, during the rest season, the mineral crystals are more organized but scarcer and more densely packed, creating an opaque band with lower mineral intensities.

Finally, for our specific purpose of physiological variations, another trade-off (Chapter 8) predicts that stressors will deplete the growth pathway in favor of the immune or regeneration systems, creating translucent *hypomineralized* bands (BTA). However, a pregnancy is a period where the mother's mineral production is significantly increased to the fetus' benefit, but not necessarily to the detriment of the mother, who is supposed to be adapted to such events.

However, the microstructure of calcified tissues is complex. Under polarized light microscopy, cortical bone is birefringent (alternation of light and dark lines) (Giraud-Guille, 1988; Giraud-Guille et al., 2003). In bone, the birefringence is due to the orientation of mineralized collagen fibers. Cementum shows a similar pattern. The orientation of mineralized collagen fibers may also explain the birefringence observed in TLM. The question of the fibers' orientation is thus again raised and requires a further analysis that goes beyond the current possibilities of Raman spectrometry.

14.5 Conclusion

This work on two documented samples with one and two live pregnancies demonstrated that accentuated AEFC increments could be identified and precisely attributed to the pregnancies with relatively simple tools. In both samples, these AEFC variations were the most outstanding optically and chemically. This is notable because such a method's ultimate purpose is to identify fertility events in archaeological samples blindly. In this context, it will be necessary to discriminate between pregnancies and other "stressors" and improve the micrograph BA detection sensibility and specificity.

Acknowledgments

We would like to thank Philippe Recourt for his precious help with ESEM analysis.

References

Alqahtani, S. J., M. P. Hector, and H. M. Liversidge. 2010. Brief communication: The London atlas of human tooth development and eruption. *American Journal of Physical Anthropology* 142(3): 481–90.

Boyde, A., 1963. Estimation of age at death from young human skeletal remains from incremental lines in dental enamel. Third International Meeting in Forensic Immunology, Medicine, Pathology and Toxicology, London, 36–46.

Buikstra, J. (2022). A brief history of cemental annuli research, with emphasis upon anthropological applications. In S. Naji, L. Gourichon, & W. Rendu, eds., *Cementum in Anthropology: Back to the Root*. Cambridge: Cambridge University Press, ch. 1.

Cool, S. M., M. R. Forwood, P. Campbell, and M. B. Bennett. 2002. Comparisons between bone and cementum compositions and the possible basis for their layered appearances. *Bone* 30 (2): 386–92.

Blondiaux, J., A. Alduc-Le Bagousse, C. Niel, et al. 2006. Relevance of cement annulations to paleopathology. *Paleopathology Newsletter* 135: 4–15.

Cerrito, P., S. E. Bailey, B. Hu, et al. 2020. Parturitions, menopause and other physiological stressors are recorded in dental cementum microstructure. *Scientific Reports* 10(1): 1–10.

Colard, T., B. Bertrand, S. Naji, Y. Delannoy, and A. Bécart. 2015. Toward the adoption of cementochronology in forensic context. *International Journal of Legal Medicine* 129: 1–8.

Colard, T., G. Falgayrac, B. Bertrand, et al. 2016. New insights on the composition and the structure of the acellular extrinsic fiber cementum by Raman Analysis. *PLoS ONE* 11(12): e0167316.

Courbebaisse, M., and J. C. Souberbielle. 2011. Phosphocalcic metabolism: Regulation and explorations. *Nephrologie & Therapeutique* 7(2): 118–38.

Dean, M. C. 1987. Growth layers and incremental markings in hard tissues: A review of the literature and some preliminary observations about enamel structure in *Paranthropus boisei*. *Journal of Human Evolution* 16: 157–72.

Dean, M. C. 2000. Incremental markings in enamel and dentine: What they can tell us about the way teeth grow. *Development, Function and Evolution of Teeth*, 119–30.

Dean, M. C., A. Le Cabec, K. Spiers, Y. Zhang, and J. Garrevoet. 2018. Incremental distribution of strontium and zinc in great ape and fossil hominin cementum using synchrotron X-ray fluorescence mapping. *Journal of the Royal Society Interface* 15: 20170626.

Falgayrac, G., et al. 2010. New method for Raman investigation of the orientation of collagen fibrils and crystallites in the Haversian system of bone. *Applied Spectroscopy* 64(7): 775–80.

Ferreira, T., M. Kota, C. Bitdeli, and J. Eglinger. 2015. Scripts: BAR 1.1.6 (Version 1.1.6). Zenodo. http://doi.org/10.5281/zenodo.28838

Giraud-Guille, M. M. 1988. Twisted plywood architecture of collagen fibrils in human compact bone osteons. *Calcified Tissue International* 42(3): 167–80.

Giraud-Guille, M. M., L. Besseau, and R. Martin. 2003. Liquid crystalline assemblies of collagen in bone and in vitro systems. *Journal of Biomechanics* 36(10): 1571–9.

Guatelli-Steinberg, D., C. S. Larsen, and D. L. Hutchsinson. 2004. Prevalence and the duration of linear enamel hypoplasia: a comparative study of Neandertals and Inuit foragers. *Journal of Human Evolution* 47(1–2): 65–84.

Kagerer, P., and G. Grupe. 2001. Age-at-death diagnosis and determination of life-history parameters by incremental lines in human dental cementum as an identification aid. *Forensic Science International* 118, 75–82.

Klevezal', G. A. 1996. *Recording Structures of Mammals: Determination of Age and Reconstruction of Life History*. Rotterdam: A. A. Balkema Series.

Kovacs, C. S. 2005. Calcium and bone metabolism during pregnancy and lactation. *Journal of Mammary Gland Biology and Neoplasia* 10(2): 105–18.

——— 2016. Maternal mineral and bone metabolism during pregnancy, lactation, and post-weaning recovery. *Physiological Reviews* 96(2): 449–547.

——— 2017. The skeleton is a storehouse of mineral that is plundered during lactation and (fully?) replenished afterwards. *Journal of Bone and Mineral Research* 32(4): 676–80.

Lieberman, D. E. 1993. Life history variables preserved in dental cementum microstructure. *Science* 261(5125): 1162–64.

Mani-Caplazi, G., G. Hotz, U. Wittwer-Backofen, and W. Vach. 2019. Measuring incremental line width and appearance in the tooth cementum of recent and archaeological human teeth to identify irregularities: First insights using a standardized protocol. *International Journal of Paleopathology* 27: 24–37.

Naji, S., et al. 2016. Cementochronology, to cut or not to cut? *International Journal of Paleopathology* 15: 113–19.

Reid, D. J. and M. C. Dean. 2006. Variation in modern human enamel formation times. *Journal of Human Evolution* 50(3): 329–46.

Ristova, M., M. Talevska, and Z. Stojanovska. 2018. Accurate age estimations from dental cementum and a childbirth indicator – A pilot study. *Journal of Forensic Science & Criminology* 6: 1–12.

Salari, P., and M. Abdollahi. 2014. The influence of pregnancy and lactation on maternal bone health: A systematic review. *Journal of Family & Reproductive Health* 8(4): 135.

Schindelin, J., I. Arganda-Carreras, E. Frise, et al. 2012. Fiji: An open-source platform for biological-image analysis. *Nature Methods* 9(7): 676–82.

Schwartz, G. T., D. J. Reid, M. C. Dean, and A. L. Zihlman. 2006. A faithful record of stressful life events recorded in the dental developmental record of a juvenile gorilla. *International Journal of Primatology* 27: 1201–19.

Skinner, M., and C. Byra. 2019. Signatures of stress: Pilot study of accentuated laminations in porcine enamel. *American Journal of Physical Anthropology* 169(4): 619–31.

Stock, S. R., et al. 2017. Cementum structure in beluga whale teeth. *Acta Biomaterialia* 48: 289–99.

Surarit, R., N. Krishnamra, and D. Seriwatanachai. 2016. Prolactin receptor and osteogenic induction of prolactin in human periodontal ligament fibroblasts. *Cell Biology International* 40(4): 419–27.

Wittwer-Backofen, U. 2012. Age estimation using tooth cementum annulation. In *Forensic Microscopy for Skeletal Tissues*. L. S. Bell (ed.). Totowa, NJ: Humana Press, 129–43.

15 Toward the Nondestructive Imaging of Cementum Annulations Using Synchrotron X-Ray Microtomography

Adeline Le Cabec, Nancy K. Tang, Valentin Ruano Rubio, and Simon Hillson

In modern humans, counts of tooth cementum annulations (TCA) have been widely used to estimate adult age at death using classical histology (Chapter 1). This destructive technique requires physically thin sectioning the teeth, which may not be an option for valuable fossil and subfossil specimens (e.g., Le Cabec and Toussaint 2017). So far, only two techniques have attempted to image *nondestructively* TCA: OCT (optical coherence tomography) and terahertz imaging (Leiss-Holzinger et al. 2015). Although both provide 2D and 3D data, OCT has a limited spatial resolution (axial resolution at best of 1.7 µm by 4.4 µm) and a penetration depth of at most 3 mm (Leiss-Holzinger et al. 2015). Terahertz imaging has the advantages of using non-ionizing radiations, providing chemical and structural information about the sample, and allowing a larger penetration depth (up to 1 cm). However, data acquisition time is very long (e.g., seventeen hours for a bear tooth), and the resolution obtained is insufficient for visualizing yearly TCA.

For more than a decade, propagation phase-contrast synchrotron X-ray microtomography (PPC-SR-µCT) at the European Synchrotron Radiation Facility (ESRF, Grenoble, France) has paved the way for *nondestructive* visualization of dental microstructures that remain otherwise invisible to conventional X-ray absorption-based µCT (Tafforeau et al. 2006; Zabler et al. 2006; Tafforeau and Smith 2008). PPC-SR-µCT has successfully been employed on the developing dentition of fossil juveniles to determine their age at death and to study the evolution of primate dental development, including several species of *Australopithecus*, early *Homo*, Neanderthals, and the stem catarrhine *Anapithecus hernyaki* (Smith et al. 2007, 2010; Tafforeau and Smith 2008; Le Cabec, Dean, and Begun 2017; Smith et al. 2015). This mainly relies on the visualization of enamel and dentine growth increments, particularly those deposited during discrete stress events, in 2D and 3D images (e.g., Le Cabec, Tang, and Tafforeau 2015; Le Cabec, Dean, and Begun 2017).

Here we extend PPC-SR-µCT to the nondestructive visualization of TCAs in known-age archeological modern human teeth for adult age at death estimation (Chapter 16). Further technical and analytical details employed are available in Le Cabec et al. (2019).

15.1 Sample and Data Production

Twenty known-age permanent canines (archeological assemblage, St. Luke's Church, London, England; Boyle, Boston, and Witkin 2005) were scanned at isotropic voxel sizes of 0.615 µm, on the beamline BM05 at the ESRF. The experiment took place from November 16 to November 19, 2013. The beamtime available within consecutive days was a major constraint that limited the number of teeth we could scan. We scanned transverse segments of acellular cementum (AEFC) in regions of interest (ROI) chosen using a standardized protocol for location in the apical region of the middle third of the buccal aspect of the root (see Le Cabec et al. 2019, for details about data acquisition and reconstruction).

Since the PPC-SR-µCT reconstruction uses single distance phase retrieval (Paganin et al. 2002), reconstructions are sensitive to fine modulations in material density. This process requires the user to define the ratio between the values of "δ" and "β," which relate to the decrement of the complex X-ray refractive index and absorption coefficient of the sample, respectively (Paganin et al. 2002; Weitkamp et al. 2011, 2013). These values are specific to each material within the sample that is assumed to be quasi-homogeneous, which explains the large and saturated white band at the root's surface (Figure 15.1). This is a phase-contrast fringe, which was not retrieved during the reconstruction because the δ/β value chosen was not adapted to account for the very different material properties existing between air and dental tissues. Finally, this means that the fine dark and light pattern observed in the produced images are fine variations in density in the cementum and not fringes of phase contrast.

The scans are made available for free at http://paleo.esrf.fr/picture.php?/2810/category/2197. The main result regarding adult age at death lies in a positive, significant linear correlation of estimated age to chronological age ($r = 0.76$, $p < 0.001$; see Le Cabec et al. 2019 for details). We show that, for TCA visualization, virtual histology proves to be advantageous in several aspects. This mainly involves its nondestructive nature and the greater degree of freedom for choosing slice orientation and thickness. This allows optimization of visualization of the structures of interest and makes it possible to avoid areas of taphonomic/diagenetic damage to the dental tissues.

15.2 Methodological Advantages for Using Virtual Histology to Identify TCA

Locally TCAs can be considered as 3D planes, parallel between each other, but also to the cementum-dentin junction (CDJ) and the root surface. The precise alignment of the whole volume along the incremental lines (Figure 15.1) is critical to locally improve TCA visibility while reducing the contribution of the rest of the structures to the image (see details in Le Cabec et al. 2019): (1) The center of rotation of the volume is set in an area where the TCAs are best visible. (2) By fine rotation in the three planes of space, the volume is orientated so that the CDJ, TCA, and root surface appear horizontal in the transverse axis (in virtual 2D sections) and roughly vertical in the sagittal axis.

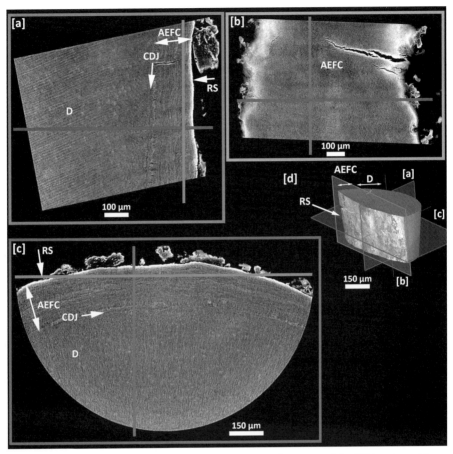

Figure 15.1 Protocol for aligning a PPC-SR-µCT reconstruction to reveal the TCA, using a 15 µm thick slab. Fine-tuning of the orientation by minute rotation and translation in the sagittal (a), frontal (b), and transverse (c) planes optimizes the visibility of TCA in 3D space (d). D: dentin, CDJ: cemento-dentin junction, AEFC: acellular extrinsic fiber cementum, RS: root surface. (78-year-old man; based on data from Le Cabec et al. 2019)

Thus, the frontal plane should be parallel to the root surface and the TCA (Figure 15.1). (3) Several contiguous µCT slices (each being 0.615 µm thick) may be overlaid to generate a slab of various thicknesses to optimize the visibility of the structures of interest (15 µm in our study; see extensive examples in Figure 15.2). Thus, the cementum microstructure will appear blurry around the defined ROI. Virtual transverse sections were saved from the properly aligned scans in VGStudio Max 2.2.3 (Volume Graphics GmbH, Heidelberg, Germany).

Notably, these virtual sections also allow greater freedom in choosing the plane of section, section thickness, and image enhancement compared to histological methods, all of which increase flexibility in examining TCAs. Regarding slice thickness, several contiguous µCT slices (each being 0.615 µm thick) may be overlaid (Figure 15.2) to reach a slab thickness of 4 to 15 µm as used in Le

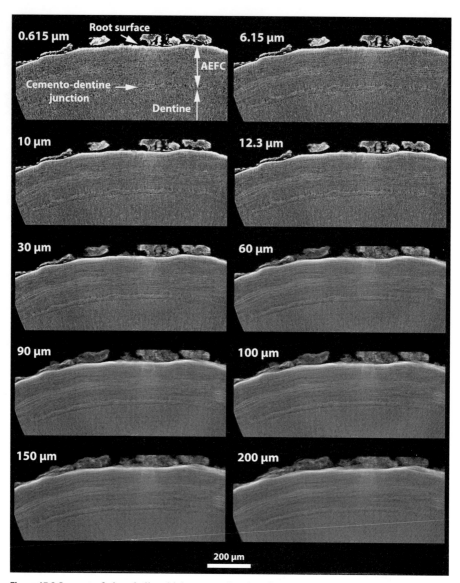

Figure 15.2 Impact of virtual slice thickness on the visualization of TCA in PPC-SR-μCT data. The thickness values are indicated above the images: 0.615 μm corresponds to one slice, whereas 12.3 μm results from the superimposition of 20 slices ("thick slab"). Abbreviations as in Figure 15.1. (78-year-old man; based on data from Le Cabec et al. 2019)

Cabec et al. (2019). In virtual histology (~5–15 μm), the optimal slice thickness is much smaller than in classical histology (~100 μm), which is limited by physical constraints of section making. In addition, minute rotations in the three planes of space and a limited translation in-depth (that is, scrolling through the scan after the optimal thickness has been determined) will help find the position where TCAs are best visible.

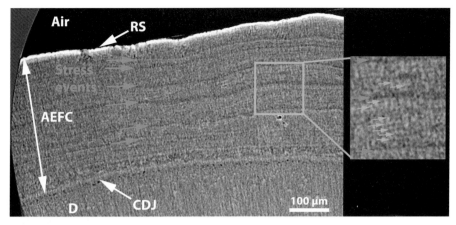

Figure 15.3 Note that accentuated lines (arrows) can be easily differentiated from TCA (smaller arrows in the right close-up). Abbreviations as in Figure 15.1. (76-year-old man; based on data from Le Cabec et al. 2019)

From the saved digital images, increments may be drawn as identified on individual layers in Adobe Photoshop CS6 (Adobe Systems, San Jose, CA). In Photoshop, iterative counting sessions may be overlaid to discuss potential disagreement (e.g., cracks affecting some areas of the slice, thick phase-contrast fringes at the root surface) and harmonize the inferred definition of the spacing between TCA. Most importantly, accentuated lines should not be mistaken for TCA (Chapter 14), as they are much fatter in appearance and do not occur periodically or on every slice investigated (Figure 15.3). One of the challenges, in common with classical histology, lies in identifying clear increments that continue throughout the whole thickness of cementum from the CDJ to the root surface, potentially by counting in different places where the increments are clearest and joining those counts by following one accentuated line that runs parallel to the CDJ.

15.3   Current Limitations and Future Directions

Validation by Combining Thin-Sectioning with Virtual Histology

This pilot study has shown that PPC-SR-µCT may be successfully used to image nondestructively yearly increments in the AEFC of modern human teeth. However, a quantitative evaluation of the accuracy of PPC-SR-µCT imaging for counting human TCAs would require a validation step involving physically sectioning scanned teeth to count the TCA using classical microscopy and then comparing these thin sections with the corresponding virtual slices of the same ROI (Chapter 16). However, due to this known-age sample's uniqueness, we were not authorized to perform destructive analyses after the PPC-SRµCT scanning. Nonetheless, these preliminary results have major implications for studying fossil remains or historical specimens for which destructive sampling is not allowed.

Prior Optimization for Choosing the ROI to Scan

In archeological and paleoanthropological teeth, diagenetic processes can confuse and lead to false interpretations of annulation counts (Chapter 1). For example, collagen dissolution can reduce the number of bands, making them look thicker, while microbes and physical damage can remove outer increments, giving the edge a scalloped appearance (Lieberman 1994). In this context, a potential drawback of PPC-SR-µCT thus far concerns the prescreening for potential areas of interest prior to scanning. Different magnifications may be used in standard (microscopy) histology to screen an area of interest on the section's whole surface. Here, the volume scanned at ~0.6 µm is very small and thus may well be affected entirely by a crack or taphonomic damage. Unless a middle-resolution scan (~5 µm) is performed on the portion of interest of the root before scanning at high resolution (~0.6 µm), identifying an ROI exempt of fine cracks or alterations is difficult. The major areas of damage can, however, be detected in radiography mode when aligning the sample. In addition to the nondestructive nature of synchrotron scans and virtual histology, it is possible to scroll through the depth of a scan and work at variable section thicknesses to locate areas where annulations are clearest. Furthermore, orientation control (i.e., translation and rotation through the scan) allows optimization of the visibility of the targeted structures (see technical details about the protocol of alignment in Le Cabec et al. 2019). Figure 15.4 shows an example on the canine of a 78-year-old man in which scrolling through the scan allows to avoid damage (pits, irregularities) and optimize the visibility of the annulations for counting.

Future Improvements in Scanning and Fine-Tuning Reconstruction

Since this exploratory data was acquired in 2013, the beamline setup has already undergone significant technical improvements to increase the spatial and contrast resolution at the ESRF (especially on the ID19 beamline) and at other synchrotron facilities (e.g., at SLS, see Newham et al. 2017), in order to define more clearly the cementum annulations. Some further fine-tuning may be possible in the post-scanning processing steps, such as during the tomographic data reconstruction. Paganin's (2002) algorithm significantly improves the contrast of the structures of interest, and further optimization of "δ" and "β" values may provide additional image contrast in PPC-SRµCT reconstructions. When fossils potentially preserving ancient DNA are considered for nondestructively imaging TCA using PPC-SR-µCT, special care should be taken to keep the dose as low as achievable (Immel et al. 2016) to avoid damaging the DNA molecules. Newham and colleagues (Chapter 16) also present data with finer processing procedures that partially circumvent the limitations encountered in this pilot study.

15.4 Conclusion

In this pilot study, we investigated the potential of phase-contrast synchrotron X-ray tomography (PPC-SR-µCT) to resolve nondestructively human tooth cementum

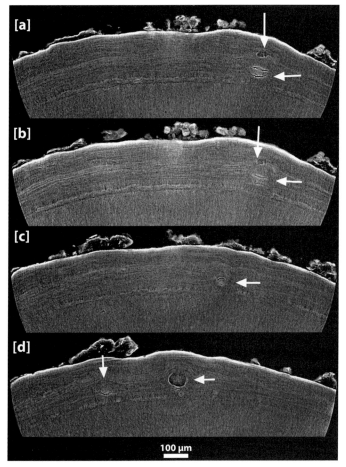

Figure 15.4 Illustration of how taphonomic/diagenetic damage can be avoided with virtual thin sections by scrolling through the scan: (a) virtual section located 27.5 μm before the virtual section used for the TCA counting (b). Virtual sections (c) and (d) are respectively 97.2 μm and 173.9 μm beyond (b). (78-year-old man; arrows point at various defects; based on data from Le Cabec et al. 2019)

annulations in a known-age historical assemblage. Based on the comparison between estimated adult age and actual age (see Le Cabec et al. 2019), it may be inferred that virtual sections can elucidate true cementum annulations even if their visibility is often close to the resolution limit of the setup used for this study. PPC-SR-μCT increment analysis shows sufficient precision but low accuracy. This inhibits the practical adoption of the methods employed here for aging fossil material of unknown age, but it is a promising step in nondestructive adult age at death estimation. Future technical developments will certainly improve the accuracy of adult age at death calculations and allow us to investigate the yet unexplored adult life-history of fossil hominins. Data acquired by Newham et al. (Chapter 16) at the Swiss Light Source synchrotron already demonstrate the wide-ranging possibility available from more highly resolved scans.

Acknowledgments

We are very grateful to S. Naji, W. Rendu, and L. Gourichon for inviting us to contribute to this book and anonymous reviewers for improving this chapter. We thank P. Tafforeau, A. Rack, and the ID19 and BM05 staff (ESRF, France) for technical support; C. Dean (UCL, UK) and T. Colard (University of Lille, France) for constructive discussions. Funding: ESRF, Max Planck Society.

References

Boyle, Angela, Ceridwen Boston, and Annsofie Witkin. 2005. *The Archaeological Experience at St. Luke's Church, Old Street, Islington*. (unpublished report). Oxford: Oxford Archaeology.

Immel, Alexander, Adeline Le Cabec, Marion Bonazzi, Alexander Herbig, Heiko Temming, Verena J. Schuenemann, Kirsten I. Bos, et al. 2016. "Effect of X-Ray Irradiation on Ancient DNA in Sub-Fossil Bones – Guidelines for Safe X-Ray Imaging." *Scientific Reports* 6: 32969.

Le Cabec, Adeline, M. Christopher Dean, and David R. Begun. 2017. "Dental Development and Age at Death of the Holotype of *Anapithecus hernyaki* (RUD 9) Using Synchrotron Virtual Histology." *Journal of Human Evolution* 108: 161–75.

Le Cabec, Adeline, Nancy K. Tang, Valentin Ruano Rubio, and Simon W. Hillson. 2019. "Non-Destructive Adult Age at Death Estimation: Visualizing Cementum Annulations in a Known Age Historical Human Assemblage Using Synchrotron X-Ray Microtomography." *American Journal of Physical Anthropology* 168: 25–44

Le Cabec, Adeline, Nancy K. Tang, and Paul Tafforeau. 2015. "Accessing Developmental Information of Fossil Hominin Teeth Using New Synchrotron Microtomography-Based Visualization Techniques of Dental Surfaces and Interfaces." *PLoS ONE* 10 (4): e0123019.

Le Cabec, Adeline, and Michel Toussaint. 2017. "Impacts of Curatorial and Research Practices on the Preservation of Fossil Hominid Remains." *Journal of Anthropological Sciences* 95: 7–34.

Leiss-Holzinger, Elisabeth, Karin Wiesauer, Henrike Stephani, Bettina Heise, David Stifter, Benjamin Kriechbaumer, Stefan J. Spachinger, Christian Gusenbauer, and Gerhard Withalm. 2015. "Imaging of the Inner Structure of Cave Bear Teeth by Novel Non-Destructive Techniques." *Palaeontologia Electronica* 18 (1): 1–15.

Lieberman, Daniel E. 1994. "The Biological Basis for Seasonal Increments in Dental Cementum and Their Application to Archaeological Research." *Journal of Archaeological Science* 21 (4): 525–39.

Newham, Elis, Kate Robson-Brown, Pamela Gill, and Ian Corfe. 2017. "Sexual Dimorphism in Primate Dental Cementum Microstructure." ISDM-IAPO Program. Bordeaux, France, 166.

Paganin, David., Sherry. C. Mayo, T. E. Gureyev, P. R. Miller, and S. W. Wilkins. 2002. "Simultaneous Phase and Amplitude Extraction from a Single Defocused Image of a Homogeneous Object." *Journal of Microscopy* 206 (1): 33–40.

Smith, Tanya M., Paul Tafforeau, Donald J. Reid, Joane Pouech, Vincent Lazzari, John P. Zermeno, Debbie Guatelli-Steinberg, et al. 2010. "Dental Evidence for Ontogenetic Differences between Modern Humans and Neanderthals." *Proceedings of the National Academy of Sciences* 107 (49): 20923–28.

Smith, Tanya M., Michel Toussaint, Donald J. Reid, Anthony J. Olejniczak, and Jean-Jacques Hublin. 2007. "Rapid Dental Development in a Middle Paleolithic Belgian Neanderthal." *Proceedings of the National Academy of Sciences* 104: 20220–25.

Smith, Tanya M., Paul Tafforeau, Adeline Le Cabec, Anne Bonnin, Alexandra Houssaye, Joane Pouech, Jacopo Moggi-Cecchi, et al. 2015. "Dental Ontogeny in Pliocene and Early Pleistocene Hominins." *PLoS ONE* 10 (2): e0118118.

Tafforeau, Paul, Renaud Boistel, E. Boller, A. Bravin, M. Brunet, Y. Chaimanee, P. Cloetens, M. Feist, J. Hoszowska, and J. J. Jaeger. 2006. "Applications of X-Ray Synchrotron Microtomography for Non-Destructive 3D Studies of Paleontological Specimens." *Applied Physics A: Materials Science & Processing* 83 (2): 195–202.

Tafforeau, Paul, and Tanya M. Smith. 2008. "Non-Destructive Imaging of Hominoid Dental Microstructure Using Phase Contrast X-Ray Synchrotron Microtomography." *Journal of Human Evolution* 54 (2): 272–78.

Weitkamp, Timm., David Haas, D. Wegrzynek, and Alexander Rack. 2011. "ANKAphase: Software for Single-Distance Phase Retrieval from Inline X-Ray Phase-Contrast Radiographs." *Journal of Synchrotron Radiation* 18 (4): 617–29.

2013. "ANKAphase: Software for Single-Distance Phase Retrieval from Inline X-Ray Phase-Contrast Radiographs. Erratum." *Journal of Synchrotron Radiation* 20 (1): 205.

Zabler, Simon Andreas, H. Riesemeier, P. Fratzl, and P. Zaslansky. 2006. "Fresnel-Propagated Imaging for the Study of Human Tooth Dentin by Partially Coherent X-Ray Tomography." *Optics Express* 14 (19): 8584–97.

16 Noninvasive 3D Methods for the Study of Dental Cementum

Elis Newham, Kate Robson Brown, Ian J. Corfe, Pamela G. Gill, Philippa Brewer, Priscilla Bayle, and Philipp Schneider

Several publications discuss recent forays into noninvasive three-dimensional (3D) imaging techniques, specifically propagation-based phase-contrast imaging (PPCI) through synchrotron radiation-based computed tomography (SR CT) for studying cementum increments and suggest future avenues for the development and application of these methods (Chapter 15). Here, we outline the principal advantages of these methods over traditional histological imaging and describe several aspects of 3D imaging that may offer novel information regarding cementum growth and structure that are unavailable using traditional histological methods. The practicalities of PPCI through SR CT (herein referred to as PPSRCT) imaging are also discussed in order to provide an up-to-date case study of high-resolution 3D cementum imaging.

16.1 Advantages of PPSRCT versus Histological Imaging of Cementum Increments

The overwhelming majority of cementum studies rely on traditional methods of creating ground-and-polished thin sections to view, and often image, cementum increments using transmitted/reflected light microscopy (Klevezal', 1996; Naji et al. 2016; Chapter 1). The creation of thin sections follows a wide range of techniques, and although several attempts have been made to establish a global standard for their production, several laboratories professionally produce thin sections of comparable quality, using markedly different techniques (Rolandsen et al. 2008; Naji et al. 2016; Chapter 9). The thin-sectioning technique offers a range of opportunities to enhance image contrast between increments, including chemical staining and controlled section thickness (Kvall and Solheim, 1996; Foster, 2012). Optical microscopy viewing of such thin sections allows submicrometer resolution, and further image contrast enhancement and identification of diagenetic alteration of the cementum in archaeological specimens is possible using polarizing plates (Stutz, 2002). Digital micrographs of cementum thin sections have been studied using a range of image-processing techniques now commonly available in image-processing software packages (e.g.,

ImageJ/Fiji; Schneider et al. 2012) (see Lieberman et al. 1990; Wall-Scheffler and Foley, 2008 for examples).

However, thin sections can only offer a restrictive two-dimensional (2D) window onto cementum tissue, based on a limited number of sections produced along a single axis through the cementum. This limits the interpretation of complexities in cementum increment patterns that are commonly seen in micrographs (Renz and Radlanski, 2006). Increments are known to both split and coalesce, which can obstruct attempts at increment counting, and negatively affect the accuracy and precision of increment counts (Lucas and Loh, 1986; Renz and Radlanski, 2006; Dias et al. 2010). These complexities are difficult to resolve in thin sections as they cannot be interpreted in the context of the entire tissue, so "genuine" circum-annual increments cannot be easily distinguished from accessory increments formed by increment splitting. Likewise, reduced counts due to coalescence cannot be identified unless the point of coalescence is visible on the section. The thin-sectioning process itself can also create artifacts that can obscure cementum increments, including surface scratches and topographic artifacts along the section surface (Naji et al. 2016). Because sectioning is a destructive process, these artifacts cannot be rectified without further grinding/polishing, which may affect increment visibility. Finally, increments are usually counted by eye in regions chosen by the researcher as displaying the highest image contrast between increments. This selection is inherently limited by the number and quality of thin sections available per tooth (Renz and Radlanski, 2006), the experience of the researcher (Rolandsen et al. 2008; Frie et al. 2011, 2013), and the quality of incrementation in the tooth under study (Spinage, 1973).

Noninvasive imaging techniques offer a means of overcoming the majority of these caveats and have drawn considerable interest from cementum researchers. Although optical coherence tomography (Liess-Holzinger et al. 2015) has been attempted, only synchrotron radiation-based approaches currently offer the ability to noninvasively image the entire cementum tissue at the submicrometre resolutions and at image contrast levels required for increment analysis.

Synchrotron light sources are large cyclic accelerators in which electrons are accelerated close to the speed of light to emit X-rays in magnetic fields that are created by so-called insertion devices located around the electron storage ring. These X-rays can be used for different experiments, including X-ray–based CT (Chapters 6 and 7; see Stock et al. 2017 and Dean et al. 2018 for examples of X-ray fluorescence study of cementum). The exceptional brilliance of X-rays generated by SR sources allows the capture of high-quality CT data at submicrometer resolutions, with typical scanning times significantly faster than laboratory-based X-ray light sources with superior image quality in terms of signal-to-noise ratio (SNR), contrast-to-noise ratio (CNR), and image sharpness. The optical coherence of synchrotron beams also allows reconstruction of changes in the phase of X-rays as they encounter materials of different refractive properties. Phase-contrast retrieval algorithms are now commonly used to reconstruct the phase information in X-ray projections before actual CT reconstruction and offer exponentially higher image contrast between materials with otherwise minor differences in X-ray absorption (Paganin et al. 2002) – in this case, between individual cementum increments.

PPSRCT data sets are volumetric in nature (Figure 16.1) and offer the opportunity to image the entire cementum tissue at isotropic spatial resolutions. Data sets can be investigated in any orientation, and individual increments can be followed through the cementum along both their transverse and longitudinal axes (Figure 16.1). This places increment splitting and coalescence in a broad spatial context, effectively untangling

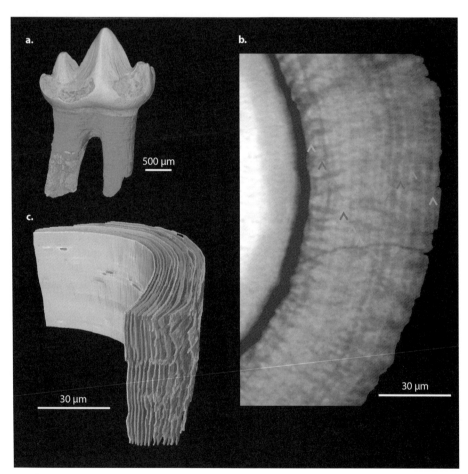

Figure 16.1 2D and 3D analyses of cementum structure using CT imaging. (a) 3D volume rendering of the m2 tooth of Early Jurassic fossil mammal Morganucodon (NHMUK PV M104134; voxel size 2 μm, laboratory-based μCT). (b) PPSRCT slice of Morganucodon cementum (specimen NHMUK PV M104127) with 14 circum-annual increments highlighted using colored arrows. (c) 3D segmentation of increments highlighted in b (colors of increments correspond to arrows in (b) through the fossilized cementum tissue. (A black and white version of this figure will appear in some formats. For the color version, please refer to the plate section.)

their complexities in 3D patterns of "genuine" circum-annual increments. The entire tissue can also be reviewed when searching for regions of highest increment image contrast, and these regions can be rotated in 3D to analyze along the axis in which increments are most easily distinguished (Le Cabec et al. 2019).

The grayscale nature of CT data makes it amenable to various image-processing protocols that can enhance increment contrast and standardize analyses of shape and texture. When studying PPSRCT cementum data, we commonly first isolate and straighten cementum. Straightening can be performed via cubic-spline interpolation, using the "straighten" tool in ImageJ/Fiji (Schneider et al. 2012) with the cemento-dentine junction as a guide for the direction of straightening (Figure 16.2). This provides a new image of the cementum isolated from the dentine, with all increments straightened relative to the cemento-dentine boundary. The use of simple macros can automate this process in ImageJ/Fiji, allowing significant portions or even the whole tissue, to be straightened. Image-processing routines can be implemented to isolate individual cementum increments using grayscale values (Lieberman and Meadow, 1992) in both 2D (Figure 16.1b) and 3D (Figure 16.1c) estimates that characterize the cementum to retrieved (Klevezal' and Stewart, 1994; Mani-Caplazi et al. 2017).

Several studies have created "virtual thin sections" of PPSRCT data by summing or averaging the grayscale values of an arbitrary number of neighboring PPSRCT slices (Figure 16.3) (Chapter 15; Le Cabec et al. 2019; Newham et al. 2020). This technique can considerably enhance image contrast between increments when an optimum number of slices are combined (Figure 16.3). This optimum can be found by systematically increasing and decreasing the number of combined slices to find a "sweet spot" that maximizes increment contrast without blurring individual increments. A comparable approach for thin sections is difficult, can only be carried out with a progressive reduction in section thickness, and can irreparably damage the section or the ability to accurately view increments if slice thickness is reduced beyond a certain point.

CT data does not suffer from such physical limitations and is unaffected by tissue preparation artifacts. Grayscale values are also directly linked to material and chemical properties (Paganin et al. 2002) and are unaffected by the refraction of visible light that occurs at the polished surface of a thin section. So PPSRCT slices offer a source of novel information regarding the structure of cementum and the shape, width, and material density of increments. Increments can be isolated and studied in 2D or 3D (Figure 16.1 and Figure 16.2) and allow exploitation of measures previously used in profiling of engineered surfaces (Dong, Sullivan, and Stout, 1992; Purnell, Seehausen, and Galis, 2012) to be used here to characterize aspects of cementum structure and texture (Figure 16.2; Table 16.1).

Several studies have sought to identify a relationship between the structure, shape, and opacity of individual cementum increments and various life-history variables (Chapter 8; Kagarer and Grupe, 2001; Mani-Caplazi et al. 2017, 2019). The majority of studies have struggled to accurately correlate the chronological estimate of individual increments of anomalous properties with known life-history events, including pregnancies (but see Kagarer and Grupe (2001) for an example of high precision and accuracy of post-hoc assignation of stress events to increments of anomalous

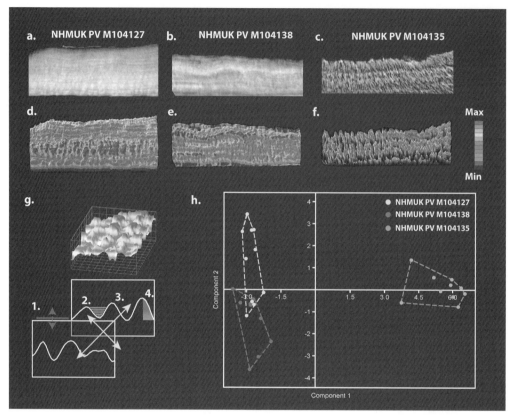

Figure 16.2 Analysis of cementum "texture" using PPSRCT grayscale values as a third dimension. (a–c) Straightened cementum data from the three Morganucodon fossil specimens. (d–f) 3D blue-red heat maps of each straightened image, with 3D height and color representing grayscale values in a–c (created using the "3D surface plot" tool in ImageJ/Fiji; Schneider et al. 2012). (g) Schematic diagram highlighting the nature of measures that can be applied to 3D heat maps of cementum increments. Numbers correspond to the four principal types of measures outlined in Table 16.1. [1: height measures that estimate grayscales above and below (blue arrows) the mean value of the surface (red line); 2: functional measures that characterize volumetric information based on the material ratio of the surface in question (the ratio between the intersecting area of a hypothetical plane passing through the surface at a given height, and the cross-sectional area of the surface – highlighted by blue infill into trough); 3: spatial measures that estimate the direction and anisotropy of grayscale values across the surface highlighted with yellow arrows; 4: hybrid measures that combine spatial and height measures.] (h) Principal components analysis of values for all measures in Table 16.1 performed for 10 PPSRCT slices for each specimen. PCA scores for measures performed for each specimen cluster in their own region of "texture space," with the specimen showing the most significant diagenetic alteration of original cementum microstructure (NHMUK PV M104135) significantly separated from the two other specimens. (A black and white version of this figure will appear in some formats. For the color version, please refer to the plate section.)

properties). Surface profiling measurements can be used to characterize the entire cementum tissue rather than looking for specific increments. This sidesteps the prerequisite of other techniques for estimating physiological properties from cementum

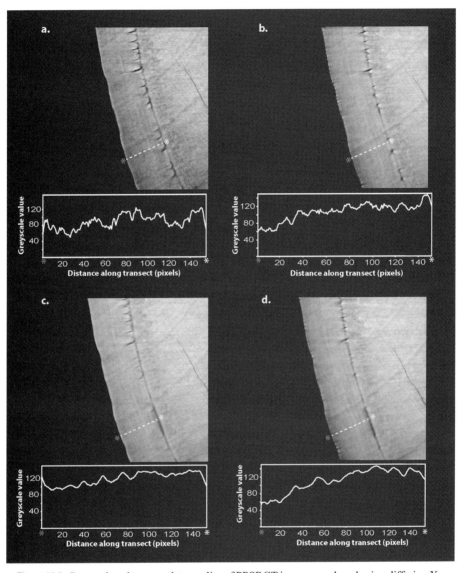

Figure 16.3 Comparison between data quality of PPSRCT images produced using differing X-ray exposure times and between single PPSRCT slices and "virtual thin sections." (a) PPSRCT slice of Macaca mulatta cementum created using 100 ms exposure time per projection and accompanying grayscale plot measured along the yellow dashed transect. (b) PPSRCT slice of the same region created using 200 ms exposure time. The grayscale transect measured for b is significantly less noisy than a, with more clear incremental patterns representing cementum increments. (c) Virtual thin section created by summation of the grayscale values of 10 images (the four slices below and five slices above the slice shown in a). (d) Virtual thin section created by summation of the grayscale values of 10 images from the region of the PPSRCT data set shown in b. Accompanying grayscale transects for both c and d are less noisy than either single PPSRCT slice. The transect for (d) also has higher increment image contrast than c, with clearer peak-trough systems representing light and dark cementum increments (respectively).

Table 16.1 3D surface profiling measures used to compare cementum in Figure 16.2

Parameter	Category	Description
Absolute average height of surface	1. Height	Average grayscale value
Relative average height of surface	1. Height	Average difference between grayscale values above the mean grayscale value and the mean grayscale value
Root mean square height of surface	1. Height	Root mean square grayscale value
Maximum peak height of surface	1. Height	Value of maximum grayscale peak above average
Average maximum peak height	1. Height	Average value of 10 highest grayscale peaks above average
10-point average maximum peak height	1. Height	10-point moving average value of 10 highest grayscale peaks above average
Minimum valley depth	1. Height	Value of lowest grayscale trough below average
Average minimum valley depth	1. Height	Average value of 10 lowest grayscale troughs above average
10-point average minimum valley depth	1. Height	10-point moving average value of 10 highest grayscale peaks above average
Surface area ratio	2. Functional	Ratio between absolute surface area and pixel number
Core roughness depth	2. Functional	Proportion of material occupied by the core
Average peak height above core	2. Functional	Average difference in grayscale between peaks above the maximum core grayscale value and the maximum core grayscale value
Average valley depth below core	2. Functional	Average difference in grayscale between troughs below the minimum core grayscale value and the minimum core grayscale value
Surface bearing area ratio	2. Functional	Proportion of the surface that consists of peaks above the core material
Autocorrelation length	3. Spatial	Horizontal distance of the autocorrelation function (ACF) that has the fastest decay to the value 0.2. Large value: surface dominated by low frequencies; low value: surface dominated by high frequencies
Texture aspect ratio	3. Spatial	Ratio from the distance with the fastest to the distance with the slowest decay of the ACF to the value 0.2–0.3
Maximum skew	4. Hybrid	The degree of symmetry of the surface heights about the mean plane
Summit density	4. Hybrid	Number of grayscale peaks per unit area
Maximum kurtosis	4. Hybrid	The prominence of inordinately high peaks and/or deep valleys
Root mean square gradient of surface	4. Hybrid	Root mean square of grayscale slopes, evaluated over all directions
Developed interfacial area ratio	4. Hybrid	Percentage of additional surface area contributed by the texture as compared to an ideal plane the size of the measurement's region

by quantitatively identifying individual increments of anomalous properties. The presence and predominance of anomalous increments will, in turn, affect the values of certain types of these measures. For instance, increments of anomalous density will affect height measures and functional measures, whereas increments of anomalous shape will affect spatial measures (see Table 16.1 for the definition of tribological or surface profiling measures). A diverse range of these measures can be derived algorithmically using image processing, and the variation that they capture can be distilled using principal components analysis (PCA). The separation of specimens representing samples of differing life-histories within the resulting PCA "texture space" has the potential to provide novel measures for estimating physiological properties from cementum. Alternatively, measures can quantify the nature and extent of diagenesis between fossil specimens (Figure 16.2). Although these measures can also be derived from thin-section data, after conversion to grayscale images, they cannot directly be compared to the same measures retrieved from X-ray image data. This is because the physical principles for image formation in light microscopy and X-ray imaging are distinct, which gives rise to the respective image brightness, and hence image contrast levels, and how they correspond to the underlying cementum microstructure.

16.2 Current Limitations of PPSRCT Imaging of Cementum Increments

PPSRCT imaging of cementum is still in its infancy, compared to decades of development of conventional histological techniques. The few studies that have attempted PPSRCT imaging have been based on significantly different samples, using different synchrotron sources and different experimental settings (Chapter 15; Le Cabec et al. 2019; Newham et al. 2020). Comparison between these studies highlights several practicalities that must be addressed in order to assess the true potential of this imaging modality.

Two of the earliest PPSRCT cementum increment studies (Mani-Caplazi et al. 2017; Le Cabec et al. 2019) focused on imaging archaeological human cementum and counting individual cementum increments by eye. Although the authors of both studies acknowledged many of the advantages of PPSRCT study over conventional thin-section histology discussed here, neither study was able to report high accuracy of cementum increment counts. In Mani-Caplazi et al. (2017), the principal difficulties were in identifying increments at all (only two of four teeth showed visible increments) and in identifying the dentine-cementum boundary and the position to start counting increments. These difficulties were primarily due to the fairly high degree of taphonomic alteration of specimens, even in those prescreened using laboratory microcomputed CT to identify such alteration. The single specimen with fully countable increments underestimated known age at death, but the underestimation was not quantified. Le Cabec et al. (2019) similarly reported a consistent underestimation of known age in their sample, especially for individuals older than fifty years of age. Across hundreds of Early Jurassic fossil mammal specimens, we have found that taphonomic and diagenetic obliteration of cementum increments and the cemento-dentine boundary affects roughly one-third to two-thirds of samples, dependent on locality (Newham et al. 2020).

Cementum increments in long-living humans are known to be difficult to count in thin sections (Rolandsen et al. 2008). However, PPSRCT data was not compared to thin-section data of the same specimens in either archaeological study where the cause of this is not known. Therefore, it is not clear whether the reported low accuracy is due to taphonomy, inherently low image contrast between increments making them difficult to distinguish, physically missing increments due to disease or biological thinning and skipping of increments in old age, or poor accuracy of PPSRCT data.

Although we are unable to compare our Jurassic fossil mammal age estimates from PPSRCT cementum increment counts to known ages, the knowledge that previous PPSRCT cementum increment counts tend to underestimate known age suggests our conclusions of long life spans and hence reptile-like physiology are conservative and robust.

Unlike optical microscopic imaging, the effective resolution of PPSRCT reconstructions is limited by the theoretic size of each voxel in the PPSRCT reconstruction. Voxel/pixel-based imaging techniques average information stored within each pixel, leading to a so-called partial volume effect, obscuring features that are thinner/smaller than one pixel/voxel. As a rule of thumb, a feature must be larger than two voxels/pixels to be imaged using such techniques. The voxel size used for PPSRCT imaging must therefore account for the absolute size and material density of increments within the cementum of the respective sample (the range of which is exemplified when comparing PPSRCT data of shrew-sized Early Jurassic fossil mammals living <20 years presented in Newham et al. (2020) versus humans living 20–81 years in Le Cabec et al. (2019).

X-ray imaging utilizes a series of core experimental settings that control the interaction between the synchrotron X-ray beam and the specimen and directly affect the quality of subsequent phase retrievals and CT reconstructions. The principal settings that can be controlled by the user are the X-ray energy, the integration time per X-ray projection, the number of angular projections taken per scan, and the sample-to-detector distance, which corresponds to a similar effective propagation distance of X-rays in cases of a parallel X-ray beam geometry found at X-ray imaging beamlines of synchrotron facilities. The optimum experimental settings are specific to the dimensions and the material properties of the specimen.

We have found that the image quality, namely SNR and CNR, and image sharpness of PPSRCT cementum data are significantly affected by these experimental settings (Figure 16.3), and distinct settings are needed for different samples. For instance, larger teeth require higher energy X-rays for sufficient transmission through the relatively thicker, dense dentine tissue, with increased exposure times to guarantee acceptable SNR levels and longer propagation distances to enhance image contrast. These image quality metrics are also dependent on the X-ray spectrum of the insertion device and the monochromator specifications and settings of a particular synchrotron's experimental station (beamline) for X-ray imaging. The available X-ray flux and coherence can change significantly with the selected X-ray energy and level of X-ray monochromaticity or energy bandwidth. We suggest that to ensure optimal image quality, each PPSRCT experiment should begin with a quantitative optimization procedure of the experimental settings when imaging a new sample at a specific synchrotron beamline. As synchrotron beamlines accumulate data from different PPSRCT imaged samples, future experiments will benefit from this crucial information.

Though CT imaging is in itself a noninvasive technique, the mounting, replacing, and transport of specimens are not without their own inherent risks. The transport of any fragile specimen such as archaeological or fossil teeth must be attempted with the utmost care, as international journeys are often required that present risk of physical damage. There is currently no suggested standard for the mounting of specimens. We have mounted teeth onto a wide variety of platforms, depending on the size of the tooth and stage design of the respective beamline. For example, we mounted millimeter-scale fossil mammal teeth onto a thin (most commonly 2 mm diameter) carbon fiber rod, while we mounted primate teeth onto a scanning electron microscopy (SEM) stub of suitable size for the particular tooth. Specimens were affixed to the mount using either glue or wax. Both mediums pose a series of risks for the specimen. These are primarily the risk of leaving a physical and chemical residue on the specimen surface, the risk of damage to the affixed surface of the specimen, and the risk of small specimens falling off mounts and becoming lost in the machinery. Although there is little standardization of mounting systems between beamlines, the majority that we have experienced commonly cater to SEM stubs. PPSRCT beamlines often use a series of magnets to affix mounted specimens to the specimen stage. If the magnetic force is too strong, the magnets can pull the mount with sufficient force for the reverberations to dislodge and even remove specimens from the mount.

Finally, the "dose" of synchrotron X-rays delivered to a specimen is known to damage several aspects of hard tissue biology. Doses of >70 kGrays (kGy) have been shown to negatively affect several mechanical aspects of human cortical bone, including strength, ductility, and fracture resistance (Barth et al. 2010). Because Ramen spectroscopy has shown that these effects are likely related to degradation of the collagen matrix, they should also be examined as a potential impact of X-ray imaging of cementum. Cementum is also known to preserve degraded ancient DNA (aDNA) in some archaeological and subfossilized remains. PPSRCT imaging has recently been shown by Immel et al. (2016) to damage this important substance when certain experimental settings are used. Although only a single beamline has been investigated, the authors quantified an effective X-ray dose of 2 (kGy) that risks damaging aDNA if exceeded in any PPSRCT experiment.

16.3   A Time Line and Guide to a PPSRCT Cementum Imaging Experiment

Here, we describe the planning, logistics, and practicalities of a typical PPSRCT experiment based on our own experience. We hope this will be a useful guide to those planning their own PPSRCT experiments and help establish a standardized approach for comparing X-ray CT data and results for cementum. The first stage in any X-ray imaging experiment at a synchrotron source is to ensure that it is capable of imaging cementum increments at a sufficiently high level for spatial resolution, SNR, and CNR levels in order to identify individual cementum increments. The tomographic/hard X-ray imaging beamline (not all synchrotrons have such a beamline) must be capable of achieving submicrometer voxel sizes and sufficient X-ray coherence for (propagation-based) phase-contrast imaging.

Unless working with industrial sponsors (who can sometimes book beamtime at industrial access rates), the allocation of synchrotron "beamtime" (experimental allocation free of charge) to a user (group) is achieved following a successful proposal to the review panel of the respective synchrotron, where calls for proposals are typically open every half-year. Proposals usually consist of a brief summary of the goals of the experiment, the scientific background, and experimental design, and the expected outcome, including how much experimental time (beamtime) is required. It is recommended to present examples of PPSRCT data of the respective sample/population in the proposal to illustrate the feasibility of obtaining the desired data. This data is normally acquired during previous experiments and in turn must be factored in when timetabling future experiments so that the pipeline of obtaining "pilot" data is maintained. Proposals are judged based on scientific merit (relevance, impact, innovation), technical feasibility (the ability of the requested beamline to achieve the expected results of the experiment), the previous record of the proposers (this includes both their publication record, including, but not exclusively, relating to synchrotron experiments, record of successful previous experimental sessions, and experimental feedback from previous experimental sessions), and availability of the resources required (i.e., the amount and quality of other proposals requesting the use of the respective beamline). This evaluation of the proposal will determine whether or not it is accepted and, if so, how much of the requested beamtime will be allocated (it is possible to receive less than the full amount of the requested beamtime).

Following acceptance of a proposal, the researcher will be given a provisional date for the experiment (usually three to nine months after proposal submission). The experiment usually requires up to eight hours of experimental setup by the in-house beamline scientist, including changing microscope objectives, focusing the camera, and establishing the correct experimental settings, with trial images to determine whether cementum increments can be identified. We suggest that a quantitative parameter optimization procedure should be implemented at this point. From here, scheduling can be based on the nature of the samples being scanned and experimental settings chosen. For instance, for each specimen, time will be required for closing the beamline shutters, physically changing the specimen, performing a compulsory safety search of the experimental hutch, opening the shutters, and physically locating the region of interest (ROI) within the cementum by aligning the sample stage. This process can often take longer than the scan itself (sometimes only a few minutes) for certain samples and needs to be factored into the scanning schedule.

A major logistical concern of PPSRCT imaging is the sheer amount of image data that can be produced during an experiment and the methods used to transport and transfer these data to the home research facility. With standard settings, a typical reconstructed CT volume is around 30 Gb in size, and the data set of original X-ray projections around 20 Gb. Given an approximate total imaging time (specimen change, ROI location, and scanning) of thirty minutes, this can easily create total data sets of more than ten terabytes from a three-day experiment. Though the data can often be downloaded remotely from the synchrotron data servers, it is, in general, a very slow process, so data can alternatively be transferred and stored using external hard drives that can cost around £20 or €20 per terabyte at current prices. Although synchrotron facilities sometimes automatically back up data and make space available for open data before or after the publication of results, this is not the case for all synchrotron facilities. The researcher should therefore also back up their own copy of the data, doubling the required storage capacity for every experiment conducted.

Following experimentation and data acquisition, PPSRCT cementum data can be studied using a variety of 2D/3D image processing and analysis software. These range from freeware (e.g., ImageJ/Fiji; Schneider et al. 2012) to commercial license–based packages (e.g., Avizo; Thermo Fisher Scientific). The choice of software is dependent on the design and goals of the respective analysis. Image processing tasks such as contrast optimization and the creation of virtual thin sections can be batch processed in ImageJ/Fiji by constructing simple macros using the "Macro recorder" tool. Stacks of these virtual thin sections can then be examined volumetrically using specialized 3D data analysis software such as Avizo to measure, isolate, and count individual increments in 3D. We have also created dedicated analysis tools in the MATLAB environment (The MathWorks, Inc., Natick, MA, USA) that isolate specific elements of PPSRCT cementum data using solely computer vision in an attempt to minimize the subjectivity in increment analysis. Although the learning curve for developing such tools is steep, their validation and public release following peer review will ensure their availability to other researchers exploring the use of PPSRCT for cementum analysis.

16.4 Conclusions

Noninvasive 3D methods for imaging cementum increments using synchrotron radiation sources are one of the most promising new avenues for cementum research. This technique offers the opportunity to overcome the major caveats to traditional thin-section imaging and provides volumetric data sets of submicrometer resolution that can be investigated in new ways. Such studies can unlock the 3D structure of cementum increments, and 3D measures may allow for new inferences on the relationship between cementum growth and life-history. However, as a new field of research, synchrotron X-ray imaging of cementum must ensure reproducibility by employing quantitative approaches to develop optimal experimental procedures and settings for imaging cementum in different samples. The quantitative parameter optimization procedure we introduce in this chapter should form a crucial part of the imaging protocol that we present here, in which we outline the major steps in preparing for, performing, and concluding a synchrotron imaging experiment based on our own experience.

Acknowledgments

We would like to thank the Natural Environmental Research Council (UK), the Engineering and Physical Sciences Research Council (UK), the Natural History Museum London, the University of Bristol, and Ginkgo Investments LTD for partial funding of this project and two anonymous reviewers. The *Morganucodon* cementum data presented here is the result of a PPSRCT experiment conducted at Beamline ID19 of the European Synchrotron Radiation Facility (project ES152 awarded to IC), and we thank Paul Tafforeau, Vincent Fernandez, Aki Kallonen, and Tuomas Kankanpää for their assistance during this experiment. The *Macaca mulatta* cementum data presented here is the result of a PPSRCT experiment conducted at the TOMCAT beamline of the Swiss Light Source Synchrotron (Paul Scherrer Institute) (project 20151391 awarded to PG), and we thank Pablo Villanueva, Alessandra Patera, Iwan Jerjen, Orestis Katsamenis, Mark Mavrogordato, Sharif Ahmed, Juan Núñez, and Christianne Fernee for their assistance during our beamtime.

References

Barth, H. D., Launey, M. E., MacDowell, A. A., Ager, J. W., and Ritchie, R. O. (2010). On the effect of x-ray irradiation on the deformation and fracture behavior of human cortical bone. *Bone* 46(6): 1475–85.

Dean, C., Le Cabec, A., Spiers, K., Zhang, Y., and Garrevoet, J. (2018). Incremental distribution of strontium and zinc in great ape and fossil hominin cementum using synchrotron x-ray fluorescence mapping. *Journal of The Royal Society Interface* 15(138): 20170626.

Dias, P. E., Beaini, T. L., and Melani, R. F. (2010). Age estimation from dental cementum incremental lines and periodontal disease. *Journal of Forensic Odontostomatology* 28: 13–21.

Dong, W. P., Sullivan, P. J., and Stout, K. J. (1992). Comprehensive study of parameters for characterizing three-dimensional surface topography I: Some inherent properties of parameter variation. *Wear* 159(2): 161–71.

Foster, B. L. (2012). Methods for studying tooth root cementum by light microscopy. *International Journal of Oral Science* 4(3): 119.

Frie, A. K., Fagerheim, K. A., Hammill, M. O., Kapel, F. O., Lockyer, C., Stenson, G. B., and Svetochev, V. (2011). Error in age estimation of harp seals (*Pagophilus groenlandicus*): Results from a transatlantic, image-based, blind-reading experiment using known-age teeth. *ICES Journal of Marine Science* 68(9),1942–53.

Frie, A. K., Hammill, M. O., Hauksson, E., Lind, Y., Lockyer, C., Stenman, O., and Svetocheva, O. (2013). Error patterns in age estimation and tooth readability assignment of grey seals (*Halichoerus grypus*): Results from a transatlantic, image-based, blind-reading study using known-age animals. *ICES Journal of Marine Science* 70(2): 418–30.

Immel, A., Le Cabec, A., Bonazzi, M., Herbig, A., Temming, H., Schuenemann, V. J., Bos, K.I., Langbein, F., Harvati, K., Bridault, A., Pion, G., Julien, M-A., Krotova, O., Conard, N. J., Münzel, S. C., Drucker, D. G., Viola, B., Hublin, J-J., Tafforeau, P., and Krause, J. (2016). Effect of ancient DNA in sub-fossil bones – guidelines for safe x-ray imaging. *Scientific Reports* 6: 32969.

Kagerer, P., and Grupe, G. (2001). Age-at-death diagnosis and determination of life-history parameters by incremental lines in human dental cementum as an identification aid. *Forensic Science International* 118(1): 75–82.

Klevezal, G. A. (1996). *Recording Structures of Mammals*. Boca Raton, FL: CRC Press.

Klevezal, G. A., and Stewart, B. S. (1994). Patterns and calibration of layering in tooth cementum of female northern elephant seals, *Mirounga angustirostris*. *Journal of Mammalogy* 75(2): 483–7.

Kvaal, S. I., and Solheim, T. (1996). Incremental lines in human dental cementum in relation to age. *European Journal of Oral Sciences* 103(4): 225–30.

Le Cabec, A., Tang, N. K., Ruano Rubio, V., and Hillson, S. (2019). Nondestructive adult age at death estimation: Visualizing cementum annulations in a known age historical human assemblage using synchrotron x-ray microtomography. *American Journal of Physical Anthropology* 168(1): 25–44.

Leiss-Holzinger, E., Wiesauer, K., Stephani, H., Heise, B., Stifter, D., Kriechbaumer, B., Spachinger, S. J., Gusenbauer, C., and Withalm, G. (2015). Imaging of the inner structure of cave bear teeth by novel non-destructive techniques. *Palaeontologia Electronica* 18(1): 1–15.

Lieberman, D. E., Deacon, T. W., and Meadow, R. H. (1990). Computer image enhancement and analysis of cementum increments as applied to teeth of *Gazella gazella*. *Journal of Archaeological Science* 17(5): 519–33.

Lieberman, D. E., and Meadow, R. H. (1992). The biology of cementum increments (with an archaeological application). *Mammal Review* 22(2): 57–77.

Lucas, P. W., and Loh, H. S. (1986). Are the incremental lines in human cementum laid down annually? *Annals, Academy of Medicine Singapore* 15: 384–86.

Mani-Caplazi, G., Hotz, G., Wittwer-Backofen, U., and Vach, W., (2019). Measuring incremental line width and appearance in the tooth cementum of recent and archaeological human teeth to identify irregularities: First insights using a standardized protocol. *International Journal of Paleopathology* 27: 24–37.

Mani-Caplazi, G., Schulz, G., Deyhle, H., Hotz, G., Vach, W., Wittwer-Backofen, U., and Müller, B. (2017). Imaging of the human tooth cementum ultrastructure of archaeological teeth, using hard x-ray microtomography to determine age-at-death and stress periods. *Developments in X-Ray Tomography XI* 10391: 103911 C. International Society for Optics and Photonics.

Naji, S., Colard, T., Blondiaux, J., Bertrand, B., d'Incau, E., and Bocquet-Appel, J.-P. (2016). Cementochronology, to cut or not to cut? *International Journal of Paleopathology* 15: 113–19.

Newham, E., Gill, P. G., Brewer, P., . . ., and Corfe, I. J. (2020). Reptile-like physiology in Early Jurassic stem-mammals. *Nature Communications* 11(1): 5121.

Paganin, D., Mayo, S. C., Gureyev, T. E., Miller, P. R., and Wilkins, S. W. (2002). Simultaneous phase and amplitude extraction from a single defocused image of a homogeneous object. *Journal of Microscopy* 206: 33–40.

Purnell, M., Seehausen, O., and Galis, F. (2012). Quantitative three-dimensional microtextural analyses of tooth wear as a tool for dietary discrimination in fishes. *Journal of The Royal Society Interface* 9(74): 2225–33.

Renz, H., and Radlanski, R. J. (2006). Incremental lines in root cementum of human teeth – A reliable age marker? *HOMO- Journal of Comparative Human Biology* 57(1): 29–50.

Rolandsen, C. M., Solberg, E. J., Heim, M., Holmstrøm, F., Solem, M. I., and Sæther, B. E. (2008). Accuracy and repeatability of moose (Alces alces) age as estimated from dental cement layers. *European Journal of Wildlife Research* 54(1): 6–14.

Schneider, C. A., Rasband, W. S., and Eliceiri, K. W. (2012). NIH Image to ImageJ: 25 years of image analysis. *Nature Methods* 9(7): 671.

Spinage, C. A. (1973). A review of age determination of mammals by means of teeth, with especial reference to Africa. *African Journal of Ecology* 11(2): 165–87.

Stock, S. R., Finney, L. A., Telser, A., Maxey, E., Vogt, S., and Okasinski, J. S. (2017). Cementum structure in Beluga whale teeth. *Acta Biomaterialia* 48: 289–99.

Stutz, A. J. (2002). Polarizing microscopy identification of chemical diagenesis in archaeological cementum. *Journal of Archaeological Science* 29(11): 1327–47.

Wall-Scheffler, C. M., and Foley, R. A. (2008). Digital cementum luminance analysis (DCLA): A tool for the analysis of climatic and seasonal signals in dental cementum. *International Journal of Osteoarchaeology* 18(1): 11–27.

Part III
Applications

17 Using Cementochronology to Discuss the Organization of Past Neanderthal Societies

William Rendu, Eric Pubert, and Emmanuel Discamps

17.1 Introduction

The spatial organization of activities in the Neanderthal's territory has often been explored by studying stone tool production and the economy of raw material acquisition and use (Faivre et al. 2014). However, Neanderthal spatial organization has seldom been studied in detail with regard to their hunting behavior (Farizy, David, and Jaubert 1994; Rendu et al. 2012; Costamagno et al. 2006; Meignen et al. 2006). These rare studies have questioned the validity of the hypothesis that Neanderthals lacked planning potential and have proposed the existence of complex land-use strategies during the Mousterian. These strategies are characterized by the use of collaborative hunting and reliance on food storage to anticipate future needs. Moreover, the organization of these activities would have been clearly structured in both time and space.

In this context, hunting seasonality is a key factor for identifying and understanding both the spatial and temporal organization of the Mousterian subsistence economy. To consider hunting and managing food resources without first considering the seasonality of their procurement severely limits any attempt to study hunter-gatherers' subsistence economy. However, for Neanderthals, this issue has rarely been addressed (Lieberman 1993; Armand, Pubert, and Soressi 2001; Rendu 2010).

Southwestern France Context

Throughout the year, and depending on their age and sex, ungulates go through several physiological phases, including rut, antler shedding and regrowth, pregnancy, and parturition. These biologically driven phases influence the animals' physical condition and, consequently, the quality and quantity of meat, grease, marrow, hides, antlers, and other products the hunters can use.

The social behavior of the prey also varies significantly with the season. Gathering and dispersal of the herds, distance of daily movements, and the individuals' wariness will vary in relatively predictable ways over the year within a population. Taken together, the variability of these seasonally linked behaviors would have significant implications for the hunting strategies and settlement patterns of Neanderthal foragers.

Human populations have learned to anticipate these fluctuations, as exemplified by the development of task-specific locations dedicated to the acquisition, transformation, and consumption of predation resources (sensu Binford 1980) in different parts of the territory. During the late Middle Paleolithic, the spatiotemporal segmentation of the hunting *chaîne opératoire* emerges in Southwestern Europe, parallel to the development of kill sites (Farizy, David, and Jaubert 1994; Rendu et al. 2012), butchery sites (Costamagno et al. 2006), and corresponding base camps.

Thus, based on the existence of task-specific locations associated with specific techno-complexes, some authors (Delagnes and Rendu 2011) proposed that several Neanderthal societies developed a logistic mobility pattern during the late Mousterian to cope with the specificity of local prey. In particular, the Quina Mousterian and the Discoidal Denticulate Mousterian (Thiébaut et al. 2010), which developed at the end of the Middle Paleolithic in Southwestern France (Jaubert 2009), are noteworthy.

A Logistic Organization during the Late Middle Paleolithic?

The Quina Mousterian (Figure 17.1) is a techno-complex identified in a large part of southwestern France, loosely correlated to the cold Heinrich Stadial 6 of the MIS 4, around 60 kA (for a discussion, see Discamps and Royer 2017). One of the Quina Mousterian characteristics in the northern part of the Aquitaine Basin is its recurrent association with reindeer hunting. On a corpus of twenty-nine Quina Mousterian stratigraphic units with associated fauna, twenty-four are primarily dominated by the arctic deer's remains, with more than half of them (18/29) presenting a specialized faunal spectrum (sensu Mellars 2004) for this taxa. In total, 73 percent of the remains found in Quina context are attributed to reindeer.

The reindeer abundance in the environment may be linked to the significant climatic pejoration characterizing the Heinrich Stadial 6 (Discamps and Royer 2017; Discamps, Jaubert, and Bachellerie 2011). During this period, we observe a major drop of the ungulate biomass (Discamps 2014). The sedentary preys that were present just before this event are abruptly replaced by reindeer, identified as a migratory species at that time (Britton et al. 2011).

Consequently, the number and kind of game had varied in this environment, but most importantly, hunters had to adapt to the major change in prey's migratory behavior and their seasonal distribution.

The Discoidal Denticulate Mousterian developed at the end of the Middle Paleolithic in Southwestern France during the first part of MIS 3. Based on faunal assemblages, two groups can be identified: sites with a diverse faunal spectrum and sites with a faunal spectrum specialized in *Bison* (Figure 17.2). The first group seems to have functioned as living camps with a large diversity of prey. Part of the second group would have been used as task-specific sites mainly dedicated to the capture of a large number of bisons (Farizy, David, and Jaubert 1994).

Although some task-specific locations were developed during these two distinct phases of the late Mousterian, their place in the annual calendar of hunter-gatherers has

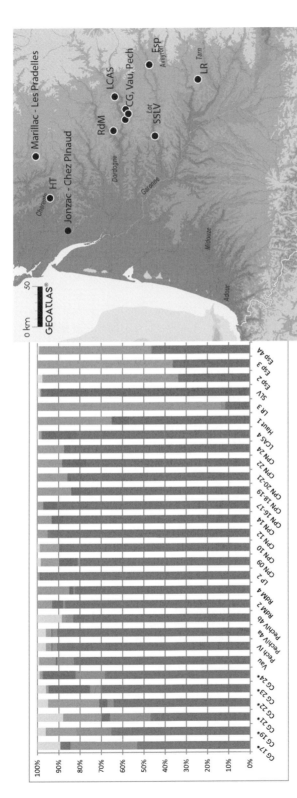

Figure 17.1 Distribution of the main Quina sites yielding faunal assemblages in Southwestern France and contribution of the main prey to the faunal spectra (in %NISP; blue = reindeer, green = red deer; red = bison; yellow = horse; gray = others). (A) CG: Combe Grenal (Guadelli 1987; Laquay 1981); Vau: Vauffrey (Delpech 1996); PechIV: Pech de l'Azé IV (Laquay 1981; Niven 2013); RdM: Roc de Marsal (Castel et al. 2017); LP: Les Pradelles (Costamagno et al. 2006); CPN: Chez Pinaud-Jonzac (Airvaux 2004; Jaubert et al. 2008; Niven 2013); LCAS: La Chapelle-aux-Saints (Rendu et al. 2014); Haut: Hauteroche (Paletta 2005); LR: La Rouquette (Rendu et al. 2011); SLV: Sous Les Vignes (Turq, Guadelli, and Quintard 1999); ESP: Espagnac (Jaubert 2001). Numbers correspond to the different stratigraphic units. *For Combe Grenal, reindeer was underevaluated in previous excavations due to selective sampling (Discamps and Faivre 2017). Based on data from Discamps and Royer 2017.

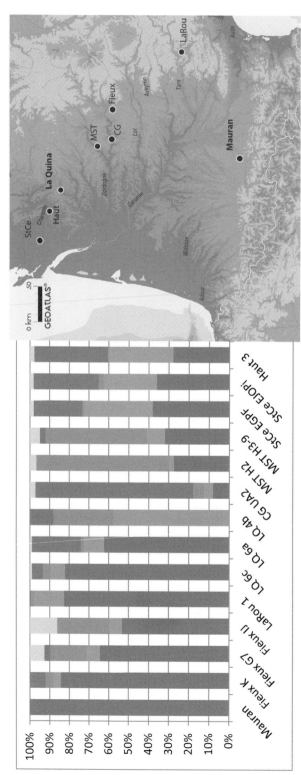

Figure 17.2 Distribution of the main Denticulate Discoidal Mousterian sites yielding faunal assemblages in Southwestern France and their faunal spectra (in %NR; blue = reindeer; green = red deer; red: bison; yellow: horse; gray: other). Mauran (Farizy, David, and Jaubert 1994); Les Fieux (Gerbe 2010); LaRou: La Rouquette (Rendu et al. 2011); LQ = La Quina (Debénath and Jelinek 1998); CG = Combe Grenal (Discamps and Faivre 2017); MST = Le Moustier (Gravina and Discamps 2015); StCE = Saint Césaire (Morin 2012); Haut = Hauteroche (Paletta 2005). Based on data from Discamps and Royer 2017.

not been discussed. As a result, their consequence on Neanderthal societal organization has been generally eluded.

Thus, the question of the seasonal organization of the sites during these periods is of prime interest to better understand their mobility strategies. In this chapter, we propose to tackle this issue by interrogating the cementochronological data available for the task-specific locations of the Quina and Discoidal Denticulate techno-complexes. Two sites for each period have been selected, three of them interpreted as kill sites and one as a secondary butchery site.

The Quina Assemblages

Level 22 at Jonzac is one of several layers from a 2-meter-high stratigraphy of reindeer bone beds (Jaubert et al. 2008). At least twenty-two reindeer have been identified from an excavation area corresponding to a small fraction of the site (maybe less than 2 percent). The site was interpreted as a task-specific location dedicated to the capture of reindeer in large numbers, based on the numerous anatomical articulations and the possible exportation of some rich elements associated with the absence of fire evidence and the presence of ready-to-use tools.

Facies 2 at *Les Pradelles* (Marillac) yielded at least sixty-nine reindeer even though less than 50 percent of the site was excavated (Costamagno et al. 2006). Moreover, it is only one of the numerous Quina units from this several-meter-deep stratigraphy. In *Les Pradelles*, Costamagno and colleagues (2006) have proposed that incomplete carcasses were brought into the site for a second butchery sequence before exportation to the base camp. The very low density of the lithic material and the systematic presence of ready-made stone tools, heavily currated, are evidence of short-term occupations. For these reasons, *Les Pradelles* was defined as a secondary butchery site. Considering both site extensions, it is possible to suggest that several hundred reindeer were processed in these two sites for an extended period.

The Discoidal Denticulate Assemblages

Mauran is located in the southern part of the Aquitaine Basin against a dismantled limestone ridge. The faunal assemblage is dominated at 99 percent by bison remains, dated from the MIS3 (Farizy, David, and Jaubert 1994). Based on the site extension and the MNI of more than 137 bison, Farizy and colleagues (Farizy, David, and Jaubert 1994) suggested that Neanderthals may have processed more than 2,000 bison.

La Quina (Gardes-le-Pontaroux, Charentes) is a large site at the base of an important limestone cliff. The site, initially excavated by L. Henri-Martin, and more recently by Debénath and Jelinek (Henri-Martin, 1909; Debénath and Jelinek 1998; Jelinek, Debénath, and Dibble 1989), yielded several stratigraphic units dated from the MIS 3. Among them, Layer 6c is largely dominated by bison remains (%NISP = 82 percent; MNI = 22).

On these two sites, the exportation of the richest elements, the expedient butchery, and the articular connections (at least at Mauran) are central evidence to interpret them as bison kill sites, where collective hunting was conducted (Rendu et al. 2011).

17.2 Materials and Methods

The cementochronological analysis of these different collections was organized under different projects but under the same protocol and with the same analysts (Table 17.1). MNI was calculated on all faunal assemblages, and one tooth per reconstructed individual was selected whenever possible to ensure that no individual would be analyzed twice. Six pictures of each tooth were recorded for preservation purposes, and each sample was molded and replicated. The teeth were embedded in an epoxy resin under a vacuum chamber. A longitudinal section was cut with a low-velocity saw (Buehler Isomet saw) following the mesiodistal plane. The sections were polished and glued to a glass slide, ground to a thickness of 100 μm, and polished. Photomicrographs were taken with a Progress CT3 camera mounted on a MOTIC BA 300 polarized microscope, with the Progress CapturePro2.10 software. Images were processed with the ImageJ software (Lieberman, Deacon, and Meadow 1990; Schneider, Rasband, and Eliceiri 2012). Thin sections were observed under natural and polarized transmitted light microscopy (x40, x100, and x400) with and without a lambda plate's insertion (Stutz 2002a,b; Rendu et al. 2009). Weathering alterations, microbial (Geusa et al. 1999), and diagenesis modifications were systematically identified with the use of the lambda (λ) plate following Stutz (2002a, 2002b). Finally, the integrity of the outermost cementum increment was evaluated.

We estimated the season of death following standard methods (Pike-Tay 1991; Martin 1909). First, we identified the nature of the last deposit as either (i) a growth zone, usually formed during the summer (wide, translucent in natural light, or light in cross-polarized light), or (ii) a "rest" layer or "annulus," usually formed in winter (thin, opaque in natural light or dark in cross-polarized light). Second, we estimated the

Table 17.1 Number of samples analyzed for each site and related references

Sites	Chronological Attribution (in MIS)	Cultural Attributions	Species Selected	Number of Samples	References
Chez-Pinaud (Jonzac)	4	Quina Mousterian	Reindeer	12	(Niven et al. 2012)
Les Pradelles (Marillac)	4	Quina Mousterian	Reindeer	12	(Rendu et al. 2012)
Mauran	3	Discoidal Denticulate	Bison	23	(Rendu et al. 2012)
La Quina	3	Discoidal Denticulate	Bison	12	(Rendu and Armand 2009)

growth stage of the last deposit. For a growth zone, three stages are defined by comparing the thickness of the last increment proportionally to the previous growth zone: Z1 – *beginning* (width lesser than 1/3 of the previous one); Z2 – *middle* (width lesser than 2/3 and greater than 1/3); and Z3 – *late* (width greater than 2/3). For an annulus, the increment's width is usually too thin to subdivide.

17.3 Results

For the two Quina sites, a total of twenty-four individuals were selected. Cementum was mostly well preserved even if some weathering alterations (longitudinal cracks) and microbial tunnels (Geusa et al. 1999) impacted three teeth's seasonal records in Jonzac. For both sites, every tooth exhibited the same increment's nature and growth stage. At Jonzac, the last increment was always an annulus, while at Les Pradelles, the last increment was a growth zone at the end of its growth (Rendu et al. 2012).

We can conclude that the killing in these two sites happened at two different moments of the seasonal growth cycle. Compared with modern data (Pike-Tay 1995), these periods correspond to the winter/early spring for Jonzac and the late summer/fall for Les Pradelles. The other seasonal proxies (tooth wear and eruption sequences and presence of fetal bones at Jonzac) support this seasonal interpretation (Costamagno et al. 2006; Niven et al. 2012). Therefore, it seems that both sites were used seasonally but at different seasons of the year.

For the Discoidal Denticulate Mousterian sites, several preservation issues were identified. Mauran teeth were primarily affected by microbial alterations and tunnels (Geusa et al. 1999), going from the dentin to the cementum on all the teeth. For three teeth, the alterations completely destroyed the seasonal record (Figure 17.3). The intensity of the alterations could be explained by the fact that Mauran is mainly an

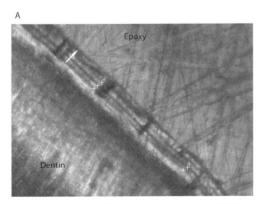 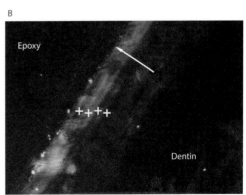

Figure 17.3 (A) Observation at X100 of cementum line of a tooth from Les Pradelles. Three annuli can be counted. The last increment is a fast-growth deposit at its end of growth. (B) Observation at high magnification (X400) of a tooth from the Mauran site. Cementum increments are challenging to see, but four annuli can be counted. The last increment is a fast-growth deposit at the end of its growth.

open-air site where the weathering also destroyed most of the cortical surfaces of numerous bones (Farizy, David, and Jaubert 1994). At La Quina, we recorded mostly longitudinal cracks within the cementum and some local recrystallization of cementum layers (Stutz 2002). Consequently, four teeth were excluded from the analysis.

For all the other teeth of these two sites, it was possible to identify the last increment as a growth zone at the end of its formation. These results agree with the other local, seasonal proxies (Farizy, David, and Jaubert 1994). We can conclude that, for both kill sites, all the bison were killed during the same period of the cementum growth cycle.

17.4   Discussion

Two different patterns seem to emerge in the Aquitaine Basin. First, during the Quina, the faunal spectra dominated by reindeer remains seem to result from occupations at different moments of the year (Figure 17.4). Unfortunately, there are very few other sites providing seasonal data for this period. However, layer 4 at La Chapelle-aux-Saints yielded a Quina assemblage associated with reindeer. In this layer, interpreted as a potential residential camp, the seasonal proxies indicate that the carcasses were accumulated during the spring to early summer period (Rendu et al. 2014). For Roc-de-Marsal layer 4, a Quina assemblage that is also dominated by reindeer, zooarchaeological analysis favors the hypothesis of a base camp or second butchery site potentially used throughout the year (Castel et al. 2017). Therefore, whatever the season, reindeer always dominate the faunal spectra in the Quina Mousterian in the north of the Aquitaine Basin. Thus, the overrepresentation of reindeer remains is likely not linked

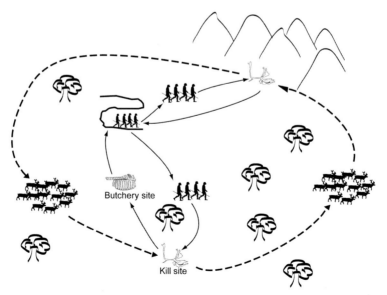

Figure 17.4 Reconstruction of the logistic mobility developed by Quina populations in the northern part of the Aquitaine Basin. Based on data from Delagnes and Rendu 2011.

to the seasonal availability of the prey nor the site function but should reflect at least in part what was available in the environment.

The recurrent use of task-specific locations over a significant period, associated with the reindeer's migratory behavior during the Quina (Britton et al. 2011), seems to suggest that reindeer movements directly influenced the settlement pattern of the Quina populations in the region and the implantation of sites within the territory. It seems that a virtual calendar of the territory occupation was established at that time, conducting the Quina society to adopt a logistic mobility (Binford 1980).

On the contrary, during the Discoidal Denticulate Mousterian, the two task-specific locations are occupied at the end of the summer or early fall. Les Fieux layer K, a contemporaneous Discoidal Denticulate site dominated by bison remains and interpreted as a task-specific location, was occupied during the same period as Gerbe (2009), demonstrated from tooth wear and eruption sequences. Thus, assemblages with a faunal spectrum specialized in bison seem to result from task-specific locations used at the same season of the year, at the moment when bison are gathering in large groups for the rut and the autumn migration (Berger and Cunningham 1991; Peck 2004). Neanderthals would have come back every end of summer to perform their collective hunts using the predictable bison's habit to optimize their capture.

Simultaneously, the Discoidal Denticulate layer EGPF at Saint-Césaire interpreted as a residential camp with a diversified faunal spectrum shows evidence of occupation during winter and spring (Morin 2012). In the similarly diverse fauna of layer H2 from Le Moustier, seasonal data is sparse but point to occupations at least in the spring and fall (Discamps and Lemeur 2019). These results are, for now, the only available seasonal data for sites with diversified faunal spectra. However, it highlights that although bison were hunted in large numbers at the end of summer/early fall, the rest of the year the Discoidal Denticulate population would have a less selective hunting activity.

Discoidal Denticulate hunting would have thus been diversified and seasonally completed by bison-specialized hunts (Figure 17.5). Therefore, Neanderthals would have taken advantage of bison's seasonal behavior to develop some task-specific locations dedicated to their capture. The exploitation of diversified prey would have counterbalanced the seasonal fluctuation of the bison concentration within the environment.

17.5 Conclusion

Within the Quina and Discoidal Denticulate, the repeated use of specific sites at a precise time of the year for the same hunting purpose attests to a scheduling of hunting activities according to a year-round pattern that influenced the movements of Neanderthal populations.

However, although the Quina Mousterians inhabiting the north of the Aquitaine Basin might have been forced to follow reindeer migrations, the Discoid Denticulate populations seems to have exploited a broader range of prey and practiced specialized hunting only during a restricted period of the year.

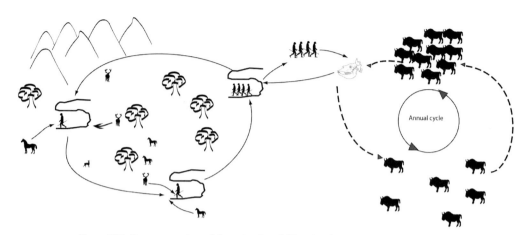

Figure 17.5 Reconstruction of the mixed mobility developed by Discoidal Denticulate populations. Based on data from Delagnes and Rendu 2011.

What seems important is the development during this late Middle Paleolithic of landmark sites that would have been used every year at the same moment. It appears that the predation system begins to structure the organization of hominid activities within their territory in both time and space and that prey behavior directly impacted the social organization of human groups.

Acknowledgments

This research was carried out as part of the CemeNTAA project – funded by the French National Agency for Research ANR (ANR-14-CE31-0011 dir. W. Rendu and L. Gourichon) and the DeerPal project – funded by the French National Agency for Research ANR (ANR-18-CE03-0007 dir. E. Discamps).

The Jonzac results were obtained in the framework of the excavation project funded and supervised by the French Ministry of Cultural Heritage (MC) SRA Nouvelle-Aquitaine-Poitiers.

References

Airvaux, J. (2004). Le site paléolithique de chez-Pinaud à Jonzac, Charente-Maritime. *Prehistoire Du Sud-Ouest* (Suppl. 8).

Armand, D., Pubert, É., & Soressi, M. (2001). Organisation saisonnière des comportements de prédation des Moustériens de Pech-de-l'Azé I. Premiers résultats. *PALEO. Revue d'archéologie préhistorique* **13**: 19–28.

Berger, J., & Cunningham, C. (1991). Bellows, copulations, and sexual selection in bison (Bison bison). *Behavioral Ecology* **2**(1): 1–6.

Binford, L. R. (1980). Willow smoke and dogs' tails: Hunter-gatherer settlement systems and archaeological site formation. *American Antiquity* **45**(1): 4–20.

Britton, K., Grimes, V., Niven, L., . . . Richards, M. P. (2011). Strontium isotope evidence for migration in late Pleistocene Rangifer: Implications for Neanderthal hunting strategies at the Middle Palaeolithic site of Jonzac, France. *Journal of Human Evolution* **61**(2): 176–85.

Castel, J. C., Discamps, E., Soulier, M.-C., . . . Turq, A. (2017). Neandertal subsistence strategies during the Quina Mousterian at Roc de Marsal (France). *Quaternary International* 43, 140–56.

Costamagno, S., Liliane, M., Cédric, B., Bernard, V., & Bruno, M. (2006). Les Pradelles (Marillac-le-Franc, France): A mousterian reindeer hunting camp? *Journal of Anthropological Archaeology* **25**(4): 466–84.

Debénath, A., & Jelinek, A. J. (1998). Nouvelles fouilles à La Quina (Charente): résultats préliminaires. *Gallia Prehistoire* **40**: 29–74.

Delagnes, A., & Rendu, W. (2011). Shifts in Neandertal mobility, technology and subsistence strategies in western France. *Journal of Archaeological Science* **38**(8), 1771–83.

Delpech, F. (1996). L'environnement animal des Moustériens Quina du Périgord. *Paléo* **8**: 31–46.

Discamps, E. (2014). Ungulate biomass fluctuations endured by Middle and Early Upper Paleolithic societies (SW France, MIS 5-3): The contributions of modern analogs and cave hyena paleodemography. *Quaternary International* **337**: 64–79.

Discamps E., & Faivre J.-P. (2017). Substantial biases affecting Combe-Grenal faunal record cast doubts on previous models of Neanderthal subsistence and environmental context. *Journal of Archaeological Science* **81**: 128132.

Discamps, E., Jaubert, J., & Bachellerie, F. (2011). Human choices and environmental constraints: Deciphering the variability of large game procurement from Mousterian to Aurignacian times (MIS 5-3) in southwestern France. *Quaternary Science Reviews* **30** (19): 2755–75.

Discamps, E., & Lemeur, C. (2019). Variabilité des proies chassées et modalités d'exploitation du Cerf au Moustérien: L'apport des collections récentes du Moustier (Dordogne, France, Couches G et H). *Paléo*, 318–29.

Discamps, E., & Royer, A. (2017). Reconstructing palaeoenvironmental conditions faced by Mousterian hunters during MIS 5 to 3 in southwestern France: A multi-scale approach using data from large and small mammal communities. *Quaternary International* **433**: 64–87.

Faivre, J.-P., Discamps, E., Gravina, B., Turq, A., Guadelli, J.-L., & Lenoir, M. (2014). The contribution of lithic production systems to the interpretation of Mousterian industrial variability in south-western France: The example of Combe-Grenal (Dordogne, France). *Quaternary International* **350**: 227–40.

Farizy, C., David, F., & Jaubert, J. (1994). *Hommes et Bisons du Paléolithique Moyen à Mauran (Haute-Garonne)*, CNRS éditions.

Gerbe, M. (2010, December 13). Économie alimentaire et environnement en Quercy au Paléolithique. Étude des assemblages fauniques de la séquence des Fieux (Lot) (PhD thesis). Université Aix-Marseille I.

Geusa, G., Bondioli, L., Capucci, E., . . . Macchiareli, R. (1999). Dental cementum annulations and age at death estimates. In L. Bondioli & R. Macchiarelli (eds.), *Osteodental Biology of the People of Portus Romae (Necropolis of Isola Sacra, 2nd–3rd cent. AD)*, 2, Roma: Museo Naz. "L Pigorini."

Gravina, B., & Discamps, E. (2015). MTA-B or not to be? Recycled bifaces and shifting hunting strategies at Le Moustier and their implication for the late Middle Palaeolithic in southwestern France. *Journal of Human Evolution* **84**: 83–98.

Guadelli, J.-L. (1987). Contribution a l'etude des zoocenoses prehistoriques en Aquitaine (Würm ancien et interstade würmien) (PhD thesis), Universite Bordeaux 1.

Jaubert, J. (2001). Un site moustérien de type Quina dans la vallée du Célé: Pailhès à Espagnac-Sainte-Eulalie. *Gallia Préhistoire* **43**: 1–100.

  (2009). Les archéoséquences du Paléolithique moyen du Sud-Ouest de la France: Quel bilan un quart de siècle après François Bordes? Presented at the François Bordes et la Préhistoire. Colloque International François Bordes, Bordeaux 22–24 avril 2009, Paris: Ed. du CTHS: 235–53.

Jaubert, J., Hublin, J.-J., Mcpherron, S. P., . . . Thiébaut, C. (2008). Paléolithique moyen récent et Paléolithique supérieur ancien à Jonzac (Charente-Maritime).

Jelinek, A. J., Debénath, A., & Dibble, H. L. (1989). A preliminary report on evidence related to the interpretation of economic and social activities of neandertals at the site of La Quina (Charente), France. In *La Subsistance*, Eraul: Liège, 99–106.

Laquay, G. (1981). Recherches sur les faunes du Würm I en Périgord (PhD thesis), Universite Bordeaux 1.

Lieberman, D. E. (1993). The rise and fall of seasonal mobility among hunter-gatherers: The case of the southern levant [and comments and replies]. *Current Anthropology* **34**(5) 599–631.

Lieberman, D. E., Deacon, T. W., & Meadow, R. H. (1990). Computer image enhancement and analysis of cementum increments as applied to teeth of *Gazella gazella*. *Journal of Archaeological Science* **17**(5): 519–33.

Martin, H. 1909. La faune moustérienne de la Quina, Bulletin de l'Association Française pour l'Avancement des Sciences, 37e session, Clermont-Ferrand, 727–30.

Meignen, L., Bar-Yosef, O., Speth, J. D., & Stiner, M. C. (2006). Changes in settlement patterns during the Near Eastern Middle Paleolithic. In E. Hovers & S. Kuhn (eds.), *Transitions before the Transition: Evolution and Stability in the Middle Paleoithic and Middle Stone Age*. New York, Boston: Springer, 149–70.

Mellars, P. A. (2004). Reindeer specialization in the early Upper Palaeolithic: The evidence from south west France. *Journal of Archaeological Science* **31**(5): 613–17.

Morin, E. (2012). *Reassessing Paleolithic Subsistence*. Cambridge: Cambridge University Press.

Niven, L. (2013). A diachronic evaluation of Neanderthal cervid exploitation and site use at Pech de l'Azé IV, France. In J. L. Clark and J. D. Speth (eds.), *Zooarchaeology and Modern Human Origins: Human Hunting Behavior during the Later Pleistocene*. The Netherlands: Springer, 151–61.

Niven, L., Steele, T. E., Rendu, W., . . . Hublin, J.-J. (2012). Neandertal mobility and large-game hunting: The exploitation of reindeer during the Quina Mousterian at Chez-Pinaud Jonzac (Charente-Maritime, France). *Journal of Human Evolution* **63**(4): 624–35.

Paletta, A. (2005). L'évolution des comportements de subsistance des hommes du Moustérien au Solutréen dans la région Poitou-Charentes (France) (PhD thesis), Muséum national d'histoire naturelle, Paris.

Peck, T. R. (2004). *Bison Ethology and Native Settlement Patterns during the Old Women's Phase on the Northwestern Plains*. Oxford: Archaeopress.

Pike-Tay, A. (1991). *Red Deer Hunting in the Upper Paleolithic of Southwest France: A Study in Seasonality*. Oxford: Tempus Reparatum.

  (1995). Variability and synchrony of seasonal indicators in dental cementum microstructure of the Kaminuriak caribou population. *Archaeofauna* **4**: 273–84.

Rendu, W. (2010). Hunting behavior and Neanderthal adaptability in the Late Pleistocene site of Pech-de-l'Azé I. *Journal of Archaeological Science* **37**(8): 1798–1810.

Rendu, W., & Armand, D. (2009). Saisonnalité de prédation du Bison du gisement moustérien de la Quina (Gardes-le-Pontaroux, Charente), niveau 6c. Apport à la compréhension des comportements de subsistance. *Bulletin de La Société Préhistorique Française* **106**(4): 679–90.

Rendu, W., Armand, D., Pubert, E., & Soressi, M. (2009). Approche taphonomique en cémentochronologie : Réexamen du niveau 4 du Pech-de-l'Azé I (Carsac, Dordogne, France). *Paléo* **21**: 223–36.

Rendu, W., Beauval, C., Crevecoeur, I., . . . Maureille, B. (2014). Evidence supporting an intentional Neandertal burial at La Chapelle-aux-Saints. *Proceedings of the National Academy of Sciences* **111**(1): 81.

Rendu, W., Bourguignon, L., Costamagno, S., . . . Park, S.-J. (2011). Mousterian hunting camps: Interdisciplinary approach and methodological considerations. *P@lethnologie* (3): 63–76.

Rendu, W., Costamagno, S., Meignen, L., & Soulier, M.-C. (2012). Monospecific faunal spectra in Mousterian contexts: Implications for social behavior. *Quaternary International* **247**: 50–8.

Schneider, C. A., Rasband, W. S., & Eliceiri, K. W. (2012). NIH Image to ImageJ: 25 years of image analysis. *Nature Methods* **9**(7): 671–75.

Stutz, A. J. (2002). Polarizing microscopy identification of chemical diagenesis in archaeological cementum. *Journal of Archaeological Science* **29**(11): 1327–47.

Thiébaut, C., Claud, É., Deschamps, M., . . . Colonge, D. (2010). Diversité des productions lithiques du Paléolithique moyen récent (OIS 4-OIS 3): Enquête sur le rôle des facteurs environnementaux, fonctionnels et culturels.

Turq, A., Guadelli, J.-L., & Quintard, A. (1999). A propos de deux sites d'habitat moustérien de type Quina à exploitation du bison: l'exemple du Mas-Viel et de Sous-les-Vignes. In J.P. Brugal, F. D. Enloe & J. G. Jaubert (eds.), *Le Bison: Gibier et Moyen de Subsistance des Hommes du Paléolithique aux Paléoindiens des Grandes Plaines*, Edition APDCA, Antibes, 143–58.

18 Investigating Seasonal Competition between Hominins and Cave Hyaenas in the Belgian Ardennes during the Late Pleistocene: Insights from Cementum Analyses

Elodie-Laure Jimenez and Mietje Germonpré

18.1 Introduction

Seasonal organization of subsistence activities has long been recognized as a key question in studying hunter-gatherer societies, including in Palaeolithic archaeology (Chapter 17). Gathering seasonal data on archaeological sites from a given region allows us to grasp the complex spatiotemporal strategies that human groups adopted to overcome fluctuating ecological and environmental pressures throughout the year. This variability in seasonal subsistence behavior can be due to multiple factors, such as climatic constraints, local depletion of prey, migratory prey behavior, or avoidance strategies when the degree of interspecific competition among predators increases (Begon, Townsend, and Harper 2006).

Within northwestern Europe, the mountainous region of the Belgian Ardennes (south to the Sambre-and-Meuse furrow, Figure 18.1) has yielded much evidence of Pleistocene human presence (Posth et al. 2016; Rougier et al. 2016; Semal et al. 2009; Toussaint et al. 2010; Toussaint and Pirson 2006) despite regular harsh environmental conditions (e.g., cold temperatures, northerly winds, fluctuations in raw material access). This karstic region of southern Belgium is characterized by a dense network of deep valleys and rivers and is situated at the crossroads of contrasting landscapes, right at the North European Plain limit. In this subregion, both Neanderthals and the first anatomically modern humans (AMH, henceforth) took advantage of the ungulate reservoir and the numerous natural shelters. However, recent zooarchaeological studies showed that these hominins also had to share this region with an exceptionally high number of other large predators, particularly cave hyaenas (fully carnivore diet) and cave bears (variable dietary preferences), with which they were in direct and indirect competition for food and habitat (Daujeard et al. 2016; Jimenez 2017). The spatial and temporal variability of these top predators' subsistence strategies should be investigated to better identify ecological and environmental pressures and understand the dynamics of their trophic relationships.

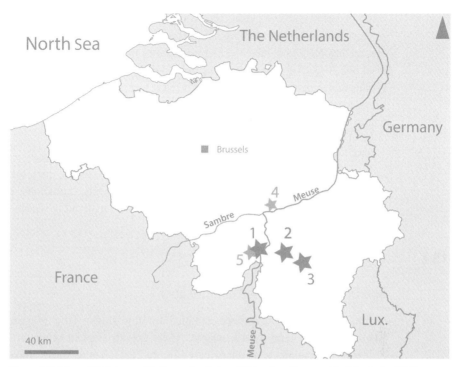

Figure 18.1 Map of Belgium with the major Palaeolithic sites discussed in this study. (1) Caverne Marie-Jeanne; (2) Trou Magrite; (3) Tiène des Maulins; (4) Scladina; (5) Trou du Diable. Black stars refer to the site sampled for this study.

Unfortunately, the very early interest in prehistoric findings brought nineteenth-century scholars to lead extensive excavations in this region, as the geologist Édouard Dupont, the first pioneers emptied most of the important Palaeolithic sequences in the area. The now-outdated recovery strategies in use hinder the possibility of offering a good context to the discoveries. Moreover, recent studies show that taphonomic processes in these caves are intensely intricate and, consequently, the sedimentary dynamics are particularly complex to decipher. Thus, albeit rich and abundant, the archaeological record in southern Belgium lacks high-quality data resolution. This study aims to examine the potential of cementum analysis to shed new light on the seasonal organization of hominin activities and one of their main competitors, cave hyaena (*Crocuta crocuta spelaea*). Therefore, we undertook a multitaxon, multisite cementochronological study in the region and tested season at death of different prey accumulated by either hyaenas or hominins during the second half of MIS 3 in the Belgian Ardennes. In conjunction with a classic seasonal study conducted on ungulate species, this study's specificity resides in the fact that carnivore dental cementum has been tested.

Since the 1970s, cementum analysis has become common practice in zoological science (Chapter 1; Grue and Jensen 1979; Medill et al. 2009) as well as in archaeology (Gourichon 2004; Jaarsveld, Henschel, and Skinner 1987; Martin 1994; Niven and Martin 2018; Pike-Tay 1991; Rendu et al. 2012; Stutz 2002). In Belgium, for example, some experimental work using cementum analysis was carried out in the 1990s by A. Stutz and collaborators (Stutz, Lieberman, and Spiess 1995). Nonetheless, only very few studies have undertaken cementum studies on ancient carnivores (e.g., Nývltová Fišáková 2013, 2014, on Pleistocene foxes, bears, and cave lions from Central Europe). If other zooarchaeological methods are used to test seasonality on other predators – like bears, for example (Germonpré and Sablin 2001; Kitagawa et al. 2012) – it still appears that questions about carnivore behavior as a proxy to reconstruct ecological pressures are widely under-investigated (but see Discamps 2014).

This chapter presents the results of cementum analyses directly conducted on several hyaena canine teeth to obtain seasonal data. Because such an approach is unprecedented, we will quickly overview the achievements, limitations, and prospects of this experiment and the validity of using carnivore material in seasonality studies.

18.2   Materials and Methods

Site Description and Research History

Three Belgian sites have been sampled for this study: Trou Magrite, Tiène des Maulins, and Caverne Marie-Jeanne. There are all situated within a 20-kilometer radius in the country's southern part (Figure 18.1). These sites' faunal collections have been analyzed as part of a PhD dissertation (Jimenez 2017).

Trou Magrite
Trou Magrite is a cave and rock shelter located in Pont-à-Lesse, province of Namur. The site lies on the Condroz plateau at the Lesse River's confluence and the Meuse River. Discovered by the Belgian geologist É. Dupont in 1864, the site has been intensively excavated for several years in the second half of the nineteenth century. É. Dupont uncovered thousands of Palaeolithic lithic artifacts and faunal remains, as well as works of portable art (Dewez 1985; Dupont 1867). Despite good intuitions and an honorable interest in the stratigraphy for this time, É. Dupont omitted to mention the spatial origin of each archaeological remain. However, the site quickly became one of the most famous Palaeolithic sites in Western Europe. It served, for instance, as a baseline for H. Breuil's subdivision of the Upper Palaeolithic (Breuil 1912). During the early 1990s, M. Otte and L. Straus conducted new controlled excavations on a peripheral zone of the cave entrance to identify "intact deposits" and characterize the Early Upper Palaeolithic levels (Otte and Straus 1995). Unfortunately, it appears that they presumably only found disturbed layers.

Although most of the Palaeolithic material derives from É. Dupont's excavations, several lithic studies have been done but only based on typological analyses (Di Modica 2009, 2010; de Sonnevilles-Bordes 1961; Dinnis 2009, 2012; Dinnis and Flas 2016; Flas 2008; Otte 1979; Ulrix-Closset 1975). Consequently, Trou Magrite has been recognized as one of the most important Middle Palaeolithic sites in Belgium (Di Modica 2010; Ulrix-Closset 1975) and Belgium's third-largest Aurignacian site (Dinnis 2015). However, scarce evidence of Magdalenian lithic material has also been found in the collection (Dewez 1985; Dinnis 2012; Flas 2008). The faunal material from Otte & Straus' excavations (about 13,000 remains, including microfauna) has been analyzed by A. Gautier and J.-M. Cordy (Cordy 1995; Gautier 1995; Gautier et al. 1997). They reported the faunal collection as being "very fragmented," with no clear evidence of anthropogenic or carnivore activities. The 50,451 faunal remains coming from Dupont's excavations, still housed in paleontology collections in the Royal Belgian Institute of Natural Sciences (RBINS), have only been studied recently (Jimenez 2017). About 1,000 bones with anthropogenic marks have been observed, associated with a faunal spectrum dominated by horse, reindeer, and rhinoceros. A scanty presence of hyaenas and their limited impact on the assemblage shows that large carnivores made short incursions on the site, probably to scavenge human leftovers. Radiocarbon dates on anthropogenically modified material provided ages ranging between 39,690 ± 320 BP (43,920 à 42,870 cal BP) for a bone *retoucher* (Smolderen 2016) to 25,080 ± 320 BP (30,340 à 29,619 cal BP) for a lozangic bone point made of reindeer antler (Charles, Hedges, and Jadin 2003). None of the twenty-three dates seems to go beyond the radiocarbon limit, which confirms that most of the archaeological material was accumulated between the end of the Middle Palaeolithic and the beginning of the Upper Palaeolithic (Aurignacian/Gravettian).

Tiène des Maulins

Tiène des Maulins is a small rock shelter situated in Rochefort, province of Namur. The low terrace and entrance of this rock shelter are situated a few meters away from the Lomme River, a small tributary of the Lesse River. B. Marée, a speleologist and amateur archaeologist, first discovered the site in the early 1970s. Between 1978 and 1985, he excavated the main chamber of the shelter with a team of volunteers and collected nearly 8,000 Pleistocene and Holocene faunal remains, as well as a small lithic assemblage. A new field program directed by M. Groenen (Université Libre de Bruxelles) started in 2000 and lasted until 2011. Hence, between 1979 and 2011, this site has been excavated for eighteen years, and this fieldwork permitted to unearth more than 11,000 faunal remains (from both Pleistocene and early Holocene periods, microfauna included) and 102 lithic artifacts (Groenen and Marée 2000). However, in the absence of consistent geoarchaeological studies during the excavations, the stratigraphy and sedimentary processes are poorly known. A recent taphonomic and spatial study combined with a critical review of the excavation archives has recovered a significant amount of missing spatial data. The zooarchaeological study on 2,555 Pleistocene faunal remains (including 1,300 dental remains) sheds light on the site function (Jimenez 2017). First, this study highlighted that the site was used as a hyaena den several times during the Late Pleistocene (<43 to 26 kA BP). Besides, the very small "Early Upper Palaeolithic"-type lithic assemblage and the ten dated horse bones (MNI = 1) with cut marks that were *a priori* associated with it show that the shelter also hosted an ephemeral butchery site circa 28,5–25 kA BP/34–28,5 kA cal. BP (Jimenez 2017 and unpublished data).

Caverne Marie-Jeanne

Last, we included in this study Caverne Marie-Jeanne, level 4. This rock crevice filled with Pleistocene sediments is situated in Hastière-Lavaux, province of Namur. The site is located about 25 m above the Féron River, a small tributary of the Meuse River. During the summer of 1943, a team from the RBINS directed by M. Glibert excavated about 40 m^3 of sediment. The totality of the filling sediment under the calcareous arch was extracted during this field campaign and this yielded a large quantity of Quaternary fauna (Gautier and De Heinzelin 1980). The faunal spectrum is dominated by cave hyaena, woolly rhinoceros, horses, and bovines. Their remains display extent carnivore activities (Jimenez 2017). Besides, the number of lithic artifacts is minimal (n = 14), and their edge damage (high degree of abrasion, rounded edges) and the absence of reduction sequence suggest that lithics have been introduced by natural transport processes and, therefore, that bones and stones have accumulated independently with no anthropogenic intention. Moreover, the complete absence of anthropogenic marks on the faunal material and the overwhelming presence of hyaena remains or evidence of its activity have led different authors to interpret this site as a hyaena/carnivore den (Gautier and De Heinzelin 1980; Jimenez 2017). Radiocarbon dating on micromammals suggested deposition of level 4 during the MIS 3, from about 43 ±1.9 kA (49,972–44,453 cal BP) to >43.9 kA BP (Brace et al. 2012).

Sampling Strategy and Analyzed Material

For this cementochronological study, we analyzed fifteen ungulate teeth from these sites: five teeth from Trou Magrite (only from É. Dupont's collection), two teeth from Tiène des Maulins, and eight teeth from Caverne Marie-Jeanne. The targeted species differ from site to site, depending on the dominant species in the faunal spectrum, the teeth available, and their state of preservation (Table 18.1).

Due to the context of their recovery and particularly complex taphonomy, samples have been selected carefully to avoid sampling the same individual twice and to increase our sample size. Thus, criteria like tooth rank, its side, as well as its size, shape, use wear, and age estimation, have been taken into account in the sampling process so that all the teeth selected belong to different individuals. Site functions (e.g., hyaena den) and taphonomic origins (samples extracted from the mandibular bone with clear marks of the accumulating agent like heavy gnawing or presence of butchery marks) have also been considered to answer different questions like predator's season(s) of occupation at the site or seasonal presence of prey species around the site.

From Tiène des Maulins, the four selected teeth are from one bison, one reindeer, and two hyaenas. Despite the absence of clear taphonomic indicators of the accumulating agent on the bison and reindeer teeth, they were selected for their good preservation and to test the seasonal presence of this species around the site. Additionally, we selected two hyaena's canine teeth to assess their season of occupation on this site.

From Trou Magrite, seven teeth from six individuals were analyzed. Three LM2 and two LP3 of reindeer were selected because the mandibular bone from which they were extracted showed clear marks of anthropogenic activities (e.g., cut marks, green breaks

Table 18.1 Details of the fifteen ungulate teeth included in this cementochronological study (Cmj = Caverne Marie-Jeanne; Mag. = Trou Magrite; Tdm = Tiène Des Maulins; L = left; R = right)

Site	ID Number	Nature	Species	Tooth Rank	Side	RBINS ID Number	Accumulating Agent
CMJ	CMJ.4.3208	Isolated tooth	Bos/Bison	LM2	L	VERT_00485	Probable hyaena
CMJ	CMJ.4.3212	Isolated tooth	Bos/Bison	LM1	L	VERT_00486	Probable hyaena
CMJ	CMJ CMJ.4.3190	Tooth + mandibular bone	Bison	LM3	R	VERT_00487	Hyaena
CMJ	CMJ.4.3187	Tooth + mandibular bone	Bison	LP3	L	VERT_00488	Hyaena
CMJ	CMJ.4.3186	Tooth + mandibular bone	Bos/Bison	LP4	L	VERT_00489	Hyaena
CMJ	CMJ.4.3188	Tooth + mandibular bone	Bos/Bison	LP3	L	VERT_00490	Probable hyaena
CMJ	CMJ.4.3197	Isolated tooth	Bos/Bison	LM1	R	VERT_00491	Probable hyaena
CMJ	CMJ.4.3207	Isolated tooth	Bos/Bison	LM1	L	VERT_00492	Hyaena
Mag	168	Tooth + mandibular bone	Rangifer	LP3	R	VERT-00493	Human
Mag	166	Tooth + mandibular bone	Rangifer	LP3	R	VERT_00494	Human
Mag	165	Tooth + mandibular bone	Rangifer	LM2	L	VERT_00495	Human
Mag	178	Tooth + mandibular bone	Rangifer	LM2	R	VERT_00496	Human
Mag	181	Tooth + mandibular bone	Rangifer	LM2	R	VERT_00497	Human
TDM	TM.81.V.36	Isolated tooth	Bison	UM	R	–	Unknown
TDM	TM.79.II.4.27	Isolated tooth	Rangifer	LM3	L	–	Unknown

Table 18.2 Details of the four cave hyaena canines included in this cementochronological study

Site	ID Number	Nature	Species	Element	Side	Reference
Trou Magrite	VERT_00498	Isolated tooth	*C. crocuta spelaea*	LC	R	Jimenez, 2017
Trou Magrite	VERT_00499	Isolated tooth	*C. crocuta spelaea*	LC	R	Jimenez, 2017
Tiène-des-Maulins	TM.80.II.45	Isolated tooth	*C. crocuta spelaea*	LC	L	Jimenez, 2017
Tiène-des-Maulins	TM.81.III.33	Isolated tooth	*C. crocuta spelaea*	LC	R	Jimenez, 2017

associated with other anthropogenic marks like scrapping and absence of carnivore marks) and could reveal the season of their exploitation. Two hyaena's canine teeth were selected to assess the carnivore presence on the site.

Last, eight teeth of *Bos/Bison* from Caverne Marie-Jeanne have been analyzed for this study. Four of them have been extracted from mandibles presenting clear evidence of hyaena activities (e.g., Binford 1981; Fourvel 2013), and four were isolated teeth with no obvious indication of the accumulating agent. No hyaena teeth were selected for this study.

In addition, four hyaena canines were analyzed, two from Trou Magrite and two from Tiène des Maulins (Table 18.2).

Methods

All of the samples presented in this study were prepared in a geology laboratory in Dijon (France). The thin sections have been analyzed in the PACEA laboratory (Bordeaux). The thin sections on ungulate specimens have been made following the protocol adapted to pluriradicular teeth (Chapters 9 and 11). For the analysis of cave hyaena specimens, we selected the standard tooth type advised by Matson's lab on modern carnivores (i.e., the canines)[1] and applied the protocol commonly used for monoradicular teeth (Chapter 1). The cutting angle of the sections is transverse, just under the collar neck, and the rest of the crown is left undamaged (Figure 18.2).

18.3 Results – Prey Selection and Mobility of the Predators

Out of the nineteen teeth analyzed, we have been able to identify a season of death on fourteen teeth (Table 18.3). Indeed, due to weathering problems and remobilizations of the mineralized increment, no convincing ROI (region of interest) could be found in five of them. We will first present the results of prey-species seasonality and then disclose the test outcome on hyaena.

Prey-Species Seasonality at Trou Magrite

At Trou Magrite, the five reindeer teeth analyzed were extracted from their mandibular bone for this study. All of them were bearing evidence of anthropogenic activities,

---

[1] www.matsonslab.com/the-science/cementum-aging

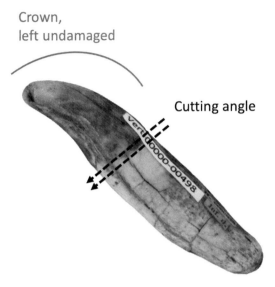

Figure 18.2 Cutting protocol used in this study for carnivore canine teeth

showing that hominins butchered the individuals. For four of the analyzed specimens, the thin sections' microscopic analysis reveals that the last increment was a slow-growth deposit, indicating the death occurred during the cold season (CS). The fifth specimen analysis shows that the last increment was a fast-growth deposit, but the growing process was still at an early age (Figure 18.3A), which suggests a season of death at the beginning or during the warm season (BWS-MWS).

Prey-Species Seasonality at Caverne Marie-Jeanne

From the eight bovine teeth sampled from Caverne Marie-Jeanne, two teeth were unreadable. The seasonal signals obtained from the analysis of the six other teeth are diverse. The analysis of one individual revealed that a slow-growth deposit ends the sequence, suggesting that its death occurred during the cold season. Two others died at an undefined stage of the warm season, two died at the beginning of the warm season, and last, the death of the individual VERT_00491 occurred between the late stage of the warm season and the end of the cold season (Figure 18.3B).

Prey-Species Seasonality at Tiène des Maulins

At Tiène des Maulins, the combination of a production defect of the thin sections and highly weathered cementum impeded us from finding a suitable ROI on the reindeer specimen. The mineralized increments of the bison specimen were in a better state of preservation (Figure 18.3D), but only a broad estimation of its season of death has been possible, from the end of the warm season to the end of the cold season (EWS-CS). However, we have to keep in mind that the taphonomic agent responsible for its death/accumulation is not identifiable since the teeth were found isolated.

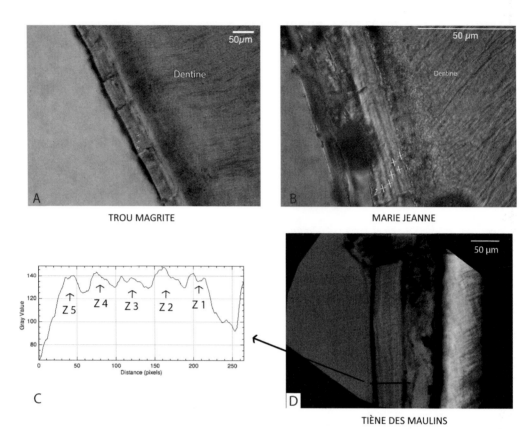

Figure 18.3 Cementum increments from (A) Reindeer tooth (VERT-00493) from Trou Magrite. Three slow-growth deposits are visible in natural light (white crosses). The last deposit is translucent, indicating a season-of-death during the warm season; (B) Cementum increments from a bovine molar (VERT-00491) from Caverne Marie-Jeanne. At least six slow-growth deposits are countable (white crosses) in natural light. Alterations are observable on the outermost deposits; (C and D) Bovine tooth (TM.81.V.36) from Tiène des Maulins; (D) Analyzed with ImageJ; (C) Five fast-growth deposits (Z1 to Z5) and four slow-growth deposits.

18.4 Cementum Analysis on Cave Hyaena: Test Outcome

Overall, the thin sections' observation made from the four hyaena teeth reveals quite a poor state of preservation of the dental structure, with many visible transversal fractures (Figure 18.4). Cementum increments, when found, clearly suffered from remobilization (see cementum on the top side of Figure 18.4). Satisfactory ROIs have been hard to diagnose.

The age of this material and its complex taphonomy could explain poor cementum preservation. It would also be worth considering that hyaenas' specific feeding behaviors (i.e., gnawing, cracking, and eating bones) could impede the long-term preservation of the cementum because the forces applied to their dentition when feeding is substantial (Binder and Van Valkenburgh 2000; Van Valkenburgh 2009) or affect the

Table 18.3 Summary of results from cementochronological study of ungulates and hyaena teeth; (CS = cold season; WS = nonidentified stage of the warm season; BWS = beginning of warm season; MWS = mid-warm season; EWS = end of warm season)

Site	ID Number	Species	Taphonomic Agent	Alterations/ Remobilization	N. Translucent Lines	N. Opaque Lines	Season at Death
CMJ	VERT_00485	Bos/Bison	Large carnivore	None	6	5	BWS
CMJ	VERT_00486	Bos/Bison	Large carnivore	None	6	6	CS
CMJ	VERT_00487	Bison	Hyaena	High presence of cellular cementum	>9	>8	BWS–MWS
CMJ	VERT_00488	Bison	Hyaena	High presence of cellular cementum	–	–	Unreadable
CMJ	VERT_00489	Bos/Bison	Hyaena	High presence of cellular cementum	–	–	Unreadable
CMJ	VERT_00490	Bos/Bison	Hyaena	High presence of cellular cementum	>13	>12	WS
CMJ	VERT_00491	Bos/Bison	Large carnivore	Hypercementosis/ Mixed cementum?	7?	6 ?	EWS–CS
CMJ	VERT_00492	Bos/Bison	Large carnivore	Weathered	>6	>6	BWS
Mag	VERT-00493	Rangifer	Anthropogenic	Weathered cementum; transversal cracks	4	3	BWS–MWS
Mag	VERT_00494	Rangifer	Anthropogenic	High presence of cellular cementum	4	4	CS
Mag	VERT_00495	Rangifer	Anthropogenic	-	4	4	CS
Mag	VERT_00496	Rangifer	Anthropogenic	Few well-preserved cementum	3	3	CS
Mag	VERT_00497	Rangifer	Anthropogenic	Little well-preserved cementum	2	1	CS
Mag	VERT_00498	Hyaena	Hyaena	Little well-preserved cementum; thin sections too thick	–	–	Unreadable
Mag	VERT_00499	Hyaena	Hyaena	Weathered cementum; transversal cracks	>5	>5	CS
TDM	TM.80.II.45	Hyaena	Hyaena	None	>6	>5	EWS–CS
TDM	TM.81.III.33	Hyaena	Hyaena	Transversal cracks; no ROI?	–	–	Unreadable
TDM	TM.81.V.36	Bison	Unknown	None	>5	>4	EWS–CS
TDM	TM.79.II.4.27	Rangifer	Unknown	Weathered cementum; glue problem in the thin sections	–	–	Unreadable

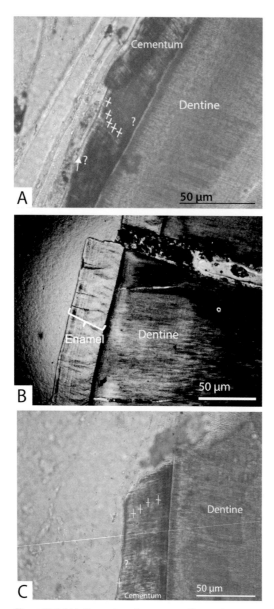

Figure 18.4 (A) Cementum increments from a hyaena canine tooth (TM.80.II.45) from Tiène des Maulins. At least five slow-growth deposits are visible; (B) Hyaena canine tooth (TM.81.III.33) from Tiène des Maulins in polarized light with enamel increments but no legible cementum; (C) Cementum increments from a hyaena's canine tooth (Vert-00499) from Trou Magrite.

dynamics of cementogenesis (e.g., hypercementosis). That being said, we could not identify any significant structural difference in the cementum increments between cave hyaena and other ungulates as they both display a "rhythmic" and consistent alternation between fast-growth and slow-growth increments.

Even though no good ROI of acellular cementum could be isolated on two hyaena specimens, a seasonal signal was identified on the two other individuals, one from Tiène des Maulins, the other from Trou Magrite. A good ROI has been identified for the individual TM.80.II.45 from Tiène des Maulins (Figure 18.4A). The last fast-growth increment of the sequence looks complete or nearly complete, and a slow-growth deposit may have even started to grow on top of it. Hence, we cautiously suggest that the individual died between the end of the warm season or during the cold season. On the second analyzed individual from the same site, TM.81.III.33, none of the thin sections permitted to find a satisfying ROI (Figure 18.4B).

At Trou Magrite, two other hyaena canines have been analyzed. Unfortunately, one of the specimens (VERT-00498) did not provide any satisfying ROI. However, these thin sections seem uneven and thicker than expected (Chapter 9), and maybe the lab preparation did not strictly follow the recommended protocol. On the contrary, the second canine tooth from specimen VERT-00499 revealed a satisfying ROI despite a poorly preserved cementum. As shown in Figure 18.4C, we can identify a minimum of five translucent and five opaque increments, indicating that the individual died during the cold season.

18.5 Discussion

Hominin Strategies in Southern Belgium

Although small (NMI = 5) and coming from a single site (Trou Magrite), our sample related to human seasonality shows that four of the five analyzed reindeer individuals were exploited during the cold season. Besides, all the dates carried out on the analyzed material confirm human occupation at the end of the Middle Palaeolithic and the Early Upper Palaeolithic. Incidentally, these results also seem to match the previous zooarchaeological study conducted by A. Gautier at Trou Magrite, showing that six reindeer were killed during the cold season. As part of the monograph on Otte & Straus' 1991–1992 excavations, Stutz and collaborators conducted a cementochronological study on archaeological faunas from the same region, consisting of the analysis of twenty-three ungulate teeth from five sites dated from the Late Pleistocene (Stutz, Lieberman, and Spiess 1995). This former study showed that ungulates at Trou Magrite "Aurignacian levels" (MNI = 4) were killed between the cold season and the beginning of the warm season. The results obtained for other sites with late MIS 3 mixed deposits or Mousterian deposits confirm this general pattern, for example, at Trou du Diable (mixed "Mousterian-Aurignacian" deposits; Figure 18.1), where data on reindeer and ibex (MNI = 8) indicate death during the cold season/beginning of the warm season. Season-of-death information from several specimens of reindeer and red deer (MNI = 6) from Scladina (Mousterian level V; Figure 18.1) also suggested that they were killed during the cold season/beginning of the warm season for four individuals and "summer/fall" for two individuals.

However, we still have to bear in mind that no evidence of anthropogenic (or carnivore) activities has been reported on these specimens, therefore questioning the nature of their accumulating agent. Nonetheless, the apparent consistency in the data from both the present study and previous works (Stutz, Lieberman, and Spiess 1995) could suggest that Trou Magrite could have possibly served as a "satellite" location for winter reindeer hunting events during the Middle to Upper Palaeolithic transition.

This seasonal subsistence strategy could have been suitable for highly mobile groups (Delagnes and Rendu 2011), as already proposed for other reindeer-dominated Mousterian assemblages like Jonzac (Niven et al. 2012) or Abri du Maras level 4.1 (Daujeard et al. 2019) or Châtelperronian-Aurignacian assemblages like Roc-de-Combe (Soulier and Mallye 2012). At Trou Magrite, and in line with the lithic studies conducted in southern Belgium, we could hypothesize that hominins planned hunting trips in the region, possibly organizing specialized hunting or mass kills of ungulates whose meat and fat could have been transported to a residential camp and stored over the winter (Enloe 2003). Even though these preliminary results and those obtained previously seem to point toward seasonal occupations of hominins at Trou Magrite and other sites in the region, further investigation will be necessary to better understand change or continuity in hominin subsistence strategies across the Middle to Upper Palaeolithic transition in the Belgian Ardennes.

Hyaena Seasonality

This work was also the opportunity to conduct a comparative seasonal study on hyaenas and test their mobility patterns and land use during MIS 3, specifically across the Middle to Upper Palaeolithic transition. In comparison to the seasonal data obtained on the archaeological record – suggesting that Palaeolithic humans seem to have preferred the warm season to hunt in the region (Jimenez et al. 2017; Stutz, Lieberman, and Spiess 1995) – the data obtained on cave hyaenas' cementum is quite different (Table 18.3). At Caverne Marie-Jeanne, our results from cementum analysis have shown that cave hyaenas hunted bovines all year-round (Table 18.3). Regarding the analyses conducted directly on hyaena specimens from Tiène des Maulins and Trou Magrite, the data obtained from two specimens show seasons at death during the cold season or at the end of the warm season. Thus, despite a relatively small number of analyzed teeth, our preliminary results on hyaena land-use strategy show no specific pattern in their seasonal distribution, suggesting that cave hyaena might have been present all year-round in southern Belgium at the end of the Late Pleistocene.

Implications for Interspecific Competition among Top Predators

Investigating differential seasonal behaviors of the two main top predators of the Pleistocene allows us to better understand their respective responses to the same environment and how they managed interspecific competition or other ecological pressures. If cave hyaenas were present all year-round within southern Belgium territory, they probably did find enough resources to subsist in terms of shelter, water, and prey. By contrast, our results on hominins could indicate that they did not exploit this same region on a year-round basis but set up more composite land-use strategies. Based on current knowledge, we can venture an assumption on the spatio-temporal organization of these two top-predators.

1. The many Neanderthal and AMH remains found in southern Belgium dated from the Middle to Upper Palaeolithic transition show that they were highly present in this region, highlighting a great interest in the available resources. However, as high-quality lithic resources were scarce in southern Belgium, human populations may have preferred alternate missions to obtain food (in the south) and other resources like lithic raw material (in the north), going back and forth between the two subregions. Our preliminary results on seasonality show that these southern incursions were more likely to happen during the cold season, perhaps to find cave shelters. This season also coincides with some prey-species' migration, like reindeer, who were migrating southward to reach their winter range.
2. Cave hyaenas, hominins' top competitors, were probably present in southern Belgium all year-round. Hominins were thus traveling to this region *despite* many carnivores being present in this same territory. Cave bears (taking advantage of the numerous deep karstic cavities to hibernate during the cold season) and cave hyaenas (present all year-round) were indeed the most common big-size predators in the environment of southern Belgium (Daujeard et al. 2016; Jimenez 2017). Regardless of this very high density of top predators present during the cold season, hominins kept coming, consequently increasing the level of interspecific competition for food and shelter. The cost-benefit ratio was thus probably favorable, either because it was an efficient, economically viable way to obtain animal-derived resources (e.g., meat, fat, skins) or because the North European Plain was too hostile during the cold season and hominins had no other choice than migrating southward to ensure their survival.

18.6 Conclusion

This study is a preliminary attempt to explore settlement patterns' variability of the two main top predators in Belgium at the end of the Late Pleistocene. Using the potential of cementum analyses, we conducted a multitaxon, multisite seasonal study on a key region of northwestern Europe. This work has gone some way toward enhancing our understanding of the northern last Neanderthals and first AMH behaviors. However, given the small sample size involved in this preliminary study, caution is warranted. Our investigations into this area are ongoing, and a combination of other zooarchaeological methods will soon be used to address questions related to seasonal behaviors. Future dating campaigns will also help to define a more precise chronological context.

To overcome taphonomic problems and increase our sample size of the carnivore record, we also performed an unprecedented cementum analysis on cave hyaena. Despite quite a low proportion of interpretable data (two out of four), this attempt showed that cave hyaenas *can* yield seasonal information. We believe that cementum analysis on this species can indeed be helpful in many contexts frequently encountered in Palaeolithic studies, notably when no seasonal signal from hyaena's prey can be obtained by other methods. Future work will concentrate on building a reference collection on modern hyaena, strengthening the protocol applied to cave hyaenas, and providing technical keys to optimize the method.

By combining criteria like (1) identifying a clear taphonomic agent for the studied specimens and (2) developing a new way to access seasonal information on complex material, this work is another step toward a better knowledge of the adaptive and interdependent behaviors of the top predators during the Late Pleistocene.

Acknowledgments

This work has been funded by the Belgian Fund for Scientific Research-FNRS as part of a fully funded PhD project; the French National Agency for Research (ANR CE14-31-0011); and the Royal Belgian Institute of Natural Sciences (BRAIN-be). I am very grateful to the CemeNTAA project and its coordinators, Dr. William Rendu, Dr. Lionel Gourichon, and Dr. Stephan Naji, for their trust and support and for allowing me to spend time working at NYU. Thank you to our local research host institutions, CIRHUS, as well as Professor Randall White. Thanks are also due to the RBINS team and its curators, Dr. Patrick Semal, Dr. Annelise Folie, and Cécilia Cousin. I am grateful to Dr. Mietje Germonpré (RBINS) and Dr. Marc Groenen (ULB) for their help, discussions, and advice. Special thanks to Alison Smolderen for her precious contribution to the study of Trou Magrite's material.

References

Begon, Michael, Colin R. Townsend, and John L. Harper. 2006. *Ecology: From Individuals to Ecosystems*, 4th ed. Malden, MA: Blackwell Publishing.
Binder, Wendy, and Blair Van Valkenburgh. 2000. "Development of Bite Strength and Feeding Behaviour in Juvenile Spotted Hyenas (*Crocuta crocuta*)." *Journal of Zoology* 252: 273–83.
Binford, Lewis. R. 1981. *Bones: Ancient Men and Modern Myths*. Studies in Archaeology. Orlando, FL: Academic Press.
Brace, S. et al. 2012. Serial Population Extinctions in a Small Mammal Indicate Late Pleistocene Ecosystem Instability. *Proceedings of the National Academy of Sciences* 109 (50): 20532–6.
Breuil, Henri. 1912. "Les Subdivisions Du Paléolithique Supérieur et Leur Signification." In *Bulletin de l'Académie Royale Des Sciences, Des Lettres et Des Beaux-Arts En Belgique*, Albert Kundig, XIVe session: 165–238. Genève, Switzerland.
Charles, Ruth, Robert E. M. Hedges, and Ivan Jadin. 2003. "Aurignacian Point, Butchery Remains and Radiocarbon Accelerator Dates from the Trou Magrite at Pont-à-Lesse (Commune of Dinant, Province of Namur, Belgium)." *Anthropologica et Praehistorica* 114: 81–84.

Cordy, Jean-Marie. 1995. "Étude de Restes Microfauniques Provenant du Trou Magrite." In *Le Trou Magrite. Fouilles 1991–1992. Résurrection d'un Site Classique En Wallonie*, Marcel Otte and Lawrence G. Straus (eds.). Liège: Eural 69: 159–66.

Daujeard, Camille, D. Vettese, K. Britton, P. Béarez, N. Boulbes, E. Crégut-Bonnoure, E. Desclaux et al. 2019. "Neanderthal Selective Hunting of Reindeer? The Case Study of Abri du Maras (South-Eastern France)." *Archaeological and Anthropological Sciences* 11 (3): 985–1011.

Daujeard, Camille, Grégory Abrams, Mietje Germonpré, Jeanne-Marie Le Pape, Alicia Wampach, Kevin Di Modica, and Marie-Hélène Moncel. 2016. "Neanderthal and Animal Karstic Occupations from Southern Belgium and South-Eastern France: Regional or Common Features?" *Quaternary International* 411 (August): 179–97.

Delagnes, Anne, and William Rendu. 2011. "Shifts in Neandertal Mobility, Technology and Subsistence Strategies in Western France." *Journal of Archaeological Science* 38 (8): 1771–83.

Dewez, M. 1985. "L'art Mobilier Paléolithique du Trou Magrite Dans son Contexte Stratigraphique." *Bulletin de la Société Royale Belge d'Anthropologie et de Préhistoire* 96: 117–33.

Di Modica, Kévin. 2009. "Le Trou Magrite à Walzin." In *Paléolithique Moyen En Wallonie. La Collection Louis Eloy*, Kévin Di Modica and Cécile Jungels (eds.). Belgium: Édition du Service du Patrimoine Culture, 145–58.

———. 2010. "Les Productions Lithiques du Paléolithique Moyen de Belgique: Variabilité des Systèmes d'Acquisition et des Technologies en Réponse à Une Mosaïque d'Environnements Contrastés." (dissertation), Université de Liège.

Dinnis, Rob. 2009. "Understanding the British Aurignacian." (unpublished dissertation), University of Sheffield.

———. 2015. "A Survey of Northwestern European Aurignacian Sites and Some Comments Regarding Their Potential Chrono-Cultural Significance." In *No Stone Unturned: Papers in Honour of Roger Jacobi*, N. Ashton & C. Harris (eds.). London: Lithics Studies Society Occasional Paper 9, 59–76.

Dinnis, Rob, and Damien Flas. 2016. "Trou Du Renard and the Belgian Aurignacian." *Proceedings of the Prehistoric Society* 82 (December): 1–25.

Discamps, Emmanuel. 2014. "Ungulate Biomass Fluctuations Endured by Middle and Early Upper Paleolithic Societies (SW France, MIS 5-3): The Contributions of Modern Analogs and Cave Hyena Paleodemography." *Quaternary International* 337 (July): 64–79.

Dupont, Édouard. 1867. "Découverte d'Objets Gravés et Sculptés Dans Le Trou Magrite à Pont-à-Lesse." *Bulletin de l'Académie Royale Des Sciences, Des Lettres et Des Beaux-Arts En Belgique* XXIV (36): 129–32.

Enloe, James G. 2003. "Acquisition and Processing of Reindeer in the Paris Basin." In *Mode de Vie Au Magdalénien: Apports de l'Archéozoologie/Zooarchaeological Insights into Magdalenian Lifeways*, Sandrine Costamagno and Véronique Laroulandie (eds.). Oxford: BAR International, 23–31.

Flas, Damien. 2008. *La Transition Du Paléolithique Moyen au Supérieur Dans la Plaine Septentrionale de l'Europe*. Belgium: Anthropologica et Praehistoricae, 119.

Fourvel, Jean-Baptiste. 2013. "Hyenidés Modernes et Fossiles d'Europe et d'Afrique: Taphonomie Comparée de Leurs Assemblages Osseux." Unpublished PhD thesis, Toulouse University.

Gautier, Achilles. 1995. "The Faunal Remains of Trou Magrite." In *Le Trou Magrite. Fouilles 1991–1992. Résurrection d'un Site Classique En Wallonie*, Marcel Otte and Lawrence G. Straus (eds.). Liège: Eural, 137–58.

Gautier, Achilles, Jean-Marie Cordy, Lawrence G. Straus, and Marcel Otte. 1997. "Taphonomic, Chronostratigraphic, Paleoenvironmental and Anthropogenic Implications of the Upper Pleistocene Faunas from Le Trou Magrite, Belgium." *Anthropozoologia* 25–26: 343–54.

Gautier, Achilles, and Jean de Heinzelin, eds. 1980. *La Caverne Marie-Jeanne (Hastière-Lavaux, Belgique)*, vol. 177. Bruxelles: Mémoires de l'Institut royal des Sciences naturelles de Belgique.

Germonpré, Mietje, and Mikhail Sablin. 2001. "The Cave Bear (*Ursus Spelaeus*) from Goyet, Belgium. The Bear Den in Chamber B (Bone Horizon 4)." *Bulletin de l'Institut Royal Des Sciences Naturelles de Belgique*, Série Sciences de la Terre, 71: 209–33.

Gourichon, Lionel. 2004. "Faune et saisonnalité: L'organisation temporelle des activités de subsistance dans l'Epipaléolithique et le Néolithique précéramique du Levant nord (Syrie)." PhD thesis, Université Lumière Lyon 2.

Groenen, Marc, and Bruno Marée. 2000. "La Grotte-Abri du Tiène des Maulins: Premier Bilan." *Notae Praeistoricae* 20: 61–72.

Grue, H., and B. Jensen. 1979. "Review of the Formation of Incremental Lines in Tooth Cementum of Terrestrial Mammals." *Danish Review of Game Biology* 11 (3): 1–48.

Jaarsveld, A. S. van, J. R. Henschel, and J. D. Skinner. 1987. "Improved Age Estimation in Spotted Hyaenas (*Crocuta Crocuta*)." *Journal of Zoology* 213 (4): 758–62.

Jimenez, Elodie-Laure. 2017. "Modalités d'Occupation du Territoire et Relations Humains-Grands Carnivores durant le Pléistocène Supérieur: Approche Archéozoologique, Taphonomique et Paléoécologique du Bassin Mosan Belge dans son Contexte Nord-Ouest Européen." PhD thesis, Brussels, Université Libre de Bruxelles.

Kitagawa, Keiko, Petra Krönneck, Nicholas J. Conard, and Susanne C. Münzel. 2012. "Exploring Cave Use and Exploitation among Cave Bears, Carnivores and Hominins in the Swabian Jura, Southwestern Germany." *Journal of Taphonomy* 10 (3–4): 439–61.

Martin, Hélène. 1994. "Nouveaux Milieux, Nouveaux Chasseurs: Une Approche des Comportements au Post-Glaciaire à Travers l'Etude des Saisons de Capture du Gibier." PhD thesis, Université Toulouse 2.

Medill, Sarah, Andrew E. Derocher, Ian Stirling, Nick Lunn, and Richard A. Moses. 2009. "Estimating Cementum Annuli Width in Polar Bears: Identifying Sources of Variation and Error." *Journal of Mammalogy* 90 (5): 1256–64.

Niven, Laura, and Hélène Martin. 2018. "Zooarcheological Analysis of the Assemblage from the 2000–2003 Excavations." In *The Middle Paleolithic Site of Pech de l'Azé IV*, Harold L. Dibble, Shannon J. P. McPherron, Paul Goldberg, and Dennis M. Sandgathe (eds.). Cham, Switzerland: Springer International Publishing, 95–116.

Niven, Laura, Teresa E. Steele, William Rendu, Jean-Baptiste Mallye, Shannon P. McPherron, Marie Soressi, Jacques Jaubert, and Jean-Jacques Hublin. 2012. "Neandertal Mobility and Large-Game Hunting: The Exploitation of Reindeer during the Quina Mousterian at Chez-Pinaud Jonzac (Charente-Maritime, France)." *Journal of Human Evolution* 63 (4): 624–35.

Fišáková, Miriam N. 2013. "Seasonality of Gravettian Sites in the Middle Danube Region and Adjoining Areas of Central Europe." *Quaternary International* 294 (April): 120–34.

———. 2014. "Seasonality of Use of Za Hájovnou Cave by Bears and Lions." *Acta Musei Nationalis Pragae*, B, 70 (1–2): 103–6.

Otte, Marcel. 1979. *Le Paléolithique Supérieur Ancien En Belgique*. Bruxelles: Musées Royaux d'Art et d'Histoire. Monographies d'Archéologie Nationale 5.

Otte, Marcel, and Lawrence G. Straus. 1995. *Le Trou Magrite, Fouilles 1991–1992. Résurrection d'un Site Classique En Wallonie*. Eraul: Liège.

Pike-Tay, Anne. 1991. "L'Analyse du Cément Dentaire Chez les Cerfs: L'Application en Préhistoire." *Paléo* 3 (1): 149–66.

Posth, Cosimo, Gabriel Renaud, Alissa Mittnik, Dorothée G. Drucker, Hélène Rougier, Christophe Cupillard, Frédérique Valentin et al. 2016. "Pleistocene Mitochondrial Genomes Suggest a Single Major Dispersal of Non-Africans and a Late Glacial Population Turnover in Europe." *Current Biology* 26 (6): 827–33.

Rendu, William, Sandrine Costamagno, Liliane Meignen, and Marie-Cécile Soulier. 2012. "Monospecific Faunal Spectra in Mousterian Contexts: Implications for Social Behavior." *Quaternary International* 247 (January): 50–58.

Rougier, Hélène, Isabelle Crevecoeur, Cédric Beauval, Cosimo Posth, Damien Flas, Christoph Wißing, Anja Furtwängler et al. 2016. "Neandertal Cannibalism and Neandertal Bones Used as Tools in Northern Europe." *Scientific Reports* 6 (1).

Semal, Patrick, Hélène Rougier, Isabelle Crevecoeur, Cécile Jungels, Damien Flas, Anne Hauzeur, Bruno Maureille et al. 2009. "New Data on the Late Neandertals: Direct Dating of the Belgian Spy Fossils." *American Journal of Physical Anthropology* 138 (4): 421–28.

Smolderen, Alison. 2016. "Cinquante Nuances de Noir. Problèmes de Diagnostic En Archéologie Du Feu: Études de Cas Du Bassin Mosan Belge Au MIS 3." PhD thesis, Université Libre de Bruxelles.

Sonnevilles-Bordes, Denise de. 1961. "Le Paléolithique Supérieur En Belgique." *L'Anthropologie* 65: 421–43.

Soulier, Marie-Cécile, and Jean-Baptiste Mallye. 2012. "Hominid Subsistence Strategies in the South-West of France: A New Look at the Early Upper Palaeolithic Faunal Material from Roc-de-Combe (Lot, France)." *Quaternary International* 252 (February): 99–108.

Stutz, Aaron Jonas. 2002. "Polarizing Microscopy Identification of Chemical Diagenesis in Archaeological Cementum." *Journal of Archaeological Science* 29 (11): 1327–47.

Stutz, Aaron Jonas, Daniel E. Lieberman, and A. E. Spiess. 1995. "Toward a Reconstruction of Subsistence Economy in the Upper Pleistocene Mosan Basin: Cementum Increment Evidence." In *Le Trou Magrite, Fouilles 1991–1992*. Liège: Eraul, 167–87.

Toussaint, Michel, Anthony J. Olejniczak, Sireen El Zaatari, Pierre Cattelain, Damien Flas, Claire Letourneux, and Stéphane Pirson. 2010. "The Neandertal Lower Right Deciduous Second Molar from Trou de l'Abîme at Couvin, Belgium." *Journal of Human Evolution* 58 (1): 56–67.

Toussaint, Michel, and Stéphane Pirson. 2006. "Neandertal Studies in Belgium: 2000–2005." *Periodicum Biologorum* 108 (3): 15.

*Ulrix-Closset, M. 1975. *Le Paléolithique Moyen Dans Le Bassin Mosan En Belgique*. Wetteren, Belguim: Universa.

Van Valkenburgh, Blair. 2009. "Costs of Carnivory: Tooth Fracture in Pleistocene and Recent Carnivorans." *Biological Journal of the Linnean Society* 96: 68–81.

19 Cementochronology to the Rescue: Osteobiography of a Middle Woodland Woman with a Combined Skeletal Dysplasia

Aviva A. Cormier, Jane E. Buikstra, and Stephan Naji

19.1 Introduction

Accurate age-at-death estimates are essential for inferring health, identity, diversity, and demography within archaeological skeletal samples. Unfortunately, the macroscopically visible skeletal structures most informative for estimating the ranges of age at death may be compromised by dysplastic, endocrine, and circulatory disorders. Cementochronology or the "tooth cementum annulations (TCA)" technique provides an alternative approach for evaluating acellular cementum banding without requiring a reference sample or complex statistical calculations (Chapter 1). In 1980, an individual (EZ 3–7–1) was excavated from Mound 3 at the Elizabeth site (11PK512) in the Lower Illinois Valley by the Center for American Archeology Contract Archeology Program and the Northwestern University Archeological Field Schools (Charles et al. 1988). The differential diagnosis suggests that EZ 3–7–1 has many of the osteological traits of a combined skeletal dysplasia of achondroplasia and Leri-Weill dyschondrosteosis (Cormier et al. 2017). Preliminary age-at-death estimates were tentative, relying only on the presence of *in situ* fetal remains (EZ 3–7–2) within her pelvis that indicate a biologically mature female and the occlusal dental wear that corresponds to that of older adults. Cementochronology has provided a more refined age-at-death estimation to the biological profile and has allowed for a more nuanced osteobiography to be presented for this pregnant female with activity limitations in her Middle Woodland social context.

Identity and Osteobiographies

Bioarchaeologists can explore the complexities and the variability of identity formation and manipulation by interacting with multiple fields and utilizing various lines of evidence, including social theory, bioarchaeology, archaeology, mortuary analysis, chemistry, and ethnographic data. Further, the archaeology and bioarchaeology of identities aim to understand the construction of identity at various levels, including public, private, group (e.g., nationality, ethnicity), community, household, family, and individual (e.g., age, gender, disability). Typically, these dimensions of identity are considered separately, although Meskell (2001) has called for scholars to "break the boundaries of identity categories themselves, blurring the crucial domains of identity formation ... " (188). This consideration has led to the use of osteobiographies and life-histories to understand the socially constructed and fluid narratives of identity, not merely the components therein.

In 1961, Frank Saul proposed the analytical approach of osteobiography to engage with past life-histories and as an alternative to merely documenting uninterpreted skeletal measurements (Saul & Saul 1989). Scholars (Boutin 2008; Knüsel et al. 2010; Mayes & Barber 2008; Renschler 2007) have advanced the osteobiographical methods through the combination of biogeochemistry, archaeological sciences, and unique theoretical and contextual approaches. As presented in a special issue of the *Journal of Anthropological Archaeology* edited by Zvelebil and Weber (2013), these methodological advances allow scholars to "(1) ... reconstruct long segments of individual life histories from birth to death; (2) to assess variation in prehistoric human behavior; and (3) to place this behavior in the context of dynamic interactions with the natural environment" (275).

Robb (2002) expanded the methodological focus of osteobiography (and life-histories) to consider the theoretical and cultural aspects of life. He refers to osteobiography as "the study through human skeletons of the biography as a cultural narrative" (Robb 2002, 160). Robb aims to understand the meaning of life and death within a particular social context, which aligns with the intentions of White and colleagues (2009) to "promote the movement from traditional osteobiography to social biography for the purpose of better understanding social identity" (155). This aim is illustrated in the seminal volume *Bioarchaeology of Individuals*, where Stodder and Palkovich (2012) present each chapter as an osteobiography of an individual, where scholars use a diverse amalgamation of methods and theoretical approaches to present the story of people, not just bones. Bioarchaeologists are now approaching the analysis of an individual's life and death, often veiled and imperceptible in the archaeological record, through the more nuanced and contextualized osteobiographical narratives to understand the development and transformation of identities in the past.

Biological Age Estimation

With many bioarchaeological collections and current excavations dealing with poor preservation and fragmentary remains, there is an ever-increasing need for updated age estimation techniques that do not rely on complete bones. Even though some scholars have proposed new statistical ways to use traditional methods for estimating age at death (Boldsen et al. 2002; Milner & Boldsen 2012), others have focused on the potential of tooth cementum annulations (TCA) (Part III; Colard et al. 2015; Naji et al. 2016; Wedel 2007; Wittwer-Backofen et al. 2004). The formation of acellular cementum banding is correlated to an annual cycle (Introduction; Chapters 1–3), and the histological age at death is calculated by adding the number of visible lines to the age of tooth eruption (Chapter 1). Because TCA estimation may assist in the age-at-death estimation of poorly preserved or fragmentary remains, it also may be invaluable in cases where pathological or genetic conditions obscure or hinder the macroscopic skeletal evaluation of gross morphological changes related to aging (Bertrand et al. 2016). An important caveat remains that the pathological or genetic conditions must not have obstructed the individual's odontogenesis so that an accurate histological age at death can be discerned. For skeletal dysplasias, including achondroplasia and Leri-Weill dyschondrosteosis, little has been published regarding the associated dental development.

Age Identities

As the bioarchaeology of childhood and the bioarchaeology of disability become increasingly popular subjects in archaeology and anthropology, it becomes essential that scholars acknowledge the complexity of age identities, recognizing the lives and agency of the young and old (Lucy 2005; Sofaer 2006). Similar to the acknowledgment of the difference between biological sex and the social construct of gender, scholars are now differentiating between chronological age (time since birth), physiological or developmental age (biological stage), or social age (socially constructed appropriate behavior for cultural age category) (Halcrow & Tayles 2008; Knudson & Stojanowski 2008). It is the intersection of these various age categories, as well as other identity constructs, that inform age identities.

19.2 The Osteobiography of EZ 3–7–1

Archaeological Context

In 1980, an adult individual (EZ 3–7–1) and perinate (EZ 3–7–2) were excavated from the Elizabeth site in the Lower Illinois Valley. They were buried in an intrusive pit burial in Mound 3. EZ 3–7–1 was interred in a supine position with partially flexed knees and elbows and the head to the north (Charles et al. 1988). The archaeologists described the positions of the fetal remains as in breech position and "partially lodged in the birth canal of Skeleton 1 [EZ 3–7–1] . . . [with the] upper-body elements rested on [the] sacrum of Skeleton 1" (Charles et al. 1988, 256). Preliminary age estimation for EZ 3–7–2 suggests an age of 28 to 30 fetal weeks (Cormier & Buikstra 2016), with further refinement and discussion appearing in a forthcoming publication. They described the adult individual as "achondroplastic" and suggested that the fetal remains indicated that EZ 3–7–1 was a female who may have died in childbirth (Charles et al. 1988, 256). In 2011, EZ 3–7–1 was radiocarbon dated to AD 132–388, suggesting a Middle Woodland context (King et al. 2011).

Osteological Evaluation

The skeleton of EZ 3–7–1 was mostly complete, with only a portion of the frontal bone, the smaller facial bones, the right parietal, patellae, most of the right os coxa, and some hand and feet bones missing. The macroscopic evaluation for estimating the age and sex was hindered by the evidence of various pathological processes. The estimation of an adult female was supported by the presence of fetal remains, seemingly *in situ* near the pelvic bones and the prominent ventral arc of the left os coxa.

The pathological observations and differential diagnosis revealed that the female may have been experiencing a combined skeletal dysplasia and a disseminated bone infection at the time of death (Cormier et al. 2017). The differential diagnosis suggests that EZ 3–7–1 has many of achondroplasia's osteological traits (Cohen 1998; Hecht et al. 1989; Henderson et al. 2000; Hunter et al. 1998; Mackie et al. 2008; Wynne-Davies et al. 1981). These indicators include a small foramen magnum, reduced interpedicle distance, spinal stenosis, lumbar lordosis, postural kyphosis, incomplete elbow extension, and "trident" hands (short, widespread fingers). Unusual elbow and wrist articulations support an additional differential diagnosis of Leri-Weill dyschondrosteosis (LWD), which is characterized by short stature, mesomelia, Madelung's deformity, increased carrying angle at the elbow, high arched palate, and scoliosis (Berdon et al. 1965; Cormier-Daire et al. 1999; Hamosh 2013; Leri & Weill 1929; Munns & Glass 2008). Thus, EZ 3–7–1 may have had a combined skeletal dysplasia (Ross et al. 2003) of achondroplasia and Leri-Weill dyschondrosteosis (Cormier et al. 2017).

Revised Age Estimation for EZ 3–7–1

The fetal remains of EZ 3–7–2 indicate that EZ 3–7–1 was biologically capable of being pregnant, thus older than her first menarche. Because of the pathology and morphology of EZ 3–7–1, most traditional age estimation methods using the os coxae cannot be used to refine that observation. The eruption of the third molars (Figure 19.1) suggests that the dental age of EZ 3–7–1 was older than seventeen years (Haavikko 1970), which is an expression of the development and eruption of the dentition and not necessarily reflective of her skeletal age or chronological age (Hillson 2005).

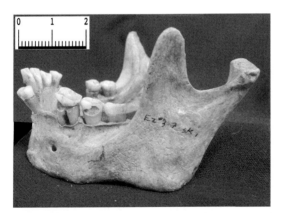

Figure 19.1 Mandible of EZ 3–7–1. Note the eruption of the third molars, the occlusal wear, and the periodontal disease. (Photo by A. Cormier)

Table 19.1 Occlusal wear of EZ 3–7–1, using Lovejoy's (1985) patterns of occlusal attrition

Dentition	Phase	Age Range (years)
Maxillary anterior (left)	D	20–24
Maxillary posterior (left and right)	H+	40–50
Mandibular anterior (right)	E	24–30
Mandibular posterior (left)	I	45–55
Mandibular posterior (right)	D	20–24

We used Lovejoy's (1985) patterns of occlusal attrition (Table 19.1) to assess the maxillary and mandibular dentition. One of the benefits of estimating age from wear patterns is that it is a method weakly influenced by the pathological conditions of EZ 3–7–1. However, the results suggest a wide possible age range (20 to 55+ years). This wide range is, of course, inherent to the method itself but also is most likely because of the asymmetrical occlusal wear that followed the antemortem loss of both the right maxillary and mandibular first molars. This bias most likely skews the estimate toward an older age range. Accounting for this skew, the more probable age range is between twenty-five and forty years.

To obtain a more precise and accurate age-at-death estimate, we applied the TCA protocol published in Colard and colleagues (2015) and Chapter 1, Figure 1.5. The left first mandibular premolar was sectioned, and five optimal regions of interest were recorded to count the acellular cementum increments (Figure 19.2).

Most studies focus on obstructive apnea and breathing difficulties of those with skeletal dysplasias, considering only the craniofacial morphology and airway morphology (Afsharpaiman et al. 2013; Pauli et al. 1984; Sisk et al. 1999; Stokes et al. 1983; Tenconi et al. 2017; Waters et al. 1995). Some publications reported oral manifestations of achondroplasia as malocclusion and the absence of teeth erupting or disturbed eruption sequences (Miller 1937; Sherry & Aponte 2015). However, Onodera and colleagues (2005) found no statistical differences in the mean chronological age at the initiation of deciduous or permanent teeth between children with achondroplasia and children without. Instead, any underlying cause for dental eruption variation is related to the small jaw structure and small stature (Sherry & Aponte 2015), not genetic or metabolic dental development disruption. For individuals with skeletal dysplasias, such as achondroplasia and Leri-Weill dyschondrosteosis, with typical odontogenesis, TCA may thus be invaluable in assisting in age-at-death estimation, which was previously deemed highly inaccurate based on morphological observations alone.

A semiautomated counting package (*Find Peaks*) was used in the ImageJ/FIJI[(R)] software to count the black and white luminescence variations of AEFC. Counts were recorded along a transect divided into three parts to minimize grayscale background noise. For each third of the transect, the minimum peak amplitude had to exceed one standard deviation in the Y-axis gray value for a peak to be included. The average (μ_1) and standard deviation (σ_1) of the five counts (22.5 ± 2.18) were added to the average (μ_2) and standard deviation (σ_2) of the age at eruption for LP1 for biologically female

Table 19.2 Summary of the age estimations of EZ 3-7-1

Method/Line of Evidence	Skeletal Element	Age Estimation	Age Identity Type
Pregnancy	Fetal remains of EZ 3-7-2	> age at first menarche	Biological
Dental eruption (Haavikko 1970)	M3s	>17 years	Biological
Occlusal wear (Lovejoy 1985)	Dentition	20–55+ years	Chronological
Cementochronology	First mandibular premolar	30–34 years	Biological

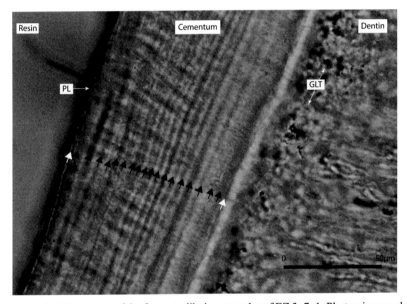

Figure 19.2 Cementum of the first mandibular premolar of EZ 3-7-1. Photomicrograph of twenty acellular cementum increments in transmitted light. Black arrows: opaque cementum increments. White arrows: first and last increments. PL: periodontal ligament; GLT: granular layer of Tomes. Magnification X400

individuals (9.6 ± 1.48) (Liversidge et al. 1998) using the formula $(\mu_1 + \mu_2)/2 \pm \sqrt{(\sigma_1^2 + \sigma_2^2)}$. The resulting estimated age atadeath is $(22.5 + 9.6)/2 \pm \sqrt{(2.18^2 + 1.48^2)} = 32.1 \pm 2.63$ (Table 19.2).

19.3 Age, Achondroplasia, and Pregnancy in the Middle Woodland Period

With the refined estimated age at death from cementochronology, we can construct a more nuanced osteobiography for EZ 3-7-1 and discuss the connection between age, achondroplasia, and pregnancy in her Middle Woodland context. Unfortunately, there is a lack of artistic, archaeological, and ethnographic material involving individuals with short stature during the Woodland periods (Cormier & Buikstra 2017), thus requiring the consideration of individuals from various temporal and geographic contexts. To understand the construction and interpretation of the various age identities of EZ 3–7–1 (i.e., chronological age, biological age, and social age), we must consider the mortality rates of infants and adults with achondroplasia, obstetric and gynecologic complications for females with achondroplasia, and the paleodemography of the Middle Woodland period.

Mortality and Achondroplasia

Because achondroplasia is the most common heritable skeletal dysplasia in modern populations with a prevalence of 1/25,000 live births (Oberklaid et al. 1979; Waller et al. 2008), there have been many publications regarding the infant mortality of those born with achondroplasia (Bland & Emery 1982; Pauli et al. 1984, 1995; Simmons et al. 2014) and preventative surgical interventions (Keiper Jr et al. 1999; Shimony et al. 2015; Tenconi et al. 2017; Unger et al. 2017; White et al. 2016). On the contrary, few publications exist regarding the mortality rates after the birth of individuals with achondroplasia. Using a sample from Texas and Maryland, Hecht and colleagues (1987) found a significantly increased age-related mortality for individuals with achondroplasia under thirty-five years due to sudden death of those under five and cardiovascular disease of young adults. Wynn and colleagues (2007) followed up on this earlier study with a larger sample and found that the mortality rate relating to heart disease was more than twice that for the general population, specifically in the age ranges of 25 to 55 and 65 to 75 years. The mortality rate for accidental causes of death was also twice that of the general population, while neurological-related deaths were more than eight times that of the general population (Wynn et al. 2007). Further, they found that, even with the advances in health care since 1987, the infant and childhood mortality was still increased compared to that of the general population (Wynn et al. 2007) with an intermediate median survival age of sixty-seven years, compared to the referent population life expectancy of seventy-eight years. Their results confirm that these ages were not skewed younger due to the high infant mortality rates (Wynn et al. 2007).

Paleodemography of the Middle Woodland Period

From these modern life expectancy studies, it can be extrapolated that individuals with achondroplasia in past populations also had a shorter life expectancy than typical morphology and stature. However, in inferring and studying life expectancy in the past, the osteological paradox (DeWitte & Stojanowski 2015; Wood et al. 1992; Wright & Yoder 2003) must be acknowledged and considered as those excavated are a very small sample of the past population and just a representation of the deceased individuals, not the living population. Further, small sample sizes of fewer than 100 individuals result in the high probability that the mortality profiles constructed are not an accurate reflection of the population (Hoppa & Saunders 1998).

Charles and colleagues (1988) present the lifetables and estimations of age at death and biological sex for the eighty-two individuals dating to the Middle Woodland

(c. 50 BC–AD 400) period excavated from the Elizabeth site, as well as from the Late Woodland (n = 74) and Archaic (n = 68) periods. They report the life expectancies from birth of the Middle Woodland sample to be 40.14 years (using Bocquet-Appel and Masset's (1982) regression) and 36.1 years (using Weiss's (1973) regression). Due to the small sample size, these means are difficult to use for site and period comparisons. However, they are similar to Blakely's (1971) findings from a larger sample size of 294 for a Middle Woodland population from the Klunk Mounds, Illinois, of a mean age at death of thirty years (33.5 years for males and 26.5 years for females). This lower mean age at death for female individuals in the Middle Woodland period corresponds with the conclusions of Wilson (2014) of an increased risk of death among reproductive-age females throughout the Late Woodland (c. AD 400–1050) and Mississippian (c. AD 1050–1500) periods. Further, they found that females surviving reproductive age had a higher probability of surviving into old age than males (Wilson 2014).

These life expectancies of the Woodland periods correspond broadly to the general estimates of global preindustrial mortality of thirty to forty years (Finch 2007), which allow for the proposal that EZ 3–7–1, ages 30–34 years at death, may have had the social age of a mature or older adult. Further, considering a shorter life expectancy for those with achondroplasia, her life expectancy could have been much younger. It may have been particularly significant that an individual with her skeletal dysplasia lived into her thirties and gained the social age of an older adult.

Age and Pregnancy

In addition to her possible social age identity, EZ 3–7–1 also may have had the identity of a pregnant female with short stature. The obstetric and gynecologic complications for those pregnant with achondroplasia are numerous, including increased incidence of menstrual complications, problems with contraception, reduced fertility, premature menopause, and increased incidence of leiomyomata (Allanson & Hall 1986; Chetty et al. 2011; Ghumman et al. 2005; Lattanzi & Harger 1982; Roopnarinesingh et al. 1983; Sharma & Kumar 2014). Further, pelvic narrowing results in a space too narrow to carry the fetus, resulting in the fetus' positioning high in the abdominal region, increasing complications due to maternal respiratory distress, early delivery, neonatal death, and cephalopelvic disproportion (Allanson & Hall 1986). Cephalopelvic disproportion (Maharaj 2010), when the fetal head cannot pass through the mother's pelvis, is common due to the small pelvic size of an individual with achondroplasia and the large head size of a baby with achondroplasia (Allanson & Hall 1986). Most, if not all, modern deliveries of pregnant individuals with achondroplasia are assisted by Caesarian sections to limit the complications of cephalopelvic disproportion. This modern surgical intervention would not have been available during the Middle Woodland period and may have resulted in the deaths of both EZ 3–7–1 and the fetus (EZ 3–7–2).

Because of the small size of fetal remains, varying burial customs, excavation techniques, and taphonomic processes, there are few archaeologically recorded examples of females buried with fetal remains who may have died near or during childbirth throughout the world. Of the published cases, there were twenty-two archaeological examples worldwide of these mother/fetus pairs with specific age-at-death estimations, including EZ 3–7–1 (Table 19.3). In addition to two North American examples from seventeenth- to nineteenth-century South Dakota (Owsley & Bradtmiller 1983) and four from the Late Archaic (ca. 5500–1500 BC) Indian Knoll site in Kentucky (Finkenstaedt 1984), the closest comparative case, temporally and geographically, is that of a female aged sixteen to nineteen years from the Late Woodland (ca. AD 500–1000) Helton site, Illinois (Valerie Sgheiza, Maria Cox, and Kelsie Hart, unpublished data). The only published case of an individual with a skeletal dysplasia excavated with associated fetal remains is from the Old Kingdom (ca. 2575–2130 BC) in Egypt, and the age estimation is merely mentioned as adult (Filer 1995).

Tague (1994, 28) suggests (in a footnote) that "if the first menarche occurred at mid-adolescence in prehistory, then reproductive maturity would not have been attained until late adolescence." In other words, the possible age at first birth would be in the late teens or early twenties (Tague 1994). Ethnographically, this age corresponds with the mean age at first birth of the Dobe !Kung of 18.8 years (Howell 2017) and the Hadza of nineteen years (Burton Jones 2016). The mean age at final birth for the Dobe !Kung was 34.4 years (Howell 2017), while that for the Hadza was thirty-seven years (Burton Jones 2016).

For modern female individuals with achondroplasia, a study by Allanson and Hall (1986) of eighty-seven individuals found a mean age of menarche of 13.3 years compared to the US mean of 12.8 years. The mean age of menopause was 47.4 years compared to the US mean of 51.4 years (Allanson & Hall 1986). Though the mean age of onset of menarche was slightly delayed, the timing and puberty sequence was typical. As Allanson and Hall (1986) state, "reproductive fitness in achondroplasia has been considered reduced," and many other publications list "reduced fertility" in the list of complications, but even today, few studies have evaluated the question of fertility in individuals with achondroplasia. Taking into account the slight delay of the first menarche, slightly early age of menopause, possible fertility complications, and the highly probable death of the mother and fetus without Caesarian section, it seems likely that EZ 3–7–1 was experiencing her first pregnancy in her early thirties with a possible social age of mature or older adult.

19.4 Conclusions: The Age and Identity of EZ 3–7–1 in the Middle Woodland Period

Although the skeletal dysplasias of EZ 3–7–1 obscure the macroscopic evaluation of morphological changes related to aging, her dental development and eruption are typical, allowing cementochronology to redefine the estimation of her age at death to be approximately thirty to thirty-four years. This biological age is one component of her age identity that allows for a more nuanced osteobiography for this Middle Woodland individual. The consideration of modern mortality rates, obstetric and gynecologic complications for females with achondroplasia, and the paleodemography of the Middle and Late Woodland period allows for the supposition that EZ 3–7–1 was

Table 19.3 Archaeologically excavated mother and fetus pairs with provided age estimations

Individuals	Burial Location	Period	Estimated Age of the Adult	Source
EZ 3–7–1 & EZ 3–7–2	Elizabeth Site, Illinois, USA [11PK512]	Middle Woodland AD 132–388	30–34 years	(Sgheiza et al. n.d.)
Burial 2A	Helton Site, Illinois, USA	Late Woodland ca. AD 500–1000	16–19 years	(Owsley & Bradtmiller 1983)
	Larson [39WW2], South Dakota	AD 1600–1832	17–19 years	(Owsley & Bradtmiller 1983)
Burial 11 F	Mobridge [39WW1], South Dakota	AD 1600–1832	30–34 years	(Owsley & Bradtmiller 1983)
Burials 242 & 243	Indian Knoll, Kentucky	Late Archaic ca. 5500–1500 BC	23–24 years	(Finkenstaedt 1984)
Burials 340 & 341	Indian Knoll, Kentucky	Late Archaic ca. 5500–1500 BC	17–18 years	(Finkenstaedt 1984)
Burials 240 & 241	Indian Knoll, Kentucky	Late Archaic ca. 5500–1500 BC	18–21 years	(Finkenstaedt 1984)
Burials 146 & 147	Indian Knoll, Kentucky	Late Archaic ca. 5500–1500 BC	23–24 years	(Finkenstaedt 1984)
PLM-9 T-13A	San Miguel, Chile	ca. AD 1200	25–26 years	(Arriaza et al. 1988)
AZ-71 T-249	Cabuza, Chile	ca. AD 380	25–30 years	(Arriaza et al. 1988)
AZ-71 T-NMT3	Tiwanaku, Chile	ca. AD 500–600	18–20 years	(Arriaza et al. 1988)
AZ-8 T-3	Gentilar, Chile	ca. AD 1400	39–42 years	(Arriaza et al. 1988)
Grave 52	Baza Necropolis, Granada, Spain	11th–14th century AD	21–25 years	(Rascón Pérez et al. 2007)
Grave 1	Costebelle Site, Hyeres, Var, France	4th century AD	52.75 ± 2.5 years	(Pálfi et al. 1992)
Ostuni 1	Ostuni, Apulia, Italy	Upper Paleolithic ca. 27 kA	20 years or younger	(Nava et al. 2017)
US 2614 SN06 ind. A & US 2617 SN06, ind. D/F	San Nicolao di Pietra Colice, Genova, Italy	14th century AD	30–39 years	(Cesana et al. 2017)
LOR 11.1	Lokomotiv, Siberia	7725–7630 cal BP	20–25 years	(Lieverse et al. 2015)
Grave 57	Cambridgeshire, England	AD 450–700	25–30 years	(Sayer & Dickinson 2013)
Inhumation 1	Portugal	19th century AD	25–30 years	(Cruz & Codinha 2010)
CV 96MN-1	Lorca, Murcia, Spain	1500–1000 BC	25–26 years	(Malgosa et al. 2004)
No. 81	Vedrovice, Moravia	Early Neolithic	20–23 years	(Jelínek 1992)
AS07H1M3a	Southern Vietnam	2100–1050 BC	15–23 years	(Willis & Oxenham 2013)

considered a mature or older individual experiencing her possibly first and final pregnancy. Unlike modern individuals with achondroplasia, she had reached the mean life expectancy for the population at the time and beyond the mean age for female individuals (possibly influenced by deaths associated with pregnancy). Possible reduced fertility linked to her skeletal dysplasias may explain why EZ 3–7–1 was pregnant at this age, although it is also possible that her complex identity within this social context may have contributed to a later onset of sexual activity.

References

Afsharpaiman, S., Saburi, A., & Waters, K. A. (2013). Respiratory difficulties and breathing disorders in achondroplasia. *Paediatric Respiratory Reviews* **14**(4), 250–5.

Allanson, J. E., & Hall, J. G. (1986). Obstetric and gynecologic problems in women with chondrodystrophies. *Obstetrics and Gynecology* **67**(1), 74–8.

Arriaza, B., Allison, M., & Gerszten, E. (1988). Maternal mortality in pre-Columbian Indians of Arica, Chile. *American Journal of Physical Anthropology* **77**(1), 35–41.

Berdon, W. E., Grossman, H., & Baker, D. H. (1965). Dyschondrostéose (Léri-Weill Syndrome): Congenital short forcarms, Madelung-type wrist deformities, and moderate dwarfism. *Radiology* **85**(4), 677–80.

Bertrand, B., Schug, G. R., Polet, C., Naji, S., & Colard, T. (2016). Age-at-death estimation of pathological individuals: A complementary approach using teeth cementum annulations. *International Journal of Paleopathology* **15**, 120–7.

Blakely, R. L. (1971). Comparison of the mortality profiles of Archaic, Middle Woodland, and Middle Mississippian skeletal populations. *American Journal of Physical Anthropology* **34**(1), 43–53.

Bland, J. D., & Emery, J. L. (1982). Unexpected death of children with achondroplasia after the perinatal period. *Developmental Medicine & Child Neurology* **24**(5), 489–92.

Bocquet-Appel, J.-P., & Masset, C. (1982). Farewell to paleodemography. *Journal of Human Evolution* **11**(4), 321–33.

Boldsen, J. L., Milner, G. R., Konigsberg, L. W., & Wood, J. W. (2002). Transition analysis: A new method for estimating age from skeletons. *Cambridge Studies in Biological and Evolutionary Anthropology*, 73–106.

Boutin, A. T. (2008). Embodying life and death: Osteobiographical narratives from Alalakh. Ph.D. thesis, University of Pennsylvania, United States.

Burton Jones, N. (2016). *Demography and Evolutionary Ecology of the Hadza Hunter-Gatherers*. Cambridge: Cambridge University Press.

Cesana, D., Benedictow, O. J., & Bianucci, R. (2017). The origin and early spread of the Black Death in Italy: First evidence of plague victims from 14th-century Liguria (northern Italy). *Anthropological Science* **125**(1), 15–24.

Charles, D. K., Leigh, S. R., & Buikstra, J. E. (1988). *The Archaic and Woodland Cemeteries at the Elizabeth Site in the Lower Illinois Valley*, Kampsville, IL: Center for American Archeology.

Chetty, S. P., Shaffer, B. L., & Norton, M. E. (2011). Management of pregnancy in women with genetic disorders, part 1: Disorders of the connective tissue, muscle, vascular, and skeletal systems. *Obstetrical & Gynecological Survey* **66**(11), 699–709.

Cohen, M. M. (1998). Achondroplasia, hypochondroplasia and thanatophoric dysplasia: Clinically related skeletal dysplasias that are also related at the molecular level. *International Journal of Oral and Maxillofacial Surgery* **27**(6), 451–5.

Colard, T., Bertrand, B., Naji, S., Delannoy, Y., & Bécart, A. (2015). Toward the adoption of cementochronology in forensic context. *International Journal of Legal Medicine* **129**, 1–8.

Cormier, A. A., & Buikstra, J. E. (2016). A case study of skeletal dysplasia inheritance and maternal/fetal health from a Middle Woodland context at the Elizabeth Site (11PK512), Illinois. 85th Annual Meeting of the American Association of Physical Anthropologists, San Francisco, CA.

(2017). Impairment, disability, and identity in the Middle Woodland Period: Life at the juncture of achondroplasia, pregnancy, and infection. In J. Byrnes & J. Muller (eds.), *Bioarchaeology of Impairment and Disability: Theoretical, Ethnohistorical, and Methodological Perspectives*. Cham, Switzerland: Springer International Publishing, 225–48.

Cormier, A. A., Buikstra, J. E., & Osterholtz, A. (2017). Overlapping genetic pathways in the skeletal dysplasias of a Middle Woodland individual: A case study. *International Journal of Paleopathology* **18**, 98–107.

Cormier-Daire, V., Belin, V., Cusin, V., ... Munnich, A. (1999). SHOX gene mutations and deletions in dyschondrosteosis or Leri-Weill syndrome. *Acta Pædiatrica* **88**, 55–59.

Cruz, C. B., & Codinha, S. (2010). Death of mother and child due to dystocia in 19th century Portugal. *International Journal of Osteoarchaeology* **20**(4), 491–6.

DeWitte, S. N., & Stojanowski, C. M. (2015). The osteological paradox 20 years later: Past perspectives, future directions. *Journal of Archaeological Research* **23**(4), 397–450.

Filer, J. (1995). *Disease. Egyptian Bookshelf*. London: British Museum.

Finch, C. E. (2007). *The Biology of Human Longevity: Inflammation, Nutrition, and Aging in the Evolution of Lifespans*. Cambridge, MA: Elsevier.

Finkenstaedt, E. (1984). Age at first pregnancy among females at the Indian Knoll Oh-2 Site. *Transactions of the Kentucky Academy of Science* **45**, 51–4.

Ghumman, S., Goel, N., Rajaram, S., Singh, K. C., Kansal, B., & Dewan, P. (2005). Pregnancy in an achondroplastic dwarf: A case report. *Journal of the Indian Medical Association* **103**(10), 536–8.

Haavikko, K. (1970). The formation and the alveolar and clinical eruption of the permanent teeth. An orthopantographic study. *Proceedings of the Finnish Dental Society* **66**, 101–70.

Halcrow, S. E., & Tayles, N. (2008). The bioarchaeological investigation of childhood and social age: Problems and prospects. *Journal of Archaeological Method and Theory* **15**(2), 190–215.

Hamosh, A. (2013). OMIM Entry – # 127300 – Leri-Weill Dyschondrosteosis; LWD. www.omim.org/entry/127300 (January 14, 2015).

Hecht, J. T., Francomano, C. A., Horton, W. A., & Annegers, J. F. (1987). Mortality in achondroplasia. *American Journal of Human Genetics* **41**(3), 454.

Hecht, J. T., Horton, W. A., Reid, C. S., Pyeritz, R. E., & Chakraborty, R. (1989). Growth of the foramen magnum in achondroplasia. *American Journal of Medical Genetics* **32**(4), 528–35.

Henderson, J. E., Naski, M. C., Aarts, M. M., ... Ornitz, D. M. (2000). Expression of FGFR3 with the G380R: Achondroplasia mutation inhibits proliferation and maturation of CFK2 chondrocytic cells. *Journal of Bone and Mineral Research* **15**(1), 155–65.

Hillson, S. (2005). *Teeth*. Cambridge: Cambridge University Press.

Hoppa, R., & Saunders, S. (1998). The MAD legacy: How meaningful is mean age-at-death in skeletal samples. *Human Evolution* **13**(1), 1–14.

Howell, N. (2017). *Demography of the Dobe !Kung*. London: Routledge.
Hunter, A. G., Bankier, A., Rogers, J. G., Sillence, D., & Scott, C. I. (1998). Medical complications of achondroplasia: A multicentre patient review. *Journal of Medical Genetics* **35**(9), 705–12.
Jelínek, J. (1992). Two early neolithic female burials with foetal remains. *Anthropologie (1962–)* **30**(2), 165–8.
Keiper Jr, G. L., Koch, B., & Crone, K. R. (1999). Achondroplasia and cervicomedullary compression: Prospective evaluation and surgical treatment. *Pediatric Neurosurgery* **31**(2), 78–83.
King, J., Buikstra, J., & Charles, D. (2011). Time and archaeological traditions in the Lower Illinois Valley. *American Antiquity* **76**(3), 500–28.
Knudson, K. J., & Stojanowski, C. M. (2008). New directions in bioarchaeology: Recent contributions to the study of human social identities. *Journal of Archaeological Research* **16**(4), 397–432.
Knüsel, C. J., Batt, C. M., Cook, G., ... Wilson, A. S. (2010). The identity of the St Bees Lady, Cumbria: An osteobiographical approach. *Medieval Archaeology* **54**(1), 271–311.
Lattanzi, D. R., & Harger, J. H. (1982). Achondroplasia and pregnancy. *The Journal of Reproductive Medicine* **27**(6), 363–6.
Leri, A., & Weill, J. (1929). Une affection congénitale et symétrique du développement osseux: la dyschondrostéose. *Bulletins et Mémoires de la Société Médicale des Hôpitaux de Paris*, 1491–4.
Lieverse, A. R., Bazaliiskii, V. I., & Weber, A. W. (2015). Death by twins: A remarkable case of dystocic childbirth in Early Neolithic Siberia. *Antiquity* **89**(343), 23–38.
Liversidge, H. M., Herdeg, B., & Rösing, F. W. (1998). Dental age estimation of non-adults. A review of methods and principles. In K. W. A. Priv-Doz, F. W. Rösing, & M. Teschler-Nicola (eds.), *Dental Anthropology*. Vienna: Springer, 419–42.
Lovejoy, C. O. (1985). Dental wear in the Libben population: Its functional pattern and role in the determination of adult skeletal age at death. *American Journal of Physical Anthropology* **68**(1), 47–56.
Lucy, S. (2005). The archaeology of age. In M. D.-A. García, S. Lucy, S. Babic´, & D. Edwards (eds.), *The Archaeology of Identity: Approaches to Gender, Age, Status, Ethnicity and Religion*. London: Routledge, 43–66.
Mackie, E. J., Ahmed, Y. A., Tatarczuch, L., Chen, K.-S., & Mirams, M. (2008). Endochondral ossification: How cartilage is converted into bone in the developing skeleton. *The International Journal of Biochemistry & Cell Biology* **40**(1), 46–62.
Maharaj, D. (2010). Assessing cephalopelvic disproportion: Back to the basics. *Obstetrical & Gynecological Survey* **65**(6), 387–95.
Malgosa, A., Alesan, A., Safont, S., Ballbé, M., & Ayala, M. M. (2004). A dystocic childbirth in the Spanish Bronze Age. *International Journal of Osteoarchaeology* **14**(2), 98–103.
Mayes, A. T., & Barber, S. B. (2008). Osteobiography of a high-status burial from the lower Río Verde Valley of Oaxaca, Mexico. *International Journal of Osteoarchaeology* **18**(6), 573–88.
Meskell, L. (2001). Archaeologies of identity. In I. Hodder (ed.), *Archaeological Theory Today*, Cambridge: Polity, 187–213.
Miller, H. A. (1937). Dental abnormalities in a patient with achondroplasia. *International Journal of Orthodontia and Oral Surgery* **23**(3), 296–9.

Milner, G. R., & Boldsen, J. L. (2012). Transition analysis: A validation study with known-age modern American skeletons. *American Journal of Physical Anthropology* **148**(1), 98–110.

Munns, C., & Glass, I. (2008). SHOX-related haploinsufficiency disorders. In R. A. Pagon, M. P. Adam, H. H. Ardinger, ... K. Stephens (eds.), *GeneReviews(®) [Internet]*, Seattle: University of Washington.

Naji, S., Colard, T., Blondiaux, J., Bertrand, B., d'Incau, E., & Bocquet-Appel, J.-P. (2016). Cementochronology, to cut or not to cut? *International Journal of Paleopathology* **15**, 113–19.

Nava, A., Coppa, A., Coppola, D., ... Bondioli, L. (2017). Virtual histological assessment of the prenatal life history and age at death of the Upper Paleolithic fetus from Ostuni (Italy). *Scientific Reports* **7**(1), 9427.

Oberklaid, F., Danks, D. M., Jensen, F., Stace, L., & Rosshandler, S. (1979). Achondroplasia and hypochondroplasia. Comments on frequency, mutation rate, and radiological features in skull and spine. *Journal of Medical Genetics* **16**(2), 140–6.

Onodera, K., Sakata, H., Niikuni, N., Nonaka, T., Kobayashi, K., & Nakazima, I. (2005). Survey of the present status of sleep-disordered breathing in children with achondroplasia: Part I. A questionnaire survey. *International Journal of Pediatric Otorhinolaryngology* **69**(4), 457–61.

Owsley, D. W., & Bradtmiller, B. (1983). Mortality of pregnant females in Arikara villages: Osteological evidence. *American Journal of Physical Anthropology* **61**(3), 331–6.

Pàlfi, G., Dutour, O., Borreani, M., Brun, J.-P., & Berato, J. (1992). Pre-Columbian congenital syphilis from the late antiquity in France. *International Journal of Osteoarchaeology* **2**(3), 245–61.

Pauli, R. M., Horton, V. K., Glinski, L. P., & Reiser, C. A. (1995). Prospective assessment of risks for cervicomedullary-junction compression in infants with achondroplasia. *American Journal of Human Genetics* **56**(3), 732–44.

Pauli, R. M., Scott, C. I., Wassman, E. R., ... Lebovitz, R. (1984). Apnea and sudden unexpected death in infants with achondroplasia. *The Journal of Pediatrics* **104**(3), 342–8.

Rascón Pérez, J., Cambra Moo, Ó., & González Martín, A. (2007). A multidisciplinary approach reveals an extraordinary double inhumation in the osteoarchaeological record. *Journal of Taphonomy* **5**(2), 91–101.

Renschler, E. S. (2007). An osteobiography of an African diasporic skeletal sample: Integrating skeletal and historical information. Ph.D. thesis, University of Pennsylvania, United States.

Robb, J. (2002). Time and biography. In Y. Hamilakis, M. Pluciennik, & S. Tarlow (eds.), *Thinking through the Body*. New York: Springer, 153–71.

Roopnarinesingh, S. S., Naraynsingh, V., & Woo, J. (1983). Achondroplasia and pregnancy. *West Indian Medical Journal* **32**(2), 112–13.

Ross, J. L., Bellus, G., Scott, C. I., Abboudi, J., Grigelioniene, G., & Zinn, A. R. (2003). Mesomelic and rhizomelic short stature: The phenotype of combined Leri-Weill dyschondrosteosis and achondroplasia or hypochondroplasia. *American Journal of Medical Genetics Part A* **116A**(1), 61–65.

Saul, F. P., & Saul, J. M. (1989). Osteobiography: A Maya example. In M. Y. Iscan & K. A. R. Kennedy (eds.), *Reconstruction of Life from the Skeleton*. New York: Liss, 287–302.

Sayer, D., & Dickinson, S. D. (2013). Reconsidering obstetric death and female fertility in Anglo-Saxon England. *World Archaeology* **45**(2), 285–97.

Sgheiza, V., Cox, M., & Hart, K. (2016). A comparison of two Late Woodland features: Helton 20-36 and Carter 2-15. Presented at the 81st annual meeting of the Society for American Archaeology. Orlando, FL.

Sharma, R., & Kumar, A. (2014). Achondroplasia and pregnancy. *Journal of Evolution of Medical and Dental Sciences* **3**(16), 4237–41.

Sherry, J. S., & Aponte, S. (2015, August 26). Achondroplasia: Oral health concerns associated with genetic disorder commonly referred to as dwarfism. *Registered Dental Hygienist*. www.rdhmag.com/career-profession/students/article/16405429/achondroplasia-oral-health-concerns-associated-with-genetic-disorder-commonly-referred-to-as-dwarfism

Shimony, N., Ben-Sira, L., Sivan, Y., Constantini, S., & Roth, J. (2015). Surgical treatment for cervicomedullary compression among infants with achondroplasia. *Child's Nervous System* **31**(5), 743–50.

Simmons, K., Hashmi, S. S., Scheuerle, A., Canfield, M., & Hecht, J. T. (2014). Mortality in babies with achondroplasia: Revisited. *Birth Defects Research Part A: Clinical and Molecular Teratology* **100**(4), 247–9.

Sisk, E. A., Heatley, D. G., Borowski, B. J., Leverson, G. E., & Pauli, R. M. (1999). Obstructive sleep apnea in children with achondroplasia: Surgical and anesthetic considerations. *Otolaryngology–Head and Neck Surgery* **120**(2), 248–54.

Sofaer, J. R. (2006). *The Body as Material Culture: A Theoretical Osteoarchaeology*. Cambridge: Cambridge University Press.

Stodder, A. L. W., & Palkovich, A. M. (2012). *Bioarchaeology of Individuals*. Gainsville, FL: University Press of Florida.

Stokes, D. C., Phillips, J. A., Leonard, C. O., . . . Brown, D. L. (1983). Respiratory complications of achondroplasia. *The Journal of Pediatrics* **102**(4), 534–41.

Tague, R. G. (1994). Maternal mortality or prolonged growth: Age at death and pelvic size in three prehistoric Amerindian populations. *American Journal of Physical Anthropology* **95**(1), 27–40.

Tenconi, R., Khirani, S., Amaddeo, A., . . . Fauroux, B. (2017). Sleep-disordered breathing and its management in children with achondroplasia. *American Journal of Medical Genetics Part A* **173**(4), 868–78.

Unger, S., Bonafé, L., & Gouze, E. (2017). Current care and investigational therapies in achondroplasia. *Current Osteoporosis Reports* **15**(2), 53–60.

Waller, D. K., Correa, A., Vo, T. M., . . . Hecht, J. T. (2008). The population-based prevalence of achondroplasia and thanatophoric dysplasia in selected regions of the US. *American Journal of Medical Genetics Part A* 146A(18), 2385–9.

Waters, K. A., Everett, F., Sillence, D. O., Fagan, E. R., & Sullivan, C. E. (1995). Treatment of obstructive sleep apnea in achondroplasia: Evaluation of sleep, breathing, and somatosensory-evoked potentials. *American Journal of Medical Genetics* **59**(4), 460–6.

Wedel, V. L. (2007). Determination of season at death using dental cementum increment analysis*†. *Journal of Forensic Sciences* **52**(6), 1334–7.

Weiss, K. (1973). Demographic models for archaeology. *Memoirs of the Society for American Archaeology*. Washington, D.C.: Society for American Archaeology, 27.

White, C., Longstaffe, F., Pendergast, D., & Maxwell, J. (2009). Cultural embodiment and the enigmatic identity of the lovers from Lamani. In K. J. Knudson & C. M. Stojanowski (eds.), *Bioarchaeology and Identity in the Americas*. Gainesville, FL: University Press of Florida, 155–76.

White, K. K., Bompadre, V., Goldberg, M. J., ... Savarirayan, R. (2016). Best practices in the evaluation and treatment of foramen magnum stenosis in achondroplasia during infancy. *American Journal of Medical Genetics Part A* **170**(1), 42–51.

Willis, A., & Oxenham, M. F. (2013). A case of maternal and perinatal death in Neolithic Southern Vietnam, c. 2100–1050 BCE. *International Journal of Osteoarchaeology* **23**(6), 676–84.

Wilson, J. J. (2014). Paradox and promise: Research on the role of recent advances in paleo-demography and paleoepidemiology to the study of "health" in Precolumbian societies. *American Journal of Physical Anthropology* **155**(2), 268–80.

Wittwer-Backofen, U., Gampe, J., & Vaupel, J. W. (2004). Tooth cementum annulation for age estimation: Results from a large known-age validation study. *American Journal of Physical Anthropology* **123**(2), 119–29.

Wood, J. W., Milner, G. R., Harpending, H. C., ... et al. (1992). The osteological paradox: Problems of inferring prehistoric health from skeletal samples [and comments and reply]. *Current Anthropology* **33**(4), 343–70.

Wright, L. E., & Yoder, C. J. (2003). Recent progress in bioarchaeology: Approaches to the osteological paradox. *Journal of Archaeological Research* **11**(1), 43–70.

Wynn, J., King, T. M., Gambello, M. J., Waller, D. K., & Hecht, J. T. (2007). Mortality in achondroplasia study: A 42-year follow-up. *American Journal of Medical Genetics Part A* **143**(21), 2502–11.

Wynne-Davies, R., Walsh, W. K., & Gormley, J. (1981). Achondroplasia and hypochondroplasia. Clinical variation and spinal stenosis. *The Journal of Bone and Joint Surgery* **63B**(4), 508–15.

Zvelebil, M., & Weber, A. W. (2013). Human bioarchaeology: Group identity and individual life histories – Introduction. *Journal of Anthropological Archaeology* **32**(3), 275–9.

20 Estimating a Mortality Profile of Fisher-Gatherers in Brazil Using Cementochronology

Stephan Naji, Joël Blondiaux, Sheila Mendonça de Souza, Iris Zeng, and Jean-Pierre Bocquet-Appelt

> [...] sedentism can set into motion a number of interrelated biological, behavioral, and psychological changes that can result in increased fertility and decreased child mortality, and an increase in the population growth rate, even if such growth increases work efforts in the long term. The scenario we have outlined here, however, is speculative and requires testing against archaeological data.
>
> (Kelly 2013, 212)

One of the ongoing questions in demography has been to understand the evolution of demographic regimes, especially the pre-farming demographic system of nomadic food collectors preceding the invention of agriculture in many independent centers around 10,000 years ago (Bellwood 2005). In contrast, preindustrial sedentary farming communities, characterized by a high-fertility/high-mortality demographic regime until the eighteenth-century industrial revolution and the development of vaccination and effective contraception, are relatively well described in various parts of the world (Séguy & Buchet 2013).

As early as the 1920s V. Gordon Childe (1925) proposed that the "Neolithic Revolution" was probably the root of the cultural or population diffusion, ultimately leading to a "high-pressure" farming demographic system. Decades of archaeological research support this hypothesis and consistently demonstrate a sharp increase in various archaeological features, including skeletal remains (Bocquet-Appel 2008b; Hassan 1980). Of course, local narratives in different world regions are more complex than Childe's broad depiction. Notably, group mobility has become a major explicative co-variable to understand fertility variations and the shift in food production. Considering Childe's hypothesis and the archaeological record, what could we expect to observe from well-adapted, less mobile groups living in areas of abundant economic resources?

Starting from this hypothesis of population growth with the advent of agriculture, we are interested in nomadic food collectors' fertility and mortality schedules *before* the "Neolithic transition." Demographers refer to populations not influenced by modern medicine and contraceptive as following a "natural" fertility and mortality demographic regime. These populations include all humans before the invention of agriculture and groups of food collectors cohabiting with farming communities before the Industrial Revolution, including so-called contemporary hunter-gatherer groups. The main body of data for the latter is problematic on many levels. The demonstration that these populations were free of any influence from agriculturist neighbors, or colonialist interaction, is inconclusive at best (for examples and discussions, see Early & Headland 1998; Hill et al. 2007; Hurtado & Hill 1996; Kelly 2013).

Paleodemography, the study of demographic variables of populations with no written sources, has also been fraught with methodological biases and misconceptions (for a review, see Bocquet-Appel 2008b; Frankenberg & Konigsberg 2006; Séguy & Buchet 2013). However, archaeological evidence from skeletal samples is the only direct way to observe mortality/fertility patterns of pre-farming populations. Because these groups are often characterized by high residential mobility, it is difficult to find large enough samples of skeletons to test demographic hypotheses robustly.

Therefore, each skeletal assemblage becomes a critical piece of the prehistoric human demography puzzle and requires direct investigation whenever possible (Kelly 2013).

20.1 Cementochronology

The paleodemographic narratives of cemeteries have historically been in advance over the techniques of age-at-death estimates of adult skeletons, both regarding the quality of the age indicators and their statistical treatment (Bocquet-Appel 2008b; Frankenberg & Konigsberg 2006; Séguy & Buchet 2013). This is no longer the case, with the recent advances through the adoption of a Bayesian framework, or the use of a maximum likelihood approach, to estimate a "collective" age-at-death structure in anthropology, with parametric on nonparametric models (Bocquet-Appel & Bacro 2008; Caussinus & Courgeau 2013, 201; Gage & Dyke 1986; Séguy & Buchet 2013; Wood et al. 1992; Chapter 22). A third solution exists to assess demographic variables from skeletal data using cementochronology. A direct estimate of the mortality structure is possible with a precise and accurate anthropological age indicator because age is one of the most influential variables (Konigsberg & Herrmann 2006). Of course, other parameters have to be considered to mitigate estimation errors: (a) the biological uniformity hypothesis; (b) the population growth rate (stationary or not); (c) group homogeneity (i.e., are excavated skeletons close biologically and socioeconomically?); (d) random sampling (i.e., are all age groups adequately represented, and thus statistically representative of the entire population?) (Séguy & Buchet 2013, 99).

Cementochronology is the analysis of the seasonal incremental deposition of acellular cementum on the tooth root's surface, from the time of dental eruption to the time of death (Chapter 2). Cementochronology is the only anthropology technique relying on a continuous growth process throughout life (Chapter 1). With the recent advances in methodology (Chapter 24), cementochronology is the only anthropological method consistently achieving the theoretical minimum requirement for a valid age distribution estimation – a correlation between the biological indicator and the age at death, higher than $r = 0.9$ (Bocquet-Appel & Masset 1982; Kemkes-Grottenthaler 2002). This threshold allows estimating, without considerable risk of error, the individual age of a skeleton and the death structure to which it belongs (Bocquet-Appel & Masset 1982, 325, table 1). This is because "the effect of the anthropological reference population on the estimated structure asymptotically decreases as the correlation between age and biological indicator converges towards one" (Bocquet-Appel & Masset 1982, 326).

This chapter builds upon a preliminary analysis of the Cabeçuda age-at-death distribution presented at the 78th annual meeting of the American Association of Physical Anthropology (Blondiaux et al. 2009) and integrates recent advances in cementum diagenetic alterations. If some samples of age-at-death distributions of hunter-gatherers are known ethnographically, it is not the case for fisher-gatherers, who are now extinct. The estimation of their age-at-death distribution is the starting point of a paleodemographic narrative.

20.2 Material and Method

The Brazilian *Sambaqui*

Sambaqui, meaning "pile of shells" in the native Tupi language, are shell mounds found along the Atlantic coast of Brazil, from Espírito Santo State to Santa Catarina State (Gaspar et al. 2008). There are more than 1,000 registered *sambaquis* to attest over 6,500 years of prehistoric adaptation (Kneip et al. 2018). However, most of the Brazilian *sambaquis* were totally or partially destroyed by economic activities during the first half of the twentieth century (Gaspar et al. 2008). *Sambaquis* vary from 5 m to 60 m in height and can reach more than 400 m in length. The mounds typically consist of shells, sand, clay, charcoal, and ashes, among other materials, representing typical cultural traces, besides burying the dead on the mounds' surface (Gaspar et al. 2008). Although there are some signs of cultural and economic variation in newer layers (e.g., potsherds, ritual fireplaces), most sites lack evidence of settlement. Most of the *sambaquis* have been interpreted exclusively as mortuary monuments within regional settlement systems (De Blasis et al. 1998; Souza 2014a).

The *sambaqui* culture explored the abundant maritime and terrestrial resources that can be obtained all year-round from the affluent economic coastal ecotones of the Atlantic Forest following the growth burst of the Holocene climatic changes. Isotope analyses of bones and shells suggest that fish was the primary food source in the *sambaqui* (Figuti 1989). Recent oxygen isotope analyses of skeletons from a Santa Catarina *sambaqui* confirmed a strong dependence on marine animal resources and scarcely from plants, reinforcing an interpretation of substantial year-round catches (Colonese et al. 2014; De Blasis et al. 1998). This conclusion seems to hold, despite the decline of large shell mounds and the arrival of a new subsistence strategy around 1,500 calBP involving domesticated plants and pottery technology from inland areas (Colonese et al. 2014; Wesolowski et al. 2010). These results imply that the productive maritime economy was highly resilient to social and cultural change (Colonese et al. 2014).

The bioarchaeology of the *sambaqui* groups strengthens a model of well-adapted coastal populations. Nonspecific stress indicators, such as linear enamel hypoplasia (LEH), porotic hyperostosis, cribra orbitalia, or periostitis, have a relatively high prevalence in some *sambaquis*. These lesions suggest an increasing infectious or nutritional stress among those groups compared to other contemporary areas (Souza 2014b). Such findings support low mobility and elevated population density in some areas. This hypothesis is reinforced by the low frequency of violent trauma in most skeletal series from *sambaquis* (Lessa & Medeiros 2011; Rodrigues-Carvalho et al. 2009).

The notion of groups using affluent coastal resources, managing the same *sambaquis* requiring an enormous amount of manual labor, and burying their dead in them for centuries suggests a high level of social organization and sustainable stability (Gaspar et al. 2008). The concentration of sites, burials, and the monumental aspect of some *sambaquis* around Santa Catarina State support increasing population size or density. This context creates the necessary components for a local atypical demographic transition (Souza 2014b) from a singular emphasis on nomadic, highly mobile shellfish collectors to denser, less mobile societies with an intricate social organization (De Blasis et al. 1998).

The Cabeçuda Skeletal Sample

Cabeçuda is a monumental funerary mound located between the lagoons of Imaruí and Santo Antonio dos Anjos, in Laguna County, South of Santa Catarina State, Brazil. Archaeological investigations evidenced a continuous occupation of Cabeçuda for more than 3,000 years. Its size and position with smaller *sambaquis* suggest its prominent social position. The first report of Cabeçuda (Abreu 1929) describes an intact monumental mound, 22 m high and 400 m long. When Castro Faria (National Museum of Rio de Janeiro) excavated the site in the fifties, only one-tenth of the 53,000 m^3 of archaeological layers remained (Faria 1959). Recent excavations of the mound confirmed a continuous occupation with minor cultural changes (Scheel-Ybert et al. 2020).

According to Scheel-Ybert and colleagues (2020), radiocarbon dates place the construction and use of the Cabeçuda shell mound from 4,180 ± 60BP (4,766–4,325 years calBP) to 1,800 ± 40BP (1,711–1,519 years calBP) (Kneip et al. 2018). Direct radiocarbon dating of human bones ranges from 3,870 ± 50calBP (Rodrigues-Carvalho et al. 2011) at the mound base to 1,800 ± 40 calBP (Scheel-Ybert et al. 2020). This period corresponds to the *sambaqui* expansion peak and the start of the *sambaqui* density decline with contemporary horticulturalists' arrival in the region (Kneip et al. 2018).

Among 280 skeletons in Cabeçuda's collection, ninety-three have been excavated from the area corresponding to the central part of the original *sambaqui*. The people buried in Cabeçuda were robust individuals (Alvim et al. 1975), with no violent trauma

Table 20.1 Cabeçuda skeletal sample distribution by age category

Age	0–4.9	5–9.9	10–14.9	15–19.9	20+	Total
N	8,0	6,5	5,5	4,0	69	93

(Lessa & Medeiros 2011) and few joint diseases (Rodrigues-Carvalho et al. 2009). Approximately 35 percent showed evidence of environmental or nutritional stress lesions (Alvim & Gomes 1989). Also, LEHs were notable, but almost no signs of periosteal reactions were recorded (Souza 1995). The heavily worn teeth were free of dental caries (Souza 1995, 1999). Dental calculi were voluminous, but only a few tiny starch grains were identified (Jorge 2016). These results suggest periods of stress/recovery not uncommon to groups exposed to tropical pathogens.

Only thirty-eight adult skeletons (twenty-two males, sixteen females) could be assigned a morphological sex (Souza 1991). The null hypothesis of proportion equality between Cabeçuda sex ratio of 1.375 and the theoretical natural sex ratio of one (Orzack et al. 2015) is not rejected at the 0.05 significance level (z-test for two population proportions, $p = 0.4899$). Of course, for such a small sample size, the 95 percent confidence interval for p ranges from –0.144 to 0.302 and thus includes both the null and alternative hypotheses. As a working premise, we will accept that the sample's sex ratio is close enough to the expected value.

Age categories were assigned by the anthropologists using dental development and skeletal maturation (Souza 1991). Twenty-four skeletons were identified as subadults below twenty years of age, and sixty-nine as adults over twenty years old (Table 20.1).

The proportion of "0–15" in the total Cabeçuda sample is 21,50 percent (20/93). This frequency is far below the ratio observed in contemporary hunter-gatherer groups, averaging around 60 percent (Gurven & Kaplan 2007, table 5). The lack of children could be indicative of several selection biases: *ritual* – some of the children were buried elsewhere; *archaeological* – the excavation didn't include part of the cemetery containing children; *taphonomic* – subadult bones were not preserved homogeneously; *misclassified* as faunal remains (Klökler 2014) or a combination of factors. In fact, Faria's notes mention the abundance of children's bones and explain his decision to select individuals based on skeletal preservation or anthropological value (Ederly 2014). This selection bias is a common problem that some techniques can circumvent, most notably the use of skeletal ratios.

Adult Age Estimation Using Cementochronology

To get a more precise sense of the adult mortality profile, we estimated the age-at-death distribution of the sample using cementochronology. One tooth was extracted from seventy-one individuals. Two adults didn't have teeth. One was age fifteen to nineteen years old, and the other over twenty (Souza 1991, 1995, 95). All teeth sampled from the Cabeçuda site were prepared and analyzed initially by one of the coauthors (JB), following a protocol comparable to the one published in this volume (Chapter 1, Figure 1.5).

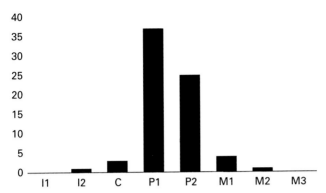

Figure 20.1 Adult sample teeth distribution by tooth type (I: incisor; C: canine; P: premolar; M: molar); mandibular and maxillary

Samples were then reviewed at the New York University Dental School by two of the authors (SN, IZ) using a quarter-plate lambda filter in polarized light. This later analysis was done to discriminate diagenetic cementum layers from natural ones (Stutz 2002).

The maximum number of cementum layers was added to the average sex-specific year of tooth eruption (Liversidge 2015) to obtain the estimated age. This choice was motivated by the heavy diagenetic influence observed on many samples. In other words, if our counts are biased, they would be toward an under-counting (omitting) of cementum layers. Using the maximum number of increments (instead of the average) is one option to account for this bias. The only way to properly avoid these statistical biases would be to infer the collective age distribution directly from the increment counts within a Bayesian framework (Naji et al. 2016; Séguy & Buchet 2013). For this study, various tooth types were collected (Figure 20.1), preventing us from using a Bayesian approach because all of the valid methods are currently based on a single homogenous indicator. The Bayesian algorithm for multiple teeth still does not exist.

20.3 Results

In the absence of a collective age-at-death technique, we must implement a less satisfactory method, namely aggregating the individuals in demographic age categories. To deal with overlapping estimate ranges across age categories, we distributed the adult age using a normal distribution model (Bocquet-Appel 2005; Lanteri 2016). We recognize this is also a potential problem. However, because we do not have prior information regarding the age structure of pre-farming, seminomadic populations, this is the less biased option (Table 20.2).

The adult age-at-death frequency distribution (Figure 20.2) illustrates two mortality modes: at 20–29 years (lowest) and 40–49 years (highest). The lowest mortality is in the youngest (15–19) and oldest (70+) age categories.

Table 20.2 Probabilities (p.) of the adult age-at-death distribution of the Cabeçuda dental sample, redistributed across age categories

	p.15–19.9	p.20–29.9	p.30–39.9	p.40–49.9	p.50–59.9	p.60–69.9	p.70–79.9	p.80+	Total
N	4,0	14,0	13,0	26,0	9,0	5,0	2,0	0,0	73
%	0,04	0,15	0,14	0,28	0,10	0,05	0,02	0,00	1

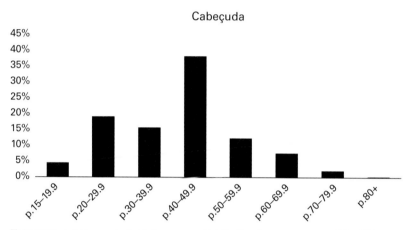

Figure 20.2 Adult age-at-death frequency distribution by age category (N = 73)

If the cementochronology analysis is representative, this is the first demographic sample directly estimated from a skeleton sample of fisher-gatherers in South America. The high frequency of young adults departs quite clearly from attritional age structures observed in contemporary hunter-gatherers' models. Since Howell (1982), many paleodemographers noted that prehistoric analyses tended to produce incongruous age-at-death structure with mortality rates never observed in recent mortality studies of isolated groups (Gage & Leslie 1989, 89; Hurtado & Hill 1996).

Even though individuals are present in every age category, there is a notable lack of older adults past the sixth decade of life. Conversely, there is an unusually high proportion of young adults. This pattern is more commonly seen in catastrophic samples from events such as wars or epidemics (Blondiaux et al. 2016; Naji 2010).

20.4 Discussion

Interpreting the Age-at-Death Distribution

The archaeological evidence suggests that Cabeçuda was used at the peak of the *sambaqui* growth period (Kneip et al. 2018). Therefore, the assumption of an average stationary growth rate across this transition is not unrealistic. Likewise, *sambaqui* population distribution and movements in the area have been described as a stable territorial partitioning around central mounds such as Cabeçuda (Kneip et al. 2018), suggesting little or no significant migrations occurred outside the area.

To interpret our age-at-death distribution comparatively, we can use available age structures of preindustrial populations documented through historical and ethnographic data. For preindustrial farming populations, Séguy and Buchet (2013) defined a standard preindustrial demographic regime by selecting and correcting 167 documented life tables of groups characterized by very high rates of fertility and child mortality, with a low life expectancy at birth, similar to life expectancy at age twenty (Séguy & Buchet 2013, 314). Building on previous works by Bocquet-Appel and Masset (1977), Séguy and Buchet (2013) describe a preindustrial mortality hazard pattern observed in extant populations. This standard preindustrial model (Séguy & Buchet 2013, 314) describes the lowest mortality risk between ten to forty years of age, followed by a steady increase peaking around seventy years, and concluded by a rapid decline in the last decades of life (Figure 20.3).

For "natural" hunter-gatherer populations, the data exists for only five groups: the Botswana-Namibia !Kung (Howell 1979), the Tanzanian Hadza (Blurton Jones 2016), the Ache of Paraguay (Hurtado & Hill 1996), the Agta of the Philippines (Early & Headland 1998), and the Hiwi of Venezuela (Hill et al. 2007). All other study implies some level of food production (horticulturalists) or some contact with neighboring farmers or colonial posts (Gurven & Kaplan 2007, figure 1). These populations are an interesting window into contemporary hunter-gatherer population demography. Distributions for preindustrial farmers and contemporaneous hunter-gatherers are compared in Figure 20.3.

The evidence describes a comparable pattern with very little increase in mortality hazard between fifteen and forty, followed by a steady rise of Gompertz fashion (rapid increase with very high death rates) with a modal ages of adult death between sixty-five

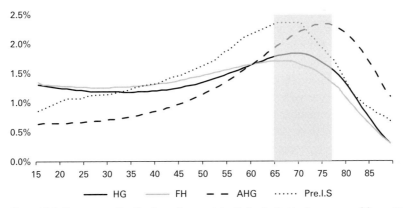

Figure 20.3 Frequency distribution of ages at death for individuals over age fifteen. HG: hunter-gatherer – solid black line; FH: fisherman horticulturist – solid gray line; AHG: acculturated hunter-gatherer – black dash line (based on data from Gurven and Kaplan 2007, figure 4, using DataThief); Pre.I.S: preindustrial farmer, standard – gray dot line (based on data from Séguy and Buchet 2013)

and seventy-five years of age (Gurven & Kaplan 2007, 337, figure 4). This pattern is also in line with revised estimates of life expectancies in several archaeological sites using a maximum likelihood model (Konigsberg & Herrmann 2006). Of course, most studies on contemporary preindustrial groups suffer from cofactors and sampling dependency that limit the interpretative value of their conclusions.

Also, in all ethnographic models, the effect of sedentism on mortality has not been explored in detail for lack of quantifiable data. The most notable studies include the Nunamiut (Binford & Chasko 1976), the !Kung (Harpending & Wandsnider 1982), the Kutchin Athapaskans (Roth 1981), and the Turkana pastoralists (Brainard 1986). After the change toward decreased mobility pattern and its consequences in terms of diet and division of labor, all these studies conclude to a general decrease in child mortality and an increase in fertility.

The Cabeçuda age-at-death distribution obtained from cementochronology does not fit with the hypothetical pre-farming pattern described here. If unbiased, this distribution could only be interpreted in the context of a catastrophic event or major migratory movements. Because the archaeological record does not support such hypotheses, the most probable conclusion is that the distribution is not representative of the underlying adult "burying" population (Bocquet & Masset 1977).

Demographic Proxy Indicator of Fertility

Another approach to refine our interpretation is to use a proxy indicator of the birth rate using skeletons ratio. Several ethnographic studies have documented the shift from mobility to sedentism with an increase in fertility (Binford & Chasko 1976; Ellanna 1990; Gomes 1990; Hitchcock 1982; Roth & Ray 1985). There is a potential confounding factor in the availability of modern medicine and antibiotics, however. The changes all occurred in postindustrial contexts, where sexually transmitted diseases significantly impacted sterility (up to 40 percent) and fertility rates (Pennington 2001). The availability of modern medicine makes the archaeological study of mobility and demography all the more essential to obtain a clearer understanding of pre-farming population demography (Kelly 2013). Because of the inherent bias in skeletal age estimation, Bocquet-Appel and Masset developed a demographic proxy indicator, the Juvenility Index (Bocquet & Masset 1977; Bocquet-Appel & Masset 1982) later updated to the $_{15}P_5$ ratio (Bocquet-Appel 2002). The $_{15}P_5$ ratio is calculated by dividing the number of skeletons ages five to nineteen by the number of skeletons ages five and over: $_{15}P_5 = d(5-i)/d(5+)$. This $_{15}P_5$ ratio has the benefit of (a) taking into account the taphonomic and ritual variations linked with the lack of subjects aged below five in archaeological sites; (b) using a cutoff point (twenty years of age) easily estimated using anthropological aging standards, and (c) being a continuous ratio (Séguy & Buchet 2013). The $_{15}P_5$ ratio is highly correlated with the birth rate (adjusted $r^2 = 0.963$) and strongly correlated with the growth rate and the life expectancy at birth (Bocquet-Appel 2002).

When applied to 138 archaeological sites (Bocquet-Appel 2008a, 39, table 1), the use of the $_{15}P_5$ *ratio* clearly differentiated nomadic hunter-gatherers ($_{15}P_5 = 0.2228$)

Table 20.3 Summary table for the estimation of the birth rate (b), growth rate (r), and life expectancy at birth (e0) from the $_{15}P_5$ ratio, with two standard errors (±2σ) (see Bocquet-Appel 1996 for the calculations)

$_{15}P_5 = 0{,}1882$		−2σ	+2σ
b	0,0384	0,0323	0,0445
r	0,0026	−0,0080	0,0133
e₀	28,412	24,033	32,790

from sedentary farmers ($_{15}P_5$ = 0.2536), with semisedentary shell mound foragers in between ($_{15}P_5$ = 0.2292). Also, in contemporary hunter-gatherers, the average life expectancy at birth varies from twenty-one to thirty-seven years (Gurven & Kaplan 2007, 326).

For the Cabeçuda sample, the $_{15}P_5$ ratio is $_{15}P_5 = p_{5-19.9}/p_{5+} = 16/85 = 0{,}18824$. The estimated growth rate (Bocquet-Appel & Masset 1996) ranges from −0.00804 to 0.0133 (95 percent confidence interval) and includes the stationary hypothesis, $r = 0$ (Table 20.3).

The Cabeçuda ratio falls below all the other observed groups. However, the small sample size makes the indicator very sensitive to any missing data, and we have acknowledged that some children were not excavated. Nevertheless, we do not know which age category is most affected by this problem. Because the $_{15}P_5$ ratio was designed to cope with the youngest age category bias, we must consider that the skeletons could still be a random sample of the living group and thus representative of Cabeçuda's birth rate.

The Total Fertility Rate

Few data exist on natural fertility for Pleistocene populations. The only proxies demographers have been using are contemporary groups defined by their subsistence strategies as Hunter-Gatherers, Farmers, or Transitional (from Collectors to Producers). Campbell and Wood (1988) looked at seventy of these populations and found that the average number of children from females surviving to mean childbearing age, represented by the total fertility rate (TFR), varies significantly from 3.5 to 9.8.

This variation is more than three times the variance observed in "controlled-fertility" populations (TFR = 1.5–4.5). Wood concludes that "there is no typical level of natural fertility" (Wood 1994, 32). However, other analyses identified a significant difference between agriculturalists (TFR > 6.6) and nonagriculturalists (TFR < 5.5) (Bentley et al. 1993; Blurton Jones 2016; Hewlett 1991). All these studies point out that hunter-gatherers do not necessarily have fertility as low as the level we see after the Contemporary Demographic Transition (Campbell & Wood 1988).

Sellen and Mace (1997) tried to tease out these differences by distinguishing each subsistence strategy and relate them to fertility. They concluded that "differences in dependence on agriculture were the strongest predictors of the differences in fertility between closely related cultures" (Sellen & Mace 1997, 886).

Bocquet-Appel and Naji (2006) directly tested the metabolic load hypothesis in the archaeological record and 172 ethnographic populations of North American Indians (Bocquet-Appel 2008a, table 1). In both data sets, results support the prediction that energy intake (diet) and energy expenditure (mobility and lactation) are good predictors of low fertility for female nomadic hunter-gatherers (high mobility, high carrying loads, and low-calorie diet) and high fertility for sedentary farmers (low mobility, no carrying load, and calorie-dense food).

Therefore, this model predicts that the Cabeçuda sample (partly sedentary and consuming a calorie-poor/nutrient-dense diet) should have a TFR between fully nomadic hunter-gatherers and entirely sedentary farmers.

Using the preindustrial table's function describing the relationship between $_{15}P_5$ and the total fertility rate, we can infer the TFR in the Cabeçuda sample if we assume a stationary population hypothesis. For a $_{15}P_5$ ratio of 0.1883, the corresponding TFR equals 5.44 (Bocquet-Appel & Naji 2006, figure 6). Cabeçuda's TFR does fall within the observed values of contemporary pre-farming groups.

20.5 Conclusion

If the data are valid, the Cabeçuda sample represents a group with low fertility but not as low as the one observed after the CDT. The metabolic load model predicts that a population of fisher-gatherers (nutrient-rich, calorie-poor diet), probably seminomadic (average mobility and lactation), should display a transitional level of fertility (lower than full sedentary farmers, but higher than full nomadic hunter-gatherers). This is the case for Cabeçuda. However, within a quasi-stable hypothesis, we should also expect a corresponding low mortality hazard. Even though several variables can produce the same output, we lack the data to evaluate the death structure in the Cabeçuda sample.

The limits of our results can come from several sources:

(1) *Ritual*: The skeletal sample is biased and not representative of the underlying living population. Territorial distribution around Cabeçuda is clustered and includes several other smaller mounds. Any selective funerary process splitting the members in different mounds for burial could bias any single sample.
(2) *Archaeological*: We have direct testimony that children's burials were present and not systematically excavated.
(3) *Demographic*: Any population movements between adjacent mounds or from outside the Cabeçuda group, for economic or social reasons, would skew the distribution.
(4) *Demographic*: The growth rate, fueled by high births or immigration, is much higher than expected.

(5) *Taphonomic*: The age indicator was severely biased by diagenetic processes and led to a biased age-at-death distribution.
(6) *Health*: (a) The sample comes from a catastrophic event, even though the archaeological record cannot suggest any particular type (war, epidemics) and supports a somewhat "healthy" sample; (b) increased sedentism and population growth may also lead to an increase in childhood metabolic stress and consequent adults' higher mortality.
(7) *Metabolic*: Cabeçuda represents some other combination of diet/mobility within pre-farming populations, unobserved before in the archaeological record, and maybe related to the unique energy expenditure related to mound life.

The demographic transition in the Cabeçuda area, from the end of the expanding period-2 to the initial declining periods-3 (Kneip et al. 2018, figure 2), is a theme for future investigations. Additional funerary sites should be included to increase the sample size and representativity. Categorizing sites by mobility (from nomad to sedentary) and diet (calorie-poor or calorie-dense) gradients in various environmental contexts is thus central to making accurate predictions on demographic outcomes, understanding demographic transitions within their local ecological contexts, and directly testing the hypothesis of a pre-farming, low-fertility, and mortality demographic regime.

Acknowledgments

This chapter is dedicated to the memory of Jean-Pierre Bocquet-Appel, who initiated this study and funded part of the analysis of Cabeçuda human remains. Part of this work was funded by the NYU Dean Undergraduate Research Fund.

References

Abreu, S. F. (1929). Sambaquis de Imbituba e Laguna (Santa Catharina). *Revista da Sociedade de Geografia do Rio de Janeiro* **1**, 8–50.
Alvim, M. E. M. C. & Gomes, J. C. O. (1989). Análise e interpretaçãodascondiçõespatológicas – Órbitacrivosa, osteoporosepuntiforme e hiperostoseesponjosa – emcrânioshumanosprovenientes de sítioarqueológico Sambaqui de Cabeçuda, Laguna, SC, Brasil. São Paulo. *Revista de Pré-História* **7**, 127–43.
Alvim, M. E. M. C., Vieira, N., & Cheuiche, L. N. (1975). Os construtores dos sambaquis de Cabeçuda, SC e de Piaçaguera, SP:EstudoMorfológicoComparativo. Rio de Janeiro. *Arquivos de Anatomia e Antropologia* **1**, 393–406.
Bellwood, P. (2005). *First Farmers: The Origins of Agricultural Societies*. Oxford: Blackwell.
Bentley, G. R., Goldberg, T., & Jasienska, G. (1993). The fertility of agricultural and nonagricultural traditional societies. *Population Studies* (47), 269–81.
Binford, L. R., & Chasko, W. J. (1976). Nunamiut demographic history. In *Demographic Anthropology: Quantitative Approaches*. Albuquerque: University of New Mexico Press, 63–143.

Blondiaux, J., Bocquet-Appel, J.-P., Souza, S. M. de, & Naji, S. (2009). First demographic profile of South American fisherman-horticulturists estimated from TCA technique. *Implications for Paleopathology*, vol. S48. Presented at the American Association of Physical Anthropology, Chicago, IL, 106–7.

Blondiaux, J., Naji, S., Bocquet-Appel, J.-P., Colard, T., de Broucker, A., & de Seréville-Niel, C. (2016). The leprosarium of Saint-Thomas d'Aizier: The cementochronological proof of the medieval decline of Hansen disease in Europe? *International Journal of Paleopathology* **15**, 140–51.

Blurton Jones, N. (2016). *Demography and Evolutionary Ecology of Hadza Hunter-Gatherers*. Cambridge: Cambridge University Press.

Bocquet, J.-P., & Masset, C. (1977). Estimateurs en paléodémographie. *L'Homme* **17**(4), 65–90.

Bocquet-Appel, J.-P. (2002). Paleoanthropological traces of a neolithic demographic transition. *Current Anthropology* **43**(4), 637–50.

(2005). La paléodémographie. In O. Dutour, J.-J. Hublin, & B. Vandermeersch (eds.), Editions du Comité des Travaux Historiques et Scientifiques. *Objets Et Methodes En Paleoanthropologie*. Paris, 271–313.

(2008a). Explaining the Neolithic demographic transition. In J.-P. Bocquet-Appel & O. Bar-Yosef (eds.), *The Neolithic Demographic Transition and its Consequences*. Dordrecht: Springer Netherlands, 35–55.

(2008b). *Recent Advances in Paleodemography. Data, Techniques, Patterns*. Dordrecht/London: Springer Verlag.

Bocquet-Appel, J.-P., & Bacro, J.-N. (2008). Estimation of an age distribution with its confidence intervals using an iterative Bayesian procedure and a bootstrap sampling approach. In J.-P. Bocquet-Appel (ed.), *Recent Advances in Palaeodemography*. The Netherlands: Springer, 63–82.

Bocquet-Appel, J.-P., & Masset, C. (1982). Farewell to paleodemography. *Journal of Human Evolution* **11**, 321–33.

(1996). Paleodemography: Expectancy and false hope. *American Journal of Physical Anthropology* **99**, 571–83.

Bocquet-Appel, J.-P., & Naji, S. (2006). Testing the hypothesis of a worldwide Neolithic demographic transition corroboration from American cemeteries (with comments). *Current Anthropology* **47**(2), 341–65.

Brainard, J. (1986). Differential mortality in Turkana agriculturalists and pastoralists. *American Journal of Physical Anthropology* **70**(4), 525–36.

Campbell, K. L., & Wood, J. W. (1988). Fertility in traditional societies: Social and biological determinants. In P. Diggory, M. Potts, & S. Teper (eds.), *Natural Human Fertility: Social and Biological Determinants*. London: MacMillan, 36–69.

Caussinus, H., & Courgeau, D. (2013). A new method for estimating age-at-death structure. In *Handbook of Palaeodemography*. Cambridge, MA: Springer International Publishing, 255–286.

Childe, V. G. (1925). *The Dawn of European Civilization*. New York: Alfred A. Knopf.

Colonese, A. C., Collins, M., Lucquin, A., ... Craig, O. E. (2014). Long-term resilience of Late Holocene coastal subsistence system in Southeastern South America. *PLoS ONE* **9**(4), e93854.

De Blasis, P., Fish, S. K., Gaspar, M. D., & Fish, P. R. (1998). Some references for the discussion of complexity among the Sambaqui mound builders from the southern shores of Brazil. *Revista de Arqueología Americana* (15), 75–105.

Early, J. D., & Headland, T. N. (1998). *Population Dynamics of a Philippine Rain Forest People: The San Ildefonso Agta*. Gainesville: University Press of Florida.

Ederly, T. (2014). *Sambaqui de Cabeçuda: de Monte de Lixo a Monumento de Vida e Morte. Monografia de Conclusão de Curso* (LicenciaturaemHistória). Rio de Janeiro: Universidade do Grande Rio.

Ellanna, L. (1990). Demographic change, sedentism, and western contact: An inland Dena'ina Athabaskan case study. In B. Meehan & N. White (eds.), *Hunter-Gatherer Demography Past and Present*, Oceania Monograph, vol. 19. Sydney: University of Sydney, 101–16.

Faria, L. de C. (1959). Le problème des sambáquis du Brésil: Récents excavations du gisement de Cabeçuda (Laguna, Santa Catarina). In *Proceedings of the 30th International Congress of Americanists*. Cambridge: Royal Anthropological Institute.

Figuti, L. (1989). Estudo dos vestígiosfaunísticos do Sambaqui Cosipa-3, Cubatão, SP. São Paulo. *Revista de Pré-História* **7**, 112–26.

Frankenberg, S., & Konigsberg, L. W. (2006). A brief history of paleodemography from Hooton to Hazard Analysis. In J. E. Buikstra & L. A. Beck (eds.), *Bioarchaeology. The Contextual Analysis of Human Remains*. Boston: Academic Press, 262–80.

Gage, T. B., & Dyke, B. (1986). Parameterizing abridged mortality tables: The Siler three-component hazard model. *Human Biology* (58), 275–91.

Gage, T. B., & Leslie, P. (1989). Demography and human population biology: Problems and progress. In M. Little & J. D. Haas (eds.), *Human Biology: A Transdisciplinary Science*. Oxford: Oxford University Press, 15–44.

Gaspar, M. D., Deblasis, P., Fish, S. K., & Fish, P. R. (2008). Sambaqui (Shell Mound) societies of coastal Brazil. In H. Silverman & W. Isbell (eds.), *Handbook of South American Archaeology*. New York: Springer Science & Business Media, 319–35.

Gomes, A. (1990). Demographic implications of villagisation among the Semang of Malaysia. In B. Meehan & N. White (eds.), *Hunter-Gatherer Demography Past and Present*, Oceania Monograph, vol. 19. Sydney: University of Sydney, 126–48.

Gurven, M., & Kaplan, H. (2007). Longevity among hunter-gatherers: A cross-cultural examination. *Population and Development Review* **33**(2), 321–65.

Harpending, H., & Wandsnider, L. (1982). Population structures of Ghanzi and Ngamiland! Kung. In M. H. Crawford & J. H. Mielke (eds.), *Current Developments in Anthropological Genetics: Ecology and Population Structure*. Boston, MA: Springer US, 29–50.

Hassan, F. (1980). The growth and regulation of human populations in prehistoric times. In M. N. Cohen, R. S. Malprass, & H. G. Klein (eds.), *Biosocial Mechanisms of Population Regulation*. New Haven: Yale University Press, 305–20.

Hewlett, B. S. (1991). Demography and childcare in pre-industrial societies. *Journal of Anthropological Research* **47**(1), 1–37.

Hill, K., Hurtado, A. M., & Walker, R. S. (2007). High adult mortality among Hiwi hunter-gatherers: Implications for human evolution. *Journal of Human Evolution* **52**(4), 443–54.

Hitchcock, R. (1982). Patterns of sedentism among the Basarwa of eastern Botswana. In E. Leacock & R. B. Lee (eds.), *Politics and History in Band Society*. New York: Cambridge University Press, 223–67.

Howell, N. (1979). *Demography of the Dobe !Kung*. New York: Academic Press.

(1982). Village composition implied by paleodemographic life table: The Libben site. *American Journal of Physical Anthropology* **59**, 263–9.

Hurtado, A. M., & Hill, K. (1996). *Ache Life History: The Ecology and Demography of a Foraging People*. New York: Aldine Transaction.

Jorge, A. C. F. Viana. (2016). Análise de microvestígiosvegetaisemcálculosdentárioshumanos do Sambaqui de Cabeçuda. Dissertação de Mestrado, Escola Nacional de SaúdePública, Fiocruz.

Kelly, R. L. (2013). *The Lifeways of Hunter-Gatherers: The Foraging Spectrum*. Cambridge; New York: Cambridge University Press.

Kemkes-Grottenthaler, A. (2002). Aging through the ages: Historical perspectives on age indicator methods. In R. D. Hoppa & J. W. Vaupel (eds.), *Paleodemography: Age Distributions from Skeletal Samples*. Cambridge: Cambridge University Press, 48–72.

Klökler, D. (2014). Adornos em concha doSítio Cabeçuda: revisitaàsamostras de Castro Faria. São Paulo. *Revista de Arqueologia* **27**(2), 150–69.

Kneip, A., Farias, D., & De Blasis, P. (2018). Longaduração e territorialidade da ocupaçãosambaquieira na laguna de Santa Marta, Santa Catarina. *Revista de Arqueologia* **31**(1), 25–51.

Konigsberg, L., & Herrmann, N. P. (2006). The osteological evidence for human longevity in the recent past. In K. Hawkes & R. R. Paine (eds.), *The Evolution of Human Life History*. Santa Fe: School of American Research Press, 267–306.

Lanteri, L. (2016). Recrutement, paléodémographie et cémentochronologie. Application à un contexte d'inhumation paroissial d'Ancien Régime: Notre-Dame du Bourg à Digne-les-Bains . PhD thesis, Aix-Marseille.

Lessa, A., & Medeiros, J. C. de. (2011). Reflexõespreliminares sobre a questão da violênciaempopulaçõesconstrutoras de sambaqui: Análisedos sítiosArapuã (RJ) e Cabeçuda (SC). São Paulo. *Revista Do Museu de Arqueologia e Etnologia* **11**, 77–93.

Liversidge, H. M. (2015). Tooth eruption and timing. In J. D. Irish & G. R. Scott (eds.), *A Companion to Dental Anthropology*. Oxford: John Wiley & Sons, Inc., 159–71.

Naji, S. (2010). Analyse spatio-temporelle des données bioarchéologiques de la population médiévale de l'église Saint-Laurent de Grenoble, Isère: IVe–XVe siècle. Thèse de Doctorat. Paris: EHESS.

Naji, S., Bertrand, B., & Colard, T. (2016). Archaeological application of three age-at-death estimation techniques to the Medieval site of La Granède, France: Cementochronology, new life tables and Caussinus-Courgeau bayesian procedure. *American Journal of Physical Anthropology* S.62, 238.

Orzack, S. H., Stubblefield, J. W., Akmaev, V. R., . . . Zuckerman, J. E. (2015). The human sex ratio from conception to birth. *Proceedings of the National Academy of Sciences of the United States of America* **112**(16), E2102–E2111.

Pennington, R. (2001). Hunter-gatherer demography. In C. Panter-Brick, R. Layton, & P. Rowley-Conwy (eds.), *Hunter-Gatherers: An Interdisciplinary Perspective*. Cambridge: Cambridge University Press, 170–204.

Rodrigues-Carvalho, C., Lessa, A., & Souza, S. M. de. (2009). Bioarchaeology of the Sambaqui groups: Skeletal morphology, physical stress and trauma. *BAR International* (S2026), 15–20.

Rodrigues-Carvalho, C., Scheel-Ybert, R., Gaspar, M. D., . . . Borges, D. S. (2011). Cabeçuda II: Um conjunto de amoladores-polidoresevidenciadosem Laguna, Santa Catarina. São Paulo. *Revista Do Museu de Arqueologia* **21**, 389–93.

Roth, E. A. (1981). Sedentism and changing fertility patterns in a Northern Athapaskan isolate. *Journal of Human Evolution* (10), 413–25.

Roth, E. A., & Ray, A. K. (1985). Demographic patterns of sedentary and nomadic Juang of Orissa. *Human Biology* **57**(3), 319–25.

Scheel-Ybert, R., Rodrigues-Carvalho, C., DeBlasis, P., Gaspar, M. D., & Klökler, D. (2020). Mudanças e permanências no Sambaqui de Cabeçuda (Laguna, SC): Dasescavações de Castro Faria àsquestõesatuais. *Revista de Arqueologia* 33(1), 169–97.

Séguy, I., & Buchet, L. (2013). *Handbook of Palaeodemography*, vol. 2, Cham: Springer International Publishing.

Sellen, D. W., & Mace, R. (1997). Fertility and mode of subsistence: A phylogenetic analysis. *Current Anthropology* **38**(5), 878–89.

Souza, S. M. de. (1991). Aplicação de funções discriminantes na estimativa de sexoemossoshumanospre-históricos. Dissertação de Mestrado. Rio de Janeiro: UniversidadeFederal do Rio de Janeiro.

(1995). *Estresse, Doença e Adaptabilidade. EstudoComparativo de Dois Grupos Pré-históricosemPerspectivaBiocultural*. (Tese de Doutorado), Escola Nacional de SaúdePública, Fiocruz.

(1999). Anemia e adaptabilidadeemum grupo costeiro pré-histórico: UmaHipótesePatocenótica. In M. C. Tenório (ed.), *Pré-história da Terra Brasilis*, Rio de Janeiro:Editora UFRJ, 171–88.

(2014a). Bioarchaeology in Brazil. In B. O'Donnabhain & M. C. Lozada (eds.), *Archaeological Human Remains: Global Perspectives*. Cham: Springer International Publishing, 53–63.

(2014b). Sambaqui people, the Shell Mound Builders of Brazil. A challenge for paleodemographers. In M. Roksandic, S. M. de Souza, S. Eggers, & M. Burchell (eds.), *The Cultural Dynamics of Shell-Matrix Sites*. Albuquerque, NM: University of New Mexico Press, 163–71.

Stutz, A. J. (2002). Polarizing microscopy identification of Chemical Diagenesis in archaeological cementum. *Journal of Archaeological Science* **29**(11), 1327–47.

Wesolowski, V., Souza, S. M. de, Reinhard, K. J., & Ceccantini, G. (2010). Evaluating microfossil content of dental calculus from Brazilian sambaquis. *Journal of Archaeological Science* **37**(6), 1326–38.

Wood, J. W. (1994). *Dynamics of Human Reproduction, Biology: Biology, Biometry, Demography*. Hawthorne/New York: Aldine de Gruyter.

Wood, J. W., Holman, D. J., Weiss, K. M., Buchanan, A. V., & LeFor, B. (1992). Hazards models for human population biology. *American Journal of Physical Anthropology* **35** (supplement 15), 43–87.

21 Cementochronology: A Solution to Reconstructing Past Populations' Mortality Profiles Using Individual Age-at-Death Estimates

Laëtitia Lanteri, Bruno Bizot, Bérengère Saliba-Serre, and Aurore Schmitt

21.1 Cementochronology

Reconstructing a paleodemographic mortality profile of a complete human skeletal collection that includes both subadult and adult individuals is problematic because current methods fail to provide a valid solution for estimating unbiased adult age distributions, despite continuous complex mathematical and statistical improvements. Consensually, individual adult age estimation has been discarded from paleodemographic studies because of its methodological biases and inaccurate results (Bocquet-Appel 2008; Buchet and Séguy 2013; Hoppa and Vaupel 2002). Among these issues is the use of different indicators according to the skeleton's preservation that is not similar from one individual to another. The use of multifactorial methods to maximize accuracy and precision is also recommended. Both approaches induce a bias related to the aggregation of different methods based on different populations' standards. This limit was partially encountered by the use, for instance, of transition analysis (Boldsen et al. 2002), which was finally revealed to perform more poorly than expected (Milner and Boldsen 2012). The combined age estimate method deserves further research (Buckberry 2015). The recently developed Bayesian inference procedure still requires a prior age distribution that is not estimated from individual skeletal samples (Caussinus and Courgeau 2010; Buchet et al. 2017).

Some past population demographic parameters have been estimated using paleodemographic estimators based on subadult age category ratios (Bocquet and Masset 1977). Although considered more reliable and accurate than other estimation techniques, subadult age estimation encounters two unresolved issues, namely (1) the question of how to classify the individuals whose estimated age intervals overlap two demographic age categories and (2) the fact that subadult age-at-death assessment requires different indicators depending on the state of growth and maturity. For instance, the assessment methods based on teeth are appropriate until mineralization and eruption are complete. Then, the assessment is based on the chronology of fusion of the secondary point of ossification. However, as already mentioned, the aggregation of several age estimates obtained by different skeletal and dental aging methods to

Supplemental online materials are available at www.cambridge.org/naji.

build an age distribution introduces uncontrolled methodological biases. As a consequence, we suggest reconsidering that individual age estimates be provided by a method that was previously considered appropriate only for adult individual age assessment, namely, cementochronology.

Composed of the three hardest tissues of the human body, teeth are particularly relevant to maximizing representativeness in archaeological contexts. Recently, cementochronology has been greatly improved and has reached a high-performance level for age-at-death estimation (Chapter 1; Colard et al. 2018). Superior to all existing conventional age-at-death assessment techniques, cementochronology consists of counting the histological annual recording structures (tooth cementum annulations) in cementum. Dental cementum is a unique aging indicator considering its continuous growth throughout the life cycle (Introduction, Chapters 1–3). Its first layer of mineralization starts immediately after the Hopewell-Smith hyaline layer of mineralization on deciduous teeth roots before dental eruption (D'Incau 2012; Hillson 2000), and the process continues until natural deciduous tooth loss. According to the same biological process, dental cementum annulations continue to be mineralized on permanent teeth until antemortem tooth loss or death.

Cementochronology has rarely been applied in paleodemographic studies until recently (Blondiaux et al. 2016; Robbins-Schug, Brandt, and Lukacs 2012; Lanteri et al. 2018; Chapters 20–23). However, the method has never been used at an individual level to estimate the age distributions of an entire skeletal sample, including subadults. However, the method yields the opportunity to reconstruct paleodemographic mortality profiles from a single skeletal indicator. We are aware that the process requires teeth preservation (skull and mandible), which is a parameter that is likely to reduce the representativeness of a series. In the present prospective study, better accuracy and precision were preferred to a biased assessment of age at death.

This chapter aims to test the reliability of cementochronology in reconstructing the mortality profile and the life table of an archaeological sample using a single age indicator and no reference population. For this purpose, we applied cementochronology on a skeletal series for which some demographical parameters, such as the mortality profile, could be assessed by historical archives.

21.2 Materials and Methods

Because reference collections are rarely available for histological analyses, we selected a recent archaeological site dating from the modern period with documented historical and archaeological contexts and corresponding textual archives to demonstrate our method's reliability. The osteological collection of Notre-Dame du Bourg Cathedral (Digne-les-Bains, France) provided one of the largest skeletal samples ever excavated in southeastern France, totaling 1,700 burials dating from the fourth to the eighteenth century. During the 1984–1988 excavation campaigns, 421 adult and 142 subadult skeletons dating from the sixteenth to the eighteenth centuries were excavated from primary burials located inside the cathedral (Démians d'Archimbaud, Pelletier, and Flavigny 2010). We chose to focus on this period because the historical archives allow us to access this population's accurate mortality profile. Except for a few specific pathological analyses, no extensive anthropological research has been conducted on this collection before the present one. We compared two independent data sets to validate our study: individual age estimates obtained by cementochronology and the ages at death recorded in the death registers.

Historical Archives Analysis

To assess the mortality rates for the modern period, we examined the death registers of the individuals buried in Notre-Dame du Bourg Cathedral between 1671 and 1721 (for more details, see Lanteri et al. 2018). Demographers and historians have well identified the issue of unreliable reported age-at-death data in death registers. One of the observed trends is to preferentially round ages in multiples of five or ten (e.g., Henry 1984). To correct the age structures obtained from historical sources, historical demographers redistribute individuals into age categories using a moving average (Henry 1984; Soladay Shryock et al. 1973). We applied this consensual solution to our adult data set, centered on the examined age and spread over a five-year age range. The corrected age-at-death distribution from the death registers revealed that 2,854 individuals of known ages were buried in Notre-Dame du Bourg Cathedral and its cemetery between 1671 and 1721 (Figure 21.1).

Dental Material Selection

In the Notre-Dame du Bourg Cathedral, the ratio between the number of individuals discovered during archaeological excavations and the number of deaths in the entire parish during the period considered is low (563/4,903 = 11.48 percent). However, most of the deceased (65 percent) from all social categories have been buried in Notre-Dame du Bourg Cathedral and its cemetery since the seventeenth century. Therefore, we considered that this osteological sample is representative of the population inhabiting the city during the modern period.

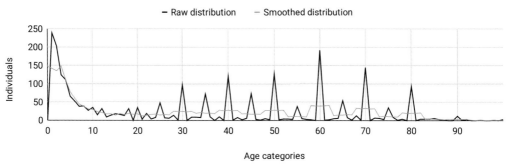

Figure 21.1 Raw age distribution of reported ages at death in the death registers and the smoothed-age distribution after using a five-year age range moving average

After inventorying every tooth of the 563 individuals, we focused on the best-preserved anterior tooth class of the adults to minimize the methodological variations of the dental eruption age estimates. The canine was the most represented tooth, as 109 adults had at least one tooth of this type. The results of this study are developed in Lanteri et al. (2018). However, this sample strategy that we intended to extend to the subadults was not relevant because the samples would have been too small. Therefore, we decided to select the best-preserved anterior deciduous or permanent tooth of each subadult individual. Subadult dental age can be estimated by the Hopewell-Smith hyaline layer deposit, which is anterior to the first cementum annulation and contemporaneous of the eruption of the median radicular area (Chapter 2).

For this reason, only deciduous and permanent teeth with a degree of root mineralization of at least 50 percent were eligible. The deciduous teeth that had started the rhizolysis process were discarded because of the biological destruction of the age information contained in the cementum. Our subadult dental sample comprised forty-three healthy monoradicular anterior deciduous and permanent teeth.

The dental preservation rate was low in the analyzed sample (28.2 percent) because of the skeletons' craniofacial region fragmentation due to considerable and multiple burial overlapping. The 563 individuals were superimposed on three levels of graves that constituted a homogeneous stratigraphic layer and were distributed over a surface of 300 m². This is the only information known about the taphonomy at this archaeological site because the recording of the taphonomical changes only began in the 1980s. The intense burial overlapping reflects the fact that *ad ecclesiam* burials were particularly sought after during the modern period to ensure the salvation of Christian souls (Ariès 1977a, b; Bertrand 1994). However, the random nature of postmortem tooth loss is not correlated with any cultural or taphonomic process. It is simply the consequence of the continuous and dense use of burial ground during the cemetery's occupation. Because there is no spatial or temporal patterning to this phenomenon, we considered it random. Consequently, we assumed that our sample was randomly selected from the total number of buried skeletons and, thus, we retained the hypothesis that our sample is representative of the underlying buried population.

Dental Material Analysis

An adapted version of the standardized thin-sectioning cementochronology preparation procedure (Colard et al. 2018) and incremental line counting was carried out by one single operator (L.L.) at the UMR 7268 ADES laboratory in Marseille, France (for details of the entire adapted protocol, see Lanteri et al. 2018). We applied the same procedure to subadult and adult dental material, except that we extracted five cross-sections from each subadult's tooth and eight from each adult's tooth.

Individual age at death was estimated by adding the mean paired incremental lines of dental cementum to the age-at-eruption range. Contrary to traditional age-at-eruption methods, such as those of Moorrees, Fanning, and Hunt (1963a, b) or AlQahtani, Hector, and Liversidge (2010), who did not publish exhaustive, precise tooth eruption standard deviations, we chose to use Liversidge and Molleson's reference (2004). This publication provides precise mean age and standard deviations specific to the ongoing and effective occlusion stage of every deciduous tooth. We chose Hurme's (1949) reference regarding permanent teeth because it provides precise mean age and standard deviations specific to maxillary and mandibular teeth.

Probabilistic Method

We developed a cumulative probabilistic method (Appendix 21.1) to propose a solution to the overlapping age range issue and assign the individuals to specific demographic age categories (Lanteri et al. 2018). After calculating the densities of the probability that every individual's estimated age at death belonged to each subadult age class (0–1, 1–4, 5–9, 10–14, 15–19) and adult ten-year age category, we established the matrix of probabilities. The vector comprising the different probability totals by age category is the probabilistic age-at-death distribution of the skeletal sample. As the variability of both the cementum-paired incremental line counts and the age at eruption are included in this distribution, we can construct the corresponding abridged life table after assuming the population's stationarity. This hypothesis is valid for the modern population of Digne-les-Bains as reported by baptismal and death records analysis (Lanteri 2016).

Data Set Comparisons

To determine whether the probabilistic age composition is consistent with the Notre-Dame du Bourg Cathedral's death register data, we performed a chi-square test using the "chisq.test" function of the R statistical freeware.

We constructed the corresponding life table based on the hypothesis that the cemetery population is the total sum of all living individuals who used the Notre-Dame du Bourg Cathedral and its cemetery as a burial place. To properly compare the data sets, we calculated a five-year age range probabilistic age distribution from the cementum age estimates. The five-year mortality rates fitting the probabilistic age-at-death distribution were compared to the death register records and a model life table illustrating the preindustrial mortality pattern presented in Table 21.1 (Séguy et al. 2006, 315, figure 11). Using the supplementary information in Buchet and Séguy (2013), we calculated the preindustrial mortality pattern from two entry parameters: the value of life expectancy at twenty years of age and the juvenility index's value, which were both calculated from historical records.

21.3   Results

We excluded nineteen adults and fourteen subadults for whom we could not record at least five counts per tooth because of taphonomy alterations. Obscure artifacts were observed on thirty-three teeth and prevented cementum line counts on seventy histological transverse sections. Two individuals were rejected because many

Table 21.1 Preindustrial life table calculated using the two entry parameters of the "best" model recommended by the authors are the life expectancy at twenty years of age value (31.9 years) and the juvenility index (0.26) from parish registers (Séguy et al. 2006, 315, figure 11, both sexes)

Mortality Rate	Mean	SD	−2SD	2SD	R² ajusté
1q0	248	58	132	364	0,993
4q1	261	57	147	375	0,806
5q5	142	57	28	256	0,968
5q10	64	48	−32	160	0,913
5q15	52	52	−52	156	0,814
5q20	69	52	−35	173	0,828
5q25	80	55	−30	190	0,821
5q30	89	44	1	177	0,999
5q35	103	37	29	177	0,999
5q40	110	37	36	184	0,999
5q45	136	37	62	210	0,903
5q50	160	38	84	236	0,885
5q55	211	42	127	295	0,846
5q60	248	32	184	312	0,998
5q65	332	29	274	390	0,997
5q70	1,000	27	946	1054	0,987

sections were unavailable for assessing their age at death. Assuming that cementum is subject to the same diagenetic processes as those of bone, Bondioli and Macchiarelli (1999) and Roksandic et al. (2009) identified these obscure artifacts as inclusions and infiltrations of diagenetic origin, probably due to a chemical reaction and to the degradation by microorganisms of groundwater, which facilitates the impregnation of minerals leached by the soil. This hypothesis is consistent with our archaeological context because the cathedral foundations, built in the thirteenth century, were regularly flooded.

The age-at-death estimates and probabilities for fitting the demographic age categories using the remaining ninety adults' canines and the twenty-nine subadults' teeth (119 individuals; i.e., 21 percent of the initial 563 individuals' sample) are presented in Supplemental Table ST.21.1. The standard deviations span from 0.11 to 4.57 years, except for two outliers, probably due to a duplicate effect of the cementum incremental lines (Condon, Charles, Cheverud, and Buisktra 1986; Wittwer-Backofen, Gampe, and Vaupel 2004).

As shown in Figure 21.2, the standard deviation values do not increase with age because the data dots remain concentrated between 0 and 4, and the regression line's slope of the entire cloud is very close to 0.

The probable age-at-death distribution (Figure 21.3) obtained by using cementum analysis reveals the low representation of the 0–1 age category, the strong representation of the 1–4 age category, and a decrease in following subadult age groups. The proportion of deaths between the ages of fifteen and nineteen increases slightly based on cementum analysis, which differs from the historical records trend. Regarding

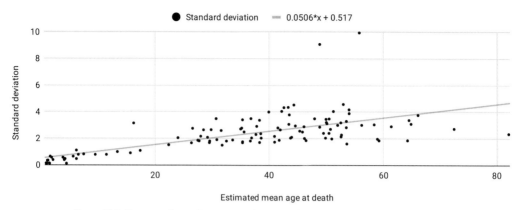

Figure 21.2 Cementochronology age estimates: distribution of the standard deviation values by estimated mean age at death

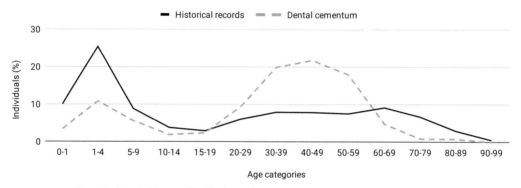

Figure 21.3 Probable age distributions obtained by the cementum analysis and age repartition from the historical records

adult individuals, the 30–59 age category is overestimated compared to the archives, with the 40–49 age category being the most represented. Finally, individuals more than sixty years of age are strongly underestimated compared to the death record data.

A chi-square homogeneity test comparing the overall age distributions obtained by cementum analysis and death records showed a statistically significant difference ($\chi2 = 91.777$, df = 12, p-value < 0.001). However, the difference between the two 5–59 age-at-death distributions is not statistically significant ($\chi2 = 5.9468$, df = 4, p-value = 0.2032).

The life expectancy at twenty years calculated from the cementum data is underestimated by 7.8 years compared to the same value calculated from the historical records. Regarding the mortality rates (Table 21.2), the pattern of the probabilistic mortality profile produced by cementochronology is similar to the pattern based on the historical archives (Figure 21.4). The dental cementum method overestimates death probability for individuals older than thirty-five, compared with the historical archives' mortality profiles and the preindustrial mortality pattern.

Table 21.2 Estimated life tables of the probabilistic age-at-death distribution provided by cementochronology analysis (C) and the age-at-death distribution obtained from death registers (A)

Age Category	Age Distribution C	Age Distribution A	Calculated Mortality Rates C	Calculated Mortality Rates A	Survivals (Sx) C	Survivals (Sx) A	Dead (Dx) C	Dead (Dx) A	Number of Individuals by Age Category (Vx) (stationary population) C	Number of Individuals by Age Category (Vx) (stationary population) A	Total Number (Tx) (stationary population) C	Total Number (Tx) (stationary population) A	Life Expectancy C	Life Expectancy A	Mortality Rates C	Mortality Rates A
0–1	4,13	288	0,035	0,101	119	1392	4	140	585	6610	4714	45063	39,6	32,4	34,7	100,9
1–4	12,98	726	0,113	0,283	115	1252	13	354	542	5374	4130	38453	36,0	30,7	113,0	282,9
5–9	6,72	254	0,066	0,138	102	898	7	124	493	4179	3588	33079	35,2	36,8	66,0	138,0
10–14	2,29	110	0,024	0,069	95	774	2	54	470	3735	3095	28900	32,5	37,3	24,1	69,3
15–19	2,86	84	0,031	0,057	93	720	3	41	457	3498	2625	25165	28,3	34,9	30,8	56,9
20–24	2,1	77	0,023	0,056	90	679	2	38	445	3301	2168	21667	24,1	31,9	23,3	55,6
25–29	9,1	95	0,104	0,073	88	641	9	47	417	3091	1723	18365	19,6	28,6	103,5	72,6
30–34	9,55	114	0,121	0,093	79	595	10	56	370	2836	1307	15274	16,6	25,7	121,2	93,3
35–39	14,18	113	0,205	0,102	69	539	14	55	311	2559	937	12439	13,5	23,1	204,8	102,0
40–44	13,54	118	0,246	0,119	55	484	14	58	241	2277	626	9880	11,4	20,4	245,9	119,2
45–49	12,39	106	0,298	0,122	42	427	12	52	177	2003	385	7602	9,3	17,8	298,4	121,7
50–54	15,61	105	0,536	0,136	29	375	16	51	107	1746	208	5599	7,1	14,9	535,9	136,4
55–59	5,79	110	0,428	0,166	14	324	6	54	53	1483	101	3853	7,5	11,9	428,3	166,4
60–64	3,99	149	0,516	0,270	8	270	4	73	29	1167	48	2370	6,2	8,8	516,2	269,8
65–69	1,72	112	0,460	0,278	4	197	2	55	14	848	19	1203	5,2	6,1	459,9	277,9
>70	2,02	292	1,000	1,000	2	142	2	142	5	356	5	356	2,5	2,5	1000,0	1000,0

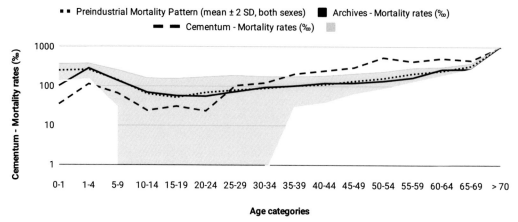

Figure 21.4 Estimated mortality rates of the probabilistic age-at-death distribution compared to the probabilities of dying at every age group obtained from the archives and the preindustrial mortality profile calculated with Séguy and Bouchet's model (2013).

21.4 Discussion

As a single age indicator, dental cementum successfully reconstructed the mortality profile and the life table of an archaeological sample from individual age-at-death estimates. By combining cementochronology with probability density analysis, our results revealed that we correctly assessed individuals' mortality profiles under the age of thirty-five from 21 percent of the initial 543-individual sample. Currently, cementochronology is the only aging method that can be used to reconstruct paleodemographic mortality profiles by including subadult and adult individual age estimates from a single skeletal indicator.

Our probabilistic method revealed that few subadults aged less than one year were buried in Notre-Dame du Bourg Cathedral. Confirmed by the historical records, this result does not indicate low natality in the modern Digne-les-Bains population but rather a Christian funeral practice. Unbaptized newborns were excluded from consecrated ground, *a fortiori* inside the cathedral and, therefore, they are not mentioned in the parish registers.

However, the difference between our estimations and the total number of 0–1 individuals buried in the cathedral according to the parish registers can be explained by the biological limitations of dental cementum and, without a doubt, by the issues related to the preservation of dental and osseous remains. Cementochronology is a relevant aging method provided that the first cementum layer has undergone mineralization, which is contemporaneous with dental eruption (Chapter 3). Consequently, cementochronology can estimate a subadult age at death from 0.72 ± 0.12 years of age (7.2 months of age at best), which corresponds to the deciduous upper-central incisor age at eruption, according to Liversidge and Molleson's reference (2004).

Regarding the slight overestimation of the 15–19 age group using cementochronology, this anomaly most likely results from the small sample size bias (2.86 individuals; i.e., 2.4 percent of the analyzed sample).

Under the age of thirty-five, the estimated mortality rates are consistent with those taken from the historical records. Over the age of thirty-five, individuals are overrepresented compared to the death record data. However, elderly individuals are strongly underrepresented. Although some researchers have observed a tendency of cementochronology to underestimate the age of middle-aged adults, especially after forty years of age (e.g., Aggarwal, Saxena, and Bansal 2008; Dias, Beaini, and Melani 2010), cementochronology has already shown to be applicable for accurately estimating the age at death of elderly individuals (Wittwer-Backofen and Buba 2002; Wittwer-Backofen et al. 2012).

In our study, the most plausible explanation for the underrepresentation of the elderly population is that this group was originally lacking in the sample due to a high prevalence of antemortem tooth loss reported in the modern population (Chazel et al. 2005; Perrin et al. 2019). Moreover, taphonomic alterations such as burial overlapping and skull fragmentation that induced postmortem tooth loss may also have biased the sampling. Further research on postmortem tooth loss patterns may provide a helpful reference in better understanding these issues.

To ensure reliable paleodemographic results, our study suggests that cementochronology must be carried out in documented archaeological contexts with a paleodemographic objective that is defined prior to archaeological excavation and regularly updated according to the preservations and the taphonomy impacting the remains.

Although the statistical application of our probabilistic method is particularly efficient when combined with cementochronology, it can be applied to any other aging method providing both a mean age at death and a standard deviation.

21.5 Conclusion

This chapter's main goals were to assess the age at death of both subadults and adults using a single aging method, namely, cementochronology, and to test the value of cementochronology as a paleodemographic tool in assessing mortality profiles from individual age-at-death estimates.

Combining cementochronology and paleodemography provides satisfying results. This innovative approach leads to new prospects for studying past mortality. However, for the moment, the method is more appropriate for series composed of undisturbed primary burials that have a higher probability of providing skulls and mandibles. Two significant issues must be solved. The first is the underrepresentation of the oldest age group. As antemortem tooth loss particularly affects these individuals, their underrepresentation is predictable in archaeological samples and will thus be encountered. To ensure that this underrepresentation is not due to a bias related to the method's incapacity to identify these individuals, additional testing on elderly individuals of known age is necessary. The second limitation is using a single type of tooth, as it reduces the number of adult individuals available in the analysis. As a future research perspective, dental representativeness should be maximized by including several teeth per individual, especially multirooted ones that are less prone to taphonomical alterations due to their stronger anchorage in the jawbone.

Acknowledgments

The authors acknowledge the two anonymous reviewers and the editors of the book for their valuable comments.

References

Aggarwal, P., Saxena, S., and Bansal, P. 2008. Incremental lines in root cementum of human teeth: An approach to their role in age estimation using polarizing microscopy. *Indian Journal of Dental Research* 19: 326–30.

AlQahtani, S. J., Hector, M. P., and Liversidge, H. M. 2010. Brief communication: The London atlas of human tooth development and eruption. *American Journal of Physical Anthropology* 142: 481–90.

Ariès, P. 1977a. *Essais sur L'Histoire de la Mort en Occident du Moyen Âge à Nos Jours*. Paris: Editions du Seuil.

1977b. L'Homme devant la mort. *Tome I*. Paris: Editions du Seuil.

Bertrand, R. 1994. Les Provençaux et leurs morts – Recherches sur les pratiques funéraires, les lieux de sépultures et le culte du souvenir des morts dans le Sud-Est de la France depuis la fin du XVIIe siècle. Unpublished doctoral dissertation, vol. 5. Paris: Université de Paris I.

Blondiaux, J., Naji, S., Bocquet-Appel, J.-P., Colard, T., de Broucker, A., and de Seréville-Niel, C. 2016. The leprosarium of Saint-Thomas d'Aizier: The cementochronological proof of the medieval decline of Hansen disease in Europe? *International Journal of Palaeopathology* 15: 140–51.

Bocquet, J.-P., and Masset, C. 1977. Estimateurs en paléodémographie. *L'Homme* 17:65–90.

Bocquet-Appel, J.-P. 2008. *Recent Advances in Palaeodemography. Data, Techniques, Patterns*. The Netherlands: Springer.

Boldsen, J., Milner, G., Konisberg, L. W., and Wood, J. W. 2002. Transition analysis: A new method for estimating age from skeletons. In *Paleodemography. Age Distributions from Skeletal Samples*. R. D. Hoppa and J. W. Vaupel (eds.). Cambridge: Cambridge University Press, 73–106.

Bondioli, L., and Macchiarelli, R., eds. 1999. *Osteodontal Biology of the People of Portua Romae (Necropolis of Isola Sacra, 2nd–3rd cent AD) II. Digital Archives of Human Palaeobiology*. Milan: E-LISA Sas.

Buchet, L., and Séguy, I. 2013. *Handbook of Palaeodemography*. Cham, Switzerland: Springer.

Buchet, L., Caussinus, H., Courgeau, D., and Séguy, I. 2017. Atouts d'une procédure récente d'inférence bayésienne pour l'étude de l'impact des crises démographiques. Application à trois sites médiévaux bas-normands. *Bulletins et Mémoires de la Société d'Anthropologie de Paris* 29: 70–84.

Buckberry, J. 2015. The (mis)use of adult age estimates in osteology. *Annals of Human Biology* 42(4): 323–31.

Caussinus, H., and Courgeau, D. 2010. Estimer l'âge sans le mesurer en paléodémographie. *Population* 65: 117–45.

Chazel, J.-C., Valcarcel, J., Tramini, P., Pelissier, B., and Mafart, B. 2005. Coronal and apical lesions, environmental factors: Study in a modern and an archeological population. *Clinical Oral Investigations* 9: 197–202.

Colard, T., Bertrand, B., Naji, S., Delannoy, Y., and Bécart, A. 2018. Toward the adoption of cementochronology in forensic context. *International Journal of Legal Medicine* 132(4): 1117–24.

Condon, K., Charles, D. K., Cheverud, J. M., and Buikstra, J. E. 1986. Cementum annulation and age determination in *Homo sapiens*. II. Estimates and accuracy. *American Journal of Physical Anthropology* 71: 321–30.

D'Incau, E. 2012. Hypercémentose: définition, classification et fréquence. Apport des résultats à la lignée néandertalienne. Unpublished doctoral dissertation. France: Université Bordeaux I.

Démians d'Archimbaud, G., Pelletier, J.-P., and Flavigny, F. 2010. *Notre-Dame du Bourg à Digne*. Digne: Agence pour le Développement et la Valorisation du Patrimoine et Ville de Digne-les-Bains.

Dias, P. E. M., Beaini, T. L., and Melani, R. F. H. 2010. Age estimation from dental cementum incremental lines and periodontal disease. *Journal of Forensic Odontostomatology* 28: 13–21.

Henry, L. 1984. *Démographie. Analyse et Modèles*. Paris: Édition de l'INED.

Hillson, S. (2000) Dental cement. In *Dental Anthropology*. S. Hillson (ed.). Cambridge: Cambridge University Press, 198–206.

Hoppa, R. D., and Vaupel, J. W., 2002. *Palaeodemography: Age Distributions from Skeletal Samples*. Cambridge: Cambridge University Press.

Hurme, V. O. 1949. Ranges of normalcy in the eruption of permanent teeth. *Journal of Dentistry for Children* 16: 11–15.

Lanteri, L. 2016. Recrutement, paléodémographie et cémentochronologie. Application à un contexte d'inhumation paroissial d'Ancien Régime: Notre-Dame du Bourg à Digne (04, France). Unpublished doctoral dissertation. Marseille: Aix-Marseille Université.

Lanteri, L., Bizot, B., Saliba-Serre, B., Gaudart, J., Signoli, M., and Schmitt, A. 2018. Cementochronology: A solution to assess mortality profiles from individual age-at-death estimates. *Journal of Archaeological Science: Reports* 20: 576–87.

Liversidge, H. M., and Molleson, T. 2004. Variation in crown and root formation and eruption of human deciduous teeth. *American Journal of Physical Anthropology* 123(2): 172–80.

Milner, G. R., and Boldsen, J.L. 2012. Transition analysis estimates do not perform as well as experience-based assessments, indicating the existing procedure is too narrowly focused on commonly used pelvic and cranial structures. *American Journal of Physical Anthropology* 148(1): 98–110.

Moorrees, C. F. A, Fanning, E. A, and Hunt, E. E. (1963) Age variation of formation stages for ten permanent teeth. *Journal of Dental Research* 42(6): 1490–1502.

(1963) Formation and resorption of three deciduous teeth in children. *American Journal of Physical Anthropology* 21(2): 205–13.

Perrin, M., Ardagna, Y., Richier, A., and Schmitt, A. 2019 Paléopathologie dentaire et époque contemporaine: Le cimetière des Crottes à Marseille, 1784–1905. *Bulletins et Mémoires de la Société d'Anthropologie de Paris* 31(3–4): 153–70.

Robbins Schug, G., Brandt, E. T., and Lukacs, J. R. 2012. Cementum annulations, age estimation, and demographic dynamics in mid-Holocene foragers of North India. *Journal of Human Biology* 63: 94–109.

Roksandic, M., Vlack, D., Schillaci, M. A., and Voicu, D., 2009. Technical note: Applicability of tooth cementum annulation to an archaeological population. *American Journal of Physical Anthropology* 140: 583–88.

Séguy, I., and Buchet, L. 2013. *Handbook of Palaedemography*, vol 2. INED Population Studies. Cham: Springer International Publishing.

Séguy, I., Buchet, L., Belaigues-Rossard, M., Couvert, N., and Perraut, C. 2006. Des tables-types de mortalité pour les populations pré-industrielles. In *La Paléodémographie. Mémoire d'os, Mémoire d'Hommes*. L. Buchet, C. Dauphin, and I. Séguy (eds.). Sophia Antipolis: Editions APDCA, 303–21.

Soladay Shryock, H., Siegel, J. S. et. al. 1973. Age composition. In *The Methods and Materials of Demography*, 2nd ed., vol. 1. H. Soladay Shryock and J. S. Siegel (eds.). Washington DC: US Government Printing Office, 201–51.

Wittwer-Backofen, U. 2012. Age estimation using tooth cementum annulation. In *Forensic Microscopy for Skeletal Tissues: Methods and Protocols. Methods in Molecular Biology*, vol. 915. L. S. Bell (ed.). New York: Humana Press, Springer, 129–43.

Wittwer-Backofen, U., and Buba, H. 2002. Age estimation by tooth cementum annulation: Perspectives of a new validation study. In *Paleodemography. Age Distributions from Skeletal Samples*. R. Hopa and J. Vaupel (eds.). Cambridge: Cambridge University Press, 107–28.

Wittwer-Backofen, U., Gampe, J., and Vaupel, J. W. 2004. Tooth cementum annulation for age estimation: Results from a large known-age validation study. *American Journal of Physical Anthropology* 123: 119–29.

22 Assessing Age-Related Mortality at Petra, Jordan, Using Cementochronology and Hazard Modeling

Akacia Propst, Michael Price, and Megan Perry

The city of Petra, located in southwestern Jordan (Figure 22.1), was the political and economic center of the Nabataean kingdom (300 BC–AD 106). The Nabataeans played a crucial role in the international trade of aromatics in antiquity, but their capital city Petra is better known today for its striking funerary architecture and landscape. Hidden among Petra's famous façade tombs are the less visible and less well-known shaft and pit tombs, of which Petra is generously littered with more than 800 (Nehmé 2003, 157–8). Despite centuries of looting from antiquity into the modern era, the excavation of shaft tombs located on Petra's North Ridge has shown that these structures remain a rich source of data in the form of architectural data, material goods, and skeletal remains (Bikai and Perry 2001; Parker and Perry 2013, 2017; Perry 2017; Perry and Walker 2018). Although the North Ridge shaft tombs contain some primary, articulated inhumations, the majority of skeletal remains are fragmented and commingled due to taphonomic processes, Nabataean funerary practices, and intermittent looting. The poor preservation of the skeletal remains, particularly those skeletal elements necessary for age-at-death estimation, has posed substantial challenges for determining the demographic profile of Petra's North Ridge population. Teeth, one of the most durable components of the human skeleton, have survived in greater numbers and in better conditions in the North Ridge assemblage than the os coxae. Age estimation methods utilizing the teeth provide an alternative method that can help better reconstruct demographic profiles in highly fragmented and commingled skeletal samples.

This study uses cementochronology (Chapter 1) to establish age-specific mortality risk for the individuals buried on Petra's North Ridge using the Gompertz-Makeham hazard model. One challenge that must be overcome in deriving age-specific mortality is the confounding influence of population growth (or shrinkage) on the archaeological age-at-death distribution. In a growing population, the age distribution is skewed toward younger individuals. Hence, two populations with identical age-specific mortality rates but different growth rates (arising from different age-specific fertility rates) will have different assemblage age-at-death distributions. If zero growth is assumed for both, the growing population will, paradoxically, appear to have higher mortality.

Supplemental online materials are available at www.cambridge.org/naji.

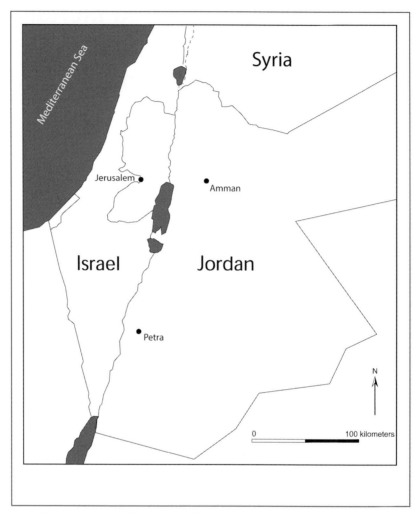

Figure 22.1 Map marking the location of Petra in Jordan

To account for this, we provide maximum-likelihood estimates of the age-specific mortality with different choices for the population growth rate.

An equally important challenge when using archaeological age-at-death data is sampling. There are two primary, salient difficulties: low sample sizes and bias. The use of a parametric mortality model with a small number of parameters (Gompertz-Makeham) helps regularize the reconstructed mortality hazard and improves reconstructions with small sample sizes (Gage 1988; Wood et al. 2002). By bias, we are specifically concerned with age bias, which can occur for cultural reasons (e.g., young people are less likely to be buried) or taphonomic reasons (the bones and teeth of the very young and very old do not preserve as well). Although adopting a simple parametric model, such as Gompertz-Makeham, may help somewhat to regularize the reconstructed mortality hazard and thus mitigate bias, a Bayesian framework has much more appeal. We return to this in the conclusion, when we discuss future directions.

22.1 Background

At its height in 100 BC–AD 100, the Nabataean kingdom spanned from southern Syria to northern Saudi Arabia and west across the Negev desert into modern-day Israel. The kingdom flourished economically during this period, with Petra serving as an *entrepôt* in the trade of incense (frankincense and myrrh) between production centers in Arabia and the circum-Mediterranean region (Durand 2007). It was during the beginning of this period that rapid development of major architectural complexes, temples, and the water system occurred, including heterogeneity in house and tomb construction, perhaps reflecting social or economic differentiation, in Petra (see Kolb 2007; Tholbecq 2007).

The shaft tombs in the upper sector of Petra's North Ridge were constructed at this point of the city's florescence, dated based on finely tuned chronologies of Nabataean painted fine-ware (Parker and Perry 2013, 2017; Schmid 2000). The difference in scale and visibility between these tombs and those associated with Petra's famous façade tombs suggests they contained the city's non-elite inhabitants or elite residents uninterested in displaying their socioeconomic or political status through mortuary structures. The skeletal remains from the North Ridge (MNI = 121) display almost no skeletal lesions related to infection, malnutrition, or trauma compared to other regional sites, potentially suggesting that this urban population experienced a significantly lower prevalence of these conditions compared to their rural and nomadic counterparts (Canipe 2014). Paleopathological data can be difficult to interpret without accompanying age-at-death and mortality data, however. Low frequencies of skeletal lesions may be the result of both a low frequency of the conditions they indicate in a population or the result of increased frailty within a population resulting in individuals perishing before an observable skeletal response can form (Wood et al. 1992).

Examining skeletal lesions within the context of mortality data allows us to explore how the presence or absence of skeletal lesions is connected to mortality risk (Wood et al. 1992; see DeWitte 2014). Though the preservation of the North Ridge population does not allow us to examine direct associations between skeletal lesions and mortality risk in individuals, the overall demographic structure of a mortuary sample can help categorize the events that led to its creation (i.e., attritional versus catastrophic) (see Gowland and Chamberlain 2005). Here, we turn to cementochronology to provide age-at-death estimates in order to understand age-related mortality and the processes that helped create this mortuary sample. The relatively high correlations between known age and cementochronology-derived ages suggest that cementochronology is a promising method for age-at-death estimation (Naji et al. 2016).

Reconstructing a paleodemographic profile from a cemetery sample has vexed biological anthropologists seeking to understand age-related mortality, including imprecise age estimation techniques, "mimicry" of reference population age structures, heterogeneity in mortality patterns within the sample, and assumptions of demographic nonstationarity (Bocquet-Appel and Masset 1982, 1985, 1996; Sattenspiel and Harpending 1983; Wood et al. 1992). Cementochronology can alleviate issues related to age estimation precision; however, they also fundamentally rely on studies of dental formation in reference samples with varying age structures and may reflect dynamics such as immigration and fertility as opposed to mortality. Hazard models such as the Gompertz-Makeham incorporate parameters such as the probability of death at a particular age, potentially ameliorating issues due to gaps or errors in the age-at-death pattern (Wood et al. 2002). Additionally, applying transition analysis and a Bayesian approach to calculating the probability of being a particular age if a particular age-related characteristic is present [$Pr(a|c)$] may alleviate the "mimicry" of reference population age distributions (Boldsen et al. 2002; Hoppa and Vaupel 2002). Here we focus on applying a Gompertz-Makeham hazard model to our cementochronology-produced age estimates to smooth the age-at-death mortality data to mitigate the effects of small sample sizes other sources of bias.

Two major assumptions in paleodemography remain unmet, thus potentially biasing our interpretations. The first, the assumption that our sample comes from a population experiencing no immigration or changes in fertility, is simply unrealistic, especially in a cemetery used for a relatively short period of time in an urban trade center. The second – that all individuals in the sample had the same chance of dying at particular ages due to host or environmental factors – also remains unmet. However, scholars have developed a greater understanding of how Petra's social and political structure was mirrored in the city's geography, potentially including its cemeteries (Nehmé 2013; Perry and Lieurance 2020; Tholbecq 2016; Wadeson 2012, 2013). These five tombs come from a circumscribed area within the northern sector of the city and likely constitute a sample more homogeneous than one drawn from different locations across the urban center (see Perry and Lieurance 2020 for a comparison of dental disease between different Petra communities). However, the possibility of heterogeneity in frailty and mortality risk must be acknowledged in our interpretations.

22.2 Materials and Methods

The commingled and fragmented nature of the Petra North Ridge sample required careful sample selection that took archaeological context and tooth characteristics into consideration in order to prevent double sampling of individuals. Teeth within each tomb context (based on stratigraphic and taphonomic evidence) were sorted based on type, side, position, morphology, and wear patterns to establish which teeth could be safely attributed to separate individuals. In addition, a few primary, articulated burials and alveolar bone containing more than one tooth produced dentition clearly from the same individual. When possible, at least two teeth were selected from each identifiable individual in order to increase the probability that a viable section of cementum would be collected and help account for intra-observer error. Following the findings of Charles et al. (1986) and Wittwer-Backofen et al. (2004), incisors and first premolars

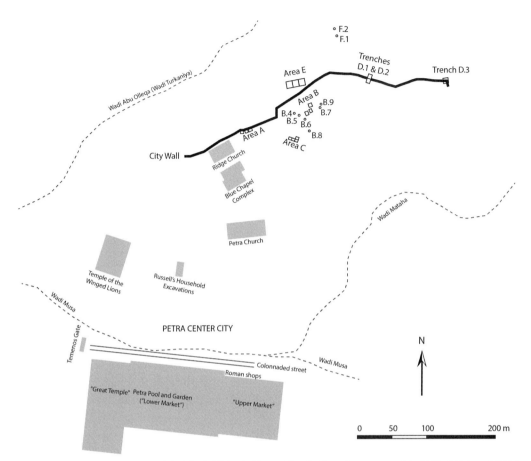

Figure 22.2 Map of the North Ridge in Petra. The shaft tombs excavated in 2012, 2014, and 2016 field seasons are in Area B and Area F. Tombs 1 and 2 from the 1999 season are located by the Ridge Church.

were preferentially selected. Third molars were completely omitted from selection due to the large standard deviation of the average age of tooth eruption.

The final sample size was 110 teeth recovered from six shaft tombs (MNI represented = 66; Figure 22.2). Of the 110 teeth sampled, four teeth were found not to have any viable cementum to count after sectioning (Table 22.1). An additional seven teeth were omitted during the final analysis as they were determined to most likely be double sampled. Almost no subadult remains (i.e., < 20 years of age) are represented in the North Ridge tombs and were not represented in this analysis. Photographs were taken of all teeth selected for this study to ensure that a complete record is available after processing for analysis, and basic dental pathology, morphology, and metric data were recorded following *Standards* (Buikstra and Ubelaker 1994).

Many tooth roots were highly friable, and different resin concentrations for embedding teeth were tested. Caroplastic resin was found to provide the preferred level of rigidity and plasticity. The tooth roots were embedded in resin within either

Table 22.1 Breakdown of the number of teeth used for cementochronology and the minimum number of individuals by tomb

Tomb	Number of Teeth	Omitted Teeth	MNI Represented by the Sampled Teeth
B.4	8	1	5
B.5	42	1	22
B.6	23	0	14
B.7	24	4	14
F.1	9	1	7
Tomb 2	4		4
Total:	110	7	66

a 5 ml or 30 ml syringe, leaving the crown exposed for future research. The hardness of the resin was determined by using the preparation guidelines for gross anatomy samples. Once the resin was set, the teeth were sectioned using a Buehler Isomet Low Speed Saw with a diamond wafering blade. Although 100 μm sections are required for analysis, the fragility and friability of the teeth necessitated cutting sections of 400 μm thick or thicker for some very fragile teeth. After sectioning, the individual sections were gently cleaned with alcohol and distilled water to remove any debris left from the low-speed saw. The sections were mounted onto a glass slide using Crystal Bond™ adhesive. The sections were then lapped until they measured 100 μm and polished using Buehler Alpha Micropolish II (0.3-micron particle size) and wiped clean with an alcohol swab and lens cloth to remove any polish residue.

The slides were viewed at 20X and 40X magnification with a transmitted light microscope, and multiple photographs were taken for each slide. The photos were uploaded to Adobe Photoshop in order to increase the contrast between the dark and light annulations and facilitate counting using the Auto Tone, Auto Contrast, Auto Color, Level Adjustment, and Unsharp Mask tools. The annulations were then counted, and the age ranges of tooth development stages, taken from the *Atlas of Human Tooth Development and Eruption* (AlQahtani et al. 2010), were added to these counts to provide an age-at-death range

Parametric hazard analysis was used to estimate age-specific risk of mortality using the age-at-death estimates. Because no subadults were included in the sample, a Gompertz-Makeham hazard model was used to estimate adult mortality. The Gompertz-Makeham mortality hazard is $\mu(x) = b_1 + b_2 e^{b_3 x}$, where x is age. The model includes two terms: (1) a constant, age-independent term, b_1 (Makeham 1860) and (2) an accelerating mortality term, $b_2 e^{b_3 x}$ (Gage 1988; Gompertz 1825). A major challenge when fitting mortality models using archaeological age-at-death data is that the assemblage age-at-death distribution is also influenced by the population growth rate (here and elsewhere stable, but not stationary demography is assumed; Wood et al. 2002). To be precise, the age-at-death probability density of an archaeological assemblage is proportional to the stable age distribution, $c(x)$, times the mortality hazard [notation follows Caswell (2010) and further details are available in the Supplemental Mathematical Appendix (SMA.22.1)]:

$$g(x) \propto c(x)\mu(x)$$

In contrast, the age-at-death distribution faced by an individual is proportional to the survivorship function, $l(x)$, times the mortality hazard,

$$f(x) \propto l(x)\mu(x)$$

The survivorship and stable age distribution are linked by

$$c(x) \propto e^{-rx}l(x)$$

where r is the population growth rate.

Hence, earlier ages at death in the archaeological assemblage can result from either a high population growth rate or high mortality (or some combination of the two). One way of accounting for this is to fit separate curves for different population growth rates – the approach followed in this chapter.

One additional complication of the data used in this chapter is that multiple teeth were cross-sectioned for some individuals, yielding multiple age estimates from some individuals. To account for this, each sample $x^{(s)}$ for an individual of age a is assumed to be drawn from a normal distribution with a mean of a and a standard deviation of σ. Tailor-written R code was used to obtain maximum likelihood estimates for the parameters, b_2, b_3, and σ given different growth rates, r. Again, full details are provided in the Supplemental Mathematical Appendix (SMA.22.1).

22.3 Results

Figure 22.3 summarizes the results of the maximum-likelihood estimation of the mortality hazard. The top and middle graph in Figure 22.3 show, respectively, the archaeological and individual age-at-death distributions. The gray histograms show the observed age-at-death distribution; for individuals with more than one age estimate, the mean is used. The bottom graph shows the individual mortality hazard. The shading arises from the three maximum-likelihood estimates of the Gompertz-Makeham mortality hazard for per annum growth rates of –3 percent, 0 percent, and +3 percent. The central line assumes 0 percent per annum growth (the typical assumption in paleodemographic analyses). The red band shades the area between the – 3 percent and 0 percent curve, and the blue band shades the area between the 0 percent and +3 percent curve. Because these are plausible ranges for population growth, the three curves demarcate plausible ranges of the reconstructed age-specific demographic variables.

Table 22.2 gives parameter values for the maximum-likelihood fits for each growth rate, along with mean expected age at death for individuals who have survived to

Table 22.2 The parametric fit for each population growth rate (−3%, 0%, and +3% per annum). The fit parameters are b_1, b_2, b_3, and σ. The final column gives the mean expected age-at-death for an individual of 20 years.

Population Growth Rate					Mean Age at Death at 20 Years
r	b_1	b_2	b_3	sig	le20
−0.03	1.74E-09	0.014312	0.048353	2.729898	34.55265
0	7.20E-12	0.007901	0.056796	2.721128	37.64672
0.03	3.49E-08	0.003767	0.067752	2.731785	41.27554

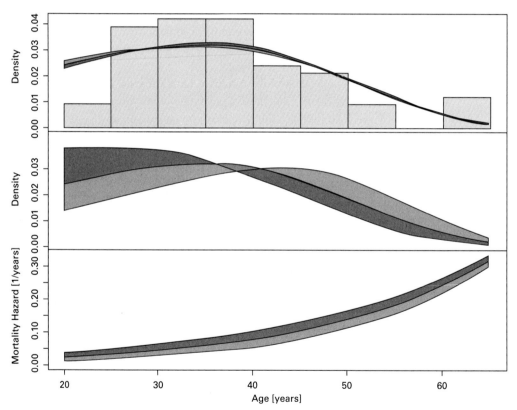

Figure 22.3 The top plot shows the assemblage age-at-death distribution (which accounts for the population growth rate), the middle plot shows the individual age-at-death distribution, and the bottom plot shows the individual mortality hazard. The gray histograms show the observed age-at-death distribution (for individuals with more than one age estimate, the mean is used); the two histograms are identical. The dark/light shading in the plots arises from the three separate maximum-likelihood fits for −3 percent, 0 percent, and +3 percent per annum population growth. The dark band shades the space between the −3 percent and 0 percent curve, and the light band shades the space between the 0 percent and 3 percent curve.

twenty years of age. The uncertainty parameter for the age-at-death estimates is about 2.7 for all three models. The mean ages of death for the three models are 34.6, 37.6, and 41.3 years for –3 percent, 0 percent, and +3 percent per annum growth. This is consistent with the plots in Figure 22.3, for which higher mortality (and an earlier individual age at death) characterize the –3 percent growth case.

Young adults thirty to forty years of age represent a large portion of this adult sample, with a gradual decline seen in the number of individuals dying at older ages. The 40+ pattern of decreased representation in the sample is typical for an attritional age-at-death profile of senescent mortality. The maximum-likelihood fits for different growth rates further suggest that the age-at-death distribution most resembles that with 0–3 percent population growth rather than population decline.

22.4 Discussion

The fragmentation and commingling of the sample prevented the direct analysis of the relationship between skeletal lesions and mortality risk. However, the age-specific mortality pattern generated from these data shows that the North Ridge tombs contained an attritional sample rather than a catastrophic one due to a mass-fatality event. This does not exclude the possibility that the low frequency of skeletal lesions in the North Ridge sample results from greater frailty and mortality risk, however. Disease epidemics and other significant events, such as famine, impacting mortality can still result in attritional mortality patterns (Chamberlain 2006; Yaussy et al. 2016).

The maximum-likelihood estimates for the age-at-death distribution assuming different fertility rates suggest that the age-at-death distribution better resembles that of a population with 0–3 percent growth. The peak in the age-specific mortality profile between thirty and forty years of age likely demonstrates the impact of immigration and population growth at Petra, not higher actual mortality risk within these age categories. The North Ridge sample dates to the period of Petra's peak as a Nabataean political and economic center, and an overrepresentation of thirty-to-forty-year-olds in this sector of the city could result in inflated mortality rates in these age categories. Increased fertility also could have stimulated this population growth, resulting in increased infant and childhood mortality. The Petra North Ridge tombs, unfortunately, suffer from infant under-enumeration either due to burial practices or taphonomic processes, significantly biasing any age-specific mortality patterns for these age classes.

The parametric hazard analysis sheds more light on mortality and age-specific mortality risk than can be achieved by just examining the age-at-death distribution. The Gompertz-Makeham hazard model indicates that many individuals at Petra would have lived well into older adulthood, with more individuals inferred as surviving if higher population growth rates are assumed. This does not indicate high rates of mortality or age-specific mortality risk. The results of the hazard modeling thus suggest that the low frequencies of skeletal lesions are not associated with high rates of age-specific mortality risk that might imply that individuals were perishing from conditions before skeletal lesions could form in this sample. The available paleopathological evidence does not reflect any clear factors affecting morbidity and mortality at Petra.

Although the three different models (i.e., assuming different population growth rates) yield similar assemblage age-at-death distributions, they yield quite different mortality hazards and individual age-at-death distributions. For each additional 1 percent increase assumed in the growth rate, the life expectancy at twenty increases by roughly one year. However, some caution is warranted in interpreting these results. The maximum-likelihood fit for the assemblage age-at-death distribution (top plot in Figure 22.3) overpredicts the number of deaths for all growth rates. Fundamentally, the Gompertz-Makeham hazard model is not sufficiently flexible to reconstruct the observed age-at-death distribution. Arguably, this means it is "doing its job" of regularizing the maximum-likelihood fit. That is, if individuals between twenty-five and forty years are systematically overrepresented compared to younger and older individuals (where the overrepresentation is with respect to the original population level age-at-death distribution), then the Gompertz-Makeham parametric fit is plausibly "smoothing over" this bias. However, if the age-at-death distribution is correct, the Gompertz-Makeham model is not a good model to apply.

Ultimately, there is no need to rely on simple parametric models such as the Gompertz-Makeham or Siler mortality models to regularize data. Furthermore, there is a good reason not to do so: There are human populations with age-specific mortality patterns that the Siler model (which generalizes the Gompertz-Makeham model) cannot accurately represent. There exists very good data on the demographic diversity of modern and recent human populations. Although there are many ways one might use this knowledge to improve paleodemographic reconstruction, perhaps the most appealing path forward is to adopt a fully Bayesian approach (McElreath 2018) and utilize state-of-the-art statistical methods for model selection, including but not limited to cross-validation (Arlot and Celisse 2010). That is, priors could be specified over vital demographic rates, including migration rates, as well as over key biases such as age bias, and these priors updated using appropriate demographic likelihood models. With proper regularization and model selection, quite sophisticated models can be identified that do not over- or underfit the data.

22.5 Conclusion

This application of cementochronology using the Petra North Ridge skeletal collection demonstrates this method's utility for age estimation of commingled, fragmented, and friable skeletal samples. Cementochronology provided a greater number of age-at-death estimates for the Petra population than standard morphological techniques such as degeneration of the pubic symphysis or auricular surface. In addition, age estimations of individuals more than fifty years of age could be determined, providing a better indicator of senescence and longevity at Petra. It additionally illustrates how cementochronology-produced age-at-death estimates can be used to calculate age-specific mortality risk using a Gompertz-Makeham hazard model and illuminate age-related mortality patterns. While issues of inference, such as those outlined by Wood et al. (1992), remain salient, more fundamental issues of data quality and bias are as vexing when reconstructing past demography. We have outlined briefly a vision for taking a fully Bayesian approach to address this problem, which is the topic of ongoing work by the authors.

That the Petra adults display low frequencies of nonspecific stress (see Bikai and Perry 2001; Canipe 2014; Perry and Lieurance 2020) could mean that they suffered high mortality due to acute health conditions that left no bony lesions. The age-specific mortality pattern, however, suggests that no catastrophic mortality event occurred. Results of the parametric hazard modeling suggest that age-specific mortality risk at Petra largely reflects immigration of particular age cohorts and thus higher-than-expected mortality in younger adults. Although these data do not completely preclude the possibility that the paleopathological data is the result of people perishing of conditions that do not result in skeletal involvement or before skeletal lesions could form, if this were the case, we might expect Petra's mortality rates to be higher than what was exhibited. In contrast, the data suggested individuals may have been living up to eighty years of age.

A final point to note is that these samples represent only a small percentage of large urban areas with very heterogeneous community experiences in terms of life and death. The Petra North Ridge sample includes a subset of the city's population buried on the North Ridge. However, a number of other shaft tombs in other sectors of the city, along with the monumental tombs, could present a different picture from the North Ridge burials. Therefore, these interpretations provide a baseline from which future research can build a broader and more inclusive picture of this urban population.

References

Al Qahtani, S. J., M. P. Hector, and H. M. Liversidge. 2010. Brief Communications: The London Atlas of Human Tooth Development and Eruption. *American Journal of Physical Anthropology* 142(3): 481–90.

Arlot, S., and A. Celisse. 2010. A Survey of Cross-Validation Procedures for Model Selection. *Statistics Survey* 4: 40–79.

Bikai, P., and M. Perry. 2001. Petra North Ridge Tombs 1 and 2: Preliminary Report. *Bulletin of the American Schools of Oriental Research* 324: 59–78.

Bocquet-Appel, J.-P., and C. Masset. 1982. Farewell to Paleodemography. *Journal of Human Evolution* 11(4): 321–33.

Bocquet-Appel, J., and C. Masset. 1985. Matters of Moment. *Journal of Human Evolution* 14: 107–11.

Bocquet-Appel, J., and C. Masset. 1996. Paleodemography: Expectancy and False Hope. *American Journal of Physical Anthropology* 99(4): 571–83.

Boldsen, J., G. Milner, L. Konigsberg, and J. Wood. 2002. Transition Analysis: A New Method for Estimating Age from Skeletons. In *Paleodemography: Age Distributions from Skeletal Samples*. R. Hoppa and J. Vaupel (eds.). Cambridge: Cambridge University Press, 73–106.

Buikstra, J., and D. Ubelaker, eds. 1994. *Standards for Data Collection from Human Skeletal Remains: Proceedings of a Seminar at the Field Museum of Natural History.* Arkansas: Arkansas Archeological Survey.

Canipe, C. 2014. Exploring Quality of Life at Petra Through Paleopathology. MA thesis, East Carolina University, Greenville.

Caswell, H. 2010. Life Table Response Experiment Analysis of the Stochastic Growth Rate. *Journal of Ecology* 98: 324–33.

Chamberlain, A. T. 2006. *Demography in Archaeology.* Cambridge: Cambridge University Press.

Charles, D., K. Condon, J. Cheverud, and J. Buikstra. 1986. Cementum Annulation and Age Determination in Homo Sapiens. I. Tooth Variability and Observer Error. *American Journal of Physical Anthropology* 71: 311–20.

DeWitte, S. 2014. Differential Survival among Individuals with Active and Healed Periosteal New Bone Formation. *International Journal of Paleopathology* 7: 38–44.

Durand, C. 2007. The Nabataeans and Oriental Trade: Roads and Commodities (Fourth Century BC to First Century AD). In *Studies in the History and Archaeology of Jordan.* F. al-Khraysheh (ed.). Amman: Department of Antiquities of Jordan, 405–11.

Gage, T. 1988. Mathematical Hazard Models of Mortality: An Alternative to Model Life Tables. *American Journal of Physical Anthropology* 76(4): 429–41.

Gompertz, B. 1825. On the Nature of the Function Expressive of the Law of Human Mortality, and on a New Mode of Determining the Value of Life Contingencies. *Philosophical Transactions of the Royal Society of London* 115: 513–83.

Gowland, R. L., and A. T. Chamberlain. 2005. Detecting Plague: Palaeodemographic Characterisation of a Catastrophic Death Assemblage. *Antiquity* 79: 146–57.

Hoppa, R., and J. Vaupel. 2002. The Rostock Manifesto for Paleodemography: The Way from Stage to Age. In *Paleodemography: Age Distributions from Skeletal Samples.* R. Hoppa and J. Vaupel (eds.). Cambridge: Cambridge University Press, 1–8.

Kolb, B. 2007 Nabatatean Private Architecture. *The World of the Nabataeans.* K. D. Politis (ed.). Stuttgart: Franz Steiner Verlag, 145–72.

Makeham, W. 1860. On the Law of Mortality. *Journal of the Institute of Actuaries* 13: 325–58.

McElreath, R. 2018. *Statistical Rethinking: A Bayesian Course with Examples in R and Stan.* Boca Raton: CRC Press.

Naji, S., T. Colard, J. Blondiaux, B. Betrand, E. d'Incau, and J.-P. Bocquet-Appel. 2016. Cementochronology, to Cut or Not to Cut? *International Journal of Paleopathology* 140: 1–7.

Nehmé, L. 2003. The Petra Survey Project. In *Petra Rediscovered.* G. Markoe (ed.). London: Thames & Hudson, 145–63.

——— 2013. The Installation of Social Groups in Petra. In *Men on the Rocks: The Formation of Nabataean Petra.* M. Mouton and S. G. Schmid (eds.). Berlin: Logos Verlag GmbH, 113–28.

Parker, T., and M. Perry. 2013. Petra North Ridge Project: The 2012 Season. *Annual of the Department of Antiquities of Jordan* 57: 399–407

——— 2017. Petra North Ridge Project: The 2017 Season. *Annual of the Department of Antiquities of Jordan* 58: 287–302.

Perry, M. 2017. Sensing the Dead: Mortuary Ritual and Tomb Visitation at Nabataean Petra. *Syria* 94: 99–106.

Perry, M., and J. Walker. 2018. The Nabataean Way of Death on Petra's North Ridge. In *Death and Burial in the Near East from Roman to Islamic Times.* C. Eger and M. Mackensen (eds.). Wiesbaden: Reichert Verlag, 121–38.

Perry, M., and A. Lieurance. 2020. The Nabataean Urban Experiment and Dental Disease and Childhood Stress. In *The Bioarchaeology of Urbanization: The Biological, Demographic, and Social Consequences of Living in Cities*. T. Betsinger and S. DeWitte (eds.). Cham: Springer International Publishing.

Sattenspiel, L., and H. Harpending. 1983. Stable Populations and Skeletal Age. *American Antiquity* 48(3): 489–98.

Schmid, S. G. 2000. *Petra ez-Zantur II. Ergebnisse der Schweizerisch-Liechtensteinischen Ausgrabungen, Teil I: Die Feinkeramik der Nabatäer: Typologie, Chronologie und kulturhistorische Hintergründe*. Mainz: Philipp von Zabern.

Tholbecq, L. 2007. Nabataean Monumental Architecture. In *The World of the Nabataeans*. K. D. Politis (ed.). Stuttgart: Franz Steiner Verlag, 103–43.

―― 2016. Wadi Sabra Archaeological Project. *American Journal of Archaeology* 120(4): 666–7.

Wadeson, L. 2012. The Funerary Landscape of Petra: Results from a New Study. In *The Nabataeans in Focus: Current Archaeological Research at Petra*. L. Nehme and L. Wadeson (eds.). Oxford: Archaeopress, 99–125.

―― 2013. Petra: Behind the Monumental Facades. *Current World Archaeology* 57(1): 18–24.

Wittwer-Backofen, U., J. Gampe, and J. Vaupel. 2004. Tooth Cementum Annulation for Age Estimation: Results from a Large Known-Age Validation Study. *American Journal of Physical Anthropology* 123: 119–29.

Wood, Carolann. 2004. An Investigation of the Prevalence of Rickets among Subadults from the Roman Necropolis of Isola Sacra (1st to 3rd centuries AD), Italy. PhD dissertation, McMaster University, Hamilton.

Wood, J., D. Holman, K. O'Connor, and R. Ferrell. 2002. Mortality Models of Paleodemography. In *Paleodemography: Age Distributions from Skeletal Samples*. New York: Cambridge University Press, 129–70.

Wood, J., G. R. Milner, H .C. Harpending, and K. M. Weiss. 1992. The Osteological Paradox. *Current Anthropology* 33(4): 343–70.

Yaussy, S. L., S. N. DeWitte, and R. C. Redfern. 2016. Frailty and Famine: Patterns of Mortality and Physiological Stress among Victims of Famine in Medieval London. *American Journal of Physical Anthropology* 160: 272–83.

23 Shaping Age-at-Death Distributions by Applying Tooth Cementum Analysis to the Early Medieval Graveyard of Lauchheim (Germany)

Ursula Wittwer-Backofen and Felix Engel

23.1 Introduction

Paleodemographic research investigates the life span and health status of premodern populations as a major indicator of living conditions. Knowing a population's age-at-death distribution helps to study past human demography. To obtain measures of mortality, numerous studies have aimed to improve age-at-death estimates from human skeletal remains (for an overview, see Bocquet-Appel, 2008; Chamberlain, 2006). However, the reliability of age-at-death distributions depends on the accuracy of individual age estimates. This problem has long been addressed in anthropology (for an overview, see Kemkes-Grottenthaler, 2002), leading to comparability tests of age estimation methods based on skeletal populations (Nagaoka and Hirata, 2007; Storey, 2007; Wittwer-Backofen et al. 2008). Among several methods, tooth cementum annulation (TCA) (Großkopf and McGlynn, 2011) has proved to be one of the most precise to date (Buikstra et al. 2022, Chapter 1). According to the literature, TCA-based age-at-death determination is possible within a relatively narrow range of ±3.23 years (Großkopf, 1990), ±2–3 years (Kargerer and Grupe, 2001), or two standard deviations (2sd) between ±2,5 years (Wittwer-Backofen, 2004) given optimal material preservation (Chapter 1: Table 1.1). Several studies failed to achieve such narrow age ranges (Jankauskas et al. 2001; Kvaal and Solheim, 1995; Stein and Corcoran, 1994; Renz and Radlanski, 2006) but still provided narrower ranges than other methods. Advantages over qualitative morphological approaches such as the complex method, transition analysis, or the revised auricular surface structure and quantitative methods such as osteon density or tooth root translucency have been demonstrated by a previous study that was restricted to a selection of 121 out of 1,368 individuals of the Lauchheim skeletal population (Wittwer-Backofen et al. 2008). This study focused on comparing a wide range of aging methods, but due to the lack of sample representation, it did not allow for reconstructing a mortality pattern.

Building on this previous study, we apply the TCA method, and a bundle of macroscopic age estimation (MAE) approaches, including the complex method, on the quasi-total adult skeletal sample of Lauchheim. To assess the performance of TCA analysis, we consider a thorough analysis of interobserver errors necessary. When based on known-age samples, high interobserver differences may be interpreted as an indicator of irregularities in the cementum tissue, coded differently by the involved observers. In contrast, a high degree of consistency may indicate a more regular cementum pattern, which is processed with higher reliability by the observers. On the other hand, interobserver differences might be influenced by the observers' training conditions.

The goal of this study is to estimate the most precise age-at-death distribution. Results of TCA and MAE methods are compared to each other at the level of (1) individual age-at-death deviations between TCA and MAE and (2) population-based age-at-death distributions from both approaches. TCA results are expected to reflect actual mortality distribution better than MAE as they produce narrower age ranges. (3) Finally, results derived from different aging methods applied to all skeletons, including subadults, are combined into one age-at-death distribution.

Our study aims to improve the reconstruction of age-at-death distributions by estimating individual age-at-death ranges more precisely. Thus, we hypothesize that the Lauchheim age distribution, including TCA estimates, delivers a more realistic picture than the age distribution resulting from MAE alone.

The Graveyard

The early medieval Lauchheim cemetery in the Ostalbkreis district of the German state Baden-Wuerttemberg revealed 1,308 graves dating from the second half of the fifth to the eighth century (Brather, 2016) and is among the largest contemporary graveyards in Europe. Thus, we expect more reliable paleodemographic distributions compared to small fluctuating populations.

The skeletal population of Lauchheim is from a rural population of about 250 to 300 individuals (Wahl et al. 1997). These people lived on farmsteads and in several villages with some degree of social and occupational differentiation, reflected by grave goods (Härke, 2014). Evidence of graveyard boundaries suggests that about 95 percent of the burials were excavated (Stork, 2010). Therefore, the skeletal population of Lauchheim is suitable for an intensive interdisciplinary study and promises reliable insights into medieval demography.

23.2 Material and Methods

Skeletal material preservation is generally poor. About half of the cranial bones and two-thirds of the long bones were lost due to taphonomic processes mainly caused by soil erosion, mechanical pressure from the stony sediment, and the postdepositional disturbance of about 40–90 percent of the burial contexts in antiquity and recent times (Stork, 2010).

An initial anthropological investigation of the skeletal remains from Lauchheim was conducted between 1991 and 2001 by Kunter and Wittwer-Backofen (Wittwer-Backofen et al. 2008), identifying 1,367 individual skeletons. All aging and sexing methods followed the recommended European standards of the time (Ferembach et al. 1980), suitable to cover an extensive local archaeological collection. In 2007, the initial investigation results were re-coded for the Global History of Health Project (GHHP), following the project's codebook (Steckel et al. 2018).

The present study analyzed age-at-death estimates for 1,337 skeletons from the Lauchheim graveyard. Initially, the remains of 1,039 individuals had been categorized as adults and 298 as subadults, according to bone maturation. Subadult individual age at death was then estimated by dental development, epiphyseal development, and fusion, or diaphyseal length development (Ferembach et al. 1980), associated with method-specific error bands. Adult skeleton age estimations were based on macroscopic methods, including the complex method (Ferembach et al. 1980). Also, 789 adult individuals (75.9 percent) were aged using TCA analyses in this study. TCA could not be implemented in almost 250 adults because of either lack of preserved teeth, progressive macroscopic dentine decomposition, or postmortem cementum tissue destruction. Sex determination for 946 individuals resulted in a balanced proportion of 52.5 females per 100 individuals. However, the TCA subsample (n = 789) showed a slightly higher female proportion (females: n = 390, 54.0 percent; males: n = 332, 46.0 percent; undetermined: n = 67).

The Complex Method

Based on the initial anthropological study, the complex method for age-at-death estimation (Ferembach et al. 1980) was applied to all skeletons with at least two out of four observable indicators (n = 315). Due to the skeletons' poor preservation, additional morphological age estimation (MAE) techniques had to be applied (Wittwer-Backofen et al. 2008). The MAE results were combined with all relevant individual information, leading to the narrowest expert-opinion age span. This procedure did not allow for calculating individual age-at-death using a Bayesian approach to estimate a posterior age probability as required by the Rostock manifesto (Hoppa and Vaupel, 2002), as lists of stages by trait had too many missing cells.

As the comparison of methods in the Lauchheim cemetery subsample has shown, the range of individual age estimations following the complex method did not vary from those achieved by other MAE methods (Wittwer-Backofen et al. 2008) and thus can be interpreted as a typical pattern of osteology-based age-at-death distributions when compared to TCA-based distributions.

Tooth Cementum Annulation

TCA was successfully applied by three independent observers to 789 adult individuals using one single-rooted tooth (incisor, canine, premolar) per skeleton. When possible, teeth in their alveolar bone were selected first. Otherwise, teeth were selected according to the best preservation. At least three nondecalcified transverse sections (70–80 µm) of the epoxy-embedded samples were produced from the middle third of the root following Wittwer-Backofen's (2012) protocol. The sections

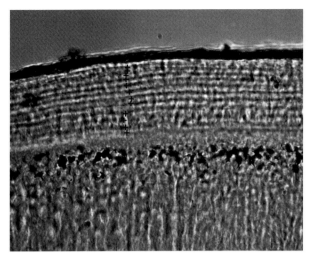

Figure 23.1 Microscopic TCA image of a Lauchheim specimen (transmitting light, magnification of 20x, contrast-enhanced)

were then analyzed at 20–40x magnification in transmitted light microscopy and recorded with a digital camera (824 x 1,026 pixel, Leica DC 250), stored in an image database (Software package: Leica IM 1000), and analyzed on a large-scale monitor. Samples were included in the TCA analysis if at least three images of different areas per tooth were evaluable. After a moderate software enhancement, images showed the typical alternating dark-and-light cementum lines between the cement–dentin junction and the periodontal ligament (Figure 23.1).

A software counting tool was used to mark each dark layer, avoid counting mistakes, and record results (Wittwer-Backofen, 2012). In several TCA studies, interobserver error influenced age results significantly. In the first study focusing on interobserver error (Charles et al. 1986), differences were identified for 5 percent of age estimation variance. In another study (Meinl et al. 2008), the interobserver error variation was 4,7 percent. Another blind study (Wittwer-Backofen et al. 2008) revealed even higher interobserver errors of up to eight years from the mean age difference.

To account for interobserver errors, we designed a new observer protocol. Before starting the project, all observers went through the same training procedure using a known-age sample. They received a series of slides from the same individual and evaluated the same tooth root sections until consistent and accurate counting was achieved. Observers were allowed to eliminate low-quality images defined by counting outliers resulting from taphonomy damages in the outer cementum layers.

Counts were performed in a blind study by three observers in two subsequent and independent counting rounds. The first observer selected the two or three best quality sections per individual and counted several times each (observer 1). An average number of incremental lines was calculated for each slide. Observers 2 and 3 counted half of the individuals several times each and delivered mean counts without any knowledge of the first observer's results. In the following text, observers 2 and 3 counts have been aggregated and are referred to as the second count of our sample.

A mean number of incremental lines per individual was calculated, and an age span of ±2,5 years was provided (2 standard deviation (SD), according to Wittwer-Backofen et al. 2004). In a subsequent step, average dental eruption age, by sex and tooth type, was added (Wittwer-Backofen et al. 2004, based on Adler, 1967) to calculate the individual estimated age at death.

Distribution of Individual Age Estimates

To obtain an age-at-death distribution, individual age estimations and associated ranges were aggregated in age categories following the proportional method for MAE (Luy and Wittwer-Backofen, 2006), starting from twenty years. Subsequently, each five-year age class received a total probability by multiplying the yearly probability based on the width of the age range with the number of years affected in the respective age group, namely between one and five. This procedure was applied to each individual, and the probabilities were subsequently added for each five-year age class. Therefore, the resulting age-at-death distribution takes into account all the individual age ranges. Both aging techniques (TCA and MAE) followed this procedure to determine a population-specific age-at-death distribution.

For all subadult individuals and those that lacked teeth for TCA investigation, MAE results were used to complete the mortality profile of the Lauchheim population.

For statistical analysis, we applied the Pearson two-tailed correlation test based on the assumption that TCA delivers a more precise age-at-death distribution compared to MAE. For interobserver error, we used a t-test to test for significant deviations of count results. To test whether the age profiles derived from TCA differ from those based on MAE, we performed chi-squared tests. Significance was assumed for probabilities $p < 0.05$. Statistical tests were performed with R (version 3.6.3).

23.3   Results

Interobserver Variation

TCA was successfully applied to 789 individuals. The interobserver error based on the mean individual TCA count does not exceed twelve increment counts. The arithmetic mean of interobserver variance is 2.84 years, and the standard deviation of interobserver error is 2.45. In 12.67 percent (n = 100) of all counts, both observers arrived at the same count (Figure 23.2A).

Almost 25 percent of all individuals were determined within an interobserver error of up to one year, and 84 percent of the total TCA counts are within a five-year interobserver error range. Consequently, 16 percent had an interobserver variance of more than five years, which means that there is no overlap of the age ranges provided by

Shaping Age-at-Death Distributions 369

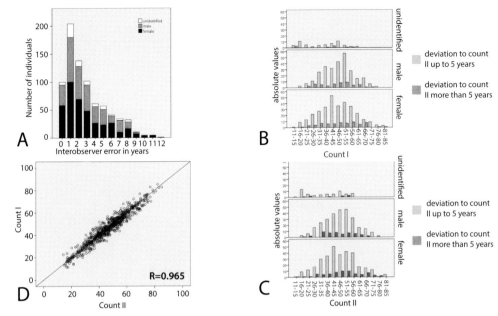

Figure 23.2 (A) Lauchheim TCA interobserver error in years by sex: male = 332, female = 390; (B, C) Number of individuals in five-year age categories for males, females, and unidentified individuals. B: count I (observer 1, left); C: count II (observers 2/3, right), showing the interobserver error of up to five years (bright columns) and more than five years (dark columns). (D) Regression of both counts (observer 1, observers 2/3). Each value (n = 789) represents one individual.

the two observers when considering the 2sd (+/–2.5 years) error in the method evaluation (Wittwer-Backofen et al. 2004). There is no significant count difference by sex.

Figure 23.2B & C shows the deviations smaller and greater than five years by sex and five-year age group for each observer's mean TCA age for age-category-specific interobserver deviations. All observers counted the highest ages in female individuals, with no evident interobserver error.

The correlation of the two TCA counts using the Pearson (two-tailed) test was highly significant at a 0.965 level (Figure 23.2D), suggesting that both Gaussian distributions are equal, with a homogeneous distribution pattern around the trend.

Method Comparison – Individual Age Interval

Based on all individuals with MAE and TCA estimations (n = 789), the calculated MAE mean age is 47,07 years; for TCA Count-I 46,22 years; and TCA Count-II 46,49 years. To compare MAE and TCA results, we combined the results of both TCA counts in a single TCA age span per individual. For this purpose, the lowest and highest values of both counts were selected to create a new age span for each individual.

Table 23.1 Statistics of individual age variations of morphological age estimations (MAE) and tooth cementum annulations (TCA)

	TCA (both counts) (n = 789) in years	MAE (n = 789) in years
Mean	7,70	19,73
Median	7,00	14,00
Standard deviation	2,42	13,40
Minimum	5,00	1,00
Maximum	16,50	61,00

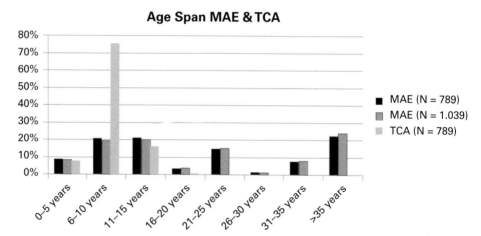

Figure 23.3 Age variation distribution for Lauchheim individuals based on TCA and MAE (both n = 789) and MAE (n = 1.039) in percent

Table 23.1 shows that TCA's age variation became larger and ranges from 5 years to 16,5 years, while the MAE values range from 1 year to 61 years. The mean MAE age variation is much higher (19,73) in comparison to the TCA (7,7). In 646 (81,88 percent) of 789 individuals, MAE has a wider age range, whereas, in 143 (18,12 percent) individuals, the range is narrower. This is mostly the case for late juvenile and young adult skeletons. The mean age variation for the MAE method, and all 1,039 adults, is 20,54 years. The aggregated TCA age variation was used in the final modeling of the age-at-death distribution of the total skeletal population.

Figure 23.3 shows a comparison between TCA and MAE age variation, including a subgroup of all individuals with MAE (n = 1.039 percent). The largest TCA age variation is visible in the six-to-ten-years error range, whereas MAE age variations show a considerable number of individuals above the thirty-five-years group for both samples. Slightly more individuals are found in the higher age-variation groups for the large sample, probably because many individuals did not have any teeth present, which was often evidence of a worse state of preservation. Consequently, the MAE age span for these individuals is wider.

Resulting Age-at-Death Distributions by MAE and TCA

Twenty-two of the 789 analyzed individuals were first classified as adults based on MAE analysis but were consequently reassigned to the juvenile group based on TCA estimates. The resulting age distributions were compared in subsequent steps. First, all age estimations based on TCA were contrasted with those from MAE based on the same 789 individuals (Figure 23.4A).

The age-at-death distribution for both TCA counts shows a matching age-at-death distribution with two mortality peaks in the 41–45 and 51–55 age groups. A Pearson's Chi-squared test was performed (χ^2(df = 14), n = 789) = 6.37, p = 0.96) to test the similarity of the two TCA distributions. The result indicates that the distributions are statistically dependent. TCA age estimations identify older individuals, namely up to eighty-five years, whereas the maximum reached by MAE estimations is eighty years.

For the MAE distribution, the highest peak is visible in the 51–55 age group. The distribution is skewed toward the older age categories. Although TCA shows an overall wider age range from eleven years to eighty-five years, the MAE curve is flattened compared to the TCA one due to the narrow individual age variations of the latter. A drastic decrease is visible between the 66–70 and the 71–75 age groups for the MAE curve. This decline might reflect method-inherent effects as many poorly preserved individuals were classified roughly between 30–70 years with the macroscopic methods. To test that the distributions from the two TCA counts differ from that of the MAE, two Pearson's Chi-squared tests were performed (χ^2 (df = 15), n = 789) = 36.24, p = 0.002 for count I and χ^2 (15, n = 789) = 49.86, p < 0.001 for count II), and demonstrates their statistical independence.

A slightly increased mortality risk for the 21–25 age group is also observed when including all individuals aged by MAE alone (n = 1.337) (Figure 23.4B). This peak results from the fact that TCA is mainly implemented for adult individuals, causing a major divergence in the number of age estimations in the age group of juveniles and young adults.

Second, to investigate whether sex influences the age-at-death distributions, we broke down all the aged, sexed individuals using MAE (n = 946). In Figure 23.4C, there is an earlier mortality peak for males in the 46–50 years age group. Females have a mortality peak in the 51–55 age group. Furthermore, an increased mortality rate for females ages twenty-one years to twenty-five years is visible. The sudden decrease in higher age categories is seen in both sexes equally. There are slightly more males than females in the oldest 76–80 age group.

To effectively compare the distributions by sex, we reduced the sample again and selected individuals with both MAE and TCA estimates and sex estimation. This subsample is comprised of 722 individuals, 332 males and 390 females. Figure 23.4D shows the same mortality peak in the 51–55 years age group for both sexes. An increased mortality risk between twenty-one and twenty-five years can also be seen for both sexes. For higher age categories, both males and females are equally represented above seventy years. Figure 23.4D illustrates the TCA age-at-death

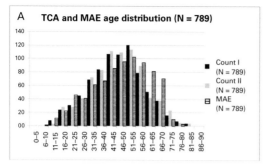
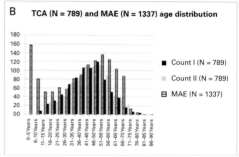
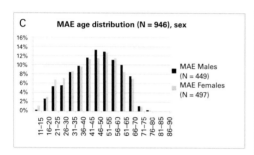
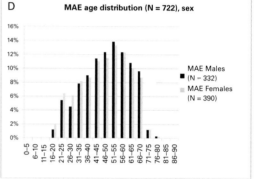
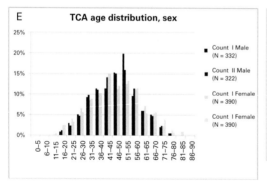
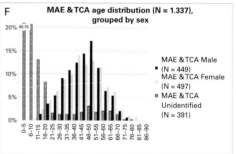

Figure 23.4 (A) TCA and MAE age-at-death distribution based on the same subgroup (n = 789); (B) Age-at-death distribution based on all MAE results (n = 1.337) including all individuals with TCA results and TCA-based results alone with an overlap of (n = 789) counts in absolute numbers; (C, D) Age-at-death distribution for all individuals by MAE. C: n = 946; D: n = 722; grouped by sex in percentage. See text for further explanations. (E) Age-at-death distribution of TCA results by sex in percentage; (F) Composite age-at-death distribution of TCA and MAE estimation by sex in percentage. TCA results of both counts are aggregated, and MAE results given when TCA results were not available.

distribution by sex for both counts (n = 722). The distributions show that males have only one outstanding peak at age 51–55 years in both counts. Females show a peak at age 41–45 in both counts, and again between fifty and sixty years of age. This suggests that females are the main driver for the overall distribution shape among the mature age group (Figure 23.4C).

Another interesting observation is the sex distribution in older categories. Both observers' TCA counts (Figure 23.4E) show that women have a wider age range (11–85 years) compared to males (16–80 years). Only very few males grew older than seventy years, and not a single man grew older than eighty years in both counts. In contrast, some females reached an age of up to eighty-five years. This sex difference is not seen in MAE results. As the sample comprises more females (n = 390) than males (n = 322), the graph displays percentages rather than absolute numbers.

Considering only the individuals with an interobserver error smaller than five years, we observe a mortality rate highest in females between forty-one and forty-five years, with a peak in the 46–50 age category and a slight increase in the following 51–55 age category. For males, both counts show a different pattern with the highest values observed for the 51–55 age group and a steep decrease in the following age category. Except for the varying mortality peaks in males and females, both counts show an approximately Gaussian distribution.

In total, TCA shows a more differentiated age-at-death distribution with probably less method-inherent effects than MAE. Thus, we modeled a final age-at-death distribution (Figure 23.4F) combining TCA results of all 789 individuals (both counts, aggregated) with MAE results for those individuals where TCA could not be applied (n = 548). The new distribution for the whole sample (n = 1.337) now displays the sex-specific mortality peaks and a wider age range of up to eighty-five years. The slight increase of the 21–25 years mortality risk seen in Figure 23.4C has shifted to the 16–20 age group. Our final age-at-death distribution shows a high infant mortality rate, an earlier mortality peak for women, and a small subgroup of women with the highest ages.

23.4 Discussion

This study compiled several macroscopic age estimation techniques, including the complex method, into an "expert opinion." However, to overcome several biases inherent to MAE, we also applied the TCA method to discuss methodological effects on the mortality profile of an early medieval graveyard population.

We introduced the TCA method here, as it is based on an incremental apposition process and thus provides a very reliable and direct age estimate. In contrast, MAE is based on gradually varying osteological aging indicators indirectly modeled from documented skeletal collections.

TCA has been proven to be a relatively stable age indicator, based on the number of annually formed incremental lines (Chapter 1). Rather than the quantity, cementum bands' quality varies with irregular increment width and appearance (see discussion in

Chapter 24). Recently, a standard protocol for the compilation of these irregularities has been provided (Mani-Caplazi et al. 2019) as the first step to link cementum band variations to life-history events such as pregnancies or disease (Chapter 8). Thus, the gap between biological and chronological age with TCA is supposed to be smaller than can be assumed for osteological MAE techniques, especially for older individuals (Chapter 24). A further advantage of TCA is the absence of over-aging individuals younger than forty years, which is observable in the complex method. However, an under-aging effect for older individuals is also documented for TCA (Wittwer-Backofen, 2004).

Interobserver variation: Our study does not confirm a significant interobserver error that influences age-at-death distribution. We presume that the study design has a significant influence on this result. This is an important finding as the interobserver error has been recognized as a significant limiting factor for the overall acceptance of the TCA method (Chapter 11). Therefore, we recommend thorough observer training before implementing TCA age estimations.

Method comparison – Age variation: Based on a previous study including a selection of 121 Lauchheim adult individuals (Wittwer-Backofen et al. 2008), the expected result of broader MAE age variation, compared to TCA age estimations, was confirmed in this study in the entire skeletal population.

In particular, diagenesis and antique grave disturbances may lead to decreased bone preservation obliterating significant aging traits and, thus, potentially causing broader individual age variations from MAE. Also, it is essential to recognize in this study that these influencing factors may also represent selective components of taphonomy, as skeletons with varying burial treatments are differentially affected. Similarly, we can assume that specific subgroups (sex, age, or social status) were targeted by postmortem reopening of graves. These changes might be significant when studying the graveyard sample of Lauchheim with its social and chronological diversity.

Compared to MAE estimates, the narrower individual TCA age intervals can be attributed to the cementum band's deposition being highly correlated to chronological age and better dental preservation against taphonomic processes.

Resulting age distributions by MAE and TCA: The results of this study show differing age-at-death distributions for MAE and TCA estimates. These patterns conform to expected method-inherent effects of MAE on age-at-death profiles:

1. The typical under-aging of older individuals, based on the demonstrated increasing gap between biological and chronological age with the increasing age of individuals known as the "attraction of the middle" (Bocquet-Appel and Masset, 1982). Comparing TCA and MAE, however, we could not support the finding of underestimation of older age categories seen in another archaeological sample (Lanteri et al. 2018).
2. The constructed right-shifted Gaussian age-at-death distribution of MAE compared to TCA results is also attributed to this phenomenon.

We also observed leveled MAE age-at-death distributions due to the large individual age intervals. Such a pattern may mask a real distribution showing clear mortality peaks and valleys. TCA age-at-death results suggest a different pattern of age distribution without leveling. When individuals are separated by sex, specific peaks for males and females suggest a more accentuated mortality regime. Although MAE distribution indicates a mortality peak of males in their early fifties, females' picture is less pronounced. TCA only shows two mortality peaks for women in their early forties and their fifties.

3. The oldest age groups in the MAE distribution contain several skeletons with broad age intervals and thus do not specifically identify individuals classified in the oldest categories. Conversely, TCA results detected specific individuals with smaller age intervals and precisely classified in the older age groups.
4. TCA estimations identified older women than men. This difference is not visible in MAE results.

In conclusion, TCA shows a more diverse age-at-death distribution. TCA method-inherent effects in this study mainly include the quality guarantee of a standardized protocol. However, the fact that the oldest individuals may suffer from extensive intra-vitam tooth loss can lead to an age selection bias by underrepresenting these oldest samples.

23.5 Outlook

The application of the TCA method illustrated the advantage of reducing age-at-death intervals and consequently reducing the leveling effects and age contraction inherent in MAE. Results also show more accented population-specific age-at-death profiles and thus confirm previous results about TCA's potential (e.g., Robbins Schug et al. 2012).

Our study suggests that TCA can complement the age-at-death distribution achieved from MAE methods. However, it has been shown that taphonomy can be a serious limitation to TCA when applied to soil-exposed teeth (Bertrand et al. 2019). Therefore, we support the need for a systematic evaluation of taphonomic processes, as illustrated in this chapter with a dedicated protocol. This protocol might need adaptation to the site and laboratory contexts to use TCA as a powerful tool for age-at-death estimates, superior to any other anthropological age indicator.

Also, the general problem of reconstructing age-at-death profiles from different skeletal indicators, which is also inherent in MAE, merits additional methodological consideration. Unfortunately, the true age of Lauchheim individuals is not known.

Despite the promising results of the TCA method, we do not suggest using this method to reconstruct age-at-death profiles of the total population solely: (1) Subadult individuals can only be estimated after forming permanent tooth roots (see Chapters 12 and 21); (2) The probability of finding teeth is reduced with increasing age; and (3) TCA analysis is costly and time-consuming compared to standard osteological methods.

Study designs need to employ various methods according to their particular strengths and weaknesses and devise methodological approaches for merging results. This requires anticipatory study designs, including budgeting of higher investment. We think this study's results justify the higher costs and higher time investment required for TCA, as valuable information about life-history parameters can be gained reliably.

We suggest taking TCA into account for outstanding populations, particularly for paleodemographic reconstructions, because a combined study design of MAE and TCA techniques, as demonstrated here, seems to overcome the shortcomings of each of the individual methods.

Acknowledgments

We especially thank Melanie Künzie for her thorough investment in TCA evaluation and analysis. The authors thank the Max Planck Institute for Demographic Research in Rostock MPIDR, Germany, for full funding of TCA lab preparation. The authors gratefully acknowledge the investment of all MAE and TCA lab staff of the MPIDR, the former Anthropology section at the University of Giessen, and the staff of Biological Anthropology at Freiburg University.

References

Adler, P. (1967). Die chronologie der gebissentwicklung. In E. Harndt and H. Weyers (eds.), *Zahn, Mund-und Kieferheilkunde im Kindesalter*. Berlin: Die Quintessenz, 38–74.

Bertrand, B., Cunha, E., Bécart, A., Gosset, D., and Hédouin, V. (2019). Age at death estimation by cementochronology: Too precise to be true or too precise to be accurate? *Am J Phys Anthropol* **169**: 464–81.

Bocquet-Appel, J.-P., ed. (2008). *Recent Advances in Palaeodemography*. The Netherlands: Springer.

Bocquet-Appel, J.-P., and Masset, C. eds. (1982). Farewell to paleodemography. *J Hum Evol* **11**: 321–33.

Brather, S. (2016). Lauchheim im frühen Mittelalter: Das DFG-Projekt und seine Perspektiven. In U. Koch, R. Prien, and J. Drauschke (eds.), *Reihengräber des Frühen Mittelalters*. Remshalden: Bernhard Albert Greiner, 47–54.

Buikstra, J. (2022). A brief history of cemental annuli research, with emphasis upon anthropological applications. In S. Naji, L. Gourichon, & W. Rendu, eds., *Cementum in Anthropology: Back to the Root*. Cambridge: Cambridge University Press, ch. 1.

Chamberlain, A. (2006). *Demography in Archaeology*. Cambridge: Cambridge University Press.

Charles, D. K., Condon, K., Cheverud, J. M., and Buikstra, J. E. (1986). Cementum annulation and age determination in Homo Sapiens. I. Tooth variability and observer error. *Am J Phys Anthropol* **71**: 311–20.

Großkopf, B. (1990). Individualaltersbestimmung mit Hilfe von Zuwachsringen im Zement bodengelagerter menschlicher Zähne. *Zeitschrift für Rechtsmedizin* **103**: 251–9.

Großkopf, B., and McGlynn, G. (2011). Age diagnosis based on incremental lines in dental cementum: A critical reflection. *Anthropologischer Anzeiger* **68**: 275–89.

Härke, H. (2014). Grave goods in early medieval burials: Messages and meaning. *Mortality*, **19** (1): 41–60.

Hoppa, R. D., and Vaupel, J. W. (2002). The Rostock manifesto for paleodemography: the way from stage to age. In R. D. Hoppa and J. W. Vaupel (eds.). *Paleodemography. Age distributions from skeletal samples. Cambridge Studies in Biological and Evolutionary Anthropology* 31. Cambridge: Cambridge University Press, 1–8.

Jankauskas, R., Barakauskas, S., and Bojarun, R. (2001). Incremental lines of dental cementum in biological age estimation. *Homo* **52/1**: 59–71.

Kargerer, P., and Grupe, G. (2001). Age-at-death diagnosis and determination of life-history parameters by incremental lines in human dental cementum as an identification aid. *Forensi +c Sci Int* **118**: 75–82.

Kemkes-Grottenthaler, A. (2002). Aging through the ages: Historical perspectives on age indicator methods. In R. D. Hoppa and J. W. Vaupel (eds.), *Paleodemography: Age Distributions from Skeletal Samples*. Cambridge: Cambridge University Press, 48–72.

Kvaal, S. I., and Solheim, T. (1995). A non-destructive dental method for age estimation. *J For Odontostomatol* **12**: 6–11.

Lanteri, L., Bizot, B., Saliba-Serre, B., Gaudart, J., Signoli, M., and Schmitt, A. (2018). Cementochronology: A solution to assess mortality profiles from individual age-at-death estimates. *J Archaeol Sci: Reports* **20**: 576–87.

Luy, M., and Wittwer-Backofen, U. (2006). Das Halley-Band für paläodemographische Mortalitätsanalysen. *Zeitschrift für Bevölkerungswissenschaften* **30**: 219–44.

Mani-Caplazi, G., Hotz, G., Wittwer-Backofen, U., and Vach, W. (2019). Measuring incremental line width and appearance in the tooth cementum of recent and archaeological human teeth to identify irregularities: First insight using a standard protocol. *Int J Paleopathology* **27**: 24–37.

Meinl, A., Huber, C. D., Tangl, S., Gruber, G. M., Teschler-Nicola, M., and Watzek, G. (2008). Comparison of the validity of three dental methods for the estimation of age at death. *Forensic Sci. Int.* **178**: 96–105.

Nagaoka, T., and Hirata, K. (2007). Reconstruction of paleodemographic characteristics from skeletal age at death distributions: Perspectives from Hitotsubashi, Japan. *Am J Phys Anthropol* **134**: 301–11.

Ferembach, D., Schwidetzky, I., and Stloukal, M. (1980). Recommendations for age and sex diagnosis of skeletons. *J Hum Evol* **9**: 517–49.

Renz, H., and Radlanski, R. J. (2006). Incremental lines in root cementum of human teeth: A reliable age marker? *Homo* **57**: 29–50.

Robbins Schug, G., Brandt, E. T., and Lukacs, J. R. (2012). Cementum annulations, age estimation, and demographic dynamics in Mid-Holocene foragers of north India. *Homo* **63**: 94–109.

Steckel, R. H., Larsen, C. S., Roberts, C. A., and Baten, J., eds. (2018). *The Backbone of Europe: Health, Diet, Work, and Violence over Two Millennia*. Cambridge: Cambridge University Press.

Stein, T. J., and Corcoran, J. F. (1994). Paradicular cementum deposition as a criterion for age in human beings. *Oral Surg. Oral Med. Oral Path* **77**: 266–70.

Storey, R. (2007). An elusive paleodemography? A comparison of two methods for estimating the adult age distribution of deaths at late Classic Copan, Honduras. *Am J Phys Anthropol* **132**: 40–7.

Stork, I. (2010). Friedhof und Dorf: der exemplarische Fall Lauchheim. In A. Gut (ed.), *Die Alamannen auf der Ostalb: Frühe Siedler im Raum zwischen Lauchheim und Niederstotzingen*. Esslingen: Landesamt für Denkmalpflege, 92–105.

Wahl, J., Wittwer-Backofen, U., and Kunter, M. (1997). Zwischen *masse* und *klasse*: Alamannen im *blickfeld* der *anthropologie*. In Die Alamannen (ed.), *Archäologisches Landesmuseum Baden-Württemberg*. Stuttgart: Theiss, 337–48.

Wittwer-Backofen, U. (2012). Age estimation using tooth cementum annulation. In L Bell (ed.), *Forensic Microscopy for Skeletal Tissues. Methods in Molecular Biology* (915). New York: Humana Press, 129–44.

Wittwer-Backofen, U., Buckberry, J., Czarnetzki, A., Doppler, S., Grupe, G., Hotz, G., Kemkes, A., Larsen, C. S., Prince, D., Wahl, J., Fabig, A., and Weise, S. (2008). Basics in paleodemography: A comparison of age indicators applied to the early medieval skeletal sample of Lauchheim. *Am J Phys Anthropol* **137**: 384–96.

Wittwer-Backofen, U., Gampe, J., and Vaupel, J. W. (2004). Tooth cementum annulation for age estimation: Results from a large known-age validation study. *Am J Phys Anthropol* **123**: 119–29.

24 Back to the Root: The Coming of Age of Cementochronology

Stephan Naji and William Rendu

Tremendous progress has been made since the 1950s when the first applications of dental cementum analysis were implemented in faunal and human remains (Chapter 1). Today, with a better understanding of cementum biology, robust, replicable protocols support promising innovative research in cementochronology. This chapter summarizes the key advances presented in this volume. We will also address recurring issues that could confuse those who are not familiar with the cementum literature. Our hope for the future is to continue expanding our understanding of cementum from a biological perspective, optimizing the various protocols, and testing broad anthropological hypotheses from the fossil record to forensic contexts.

24.1 Part I: The Biology of Cementum

Many aspects of cementum biology are confusing to nonbiologists interested in using acellular cementum's circannual growth pattern in cementochronology (Introduction, Chapter 1). The first part of the volume addressed these issues, and we will summarize what is consensual today among specialists.

Biology

Two main types of cementum are present on tooth roots. Acellular cementum (AEFC) covers cervical root surfaces, and cellular cementum (CIFC) covers apical and furcation regions, even though variations exist between species in the proportion's distribution of AEFC or CIFC along the root. For example, only CIFC is present in horses (Sahara 2014). Human disease and experimental animal models are now providing new insights into these two cementum types' functions as growth and maintenance processes, respectively (Chapters 2–5).

To further our knowledge of cementum, we argue (Introduction) that cementogenesis should be considered within a broader evolutionary framework describing the selection for the thecodont dental attachment morphology probably as early as 200 million years ago (Newham et al. 2020). Empirical evidence suggests that AEFC is under tight genetic control, with a constant growth rate *within individuals* and a consistent circannual deposit pattern (Introduction, Chapters 2–5). Cellular cementum provides the complementary adaptive system for tooth attachment against environmental influences, primarily biomechanical loadings and pathological insults (Chapters 3, 5).

Regarding AEFC composition and structure, clues to what we see when observing a semi-thin undemineralized section under transmitted light microscopy (TLM) start to emerge in Chapters 6, 7, and 14, particularly in terms of growth mineralization variation. The recent development of virtual 3D analysis combining x-ray fluorescence and x-ray diffraction mapping with synchrotron radiation microbeams was precise enough to follow individual increment oscillations across the cementum width. Independent experiments on several species of ungulates, primates, and humans evidenced the regular oscillations of calcium (Ca), phosphorous (P), zinc (Zn), strontium (Sr), and hydroxyapatite crystals (cAp) with seasons and revealed annual cementum band structure. Microtextural variation is also present across individual bands, demonstrating that the overall collagen fibril orientation undergoes subtle changes with the season. The "growth zones" creating wider and lighter (more translucent) increments should probably be interpreted as higher mineralization periods (higher mineral to organic ratio) but loosely organized. In contrast, the dark (opaque) "arrest lines" correspond to more densely packed but less mineralized events. A more comprehensive test of this hypothesis is already underway by some of the volume contributors.

Cementum: A Biological Archive of Life-History Events

The most promising research area in cementochronology is probably the potential to identify life-history events precisely. The recognition that cementum growth variations can be potentially affected by a variety of "stressors" such as pathologies (environment), parturitions (development), or fractures (traumatic) has been empirically observed in many mammal species by several authors in the past twenty years. This variation opens the door to exciting life-history studies (Chapters 7, 8).

The consensus is that at least four signals – ontogeny, phylogeny, biomechanics, and environment – are reflected in the micromorphology of skeletal and dental tissues deposited at any time during the life of an individual (Padian et al. 2013; Temple 2018). The environment part refers to the direct effects on growth and tissue expression caused by periodic, cyclical (seasonal variations), and unique environmental events or stress in a single individual (Jylhävä et al. 2017).

To address this topic reliably, broader questions must be tackled first, such as, What variables affect individual cementum deposits' width or how is individual frailty expressed in cementum growth variation throughout life? Today, we can only identify some of these changes in acellular cementum growth pattern in *documented* samples (Chapter 14). In other mammals, especially bears, these observations are routinely done (Matson & Kerr 1998). More valid protocols will be needed to translate these initial observations on documented samples to archaeological samples.

Other Considerations on Cementum Variations

We would like to address some confusing points that are lingering in the anthropology literature.

The dietary hypothesis. The change in food coarseness, and consequently in biomechanical loading to process the seasonally soft (summer) and tough (winter) food items in wild populations, and its influence on AEFC composition and optical properties specifically (Lieberman 1994), does not seem to be a robust explanatory mechanism across the large numbers of mammals that have been tested, including humans. Empirically, we know of several contexts that directly disprove this hypothesis: (1) Impacted teeth show a comparable amount of AEFC deposits than erupted teeth (Azaz et al. 1974, 1977; Nitzan et al. 1986; Rai 2009); (2) vestigial red deer canines also exhibit the same contrasted growth pattern, even though they are not functional for nutrition (unpublished data); and (3) hibernating species display similar seasonal banding even though they do not consume food during winter months (Grue & Jensen 1979; Helm & Lincoln 2017; Klevezal' 1996). Also, genetic analyses suggest that masticatory forces are probably not a driving factor (Chapter 4). Finally, this food coarseness hypothesis would predict that significant changes in the diet, such as the advent of farming (more reliable and predictable softer food) and the industrial revolution (quasi-complete homogenization of diet with processed food), should result in a clear decrease in human cementum contrast and growth worldwide. This is not the case (Klevezal' 1996; Naji et al. 2016). Similarly, the same prediction should apply to wild versus domesticated animals. However, no noticeable changes in AEFC contrasts are visible in animal studies or across human populations (Klevezal' 1996).

If the diet influences the cementogenesis of AEFC, a more likely hypothesis would be that the nutritional status (i.e., the availability of nutrients related to seasonal food) influences growth and mineralization processes, mainly via dietary metabolic pathways. Sporadic deficiencies will be accounted for through energy allocation away from growth processes and toward maintenance, probably throughout the skeleton (Bogin 2012; Temple 2018). This is essentially the hypothesis we are testing when trying to identify "stress events" in cementum layers. Overall, outside of chronic conditions or genetic defects, nutrition is not expected to affect AEFC deposition in terms of the number of layers (probably under stricter genetic control) but potentially in terms of the mineralization rate or density.

However, we would argue that the dietary hypothesis may be valid regarding CIFC growth. We hypothesize that accurate CIFC age-at-death estimates in specific taxa (Chapter 7; Matson et al. 1993) convincingly illustrate its regular and continuous adaptive function under specific conditions. When the feeding pattern and consequent biomechanical pressure are regular, with strong cyclic changes in food coarseness and nutritional value, CIFC growth can mimic the AEFC circannual deposition and be used for age estimation.

The seasonal adaptation hypothesis. The dietary hypothesis might be a covariant consequence of the dominating genetic control synchronized with a circannual periodicity (Introduction). This hypothesis is supported empirically for several species from the northernmost latitude exhibiting the most contrast in growth layers and, inversely, for the tropical/equatorial samples showing the least contrast (Klevezal' 1996, 101). For example, in tropical regions, cementum layers are more annual than seasonal and are more complex to identify than in temperate areas. Likewise, growth layer formation is inverse in the two hemispheres (Klevezal' 1996, 91) and can shift for a displaced population between the two hemispheres. Also, hibernating species still produce seasonal increments (Klevezal' 1996; Klevezal' & Kleinenberg 1967).

Overall, the complexity and variability of cementum growth layers are tied to seasonality gradient (i.e., the more seasonal, the more regular and predictable growth deposits can be identified). Today, the metabolic and endocrine pathways are understood at a much finer level. Some studies have elegantly linked bone growth to nutritional status and metabolic fitness on several ruminant species (Köhler et al. 2012). In summary, during the unfavorable seasons (dry/winter), ruminants are subject to cyclical variation in body core temperature, resting metabolic rate, and associated changes in hormonal levels (especially plasma insulin-like growth factor-1 or IGF-1). The consequence of this energy-conserving strategy is the formation of arrest growth lines. During the good season (humid/summer), the opposite happens (e.g., peak metabolic and IGF-1 levels, enhanced thyroid activity), which stimulates bouts of intense skeletal growth (Köhler et al. 2012). These cyclic growth patterns are synchronized with food availability and nutritional profile, which will dictate, in part, fat storage. Growth arrest and peak are, therefore, concurrent with hormonal and metabolic nadirs and zeniths, respectively.

From this model, we predict that the number of circannual AEFC increments is tightly controlled genetically. However, the quality (i.e., increment width, mineralization density, collagen matrix organization) may vary according to external factors or stressors.

24.2 Part II: Protocols

The main hurdle in cementochronology and one that we have argued is probably the underlying reason the method never became more ubiquitous (Naji et al. 2016) is the necessity to implement a histology protocol. Laboratory access and a cementum-specific protocol are required to optimize the observations of AEFC increments. Furthermore, numerous researchers have emphasized the critical importance of training. As Buikstra discusses in this volume (Chapter 1), standardization of a protocol has been overdue. This is no longer the case.

For freshly extracted teeth with high collagen content, observing decalcified paraffin-embedded, stained ultrathin sections (anywhere between 5 and 15 µm depending on the species) is the most accurate option today (Matson et al. 1993). Because ultrathin sections are a standard histology procedure in a forensic context, decalcified thin sections have also been used in humans with high success (Chapter 1: Table 1.1). However, for dried teeth (e.g., archaeological, osteological collections, fossils), this process will destroy the entire root. Undemineralized, embedded semi-thin ground sections (around 100 µm) are the only viable option in archaeological contexts, except for virtual 3D reconstruction.

Optimizing Thin-Section Production

For humans, Wittwer-Backofen and colleagues (Wittwer-Backofen 2012; Wittwer-Backofen et al. 2004; Wittwer-Backofen & Buba 2002) pioneered the standardization process, upon which Chapters 9–12 have improved. None exists for animals. These chapters propose systematic discussions on thin-section preparation variables and imaging parameters (Chapters 11, 12). Consequently, Chapters 1, 9, and 11 propose species-specific protocols for human and ungulate teeth. However, though the methods deliver consistent results for experienced specialists, these studies also clearly underline the need for extensive training.

Season-at-Death Validation Studies

In wildlife populations and zooarchaeology samples, estimating the season of death has been implemented reliably for the past forty years (Chapter 1). In humans, season-at-death estimation is only starting to be explored successfully (Chapter 13; Wedel 2007). In cementochronology, one of the central differences between humans and other mammals is that humans are long lived and thus accrue many cementum bands in a nonlinear pattern (Jylhävä et al. 2017). Consequently, in addition to the relatively small size of human teeth, the last deposited cementum band is challenging to identify optically. Wedel (2007) was the first to develop a method in a documented collection of freshly extracted teeth for forensic season-at-death purposes and then applied it to archaeological remains (Wedel & Wescott 2016). Chapter 12 expands cementochronology to subadults teeth, while Chapter 13 tests with success a comparable protocol on US army personnel.

However, there is a statistical sampling issue with season-at-death estimations that distinguished animal and human studies. In animal analyses, when the last band is a growth zone (summer), its large width allows for two to four subdivisions depending on the author or species (Chapters 17 and 18). Statistically, four outcomes are a critical difference over a binary outcome (summer/winter), which is the only option in humans with a thin, last band. In this scenario, the estimate would require a large sample to support its validity statistically. So far, human methods rely only on a binary (light/dark) outcome. More tests are needed to exclude random results alone and validate the prediction of season at death.

Cementum Growth Variations and Stress Markers

Several researchers are trying to systematize observations from reference collections on animal and human remains to identify the impact of "stressors" on cementum growth reliably (Edinborough et al. 2020; Mani-Caplazi et al. 2017, 2019; Newham 2018). However, if we want to build a robust method, we need to proceed with caution.

Cementum studies history (Chapter 1) should be a vivid reminder that rushed publications with oversimplified conclusions can confuse the wider anthropological community not familiar with the intricacies of cementochronology. For example, because aging processes are nonlinear and subject to local influences, using a simple growth ratio based on undefined layers in cementum seems hazardous at best (Cerrito et al. 2020). Our view is that a proper cementum-specific protocol should be used to test external influences on AEFC growth variation.

On the other hand, recent efforts by Mani-Caplazi et al. (2019), Colard et al. (2015) (Chapter 14), and Newham et al. (2020) (Chapters 8 and 16) demonstrate a desire to build a robust protocol step by step. This is the way. We hope that these combined efforts will lead to a better understanding of cementum variations.

Noninvasive Virtual Cementochronology

Groundbreaking improvements have been made using synchrotron microCT 3D reconstruction of cementum (Chapters 15 and 16). The possibility of precise and accurate noninvasive analyses, especially when fully automated (Newham et al. 2020; Chapter 16), opens a whole new research area for paleoanthropologists and paleontologists who can now extend their questions to the fossil record confidently. Even though synchrotron access remains exceptional, results from such analyses elegantly validate several hypotheses with the most precise and accurate imaging technique available today.

Automated Counting of Increments

Automated counting software is the next area where increased research will provide technological improvements to cementochronology for serial analyses. The development of an automated software has been long in the making (see discussion in Chapter 1), but it is now available for 3D imaging data (Newham et al. 2020; Chapter 16). The University of Lille and Leica have been developing a commercial software (Bertrand et al. 2017), which is unfortunately still untested and not publicly available. Conversely, Newham and Naji are currently testing the translation of Newham's 3D algorithm for 2D photomicrographs analysis in a freeware package.

Protocols – The Rise of Cementochronology

With recent methodological improvements and the rise of automation in image analysis, identifying and counting incremental layers in semi-thin/ground sections is now a reliable option for serial analysis of large collections with species-specific standardized protocols. Furthermore, the groundbreaking evolution of virtual cementochronology opens new opportunities to study the fossil record noninvasively. Applications of these new sets of tools on past hominid populations and other fossils open some of the most exciting research opportunities in cementochronology today. However, we must emphasize that these protocols require a significant learning curve to be implemented consistently. Today, few anthropology labs are adequately equipped, and the adaptation of a standardized protocol to the available equipment is counterproductive and should be avoided. By definition, changing any parameter no longer reflects the published protocol but creates a custom version that cannot guarantee tested outcomes.

24.3   Part III: Applications

The breadth of applications across disciplines is a testament to the potential of cementochronology as a tool to investigate age and season at death, seasonal mobility patterns, and eventually life-history events.

Seasonality: Discussing Mobility Pattern

In zooarchaeology, cementum increment studies have primarily focused on establishing the season of death of animal dental remains. One of the first major regional studies using cementum that significantly shifted mobility pattern interpretation discussed the seasonal hunting of reindeer during the Upper Paleolithic in France (Gordon 1988). Since then, cementochronology has mainly been used to discuss animal migrations (Burke 1993), hunting behavior (Pike-Tay 1991), and mobility patterns (Lieberman 1993). With the method's generalization, the studies have progressively expanded to answer more specific questions such as the site function or the specific hunting strategies developed by past human populations (Chapter 17). Others (Chapter 18) propose a regional paleoecological approach to reconstruct past animal coevolution with humans during the Paleolithic.

The next stage in cementochronological research applied to zooarchaeological contexts will probably include multiproxies' analyses. Recently Sánchez-Hernández and colleagues proposed a cross-study involving cementochronology and micro-wear analyses to discuss the site's seasonality of use and the environmental condition during its occupations (Sánchez-Hernández et al. 2019). Several authors of this volume obtained a sizable French grant (the ANR DeerPal project, E. Discamps) to characterize past reindeer behavior through a multiproxy analysis including isotopes, cementum, and micro-wear. We expect similar projects to start with the development of new analytical methods that allow us to directly sample elemental signatures of individual cementum increments to characterize the lives of past mammals' populations.

Life-History Events and Fertility

Many researchers have seen the circannual rhythm and continuous growth of acellular cementum throughout life as offering an exciting window of potential information of life-history recorded in the shape, texture, and chemistry of its increments. A host of studies have thus been presented studying the relationship between these factors and various life-history events affecting mammal physiology, most notably pregnancy and parturition (Chapter 8). Ongoing projects from some of this volume's contributors

(Newham, Colard, Stock, Price, and Naji) are currently funded to model past human population's fertility rigorously on modern, dedicated cementum databases.

Life Span and Mammalian Evolution

The development of noninvasive 3D methods for imaging cementum increments using synchrotron radiation sources provides volumetric datasets of submicrometer resolution and a consequent precise age estimate for hominid and mammal fossils (Chapters 15, 16).

Cementum has been imaged successfully in samples from modern humans to Neanderthals (Newham 2018). Furthermore, Newham and colleagues demonstrated that AEFC increments are still visible in the 200-million-year-old teeth of early stem-mammals (Newham et al. 2020). This unprecedented discovery about cementum preservation opens opportunities to address evolutionary questions in paleontology, such as the evolution of dental attachment and replacement among early mammals. Similarly, for our *Homo* lineage, the senescence rate and specifically the rate of osteological aging and hominid life spans can be tested directly.

For instance, despite increasing knowledge of the anatomy, ecology, and evolution of early mammals, contradictory evidence limits our understanding of their physiology and the timing in which mammalian endothermy arose. Due to the relationship between longevity and basal metabolic rate (BMR) in living mammals, age estimation using virtual cementochronology can be used as a proxy for BMR in fossil taxa. When included in a multiproxy analysis on two early Jurassic stem-mammals, cementochronology has suggested that they had maximum life spans considerably longer than comparably sized living terrestrial mammals and more similar to those of reptiles. The use of this data to estimate BMR suggests that early stem-mammals had yet to develop the elevated endothermic metabolisms of living mammals (Newham et al. 2020).

Additionally, new research perspectives in paleoecology are now foreseeable, such as reconstructing animal populations' feeding habits and mobility by analyzing trace elements and stable isotopes at the seasonal cementum increment scale. Finally, validation of the relationship between increment morphology and discrete life-history variables and events in living mammals has the potential to foster investigation of these variables in fossil taxa, promoting a new understanding of how they evolved through deep time.

The Elusive Search for the Ideal Skeletal Age Estimator

One of the research program's starting points leading to this collaborative volume was the seemingly simple question of estimating the age at death of a human adult skeleton reliably. A slightly more complex follow-up question was how to estimate the age distribution of a skeletal sample accurately. These questions are overlapping, but only in part. A unique answer with a unique age indicator would be possible if such an indicator could provide a continuous, sequential, and unidirectional aging pattern throughout the life span. Preferably, changes should be observed within a short time interval as compared with the total life span. Also, age-related alterations should not be secondary to pathological, metabolic, or nutritional changes. Finally, the indicator should be valid across species – in other words, a precise and accurate estimate with a negligible error rate for all decades of life. In this scenario, the individual age at death could be aggregated into an unbiased age distribution, and our original questions would overlap entirely.

Bocquet-Appel and Masset introduced this concept by defining a theoretical minimum requirement for estimating, without considerable risk of error, the individual age of a skeleton and the death structure to which it belongs (Bocquet-Appel & Masset 1982). The correlation between the biological indicator and the age at death must be higher than r = 0.9 (Bocquet-Appel & Masset 1982, 325, table 1). This theoretical minimum is recommended because "the effect of the anthropological reference population on the estimated structure asymptotically decreases as the correlation between age and biological indicator converges towards one" (Bocquet-Appel & Masset 1982, 326). This strong correlation between a biological feature and age is a critical point.

Unfortunately, most commonly employed anthropology methods are based on an osteological/dental age indicator staging system where the stages serve as proxies for age (Hoppa & Vaupel 2002). In other words, the determination of biological age is inferred from variables that are poorly correlated with chronological aging. The reason is that skeletal indicators are based on degenerative, wear-and-tear, senescence mechanisms. These changes are primarily correlated with biomechanical loading (lifestyle, fitness) and environmental factors (nutrition, health). However, they are only loosely correlated to an intrinsic aging mechanism (genetic) or a continuous growth process because developmental ontogeny stops in the third decade of life. This methodological distinction is central to understanding some of the underlying mechanisms distinguishing chronological and biological age.

If we step out of our discipline and consider the broader field of aging in biology, various biological clocks have been developed over the past decade to predict human health and longevity by providing a quantitative measure of the rate of aging of an individual and their overall resilience more accurately than chronological age. These clocks include DNA methylation patterns, gene expression patterns, serum proteins, and insulin growth factors glycans (Jylhävä et al. 2017). Recent developments in gerontology are starting to identify exact age estimators from living tissue samples. Some are already percolating in forensic anthropology (Lee et al. 2016). For example, the "Horvath clock" is becoming a benchmark in biomedical studies focused on aging mechanisms (Horvath & Raj 2018). More recently, plasma protein age estimation (Lehallier et al. 2019) also yielded precision levels above $r^2 = 0.95$, for all decades of life, with a small error rate. Two of these clock calculators (Hannum et al. 2013; Horvath 2013) are currently among the most robust predictors of chronological age. Both show high age correlations (r = 0.96 for Horvath and r = 0.91 for Hannum) and small mean deviations from calendar age (3.6 and 4.9 years, respectively) calculated from large validation samples (n = 8,000 for Horvath and n = 656 for Hannum). They also cover the entire adult life span and diverse populations (Jylhävä et al. 2017). These are very promising avenues of research on living tissues.

Unfortunately, in forensic anthropology and bioarchaeology, we can only rely on techniques for individual skeletal age applicable to dry osteological or dental remains, with two options: (1) Use a single, standard skeletal/dental age indicator (Buikstra & Ubelaker 1994). The resulting estimation is invariably associated with a significant standard error (>10 years at best), especially for adults above fifty. (2) Use a multifactorial method combining several skeletal indicators into an "expert opinion" (Milner & Boldsen 2012). Unfortunately, few procedures provide a viable mechanism for combining age-related information from separate anatomical structures in different parts of the skeleton in terms of point estimate or confidence intervals. From a statistical standpoint, this is problematic because the information from multiple age indicators is not independent. Without an unrealistically large reference sample, a reliable estimate is impossible, at least not without considerable simplifications (Boldsen et al. 2002). However, the transition analysis method's recent evolution (http://ta3info.com) explores an entirely new approach to the expert-opinion aging process. We are looking forward to Milner and Boldsen group's fully published method and the subsequent validation tests.

Until then, these two options are highly unsatisfactory, especially with the growing rigorous legal criteria that expert witnesses must uphold in forensic contexts. Recommendations are starting to emerge favoring a probabilistic summary of results, presenting posterior probabilities for each age (Chariot & Caussinus 2015; Konigsberg et al. 2016). We argue that this is the most rigorous approach when using standard anthropological age indicators.

In paleodemography, the debate to estimate a skeletal sample age-at-death distribution has come a long way since its initial deconstruction (Bocquet-Appel & Masset 1982). A strong consensus has emerged promoting a Bayesian approach of collective age estimation (Bocquet-Appel & Bacro 2008; Hoppa & Vaupel 2002; Konigsberg 2015; Séguy et al. 2013). In this probabilistic framework, two main trends have emerged. The English-speaking trend is mostly focused on parametric hazard models (Gage 1990; Konigsberg et al. 2016; Usher 2002; Chapter 22). In contrast, the French school is more data driven and proposes a fully Bayesian algorithm (Caussinus et al. 2017; Caussinus & Courgeau 2013). This method integrates any standard skeletal indicator into an age distribution with relatively tight credible intervals. Unfortunately, even if this should not be an excuse, both options' level of statistical proficiency prevents a broader deployment of these methods.

Back to the Root

Of course, this volume offers a third alternative. Cementochronology is, by far, the technique that complies with the most criteria defining a robust age estimation method (Kemkes-Grottenthaler 2002). Cementochronology is (1) based on a continuous growth process; (2) the most independently validated indicator, not only in humans but across eighty different species; (3) the most precise and accurate; (4) independent from any reference collection; and (5) based on teeth, one of the most available remains in archaeological samples. Cementochronology, with its high correlation to chronological age (>0.9, see Chapter 1, Table 1.1), should logically expand as a viable age indicator to estimate individual age at death or collective age distribution in all contexts (Chapters 19–23).

Nevertheless, the search for an ideal skeletal age indicator (progressive, precise, accurate, universal, and simple) continues, motivated by the multitude of applications in wildlife biology, forensic anthropology, bioarchaeology, paleodemography, paleopathology, zooarchaeology, and paleontology. Contrary to what some authors claim (Bertrand et al. 2019), cementochronology has never been described as a "perfect" age indicator. However, several authors have argued (Colard et al. 2015; Naji et al. 2016b; Introduction) that there is a clear distinction between cementochronology, which measures an actual growth process, and other skeletal adult age indicators, all based on degenerative changes. Cementum growth is subject to some aging processes and individual variations of phenotypic expression. Cementochronology estimates should thus always be assorted with an error rate. However, to date, this error rate is by far the smallest of any other skeletal or dental age indicators for any adult decade of life across species (Chapter 1: Table 1.1). Surely, this point is worth emphasizing.

Theoretically, it is probably unreasonable to believe that a perfect indicator exists considering the natural variation expressed in any biological organism's growth/senescent processes. In particular, recent discoveries on aging mechanisms (Farr & Almeida 2018; López-Otín et al. 2013) suggest that none of the visible changes associated with age is a linear process. Maintenance of body function and cohesion is context-dependent and subject-dependent, predicting a nonlinear relationship between any biological and chronological age, which we have all empirically observed (Jylhävä et al. 2017; Woodward et al. 2013). Any such pattern can and should be integrated into age estimation modeling to increase the method's precision, especially in the last decades of our life span.

Cementochronology, the Final Frontier

Traditionally, one theoretical and two practical concerns were usually invoked to dismiss cementochronology: (1) the evolutionary process explaining circannual growth cycles, (2) the subjectivity of counting the increments, and (3) the destructive nature of histological thin-section preparation.

We argue that the broader chronobiology framework (Introduction, Part I) provides the necessary hypotheses to test the first theoretical point further. Moreover, with the recent development of species-specific standardized protocols, the development of counting automation, and 3D noninvasive analysis (Part II), we argue that the two primary practical sources of concerns (subjectivity of counts and destruction of samples) have viable solutions. With these recent advances, we argue that cementochronology has the potential to renew several anthropology themes robustly (Part III).

The goal of this volume was to promote interdisciplinary discussions and stimulate new research opportunities in cementochronology. The enthusiastic collaborations resulting from this endeavor illustrate the success of the project. We hope that the Cementochronology Research Program, and anyone interested in cementum, will continue their collaborative effort and interdisciplinary approach to expand the boundaries of cementum in anthropology.

Acknowledgments

We would like to thank the ANR CemeNTAA (ANR-14-CE31-0011) and the ANR DeerPal (ANR-18-CE03-0007) for funding some of the experiments, travels, symposiums, and articles that led to the publication of this edited volume. We thank Elis Newham for help on an earlier draft. We would like to thank all the contributors who suffered our relentless reminders. We would also like to thank Daniel Antoine for his personal involvement in motivating us to seek a publisher during the 2017 AAPA symposium.

References

Azaz, B., Michaeli, Y., & Nitzan, D. (1977). Aging of tissues of the roots of nonfunctional human teeth (impacted canines). *Oral Surgery, Oral Medicine, and Oral Pathology* **43**(4), 572–78.

Azaz, B., Ulmansky, M., Moshev, R., & Sela, J. (1974). Correlation between age and thickness of cementum in impacted teeth. *Oral Surgery, Oral Medicine, Oral Pathology* **38**(5), 691–94.

Bertrand, B., Colard, T., Ramos Magalhaes, J., Cunha, E., & Hedouin, V. (2017). Computerized cementochronology taking the 16-bit between the teeth. *American Journal of Physical Anthropology* **S64**, 120.

Bertrand, B., Cunha, E., Bécart, A., Gosset, D., & Hédouin, V. (2019). Age at death estimation by cementochronology: Too precise to be true or too precise to be accurate? *American Journal of Physical Anthropology* **169**(3), 464–81.

Bocquet-Appel, J.-P., & Bacro, J.-N. (2008). Estimation of an age distribution with its confidence intervals using an iterative bayesian procedure and a bootstrap sampling approach. In J.-P. Bocquet-Appel (ed.), *Recent Advances in Palaeodemography*. The Netherlands: Springer, 63–82.

Bocquet-Appel, J.-P., & Masset, C. (1982). Farewell to paleodemography. *Journal of Human Evolution* **11**, 321–33.

Bogin, B. (2012). Chapter 11 – The evolution of human growth. In *Human Growth and Development*, 2nd ed. Boston: Academic Press, 287–324.

Boldsen, J. L., Milner, G. R., Konigsberg, L. W., & Wood, J. W. (2002). Transition analysis: A new method for estimating age from skeletons. In R. D. Hoppa & J. W. Vaupel (eds.), Paleodemography: age distributions from skeletal samples. Cambridge: Cambridge University Press, 73–106.

Buikstra, J. E., & Ubelaker, D. H. (1994). *Standards for Data Collection from Human Skeletal Remains: Proceedings of a Seminar at the Field Museum of Natural History, Organized by Jonathan Haas*. J. Haas, J. E. Buikstra, D. H. Ubelaker, & D. Aftandilian (eds.). Fayetteville: Arkansas Archeological Survey.

Burke, A. (1993). Applied skeletochronology: The horse as human prey during the Pleniglacial in Southwestern France. In G. A. Clarke (ed.), *Archaeological Papers of the American Anthropological Association* **4**, 145–50.

Caussinus, H., Buchet, L., Courgeau, D., & Séguy, I. (2017). Un problème clé de la paléodémographie: Comment estimer l'âge au décès? *Journal de la Société Française de Statistique* **158**(2), 43–71.

Caussinus, H., & Courgeau, D. (2013). A new method for estimating age-at-death structure. In *Handbook of Palaeodemography*. New York: Springer International Publishing, 255–86.

Cerrito, P., Bailey, S. E., Hu, B., & Bromage, T. G. (2020). Parturitions, menopause and other physiological stressors are recorded in dental cementum microstructure. *Scientific Reports* **10**(1), 5381.

Chariot, P., & Caussinus, H. (2015). Age estimation in undocumented migrant adolescents: Medical response to judicial authorities. *La Presse Médicale* **44**(1), 99–100.

Colard, T., Bertrand, B., Naji, S., Delannoy, Y., & Bécart, A. 2015. Toward the adoption of cementochronology in forensic context. *International Journal of Legal Medicine* **129**: 1–8.

Edinborough, M., Pilgrim, M., Fearn, S., … Edinborough, K. (2020). Mineralisation within human tooth cementum identified by secondary ion mass spectrometry. *Journal of Analytical Atomic Spectrometry* **35**(6), 1199–1206.

Farr, J. N., & Almeida, M. (2018). The spectrum of fundamental basic science discoveries contributing to organismal aging. *Journal of Bone and Mineral Research* **33**(9), 1568–84.

Gage, T. B. (1990). Variation and classification of human age patterns of mortality: Analysis using competing hazards models. *Human Biology* **62**(5), 589–617.

Gordon, B. C. (1988). *Of Men and Reindeer Herds in French Magdalenian Prehistory*. Oxford: BAR Publishing.

Grue, H., & Jensen, B. (1979). Review of the formation of incremental lines in tooth cementum of terrestrial mammals. *Danish Review of Game Biology* **11**, 1–48.

Hannum, G., Guinney, J., Zhao, L., … Zhang, K. (2013). Genome-wide methylation profiles reveal quantitative views of human aging rates. *Molecular Cell* **49**(2), 359–67.

Helm, B., & Lincoln, G. A. (2017). Circannual rhythms anticipate the Earth's annual periodicity. In V. Kumar (ed.), *Biological Timekeeping: Clocks, Rhythms and Behaviour*. New Delhi: Springer India, 545–69.

Hoppa, R. D., & Vaupel, J. W. (2002). The Rostock Manifesto for paleodemography: The way from stage to age. In R. D. Hoppa & J. W. Vaupel (eds.), *Paleodemography: Age Distributions from Skeletal Samples*. Cambridge: Cambridge University Press, 1–8.

Horvath, S. (2013). DNA methylation age of human tissues and cell types. *Genome Biology* **14**(10), 1–20.

Horvath, S., & Raj, K. (2018). DNA methylation-based biomarkers and the epigenetic clock theory of ageing. *Nature Reviews Genetics* **19**(6), 371–84.

Jylhävä, J., Pedersen, N. L., & Hägg, S. (2017). Biological age predictors. *EBioMedicine*, **21**, 29–36.

Kemkes-Grottenthaler, A. (2002). Aging through the ages: Historical perspectives on age indicator methods. In R. D. Hoppa & J. W. Vaupel (eds.), *Paleodemography: Age Distributions from Skeletal Samples*. Cambridge: Cambridge University Press, 48–72.

Klevezal', G. A. (1996). *Recording Structures of Mammals: Determination of Age and Reconstruction of Life History*. Rotterdam: A. A. Balkema Series.

Klevezal', G. A., & Kleinenberg, S. E. (1967). *Age Determination of Mammals from Annual Layers in Teeth and Bones*. S.S.S.R: Akademiya Nauk.

Köhler, M., Marín-Moratalla, N., Jordana, X., & Aanes, R. (2012). Seasonal bone growth and physiology in endotherms shed light on dinosaur physiology. *Nature* **487**(7407), 358–61.

Konigsberg, L. W. (2015). Multivariate cumulative probit for age estimation using ordinal categorical data. *Annals of Human Biology* **42**(4), 368–78.

Konigsberg, L. W., Frankenberg, S. R., & Liversidge, H. M. (2016). Optimal trait scoring for age estimation. *American Journal of Physical Anthropology* **159**(4), 557–76.

Lee, H. Y., Lee, S. D., & Shin, K.-J. (2016). Forensic DNA methylation profiling from evidence material for investigative leads. *BMB Reports*, **49**(7), 359–69.

Lehallier, B., Gate, D., Schaum, N., . . . Wyss-Coray, T. (2019). Undulating changes in human plasma proteome profiles across the lifespan. *Nature Medicine* **25**(12), 1843–50.

Lieberman, D. E. (1993). Variability in hunter-gatherer seasonal mobility in the Southern Levant: From the Mousterian to the Natufian. *Archaeological Papers of the American Anthropological Association* 4, 207–19.

  (1994). The biological basis for seasonal increments in dental cementum and their application to archaeological research. *Journal of Archaeological Science* **21**, 525–39.

López-Otín, C., Blasco, M. A., Partridge, L., Serrano, M., & Kroemer, G. (2013). The hallmarks of aging. *Cell* **153**(6), 1194–1217.

Mani-Caplazi, G., Hotz, G., Wittwer-Backofen, U., & Vach, W. (2019). Measuring incremental line width and appearance in the tooth cementum of recent and archaeological human teeth to identify irregularities: First insights using a standardized protocol. *International Journal of Paleopathology* **27**, 24–37.

Mani-Caplazi, G., Schulz, G., Deyhle, H., . . . Müller, B. (2017). Imaging of the human tooth cementum ultrastructure of archeological teeth, using hard x-ray microtomography to determine age-at-death and stress periods. Conference paper. https://doi.org/10.1117/12.2276148

Matson, G. M., & Kerr, K. D. (1998). A method for dating tetracycline biomarkers in black bear cementum. *Ursus* **10**, 455–8.

Matson, G., Van Daele, L., Goodwin, E., Aumiller, L., Reynolds, H., & Hristienko, H. (1993). *A Laboratory Manual for Cementum Age Determination of Alaska Brown Bear PM1 Teeth*. Milltown, Montana: Alaska Deptartment of Fish and Game, and Matson's Laboratory.

Milner, G. R., & Boldsen, J. L. (2012). Transition analysis: A validation study with known-age modern American skeletons. *American Journal of Physical Anthropology* **148**(1), 98–110.

Naji, S., Colard, T., Blondiaux, J., Bertrand, B., d'Incau, E., & Bocquet-Appel, J.-P. (2016). Cementochronology, to cut or not to cut? *International Journal of Paleopathology* **15**, 113–9.

Newham, E. (2018). Exploring the use of tomography for the quantification of cementum growth patterns across the mammal phylogeny. Ph.D. dissertation, University of Southampton, Southampton.

Newham, E., Gill, P. G., Brewer, P., . . . Corfe, I. J. (2020). Reptile-like physiology in Early Jurassic stem-mammals. *Nature Communications* **11**(1), 5121.

Nitzan, D. W., Michaeli, Y., Weinreb, M., & Azaz, B. (1986). The effect of aging on tooth morphology: A study on impacted teeth. *Oral Surgery, Oral Medicine, Oral Pathology* **61**(1), 54–60.

Padian, K., de Boef Miara, M., Larsson, H. C. E., Wilson, L., & Bromage, T. (2013). Research applications and integration. In K. Padian & E.-T. Lamm (eds.), *Bone Histology of Fossil Tetrapods*. Oakland: University of California Press, 265–85.

Pike-Tay, A. (1991). *Red Deer Hunting in the Upper Paleolithic of Southwest France: A Study in Seasonality.* Oxford: Tempus Reparatum.

Rai, B. (2009). Effect of nutrition on coronal displacement of cementum in impacted teeth. *Annals of Human Biology* **36**(4), 431–6.

Sahara, N. (2014). Development of coronal cementum in hypsodont horse cheek teeth: Coronal cementogenesis in horse cheek teeth. *The Anatomical Record* **297**(4), 716–30.

Sánchez-Hernández, C., Gourichon, L., Pubert, E., Rendu, W., Montes, R., & Rivals, F. (2019). Combined dental wear and cementum analyses in ungulates reveal the seasonality of Neanderthal occupations in Covalejos Cave (Northern Iberia). *Scientific Reports* **9**(1), 14335.

Séguy, I., Caussinus, H., Courgeau, D., & Buchet, L. (2013). Estimating the age structure of a buried adult population: A new statistical approach applied to archaeological digs in France. *American Journal of Physical Anthropology* **150**(2), 170–83.

Temple, D. H. (2018). Bioarchaeological evidence for adaptive plasticity and constraint: Exploring life-history trade-offs in the human past. *Evolutionary Anthropology: Issues, News, and Reviews.* https://doi.org/10.1002/evan.21754

Usher, B. M. (2002). Reference samples: The first step in linking biology and age in the human skeleton. In R. D. Hoppa & J. W. Vaupel (eds.), *Paleodemography: Age Distributions from Skeletal Samples.* Cambridge: Cambridge University Press, 29–47.

Wedel, V. L. (2007). Determination of season at death using dental cementum increment analysis. *Journal of Forensic Sciences* **52**(6), 1334–7.

Wedel, V. L., & Wescott, D. J. (2016). Using dental cementum increment analysis to estimate age and season of death in African Americans from an historical cemetery in Missouri. *International Journal of Paleopathology* **15**, 134–9.

Wittwer-Backofen, U. (2012). Age estimation using tooth cementum annulation. In L. S. Bell (ed.), *Forensic Microscopy for Skeletal Tissues*, vol. 915. Totowa, NJ: Humana Press, 129–43.

Wittwer-Backofen, U., & Buba, H. (2002). Age estimation by tooth cementum annulation: Perspective of a new validation study. In R. D. Hoppa & J. W. Vaupel (eds.), *Paleodemography, Age Distributions from Skeletal Samples.* Cambridge: Cambridge University Press, 107–28.

Wittwer-Backofen, U., Gampe, J., & Vaupel, J. W. (2004). Tooth cementum annulation for age estimation: Results from a large known-age validation study. *American Journal of Physical Anthropology* **123**(2), 119–29.

Woodward, H. N., Padian, K., & Andrew, L. H. (2013). Skeletochronology. In K. Padian & E.-T. Lamm (eds.), *Bone Histology of Fossil Tetrapods: Advancing Methods, Analysis, and Interpretation.* Berkeley: University of California Press, 195–215.

Index

acellular afibrillar cementum (AAC), 51
acellular cementum, 50–1
   evidence of onset of puberty, 245
   formation of, 47, 50
   identifying parturition lines in acellular
      cementum, 234–46
   phosphate metabolism, 67–70, 76
   potential insights from mouse genetic models,
      75–7
   pyrophosphate regulation of cementogenesis,
      70–3, 76
   role of ECM proteins, 73–5
acellular cementum increments composition study
   aim of the study, 110–11
   cementum–dentin junction identification, 116–18
   cementum mineralization front identification,
      116–18
   comparison of band structures from X-rays and
      optical microscopy, 124–9
   compositional differences and the band structure,
      135
   crystallographic texture within cementum,
      129–34
   elemental signature of cementum and dentin,
      127–9
   methods, 112–15
   protocol improvements for microstructure
      analysis, 134–5
   reasons for differences between X-ray and optical
      microscopy results, 127–34
   reference collections, 111–12
   results, 115–29
   synchrotron sample preparation and microbeam
      sampling, 112–15
   thin-section preparation and optical microscopy,
      112–13
   X-ray signals and band structure in cementum,
      118–25
   X-ray signals and the dental structures, 116–18
acellular extrinsic fiber cementum (AEFC). See
      acellular cementum
Ache people of Paraguay, 329
acromegaly
   association with hypercementosis, 100–1
adaptive cementum. *See* cellular cementum
age-at-death distribution
   Early Medieval population
      advantages and limitations of the TCA method,
         375–6
      approach to reconstruction in a past
         population, 364–5
      benefits of a study design using combined
         methods, 375–6
      comparison of aging methods, 364–5
      comparison of methods of age estimation,
         369–70
      Complex Method for age-at-death estimation,
         366
      distribution of individual age estimates, 368
      graveyard at Lauchheim, Germany, 365
      interobserver variation, 368–9
      interpretation of distributions from different
         methods, 373–5
      material and methods, 365–8
      morphological age estimation (MAE)
         methods, 366
      resulting distribution by each method, 371–3
      results, 368–73
      sample selection, 365–6
      TCA method of age-at-death estimation,
         366–8
   fisher-gatherer population in Brazil, 322–33
   for past populations
      challenges of individual age assessment,
         338–9
      considerations when using
         cementochronology, 346–8
      data set comparisons, 342
      dental material analysis, 341–2
      dental material selection, 340–1
      historical archives analysis, 340
      materials and methods, 339–42
      Notre-Dame du Bourg Cathedral death
         registers, 340
      probabilistic method, 342
      range of methods of age estimation, 338–9

reconstruction of the mortality profile, 346–7
reference collection of Notre-Dame du Bourg
    Cathedral, France, 339–40
results, 342–6
use of cementochronology for individual age
    estimation, 339
value of cementochronology as
    a paleodemographic tool, 347–8
Nabataean burials at Petra, Jordan, 351–61
age-at-death estimation
    dental eruption charts, 216
    development of cementum analysis protocol,
        30–6
    human deciduous teeth age-at-extraction study,
        215–24
    identification of US POW/MIA service members,
        226–32
    London Atlas of Human Tooth Development, 216
    search for the ideal skeletal age indicator, 386–9
    validation studies, 31–6
age estimation
    Bayesian approach, 388
    biological clocks, 387
    correlation of cementum thickness with age in
        humans, 28–9
    history of the use of cementum, 2–3
    limitations of markers of biological aging, 10–11
    use of bone remodeling in humans, 8
age identities
aging process
    influence of individual variations in cementum
        studies, 166
Agta people of the Philippines, 329
alligators, 86–7
alpacas, 87
ALPL gene, 84–5
ALPL gene mutations, 72
ALPL knock-out mice, 72
amphibians
    annual growth pattern, 7
anatomically modern humans (AMH)
    hominin strategies in southern Belgium (Late
        Pleistocene), 288–302
animal studies
    history of use of cementum for age estimation, 2
    hormonal physiology and cementum growth,
        157–9
    wildlife and zoo studies of cementum annulation,
        29–30
ANK gene mutations, 72–3
ANK mutant or knock-out mice, 72–3
annual rhythms. *See* circannual rhythms
annuli, 2
antemortem loss of antagonistic teeth
    influence on cementum deposition, 99
anthropology, 3, 7
antiresorptive therapies

risk of osteonecrosis of the jaw, 59
apical periodontitis
    influence on cementum deposition, 98
archeological studies, 30
archeology
    diagenetic and taphonomic effects on tooth
        cementum, 148–50
ARNTL gene, 86
automated counting of increments, 384

baboons, 85
bald eagles, 87
barren-ground caribou, 202
bats, 87
Bayesian approach to age estimation, 388
Bayesian inference procedure, 338
bears, 9, 30, 38, 380
beluga whales, 6
biological clocks. *See* chronobiology
bison, 29, 30, 276–80
black bears, 148, 158
Black, G. V., 26
Blake, Robert, 23–5
BMP-2 gene, 85
BMP-7 gene, 85
bone
    cyclical growth patterns, 7–8
    properties compared with cementum, dentin, and
        enamel, 54
bone deposition and mineralization
    circadian rhythms, 6
bone morphogenic protein (BMP)
    genes associated with, 85
bone sialoprotein (BSP), 49, 53–4, 73, 163
    role in cementogenesis, 73–5
Brazil
    pre-farming population demography, 322–33
broad and translucent annulations (BTAs), 159–61
BSP gene, 90
buffalo, 29
bushbuck, 29

calcinosis, 102
calcium
    concentrations in chimpanzee cellular cementum,
        142–5
Camargue cattle, 111–12
camels, 87
caribou, 30
caries
    effects on cementum, 56
caries therapy
    effects on cementum, 58
cave bears, 288, 301
cave hyaenas, 288
    carnivore cementum studies, 289
    cementum analysis, 296–9

cave hyaenas (cont.)
  land-use strategy, 300
  presence in southern Belgium (Late Pleistocene), 301
  tooth samples, 294
cellular cementum, 50–1
  cementocytes, 51
  chimpanzee cellular cementum elemental distribution, 138–51
  formation of, 47–50
cellular intrinsic fiber cementum (CIFC). *See* cellular cementum
cellular mixed stratified cementum (CMSC), 51
cementoblastoma, 58
cementoblasts, 47, 49–50, 54
  BSP as marker for, 74
cémentochronologie, 3
cementochronology, 83–4
  accounting for individual variations in the aging process, 166
  comparison with markers of biological aging, 10–11
  future of, 162–5
  hurdles preventing reliable use of cementum variations, 165–6
  influences on cementum mineralization, 163
  influences on the chemical composition of cementum increments, 163–4
  methodological issues in studies of life-history events, 165
  need for a standardized protocol, 38–9
  optimizing protocol variables, 198
  optimizing sample preparation and imaging protocols, 189
  origin of the term, 3
  preparation protocols specific to cementum studies, 195–8
  virtual cementochronology, 164–5
  See also tooth cementum annulations (TCA) method
cementochronology key advances, 379
  applications, 385–9
  automated counting of increments, 384
  cementum biology, 379–80
  dealing with concerns about cementochronology, 389–90
  dietary hypothesis, 381
  hypotheses on the influences on cementum growth, 381–2
  identification of life-history events in cementum, 380
  life span studies, 386
  mammalian evolution studies, 386
  noninvasive virtual 3D cementochronology, 384
  optimizing thin-section production, 383
  population fertility studies, 385–6
  protocols, 382–5
  search for the ideal skeletal age indicator, 386–9
  season-of-death validation studies, 383
  seasonality and mobility patterns, 385
  seasonality hypothesis, 381–2
  stress markers in cementum, 383–4
  synchrotron X-ray studies, 384
  understanding cementum growth variations, 383–4
Cementochronology Research Program, 389
cementocytes, 47, 51
cementogenesis, 46–9
  acellular cementum, 47, 50
  cellular cementum, 47–50
  cementoblasts, 47, 49–50
  cementocytes, 47
  collagen fibers, 47
  potential insights from mouse models, 75–7
  regulation by pyrophosphate, 70–3, 76
  role of ECM proteins, 73–5
  role of Hertwig's epithelial root sheath (HERS), 47
cemento-osseous dysplasia, 58
cemento-ossifying fibroma, 58
cementum
  circannual rhythms, 6
  circannual rhythms studies, 9–10
  incremental growth patterns, 9–10
  insights into the origin and evolution of, 77
  mechanisms of cementum banding, 75–6
  terms relating to, 2–3
  See also acellular cementum; cellular cementum
cementum annulation
  wildlife and zoo studies, 29–30
cementum biology, 379–80
  aspects of, 46
  cementum formation (cementogenesis), 46–9
  clinical and environmental considerations in TCA analysis, 54–9
  comparison with bone, dentin, and enamel, 54
  composition of cementum, 53–4
  types of cementum, 50–3
cementum–dentin junction
  identifying, 116–18
cementum deposition
  hypercementosis, 99–104
cementum deposition modulators
  antemortem loss of antagonistic teeth, 99
  apical periodontitis, 98
  dentoalveolar compensations, 95–7
  occlusal trauma, 98
  pathological factors, 97–9
  pathological tooth displacement, 98
  periodontal disease, 97–8
  physiological factors, 94–7
  root anatomy, 94–6
  root caries, 98–9
  tooth eruption and function, 94–5

Index

cementum formation. *See* cementogenesis
cementum mineralization front
   identifying, 116–18
cementum types, 50–3
   acellular afibrillar cementum (AAC), 51
   acellular cementum, 50–1
   cellular cementum, 50–1
   cellular mixed stratified cementum (CMSC), 51
   coronal cementum, 53
   reparative cementum, 51
Childe, V. Gordon, 322
chimpanzee cellular cementum study
   barium distribution in cementum, 140
   calcium concentrations, 142–5
   calcium distribution in cementum, 139–40
   data acquisition, 142
   experimental setup, 141–2
   incremental elemental distribution, 138–9
   mineral concentrations and incremental lines, 148–51
   phosphorus concentrations, 142–5
   phosphorus distribution in cementum, 139–40
   samples, 141
   second-order incremental markings, 147–8
   strontium concentrations, 145–6
   strontium distribution in cementum, 140
   synchrotron X-ray fluorescence, 141
   trace elements in cementum, 139–40
   zinc concentrations, 146–7
   zinc distribution in bone and dental tissues, 140
chimpanzees, 97
chondrocalcinosis (CCAL2), 72
chronic sclerosing osteomyelitis, 102
chronobiology, 1, 3, 10
   biological clocks, 387
   cycles of life, 3–4
   origin of the field, 3
chronotypes, 4
circadian clocks, 3
circadian rhythms, 4
   bone deposition and mineralization, 6
   dentin, 6
   mechanisms for, 5
   relationship to circannual rhythms, 6
   teeth, 6
   tooth enamel, 6
circannual clocks, 3
circannual rhythms, 4
   adaptive benefits of, 6–7
   cementum, 6
   chronotypes, 4
   clock-shop model, 5–6
   environmentally evoked rhythms, 5
   environmentally synchronized rhythms, 5
   epigenetic regulation, 5
   evolutionary origins, 5
   mechanisms responsible for, 4–7

   relationship to circadian rhythms, 6
   seasonal (circannual) progressive rhythms, 4
   teeth, 6
   trans-generational annual rhythms, 4
   types of, 4–5
circannual rhythms validation studies, 7–10
   amphibians, 7
   bone, 7–8
   cementum incremental growth patterns, 9–10
   fish, 7
   humans, 8
   mammals, 8
   methods of demonstrating hard tissue seasonal growth in animals, 7
   Nile crocodiles, 7–8
   sclerochronology, 7
   sharks, 8
   skeletochronology, 7–8
   teeth, 9–10
   ungulates, 8
circaseptan rhythms, 4
clock genes
   ARNTL gene, 86
clock-shop model, 5–6, 10
collagen fibers
   role in cementogenesis, 47
combined age estimate method, 338
Complex Method for age-at-death estimation, 366
Contemporary Demographic Transition, 331
coronal cementum, 53
coyotes, 30
craniometaphyseal dysplasia (CMD), 72
crocodiles, 86–7
Cuvier, Georges, 25

deciduous teeth. *See* human deciduous teeth TCA study
demographic regimes
   evolution of, 322–3
   Neolithic Revolution hypothesis, 322
demography
   pre-farming fisher-gatherer population in Brazil, 322–33
dental cementum increment analysis (DCIA), 3, 50
dental disease and trauma
   effects on cementum, 56–58
dental eruption charts, 216
dental therapies
   effects on cementum, 58
dentin
   circadian rhythms, 6
   cyclic growth, 6
   incremental growth patterns, 6
   properties compared with cementum, enamel, and bone, 54
   von Ebner's lines, 9
dentin matrix protein 1 (DMP1), 47, 51, 54, 73

dentin phosphoprotein (DPP), 47, 73
dentin sialoprotein (DSP), 47, 73
dentoalveolar compensations
    modulation of cementum deposition, 95–7
diagenesis
    effects on tooth cementum, 37
dietary hypothesis, 381
dinosaurs, 7, 8, 10, 83
disability, bioarcheology of
    osteobiography of a Middle Woodland woman, 306–16
domestic cat, 87
drugs
    effects on cementum, 59
Dupont, Édouard, 289, 290–1

ectonucleotide pyrophosphatase phosphodiesterase I (ENPP1), 72–3
ectopic calcification, 70, 72
elephant seals, 158
elephants, 25
elk, 30
enamel
    circadian rhythms, 6
    incremental growth patterns, 6
    properties compared with cementum, dentin, and bone, 54
enamel dysplasia with hamartomatous atypical follicular hyperplasia, 102
enamel renal syndrome, 102
endodontic therapy
    effects on cementum, 58
ENPP1 gene, 90
ENPP1 gene mutations, 72–3, 76
ENPP1 mutant or knock-out mice, 72–3
environmentally evoked circannual rhythms, 5
environmentally synchronized circannual rhythms, 5
European lynxes, 158
Eustachio, Bartolomeo, 23
evolution
    adaptive benefits of circannual rhythms, 6–7
    insights into the origin of cementum, 77
    mammalian evolution studies, 386
    origins of circannual rhythms, 5
evolutionary genetics of cementum
    ALPL candidate gene, 84–5
    ARNTL candidate gene, 86
    BMP-2 candidate gene, 85
    BMP-7 candidate gene, 85
    branch-specific selection patterns, 86–7
    candidate gene study methods and results, 86–91
    candidate genes, 84–6
    comparative genetic analysis approach, 84
    evidence for purifying selection, 86
    evolution of genes associated with cementum deposition, 89–90

influence of diet type, 87–8
influence of life span, 88–9
influence of tooth count and radicularity, 88–91
lineage-specific selection pressures, 87
selection pressures on the ALPL gene, 85
selection pressures on the ARNTL gene, 86
selection pressures on the BMP-2 gene, 85
selection pressures on the BMP-7 gene, 85
evolutionary history of cementum
    thecodonty, 83
external root resorption, 98
extracellular matrix (ECM) proteins
    role in cementogenesis, 73–5, 76–7
    SIBLING family of proteins, 73–5

fetuin-A (AHSG), 70
fibroblast growth factor 23 (FGF23), 68
fibro-osseous lesions of the jaw, 58
fish, 9
    otolometry, 7
    scalimetry, 7
fisher-gatherers
    pre-farming population demography, 322–33
flying foxes, 86
forensic anthropology, 3
fossil hominin tooth study
    diagenetic and taphonomic effects on the cementum, 148–50
    future directions in fossil tooth study, 151
    sample, 141
    synchrotron X-ray study, 141
fossils, 10, 29
    toothed fossil birds, 10
foxes, 157
Fränkel, Meyer, 25

Galen, 22–3
Gardner syndrome, 102
gazelle, 29
gene editing
    gene knock-in, 67
    gene knock-out, 67
    mouse models, 67
    transgenic expression, 67
generalized arterial calcification in infancy (GACI), 72
genetic disorders
    ANK gene mutations, 72–3
    ENPP1 gene mutations, 72–3
    hypophosphatasia (HPP), 72
    X-linked hypophosphatemia, 70
genetic model organisms
    mouse genetic models, 65–7
genetic mutations
    effect on cementum formation and stability, 56
gharials, 86–7
gingivitis
    during pregnancy, 155–6

goiter
  association with hypercementosis, 100
Gompertz-Makeham hazard model, 351, 352, 354, 356–7
gorillas, 140
greater kudu, 29
growth layer groups (GLG), 2
growth layer of the first order, 2
growth rest lines, 2
growth zones, 2

Hadza people of Tanzania, 329
Hannum clock, 387
Hertwig's epithelial root sheath (HERS), 47
hibernation, 9
history of cementum discovery, 2–3
history of cementum studies, 21–2
  correlation of cementum thickness with age in humans, 28–9
  development of cementum analysis protocol, 30–6
  discovery and early characterizations, 22–7
  early twentieth century, 28–30
  late twentieth and twenty-first century, 30–6
  ongoing methodological issues, 36–7
  twenty-first century developments, 36–7
  validation studies for age-at-death estimation, 31–6
  wildlife and zoo studies of cementum annulation, 29–30
Hiwi people of Venezuela, 329
hominids
  life span and evolution studies, 386
hominin strategies in southern Belgium (Late Pleistocene)
  approach to accessing seasonal information, 301–2
  carnivore cementum studies, 289
  cave hyaena cementum analysis, 296–9
  cave hyaena land-use strategy, 300
  cave hyaena tooth samples, 294
  Caverne Marie-Jeanne site, 292
  implications for competition among top predators, 300–1
  indications of seasonal occupation of sites, 299–300
  materials, 290–4
  methods, 294–5
  possible seasonal subsistence strategy, 299–300
  potential competition between top predators, 288–9
  prey selection and mobility of predators, 294–6
  prey-species seasonality at Caverne Marie-Jeanne, 295
  prey-species seasonality at Tiène Des Maulins, 295
  prey-species seasonality at Trou Magrite, 294–5
  results, 294–9
  sampling strategy and analyzed material, 292–4
  site description and research history, 290–2
  Tiène des Maulins site, 291
  Trou Magrite site, 290–1
hormonal physiology
  animal studies of cementum growth effects, 157–9
  effects on oral health and cementum growth, 155–7
  human studies of cementum growth effects, 159–62
horses, 25, 379
Horvath clock, 387
human deciduous teeth TCA study
  directions for future study, 223
  issues with age-at-extraction estimation, 223–4
  methodological challenges, 215
  methods, 219
  results, 219–20
  review of literature on age-at-death estimation, 216
  sampling limitations for deciduous teeth, 216–17
  sources of error, 220–3
  study sample, 217–18
humans
  archeological reference collection (Middle Ages), 111–12
  bone remodeling and age estimation, 8
  circannual growth patterns, 8
  correlation of cementum thickness with age, 28–9
  effects of life-history events on cementum growth, 159–62
  history of the use of cementum for age estimation, 3
  lamellar bone growth rates, 8
  strontium concentrations in dental tissues, 140
hunter-gatherers
  demography of contemporary groups, 329–30
hydroxyapatite, 53, 54, 73, 139–40
  phosphase metabolism and, 67–8
  pyrophosphate regulation, 70–3, 76
hypercementosis, 94, 95, 99–104
  association with acromegaly, 100–1
  association with Paget's disease, 100
  association with thyroid goiter, 100
  cementum ridges (spike-like projections), 103
  diffuse form, 99–103
  in past populations, 102–4
  nodular forms (cementicles), 103–4
  potential indicator of past population health, 104–5
hypophosphatasia (HPP), 72, 84–5

IBSP gene, 53
IBSP gene polymorphisms, 75
IBSP–/– mice, 75

ichthyosaurs, 10
identities in the past
  role of osteobiography, 306–7
identity
  age identities, 308
idiopathic hypoparathyroidism, 102
incremental growth layers, 2
insectivores, 30
interdisciplinary research, 1
interobserver reliability
  ungulate teeth thin sections, 201–13
intradian rhythms, 3

Juvenility Index, 330

kidney-parathyroid-bone axis, 68
!Kung people of Botswana-Namibia, 329, 330
Kutchin Athapaskan people, 330

Lamedin dentin translucence method, 38
life-histories
  osteobiography of a Middle Woodland woman, 306–16
life-history events
  animal studies of cementum growth effects, 157–9
  effects of pregnancy on cementum growth, 155–7
  hormonal effects on cementum growth, 155–7
  human studies of effects on cementum growth, 159–62
  hurdles preventing reliable use of cementum variations, 165–6
  identifying in dental cementum, 155–66, 380
  identifying parturition lines in acellular cementum, 234–46
  individual variations in the aging process, 166
  influences on cementum mineralization, 163
  influences on the chemical composition of cementum increments, 163–4
  methodological issues in cementum studies, 165
ligne d'arrêt de croissance, 2
London Atlas of Human Tooth Development, 216
lunar rhythms, 4

macaques, 8, 9, 30, 50, 96, 140, 148, 263, 270
Malpighi, Marcello, 23
mammals, 7
  circannual growth patterns, 8
  mammalian evolution studies, 386
  marine mammals, 30
marmosets, 30
matrix extracellular phosphoglycoprotein (MEPE), 73
matrix gla protein (MGP), 70
medications
  effects on cementum, 59
methyl methacrylate (MMA), 185

mink, 9
monkeys, 8
moose, 29, 30
Morganucodon, 260, 262, 270
morphological age estimation (MAE) methods, 366
mortality profile. *See* age-at-death distribution
mosasaurs, 10, 83
mouse genetic models, 65–7
  ALPL knock-out mice, 72
  ANK mutant or knock-out mice, 72–3
  ENPP1 mutant or knock-out mice, 72–3
  gene-editing techniques, 67
  HYP mouse, 68–70
  IBSP–/– mice, 74–5
  implications for vitamin D-related rickets, 76
  mouse dentition, 67
  potential insights from, 75–7
mouse lemur, 8
mule deer, 29
multidien rhythms, 4

Nabataean age-related mortality
  age-bias problem, 352–3
  challenges in deriving age-related mortality, 351–3
  challenges of reconstructing a population mortality profile, 353–4
  confounding effect of a growing or shrinking population, 351–2
  Gompertz-Makeham hazard model, 351, 352, 354
  Gompertz-Makeham hazard model applied to the sample data, 356–7
  history of Petra and the Nabataean kingdom, 353–4
  implications of the age-related mortality profile, 360–1
  interpretation of the pattern of age-related mortality, 254–5
  materials and methods, 354–7
  Petra North Ridge burials, Jordan, 351–2
  problem of small sample size, 352
  reconstruction of the age-at-death distribution, 357–9
  results, 357–9
  sample selection, 354–5
  value of cementochronology for individual age-at-death estimates, 360–1
Neanderthal spatial organization
  anticipation of prey behavior and distribution fluctuations, 275–6
  bison hunting in the Discoidal Denticulate Mousterian, 276–9
  bison kill and butchery sites, 279–80
  cementum analysis of samples, 280–1
  Discoidal Denticulate faunal assemblages, 279–80

Discoidal Denticulate Mousterian fauna, 276–9
hunting seasonality, 275
  influence of prey behavior, 283–4
  materials and methods, 280–1
  mobility strategies in the Late Middle
    Palaeolithic, 276–9
  patterns of occupation and mobility, 282–4
  Quina reindeer assemblages, 279
  reindeer butchery sites, 279
  reindeer hunting in the Quina Mousterian, 276
  results of cementum analysis, 281
  seasonal use of specific sites, 282–4
  southwest France context, 275–6
  structure related to the predation system, 283–4
  task-specific locations, 276, 282–4
Neanderthals, 103
  hominin strategies in southern Belgium (Late Pleistocene), 288–302
Neolithic Revolution hypothesis, 322
Neolithic studies, 29
Nile crocodiles
  annual growth pattern, 7–8
nomenclature
  terms relating to cementum, 2–3
nondestructive imaging of TCAs
  current limitations, 253–4
  data collection, 250–1
  future improvements in scanning and fine-tuning reconstruction, 254
  methodological advantages of virtual histology, 250–3
  nondestructive methods, 103–4
  optical coherence tomography (OCT), 249
  potential of phase-contrast synchrotron X-ray microtomography, 254–5
  prior optimization for choosing the ROI to scan, 254–5
  propagation phase-contrast synchrotron X-ray microtomography, 249
  sample, 250–1
  Terahertz imaging, 249
  validation by combining with thin sectioning, 253
noninvasive 3D imaging of cementum
  advantages of PPSRCT, 258–65
  current limitations of PPSRCT imaging, 265–7
  PPCI through SR CT (PPSRCT), 258
  quantitative approaches to synchrotron X-ray imaging, 269
  time line and guide to a PPSRCT cementum imaging experiment, 267–9
noninvasive virtual 3D cementochronology, 384
Nunamiut people, 330

occlusal trauma
  influence on cementum deposition, 98
odontocete age estimation, 2
odontochronology, 9

odontogenic tumors, 56–58
optical coherence tomography (OCT), 249
optical microscopy illumination comparison, 190
  discussion of illumination techniques, 195–7
  results, 194
  sample preparation, 192
  samples, 191–2
oral health
  effects of pregnancy on cementum growth, 155–7
orang-utans, 140
orthodontic therapy, 56
  effects on cementum, 58
osteobiography of a Middle Woodland woman
  achondroplasia and pregnancy, 313–14
  age and identity of EZ 3-7-1, 314–16
  age and pregnancy, 313–14
  age identities, 308
  archeological context, 308
  biological age (age-at-death) estimation, 307–8
  constructing the osteobiography of EZ 3-7-1, 311–14
  evidence of a combined skeletal dysplasia (achondroplasia and Leri-Weill dyschondrosteosis), 306, 308–9
  excavation of EZ 3-7-1 (female adult) and EZ 3-7-2 (fetal remains), 306
  identity and osteobiographies, 306–7
  life expectancy in the Middle Woodland period, 312–13
  mortality and achondroplasia, 311–12
  osteological evaluation, 308–9
  paleodemography of the Middle Woodland period, 312–13
  revised age-at-death estimation, 309–11
osteocalcin (OCN), 47, 49
osteological paradox, 166
osteopontin (OPN), 47, 49, 53, 54, 70, 73
osteoporosis therapy
  risk of osteonecrosis of the jaw, 59
otolometry, 7
otters, 30
Owen, Richard, 25

Paget's disease
  association with hypercementosis, 100
paleodemography, 323
paleoecology, 386
parametric hazard models, 388
Paranthropus boisei fossil tooth
  diagenetic and taphonomic effects on the cementum, 148–50
  study sample, 141
  synchrotron X-ray study, 141
parathyroid hormone (PTH), 68
parturition lines in acellular cementum
  chemical signal of pregnancy, 243–5
  effects of life-history events, 234–5

parturition lines in acellular cementum (cont.)
   environmental scanning electron microscopy, 237
   experimental design, 235
   grayscale profile analysis by Fiji software, 236
   histological preparation of samples, 235–6
   methodological approach, 243
   physical nature of broad annulations, 245–6
   protocol for identification, 246
   Raman microspectrometry and imaging analysis, 236–7
   results, 237–44
   sample collection, 235
pathological tooth displacement
   influence on cementum deposition, 98
Pendred syndrome, 102
penguins, 87
periodontal disease
   effects on cementum, 56
   influence on cementum deposition, 97–8
periodontal ligament (PDL), 51
periodontal treatment, 56
   effects on cementum, 58
periodontitis
   during pregnancy, 155–6
Petra, Jordan, North Ridge burials. See Nabataean age-related mortality
PHEX gene mutations, 68
PHEX gene mutations (mouse), 68–70
phosphate metabolism, 67–70, 76
phosphorus
   concentrations in chimpanzee cellular cementum, 142–5
pigs
   multidien (5-day) rhythms, 6
pituitary gland, 5
polar bears, 158
polyphyodonty, 87
population fertility studies, 385–6
positive selection, 85, 86
PPCI (propagation-based phase-contrast imaging) through SR CT (synchrotron-based computed tomography) (PPSRCT), 258
pre-farming population demography, 322–3
   adult age estimation using cementochronology, 326–7
   age-at-death estimation using cementochronology, 323–4
   Brazilian *sambaquis*, 324–6
   Cabeçuda skeletal sample, 325–6
   demography of contemporary hunter-gatherer groups, 329–30
   interpreting the age-at-death distribution, 328–30
   limitations of the Cabeçuda data, 332–3
   material and method, 324–7
   metabolic load hypothesis, 332
   models of preindustrial demography, 329–30
   potential influences on the demographic distribution, 332–3
   proxy indicator of fertility ($_{15}P_5$ ratio), 330–1
   results, 327–8
   total fertility rate (TFR), 331–2
pregnancy
   effects on oral health and cementum growth, 155–7
   gingivitis related to, 155–6
   identifying parturition lines in acellular cementum, 234–46
   osteobiography of a Middle Woodland woman, 306–16
   periodontitis related to, 155–6
   tooth loosening related to, 155–6
primary cementum. See acellular cementum
primates, 30
probabilistic method, 342, 388
progressive ankylosis protein (ANK), 72–3
propagation-based phase-contrast imaging (PPCI), 258
propagation phase-contrast synchrotron X-ray microtomography, 249
proteoglycans, 47
protocols
   key advances in, 382–5
   standardized protocol in cementochronology, 38–9
puberty
   evidence of onset in acellular cementum, 245
pulpal necrosis, 56
purifying selection, 85, 86
   evidence in cementum candidate genes, 86
Purkinje, Jan, 25, 46
pycnodysostosis, 102
pyrophosphate regulation of cementogenesis, 70–3, 76

rabbits, 87
rats, 8
red deer, 111–12
red foxes, 30
regenerative cementum. See reparative cementum
region of interest (ROI) selection
   age-at-death estimations from different observers, 212
   criteria for inclusion, 202–3
   importance of observer training and experience, 212–13
   methodological issues, 201
   optimal ROI selection by applying the criteria, 212
   sample set, 203
   season of death estimations from different observers, 212
   study objective, 202–3
   study results, 204–12
   testing an optimal ROI selection, 203–4

reindeer, 111–12, 276, 279, 385
renal osteodystrophy, 102
reparative cementum, 51, 58
reptiles, 7, 10
Retzius, Anders, 25, 46
rickets
   phosphate metabolism and, 76
   vitamin D-related rickets, 76
   X-linked hypophosphatemia, 70
Ringelmann, Carl Joseph von, 25
rodents, 30
root caries
   influence on cementum deposition, 98–9
root resorption, 58
   effects on cementum, 56
   external, 98
Rostock Paleodemography Workshops, 36
RSK2 gene, 90

saliva flow
   influence on oral health, 156
Saul, Frank, 307
scalimetry, 7
sclerochronology, 7
sclerostin (SOST), 51
sea otters, 158
seals, 4, 29, 86, 87, 158, 159
season at time of death
   identification of US POW/MIA service members, 226–32
   mobility patterns and, 385
   validation studies, 383
seasonal (circannual) progressive rhythms, 4
seasonal affective disorder, 4
seasonality hypothesis, 381–2
secondary cementum. *See* cellular cementum
sharks
   circannual growth patterns, 8
Sharpey's fibers, 47, 49, 51, 157
sheep, 8
Siler mortality model, 360
skeletochronology, 7–8
small integrin-binding ligand N-linked glycoprotein (SIBLING) family of proteins, 53, 54, 73–5
SOST gene mutations, 51
SPP1 gene, 54
squirrels, 30
standardized protocol in cementochronology, 38–9
stressors
   effects on cementum growth, 380
stria of Retzius, 9
strontium
   concentrations in chimpanzee cellular cementum, 145–6
suprachiasmatic nuclei, 5
synchrotron X-ray studies
   acellular cementum increments composition, 110–35
   chimpanzee cellular cementum elemental distribution, 138–51
   key advances in cementochronology, 384
   nondestructive imaging of TCAs, 249–55
   noninvasive 3D imaging of cementum, 258–69
synchrotron-based computed tomography (SR CT), 258
systemic lupus erythematosus, 102

taphonomy
   effects on tooth cementum, 37
teeth
   circadian rhythms, 6
   circannual rhythms, 6, 9–10
Tenon, Jacques-René, 25
Terahertz imaging, 249
thecodonty, 83
thin-section preparation
   diversity of approaches for nonhuman teeth, 173
   embedding materials comparison, 190, 191–3, 195, 197
   epoxy resin embedding material, 190
   issues with ungulate teeth, 201–13
   methyl methacrylate (MMA) embedding material, 190
   optimizing production, 383
   optimizing protocol variables, 198
   planes of sectioning comparison, 191–2, 193–4, 195–6, 197–8
thin-section preparation protocol
   animal and human protocol proposal, 186–7
   cutting quality, 177–81
      according to the cutting plane (height), 181
      according to the cutting plane (length), 181
      according to the cutting settings, 180
      according to the diameter of the flanges used, 180–1
      according to the model of the cutting disc used, 180
      according to the resin and catalyst dosages, 179
      according to the resin used, 179
      according to the sample position, 180
      variability with fixed parameters, 177–9
   finishing step, 184
      different methods of finishing, 184
      use or not of a coverslip, 184
   four main steps, 173
   gluing quality, 181–4
      according to pressure, 184
      according to temperature, 182
      according to the surface condition of the slide and the specimen, 182
      measures of, 182–4
   intraobserver errors, 174–5
   operations for the experimental designs

thin-section preparation protocol (cont.)
  optimization study, 173–4
  resin consolidation quality, 175–7
    according to flow height, 176
    according to flow velocity, 176
    according to mixing mode, 176
    according to the vacuum cycle, 177
    inclusion quality with or without vacuum, 177
  sections with embedded objects, 185
    air bubbles, 185
    methyl methacrylate (MMA) embedding, 185
    polymers used for embedding, 185
    resin embedding, 185
time-of-flight secondary ion mass spectrometry, 161
tissue nonspecific alkaline phosphatase (TNAP), 49–50, 72, 84
tooth cementum annulations (TCA) method, 3, 22, 50
  clinical and environmental considerations, 54–9
  effects of caries on cementum, 56
  effects of caries therapy on cementum, 58
  effects of dental disease and trauma, 56–58
  effects of dental therapies on cementum, 58
  effects of drugs on cementum, 59
  effects of endodontic therapy on cementum, 58
  effects of genetic mutations, 56
  effects of orthodontic therapy on cementum, 58
  effects of periodontal disease on cementum, 56
  effects of periodontal treatment on cementum, 58
  effects of root resorption on cementum, 56
  effects of tumoral lesions on cementum, 56–58
  human deciduous teeth, 215–24
  identification of US POW/MIA service members, 226–32
  need for a standardized protocol, 38–9
  nondestructive imaging using synchrotron X-ray microtomography, 249–55
  ongoing methodological issues, 36–7
  protocol development and validation studies, 30–6
  See also cementochronology
tooth decay. See caries
tooth loosening
  related to pregnancy, 155–6
tooth loss
  effects of loss of antagonistic teeth, 99
tooth whitening agents, 56

trans-generational annual rhythms, 4
transition analysis, 338, 388
trauma
  effects on cementum, 58
tumoral lesions
  effects on cementum, 56–58
Turkana pastoralists, 330

ungulates, 29–30
  circannual growth patterns, 8
  problem of thin-section preparation and interpretation, 201–13
US military POW/MIA recovery missions
  age and season-of-death estimation, 226–7
  age estimation by TCA, 231
  effects of dental disease and treatments on age estimations, 232
  identification of service members, 226–7
  identifying season at time of death, 231–2
  potential value of TCA analysis, 232
  protocol for TCA analysis, 230–1
  results of TCA age and season-of-extraction study, 228–31
  study sample of teeth from active service members, 227–8

Van Buchem disease, 51
Van Leeuwenhoek, Antoni, 23
Vesalius, Andreas, 23
virtual cementochronology, 164–5
vitamin D, 68, 76
vitamin D-related rickets, 76
von Ebner's lines, 9

walruses, 158
waterbuck, 29
whales, 127, 134, 140, 147
white-tailed deer, 29

X-linked hypophosphatemia, 70

zinc
  concentrations in chimpanzee cellular cementum, 146–7
  distribution in bone and dental tissues, 140
zooarchaeology, 83